PEARSON BACCALAUREATE

Economics

SEAN MALEY • JASON WELKER

Supporting every learner across the IB continuum

Pearson Education Limited is a company incorporated in England and Wales, having its registered office at Edinburgh Gate, Harlow, Essex, CM20 2JE. Registered company number: 872828.

www.pearsonglobalschools.com

Text © Pearson Education Limited 2011

First published 2011

20 19 18 17 16 15
IMP 10 9 8 7 6 5 4 3 2 1

ISBN 978 144799067 3

Edited by Penelope Lyons
Designed by Tony Richardson
Typeset by TechType
Photo research by Emily Taylor
Original illustrations © Pearson Education Limited 2011
Illustrated by TechType
Cover design by Tony Richardson
Cover photo © iStockphoto
Printed in Slovakia by Neografia

Dedications

To my parents and siblings, the echoes of conversations past, about politics and people, are found herein. Thank you for always challenging me. This book is also written with all my students, past and present, well in mind. In it you'll find everything I've wanted to say when time ran short. To Jane, Pen, and everyone at Pearson, thank you for helping us produce a book of which I am proud. And to my wife Linda, I dedicate this book to you, the source of my inspiration.

Sean Maley

As a student I was once inspired by three great economics teachers: Tim Sorenson, Dean Peterson and the late Chris Weber. Thanks to them for inspiring me to pursue a career in economics education. Thanks also to my students at ZIS, whose feedback on early drafts of this book helped me immensely. My teaching partner Joe Hauet has been a great inspiration over the years. To my family, without whose support I would never have had the energy to undertake this project, including my parents Jeff and Peggy, my brother Troy, and my wife Elizabeth, I dedicate this book.

Jason Welker

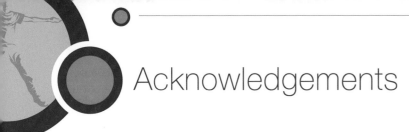

Acknowledgements

The publisher would like to thank the following for their kind permission to reproduce their photographs:

(Key: b-bottom; c-centre; l-left; r-right; t-top)

123RF.com: 123rf.com 194tr; **Alamy Images:** 427tr, 642br, 643cr, 647tr, 648tl, 427tr, 642br, 643cr, 647tr, 648tl, 427tr, 642br, 643cr, 647tr, 648tl, 427tr, 642br, 643cr, 647tr, 648tl, 427tr, 642br, 643cr, 647tr, 648tl, Greg Balfour Evans 217c, Kathy deWitt 479c, Lonely Planet Images 21c, Manor Photography 224bl, Marcelo Rudini 412tc, Open Door 638cr; **Corbis:** 249tr, 325br, 249tr, 325br, Bettmann 5bc, 5br, 196tl, 373tr, Bettmann 5bc, 5br, 196tl, 373tr, Bettmann 5bc, 5br, 196tl, 373tr, Bettmann 5bc, 5br, 196tl, 373tr, Bishop Asare / epa 621br, Bob Krist 386bl, George Grantham Bain 405br, Jim Lo Scalzo / Epa 256bl, John Carnemolla 285tl, John Van Hasselt 144c, Kim Ludbrook / epa 558cl, Luke Macgregor / Reuters 230bc, Marianna Day Massey / ZUMA 152cl, PATRICIA DOMINGUEZ / epa 196tr, Stringer / Russia / Reuters 589c, US Coast Guard / Handout 148c, Viviane Moos 334c; **EFTA:** 409tr; **Fotolia.com:** Andrey Armyagov 223tr, ErnstPieber 328cl, Jorge Chaves 85cr, Lane Erickson 130c, Pakhnyushchyy 94bl, Paul Prescott 630cl, photoclicks 431c, Richard Seeney 72t, Scott Hancock 385c, Sharpshot 98tl, Zhuang Mu 414bl; **Getty Images:** AFP 631bc, Asia Images 624tl, Brent Stirton 619br, Clive Rose 596bc, Dan Kenyon 537br, Stockbyte 123c, Time & Life Pictures 403br; **Glow Images:** 229br, 443tr, 640bl, 229br, 443tr, 640bl, 229br, 443tr, 640bl, Stock Connection 401c; **iStockphoto:** 3br, 3br, BanksPhotos 53c, Chris Hutchison 215c, Diane Diederich 132bl, FotografiaBasica 453c, Jaap Hart 141br, Jani Bryson 409cl, Mark Wragg 300bl, Ranplett 628bl, ShutterWorx 414cl, Thomas Ward 57tr; **Jamie Sinz:** 176c; **Lyons Photo Library:** 234c, 367c, 234c, 367c; **Rex Features:** 541bc; **Scala London:** White Images 404cr; **Shutterstock.com:** 196tc, Hung Chung Chih 5bl, Iakov Kalinin 139br, Luisa Puccini 4cl, Scott Latham 89tr, Stephen Coburn 11t, Tatagatta 132bc; **Jason Welker:** 1c, 565b, 616t, 1c, 565b, 616t, 1c, 565b, 616t, 1c, 565b, 616t

Cover images: *Front:* **iStockphoto**

All other images © Pearson Education

The assessment statements, assessment information and past examination questions have been reproduced from IBO documents and examination papers. Our thanks go to the International Baccalaureate Organization for permission to reproduce its intellectual copyright.

We are grateful to the following for permission to reproduce copyright material:

Figures
Figure on page 3 from based on data from OECD (2009),Unemployment rates: total, in OECD Factbook 2009, http://dx.doi.org/10.1787/factbook-2009-table75-en; Figure 14.8 from Economica, The original Phillips Curve from paper: The Relationship between unemployment and the rate of change of money wages in the UK 1861-1957 found in Economica. Phillips, 1958, http://mahalanobis.twoday.net/stories/2778677/, Reproduced with permission of Blackwell Publishing; Figure 14.9 from Economica, The short-run Phillips Curve from paper: The Relationship between unemployment and the rate of change of money wages in the UK 1861-1957 found in Economica, http://mahalanobis.twoday.net/stories/2778677/, Reproduced with permission of Blackwell Publishing; Figure 26.5 from Per capita GDP and per capita GNI, selected developed countries, 2009, http://www.worldbank.org/, based on World Bank development indicators database; Figure 26.6 from Per capita GDP and per capita GNI, selected developing countries, 2009, http://www.worldbank.org/, based on World Bank development indicators database; Figure 26.7 from Adolescent fertility rate, 2009, http://www.worldbank.org/, based on World Bank development indicators database; Figure 26.8 from Female life expectancy, 2009, http://www.worldbank.org/, based on World Bank development indicators database; Figure 26.9 from Primary pupil to teacher ratio, http://www.worldbank.org/, based on World Bank development indicators database; Figure 26.10 from Adult literacy rate / %,

Tables
Table on page 1 from Aid Statistics, Recipient Aid Charts, Afghanistan, www.oecd.org/dac/stats/data.; Table on page 2 from based on data from OECD (2008), Agricultural Policies in OECD Countries 2008: At a Glance, OECD Publishing, http://dx.doi.org/10.1787/agr_oecd-2008-en; Table on page 4 from based on data from Consumer prices - Annual inflation, under Consumer Prices (MEI), under Prices and Price Indices under Prices and Purchasing Power Parities from OECD.Stat Extracts, http://stats.oecd.org (accessed on date); Table on page 5 from "Aid targets slipping out of reach?", http://www.oecd.org/dataoecd/47/25/41724314.pdf; Table on page 6 from Net ODA disbursements, Total DAC countries, http://webnet.oecd.org/dcdgraphs/ODAhistory; Table on page 7 from Net ODA in 2009 and ODA/GNI in 2009, http://webnet.oecd.org/oda2009; Table 6.2 from Greenhouse gas emissions of countries in 2005 and ranking of their per capita

Text

CONTENTS

INTRODUCTION

 Content

This Pearson Baccalaureate economics book offers International Baccalaureate (IB) economics students a unique way to learn and prepare for the IB examinations at both higher level (HL) and standard level (SL). It will help you prepare for your examinations in a thorough and methodical way as it follows the syllabus outline, explaining and expanding on the material in the course syllabus.

But what makes this book unique? First, it's based specifically on the new IB economics curriculum (first examinations in May 2013). Links between different parts of the syllabus are noted, and key terms essential to your understanding are emphasized throughout. In most chapters, you will find general in-text exercises to test your knowledge and understanding of that part of the course. Some of the exercises are quantitative and involve numerical calculations; these have worked out solutions available in the Answers chapter at the end of the book. The quantitative exercises are mainly (but not exclusively) for higher-level students. At the end of each chapter are some practice questions of the style and weight you can expect to find in the examination papers.

But that's not all; in addition to being a printed text, this book is accompanied by many online activities and resources. There are two sorts of in-chapter links: hotlinks and online resources.

- The hotlinks boxes mostly direct you to a blog written by the authors and updated regularly with posts relating to the IB economics course.
- The online resources boxes mostly direct you to related worksheets specifically written for this course. For more information, see 'Information boxes' below.

Some of the other features you will find which set this book apart include the following.
- The relationship between syllabus units and the content of each chapter is identified in the contents list.
- Relevant learning outcomes are identified at the start of each main section of the text to help you identify what you need to know at each step of your economics journey.
- There is a clear distinction between HL and SL content. All HL content is specifically identified as HL only; exercises in HL-only sections are also clearly marked as HL only. All unmarked content is for both SL and HL students.
- The quantitative in-chapter exercises offer HL students practice solving the various quantitative problems that will appear in the new HL paper 3.
- Fully referenced tables and coloured diagrams are accompanied by clear explanations in the text.
- Over 100 practice exam questions specifically chosen for each of the main chapters reflect the appropriate form and content of examination questions you will find in the new format IBO papers.
- Interesting facts, key definitions, and connections to theory of knowledge (TOK) are conveniently highlighted in coloured boxes throughout the book to help broaden your knowledge and keep you thinking of the wider applications of your learning.
- A specific TOK chapter discusses various applications of economics, connects economics and TOK, and addresses economics in the TOK essay.
- Two additional chapters offer specific advice on writing the Internal Assessment (including sample commentaries and an example marked commentary) and the Extended Essay in economics, and preparing for the external examination.

Information boxes

Throughout the book you will see a number of coloured boxes interspersed through each chapter. Each of these boxes provides different information and stimulus as follows.

Learning outcomes
- Explain the difference between equity in the distribution of income and equality in the distribution of income.
- Explain that due to unequal ownership of factors of production, the market system may not result in an equitable distribution of income.

You will find a box like this at the start of each section in each chapter. Each contains the learning objectives for the section you are about to read and they set out what content and aspects of learning are covered in that section.

Case studies are self-contained examples in orange boxes that you can use to answer questions on specific points. They often contain photographs or other illustration.

CASE STUDY

Just how much international sporting events such as the World Cup contribute to human development is debatable.

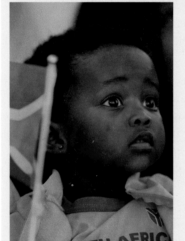

Big sporting events: real investment or all flash?

Poor and middle-income countries hoping for a taste of international prestige must have been inspired by South Africa's hosting of the World Cup in 2010. Millions of visitors streamed into the country, injecting large amounts of foreign cash and cachet. The games went off without serious incident or technical problems or violence and were, to most observers, a shining success. But to others, the allure of major competitions like the World Cup and the Olympics are more mirage than substance. Hosting such tournaments offers up all the glitter of foreign direct investment, with few of its benefits and all of its drawbacks.

Such events promise large amounts of foreign exchange, but this is usually a one-time injection. Rather than receiving foreign capital, countries typically go deeply into debt, diverting local capital away from local needs to build the necessary infrastructure to host these events. In poor countries, this may result in some new roads and mass transit links, but it also requires expensive stadium projects that are luxurious by regional standards. These hulking 'white elephants' are often barely used again, and live on as ugly memories of an expensive party the country hosted years before: Greece's white elephants from 2004 are famous, and as early as 2009 the glorious 'Bird's Nest' in Beijing was falling into disrepair from lack of use. Suspicions about the predatory nature of some FDIs were further bolstered when it was revealed by the Dutch government that FIFA, the World Cup governing body, pressed it and other bidding countries to implement special laws for the World Cup – including blanket tax exemptions for FIFA and FIFA sponsors, as well as limits on workers' rights.

If this can happen under the public spotlight of a major sporting event, critics wonder, then what kind of deals and exemptions might apply during the routine approval of more mundane investment projects in more remote places? Better to win on the pitch, it is said, than to play a losing game off of it. South Africans, who spent $5.1 billion on the games, are prepared for a spending hangover, but appear to be pleased with the results. And it is expected that the quest to host such events will continue. The cost, it is argued, is well worth it in the name of enhancing a country's 'brand.' At the same time, it could be said that such tournaments are rarely justified economically, unless one counts the losses as 'psychic income,' and believes that LDCs should have the same opportunities to misspend their money that rich ones have.

Worked examples are not really in boxes, but they have a coloured line above and below the calculation so you can see clearly where it starts and ends. These examples show you in detail how to work out some necessary calculations.

Worked example

Equilibrium is the point at which supply equals demand, so the first step is to set supply equal to demand.

$$(Q_S = -200 + 150P) = (Q_D = 600 - 50P)$$

$$-200 + 150P = 600 - 50P$$

To find the equilibrium price, simply solve for P.

Simplify by adding 200 to both sides.

$$150P = 800 - 50P$$

Simplify again by adding $50P$ to both sides.

$$200P = 800$$

Divide both sides by 200.

$$P = 4$$

The equilibrium price is \$4. Now that we have the equilibrium price, we can determine the equilibrium quantity by substituting the price into the demand and supply functions.

$$Q_S = -200 + 150(4) = -200 + 600 = 400$$

$$Q_D = 600 - 50(4) = 600 - 200 = 400$$

In addition to the Theory of knowledge chapter towards the end of the book, there are pink TOK boxes throughout. These boxes are there to stimulate thought and consideration of any TOK issues as they arise and in context. Often they will just contain questions to stimulate your own thoughts and discussion.

The government is best which governs least. This aphorism is sometimes used to argue against the active role of government in an economy. Do you agree that society is better off with less government? Would we all be better off without any government in our lives? What do governments do that contributes to our well-being? What do they do that detracts from our well-being?

Blue online resource boxes indicate that online resources are available that relate to this section of the book. These resources might be extension exercises, additional practice questions, interactive online material, suggestions for IA, EE and revision, or other sources of information. Some of the content of this site may be password protected for copyright reasons. When prompted for a password, please use PearsonBaccEco exactly as shown.

 To access Worksheet 16.1 on tax progressivity, please visit www.pearsonbacconline.com and follow the onscreen instructions.

The brown hotlinks boxes direct you to the publisher's website, which in turn will take you to a relevant website. On the webpages there, you will find additional information to support the topic you are reading about.

 To earn more about scarcity, visit www.pearsonhotlinks.com, enter the title or ISBN of this book and select weblink 1.1.

Excess capacity is the amount of output an industry can produce in the short run beyond its current level without having to expand its plant size. If large amounts of excess capacity exist, producers can be highly responsive to changes in the price. With little excess capacity, producers cannot respond quickly to changes in price.

These green boxes contain key terms which are drawn out of the main text and so highlighted. This makes them easily identifiable for quick reference.

The most heavily traded currencies in 2009 were:
· US dollar (USD)
· European euro (euro)
· Japanese yen (JPY)
· British pound (GBP)
· Swiss franc (CHF)
· Canadian dollar (CAD)
· Australian dollar (AUD)
· South African rand (ZAR)

These yellow boxes contain interesting information which will add to your wider knowledge but which does not fit within the main body of the text.

Now you are ready to start. Good luck with your studies.

1 THE FOUNDATIONS OF ECONOMICS

1.1 Economics is a social science

Learning outcomes
- Explain that economics is a social science.
- Outline the social scientific method.

Looking over the ever-changing cityscape of Singapore.

Look around you. What do you see? Are there tall buildings made of steel? Paved roads and parking lots? Strip malls? Fields of crops awaiting harvest? Homes built of wood, brick and glass? Factories producing goods for consumers? Perhaps you see a thick forest or a view of hills stretching to the distance. Or do you see school buildings? Now ask yourself, how did things get to be this way? Why are there fields of corn beyond my town? Why are there factories surrounding my city? Why do people live the way they do in my state, region or country? Why am I wearing the clothes I wear and speaking the language I speak and going to the school I attend? How did things get to be this way?

There are many ways to attempt to answer these questions. Biologists tell a story of evolution based on natural selection. Physicists answer difficult questions by studying the elemental forces of nature that shaped our universe over billions of years, while mathematicians observe the quantifiable variables of our lives and seek to understand our world through numbers. Every field of science views the world through a lens shaped by its own tools and methodologies. Economics is no different.

What distinguishes a social science from a natural science? Is there a 'social scientific method' as opposed to a 'natural scientific method'? What might be the similarities and differences?

A social science is a field of academic scholarship that examines the interactions between humans, our institutions, our organizations and the natural and social environment we inhabit.

Regardless of what continent you live on, which country you live in, what city or town you call home, what school you go to, whether you are a native English speaker, a citizen of one or more countries, or a third culture kid, economics is about you. Actually, to be more general, economics is about us and the world we live in. Economics is a social science: it is one of the fields of academic scholarship that examine the interactions between humans, our institutions, our organizations, and the natural and social environment we inhabit. Economics is specifically the field of study that addresses the problems that arise as human societies attempt to balance their infinite physical needs and wants with the finite resources of the world which are required to meet those needs and wants.

1.2 Scarcity

Learning outcomes

- Explain that scarcity exists because factors of production are finite and wants are infinite.
- Explain that economics studies the ways in which resources are allocated to meet needs and wants.
- Explain that the three basic economic questions that must be answered by any economic system are: 'What to produce?', 'How to produce?' and 'For whom to produce?'

Scarcity is the basic economic problem. Something is scarce when it is both limited in supply and desired.

Economics is not rocket science, but it does have something in common with rocket science. Think of it this way: rocket scientists dedicate their efforts to overcoming one basic problem of nature. What is it? Well, to get a rocket into space, it must overcome the problem of gravity. The existence of gravity creates a need for the field of study called rocket science. Economists also dedicate themselves and their studies to helping mankind overcome a basic problem of nature.

To learn more about scarcity, visit www.pearsonhotlinks.com, enter the title or ISBN of this book and select weblink 1.1.

Scarcity is the basic problem of economics. Rockets are the tools that enable us to overcome the problem of gravity and launch ourselves into the sky; the tools of economics help us overcome scarcity and achieve an allocation and use of the world's scarce resources to meet the needs and wants of society. The goal of rocket science is to expand the frontiers of human knowledge and our understanding of outer space. The goal of economics is to expand the frontiers of the human experience here on earth, to improve efficiency in the use of and allocation of the world's scarce resources.

CASE STUDY

Scarcity – the basic economic problem

Something is scarce when it is desired but limited. Scarce resources are those things, both natural and man-made, that are used in the production of the goods and services that humans consume to survive and to enjoy life. The problem with scarcity is that while resources are finite, the wants and needs of humans are infinite. There are simply not enough resources available in the world to satisfy the wants of the world's people. In our pursuit of our material desires, we use up more and more of the world's resources, so scarcity is intensified.

To learn more about the factors of production, visit www.pearsonhotlinks.com, enter the title or ISBN of this book and select weblink 1.2.

The scarce resources discussed below are also known as the 'factors of production' because all three are required for the production of any good or service that might be exchanged in an economy.

- **Land is scarce.** Land resources are those things that are 'gifts of nature'. The soil in which we grow food is scarce because fertile land is in limited supply but there is a huge desire for the food which grows on such land. Wood is a scarce resource because ultimately all wood comes from trees which are grown on scarce land. Minerals such as copper and tin, and resources such as oil, coal, gas and uranium are scarce. This is because these materials are all used to produce energy and other things we desire but they are all in limited supply and the supplies do not renew themselves.

- **Labour is scarce.** Labour refers to the human resources used in the production of goods and services. In a world of nearly seven billion people, it may sound silly to say labour is scarce, but it most certainly is. Labour is the human work, both physical and intellectual, that contributes to the production of goods and services. Some types of labour are more scarce than others. For example, factory workers are desirable in huge numbers in some parts of the world; in China and India they are not very limited but are greatly desired, therefore they are scarce. Medical doctors are desired in all parts of the world, but they are more limited in number than people able to work in factories; therefore, doctors are scarcer relative to factory workers.

- **Capital is scarce.** Capital refers to the tools and technologies that are used to produce the goods and services we desire. The word 'capital' is also sometimes used to refer to the money that individuals and businesses need to acquire the tools and technologies of production. More and better tools enhance the production of all types of goods and services but the amount of capital in the world is limited, so capital is a scarce resource.

A resource worth mentioning that is not scarce is entrepreneurship, which can be defined as the innovation and creativity applied in the production of goods and services. Creativity and innovation have contributed more to improvements in the well-being of the world's people than any other resource. The physical scarcity of land, labour and capital does not apply to human ingenuity, which itself is a resource that goes into the production of economic output.

The basic economic problem of scarcity has led to the development of various economic systems and their methods for allocating the resources of land, labour and capital, and distributing the output produced.

 Economics is the field of study that concerns itself with the allocation of the scarce resources between the competing needs and wants of society.

A brief history of economic thought

The study of economics as its own field of science is relatively young and can be traced back to the late 18th century. The observations of Adam Smith, a Scottish social philosopher, spawned a revolution in society's views of how we interact with one another in the commercial realm. He wrote two books that would contribute to the field that you are studying today: *The Theory of Moral Sentiments* (1759) and *An Inquiry Into the Nature and Causes of the Wealth of Nations* (1776). In these works, Smith laid out his views on the importance of liberty and the pursuit of self-interest in achieving an efficient allocation of society's scarce resources.

While he did not invent economics, Smith was the first thinker to formalize the process of observing and reflecting on humans' economic behaviour. He formulated several of the principles that still underlie our understanding of economics today.

While the revolution in social science brought on by the development of economics as a field of study occurred less than 250 years ago, a very different revolution occurred thousands of years ago that led to the development of economies. *An economy is a system of interactions between individuals in a geographical area (village, town, state; national or international) that brings together those involved in the production, distribution, exchange and consumption of resources, goods and services of that area.* The key word in this definition is 'exchange': to

Adam Smith (1723–90) – the father of modern economics.

understand how human society came to involve economies, we must understand how the need for them arose in the first place.

In his book *The Worldly Philosophers*, historian Robert L Heilbroner writes about the 'economic revolution' that occurred thousands of years ago in human society.

Since he came down from the trees, man has faced the problem of survival, not as an individual but as a member of a social group. His continued existence is testimony to the fact that he has succeeded in solving the problem; but the continued existence of want and misery, even in the richest of nations, is evidence that his solution has been, at best, a partial one.

Bushmen of the Kalahari have an economy based on tradition.

Heilbroner points out that early humans, whose survival depended on the ability to hunt and gather food, were not concerned so much with the complex web of exchanges that a modern economy exhibits, thus there would have been little need for economists in early human society. He explains how studies of the African Bushmen of the early 20th century revealed interactions that solved the economic problem in communities that were most likely to represent life in pre-agricultural and pre-industrial human societies.

[Anthropologists] describe how a gemsbok is divided among relatives and relatives' relatives, until in the end 'no person eats more than any other.' But in an advanced community this tangible pressure of the environment, or this web of social obligations, is lacking. When men and women no longer work shoulder to shoulder in tasks directly related to survival – indeed when two-thirds of the population never touches the earth, enters the mines, builds with its hands, or even enters a factory – or when the claims of kinship have all but disappeared, the perpetuation of the human animal becomes a remarkable social feat.

So remarkable, in fact, that society's existence hangs by a hair. A modern community is at the mercy of a thousand dangers: if its farmers should fail to plant enough crops; if its railroad men should take it into their heads to become bookkeepers or its bookkeepers should decide to become railroad men; if too few should offer their services as miners, puddlers of steel, candidates for engineering degrees – in a word, if any of a thousand intertwined tasks of society should fail to get done – industrial life would soon become hopelessly disorganized. Every day the community faces the possibility of breakdown – not from the forces of nature, but from sheer human unpredictability.

Robert L Heilbroner, *The Worldly Philosophers*, 1999

In today's world, argues Heilbroner, there is a need for a science that examines and develops tools to assist in the allocation of scarce resources and the goods and services which they are used to produce. This is precisely because the systems of exchange, or the economies, of modern society are so complex. And that science is economics.

Without ancient traditions governing the ways in which humans exchange with one another, and in the absence of an absolute dictator who determines how much of which resources will be used to produce what and for whom, it can appear to be a miracle that anything productive gets done in modern economies.

It is not a miracle, however, as you will see throughout your study of economics over the coming months. Complex modern economies can be understood by examining the exchanges that take place in markets that lead to the satisfaction of the wants and needs of the world's people.

The basic economic questions

The existence of scarcity in our world gives rise to some basic questions that any economic system must answer. Some economic systems rely on customs and traditions to answer these questions, some rely on the commands of a central authority or government, and some rely on free exchanges between individuals in a market system. Regardless of whether it is governed by tradition, command, or exchanges in the marketplace, there are three basic economic questions that any economic system must address.

- **What should be produced?** Should society's scarce resources (land, labour and capital) be used to grow food, make clothes, toys and tools, or should they be used to provide services such as healthcare, entertainment and haircuts? What a particular economy should produce is one of the basic questions an economic system should answer. An economy based on tradition may answer 'produce what has always been produced: food for survival'. A centrally planned economy may choose to produce whatever the government decides is most crucial to meeting society's needs, while a market economy leaves the answer up to the interactions between the supply and the demand of self-interested consumers and producers.

- **How should it be produced?** Should production be labour intensive or capital intensive? Should robots replace workers whenever possible or should workers make up the majority of inputs into the production of goods and services? To what extent will technological innovation affect the way things are produced? Economic systems must address the question of how society's output will be produced.

- **For whom should it be produced?** The allocation and use of resources for the production of goods and services is only part of the objective of economic systems. The allocation of the output of an economy is the final issue the system must address. Who will receive the output of the economy, and how much will each person receive? Should levels of consumption be based on social standing? Gender or age? Race or religion? Or should output be allocated fairly across all sections of society? Perhaps levels of consumption should be based on merit or worth or individuals' willingness and ability to pay for the things they want to consume. The question of the allocation of output is the final issue all economic systems must address.

The basic economic questions arise from the basic economic problem of scarcity. Once we recognize that scarcity exists, we must confront these questions in order to determine how to deal with the problem of scarcity in our allocation of resources and the goods and services they are used to produce.

 To learn more about the basic economic questions, visit www.pearsonhotlinks. com, enter the title or ISBN of this book and select weblink 1.3.

The Bushmen of Africa and other tribal societies answer the basic economic questions through traditions passed down from generation to generation. The feudal societies that dominated mediaeval Europe and Asia and the centrally planned, totalitarian states of the 19th and 20th centuries turned to strong leaders and the power of the state to decide on the allocation of resources, goods and services.

◀ Mao Zedong (left), Joseph Stalin (centre) and Fidel Castro (right): 20th-century rulers who executed nearly total control over the economic activities of their respective countries (China, Soviet Union and Cuba).

There are very few command economies left. China began embracing market reforms soon after Mao Zedong's death in 1976. The Soviet Union dissolved in 1991 and now consists of over a dozen separate countries, mostly with market-based economies. Even Castro's Cuba has embarked on market reforms since Fidel Castro stepped down as its leader in 2007. Only North Korea remains as a vivid example of totalitarian economic control.

The thoroughly controlled command economy of North Korea is mainly newsworthy for want and famine. In the early 1990s, from a total population of 22 million, between 900 000 and 3 million people died of starvation. Stunted by lack of food, the average North Korean is now two inches shorter than the average South Korean.

To learn more about command economies, visit www.pearsonhotlinks.com, enter the title or ISBN of this book and select weblink 1.4.

To learn more about incentives, visit www.pearsonhotlinks.com, enter the title or ISBN of this book and select weblink 1.5.

Command economies

The economic system implemented in Mao's China, Stalin's Soviet Union and Castro's Cuba is known as socialism. In each case, these leaders sought to move the economy of their country from an agricultural base to an industrial and manufacturing base. The mechanism used to pursue this goal involved total control of the nation's resources by the government. Answers to the basic economic questions were based on government priorities.

Typically, a command economy requires state ownership of the factors of production and is guided by the principles of socialism. These principles place the objective of equality above that of efficiency. Socialist economies aim to achieve fairness within society by allocating resources and output based on the common needs of humans rather than the individual pursuit of self-interest that underlies market economies. Private ownership of factors of production is therefore abolished. All agricultural and industrial output is appropriated by the central government and is re-allocated among the nation's people in what is intended to be a fair and equitable manner.

Because of the lack of individual property rights and the incentive to achieve maximum efficiency in the use of resources (which characterize private ownership), the command economies of the 20th century eventually became highly inefficient. Ultimately, they were unable to provide their nations' people with the basic necessities for a healthy and happy existence. Both Russia (the core of the former Soviet Union) and China eventually abandoned the command system of economic management. Even Cuba, under its current ruler Raul Castro, who succeeded his brother Fidel in 2007, has recently embarked on market-based economic reforms.

The failure of command economies to achieve sustainable and meaningful improvements in the well-being of their people can be tied to the lack of an effective mechanism for determining the most efficient allocation of society's scarce resources. Central planners, it turned out, were too prone to making mistakes in their determination of what was best for society. Massive inefficiencies and high levels of corruption emerged as producers in the economy focused less on producing quality products that society truly demanded, and more on meeting the strict production targets passed down from the central government.

An economic system that does not appropriately harness incentives towards achieving efficiency in production will eventually collapse under the mounting inefficiencies that emerge while attempting to manage the activities of millions of individuals across the nation. This helps explain why the command economies of the 20th century failed to thrive and why most of them eventually adopted market-based economic reforms granting individual ownership of property and encouraging the pursuit of self-interest.

So how does a modern economy answer the basic economic questions? Humans' economic exchanges today are not guided by the tradition and custom of the tribal societies nor by totalitarian commands from above. Traditional economies and command economies have largely declined in the modern era as the market system has emerged as the dominant mechanism for answering the basic economic questions. Today, most of the world's economies are guided by a system that Adam Smith described as 'the invisible hand of the market'.

The market system

Adam Smith's revolutionary observation was that society's needs and wants would be best satisfied by letting individuals pursue their own selfish objectives in an entirely free market. Smith believed that the 'market' (a place where buyers and sellers meet to engage in exchanges with one another) was the most efficient means for allocating scarce resources and therefore led to the greatest amount of gain for the largest number of people when it was left entirely free of government control.

A market is a place where buyers and sellers come together to engage in exchanges with one another.

Smith advocated a *laissez-faire* approach to the government's management of the nation's economic activity. *Laissez-faire* is a French term that translates as 'let it be'. A government, said Smith, should let an economy be free, since individual agents in a free market will interact in a manner that results in outcomes beneficial for both the individual and society.

Smith believed that freedom and the pursuit of self-gain would not lead to chaos and anarchy, but to a socially beneficial outcome whereby society's wants and needs are satisfied by an invisible hand rather than an iron fist.

Whoever offers to another a bargain of any kind, proposes to do this. Give me that which I want, and you shall have this which you want, is the meaning of every such offer; and it is in this manner that we obtain from one another the far greater part of those good offices which we stand in need of.

It is not from the benevolence of the butcher, the brewer, or the baker that we expect our dinner, but from their regard to their own self-interest. We address ourselves, not to their humanity but to their self-love, and never talk to them of our own necessities but of their advantages.

Adam Smith, *The Wealth of Nations,* **1776**

The idea that individuals pursuing their self-interest could end up contributing to the well-being of others was rooted in Smith's moral philosophy that humans' personal happiness is based to some extent on the well-being of those around them. Smith believed that in a complex society made up of thousands or millions of individuals whose interests do not always overlap, an economy governed by tradition or command could not possibly achieve a more beneficial outcome for the greatest number of people than a system in which individuals are able to pursue their own self-interest.

Are economic theories independent of culture? Can a culture remain unique while adopting an economic system shared by other cultures?

Freedom of choice was a fundamental basis for Smith's economic and social philosophy and, to this day, freedom remains a key characteristic of the economics we study and of the policies that economic theory helps shape in both national and international economies.

Most economies combine elements of the free market with some degree of government intervention – these are mixed economies. The degree to which government is involved varies greatly between countries, and is a central point of argument in each country's politics.

To learn more about free markets, visit www.pearsonhotlinks.com, enter the title or ISBN of this book and select weblink 1.6.

The circular flow of a market economy

Fundamental to the market economic system is the idea that the exchanges between individuals are voluntary and that anyone engaging in such exchanges benefits from them. This implies that when one person voluntarily gives another something that the second person wants, the first person must be getting something he or she wants in return. Thus, both parties are better off following the exchange. In other words, market economics is not a zero-sum game. When one person wins, it does not necessarily mean that someone else loses. There are winners and winners in a market economy.

All exchanges in a market economy take place in either the 'product market' or the 'resource market'. In our study of market economies, the demand for resources by firms, and for goods and services by households, is met in one of these two markets. Households are the 'owners' of productive resources, which are the inputs firms need in order to produce goods and services. To acquire the inputs for production, firms must pay households for their resources in the *resource market*. Households earn their income in the

To learn more about the circular flow model, visit www.pearsonhotlinks. com, enter the title or ISBN of this book and select weblink 1.7.

Figure 1.1
The circular flow model of the market economy.

resource market and then demand the finished products provided by firms in the *product market*. The flow of resources, money and goods and services is illustrated in a model economists call the circular flow model (Figure 1.1).

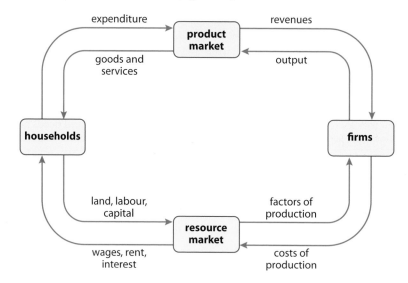

In Figure 1.1, money payments flow clockwise in the outer loop while resources, goods and services flow counter-clockwise in the inner loop. In the resource market, households provide firms with the factors of production (land, labour and capital) they demand in order to produce their output. But these inputs are not free; firms face costs in acquiring them. These costs translate into money incomes that households receive for the resources they provide; wages for labour, rent for land, and interest for capital.

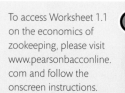

To access Worksheet 1.1 on the economics of zookeeping, please visit www.pearsonbacconline. com and follow the onscreen instructions.

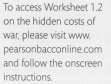

To access Worksheet 1.2 on the hidden costs of war, please visit www. pearsonbacconline.com and follow the onscreen instructions.

Once firms have acquired all the inputs necessary to produce their finished products, they sell their products to households in the product market. The money households earn in the resource market goes to pay for the goods and services they demand in the product market. Household expenditures on goods and services translate into revenue for the firms. Thus the money earned by households in the resource market is ultimately earned by firms in the product market, and the circular flow is complete. Inputs turn into outputs, income turns into revenue.

Thus Figure 1.1 illustrates at a basic level how market economies function. The exchanges between households and firms in each market are mutually beneficial, because in the absence of oppression, coercion, or forced exchange, it must be assumed that in each of the transactions between household and firm, Adam Smith's words are guiding the individuals: 'Give me that which I want, and you shall have this which you want.'

CASE STUDY

Cuba plans to lay off 500 000 workers

Cuba announced Monday it will cast off at least half a million state employees by mid-2011 and reduce restrictions on private enterprise to help them find new jobs – the most dramatic step yet in President Raul Castro's push to radically remake employment on the communist-run island.

Castro suggested during a nationally televised address on Easter Sunday that as many 1 million Cuban workers – about one in five – may be redundant. But the government had not previously laid out specific plans to reduce the work force.

The layoffs will start immediately and continue through the first half of next year, according to the nearly 3 million-strong Cuban Workers Confederation – the only labour union allowed by the government.

To soften the blow, it said the government would increase private-sector job opportunities, including allowing more Cubans to become self-employed, forming cooperatives run by employees rather than government administrators and increasing private control of state land, businesses and infrastructure through long-term leases.

It did not say which parts of the economy would be retooled to allow for more private enterprise. The union said that the state would only continue to employ people in 'indispensable' areas where the labour force is historically insufficient, such as in farming, construction, industry, law enforcement and education.

The announcement added that Cuba would overhaul its labour structure and salary systems since it will 'no longer be possible to apply a formula of protecting and subsidizing salaries on an unlimited basis to workers.'

Instead, Cubans will soon be 'paid according to results,' it said, though few details were provided. Castro has said repeatedly he sought to reform the pay system to hold workers accountable for their production, but the changes have been slow in coming.

Currently, the state employs 95 per cent of the official work force. Unemployment last year was 1.7 per cent and hasn't risen above 3 per cent in eight years – but that ignores thousands of Cubans who aren't looking for jobs that pay monthly salaries worth only $20 a month on average.

In exchange for the low salaries, the state provides free education and healthcare and heavily subsidizes housing, transportation and basic food.

Castro's government has moved to embrace some small free-market reforms. Earlier this year, it handed some barbershops over to employees, allowing them to set their own prices but making them pay rent and buy their own supplies. Authorities have also approved more licenses for private taxis while getting tough on unlicensed ones.

Associated Press /NPR News, 13 September 2010

 To learn more about economic systems, visit www.pearsonhotlinks.com, enter the title or ISBN of this book and select weblink 1.8.

EXERCISES

1 How is the basic economic problem of scarcity dealt with in a centrally planned economy such as Cuba's?

2 How are wages determined in a centrally planned economy? How will they be determined as more and more workers in Cuba begin working in the private sector?

3 How will increased private ownership of land, capital and labour lead to more efficient use of resources in Cuba?

4 The article says, 'the state would only continue to employ people in "indispensable" areas where the labour force is historically insufficient'. How does a free market system assure that 'indispensable' jobs in the economy get done? Is a central planner needed to make sure there are enough farmers, teachers and law enforcement agents?

 1.3 Choice and opportunity cost

Learning outcomes
- Explain that as a result of scarcity, choices have to be made.
- Explain that when an economic choice is made, an alternative is always foregone.

The existence of scarcity means that in humans' pursuit of material well-being, not every want and need of mankind can be simultaneously satisfied. As Heilbroner says, 'the

To learn more about opportunity cost, visit www.pearsonhotlinks. com, enter the title or ISBN of this book and select weblink 1.9.

To learn more about tradeoffs, visit www. pearsonhotlinks.com, enter the title or ISBN of this book and select weblink 1.10.

The opportunity cost is what must be given up in order to undertake any activity or economic exchange. Opportunity costs are not necessarily monetary; rather, when you buy something, the opportunity cost is what you could have done with the money you spent on that thing. Even non-monetary exchanges involve opportunity costs, as you might have chosen to do something different with your time.

continued existence of want and misery' is evidence that the economic problem has not been overcome, even in the richest of countries. So, why can't all of humans' wants and needs be satisfied? Why can't global poverty be eliminated, which would surely put an end to many of the violent social, political and economic conflicts that plague our planet?

The problem of scarcity gives rise to another fundamental reality faced by individuals everywhere: the reality that nothing is free. Every economic decision involves costs. A cost is defined as what must be given up in order to have something else. In answering the basic economic questions, choices must be made and those choices inevitably involve costs, since resources are scarce.

For example, think about your decision to sign up for this economics class. You could have studied several other subjects: geography, history, psychology, perhaps business. Your decision to study economics was your choice of how to use the scarce resource of time during your last two years in school. The cost of your decision is the foregone opportunity to study one of the other subjects, and all the skills and knowledge you would have learned had you chosen another subject.

You may be saying to yourself: 'No, the cost of me taking economics is the tuition fees or taxes my parents are paying to support my education at this school.' That is also true. But in economics, we define costs as more than just the monetary expenses involved in an economic transaction. The opportunity cost is the opportunity lost when making a decision of how to use our scarce resources, whether it's time, money, labour, land or capital.

We face trade-offs every day of our lives. On a Friday night, you may face several trade-offs: you can go to a movie with friends, have dinner at home with your parents, play video games with your brother or study for next week's exams. Trade-offs are the various opportunities you could choose to pursue in any given situation. The opportunity cost of a decision is the next best alternative to the choice you make. If you decide to play video games on Friday night, but the next best alternative was to study, then the opportunity cost of playing video games is the benefit you would have gained from studying instead.

1.4   The use of models in economics

Learning outcomes
- Explain the process of model building in economics.
- Explain that economists must use the *ceteris paribus* assumption when developing economic models.
- Distinguish between positive and normative economics.
- Explain that a production possibilities curve (production possibilities frontier) model may be used to show the concepts of scarcity, choice, opportunity cost and a situation of unemployed resources and inefficiency.

Model building in economics

A model can be used to represent a concept from the real world. Economists use models to demonstrate economic principles. An economic model is not unlike any other model you may already be familiar with. Models represent an object or situation from the real world, but do not perfectly re-create the characteristics of the real thing. For example, a model car looks similar to a real car, but you cannot use it to get to work. Likewise, a model of the solar system represents the relationship between the sun and the planets, but the relationships are not to scale nor are they realistic in the scientific sense.

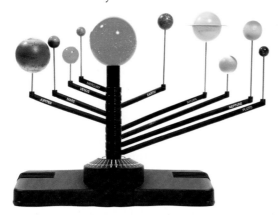

Economics models are not dissimilar to model cars and models of the solar system. Economists will simplify reality in order to analyse human interactions in a model (also referred to as diagrams or graphs in economics).

Ceteris paribus – all else equal

When using models to represent reality, economists usually hold all variables other than those illustrated in the model constant. This allows for a simple analysis of particular economic variables.

The demand diagram is a model used by economists to show the relationship between the price of a particular good and the quantity of that good demanded by consumers. To analyse how consumers respond to a change in the price of a product, economists assume that no other variables (e.g. income of consumers, price of other related products, etc.) are changing. In reality, other variables are constantly changing but economists ignore this in order to focus on how one variable (e.g. consumer demand) responds to a change in another (e.g. price of the product).

The Latin phrase *ceteris paribus* translates as 'other things being equal'. The *ceteris paribus* assumption (the assumption that all other things are unchanging) is an important requirement when examining economic models. Throughout your economics course, economic models will always assume *ceteris paribus* – that no variable other than that under investigation in a particular model is changing.

 Ceteris paribus is a Latin phrase meaning 'other things being equal'. Economists assume *ceteris paribus* when examining certain variables in an economic model. This allows us to easily examine the relationship between one variable and another without complicating our analysis with all the other things that could cause the variable in question to change.

Positive and normative economics

Economists may not always agree on everything. Whether or not an economic statement is purely an expression of factual information or whether it is an expression of values or opinions based on facts determines whether the economic statement is a positive one or a normative one.

Positive economics deals with what is. It focuses on observations and expressions based purely on factual evidence. For instance, it is a fact that when the price of doughnuts rises, the number of doughnuts that consumers demand falls. This is not an issue that economists would find it necessary to debate. In fact, the relationship between the price of a good and the quantity demanded by consumers is so widely agreed upon that it has become an economic law (the law of demand).

 What are the implications of the assumption of *ceteris paribus*? Do other areas of knowledge make a similar assumption? How do we test knowledge claims in economics? Should all knowledge claims in economics be testable? If a claim is not testable, is it meaningless?

Another example of a positive economic statement is that when a country's currency appreciates (gets stronger relative to other countries' currencies), its exports become more expensive to foreign consumers and tend to fall. This is a fact that can be supported using evidence, therefore its statement is an expression of positive economics. All economists agree that this statement is true and there is no room to debate the issue.

However, not every economic statement is irrefutable. Some are more an expression of a particular economist's opinion or the values which that economist holds dear. Consider the statement, 'Doughnuts should be taxed because at their current price they are over-consumed and contribute to obesity in the nation.' This may be true in that doughnuts can cause health problems, but the view that they 'should be taxed' is debatable. Therefore, this statement is normative. Normative economics deals with what *should be* rather than what *is*.

Positive economic analysis examines human interactions through the lens of quantifiable, irrefutable, evidence-based observations. There is no role for values or ethics in the realm of positive economics. Normative economics, on the other hand, allows for the expression of the economist's values or personal views based on the quantifiable evidence observed in a particular market or realm of social interaction.

Examples of positive economic statements

- Unemployment rose by 0.8% last quarter as 250 000 Americans lost their jobs in the public and private sectors.
- Rising pork prices have led to a surge in demand for chicken across China.
- Increased use of public transport reduces congestion on city streets and lowers traffic fatality rates.

These are all statements of fact and each can be supported by evidence based on quantifiable observations of the world.

Examples of normative economic statements

- Unemployment rates are higher among less educated workers, therefore government should include education and job-training programmes in benefits for the nation's unemployed.
- Rising pork prices harm low-income households whose incomes go primarily towards food. Therefore, to slow the rise in food prices, the Chinese government should enforce a maximum price scheme on the nation's pork industry.
- It is the government's obligation to provide public transport options to the nation's people to relieve the negative environmental and health effects of traffic congestion.

These are all statements based on observable, quantifiable variables but each includes an element of opinion or an expression of the economist's values. Each statement expresses what the economist believes should happen based on his or her observations of what is.

The production possibilities curve

The existence of scarcity and the reality that every economic decision involves trade-offs and costs can be illustrated in what will be the first of many economics models you will learn about in this course. The production possibilities curve (PPC) is a model economists employ to demonstrate the fundamental economic concepts you have been reading about so far (Figure 1.2).

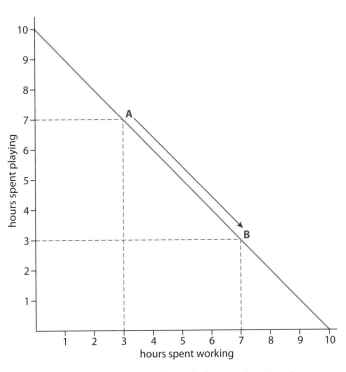

Figure 1.2

Sarah's production possibilities curve.

The PPC in Figure 1.2 illustrates the trade-off Sarah faces in deciding how to use her 10 hours of free time each week. She can spend her free time doing one of two things, playing or working.

Assume that point A represents Sarah's decision in week 1, when she allocates seven hours to playing and three hours to working. Her decision to allocate her limited time in this manner involves an opportunity cost, which is the benefit she would have gained from spending more time working and less time playing.

Assume that point B represents Sarah's decision in week 2, when she has decided to spend seven hours working and only three hours playing. The opportunity cost of working four additional hours is the four fewer hours she gets to spend playing and all the enjoyment she foregoes as a result of her decision.

This simple production possibilities curve demonstrates several concepts fundamental to economics.

- **Scarcity**. Because resources are scarce, there is a limit to the amount of production or consumption an individual (or a nation) can undertake. Time is the scarce resource in Figure 1.2. With only 10 hours of free time, Sarah must decide how to allocate her time among competing activities.
- **Trade-offs and choices**. The two axes in a PPC represent two trade-offs faced by an individual, firm, government or society. The axes may represent any economic activity that can be undertaken by an individual, firm or nation in the employment of its scarce resources. Because we face trade-offs, we must make choices, which involve costs.
- **Opportunity cost**. Nothing is free. More time playing comes at the expense of the benefits from time spent working. Likewise, a nation that chooses to produce a certain good faces costs in the form of the other goods that could have been produced with the same resources.

To learn more about the production possibilities curve, visit www.pearsonhotlinks.com, enter the title or ISBN of this book and select weblink 1.11.

What is a model in economics? What does it do? Does it matter that many of the models we use in economics do not correspond well to reality? What are the limitations of the use of diagrams and charts in economics? How important is it that as students of economics we respect the limitations of a model representing reality?

Other basic economic concepts illustrated by the PPC

The law of increasing opportunity cost

The PPC can be used to illustrate a nation faced with a decision regarding what types of goods to use its scarce resources to produce. The PPC in Figure 1.3 assumes that Country I can produce two goods – pizzas and robots.

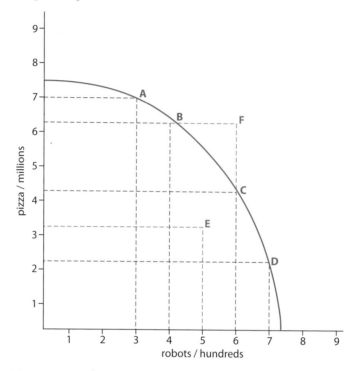

Country I's PPC in Figure 1.3 has a convex shape (it bows out from the origin). The reason for this lies in differences in the production of pizzas and robots. Pizzas and robots require very different resources in their production. Pizzas are land intensive (large amounts of land are needed to grow the ingredients). Pizzas also require a particular type of labour and capital: farmers and cooks need not have advanced degrees and extensive expertise in engineering to grow ingredients and make pizzas. The land and labour resources required to make robots are very different than those for pizza. The type of labour needed is highly skilled and educated. Because Country I's land, capital and labour resources are not equally suitable to making either robots or pizzas, the opportunity cost of increasing production of robots increases in terms of pizzas the more robots are produced.

Notice, for instance, that when robot production increases from 300 to 400 units, the cost of the additional 100 robots is just under one million pizzas (since pizza production falls from 7 million to a little over 6 million). As robot production increases, however, from 600 to 700 units, the additional 100 robots costs Country I around two million pizzas (since pizza output falls from around 4 million to 2 million pizzas).

Why did Country I have to give up twice as many pizzas to increase robot production by one hundred units from 600 to 700 than it did to increase production by one hundred units from 300 to 400? The explanation lies in the fact that as Country I started making robots (between 100 and 400) only the resources best suited for robot design and production were employed. Electrical engineers and highly educated technicians who had been employed in the pizza industry quit making pizzas (which they were never any good at anyway) and started making robots. The land, labour and capital that was best for making pizzas remained employed in the pizza industry, and at first Country I was able to increase its production of robots at a relatively low cost.

However, as robot production intensified, resources were increasingly moved out of pizza production and into the robot industry. To produce 700 robots, highly skilled pizza makers and land better suited for growing wheat and flour and tomatoes and dairy cows had to be shifted into robot production. The cost of robots in terms of pizzas increases the more robots Country I produces. The law of increasing opportunity cost explains why the PPC is bowed outwards from the origin. The law says that as the output of a particular product increases, the opportunity cost of producing additional units rises.

Not all PPCs are bowed outwards. If the two goods represented in a PPC are very similar in their production, requiring similar types of labour, capital and land resources to produce, then the PPC for the two products is a straight line, such as Country I's PPC for pizzas and calzones (Figure 1.4). A calzone is basically a pizza folded in half. Therefore, the opportunity cost of one calzone is always only one pizza, so the PPC is a constant sloping curve.

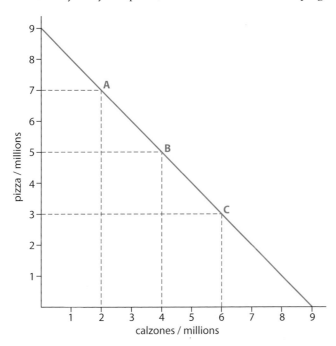

◀ **Figure 1.4**
A PPC with constant opportunity cost.

Efficiency, inefficiency and economic growth

The PPC can also be used to illustrate the economic concepts of efficiency, inefficiency and economic growth. Look again at Figure 1.3. Points A, B, C and D are all on the curve; at each of these points Country I is producing some combination of goods and using its existing resources (land, labour and capital) efficiently. This means that nearly every person of working age who wants a job has a job, the land that can be used for production of pizza ingredients and robot components is being used and the nation's existing capital (factory equipment, ovens, and other tools) is operating at full capacity – no capital is sitting idle. At these points, an increase in *total* output is not possible without an increase in inputs first. A nation achieving its production possibilities is producing at its full-employment level of output.

A nation not achieving full employment of resources is producing at a point *inside* its PPC. If Country I is producing 500 robots and 3.2 million pizzas (point E), it is under-utilizing its land, labour and capital. A country is said to be inefficient if it is producing at a point inside of its PPC. This means that unemployment is likely to be high, land that could be put into

The production possibilities curve, the most basic of economic models, can also be used to show many of the economic concepts you will learn about in this course: unemployment, recession, economic growth, economic development, inflation and deflation.

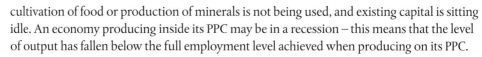

To access Worksheet 1.3 on the production possibilities curve for energy, please visit www.pearsonbacconline.com and follow the onscreen instructions.

Economic growth is an increase in the output of goods and services in a nation over time. Growth can be illustrated as an outward shift of a nation's PPC.

Productivity is the output attributable to each unit of input. Increases in the productivity of land, labour or capital lead to an overall increase in the output of a nation.

cultivation of food or production of minerals is not being used, and existing capital is sitting idle. An economy producing inside its PPC may be in a recession – this means that the level of output has fallen below the full employment level achieved when producing on its PPC.

Clearly the production possibilities curve can also illustrate the possibility of economic growth. A point *outside* the PPC is unattainable given the existing quantity and quality of resources, but it is clearly desirable. At point F in Figure 1.3, Country I would produce and consume 600 robots and over six million pizzas. This is clearly beyond the current production possibilities, but it may be attainable in the future if the economy grows.

Economic growth is defined as an increase in the total output of a nation over time, which is possible if a nation experiences an increase in the quality or the quantity of productive resources. In order to achieve a level of production and consumption corresponding with point F, Country I must increase the amount of land, labour or capital in the country or improve the productivity of these resources.

Productivity is defined as the output attributable per unit of input. If Country I's workers became better at producing pizzas and robots, either through better training and education or through an increase in the quality of the technologies used to produce these goods, then the national output of Country I would grow and the country would move towards point F. Investments in public education by the government or investments in better technology and more capital by the country's businesses could lead to economic growth. Economic growth is an objective that plays a significant role in macroeconomics.

1.5 Central themes in economics

Learning outcomes
- Explain that the economics course will focus on several themes, which include:
  - the extent to which governments should intervene in the allocation of resources
  - the threat to sustainability as a result of the current patterns of resource allocation
  - the extent to which the goal of economic efficiency may conflict with the goal of equity
  - the distinction between economic growth and economic development.
- Examine the assumption of rational economic decision-making.

So far, you have ventured into the field of economics, identified scarcity as the basic problem which economists attempt to address, and looked at the basic questions that economic systems strive to answer. You have also learned a little about the history of economic thought through the words of Adam Smith and learned about the basic model in economics, the production possibilities curve, which illustrates several fundamental economic concepts including scarcity, choice and opportunity cost. You are now going to examine four central themes of economics.

The extent to which governments should intervene in the allocation of resources

Throughout your economics course, you will visit and revisit the debate over the appropriate role of the government in the economy. You know that Adam Smith believed that the government which serves society best is the one that interferes least in the free market interactions of individuals. The *laissez-faire* view of economics believes that competitive markets, composed of individual buyers and sellers with perfect information about the goods, services and resources being bought and sold, will lead to the most efficient and desirable allocation of resources towards the types and amounts of output that benefit society most. Government, argues the *laissez-faire* school of economics, cannot possibly improve on the outcome achieved by the unfettered free market.

The classical *laissez-faire* view of the economy has come under criticism at many points throughout history by those who argue that the free market, left unchecked, results in inefficiencies in the allocation of resources, whereby certain goods are over-produced while others are under-produced. Other criticisms of *laissez-faire* include the perpetuation of poverty, inequality in the distribution of income within and across nations, and involuntary unemployment during the economic slumps that free market economies frequently experience. The critics of *laissez-faire* argue that government intervention in the free market is sometimes necessary to correct the various market failures and to offset the negative effects of macroeconomic slumps caused by falling demand for a nation's output.

One of the most influential economic theorists of the 20th century was Cambridge economist John Maynard Keynes. At the time of the Great Depression (roughly throughout the 1930s), he argued for an active government role in managing the overall level of economic activity in the nation to help achieve certain macroeconomic objectives such as full employment and economic growth. While he believed that competitive markets were necessary and beneficial, he also argued that uncertainty among economic agents would lead to major swings in the overall level of demand in an economy. He believed that, if left unchecked by the government, this would result in economic shocks that contributed to suffering and misery. Keynes therefore believed that government needed to regulate the activities of private firms and individuals and thereby minimize the level of uncertainty in the economy. This would promote an atmosphere of stability in which individuals could participate in the relatively free exchange of goods, services and resources in pursuit of Smith's ideals of freedom and the pursuit of self-gain.

Keynes's theories have an important role in our study of macroeconomics, in which the role of government is a fiercely debated topic, particularly in the aftermath of the Great Recession, as the worldwide economic slump of 2008 and 2009 has come to be known.

During the second half of the 20th century, two schools of economic thought dominated macroeconomics: the *Keynesian* school and the *Neo-classical* school. At the heart of the debate is the issue of freedom *vs* control. Neo-classical economics argues that markets are always more efficient than governments, while the Keynesian school argues for an active government providing a system of regulation and control over the free market.

The threat to sustainability as a result of the current patterns of resource allocation

Another theme central to our study of economics is the issue of sustainability in current patterns of resource allocation. Sustainability can be defined as the capacity to endure. The dominant system of economic organization in the world today is a market system that emphasizes the pursuit of self-interest. One assumption underlying this system is that all individuals are rational, self-interested agents whose ultimate objective is to improve their level of material well-being through increased incomes and consumption. The problem of scarcity, however, leads to an obvious conflict between the objective of increased output and consumption of goods and services and the continuously diminishing quantity of the natural resources needed to produce those goods and services.

To learn more about rational behaviour, visit www.pearsonhotlinks.com, enter the title or ISBN of this book and select weblink 1.12.

Some argue that 'sustainable economic growth' is a contradiction in terms since growth, which in economics means an increase in the output of goods and services over time, necessitates continued exploitation of the natural environment and the resources it provides us. Growth, argue the sceptics, is fundamentally unsustainable.

The 21st century will be characterized by growing concern regarding the effects on the earth's ecosystems, on human and social health and on the biosphere of:

- global economic growth
- the emergence of billions of the world's poor from poverty
- expansion in agricultural and industrial output.

From global warming to deforestation to over-fishing and the loss of biodiversity, the capacity of our economic system to endure must be called into question and the challenges of sustainability addressed directly by today's economics students, who will influence the economic policies of tomorrow. The issue of sustainability and the conflict that arises when the growing economies of the world encounter head-on the worsening problem of scarcity is therefore a major theme of this textbook.

The extent to which the goal of economic efficiency may conflict with the goal of equity

Fundamental to the debate over the role of government in the allocation of resources and output is the extent to which the goal of economic efficiency and the goal of equity can be achieved simultaneously.

Efficiency in economics is defined as a state in which no one can be made better off without making someone else worse off and in which more output cannot be achieved without first increasing the quantity or the quality of inputs. Increased efficiency in the allocation and use of resources ensures that total economic output can be maximized at any given time, presumably resulting in the greatest possible level of material consumption among an economy's people. Efficiency is a worthy goal in this regard, but it may conflict with the goal of equity. In economics, equity is defined as fairness in the distribution of output in a nation. An economic system that strives to maximize efficiency may result in inequality in the distribution of output, a situation deemed by many to be fundamentally inequitable. What's best for society as a whole (efficiency) may appear extremely unfair for certain groups within society (inequitable).

What are the implications of economics being based, ultimately, on human psychology? To what extent should ideas of fairness and justice inform economic thinking?

One objective of economic policy is to increase equality in the distribution of income of a nation. But to achieve this, certain individuals in society will be made worse off because redistribution requires taxing the activities or incomes of those in an economy whose ability to pay is greater. The goal of equity therefore conflicts with the goal of efficiency. This conflict will be revisited throughout this book as we evaluate the effects of various economic policies on individuals and society as a whole.

The distinction between economic growth and economic development

In the final section of this book, attention will turn away from issues relating to the behaviour of individual businesses and households, to the total output, employment and price levels of the economy as a whole. You will look at issues relating to economic development. The distinction between economic growth and economic development is another important theme in your economic studies.

Growth refers to an increase in the total output of goods and services in a nation over time. Economic growth as an objective of economics is justified by the fundamental assumption that more is always better, that increasing the output of stuff results in improvements in the well-being of people in a nation. The idea of economic growth as an end in itself can and should be challenged on many grounds.

You will investigate the concept of economic development and distinguish it from the concept of growth. Development, defined as an improvement in the well-being of a nation's people, accounts for levels of output and consumption of goods and services, and also considers matters relating to quality of life beyond the material realm. Indicators such as life expectancy, literacy rate, child mortality rate, gender and racial equality, and religious and political freedom are all aspects of economic development. In recent years, several areas of economic study have emerged which have shifted focus away from unending increases in production and consumption and instead emphasized the importance of broadening the goal of economic policies to include development indicators. It is no longer universally agreed among economists that more is always better.

Keynes, whose theories will play a major role in this book, believed that economic growth was not an end in itself, but rather a necessary means for achieving a level of material well-being at which society could begin to turn its attention towards other ends such as social harmony. This, Keynes believed, required not only a high income and full employment but, more importantly, a society in which the cultivation of environmental, cultural, religious and ethical values was the main objective, not unending growth. In a speech in Dublin in April 1933, Keynes reflected on economics' traditional focus on economic growth as an end in itself.

We destroy the beauty of the countryside because the unappropriated splendours of nature have no economic value. We are capable of shutting off the sun and the stars because they do not pay a dividend ... Today we suffer disillusion, not because we are poorer ... but because other values seem to have been sacrificed ... unnecessarily. For our economic system is not, in fact, enabling us to exploit to the utmost the possibilities for economic wealth afforded by the progress of our technique ... leading us to feel we might as well have used up the margin in more satisfying ways.

John Maynard Keynes, June 1933

Keynes attempted to focus the study of economics on issues relating to human welfare and economic development, and many contemporary economists have begun to do the same. The distinction between growth and development as means and ends in the economic sphere of human society will therefore form a framework for the evaluation of economic theories and policies throughout this book.

1.6 Theory of knowledge and economics

Economics is a part of group 3 in the International Baccalaureate diploma programme, which means the subject's focus is on individuals and societies. This means you will explore the interactions between humans and their environment in time and place. As a social science, economics explores the interactions between humans in the commercial realm, focusing on the behaviours of households, business firms, and governments in the pursuit of various individual and societal goals.

As with other subject areas in the IB programme, there are a variety of ways in which one can gain knowledge in economics. For example, historical evidence, data collection, experimentation, observation, and inductive and deductive reasoning can all be used to help explain economic behaviours and lead to knowledge claims.

Economics students are required to evaluate these knowledge claims by exploring knowledge issues such as validity, reliability, credibility, certainty, and the individual as well as cultural perspectives.

To access Worksheet 1.4 on rational behaviour, opportunity cost and marginal analysis, please visit www.pearsonbacconline.com and follow the onscreen instructions.

The relationship between economics and theory of knowledge (TOK) is of great importance and fundamental to the diploma programme. Throughout the curriculum for both higher and standard level economics, you should be able to reflect critically on the various ways of knowing, and on the scientific and other methods used in economics. In so doing, you will become one of the 'inquiring, knowledgeable and caring young people' of the IB mission statement.

During the economics course a number of issues will arise that highlight the relationships between TOK and economics. Possible theory of knowledge discussion questions are suggested in most chapters, offering you a starting point for analyzing the knowledge claims made in economics. You and your fellow students are encouraged to explore further questions of your own.

What are the roles played by abstract reasoning and concrete evidence in constructing economic theory?

What is the role of emotion and creativity in economics?

Is there a different method of justifying qualitative rather than quantitative knowledge claims? If so, does this lead to one or other being inherently more reliable?

What is meant by 'rationality' in economics? Are there different types of 'economic rationality'?

If economics studies actual human behaviour, should it also study irrational human behaviour?

To access Quiz 1, an interactive, multiple-choice quiz on this chapter, please visit www.pearsonbacconline.com and follow the onscreen instructions.

PRACTICE QUESTIONS

1 **a** 'Economics is primarily concerned with the allocation of scarce resources which have alternative uses.' Use a production possibility curve to explain this statement.
(10 marks) [AO2]

   b Discuss the view that government is more effective in the allocation of scarce resources than the free market.
(15 marks) [AO3]
© International Baccalaureate Organization 2003 (part **a** only)

2 **a** The choice between military products and the provision of healthcare illustrates the problem of 'opportunity cost'. Explain the nature of this problem, using a production possibility curve to help you.
(10 marks) [AO2]

   b To what extent does the production possibilities curve model accurately represent the scarcity faced by less developed countries in the world today?
(15 marks) [AO3]
© International Baccalaureate Organization 1999 (part **a** only)

2 COMPETITIVE MARKETS: DEMAND AND SUPPLY

2.1 The nature of markets

Learning outcomes
• Outline the meaning of the term 'market'.

◀ Direct exchange of cash for goods in a meat market.

In most languages, the term 'market' has connotations of a direct and tangible experience. One imagines buying fruit from a local grocery, or meat from a nearby butcher. These are markets in the traditional sense, but in the modern world a market can be defined more broadly as any instance where buyers and sellers come together for the exchange of goods and services.

 A market is any place, physical or virtual, where the buyers and sellers of goods and services meet.

These interactions can happen at any time or place. Direct buying and selling usually happens in a specific place, such as when trading your cash for a farmer's fresh eggs. But markets can also operate indirectly, when buyers and sellers communicate remotely. In commodity markets, buyers can purchase massive amounts of basic goods like coffee or wheat at international meetings with representatives of the coffee farmers, but never meeting the actual producers. This indirect buying and selling may also happen online – for example, when a share trader buys a stock that you have offered up for sale; in this case, the buyer and seller have no contact at all.

Markets can be local, where buyers and sellers come from the surrounding area. They can be national, where the participants are from within the market country. And they can be international, where the market participants come from any country in the world. While the distinction between these can be blurred at times, some obvious examples of each can be noted. A corner shop like a bakery or dairy, selling locally produced goods, would qualify as a local market. National markets tend to be those limited by the laws and customs policies of national governments. Labour markets, as governed by labour laws, make a reasonable example. Healthcare in the US is largely overseen by national regulation and would also fit the national market profile. The markets for commodities such as steel, oil, gas, corn, wheat or cotton may have local producers with international buyers. Likewise, the corner shop in New York city may well be selling imported English biscuits, while the vast national market for healthcare devices may see the production of goods from China, India or Europe.

EXERCISES

The great virtue of a free market system is that it does not care what colour people are; it does not care what their religion is; it only cares whether they can produce something you want to buy. It is the most effective system we have discovered to enable people who hate one another to deal with one another and help one another.

Milton Friedman

---

1   Assess the validity of Friedman's statement.
2   Cite examples where Friedman's assertion could be true, and others where it is not.

To learn more about product markets, visit www.pearsonhotlinks. com, enter the title or ISBN of this book and select weblink 2.1.

Another way to think of markets is to distinguish between product markets and resource markets. Economists view product markets as the purchase of consumer goods and services directly from producers (Figure 1.1, page 8). In the resource market, businesses make payments to the owners of resources such as land, labour, capital and entrepreneurship. In a market economy, the recipients of these payments are private individuals or households.

Competitive markets

Markets are considered free or competitive to the extent that private individuals and firms can openly attempt to win business away from each other in the hopes of earning greater profits. Free markets have a long history. Ever since labour has been divided within groups, there has been an incentive to trade the products of specialization. While early forms of exchange were done by bartering goods, eventually societies found that exchanging money was often more convenient. All the while, the jobs performed by the individual have grown more specific.

To learn more about specialization, visit www. pearsonhotlinks.com, enter the title or ISBN of this book and select weblink 2.2.

Improvements in agriculture, the growth of colonialism, and eventually the development of industrialization further expanded the depth and breadth of economic activity. A move away from government intervention in the economy occurred in the 18th century, as enlightenment ideas of reason and liberalism were applied to economics by philosophers such as Adam Smith (Chapter 1). With greater rewards at stake, this move provided greater incentives for private business to compete on the basis of innovation and productivity, as well as market dominance. Today's sophisticated global markets rest on this foundation, and on the general principle that competitive markets bring diversity of goods, efficiencies, and generally greater wealth for all.

The competitive market is the market for a good with large numbers of buyers and sellers, where the single seller has very little or no market power.

Market structures

When examining the nature of competitive markets, it is helpful to keep in mind the categories of actors who interact in the market. A *firm* is an individual or organization that combines the factors of production to create and sell goods and services on the market.

An *industry* is made up of all the firms engaged in the same market activity. For example, a number of firms such as Toshiba, Hewlett-Packard, Dell and Lenovo sell their products in the personal-and-business-computing industry.

Industries have identifiable and distinct characteristics that have allowed economists to categorize them into four general market structure groups:

- perfect competition
- monopolistic competition
- oligopoly
- monopoly.

There are four criteria by which an industry is categorized as a particular market structure.

- **The number of firms in the industry**. This tells us how many competitors are fighting for the same customers. It is logical to assume that more firms mean more competition, more consumer sovereignty and less market power exerted by the firm.
- **A firm's level of market power**. This is the ability of the firm to control the price of its product. In other words, to what degree can the firm set ever-increasing prices for its goods? When there are few competitors and few substitutes, a firm will have quite a lot of market power. Consumers may well have less power or sovereignty as a result.
- **The degree of product differentiation between goods offered by different firms**. This can tell us something about the nature of the competition in the industry. Where the items offered are identical (homogeneous) and completely substitutable, firms often have little choice but to sell at the market price and therefore seek profit by lowering costs. When firms can convince consumers that their product is actually better in important ways, it successfully differentiates itself from competitors.
- **The ease of exit and entry**. This can tell us important things about the nature of competition. When an industry grows profitable and can prevent other firms from joining in, it is enjoying the benefits of some kind of barriers to entry. Barriers to entry such as high entry costs or major technological impediments will reduce competition entering the market and stop the erosion of profits.

Perfect competition

Perfectly (or purely) competitive markets have the following traits.

- There are very many firms in the industry; no individual firm's decisions can influence the market to any significant degree.
- An individual firm's decisions about output reflect only a tiny portion of the overall market. Therefore, firms in the perfectly competitive market do not influence overall supply. This reduces their power to influence the market price.
- Firms in the industry produce completely identical products. These goods act as perfect substitutes for each other. So, from the consumers' perspective, the seller is unimportant, and adds no value to the good itself. As a result, as well as being responsible for only a tiny portion of the overall market, the individual firm has no real market power, and exerts no influence on the price set by the market.
- Firms can enter or exit the market very easily, with effectively no barriers to entry or exit.

 A market is perfectly competitive if there are a large number of firms producing identical products facing identical production costs and in which there are no barriers to entry or exit.

Perfect competition has always been considered highly theoretical, although some markets approach perfect competition and have many of these qualities. Such markets include international markets for commodities: rice, coffee, corn, and wheat; metals like gold and iron; financial instruments such as bonds, stocks, and currencies. In most of these cases, the standards of perfect competition apply: there are many small firms, selling homogeneous products with almost no power to set the price in the market.

Coffee, for example, is the single most valuable traded commodity in the world. However, a single coffee grower in Brazil is one among tens or even hundreds of thousands of other producers. As a commodity, coffee is assumed to be basically the same product wherever it is produced. The market price is determined by the interaction of buyers and sellers at commodity exchanges in New York. This means that individual growers in, say, Brazil are producing coffee beans whose price they cannot control, and which are considered perfectly substitutable for someone else's coffee beans. They have no impact on the supply or price of coffee. In these respects, a coffee grower has many of the attributes of a perfect competitor.

Monopolistic competition

Monopolistic competition fits the criteria in the following ways.

- There are many firms in the industry, though not as many as in perfect competition.
- Any firm's decisions about output will have little influence on the overall market. Changes in output will not influence the market price.
- Firms produce relatively differentiated products. While the goods are fundamentally similar, producers can alter aspects of service, quality, and packaging. These differences can be accentuated by advertising.
- There are relatively low barriers to entry, so firms can enter or exit the industry without incurring major costs.

Examples of monopolistic competition seem to be everywhere: restaurants, jewellers, furniture stores, clothing stores, bakeries, and nail salons. Perceptions of product differentiation give firms the power to charge higher than the usual price for better-than-standard versions of the same good. For monopolistic competitors, the power of the company's brand reflects the market power they hold in the market.

A market is monopolistically competitive if there are many firms producing differentiated products and in which there are no barriers to entry or exit.

A trip down Madison Avenue in New York or Oxford Street in London would showcase the power of branding to differentiate one seller's good from another in the fashion industry. Essentially similar goods like T-shirts can command wildly different prices depending on whether the seller is Sweden's H&M ($18), America's Brooks Brothers ($40), or Italy's Gucci ($215). To different degrees, all of these firms have been able to increase their market power, increasing the price they are able to charge for their goods. At the same time, their power is not limitless. They still face competition from an abundance of significantly less expensive substitutes.

Oligopoly

Again using the criteria for market structures, oligopolies can be identified by the following traits.

- There are only a few firms in the industry, and these firms tend to dominate the market.
- Because only a few firms are selling to most of the market, these firms have significant control over price, especially if they cooperate in pricing and output decisions.
- Products are can be homogeneous or heterogeneous, depending on the industry.
- Barriers to entry are high. High industry profits can be protected and maintained through these barriers to competition.

The fewer the competitors, the more likely they are to command significant market power in their industry. Economists have established standards for determining the degree of market power for oligopolistic industries. These are called concentration ratios, which measure the market share of the top few firms. A CR4, for example, would measure how much of the market was controlled by the top four firms. The higher the percentage, the greater the concentration of market power between those four firms. The higher the concentration of market power, the greater is the temptation to work together on price and output decisions.

With even a small number of firms, nearly all oligopolies tend towards this kind of interdependence in their pricing and output decisions. The industry will often earn significantly higher profits if acting together and limiting supply, rather than competing on price and producing more. This interdependence can lead to blatant collusion, an anti-competitive activity that is often considered illegal. Furthermore, oligopolies differ from the other forms of competition in that firms will act strategically, weighing the actions and reactions of the other firms.

In the case of differentiated goods, oligopolies exist in industries such as breakfast cereal, car rental, airline, and pharmaceutical companies. For relatively undifferentiated goods, oligopolies exist in some metal industries like copper and aluminium, or cement production. These oligopolies can be local (e.g. cement production). They can be national (e.g. breakfast cereal and car rental). And they can be international (e.g. copper and aluminium).

Monopoly

Monopolies fit the criteria as follows.

- There is only one firm in the industry, so that firm dominates the market.
- The firm sells to the entire market. It has exceptional power to control output and price, although this power is constrained by the limits of consumer demand.
- The goods produced by the monopolist have no substitutes. It is not possible to buy them from anyone else.
- High barriers to entry exist, protecting the monopolist from competition and ensuring long-term profits.

Monopolies appear in a variety of forms. Sometimes the barriers to entry are legal barriers that recognize the need for monopolies to exist as a means of lowering costs. For example, local monopolies on water and power might exist because giving each residence the choice of different providers could be dramatically more expensive. (Imagine that a city's water system offered several providers for each home. In theory, each company would require separate pumping facilities and its own distinct distribution system of pipes throughout the city.)

A major national industry can be a monopoly. The sugar, steel, and oil monopolies of the late 19th century in the US are famous examples. More recently, in the 1990s Microsoft was found guilty of monopolizing the market for operating systems by the US and European Union (EU) courts. More recently still, the predominance of Google in the market for internet searching has led to concerns among EU investigators. Table 2.1 summarizes the criteria used to determine market structures.

An oligopoly is a market where a few sellers dominate the market for an identical or differentiated good, and where there are significant barriers to entry.

People of the same trade seldom meet together, even for merriment and diversion, but the conversation ends in a conspiracy against the public, or in some contrivance to raise prices.
Adam Smith, *The Wealth of Nations*, 1776

A monopoly is a market where one firm dominates the market for a good that has no substitutes and where significant barriers to entry exist.

TABLE 2.1 CRITERIA AND MARKET STRUCTURES					
	Number of firms	**Market power**	**Level of differentiation**	**Barriers to entry**	**Examples**
Perfect competition	very many	none	homogeneous; no substitutes	none	agricultural commodities (e.g. wheat, coffee)
Monopolistic competition	many	varies, generally little	differentiated or heterogeneous	relatively insignificant	mechanics, restaurants, books
Oligopoly	few, interdependent	significant	heterogeneous or homogeneous, depending on industry	significant	airlines, breakfast cereal, cell phone networks
Monopoly	one	exceptional	none, no close substitutes	major	local utilities

Market structure and market power

We can attempt to summarize some of the characteristics of market structure types with regard to the power each individual firm can wield on the market. This concept is illustrated in Figure 2.1, where the industries are ranked on the amount of power an individual firm has in relation to the industry. On the bottom are the most competitive industries, perfect competition, where there's theoretically no market power over price. At the top, with the most market power, is monopoly, where the firm constitutes the entire industry, and where firms have extraordinary power over the price of their product.

It is no coincidence that competition is inversely related to market power. Where firms have to fight each other for business, profits are likely to be driven down. Where firms stand alone, or together against the consumer, the desire to maximize profits compels firms to exert their market power.

Figure 2.1
Degrees of market power of firms in different market structures.

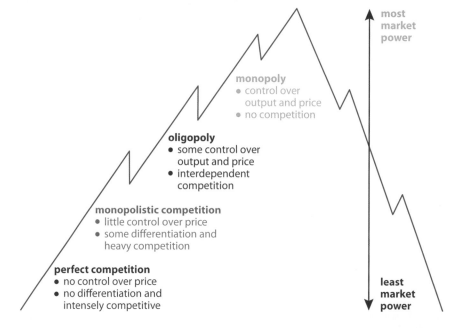

- most market power
- **monopoly**
  - control over output and price
  - no competition
- **oligopoly**
  - some control over output and price
  - interdependent competition
- **monopolistic competition**
  - little control over price
  - some differentiation and heavy competition
- **perfect competition**
  - no control over price
  - no differentiation and intensely competitive
- least market power

EXERCISES

You can always get sympathy by using the word 'small'. With little industries, you feel as you do about a little puppy.

Frances Perkins, US Secretary of Labor 1933–45

Consider the quote above. Using the terms and concepts you have just read about and your own ideas, answer the following questions.

3   Do you believe that, in business, bigger is always better?

4   Based on what you've learned so far, do you think smaller businesses provide better products and services to consumers?

5   To what extent do you agree with Perkins, that the public has too much sympathy for small business?

2.2 Demand

Every market transaction involves a buyer and a seller. The economic concept of demand takes the consumer perspective, examining what motivates and limits buyers in any given market. More specifically, consumers can be private households in the market for end-user consumer goods and services in the product market. Businesses also act as consumers in the product and resource market. Demand is defined as the quantity of a good or service that a consumer or group of consumers are willing and able to purchase at a given price, during a particular time period. Note that the quantity of demand is limited to those who are both willing and able to buy the good.

 Demand is the quantity of a good or service that consumers are willing and able to buy at a given price during a specific time period.

Individual demand

Let's start with the individual consumer. We can determine one person's demand for potato chips in a given year. A *demand schedule* is a list of prices and quantities that show the amount demanded at each price for a given time period. Table 2.2 shows the individual potato chip demand schedule for one week. For example, at a price of $2.50, five bags would be purchased.

These can be plotted as a graph to give us an individual *demand curve* (Figure 2.2).

Figure 2.2
Demand curve: potato chips.

TABLE 2.2 DEMAND SCHEDULE: POTATO CHIPS	
Price of potato chips (P) / $	**Quantity of potato chips demanded per week (Q)**
2.50	5
2.00	10
1.50	15
1.00	20
0.50	25

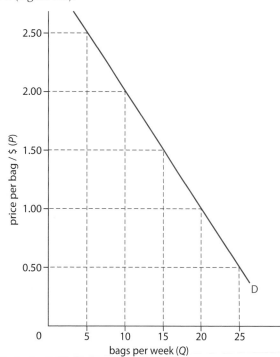

The law of demand

There appears to be a distinct pattern between the changes in price and the changes in quantity. As price declines, the quantity demanded for chips increases. This demonstrates one of the most important concepts of economics, the *law of demand*. The law of demand states that as price increases, less of a good is demanded. At the same time, as price decreases, more of a good is demanded.

The term *ceteris paribus* is a Latin term meaning that we are holding all other variables constant or frozen, while we examine how different prices change the amount demanded (Chapter 1, page 11). Many other things can influence any decision to buy goods. Holding those factors constant permits us to isolate one variable (price) and quantify the effect a change in price has on another variable (the quantity demanded).

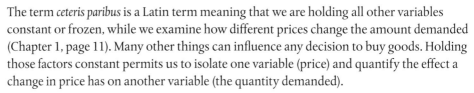

The law of demand states that as the price of a good increases, the quantity demanded of the good decreases. The converse is also true: as the price of a good decreases, the quantity demanded of that good increases.

For example, consider a school selling potato chips at a weekend sports championship tournament, priced at $1 per bag. When the tournament is over, 300 bags have been sold. So, we can say the demand for potato chips for this period was a quantity of 300 at $1 per bag, *ceteris paribus*. If we were graphing the overall demand for potato chips, this price and quantity would mark one of the points of the demand curve.

The law of demand implies a negative or indirect relationship between the two variables of price and quantity demanded. As a result, most demand curves have a downward sloping shape. This concept rises to the level of a 'law' in economics because it conforms closely to everyday reality. As individuals, we are less likely to buy any good as the price rises (exempting, for the moment, speculative goods like gold or company stocks, which may be bought with the expectation that they could be re-sold at a higher price). As the price goes up, our common sense (and budgets) generally tell us to economize and buy less. And the reverse tends to be true as well. When the price of something declines, we grow less concerned about the price and may buy a little more of it as a result, and perhaps others will start to switch to it also, increasing the amount demanded.

The following are some of the factors that underlie the law of demand.

- **The income effect**. Real income refers to income that is adjusted for price changes, and implies the actual buying power of a consumer. As the price of a good decreases, the quantity demanded increases because consumers now have more real income to spend. With more buying power, they sometimes choose to buy more of the same product.

- **The substitution effect**. As the price of a good decreases, consumers switch from other substitute goods to this good because its price is comparatively lower.

- **The law of diminishing marginal utility**. This law states that as we consume additional units of something, the satisfaction (utility) we derive for each additional unit (marginal unit) grows smaller (diminishes).

The law of diminishing marginal utility does *not* state that extra consumption causes a decline in total satisfaction. It merely states that, in this instance, a second or third bag of potato chips will be less satisfying than the first bag. It may still be delicious and add to one's total level of benefit, but the *rate* at which it satisfies has dropped from the first to the second and third bags.

For example, if satisfaction were measured in units of utility, one might say that the first bag was 10 utils, but the second bag only 8 utils. Still satisfying, but not as much as the first bag. The third consumed would provide the consumer with a smaller number of utils, and so on. In an extreme case, it is possible that a consumer eating repeated bags would find that some future bag would produce negative satisfaction, making them ill.

Why, then, would consumers buy extra bags? It is logical that a consumer would only buy a second or third unit of a good when the price was lower, reflecting their lower utility for extra units of the good. So at lower prices, more are demanded.

Figure 2.3 shows how a graph can reflect the law of diminishing marginal utility, and how the relationship mirrors that shown in the demand curve in Figure 2.2. The theory of marginal benefit says that the price we are willing to pay for a good is a reasonable approximate measure of our satisfaction of the good – that is, our benefit. If we are willing to buy 10 bags of chips at a price of $2, then we are signalling to the world that our benefit is at least $2 from the 10th bag.

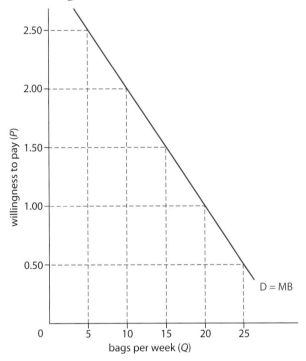

◀ **Figure 2.3**
Willingness to pay, marginal benefit.

The marginal benefit is the additional utility or satisfaction derived by an increase or a decrease in the amount of an item consumed or an activity enjoyed.

Because a demand curve reflects what we are willing to pay for a good, it is an approximate reflection of the marginal benefit (MB) we receive from consuming additional units of a good. If our consumer were to consume an 11th bag of chips, we would have to assume that his or her satisfaction from it would be less than $2-worth, and that the only way he or she would buy more than 10 bags is if the price were lowered to something below $2. Thus we see the concept of diminishing marginal utility at work in the everyday demand curve.

To learn more about the law of demand, visit www.pearsonhotlinks.com, enter the title or ISBN of this book and select weblink 2.3.

EXERCISES

6   Create a table showing the demand schedule for a product you consume. Using the figures from that table, create a demand curve.

7   Explain an example where you would demand more (or less) quantity of the product as a result of the income effect. Show this on your diagram as a movement from an original point A, to a new point B on the curve.

8   Explain an example where you would demand more (or less) quantity of the product as a result of the substitution effect. Show this on your diagram as a movement from an original point A, to a new point C on the curve.

9   Write an explanation of your downsloping demand curve in terms of the law of diminishing marginal utility.

Individual demand and market demand

If what we have seen so far is merely the demand of one person for potato chips over a single week, then what would the demand for a whole group look like? To get the total market demand for a good we take the sum of all the individual demand curves for the same good. Therefore, if we started with the demand for consumer X, and added it to the demand for an additional consumer Y, we would have the market demand for potato chips between those two people (Figure 2.4).

Figure 2.4

Individual demand to market demand: **a** consumer X; **b** consumer Y; **c** consumers X + Y + all others.

If consumer X were to buy 5 bags at $2.50 as shown on Figure 2.4a, and consumer Y were to buy 10 at $2.50 as shown on Figure 2.4b, then the market demand together would be 15 bags at a price of $2.50. At a price of $2.00, consumer X would buy 10, consumer Y would buy 14, and the market demand would be 24. This summation continues at every price until the market demand for potato chips is complete (Figure 2.4c).

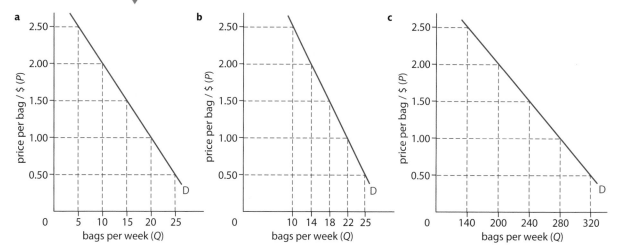

Note that the demand curve for consumer Y is steeper than that for consumer X. (This is because each has a different elasticity, a concept covered in Chapter 4.) However, the slope is still downwards, reflecting the law of demand.

2.3 Determinants of demand

Determinants of demand are the non-price variables that influence the demand for a product.

Learning outcomes

- Explain how factors including changes in income (in the cases of normal and inferior goods), preferences, prices of related goods (in the cases of substitutes and complements) and demographic changes may change demand.
- Distinguish between movements along the demand curve and shifts of the demand curve.
- Draw diagrams to show the difference between movements along the demand curve and shifts of the demand curve.

Until now, we have held constant (*ceteris paribus*) all of the other factors (variables) that could influence the demand for goods so that we could exclusively examine the effect of price changes on the amount of demand. All of those other factors can be referred to as the non-price determinants of demand, the variables that will cause demand for a good to increase or decrease.

Shift in demand and movement along a demand curve

One significant difference between changes in price and changes in the determinants of demand is that a change in price will cause only *a movement along* the demand curve. In Figure 2.5a, a change in the market price from $1.50 to $2.50 causes a movement along the demand curve and a decrease in the *quantity demanded* from 15 to 5.

However, when the non-price determinants of demand change, there is a *shift* of the entire demand curve. The quantity demanded will change at each price. In Figure 2.5b, the initial demand is indicated by curve D. If one of the determinants of demand were to change and cause an increase in demand, the new demand curve would be D_1, a shift outwards or to the right. More is being demanded at every price. For example, at $1.50, where once only 15 were demanded, now a quantity of 20 are demanded. The same is true at all prices, all because of a change in the *ceteris paribus* variables for potato chip demand. The same process works in reverse as well. If demand were to decrease, then there would be smaller quantities demanded at each price and a shift of the demand curve backwards or left would occur.

 A change in price causes a change in *quantity demanded*, with the corresponding movement along the curve, not an *increase or decrease in demand*. We use this latter phrase when referring to a shift of the demand curve, to right or left.

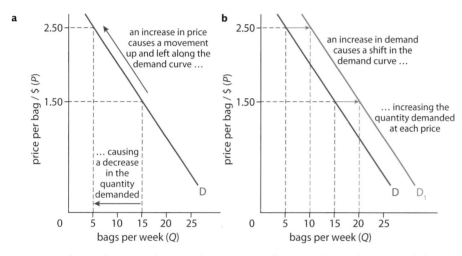

◀ **Figure 2.5**
a Movement along the demand curve; **b** shift of the demand curve.

Figure 2.6 shows the general cases of movements along the demand curve and changes in overall demand.

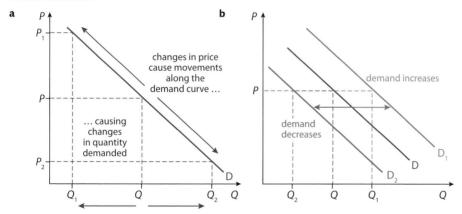

◀ **Figure 2.6**
a Movements along a demand curve; **b** shifts of demand.

Non-price determinants of demand

The most important determinants of demand include:
* income
* price of related goods

- taste and preferences
- expectations of future prices and income
- number of potential buyers.

Lesser but still noteworthy determinants include:
- demographic change
- government policy
- seasonal change.

All these determinants are discussed below.

Income

People tend to increase their spending when their income improves. But whether an increase in income actually increases demand for any particular good depends on whose income rises, and on their relationship to that good.

Normal goods

These are goods for which demand increases as income rises and falls as income falls. Examples of normal goods would be automobiles, cinema tickets and restaurant meals.

This principle is dependent on the income for a particular population. The relatively poor, given in increase in incomes, may view bicycles as a normal good, while richer populations would not.

The demand for restaurant meals is shown in Figure 2.7: an increase in income for normal goods shifts the demand curve to the right. This increases the demand for restaurant meals at every price.

A normal good is a good for which the demand increases as consumer income increases, and for which demand decreases as consumer income decreases.

Figure 2.7
Normal goods: restaurant meals.

To learn more about normal goods, visit www. pearsonhotlinks.com, enter the title or ISBN of this book and select weblink 2.4.

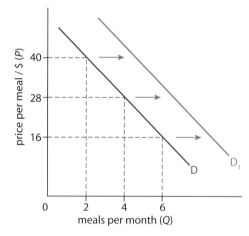

An inferior good is one for which the demand decreases as consumer income increases, and for which the demand increases as consumer income decreases.

To learn more about inferior goods, visit www. pearsonhotlinks.com, enter the title or ISBN of this book and select weblink 2.5.

Inferior goods

These are goods for which demand decreases as income rises and increases as income falls. Inferior goods are generally considered to be a cheaper alternative to higher quality goods. Examples of inferior goods could be, for middle income and richer populations, bicycles and bus tickets. Other typical examples include raw food ingredients like baking flour and millet, since richer consumers are more likely to buy the finished product. Previously used goods like used cars and clothing are also good examples. In these cases, an increase in income would result in a shift of the demand curve backwards or to the left.

Price of related goods

Goods may be substitutes for each other, complementary to each other, or not related at all.

Substitute goods

These are goods that one might easily use in place of another. Because they are so similar, an increase in the price of one may lead consumers to switch consumption to the substitute. Therefore, the price of one good and the demand for a substitute have a positive relationship. As the price of one increases, demand for the other increases. There are many examples among branded goods such as fizzy drinks, or fast-food hamburger stores. Other examples include margarine and butter, buses and train travel, and chicken and beef.

Figure 2.8 shows how an increase in the price of fizzy drink C (Figure 2.8a) causes an increase in the demand for its substitute, fizzy drink P (Figure 2.8b). The demand curve for the latter moves to the right, increasing the amount demanded at every price.

 A substitute good (demand) is one for which demand will increase when the price of another good increases. Demand for a substitute good will decrease when the price of its substitute decreases.

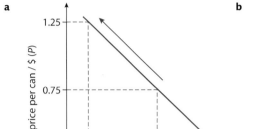

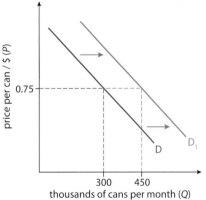

 Figure 2.8
Price of related goods: demand substitution. **a** Fizzy drink C; **b** Fizzy drink P.

 To learn more about substitutes, visit www.pearsonhotlinks.com, enter the title or ISBN of this book and select weblink 2.6.

Complementary goods

These are goods that are typically purchased and consumed together. Therefore an increase in the price of a complementary good will appear to the consumer as an increase in the price of enjoying the combined experience of both goods. As a result, the demand for the complementary good will decrease. Examples include goods such as DVD players and DVDs, computers and printers, cameras and memory cards.

In Figure 2.9, a decrease in the price of digital cameras, shown as a movement along the curve (Figure 2.9a), causes an increase in the demand for memory cards (Figure 2.9b). The demand curve for memory cards shifts forwards, or to the right, reflecting an increase in the amount of demand for memory cards at every price.

Complementary goods are typically consumed together, so the demand for one is decreased by the price increase of the other.

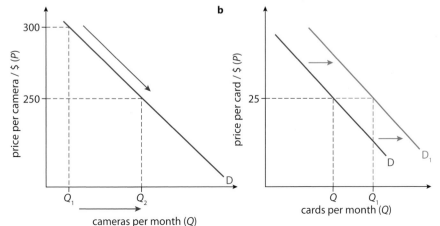

Figure 2.9
Price of related goods: complementary goods. **a** Digital cameras; **b** memory cards.

 To learn more about complements, visit www.pearsonhotlinks.com, enter the title or ISBN of this book and select weblink 2.7.

Taste and preferences

Demand changes with consumer tastes and preferences. Goods become more or less popular because of fashion, current events, and word-of-mouth recommendations between friends or co-workers.

Expectations of future prices and income

Consumers think and act according to the information they receive about the world. Sometimes consumers believe that the price of a good, or their own income, will change in the near future. This can influence their decisions about buying particular goods.

Expectation of future prices

If consumers believe that the price of a good is likely to climb rather quickly, they will be inclined to purchase more immediately. This means that an expectation of higher future prices will cause consumers to buy more now (an increase in demand now, a shift to the right). An expectation that prices will decline soon is likely to cause consumers to defer their purchases until the product becomes cheaper (a decrease in demand now, a shift to the left).

Expectation of future income

If consumers are buying in an economic climate of high growth, steadily rising wages, surging business investment, and relatively low unemployment, they may reasonably conclude that their future incomes will rise, and thus consume more. This would shift demand for most goods to the right. The reverse can be true, of course, as a recession with rising unemployment and decreasing wages can create an atmosphere of pessimism, discouraging consumers from buying goods. This is called a lack of consumer confidence. In this case, demand for most goods is likely to shift to the left.

Number of potential buyers

All businesses hope to market their goods to the widest audience possible. New markets increase potential demand. In the last two decades, many companies have relocated major operations to China partly because they hope to sell their product in the world's largest newly opened market. All of these companies are attempting to increase the number of potential buyers, because more buyers means more demand and a shift to the right of the demand curve for their goods. Correspondingly, a decrease in the potential number of buyers shrinks demand. For example, if a trade restriction were to prevent the importing of Japanese electronics into China, demand for the Japanese electronics would drop.

Demographic change

Demand can change with major shifts in the age structure, income distribution or other demographic traits. For example, a spike in birth rate creates a disproportionately large number of people in a similar age bracket, so the national demand may be skewed towards producing goods and services for that group. When the US baby-boomer generation (born between 1946 and 1964) grew to be of parenting age, a vast increase in childcare-related products flooded the market. As the same population grows into retirement and old age, it is likely that the product market will respond with more products servicing their age group (e.g. healthcare services, prescription drugs).

Demand can also be affected by the distribution of income. If the share of national income shifts towards the rich, the sellers of luxury goods will see their demand increase. Another example of demographic change is immigration patterns. If immigration increases, so will the demand for goods associated with that population, most obviously food items and other products with strong cultural ties to the immigrant population.

Government policy

Changes in taxation and subsidy policies can have an impact on demand. For example, if the government were to increase income taxes, it might cause a decrease in overall consumption as households have less income available to spend. Other policy changes, like restriction and regulation of behaviour and product safety, can also affect demand. Bar owners in many countries feared that government restrictions on smoking in public would reduce their business (although it may also possibly improve it). In Ireland, introducing a tax on plastic shopping bags increased demand for cloth reusable bags.

Seasonal change

Changes from one season to another may increase demand for particular goods. Snow recreation equipment, from snowmobiles to snowboards, is likely to increase in demand during the winter months, while swimsuits and sandals sell more during the summer.

To access Worksheet 2.1 on luxury goods, please visit www.pearsonbacconline.com and follow the onscreen instructions.

To access Worksheet 2.2 on demand, please visit www.pearsonbacconline.com and follow the onscreen instructions.

To learn more about the determinants of demand, visit www.pearsonhotlinks.com, enter the title or ISBN of this book and select weblink 2.8.

EXERCISES

10 Consider these headlines:

  i A summer heatwave affects the market for electric fans.

  ii The price of toy airplanes increases.

  iii A formerly communist country is now eligible to buy cars from the rest of the world.

  iv Consumers are expecting the price of beef to rise significantly in the coming weeks.

  v Diamond sellers are worried about the impact of the recession.

  vi The price of toothpaste drops unexpectedly.

  vii As population grows older, the market for bicycles is changing.

  For each headline:

    a state whether there is a shift or a movement along the demand curve

    b state the kind of shift

    c create a diagram to demonstrate the shift

    d identify the determinant that caused the shift.

2.4 Linear demand functions (HL only)

Learning outcomes

- Explain a demand function (equation) of the form $Q_D = a - bP$.
- Plot a demand curve from a linear function (e.g. $Q_D = 60 - 5P$).
- Identify the slope of the demand curve as the slope of the demand function $Q_D = a - bP$, that is $-b$ (the coefficient of P).
- Outline why, if the a term changes, there will be a shift of the demand curve.
- Outline how a change in b affects the steepness of the demand curve.

Demand for a good can be expressed using mathematical functions. These functions are simplifications of real-world relationships. In reality, there are likely to be many other factors that influence the demand for any particular good. However, these functions provide a more detailed understanding of how demand theory works. Demand functions demonstrate a negative relationship between price and quantity and are graphically represented by downward sloping lines, reflecting the inverse relationship between price and quantity observed by the law of demand.

Typical demand function

A typical demand function looks like this:

$$Q_D = a - bP$$

Where:

Q_D represents the quantity demanded

a represents the autonomous level of demand or the quantity demanded if the price were zero

b represents the change in quantity demanded resulting from a change in price – it is negative, which reflects the fact that quantity demanded changes inversely with the price

P represents the price of a single item

For example, take the demand for cappuccinos in a small town in a single day. The demand function for cappuccinos can be expressed as:

$$Q_D = 600 - 50P$$

The *a* value in this function is 600. This is called the autonomous level of demand, because it represents the number of cappuccinos demanded irrespective of the price. In other words, even if the price were zero, 600 cappuccinos would be demanded in this town. The *a* value will change if any of the determinants of demand for cappuccinos changes.

For instance, if the price of tea (a substitute for cappuccino) rises, consumers will demand more cappuccinos irrespective of the price, and the *a* value will increase. The demand curve shifts to the right, or 'up', when the *a* value rises; it shifts to the left, or 'down', when *a* decreases.

As the coefficient of *P*, the *b* value (50 in our demand function above) tells us the change in quantity demanded resulting from a change in the price of cappuccinos; *b* will therefore determine the slope of the demand curve. In our case, an increase in the price of cappuccinos to $1 would lead to a decrease (notice the negative sign!) in the quantity demanded by 50 drinks. A change in the value of *b* will change the steepness of the demand curve.

If the price were 0, 600 cappuccinos would be demanded. This tells us the *x*-intercept, the point where the demand curve meets the *x*-axis. It can also be called the Q-intercept for demand, because quantity is always on the *x*-axis for both supply and demand. So, for this demand function, the Q-intercept for demand is 600.

Let's now assume the price of a cappuccino is $10. (An expensive cup, but some consumers may be addicted.) At this price, the quantity demanded is:

$$Q_D = 600 - 50(10) = 600 - 500 = 100$$

At the high price of $10, consumers will demand only 100 cappuccinos. According to the law of demand, a decrease in the price should lead to an increase in the quantity of cappuccinos demanded. To test this, see what happens when cappuccinos sell for only $8:

$$Q_D = 600 - 50(8) = 600 - 400 = 200$$

When the price falls to $8, consumers demand more cappuccinos. For every $1 fall in the price, 50 additional drinks were sold, evidence that the price coefficient of 50 determines the responsiveness of consumers to a change in the price. At lower prices, more cappuccinos are demanded. At $4, the quantity demanded is:

$$Q_D = 600 - 50(4) = 600 - 200 = 400$$

Remember, the *a* value in the demand function (600 in this case), tells us the *autonomous level of demand*, or the quantity demanded when the price is zero. It changes with changes to the determinants of demand. Meanwhile, *b* demonstrates the law of demand, which says that there is an inverse relationship between the price of a good and the quantity demanded by consumers. As the price of cappuccinos falls from $10 to $0, the quantity demanded increases from only 100 drinks to 600 drinks.

It is possible to construct both a demand schedule and demand curve from this demand function. Table 2.3 shows a list of possible prices and the corresponding quantities, as calculated through the above function. Figure 2.10 illustrates a demand curve for cappuccinos based on the same prices and quantities.

TABLE 2.3 LINEAR DEMAND SCHEDULE: CAPPUCCINOS, $a = 600$	
Price of cappuccinos (P) / $	**Quantity demanded per day (Q_D)**
10	100
9	150
8	200
7	250
6	300
5	350
4	400
3	450
2	500
1	550
0	600

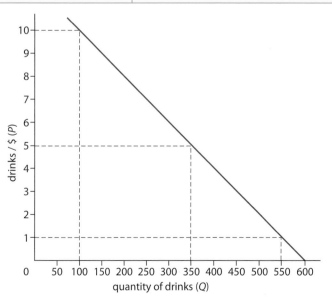

Figure 2.10
Linear demand curve: cappuccinos, $a = 600$.

Figure 2.10 shows various quantities of cappuccinos demanded (Q_D) at prices ranging from $0 to $10. A movement along the demand curve will occur any time the price of cappuccinos increases or decreases. At lower prices, more are demanded; at higher prices, fewer cappuccinos are demanded by consumers.

Changes in *a*

If any of the determinants of demand change, then the *a* value in the demand function will change and the demand curve will shift either inwards or outwards (down or up graphically). For instance, if a recession causes the incomes of consumers to fall and, therefore, the *autonomous level of demand* falls, then there are fewer people willing and able to buy cappuccinos at each price. The demand function may change to:

$$Q_D = 500 - 50P$$

Notice that the *a* value has decreased from 600 to 500 drinks. The *b* value, or the price coefficient, has not changed so the slope of our new demand curve will be the same as our original curve.

The quantities demanded resulting from the new demand function are shown in Table 2.4 and Figure 2.11.

TABLE 2.4 LINEAR DEMAND SCHEDULE: CAPPUCCINOS, $a = 500$	
Price of cappuccinos (P) / $	**Quantity demanded per day (Q_D)**
10	0
9	50
8	100
7	150
6	200
5	250
4	300
3	350
2	400
1	450
0	500

Each of the quantities demanded has decreased by the amount of the change in *a* (i.e. 100 units). As a result, there is a new demand curve, shown in Figure 2.11 as D_1. Lower incomes caused *a* to decrease, causing a shift in demand to the left by exactly 100 units. The Q-intercept for demand is now at 500 not 600.

Figure 2.11
Linear demand curve: cappuccinos, $a = 500$.

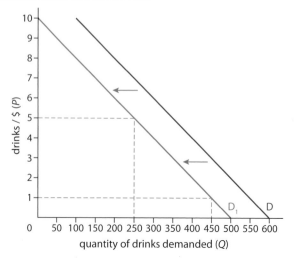

As shown above, a change in the determinants of demand cause a change in and shift of demand. In this case, demand shifts left, or 'down' by 100 units at every price.

Changes in *b*

Changes to the price coefficient *b* will change the steepness of the demand curve. Assume that consumers become less responsive to a change in the price of cappuccinos: instead of demanding 50 fewer drinks each time the price rises by $1, consumers now demand only 30 fewer drinks. The price coefficient *b* in our demand function changes from 50 to 30. So the new demand function is:

$Q_D = 600 - 30P$

The resulting values for price and quantity demanded are shown in Table 2.5 and Figure 2.12.

TABLE 2.5 LINEAR DEMAND SCHEDULE: CAPPUCCINOS, *b* = 30	
Price of cappuccinos (P) / $	**Quantity demanded per day (Q_D)**
10	300
9	330
8	360
7	390
6	420
5	450
4	480
3	510
2	540
1	570
0	600

The prices are the same as before. However, the range of quantities is smaller, from 300 units to 600, instead of 100 to 600. We can also observe the change in the slope of the demand curve. Figure 2.12 shows that the linear demand for cappuccinos becomes steeper when the *b* value changes from 50 to 30. A decrease in price of $1 increases the quantity demanded at a slower rate (30 drinks) than it did in the previous demand function where the price coefficient was 50.

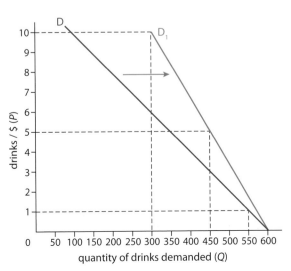

Figure 2.12
Linear demand curve: cappuccinos, *b* = 30.

A change in the price coefficient of cappuccinos from −50 to −30 represents a decrease in the responsiveness of cappuccino consumers to changes in the price. Previously, a $1 increase in price led to 50 fewer drinks being sold. Now it reduces the quantity demanded by only 30 drinks. The demand curve has become steeper, indicating that consumers are less sensitive to price changes than previously.

The overall demand for cappuccinos has now become what economists call more inelastic. Elasticity refers to the responsiveness of consumers to changes in price. Price elasticity of demand, as well as several other types of elasticity, is explored in detail in Chapter 4.

HL EXERCISES

Use the linear demand function: $Q_D = 300 - 30P$

11 Create a demand schedule with prices of $0, $3, $5, $7, and $9.

12 Create a demand curve, plotting the points from your demand schedule.

13 Decrease the value of a, the autonomous element of demand, by 30 units. Create a new demand schedule, with adjusted values for Q_D.

14 On your previous diagram, show the new demand curve.

15 Now change the value of the price coefficient in the original demand function to −10. Calculate the prices and quantities demanded, and list them on a demand schedule.

16 Create a new demand curve.

2.5 Supply

Learning outcomes
- Explain the positive causal relationship between price and quantity supplied.
- Describe the relationship between an individual producer's supply and market supply.
- Explain that a supply curve represents the relationship between the price and the quantity supplied of a product, *ceteris paribus*.
- Draw a supply curve.

> Supply is the quantity of a good or service that producers are willing to offer for sale at a given price during a specific time period.

Any market transaction requires two parties, *buyers* and *sellers*. Demand explores the buyers' side of things, while supply takes the perspective of the sellers. Supply is defined as the quantity of goods that producers will produce and sell at a given price over a particular time period, *ceteris paribus*. So in this case, a supply curve shows us the relationship between the price of the good and how much producers will send to market at that price. Again, all other variables are held constant, *ceteris paribus*, so that we may clearly see that relationship between price and quantity supplied. When the other, non-price variables change, there will be a shift of the entire curve.

Like demand, the relationship between price and quantity supplied can be shown with a table or *supply schedule*, as well as with a *supply curve*. Table 2.6, a supply schedule for potato chips, shows that as price decreases from $2.50 to $0.50, the quantity supplied decreases as well. This is consistent with the positive relationship explained by the law of supply. Figure 2.13 shows the supply curve for the schedule in Table 2.6.

TABLE 2.6 SUPPLY SCHEDULE: POTATO CHIPS	
Price of potato chips (P) / $	**Quantity of potato chips supplied per week (Q)**
2.50	25
2.00	20
1.50	15
1.00	10
0.50	5

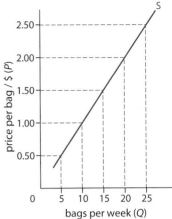

Figure 2.13
Supply curve: potato chips.

> The law of supply states that as price increases, more of a good is offered for sale by firms. As price decreases, less of a good is offered for sale.

The law of supply

The law of supply states that as price increases, more of a good is supplied by firms. As price decreases, less of a good is supplied. In Figure 2.13, the supply of potato chips reflects how output increases as price rises with an upward sloping supply curve. As price increases from $0.50 to $2.50, the quantity offered for sale rises from 5 to 25. This causes a movement upwards along the supply curve. Thus, there is a positive relationship between price and quantity supplied. Why do economists generally hold this to be true? Indeed, why is it held to be so true as to be considered a law of economics?

The profit incentive

Firms exist to maximize profits. If we hold everything else equal, a firm would prefer to sell a product at a higher price than a lower one because that will increase profits. Therefore, it is safe to say that a firm would produce more if it believed it could get higher prices for its good because it is more likely to earn extra profit as a result.

Figure 2.13 above depicts the law of supply with regard to potato chips. At $0.50 per bag, the incentive to produce is lower because the expected profits would be relatively low. However, should the price rise to $1.00, the firm has twice the incentive to supply it. This would motivate the firm to produce more. At the same time, in many instances there are additional costs to providing more of the good, so the higher prices will help to cover those costs. Generally speaking, from the firm's perspective, at higher prices greater profits are more likely, and thus firms supply more to the market.

Individual supply and market supply

As with demand, to get the overall market supply for a good is to take the sum of all the individual supply curves for the same good. Therefore, if we started with the supply for producer X and added it to the supply for an additional producer Y, we would have the market supply for potato chips, although a very narrowly defined one of just those two firms.

If producer X sells 25 bags at $2.50 (Figure 2.14a, overleaf), and producer Y sells 32 bags at the same price (Figure 2.14b), then the market supply is 57 bags at $2.50. At $2.00 per bag, producer X would sell 20, producer Y would sell 25, and the market demand would therefore be 45. This summation continues, along with all other suppliers' quantities, at every price until the market supply for potato chips is complete. Total market supply is shown in Figure 2.14c. Note that the supply curve for firm Y is not as steep as that for firm X. (This is because each has a different elasticity, a concept covered in Chapter 4.) However, the slope is still upwards, reflecting the law of supply.

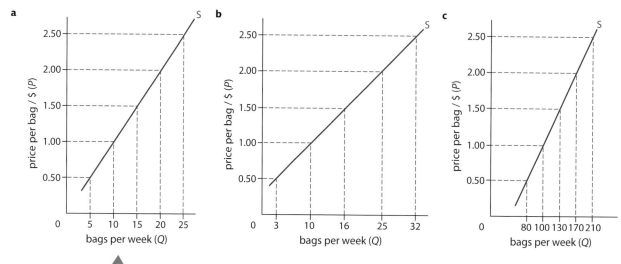

Figure 2.14
Individual supply to market supply. **a** Producer X; **b** producer Y; **c** producers X + Y + all others.

To learn more about the law of supply, visit www.pearsonhotlinks.com, enter the title or ISBN of this book and select weblink 2.9.

EXERCISES

17 In your own words, explain the law of supply.

18 Select an example product, perhaps something you use frequently. Explain how the law of supply could apply to this product.

19 With the example product you selected for exercise 18, speculate as to number of suppliers for this good. Do you think this is a local, national or international market for the good?

20 Apply your understanding: imagine and draw what the supply curve would look like if the supply of something were completely fixed.

2.6 Determinants of supply

Learning outcomes

- Explain how factors including changes in costs of factors of production (land, labour, capital and entrepreneurship), technology, prices of related goods (joint/competitive supply), expectations, indirect taxes and subsidies and the number of firms in the market can change supply.
- Distinguish between movements along the supply curve and shifts of the supply curve.
- Construct diagrams to show the difference between movements along the supply curve and shifts of the supply curve.

Determinants of supply are the non-price factors that influence the supply of a good offered for sale.

Aside from price changes, a variety of non-price factors can also affect supply. These non-price factors are called determinants, as in demand theory. They will cause the supply curve to shift outwards and inwards to reflect a change in the market at every price.

Shift in supply and movement along a supply curve

For supply (as with demand), a change in product price will cause only *a movement along* the supply curve. In Figure 2.15a, a change in the market price from $1 to $2 leads to a

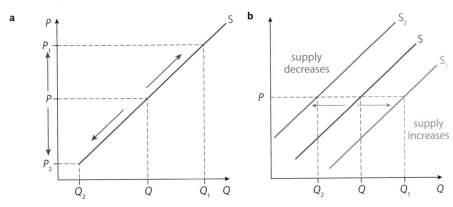

movement along the supply curve and an increase in the *quantity supplied* from 10 to 20 bags.

However, when the non-price determinants of supply actually change, there is a *shift* of the entire supply curve. All quantities of supply are changed for each price. Consider the market supply for potato chips in Figure 2.15b, where the initial supply is indicated by S. If one of the determinants of supply were to change and cause an increase in supply, the new supply curve would be S_1, a shift outwards or to the right. Price does not necessarily change at all, but more is being supplied at every price. For example, at $1.50, where previously 15 bags were supplied, now 22 bags are supplied. The same is true at all prices, because of a change in the previously *ceteris paribus* factors for potato chip supply. The process also works in reverse. If supply were to decrease, then there would be smaller quantities supplied at each price and a shift of the supply curve backwards would occur.

Figure 2.16 shows the general cases of movements along the supply curve and changes in overall supply.

Non-price determinants of supply

The most important determinants of supply include:

- costs of production
- productivity
- government intervention
- price of related goods
- supply shocks.

Costs of production

The ability of a firm to produce is intimately related to the costs of production. Higher costs obviously make it more difficult to earn profits, all other things being equal. If firms are selling potato chips for $2 per bag and costs rise from $1.50 to $1.75, profits per bag will fall by $0.25. This reduction in profits may provoke some producers to quit production, or to simply produce fewer potato chips and shift resources to the production of something else that is more profitable.

What causes the costs of production to change? Most generally, the price and availability of the factors of production will influence costs. As discussed in Chapter 1, the broad categories of the factors of production are land or natural resources, labour, financial and productive capital, as well as entrepreneurship or management. For example, if the amount of potatoes on the market shrinks, it will become more expensive to buy them. This increased resource cost will make potato chip production less profitable and the supply curve will shift left, as shown in Figure 2.17.

Figure 2.17
Costs of production, decreased supply: bags of potato chips.

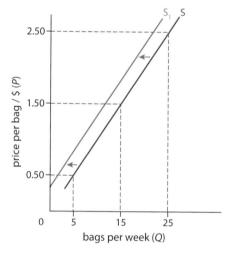

Furthermore, if the other factors of production for chips were to become less available or more expensive, supply would again shift left. For example, if the workers' wages or machine rental fees begin to rise, the profitability of chip production is diminished. Supply will therefore shift left. This would mark a decrease in the quantity supplied at every price. At all prices, firms would produce fewer bags of potato chips.

Productivity

Productivity is a concept closely related to production costs. Productivity is the amount of output per unit of input. If a firm is able to use fewer factor resources in the production process, it will spend less on those resources. If it can get more out of its resources while still getting the same prices, then it will earn more profits on each unit.

Productivity can be enhanced in different ways. Managerial insight can lead to better *methods of production*. This can also happen via the creation of better incentives for workers, changing production schedules, or adding new and specialized jobs to increase efficiency. Increased productivity can also come from *technological improvements*. For example, robotic systems can replace expensive labour. Data management can reduce accounting costs and find new ways of marketing products. Both methods and machines play an important role in reducing costs and improving efficiency.

Figure 2.18 shows productivity for a strawberry-farming business. The business has created and instituted a new incentive programme for its pickers. The goal is to improve the quantity and quality of the berries picked. The new programme proves effective, and the resulting increase in efficiency shifts supply to the right, increasing the supply of strawberries at every price.

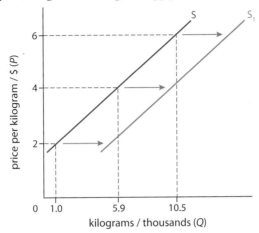

Using our initial example, if potato chip producers reorganized their workforce to improve worker efficiency, supply would shift to the right, meaning more bags would be produced at every price. This would be productivity enhanced by improved methods of production. An example of a technological improvement would be if the chip-maker retooled their processing facility with new chip fryers and bagging machines. As a result, more chips could be produced more quickly, lowering costs and shifting supply to the right.

Government intervention

So far, we have assumed that firms are operating in a purely free market, without an intrusion from government policies or rules. Even in the freest markets, however, governments intervene on some level. Government intervention, as suggested by the discussion of economic systems in Chapter 1, is when the government makes decisions regarding the essential questions of economics: what to produce, how to produce, and who should receive the benefits of production. The effect of intervention depends on the type of action the government takes.

Regulation

In any modern society, government is likely to apply some rules and regulations to even the most basic of products. This may be in the interests of protecting consumers from harm or deception. It may also be done to protect workers' health and safety. Whatever the motivation, the application of these rules is expected to cause extra costs.

Taxes and subsidies

Taxes and subsidies can also strongly influence supply decisions. Businesses view an indirect tax on their product as an increase in the cost of production. Indirect taxes are taxes on goods or services that are collected at the point of sale, and then transferred by the seller to the government. Because firms will earn smaller profits, they are likely to decrease production of the product when the taxes on it increase. Supply decreases, shifting the supply curve to the left and reducing the amount produced at every price.

More specifically, *taxes* will move the supply curve upwards by the amount of the tax. As shown in Figure 2.19 (overleaf), a tax on soft drinks of $0.45 will lift the supply curve up by the amount of the tax. This has the effect of shifting supply back, a reduction in supply determined by the size of the tax.

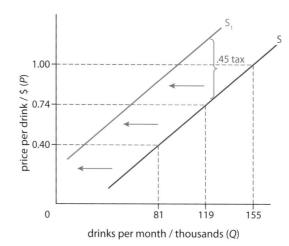

Subsidies, on the other hand, have the opposite effect. A subsidy is when the government pays a producer to make more of the good. While there are different ways to subsidize production, we will focus on per-unit subsidy. This type of subsidy pays the firm for each unit produced. This has the effect of reducing production costs. Therefore, an increase in subsidies will have the effect of shifting supply to the right, successfully encouraging more supply of the product at every price.

Price of related goods

From the producer perspective, firms have a choice as to what to produce. Firms can substitute the supply of goods from those earning lower prices to those getting better ones. This is most clearly demonstrated by goods that offer joint supply. Joint supply occurs when two or more goods are derived from the same product. Animal products are an example. The various parts of an animal can be sold for different purposes, such as skin for leather and meat for consumption.

> A supply substitute is a good that can be produced in a similar way, with similar inputs and processes, as another good.

Another example of joint supply is corn. Corn can be used to produce a variety of goods, including corn syrup and ethanol (alcohol) for fuel. Should the price of ethanol increase, corn producers may choose to sell more corn on the ethanol market and reduce the amount supplied for corn syrup.

Figure 2.20a shows an increase in the price of ethanol, perhaps in response to concerns about fuel supplies. The quantity supplied increases in accordance with the law of supply. This is shown as a movement along the supply curve for ethanol from 10 litres to 20 litres. To farmers, ethanol is relatively more profitable than before, and they switch their supply from other corn-based products to ethanol. As a result, in Figure 2.20b, the supply of corn syrup shifts to the left as producers substitute corn from the corn syrup market to the market for ethanol.

a

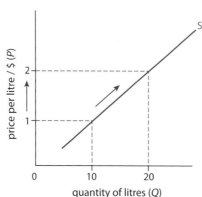

b

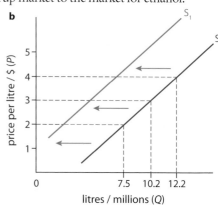

To take the potato chip example, a shift by consumers to more health-conscious living has increased the popularity (and price per gram) of 'baked' potato chips, which contain less fat. As a result, producers are shifting production to those products, and away from comparable goods like frozen French fries.

Supply shocks

Supply shocks are random events that can disrupt the normal supply of goods and services. Rarely, such events can improve supply situations, but we most typically associate random events with natural disasters like earthquakes, tsunamis, and floods. Clearly, the flooding of a great river like China's Yangtze, or Europe's Danube, can destroy significant aspects of a community's wealth: crops, homes, and infrastructure are all swept away. This kind of destruction obviously reduces the supply of certain foods or housing in that area. In the mildest sense, even bad weather can diminish agricultural production in any given year.

Many random destructive events are man-made. Environmental disasters (e.g. the Union Carbide accident in Bhopal, India, the Gulf of Mexico oil spill and the more recent Fukushima nuclear power plant explosion in Japan) have devastating effects on the supply of many goods and services. Conflict also tends to wreck the everyday business plans of most firms as well as destroying human and capital resources.

In Figure 2.21, the output of tea from Sri Lankan tea-growers is reduced by the tsunami of 2004. The effect of salt water flooding large areas of land is to destroy crops and render the land useless for agriculture.

Of course, random events need not always be negative. Indeed, on a small scale, good weather can dramatically improve crop yields. More dramatically, a country may discover that it possessed large deposits of minerals or fossil fuels that would improve the supply of those goods. In these instances, supply would shift to the right.

Events, my dear boy, events.
Harold Macmillan, UK Prime Minister 1957–63, when asked what posed the greatest challenge to a statesman.

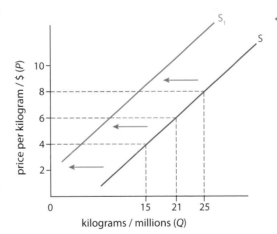

◀ **Figure 2.21**
Supply shock: effect of the tsunami on tea output from Sri Lanka.

To learn more about the determinants of supply, visit www.pearsonhotlinks. com, enter the title or ISBN of this book and select weblink 2.10.

EXERCISES

21 Consider these headlines:

i Airlines expect more rules in response to increased accident rates.

ii New teacher robots are expected to revolutionize teaching at major universities.

iii Shortage of apples expected to influence the apple juice industry.

iv To save money, the government eliminates subsidies for sugar producers.

v Cotton growers relieved that peace talks are successful in war-torn country.

For each headline:

a state whether there is a shift or a movement along the supply curve

b state the kind of shift

c create a diagram to demonstrate the shift

d identify the determinant that caused the shift.

2.7 Linear supply functions (HL only)

Learning outcomes
- Explain a supply function (equation) of the form $Q_S = c + dP$.
- Plot a supply curve from a linear function (e.g. $Q_S = -30 + 20P$).
- Identify the slope of the supply curve as the slope of the supply function $Q_S = c + dP$, that is d (the coefficient of P).
- Outline why, if the c term changes, there will be a shift of the supply curve.
- Outline how a change in d affects the steepness of the supply curve.

Supply for a good can also be expressed using mathematical functions. A supply function will demonstrate a positive relationship between price and quantity, and will be shown diagrammatically as upward sloping lines, in accordance with the law of supply.

Typical supply function

A typical supply function might look like this:

$$Q_S = c + dP$$

Where:

Q_S represents the quantity supplied

c represents the autonomous element of supply or the quantity that would be produced at a price of zero

d represents the rate at which a change in price will cause the quantity supplied to increase – in a supply function, d is always positive, in keeping with the law of supply

P represents the price of a single item

In this function, c represents the non-price factors that determine supply and indicates the quantity of output produced by the firms in a market at a price of zero. If any of the non-price determinants of supply change, then c will change, and the supply curve will shift inwards or outwards.

For example, if the number of firms in an industry increases, then the autonomous level of supply will increase, and the supply curve will shift outwards, or to the right. The corresponding value of Q_S will increase by the same amount as c at each price along the supply curve. In short, changes in c result in shifts of the supply curve.

The value of d affects the degree to which a price change will affect the quantity supplied. If d has a value of 5, for example, an increase in price of $1 will increase the quantity supplied by 5 units. Thus, d is the price coefficient for the linear supply function, determining the slope of the supply curve and therefore the responsiveness of producers to a change in the price of the good.

Returning to the market for cappuccinos, assume the following linear supply function describes the supply of cappuccinos across a small town for one day:

$$Q_S = -200 + 150P$$

If the price were $0, −200 cappuccinos would be supplied; in other words, no producers would be willing and able to sell cappuccinos at a price of zero. To determine the price at which producers would begin considering producing and selling cappuccinos (known as

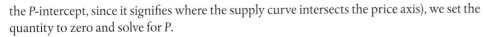

the *P*-intercept, since it signifies where the supply curve intersects the price axis), we set the quantity to zero and solve for *P*.

$0 = -200 + 150P$

$200 = 150P$

$P = 1.33$

At a price of \$1.33, producers begin to consider selling cappuccinos. This is where the supply curve begins. At any price greater than \$1.33, there is a direct relationship between the quantity supplied and the price. For example, if the price of cappuccinos were to rise to \$3, we would expect more sellers to be willing to make and sell cappuccinos.

$P = 3$

$Q_S = -200 + 150(3) = -200 + 450 = 250$

At \$3, 250 cappuccinos are produced and made available to consumers. The direct relationship between quantity and price continues at higher prices. Assume demand rises and the price increases to \$5.

$P = 5$

$Q_S = -200 + 150(5) = -200 + 750 = 550$

At \$5, 550 drinks are produced.

Of course, if the price were to decline, fewer drinks would be produced and sold. At \$4, the quantity supplied is 400.

$P = 4$

$Q_S = -200 + 150(4) = -200 + 600 = 400$

TABLE 2.7 LINEAR FUNCTION SUPPLY SCHEDULE: CAPPUCCINOS, $c = -200$	
Price of cappuccinos (P) / \$	Quantity supplied per day (Q_S)
10	1300
9	1150
8	1000
7	850
6	700
5	550
4	400
3	250
2	100
1	−50
0	−200

With our supply function of $Q_S = -200 + 150P$, it is possible to construct both a supply schedule and supply curve. Table 2.7 shows a list of possible prices and the corresponding quantities computed using this supply function.

There is a direct relationship between the price and the quantity supplied. As price falls, producers are willing to provide fewer drinks to the market. Figure 2.22 shows a supply curve for cappuccino drinks based on these prices and quantities. The *P*-intercept is where the price equals \$1.33, the price at which firms begin making cappuccinos.

As the price of cappuccinos changes, the quantity supplied changes at a rate established by the value of *d* in the original supply function (150 units). These would be seen as movements along the supply curve.

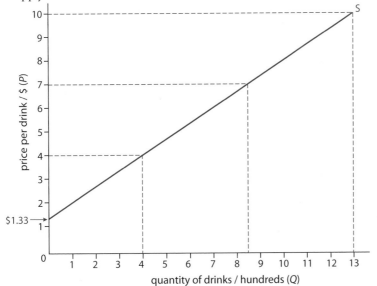

Figure 2.22
Linear supply curve: cappuccinos, *c* = 200.

Changes in c

In the above supply function, c with a value of -200 is known as autonomous level of supply. Any change in the determinants of supply will lead to a change in c, and will give us a new supply function.

Take, for instance, an increase in the number of firms selling cappuccinos in the market. More competition increases the level of supply, and the new supply function is:

$$Q_S = -100 + 150P$$

With more competition in the market, the price at which firms are willing to start producing cappuccinos falls. We can set the quantity to zero to find the new P-intercept, or the price at which firms will begin producing drinks.

$$0 = -100 + 150P$$
$$100 = 150P$$
$$P = 0.75$$

Now, at only $0.75, firms will begin thinking about making and selling cappuccinos, whereas before the new firms entered the market, a price of $1.33 was required to stimulate production.

With the new supply function, at every price we looked at previously, a greater quantity of cappuccinos is produced. For example, at a price of $3:

$$P = 3$$
$$Q_S = -100 + 150(3) = -100 + 450 = 350$$

And at a price of $4:

$$P = 4$$
$$Q_S = -100 + 150(4) = -100 + 600 = 500$$

At a price of $5:

$$P = 5$$
$$Q_S = -100 + 150(5) = -100 + 750 = 650$$

TABLE 2.8 LINEAR SUPPLY SCHEDULE: CAPPUCCINOS, $c = -100$

Price of cappuccinos (P) / $	Quantity supplied per day (Q_S)
10	1400
9	1250
8	1100
7	950
6	800
5	650
4	500
3	350
2	200
1	50
0	-100

Clearly, an increase in the c value of the supply function increases the quantity of cappuccinos produced at every price. Using the new function, Table 2.8 shows how the change in the number of suppliers has increased the quantity demanded by 100 units at every price.

These prices and quantities can be plotted on a new supply curve. Figure 2.23 shows supply shifting to the right. Because c represents all the *non-price* determinants of supply, a change in any one of them shifts supply outward or to the right. As a result, the P-intercept for supply is now at $0.75, not $1.33. Increased competition means producers are willing to sell cappuccinos at a lower price.

Besides an increase in the number of producers, other factors that could have caused the supply of coffee to increase include a fall in the price of inputs (cheaper coffee beans, cheaper milk, or lower wages for baristas) or a government subsidy to cappuccino producers.

On the other hand, factors that could shift supply to the left include an increase in input costs, a decrease in the number of producers, or a per unit tax levied on cappuccinos. If

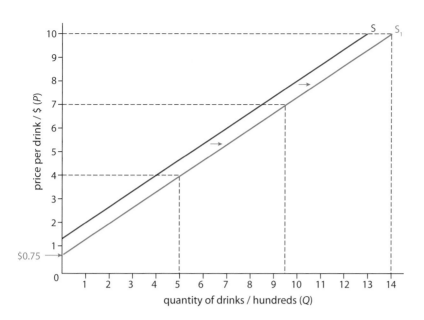

Figure 2.23
Linear supply curve:
cappuccinos, $c = -100$.

any of these occur, c will decrease and the supply curve will shift to the left, reducing the quantity supplied at each price. For example, assume the new supply function is:

$$Q_S = -300 + 150P$$

Now, at every price, the quantity of drinks sold is lower. In fact, it would take a price of $2 per drink just to get firms interested in making cappuccinos (you can calculate this by setting the Q at zero and solving for P, in other words, by finding the P-intercept). This would shift supply to the left.

Thus, if any of the determinants of supply were to change, then c would change and the number of cappuccinos supplied at each price would change as well, a shift of supply to the right or left.

Changes in d

As with linear functions for demand, it is possible for the price coefficient d to change. Changes to d change the steepness of the supply curve, and thus either increase or decrease the responsiveness of producers to a change in the price. Assume, for instance, that the price coefficient increases from 150 to 200. Now, for every $1 change in price, the quantity supplied changes by 200 drinks instead of just 150. The new supply function would be:

$$Q_S = -200 + 200P$$

Quantity supplied changes for every price. These changes are shown in Table 2.9.

Having changed the price coefficient in the supply function, we can observe the change in the slope of the supply curve. In Figure 2.24, the linear supply for cappuccinos has become a less steep slope. A $1 increase in the price of cappuccinos now leads to a larger increase in the quantity supplied than in the original supply function: 200 drinks rather than just 150. The new P-intercept is:

$$0 = -200 + 200P$$
$$200 = 200P$$
$$P = 1$$

The new supply curve begins at a price of $1 as shown in Figure 2.24 (overleaf).

TABLE 2.9 LINEAR SUPPLY SCHEDULE: CAPPUCCINOS, $d = 200$	
Price of cappuccinos (P) / $	**Quantity supplied per day (Q_S)**
10	1800
9	1600
8	1400
7	1200
6	1000
5	800
4	600
3	400
2	200
1	0
0	-200

Figure 2.24
Linear supply curve:
cappuccinos, *d* = 200.

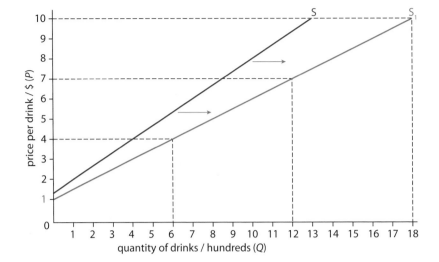

The overall supply for cappuccinos has now become what economists call *more elastic*. You will recall that elasticity refers to the responsiveness of producers to changes in price. When the price coefficient was 150, the quantity supplied increased at a slower rate following increases in the price. But with a coefficient of 200, the quantity supplied increases more rapidly over the same range of prices.

Now, for every $1 increase in the price, producers are much more responsive and will produce 200 more drinks compared to just 150. Likewise, if the *d* value of the supply function were to decrease, the responsiveness of producers to price changes would decrease, and the supply curve would become steeper.

Price elasticity of supply, along with several other types of elasticity, is explained in detail in Chapter 4.

To access Worksheet 2.3 on linear supply and demand functions, please visit www.pearsonbacconline.com and follow the onscreen instructions.

HL EXERCISES

Use the linear supply function: $Q_S = -100 + 10P$

22 Create a supply schedule with prices of $10, $20, $30, $40, and $50.

23 Create a supply curve, plotting the points from your supply schedule.

24 Increase the value of *c*, the autonomous element of supply, by 50 units. Create a new supply schedule, with adjusted values for Q_S.

25 On your previous graph, show the new supply curve.

26 Now change the value of the price coefficient in your original supply function to +30. Calculate the prices and quantities supplied, and list them on a supply schedule.

27 Create a new diagram showing the new supply curve with its new slope.

To access Quiz 2, an interactive, multiple-choice quiz on this chapter, please visit www.pearsonbacconline.com and follow the onscreen instructions.

PRACTICE QUESTIONS

1 Explain the difference between a movement along the demand curve and a shift in the demand curve. (10 marks) [AO2], [AO4]

2 Using an appropriate diagram and your knowledge of the determinants of demand, explain why the demand for meat might increase. (10 marks) [AO2], [AO4]

3 Explain the difference between a movement along the supply curve and a shift in the supply curve. (10 marks) [AO2], [AO4]

4 Using an appropriate diagram and your knowledge of the determinants of supply, explain why the supply of rice might decrease. (10 marks) [AO2], [AO4]

3 PHYSICS AND PHYSICAL MEASUREMENT

3.1 Equilibrium

- Explain, using diagrams, how demand and supply interact to produce market equilibrium.
- Analyse, using diagrams and with reference to excess demand or excess supply, how changes in the determinants of demand and/or supply result in a new market equilibrium.

Having examined demand and supply separately, we can combine them to analyse markets more completely. When demand and supply are combined, there is a tendency for the market to reach an equilibrium state.

Equilibrium is defined as the state in which all contrasting forces cancel each other out, resulting in balance or stability. Market equilibrium is defined as the state in which the quantity supplied is equal to the quantity demanded. Supply and demand are balanced. The price at which the quantity supplied and demanded are equal is called the equilibrium price. At this price, the amount purchased is exactly equal to the amount sold. There is no surplus product available on the market, nor are there shortages of supply at that price. For this reason, the equilibrium price is also called the market-clearing price. Everything put on the market, at that price, is sold.

Returning to the bags of potato chips we used in Chapter 2, the total market schedule shows the equilibrium price is $1.50 per bag (Table 3.1, overleaf). At that price, the amount

 Market equilibrium occurs at the price where the quantity demanded and quantity supplied are equal (also called the market-clearing price).

 To learn more about supply and demand, visit www.pearsonhotlinks.com, enter the title or ISBN of this book and select weblink 3.1.

supplied and demanded is 15 000 bags per week. All the chips offered on the market are purchased by consumers. Prices set above or below the market price will result in market disequilibrium, because there will be excess supply or demand.

Price of potato chips (P) / $	Quantity of potato chips demanded per week (Q_D) / thousands	Quantity of potato chips supplied per week (Q_S) / thousands
2.50	5	25
2.00	10	20
1.50	15	15
1.00	20	10
0.50	25	5

TABLE 3.1 DEMAND AND SUPPLY SCHEDULE: POTATO CHIPS

Figure 3.1 shows market equilibrium, with the equilibrium price of $1.50. At that price, an equal amount are demanded and supplied. Thus, the market clears all output at that price.

Figure 3.1
Market equilibrium.

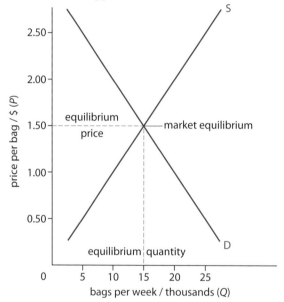

Market disequilibrium

Excess supply

A market disequilibrium is any price at which the demand and supply quantities are not equal. Let's look at specific examples of market disequilibriums, and analyse the results of attempting to set prices anywhere other than the equilibrium price.

Table 3.1 and Figure 3.1 show the market price to be $1.50. If the producers of these potato chips had an exaggerated sense of their value, they might set the price too high. Let's say, for example, that they greedily set the price at $2.50 per bag. At that price, the quantity demanded is much smaller than at the equilibrium price. Quantity demanded drops from 15 000 to 5000 bags per month. This is equivalent to a movement along the demand curve, as shown in Figure 3.2.

As price increases, the quantity demanded decreases or moves upwards and left along the demand curve. At the same time, setting the price higher induces producers to increase production as they expect higher profits at higher prices. Quantity supplied thus moves in the opposite direction, moving upwards along the curve to a quantity of 25 000.

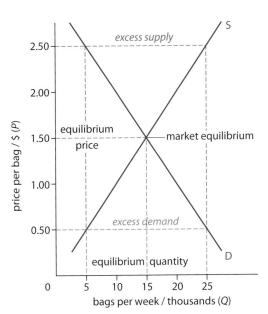

Figure 3.2
Equilibrium with shortages
and surplus.

Thus, we can say at $2.50, an *excess supply* for chips exists, with more quantity supplied than demanded. What happens to this surplus? Producers can only sell the extra goods if they lower the price. As they do so, more quantity is demanded, and producers reduce production. This narrows the gap continuously until the surplus is reduced to zero at the market-clearing, equilibrium price.

Excess demand

Let's take up the opposite case and assume that firms are not aware of the market value of their chips, and they under-price them at $0.50. At this price, the quantity demanded is much higher, now 25 000 bags, while the lower price is not well received by producers. They scale back production to only 5000 bags. This gap between relatively higher quantity demanded and lower quantity supplied is called *excess demand*.

When excess demand exists, market forces take over. With relatively scarce amounts of the good on the market at $0.50 (an excess demand of 20 000 bags) some consumers start to bid the price higher in an attempt to get more of the good. As chips quickly fly off the shelves, producers also realize they can charge a higher price. So, at the higher price of $1.00, producers make more (10 000 bags) and some consumers drop out of the market, reducing the quantity demanded to 20 000. Now the shortage is smaller (10 000 bags) but there is still a shortage. This prompts producers to raise the price again, with some consumers dropping out again. This process continues until all of the extra demand is satisfied at the market-clearing price of $1.50.

Therefore, at any price other than the market-clearing price, either excess supply or demand will exist. Furthermore, unless firms are compelled by law to keep their prices at some disequilibrium level (too high or too low), market forces will urge producers and consumers towards a market-clearing price where everything offered is purchased.

Changes in supply and demand

The tendency of a market towards equilibrium is strong. When prices are too high or too low, the market tends to clear eventually. And when markets are in balance, it requires some external force or event to change them. Shifts in either market supply or demand will change the market equilibrium, changing the market-clearing price and quantity as well.

Shifts of demand

A few years ago, consumer demand for pomegranate juice significantly increased following reports that it contained very high levels of antioxidants. As a result, demand for all products using pomegranate increased, shifting demand for pomegranates to the right. As shown in Figure 3.3, demand for pomegranates shifted to the right, causing a temporary shortage at the old equilibrium price of $4.00. The quantity demanded (Q_D) is thus far greater than the quantity supplied (Q_S). In this case, the excess demand is 40 million kilograms. As producers realize they can raise the price, they produce more, a movement upwards along the supply curve. And as consumers see the higher prices, they decrease the quantity demanded, a movement up and left along the new demand curve. The quantities of supply and demand settle at the new equilibrium price of $5 and equilibrium quantity of 110 million kilograms. As a result of the increased demand, prices are higher and quantities greater than before.

Figure 3.3

Market equilibrium, increased demand: pomegranates.

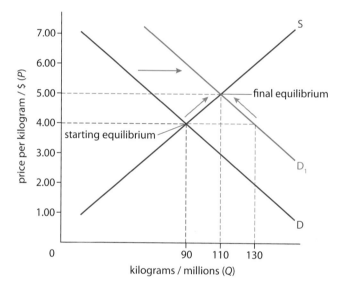

A decrease in demand can have the opposite effect. A decrease in a country's income might decrease the demand for all normal goods. Automobile sales, in particular, tend to be immediately affected by decreases in income, and a recession causes a decrease in demand for automobiles. In Figure 3.4, a decrease in demand of this type results in a temporary surplus of 6 million cars at the equilibrium price of $12 500 (fewer new cars being sold); producers cut prices to entice buyers (increasing quantity demanded, moving down along the new demand curve). Eventually, the market settles at a new, lower market price and quantity ($9000 and 5.5 million cars): fewer cars are being sold at lower prices.

Market shocks (sudden increases in supply or demand) can raise serious ethical dilemmas. After the earthquake, tsunami and radiation disaster in Japan (March 2011), thousands of people tried to leave the country. Airlines were reportedly charging four to five times the usual price to fly out of Tokyo (e.g. flights to Los Angeles at $6000). Is it unethical to charge higher prices for necessity goods during a humanitarian crisis? Or would the law of supply help ensure that more of these goods are offered for sale in the crisis zone?

Figure 3.4

Market equilibrium, decreased demand: new cars.

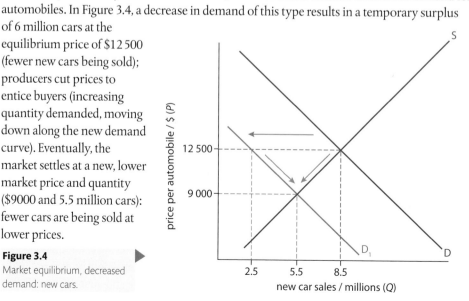

Shifts of supply

Supply shifts can also have important effects on price and quantity. In Figure 3.5, the market for rubber ducks shows the effect of synthetic rubber production. Synthetic rubber is much cheaper than rubber collected from rubber trees, so it becomes much less costly to produce rubber items, including rubber ducks. As a result, the supply of rubber ducks shifts to the right. A temporary surplus of 7 million ducks exists at the old equilibrium price of $3.75. This surplus is eliminated by cutting prices and selling off the excess supply. Consumers do their part by buying up the residual amounts at successively lower prices, an increase in quantity demanded at each lower price. The increase in supply therefore results in a lower equilibrium price for rubber ducks at $2.25, and a higher equilibrium quantity of 12 million sold.

How does production of synthetic rubber affect the price of rubber ducks?

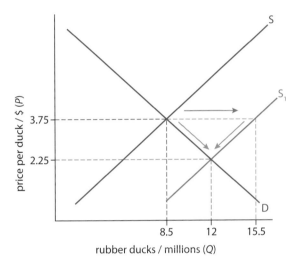

Figure 3.5
Increased supply: rubber ducks.

A decrease in supply will have the inverse result. Figure 3.6 shows the effect of a deep winter freeze across the Mediterranean which damaged orange crops in Greece, Italy, Spain and Cyprus. As a result, the number of oranges available for juice products decreased dramatically. Oranges are an input cost for orange juice, so the supply of orange juice decreases, shifting supply to the left. The reduced supply causes a temporary shortage of 700 million litres at the old equilibrium price of $1.50 per litre. Producers therefore begin to increase their prices, and consumers respond by decreasing the quantity demanded. The final price and quantity settle at $2.10 per litre and 550 million litres consumed. Thus, the decrease in supply has caused a decrease in quantity available and increased prices.

Figure 3.6
Decreased supply: orange juice.

Perhaps the greatest single supply shock in the modern era occurred with the 1973 oil crisis. The Organization of the Petroleum Exporting Countries (OPEC) launched an embargo of oil in response to US support of Israel during the Yom Kippur War. The price of oil quadrupled to a then-record $12 per barrel. This resulted in long queues, price controls and rationing in the US, Europe and Japan. It also stoked inflationary tendencies at work during this period, and is credited with starting the era of stagflation.

To learn more about equilibrium, visit www.pearsonhotlinks.com, enter the title or ISBN of this book and select weblink 3.2.

To access Worksheet 3.1 on linear functions and equilibrium, please visit www.pearsonbacconline.com and follow the onscreen instructions..

EXERCISES

1 For each of the headlines i–ix below:

a Decide the kind of shift that would occur, and create a diagram to demonstrate the shift. Diagrams should show the relevant shifts and notation that reflect the new equilibrium.

b Identify the determinant that caused the shift.

i Heavy rainfall affects the market for rubber boots.

ii Diplomatic agreements open the market for Chinese cars to several new countries.

iii Consumers learn that cars will be much more heavily taxed starting with next year's models.

iv House-building companies are gloomy about new business during the recession.

v A baby boom 15 years ago influences the market for popular music and cosmetics today.

vi The government places more regulations on food preparation after several poisoning scares.

vii A maker of MP3 players moves production to a country with significantly lower labour costs.

viii A severe winter frost decimates the crop of grapes from which French champagne is made.

ix Country X joins the EU and its wheat farmers reap massive subsidies.

3.2 Market equilibrium and linear equations (HL only)

Learning outcomes

- Calculate the equilibrium price and equilibrium quantity from linear demand and supply functions.
- Plot demand and supply curves from linear functions, and identify the equilibrium price and equilibrium quantity.
- State the quantity of excess demand or excess supply in the above diagrams.

You have already learned how linear equations can demonstrate both demand and supply functions. You can use the same type of linear equations to establish the equilibrium market price and quantity.

Using the cappuccino examples from Chapter 2 (pages 36 and 48), the demand and supply functions for cappuccinos were:

$$Q_D = a - bP = 600 - 50P$$

$$Q_S = c + dP = -200 + 150P$$

These functions can be presented as a demand and supply schedule (Table 3.2).

The equilibrium price and quantity are easily spotted as the price at which the quantity demanded equals the quantity supplied. At $4, cappuccino producers are willing to make 400 drinks, and consumers are willing to buy 400 drinks. The market is in equilibrium at $4 per drink.

TABLE 3.2 COMBINED SUPPLY AND DEMAND SCHEDULE: CAPPUCCINOS		
Price of cappuccinos (P) / $	Quantity demanded per day (Q_D)	Quantity supplied per day (Q_S)
10	100	1300
9	150	1150
8	200	1000
7	250	850
6	300	700
5	350	550
4	400	400
3	450	250
2	500	100
1	550	−50
0	600	−200

It is possible to determine equilibrium price and quantity without producing a side-by-side supply and demand schedule.

Worked example

Equilibrium is the point at which supply equals demand, so the first step is to set supply equal to demand.

$(Q_S = -200 + 150P) = (Q_D = 600 - 50P)$

$-200 + 150P = 600 - 50P$

To find the equilibrium price, simply solve for P.

Simplify by adding 200 to both sides.

$150P = 800 - 50P$

Simplify again by adding 50P to both sides.

$200P = 800$

Divide both sides by 200.

$P = 4$

The equilibrium price is $4. Now that we have the equilibrium price, we can determine the equilibrium quantity by substituting the price into the demand and supply functions.

$Q_S = -200 + 150(4) = -200 + 600 = 400$

$Q_D = 600 - 50(4) = 600 - 200 = 400$

At a price of $4 per drink, the quantity demanded and supplied is equal. There is neither a shortage nor a surplus of cappuccinos at this price. Therefore, this is the equilibrium or market-clearing price and quantity.

We can also plot the values of the demand and supply schedule to illustrate the market equilibrium, as shown in Figure 3.7 (overleaf). Again, the equilibrium price is evident at the intersection of demand and supply at a price of $4 and quantity 400 drinks.

Figure 3.7

Market equilibrium, linear demand and supply: cappuccinos.

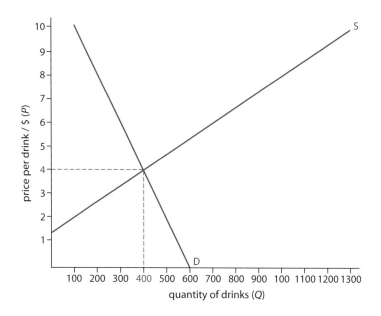

Shifts in supply and the effect on equilibrium

Using demand and supply functions, we can also demonstrate the effects on equilibrium of a change in the determinants of supply. Such a change causes a change in the value of the *c* variable of the supply function. Let's assume, for instance, that the price of coffee beans increases, adding to the costs of production of cappuccinos, and thereby reducing the supply. The new supply function is:

$Q_S = -400 + 150P$

The new supply schedule is shown in Table 3.3.

TABLE 3.3 NEW SUPPLY SCHEDULE: CAPPUCCINOS	
Price of cappuccinos (P) / $	**Quantity supplied per day (Q$_S$)**
10	1100
9	950
8	800
7	650
6	500
5	350
4	200
3	50
2	−100
1	−250
0	−400

With the new supply schedule, we can plot the new supply curve.

Worked example

First solve for the *P*-intercept by making $Q_S = 0$.

$0 = -400 + 150P$

$400 = 150P$

$P = 2.67$

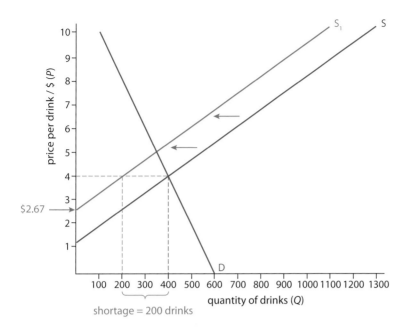

Figure 3.8
Linear functions, supply shift: cappuccinos.

Our new supply curve starts at a price of $2.67. As the *d* value has not changed, it will have the same slope as the original supply curve (Figure 3.8, above).

The *c* variable has decreased by 200 units. As shown above, the supply curve has shifted to the left, with 200 fewer units being offered for sale at every price.

With the new supply, there is a disequilibrium at the original price of $4. To determine whether there is a shortage or a surplus of cappuccinos, we must find the quantity supplied at $4 based on the new supply function:

$Q_S = -400 + 150(4) = -400 + 600 = 200$

At $4, the quantity demanded is 400 drinks but the quantity supplied following the increase in resource costs is only 200 cappuccinos. There is a shortage of 200 drinks in the market. We therefore expect the price to begin to rise in order to eliminate the excess demand in the market.

The price rises until the market is cleared, with all the excess demand eliminated. To determine the new equilibrium price following the decrease in supply, we need to make the new supply and demand functions equal to one another and solve for *P*.

Worked example

$-400 + 150P = 600 - 50P$

$150P = 1000 - 50P$

$200P = 1000$

$P = 5$

The new equilibrium quantity can be found by putting the price into the supply and demand functions:

$Q_S = -400 + 150(5) = 350$

$Q_D = 600 - 50(5) = 350$

As the market adjusts to the reduced supply of cappuccinos resulting from higher resource costs, a new equilibrium price and quantity are established (Figure 3.9).

Figure 3.9
New market equilibrium after supply shift: cappuccinos.

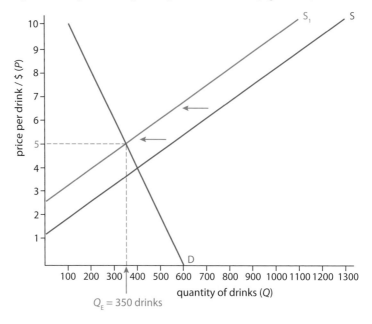

$Q_E = 350$ drinks

Shifts in demand and the effect on equilibrium

Now let's assume that one of the determinants of demand changes. In addition, demand becomes less elastic. In other words, a and b values change in the demand function. The new demand function is:

$$Q_D = a - bP = 400 - 25P$$

The decrease in demand for cappuccinos shifts the demand curve to the right. The decrease in the value of b means that consumers are less responsive to price changes, so the demand curve becomes steeper (Figure 3.10).

Figure 3.10
Linear functions, demand shift: cappuccinos.

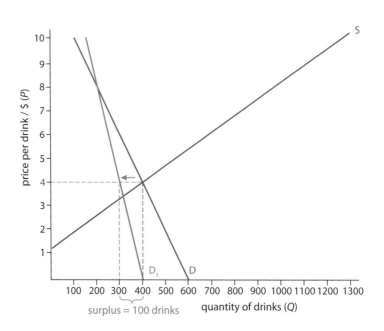

surplus = 100 drinks

At the original equilibrium price of $4, there is a surplus of cappucinos. The amount of excess supply can be found by plugging $4 into the new demand function and the original supply function.

Worked example

$Q_D = 400 - 25(4) = 300$

$Q_S = -200 + 150(4) = 400$

There is a surplus of 100 capuccinos at $4. Therefore, the price of cappuccinos is likely to fall to a new equilibrium, which reduces the quantity supplied and increases the quantity demanded until the excess supply is eliminated.

To determine the new equilibrium price and quantity, simply make supply and demand equal.

Worked example

$400 - 25P = -200 + 150P$

Solve for P.

$600 - 25P = 150P$

$600 = 175P$

$P = 3.43$

Finally, solve for Q.

$Q_S = -200 + 150(3.43) = 314$

$Q_D = 400 - 25(3.43) = 314$

The decrease in demand causes the price of cappuccinos to fall from $4 to $3.43 and the equilibrium quantity to decrease from 400 to 314 drinks. The new market equilibrium is shown in Figure 3.11.

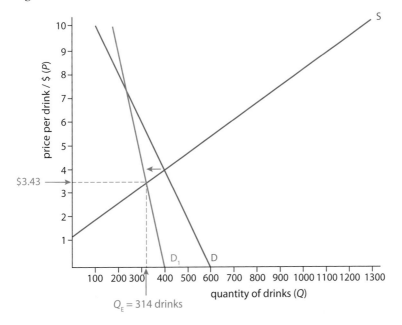

► **Figure 3.11**
New market equilibrium after demand shift: cappuccinos.

To access worksheet 3.1 on linear functions and equilibrium practice, please visit www. pearsonbacconline.com and follow the on-screen instructions.

2 Solve for P and Q_D using the following linear supply and demand functions:

    a $Q_S = -400 + 50P$; $Q_D = 800 - 30P$

    b $Q_S = -240 + 40P$; $Q_D = 660 - 20P$

    c $Q_S = -50 + 25P$; $Q_D = 90 - 10P$

3 $Q_S = 100 + 10P$; $Q_D = 300 - 30P$

    a Create a table to show the demand and supply schedule with prices of $0, $3, $5, $7 and $9.

    b Create a demand curve, plotting the points from your demand schedule.

    c Show the equilibrium quantity bought and sold.

    d Using the two functions, solve for the equilibrium price and quantity.

4 Assume that the above demand function changes to $Q_D = 380 - 30P$

    a Make a new supply and demand schedule for all the prices in exercise 3a.

    b Plot the points on this new schedule.

    c Show the excess demand at the original price.

    d Calculate the excess demand using the old equilibrium price and the current demand and supply functions.

3.3   Role of price in resource allocation

Learning outcomes

- Explain why scarcity necessitates choices that answer the 'What to produce?' question.
- Explain why choice results in an opportunity cost.
- Explain, using diagrams, that price has a signalling function and an incentive function, which result in a reallocation of resources when prices change as a result of a change in demand or supply conditions.

Signalling and incentive functions of price

In a world of finite resources, human desires run up against the fact of scarcity. Our wants are unlimited compared to the limited resources we have available, which is another way of saying that resources are scarce. With this in mind, we are faced with a choice of how to use those resources.

All such choices involve a cost – specifically, an opportunity cost. To choose one product or activity, we lose out on the opportunity to enjoy the other. This makes the system of resources allocation all the more important.

In competitive markets, we have seen that buyers and sellers come to a settlement or agreement on the appropriate market price. This is not done through any central command or by the guidance of some overseeing body of government. Instead, the establishment of a market price happens when countless buyers and sellers, each making rational choices about their scarce resources, make the best decision for themselves. Buyers are conscious of their time and income levels, while suppliers watch closely their costs and the selling potential for their goods. This decentralized, seemingly random process produces one of the most important benefits of competitive markets, an efficient rationing of resources through the price system.

When markets operate freely, the price system is the organizing principle around which all resources are allocated. Resource allocation is the manner by which society selects which resources are used for what purposes. The interaction of supply and demand tells us those goods which are most scarce (lowest supply relative to demand) because they have the highest prices, and least scarce (lowest demand relative to supply) because they have the lowest prices.

When a resource or product rises in price, buyers and producers act accordingly by using it less frequently in the case of a buyer, or trying to produce more of it in the case of the producer. Buyers are rationing their income and use of products to get the most out of all of their consumption choices. Producers may see a price increase and choose to produce more of the good because the price has revealed a scarcity in that market.

Thus, when markets act freely and competitively, the price information they emit acts as a signal to all the market actors. The signalling function of the price system allows this decentralized system of actors to make decisions for themselves and at the same time tell the world what is most important to them, what is worth producing. In this system, consumer desires rule the market. Consumer sovereignty is a term that suggests the enormous power that consumer wishes have in deciding what gets made, even if this power is diffuse and indirect. If you recall, this is the first great question any economic system must answer, 'What is to be produced?'

Figure 3.12 shows how a competitive market uses supply and demand to ration resources in this way. As demand for a good increases, a temporary shortage occurs (Figure 3.12a). Firms see the shortage and begin to raise the price of the good. This acts as incentive to produce more, helping to relieve the shortage. At the same time, consumers reduce the quantity they demand, and there is a movement up and to the left along the demand curve. Eventually, the price settles at a new equilibrium (Figure 3.12b). The rise in prices has told consumers to ration their consumption and producers to make more.

Resource allocation is the manner by which society manages and rations its resources.

Because they do a poor job of placing a value on goods, command economies are famous for producing shortages. A noteworthy shortage occurred in 1980 when, in parts of the Soviet Union, milk was in such short supply that it was rationed by medical prescription. Little or poor-quality food often led to work stoppages. A chronic lack of medical supplies and basic necessities had a long-term debilitating effect on the population. Even nurses were scarce because the job was difficult and did not pay.

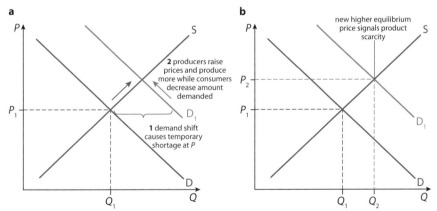

Figure 3.12
Role of prices, signalling function. **a** Temporary shortage; **b** new equilibrium.

The price system also answers the second question, 'How to produce?' A producer surveys all the resource costs for the product and constantly looks for ways to save on costs. By managing resources effectively, a firm can save money and increase profits. It may also be able to reduce prices so as to sell more competitively on the market. So, in addition to serving consumer wants, this process also helps ration resources more efficiently. In seeking out lower-priced alternatives to current resources, firms use price information to help society get more out of its scarce resources.

Figure 3.13 (overleaf) shows a resource market for capital equipment (i.e. any kind of machinery or service that is used in production). Here, an increase in the supply of this resource sends critical information to the producer, who buys the capital equipment as an input for the products. The information about lower prices says that this resource is more available and will cost less. A wise producer may look for ways to use this resource more frequently, and for ways to use other, relatively more expensive resources, less frequently. A rational reaction to this information would be for producers to look for ways to hire more capital equipment (which now costs less) and less labour.

Figure 3.13
Role of prices, signalling and rationing: resource market, capital equipment.

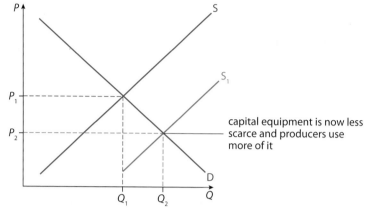

capital equipment is now less scarce and producers use more of it

To access Worksheet 3.2 on how prices allocate resources, please visit www.pearsonbacconline.com and follow the onscreen instructions.

Thus, the forces of supply and demand work towards an efficient allocation of resources. This is what Adam Smith referred to when he coined the term the 'invisible hand of the market.' Market forces, Smith argued, consistently and accurately guide us to produce and consume to get the best outcomes. Buyers and sellers are rationing resources, based on prices, to get the most from what they have. In the process, consumer wants are satisfied with the least possible cost to society.

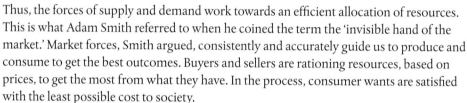

EXERCISES
5 Cite an example when the price of a good you use increased.
6 Speculate as to the reason why it increased. Was it increased demand or decreased supply?
7 Discuss how the price sends signals about the scarcity of the good.
8 Discuss how the price may cause consumers to ration the good.

 3.4 # Market efficiency

Learning outcomes
- Explain the concept of consumer surplus.
- Identify consumer surplus on a demand and supply diagram.
- Explain the concept of producer surplus.
- Identify producer surplus on a demand and supply diagram.
- Explain that the best allocation of resources from society's point of view is at competitive market equilibrium, where social (community) surplus (consumer surplus and producer surplus) is maximized (marginal benefit = marginal cost).

Consumer surplus

Competitive markets can also yield benefits beyond the efficiencies just discussed. Consumer surplus is the benefit consumers receive when they pay a price below what they are willing to pay. Let's take a sample case of a fictitious movie, *Action Hero 2*, released on DVD and for direct digital distribution (via iTunes, for example). The market schedule for this product is shown in Table 3.4.

Consumer surplus is the benefit consumers receive when they pay a price below what they are willing to pay.

TABLE 3.4 MARKET SCHEDULE FOR *ACTION HERO 2*

Price / $	Quantity demanded (Q_D) / millions	Quantity supplied (Q_S) / millions
25	5	30
20	15	25
15	20	20
10	25	15
5	30	5

In Table 3.6, it is evident that the equilibrium price is $15, where 20 million copies are sold. However, a closer look at the demand schedule tells us right away that there are many fans of *Action Hero 2* who are willing to pay considerably more than the market price. At a price of $25, nearly 5 million copies are demanded. And yet, because this is a market where all consumers pay only one price ($15), these fans will get an extra benefit worth $10 to each of them. We call this extra benefit received by consumers (here, the fans who are willing to pay $25) the consumer surplus. In this case, the consumer surplus = $25 (price willing to pay) – $15 (actual market price) = $10. The demand schedule reveals that this consumer surplus can be calculated as the difference between what consumers are willing to pay and the market price they ultimately pay (Table 3.5).

TABLE 3.5 CALCULATING CONSUMER SURPLUS

Price / $	Quantity demanded (Q_D) / millions	Market price / $	Specific consumer surplus (demand price – market price) / $
25	5	15	10
20	10	15	5
15	15	15	0

The equilibrium or market price for this movie is, as with all other markets, the intersection of supply and demand. Here it is $15, where 20 million copies are expected to be sold. The consumer surplus can also be shown on a diagram, as the area between the demand curve and the market price (Figure 3.14).

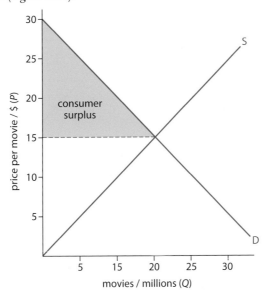

Figure 3.14
Consumer surplus: *Action Hero 2*.

It can be inferred (from the schedule or the diagram) that any decrease in price will have the effect of increasing consumer surplus, *ceteris paribus*. Any increase in the market price will shrink that difference, causing a decrease in consumer surplus.

Producer surplus

Producer surplus is the benefit producers receive when they receive a price above the one at which they were willing to supply the good.

It is also possible to see the same type of benefit accruing to producers. Producer surplus is the benefit producers receive when they receive a price above the one at which they were willing to supply the good. A close look at the supply schedule in Table 3.8 should reveal this phenomenon. Even at the lowest price listed, some producers are willing to produce. Perhaps they are very efficient. They would produce 5 million copies at a price of just $5. However, because the prevailing market price is $15, $15 is what they receive for every unit sold. Therefore, they enjoy a producer surplus of $10 per unit. Table 3.6 shows the producer surplus at each price.

TABLE 3.6 CALCULATING PRODUCER SURPLUS			
Price / $	**Quantity supplied (Q_S) / millions**	**Market price / $**	**Per-unit producer surplus (market price − supply price) / $**
15	20	15	0
10	15	15	5
5	5	15	10

These extra producer benefits can also be seen on the same supply and demand diagram. Figure 3.15 shows the producer surplus for *Action Hero 2* as the distance between the supply curve up until the market price. We can infer from this diagram, as well as from the data above, that any increase in the market price of *Action Hero 2*, *ceteris paribus*, would yield extra producer surplus at each price and increase the producer surplus area on the diagram.

Figure 3.15
Producer surplus: *Action Hero 2.*

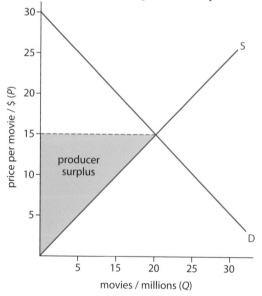

To calculate the *total amount* of consumer or producer surplus, you need the formula for calculating the area of a triangle:

$$A = \frac{1}{2}b \times h$$

Where:

A is the area

b is the length of the base

h is the height

Consumer surplus = 0.5(20 × (30 − 15)) = 0.5(20 × 15) = 0.5(300) = 150

Producer surplus = 0.5(20 × (15 − 0)) = 0.5(300) = 150

Consumer surplus + producer surplus = community surplus. Therefore, in this example, the community surplus is $300 million. It is shown in Figure 3.16 as the area of both the green and red triangles.

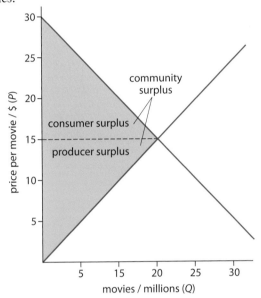

◀ **Figure 3.16**
Community surplus: *Action Hero 2*.

Allocative efficiency and competitive markets

Allocative efficiency is one of the measures of economic efficiency used by economists. Allocative efficiency is generally considered to be in effect if society is getting the goods and services it wants most. More specifically, allocative efficiency is achieved if society produces enough of a good so that marginal benefit (MB) is equal to marginal cost (MC). This most directly relates to the 'What should be produced?' question of economics. Through the price system, free and competitive markets should bring consumers what they desire. But a look back at marginal cost and benefit theory makes the case clearer.

You will recall from Chapter 2 (page 28) that the marginal benefit derived from any good tends to drop as more is consumed. In other words, satisfaction tends to decline with extra consumption, and the demand curve's downward slope reflects this principle. Also, recall that the additional cost of producing more and more units tends to increase. In other words, the marginal costs tend to rise as more is made. This explains why marginal cost (supply) tends to slope upwards, and marginal benefit (demand) tends to slope downwards.

Allocative efficiency asks whether a market produces what consumers want, and part of the answer comes from the demand/marginal benefit curve. Figure 3.17 (overleaf) reproduces the demand curve showing that what consumers are willing to pay for a good is our best guess at the value (or benefit) society places on it. A price of $15 for a copy of *Action Hero 2* tells us that a certain number of consumers value the movie at least that much (and possibly more).

 Allocative efficiency is achieved if society produces enough of a good so that the marginal benefit is equal to the marginal cost.

 In theory, markets give us what we want at the least possible costs. How would market theory explain acts of giving or charity? Is the exchange of gifts at holidays and family occasions like weddings efficient? Does it matter? Which ways of knowing (sense perception, emotion, reason, language) does your response draw on?

Figure 3.17
Allocative efficiency in competitive markets.

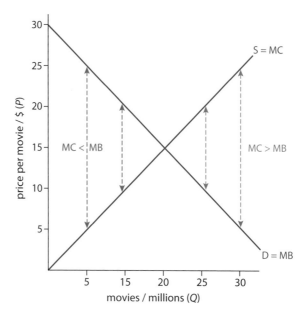

The question of whether society is producing enough of that good is further answered by the use of marginal analysis. In the example above, if society produced only 5 million copies, there would be a gap between the marginal benefit and the marginal cost. At this output level, potential consumer and producer surplus is lost. Society would clearly be better off, in terms of consumer satisfaction and producer profit, if the market level of output at the market price of $15 were produced and sold (i.e. 20 million copies).

In fact, rational decision making by both the producer (to produce more) and consumers (to consume more) is precisely what should happen to bring the market to equilibrium. Market equilibrium is best achieved whenever marginal benefit and marginal cost are equal (MB = MC). Any more production, to perhaps 25 million units for example, will bring the marginal costs beyond the marginal benefits. In short, society would be producing too much of the good, and would be paying more than marginal benefit curve shows society to value the good.

In this context, it is possible to say that competitive markets achieve allocative efficiency in this very important sense. Consumers get what they want most, as revealed by their demand and marginal benefit curves, and they get as much as they want, with the market calibrated naturally to prevent them from overpaying or overproducing as marginal costs rise.

To learn more about efficiency, visit www. pearsonhotlinks.com, enter the title or ISBN of this book and select weblink 3.3.

	EXERCISES
9	Identify a common product you use or consume.
10	What is the maximum price you would pay for that good?
11	What is the consumer surplus for that good?
12	Draw an equilibrium diagram of the market for the good, indicating consumer and producer surplus.
13	Identify the consumer, producer, and community surplus for this market.

PRACTICE QUESTIONS

1   Identify three reasons why the supply of oranges, for example, might increase and explain how this change will result in a new equilibrium.   (10 marks) [AO2], [AO4]

2   List three possible reasons why the supply for automobiles, for example, would increase and explain how this change will result in a new equilibrium.   (10 marks) [AO2], [AO4]

3   The basic economic problem is one of scarcity of productive resources. Explain how resources are allocated between competing uses in a market economy.
                                                                        (10 marks) [AO2], [AO4]

© International Baccalaureate Organization 2006

4

5   Using a diagram, explain the concept of community surplus.   (10 marks) [AO2], [AO4]

    Describe the concept of allocative efficiency and explain why it is achieved at the competitive market equilibrium.   (10 marks) [AO2], [AO4]

To access Quiz 3, an interactive, multiple-choice quiz on this chapter, please visit www.pearsonbacconline.com and follow the onscreen instructions.

4 ELASTICITIES

4.1 Defining elasticity

Like rubber bands, demand and supply can be elastic (or inelastic).

In Chapter 3, you learned about the fundamental relationships between the price of a particular good and the quantities that consumers demand and that producers supply. The laws of demand and supply hold true in almost every market for goods, services or resources. At higher prices, suppliers are willing to provide more of their good, service or resource to the marketplace while consumers demand less due to the higher opportunity cost of consumption. At lower prices, consumers are willing to purchase more of a good, service or resource while suppliers are willing and able to provide less due to the declining benefits of producing and selling at lower prices.

The relationships between price and quantity demanded and supplied are stable enough to be considered *economic laws*. To extend our analysis of supply and demand, it is useful to introduce an additional component into our analysis of the relationships between price, demand and supply.

The study of elasticities

This study examines the responsiveness of consumers or producers to a change in a variable in the marketplace. Elasticity measures how much one factor changes in response to a change in a different factor. The law of demand tells us that when the price of a good increases, the quantity demanded will decrease. Determining the price elasticity of demand (PED) tells us *how much* the quantity demanded of a good will decrease when the price of that good increases, it is a measure of the *responsiveness* of consumers to a change in price.

PED is only one type of elasticity. We will also examine the responsiveness of consumers of one good to a change in the price of a related good (cross-price elasticity); the responsiveness of a consumer's demand for a particular good to a change in the consumer's income (income elasticity of demand); and the responsiveness of producers to changes in price (price elasticity of supply).

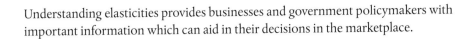

Understanding elasticities provides businesses and government policymakers with important information which can aid in their decisions in the marketplace.

Implications for businesses

- The degree to which consumers respond to changes in the price of a firm's products has major implications on a firm when it is considering raising or lowering its prices.
- Producers of some goods must be aware of the effect that changes in the prices of other goods will have on market demand for their products. A perfect example is the decision by manufacturers such as Toyota and Honda to expand their production of hybrid automobiles in the last decade as gasoline prices have risen steadily around the world.

Implications for governments

- Governments must consider elasticities when deciding which goods to place taxes on and whether or not to raise or lower income tax. Levying taxes on goods for which consumers are highly sensitive to price changes will create little tax revenue yet lead to a large decrease in the quantity sold in such markets.
- Raising or lowering income tax with the goal of stimulating or reducing overall household spending on goods and services may be futile if consumers' demand is unresponsive to changes in disposable income.

Understanding elasticities extends our ability to critically analyse the functions of the market economy. It informs our decisions as consumers, business managers, and citizens in a democratic society.

 4.2 # Price elasticity of demand (PED)

Learning outcomes
- Explain the concept of price elasticity of demand, understanding that it involves responsiveness of quantity demanded to a change in price, along a given demand curve.
- Calculate PED using the following equation.

$$PED = \frac{\text{percentage change in quantity demanded}}{\text{percentage change in price}}$$

- State that the PED value is treated as if it were positive although its mathematical value is usually negative.
- Explain, using diagrams and PED values, the concepts of price elastic demand, price inelastic demand, unit elastic demand, perfectly elastic demand and perfectly inelastic demand.
- Explain the determinants of PED, including the number and closeness of substitutes, the degree of necessity, time and the proportion of income spent on the good.
- Calculate PED between two designated points on a demand curve using the PED equation above.
- Explain why PED varies along a straight line demand curve and is not represented by the slope of the demand curve.

The law of demand states that *ceteris paribus*, there is an inverse relationship between the price of a good and the quantity demanded in the marketplace. With only a couple of exceptions, this law will hold true whenever the price of a good rises or falls. An increase in price reduces the attractiveness of a product to consumers, resulting in a decline in the quantity demanded. A fall in price, on the other hand, makes a good more attractive to consumers, who will want to buy more of it.

The price elasticity of demand (PED) is a measure of the responsiveness or sensitivity of consumers to a change in the price of a particular product. If a small increase in price leads to a proportionally large decrease in quantity demanded, consumers are said to be very *price sensitive*, and demand is therefore *price elastic*. On the other hand, if a large increase in price has little effect on the quantity of a good demanded, consumers are not very price sensitive, and demand is said to be *price inelastic*.

> Price elasticity of demand (PED) is a measure of the responsiveness of consumers to a change in the price of a particular good.

The PED coefficient

To measure the sensitivity of consumers to changes in price, we must compare the change in quantity demanded of a particular good with the particular price change of the good that led to the change in demand. To accommodate the different levels of output and price, we measure changes in *percentages*, not raw values. The formula for determining the PED coefficient is:

$$PED = \frac{\%\Delta Q_D}{\%\Delta P}$$

Where:

$\%\Delta Q_D$ is the percentage change in quantity (Δ, delta, signifies change)

$\%\Delta P$ is the percentage change in price

Thus, to calculate PED we divide the percentage change in quantity demanded of a good resulting from a particular percentage change in price.

If the price of rice rises by 15% and the quantity demanded decreases by 10%, the PED for rice is $-10/15 = -0.66$.

If the price of a digital watch falls by 20% and the quantity demanded increases by 40%, the PED is $40/20 = 2$.

However, we may not know the percentage changes in quantity and price, and would therefore be required to calculate them. The formula for calculating PED between two prices when percentage changes are not known is:

$$PED = \frac{(Q_{D2} - Q_{D1}) \div Q_{D1}}{(P_2 - P_1) \div P_1}$$

Where:

Q_{D2} is the quantity demanded following the price change

Q_{D1} is the original quantity demanded

P_2 is the new price

P_1 is the original price

Using this formula, we can determine the PED between two prices knowing only the values of quantity demanded and price.

Worked example

Let's assume a luxury sports utility vehicle (SUV) retails for £40 000 in the UK in July.

7000 SUVs are sold in July.

In August, the vehicle is marked down to £37 000.

7200 SUVs are sold in August.

Assuming no other variables changed between July and August, how responsive are UK consumers to the change in price of this SUV? To determine the price elasticity of demand for the vehicles, we can apply the price and quantity information to the equation above.

$$PED = \frac{(7200 - 7000) \div 7000}{(37\,000 - 40\,000) \div 40\,000}$$

$$PED = \frac{0.029}{-0.075} = -0.36$$

The price elasticity of demand for these SUVs between £40 000 and £37 000 in the UK is −0.36. A fall in price of 7.5% led to an increase in quantity demanded of 2.9%. Another way of interpreting this is that for every 1% decrease in price, the quantity demanded increased by 0.36%.

The PED coefficient is negative because of the inverse relationship between price and quantity. Since the law of demand applies to nearly all goods and services, we typically ignore the negative sign and express PED as an absolute value. Therefore the PED for the SUVs in the above example between the prices quoted is 0.36.

EXERCISES

1   Calculate the PED if a price increase of 50% causes the quantity demanded to fall by 40%.

2   If P = $8 and Q_D = 200, calculate the new Q_D resulting from a price increase to $10 if the PED is 1.5.

3   Explain why the PED coefficient is always negative.

Interpreting the PED coefficient

Depending on the degree to which quantity demanded changes when price changes, demand can be either price elastic, price inelastic or unit elastic. For simplicity, we will here examine the absolute value of the PED coefficient, which enables us to analyse positive numbers when comparing the elasticities of different goods.

PED < 1: → inelastic demand

A coefficient greater than zero but less than one indicates that demand for a good is inelastic. To see why, think about the example of the SUVs. When the price fell by 7.5%, consumers responded by demanding 2.9% more SUVs. The law of demand explains why consumers bought more when the price fell, while the PED coefficient of 0.36 tells us the responsiveness of consumers to the fall in price. Since the percentage change in quantity was less than the percentage change in price, the consumers are rather insensitive to changes in price in this case. Demand is price inelastic.

PED >1: → elastic demand

Now think about the example of the digital watches. When the watches fell in price by 20%, the quantity demanded increased by 40%. The PED is 40/20 = 2. A coefficient greater than one indicates that the percentage change in quantity demanded exceeds the percentage change in price. Consumers are relatively responsive or sensitive to price changes, and demand is said to be price elastic.

PED = 1: → unit elastic demand

If a particular percentage change in price results in an identical percentage change in quantity demanded, then demand is said to be unit elastic. Assume movie tickets increase from $10 to $12 and movie tickets sales drop by 20% in response. The 20% increase in price from $10 to $12 resulted in 20% fewer people buying tickets, so the coefficient is 20/20 = 1.

In the case of almost every good and service imaginable, the PED coefficient will be between 0 and infinity. But in some extreme circumstances, demand can be perfectly inelastic or perfectly elastic.

PED = 0: → perfectly inelastic demand

In this scenario, any change in price is met with no change in quantity demanded. The existence of goods for which demand is perfectly inelastic is highly unlikely, but theoretically possible. Imagine, for instance, that the price of a good such as insulin rises. Insulin is demanded by only a handful of people in the world, specifically diabetics. The quantity of insulin demanded by a particular diabetic individual is extremely constant and, without that quantity, the individual would suffer serious health consequences, maybe even death. As the price of insulin falls, diabetics will continue to demand the same amount as before, and no one else will demand insulin, so the quantity demanded will remain unchanged. As the price rises, diabetics will continue to demand the same quantity, since the risk of experiencing serious health consequences means they cannot afford to cut back on their consumption. The demand for insulin among diabetics is therefore perfectly inelastic. Of course, in the extreme case that the price rises to a level where it is beyond the means of some diabetics, the reality is that some individuals will simply not be able to afford it, so at a certain point even demand for necessities such as insulin is not perfectly inelastic.

PED = infinity: → perfectly elastic demand

The implication of a PED coefficient of infinity is that any change in price leads to an infinite change in quantity demanded. If the price of such a product increases even by 1% the quantity demanded falls to zero. A 1% decrease in price leads to an infinite increase in quantity demanded, in other words, every single consumer in the market will want to buy the product. While perfectly elastic demand is mostly theoretical, there are goods for which demand can be nearly perfectly elastic. Assume a good has thousands of perfect substitutes that are all easily available to the consumer, who has perfect information about the prices and products being sold. If one seller were to raise his price above the equilibrium level in the market, rational consumers will shun that seller and instead buy from one of the hundreds of other sellers. On the other hand, if one seller decides to lower his price below equilibrium, if only by one or two percent, all rational consumers will wish to buy from that seller and will shun all other sellers whose prices now appear too high. Such a scenario is imaginable, but extremely rare even in highly competitive markets such as agriculture, clothing, restaurants, taxis and so on.

Some of the goods for which demand is highly elastic may have very high PED coefficients, but will be less than perfectly elastic. Imagine, for instance, a company that sells phone cards. If you buy a phone card for $30, you receive $30 worth of credit for phone calls on your mobile phone. Imagine now that the price of a $30 phone card drops to $25. Almost everyone who finds out about this deal will want to buy the phone cards since it appears that they will get $5 of 'free' credit by paying $25 for a $30 card. Imagine that the number of cards sold increases from 20 000 to 500 000. Demand is highly elastic. To determine how elastic, the coefficient formula can be applied.

$$PED = \frac{(500\,000 - 20\,000) \div 20\,000}{(25-30) \div 30}$$

$$PED = \frac{24}{0.167} = 143.71$$

The PED for \$30 phone cards is 144. For every 1% decrease in price, sales increase by 144%. While this is highly elastic, it is clearly not perfectly elastic. A 1% increase in price would likely lead to an extremely large decrease in the quantity demanded, perhaps even close to zero.

Relative elasticity and the slope of the demand curve

Graphically, relative price elasticities of demand can be compared by examining the slopes of demand curves drawn on the same axes. The steeper the slope of demand for a good, the less elastic the demand for that good. The more nearly horizontal the slope, the more elastic the demand. A demand curve that is vertical is perfectly inelastic, since the quantity demanded does not change as price changes. A horizontal demand curve is perfectly inelastic since any change in price will lead to an infinite change in quantity demanded. A downward-sloping demand curve may be relatively elastic or inelastic, depending on the particular changes in price and quantity being examined, but its PED will be greater than zero and less than infinity (Figure 4.1).

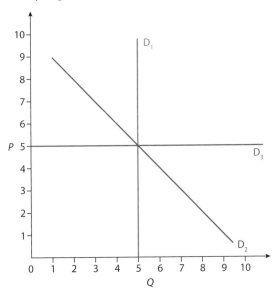

Figure 4.1
PED is reflected in the relative slope of the demand curve.

In Figure 4.1, D_1 corresponds with perfectly inelastic demand. Whether the price is 1 or 10, the quantity demanded will always remain at 5 units of this good. Consumers are totally unresponsive to changes in price. D_3 is perfectly elastic. Any change in price will lead to an infinite change in quantity demanded. If the price falls from 5 to 4, the amount of demand will be immeasurable as every consumer will wish to buy this good. If the price increases to 6, the quantity demanded will be zero as no rational consumer would continue to demand this good. The slope of D_2 is −1, indicating that demand is neither perfectly elastic nor perfectly inelastic. Depending on the price and quantity, demand for a good represented by D_2 can be relatively elastic (at higher prices) or relatively inelastic (at lower prices). D_3 and D_1 represent two extremes of elasticity that are rare if they exist at all in the real world.

The relative slopes of demand curves on the same axis indicate the relative elasticities of demand for the goods they represent. Goods for which demand is highly elastic reflect their elasticity in the flat slope of the demand curve, while goods for which demand is relatively inelastic show demand curves closer to vertical.

Worked example

The demand curves In Figure 4.2 represent more realistic ranges of elasticity.

Figure 4.2
PED can be calculated using data in a demand diagram.

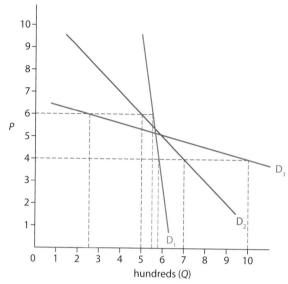

Assume the following:

- D_1 represents demand for cigarettes
- D_2 represents demand for movie tickets
- D_3 represents demand for chocolate ice cream.

To determine the elasticity for each of the three goods as their prices falls from $6 to $5, we use the PED coefficient formula.

First, we determine the percentage change in the price.

$$\%\Delta P = \frac{4-6}{6} = -0.33 \times 100 = 33\%$$

Next, we calculate the percentage change in the quantity for the three goods in response to the fall in price.

- Cigarettes: $\%\Delta Q_D = \frac{560-530}{530} = 0.056 \times 100 = 5.6\%$

- Movie tickets: $\%\Delta Q_D = \frac{700-500}{500} = 0.4 \times 100 = 40\%$

- Chocolate ice cream: $\%\Delta Q_D = \frac{1000-250}{250} = 3 \times 100 = 300\%$

Certain individuals depend on particular goods for their survival – for example, diabetics need insulin to live. Is it unethical for the producers of such necessary goods to exploit the consumers and charge as high a price as possible? Where should we draw a line on what is a fair price for goods on which individuals depend for survival?

A decrease in price of 33% from $6 to $4 led to drastically different changes in the quantity demanded for the three goods. To determine the exact PED for the three goods, we divide the percentage change in quantity by the percentage change in price.

- PED for cigarettes $= \frac{5.6}{33} = 0.17$

- PED for movie tickets $= \frac{40}{33} = 1.21$

- PED for chocolate ice cream $= \frac{300}{33} = 9.09$

Of the three goods, demand for cigarettes is the most inelastic and demand for chocolate ice cream is the most elastic. Demand for movie tickets is elastic (the coefficient is greater than one), but not nearly as elastic as for chocolate ice cream.

The determinants of PED

What determines whether demand for a particular good is elastic or inelastic? This is another way of asking what determines the sensitivity of consumers to price changes. The degree to which consumers respond to price changes depends on several factors, which can be summarized using the acronym SPLAT:

- S: substitutes
- P: proportion of income
- L: luxury or necessity
- A: addictive or not
- T: time to respond.

Number of substitutes

The number of substitutes a good has is one of the primary determinants of how elastic demand will be. Consumers will be more responsive to changes in the price of a good with a large number of substitutes than a good with very few or no substitutes. Coffee is a good with almost no perfect substitutes. Coffee consumers are therefore relatively unresponsive to changes in the price of coffee. On the other hand, any particular coffee shop has many substitutes. In a given city, there may be several dozen coffee shops, so if one unilaterally raises its prices while the others keep theirs constant, the chances are that consumers will be more responsive to that particular instance of a higher price than they would be if all coffee became more expensive.

Proportion of income

The proportion of the consumer's income the price of a good represents is another determinant of PED. Demand for goods that make up a large proportion of a consumer's income tends to be more elastic since a particular percentage change in price will appear much larger to the consumer than the same percentage change in price of a good that makes up a very small proportion of income. Take two examples: beach vacations and toothpicks. A 10% drop in the price of a family beach vacation may mean a savings of $1000 to a family of four considering an island getaway. $1000 is a significant amount of money and will therefore have a considerable impact on the number of families taking beach vacations. On the other hand, a 10% fall in the price of toothpicks may represent only a few cents savings on a box of a thousand toothpicks. Toothpicks are already so cheap and make up such a minute proportion of the typical consumer's budget that a fall in their price will have little or no effect on the overall quantity demanded.

Luxury or necessity?

Whether a good is a luxury or necessity affects its PED. Goods that are necessary to consumers will have less elastic demand than the luxuries they can do without if the price rises. Consumers are likely to be more responsive to a 20% increase in the price of fine leather handbags than a 20% increase in the price of natural gas. We depend on natural gas to heat our homes and to cook our meals, but we do not *need* fine leather handbags – we can do without them when their prices rise. Some consumers will be less responsive than others to increases in the price of luxuries – for example, those whose incomes are sufficiently high for even the price of luxury goods to be a relatively small proportion of their income.

Addictive or not?

Whether a good is addictive or not affects the PED. Addictive goods (for example, alcohol, tobacco, drugs, and fatty or salty foods) tend to have relatively inelastic demand. The reason is obvious: consumers with a physical dependence on a good will be unwilling or unable to respond to price increases to much degree. This helps explain why certain illicit drugs sell for extremely high prices on the streets of many cities; once a user is addicted, he or she is willing to pay almost anything for a drug like heroine or cocaine. If tobacco were not addictive, the chances are that many more people would quit smoking in response to the often massive taxes levied on cigarettes by governments.

Time to respond

The amount of time consumers have to respond to a price change determines the price elasticity of demand. Immediately following a change in price, it is unlikely that consumers will adjust their consumption by much. It is difficult to identify suitable substitutes for a good that has increased in price in the short run, but in the long run new options can be identified and consumers can further reduce their consumption of the more expensive good. If the price of a particular good falls, it will take time for consumers to notice the price change but once they do, it is likely that market demand will respond to the change in price.

4.3   Applications of price elasticity of demand

Learning outcomes
- Examine the role of PED for firms in making decisions regarding price changes and their effect on total revenue.
- Explain why the PED for many primary commodities is relatively low and the PED for manufactured products is relatively high.
- Examine the significance of PED for government in relation to indirect taxes.

Being able to determine a good's price elasticity of demand at a particular price allows businesses that produce that good to make informed and sound decisions regarding the optimal level of output and price. A firm or industry considering a decrease in output of its product is wise to consider the effect that the resulting price increase would have on the firm's or industry's total revenues. Figure 4.3 shows that the PED for a particular good is not constant across all prices. The higher the price of a good, the more responsive consumers are to a change in price; the lower the price, the less sensitive consumers are to price changes.

The demand curve (Figure 4.3a) shows the quantity demanded for this good at a series of prices between $10 and $0. At the high price of $10, the total market demand is 0 units, so the total revenues for producers is $10 × 0 = $0. But 10 units can be sold for $8 each, generating a total revenue of $80.

Figure 4.3b plots the total revenue in the industry at each price and quantity combination. At a price of $6, 20 units are sold for a total revenue of $120. It can be assumed that at a price somewhere between $6 and $4, and a quantity between 20 and 30 units, the revenues earned by producers will be maximized.

A decrease in price from $10 to $5 leads to an increase in the quantity demanded and an increase in the total revenues earned by producers. This indicates that the percentage increase in the quantity demanded must have exceeded the percentage decrease in the price, evidence that demand is elastic between $10 and $5.

However, as the price falls below $5, the quantity demanded continues to increase but producers' revenues fall, indicating that the percentage increase in the quantity demanded is proportionally smaller than the percentage decrease in the price.

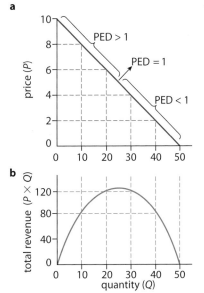

Figure 4.3
The total revenue test of PED.

The total revenue test of PED

The total revenue test of price elasticity of demand allows us to determine whether demand for a good is price elastic or price inelastic by examining the impact that a change in price has on the total revenue in the market. Generally speaking, at higher prices, demand tends to be relatively elastic for most goods. But as the price falls and the quantity demanded increases, the percentage changes in price become larger and the percentage changes in quantity become smaller, causing the PED to decrease at lower prices and higher quantities.

To confirm the concept, we can calculate the PED coefficient between two sets of prices.

Worked example

Using the example in Figure 4.3, the price first falls from $8 to $6, and then from $4 to $2. If the total revenue test holds true, we should find that PED is greater than one at the high prices and less than one at the low prices.

- PED between $8 and $6: $PED = \dfrac{(20-10) \div 10}{(6-8) \div 8} = \dfrac{1}{0.25} = 4$

- PED between $4 and $2: $PED = \dfrac{(40-30) \div 30}{(2-4) \div 4} = \dfrac{0.33}{0.5} = 0.66$

Between $8 and $6, the PED coefficient is 4, so demand is elastic, supporting our observation that an increase in total revenue following a decrease in price proves that consumers are relatively responsive to the lower price.

Between $4 and $2 the percentage decrease in price is larger than it was between $8 and $6, since the starting price is now lower. Additionally, although quantity demanded increases by the same number of units as it did following the earlier $2 price drop, the percentage increase in Q_D is smaller since the starting quantity is now larger. When price falls from $4 to $2, the total revenue in the industry declines from $120 to $80. This is evidence that consumers are no longer very responsive to lower prices, and that the percentage increase in quantity demanded must be smaller than the percentage decrease in price.

The PED coefficient of the above example at the lower price range is only 0.66, proving that a fall in price resulting in a decrease in total revenue is evidence of the inelasticity of demand between two points on a demand curve. At lower prices, consumers are no longer as responsive to price decreases as they were at higher prices. If the industry or firm were to decrease output and raise its price from $2 to $4, firms would experience an increase in total revenue because the inelastic nature of demand at low prices means that consumers are relatively unresponsive to the higher price, thus despite the lower quantity sold, the industry's revenues would rise.

EXERCISES

4   Assume the demand for a good is expressed by the function $Q_D = 500 - 20P$. Calculate the PED for this good when:

   a   the price increases from $5 to $6

   b   the price increases from $10 to $11

5   Using your answer to exercise 4, explain what happens to the PED for a good with a linear demand curve as the price of the good increases.

6   Identify two explanations for the changing price elasticity of demand along a straight line demand curve.

7   If PED = 1, what will be the effect on total revenue of a fall in the price of 5%? Explain.

For a logical explanation of the decrease in elasticity at lower prices along a straight-line demand curve, we can return to the determinants of PED. To illustrate this phenomenon, consider a top-end smartphone with touch-screen technology which, when first launched, sold for around $400. At that price, demand for the product was highly elastic.

It wasn't long before the price was brought down in most markets, which resulted in huge increases in sales and further growth in revenues. The high levels of sensitivity to changes in price when the phone was new indicated that demand was very elastic, likely due to the high price but also the perception among consumers that this was a luxury product that they could do without until the price was brought down.

It was not long before the uniqueness and luxury status of the product began to wear off. Due to market saturation, it was soon no longer the luxury product it had been in the first year of its launch. As the prestige and uniqueness waned, so did the responsiveness of consumers to changes in price. The latest generations of this phone sell for as little as $100 in most markets, and the manufacturer's unprecedented sales growth over the first year of the product's launch has slowed, even as price has continued to fall.

When the price of this luxury phone fell from $400 to $300, sales more than doubled. This reflects the highly elastic demand for the product when it was first launched. A price cut of around 25% led to sales increases of more than 100%. However, if the price now falls from $100 to $50, it is unlikely that sales will double again. Why? The product has lost its prestige, the price now represents a smaller proportion of the typical consumer's income, and there are simply not enough people out there who do not already have such a phone for the manufacturer to keep experiencing phenomenal sales growth with each new price cut.

The price elasticity of demand for most products decreases as the price decreases because when the price is lower, such goods lose their luxury status and the price is a smaller proportion of consumers' income.

For businesses making decisions about output and price, understanding price elasticity of demand is invaluable. A firm producing at a quantity and price combination along the inelastic range of its demand curve can always benefit by reducing its output and increasing its price, since consumers will be relatively unresponsive to the higher prices

To make up for the loss of prestige and the increasingly inelastic demand for their products as prices fall over time, manufacturers of items such as smartphones must continually release new models with increasingly innovative features. This may help to explain why, within four years of the first iPhone's launch, there have been four versions of this enormously popular product.

and total revenues will therefore increase. However, if a firm is producing at an output and price combination along the elastic range of its demand curve, the firm may benefit from lowering its price since consumers are relatively price sensitive and the percentage increase in quantity sold will exceed the percentage decrease in price, improving the firm's revenue figures. Table 4.1 provides a quick reference guide.

TABLE 4.1 THE TOTAL REVENUE TEST: A QUICK REFERENCE		
If ...	**Leads to ...**	**Then demand is ...**
a fall in price	an increase in total revenue	elastic
a fall in price	a decrease in total revenue	inelastic
an increase in price	a decrease in total revenue	elastic
an increase in price	an increase in total revenue	inelastic
a change in price	no change in total revenue	unit elastic

PED and indirect taxes

The price elasticity of demand of various goods also matters to economic policymakers, specifically regarding the question of what types of good should be taxed to generate government revenue. The effect that PED has on consumers, producers and the government when taxes are placed on particular goods or services is explored in depth in Chapter 5.

 To access Worksheet 4.1 on understanding price elasticity of demand, please visit www.pearsonbacconline.com and follow the onscreen instructions.

 4.4 Cross-price elasticity of demand (XED)

Learning outcomes
- Outline the concept of cross-price elasticity of demand, understanding that it involves responsiveness of demand for one good (and hence a shifting demand curve) to a change in the price of another good.
- Calculate XED using the following equation.

$$XED = \frac{\text{percentage change in quantity demanded of good X}}{\text{percentage change in price of good Y}}$$

- Show that substitute goods have a positive value of XED and complementary goods have a negative value of XED.
- Explain that the (absolute) value of XED depends on the closeness of the relationship between two goods.
- Examine the implications of XED for businesses if prices of substitutes or complements change.

 Cross-price elasticity of demand (XED) is a measure of the responsiveness of consumers of one good to a change in the price of a related good.

A second type of elasticity measures the responsiveness of consumers of a particular good to a change in the price of a related good. As you learned in Chapter 2 (pages 31–35), one of the determinants of demand for a good is the price of other related goods, both complements and substitutes. A fall in the price of a complement leads to an increase in the demand for the good in question. The XED tells us how much demand will increase for a good when the price of a complement falls. Likewise, if a substitute becomes cheaper, demand for a good will decrease since consumers will buy more of its substitutes. XED measures how much demand for a good decreases when the price of a substitute falls.

The XED coefficient

The formula for determining the XED coefficient is:

$$XED = \frac{\%\Delta Q_A}{\%\Delta P_B}$$

Where:

$\%\Delta Q_A$ is the percentage change in quantity of good A

$\%\Delta P_B$ is the percentage change in price of good B

The formula measures the responsiveness of consumers of good A to a change in the price of good B. Unlike PED, the coefficient for XED can be either negative or positive. A negative XED coefficient indicates that the two goods compared are complements for one another; a positive coefficient indicates that the goods are substitutes.

The size of the XED coefficient is an indication of how closely related the two goods in question are. For example, if a change in the price of fizzy drink C has a large effect on the quantity demanded of fizzy drink P, then the XED coefficient will be a number greater than one, and we can therefore conclude that the two goods are strong substitutes for one another. On the other hand, if fizzy drink C becomes more expensive and the quantity demanded of fizzy drink S changes only slightly, the XED is said to be relatively inelastic and the goods are not strong substitutes for one another.

The same concept applies for complementary goods. The higher the XED coefficient, the more closely related the goods in question are to one another.

To illustrate, two examples can be used: complementary goods have a negative XED coefficient; substitute goods have a positive XED coefficient.

Complementary goods: negative XED coefficient

Imagine two related goods, such as charcoal barbecues and charcoal. These two goods are complements, since the use of one requires the other. As you learned in Chapter 2 (page 33), if the price of charcoal rises, the demand for charcoal barbecues will decrease as consumers switch to gas or electric barbecues instead. There is, therefore, an inverse relationship between the price of charcoal and demand for charcoal barbecues. We can determine the responsiveness of barbecue consumers to changes in the price of charcoal by measuring the XED for charcoal and charcoal barbecues (Figure 4.4a and b).

Figure 4.4
XED for complementary goods: an increase in the price of one leads to a decrease in the demand for the other. Charcoal; charcoal barbecues.

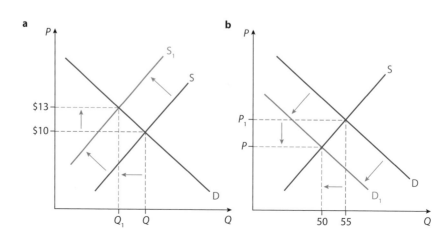

Worked example

In Figure 4.4, we see that as the price of charcoal rises from \$10 to \$13, the quantity of charcoal barbecues sold falls from 55 to 50. Using these numbers we can determine the cross-price elasticity of demand for charcoal and charcoal barbecues. If Q_B is the quantity of barbecues demanded and P_C is the price of charcoal:

$$\text{XED} = \frac{(Q_{B2} - Q_{B1}) \div Q_{B1}}{(P_{C2} - P_{C1}) \div P_{C1}}$$

$$= \frac{(50 - 55) \div 55}{(13 - 10) \div 10}$$

$$= \frac{-0.09}{0.3} = -0.3$$

We are able to determine that the cross-price elasticity of demand for charcoal barbecues and charcoal is around −0.3.

An increase in price of around 30% for charcoal leads to a decrease in quantity demanded for charcoal grills of around 9%. Barbecue consumers are relatively unresponsive to changes in the price of charcoal. The negative sign here remains as evidence of the relationship between the two goods. XED is not always negative.

Substitute goods: positive XED coefficient

Two goods that are substitutes in consumption exhibit a positive relationship between the price of one good and demand for the other. Take chicken and beef, for instance. Both meats are eaten as a source of protein. If an outbreak of bird flu leads to a fall in the supply of chicken and an increase in its price, the demand for beef rises because consumers begin to substitute the now relatively cheaper beef for the pricier chicken. The XED for beef and chicken measures the responsiveness of beef consumers to changes in the price of chicken (Figure 4.5).

Beef *vs* chicken: how responsive are the consumers of one to a change in the price of the other?

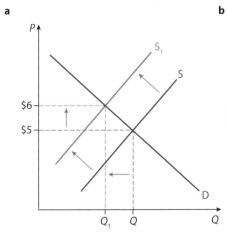

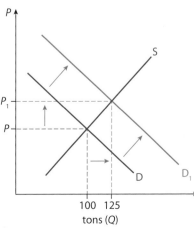

Figure 4.5
XED for substitute goods: an increase in the price of one leads to an increase in demand for the other.
a Chicken; **b** beef.

Worked example

In Figure 4.5, the price of chicken increases from \$5 to \$6 and the quantity of beef sold increases from 100 tons to 125 tons. With this information, we can calculate the cross-price elasticity of demand for beef and chicken.

$$\text{XED} = \frac{(125 - 100) \div 100}{(6 - 5) \div 5}$$

$$\text{XED} = \frac{0.25}{0.2} = 1.25$$

Beef consumers are relatively responsive to changes in the price of chicken. The cross-price elasticity coefficient of 1.25 indicates that a particular percentage increase in the price of chicken leads to a larger percentage increase in the demand for beef. The fact that the coefficient is positive is evidence of the relationship between beef and chicken. The two goods are substitutes, meaning that there is a direct relationship between the price of one and the demand for the other, hence the positive XED coefficient.

Interpreting the XED coefficient

The recent rise in demand for hybrid cars, electric cars and compact, fuel-efficient cars is almost certainly a demonstration of the concept of cross-price elasticity of demand. The demand for such vehicles is perfectly correlated with oil and fuel prices – the more expensive a tank of petrol becomes, the greater the quantity of hybrid cars demanded.

Interpretation of value of the XED coefficient is similar to interpretation of the value of the PED coefficient. A value of < 1 indicates that the two goods are cross-price inelastic, a value of 1 indicates unit elasticity and a value > 1 indicates that demand is cross-price elastic. A coefficient of zero indicates that demand between two goods is perfectly inelastic.

In the case of PED, examples of goods for which demand is perfectly inelastic are rare. But in the case of XED, perfect inelasticity indicates that the two goods are unrelated. If the price of airplane tickets rises by 10% and the demand for running socks remains constant, then the XED coefficient = 0/10 = 0. We can easily conclude that these two goods are unrelated since the change in price of one good has no effect on the demand for the other. Demand is cross-price perfectly inelastic for two goods that are neither complements nor substitutes.

EXERCISES

8   The price of good M increases by 15%, causing a fall in the Q_D of good N by 5%. Calculate the XED and comment on the relationship between the two goods. Identify an example of two goods that may demonstrate this relationship.

9   The price of good A falls from \$25 to \$20, leading to an increase in the quantity of good B demanded from 600 per week to 1000 per week. Calculate the XED for the two goods and comment on the relationship between goods A and B. Identify an example of two goods that may demonstrate this relationship.

10   Assume the XED for tennis balls and tennis rackets is –0.8. Calculate the change in quantity of tennis rackets demanded if the price of a can of tennis balls increases from \$4 to \$5.

CASE STUDY

Cross-price elasticity of demand in the news: camel demand soars in India

Farmers in the Indian state of Rajasthan are rediscovering the humble camel.

As the cost of running gas-guzzling tractors soars, even-toed ungulates are making a comeback, raising hopes that a fall in the population of the desert state's signature animal can be reversed.

'It's excellent for the camel population if the price of oil continues to go up because demand for camels will also go up,' says Ilse Köhler-Rollefson of the League for Pastoral Peoples and Endogenous Livestock Development. 'Two years ago, a camel cost little more than a goat, which is nothing. The price has since trebled.' The shift comes not a moment too soon for a national camel population that has fallen more than 50% over the past decade, to about 450 000, according to government figures.

Market prices for these 'ships of the desert', which crashed with the growing affordability of motorized transport, are rising again as oil prices soar. A sturdy male with a life expectancy of 60–80 years now fetches up to Rs40 000 ($973), compared to Rs5000–Rs10 000 three years ago, according to Hanuwant Singh of the Lokhit Pashu-Palak Sansthan, a non-profit welfare organization for livestock keepers. Entry-level tractors cost around $4000.

'It's very good news,' says Mr Singh, whose organization aims to dispel the image of backwardness associated with camel ownership and tries to promote higher economic returns for breeders. 'We had started to see camels, even female ones, being slaughtered for their meat. Now they are replacing the tractor again.'

It is too soon to say that the future for camels is bright. Shrinking grazing areas and a lack of investment in fodder trees may thwart a sustainable revival. Inadequate nutrition undermines the resilience of camel herds, making them vulnerable to disease and lowering birth rates.

The LPPS is encouraging the Raika community – traditional guardians of the camel population since the days when Maharajahs rode them into battle – to diversify into products such as camel milk, optimistically dubbed 'the white gold of the desert', camel leather handbags and camel bone jewellery.

Animal-lovers hope that the surge in oil prices will enhance the status of camel-breeders, who resent the lack of respect society has accorded their traditional knowledge, and give the Raika a strong incentive to stop selling female camels for slaughter.

Jo Johnson for the *Financial Times*, 2 May 2008

EXERCISES

11 How are camels and oil related goods? What should be true about the XED coefficient of camels and oil based on the relationship between these two goods?

12 As the price of oil rose from $110 to $130 per barrel, the quantity of camels in Rajasthan increased from 250 000 to 350 000. Calculate the cross-price elasticity of demand for camels and oil.

13 Other factors may affect the return of camels as a beast of burden in India. How might 'shrinking grazing areas and a lack of investment in fodder trees' counteract the effect of higher oil price on the camel market?

Income elasticity of demand (YED)

Learning outcomes

- Outline the concept of income elasticity of demand, understanding that it involves responsiveness of demand (and hence a shifting demand curve) to a change in income.
- Calculate YED using the following equation.

$$YED = \frac{\text{percentage change in quantity demanded}}{\text{percentage change in income}}$$

- Show that normal goods have a positive value of YED and inferior goods have a negative value of YED.

- Distinguish, with reference to YED, between necessity (income inelastic) goods and luxury (income elastic) goods.
- Examine the implications for producers and for the economy of a relatively low YED for primary products, a relatively higher YED for manufactured products and an even higher YED for services.

Income elasticity of demand (YED) is a measure of the responsiveness of consumers' demand for a particular good to a change in their income.

Income elasticity of demand (YED) measures the responsiveness of consumers' demand for a particular good to a change in income. As a determinant of demand introduced in Chapter 2 (page 32), changes in income have different effects on demand for different goods depending on the nature of the good in question.

The YED coefficient

If a good is a normal good, then rising income leads to greater demand. Normal goods may include restaurant meals, taxi rides, clothes, air travel, DVDs or anything else consumers tend to buy more of as their incomes rise.

If a rise in income leads to a decrease in consumption of a particular good, that good is said to be inferior. Inferior goods may include items such as fast food, generic brand groceries, public transport, second-hand clothes or any other product consumers tend to consume less of as incomes rise. Because consumers' demand for certain goods responds differently to changes in income, the YED coefficient can be either negative or positive.

YED is found by dividing the percentage change in quantity demanded for a good by the percentage change in the consumer's income.

$$YED = \frac{\%\Delta Q_D}{\%\Delta Y}$$

$\%\Delta Q_D$ is the percentage change in quantity demanded

$\%\Delta Y$ is the percentage change in income

If the percentage changes in quantity and price are not known but the values are known, then the simple YED formula can be used to determine the coefficient:

$$YED = \frac{(Q_{D2} - Q_{D1}) \div Q_{D1}}{(Y_2 - Y_1) \div Y_1}$$

Where:

Q_{D2} is the quantity demanded following the income change

Q_{D1} is the original quantity demanded

Y_2 is the new income

Y_1 is the original income

If there is a direct relationship between income and demand, then the YED coefficient will be positive, indicating that the good in question is a normal good. If, on the other hand, the relationship between income and demand is indirect, in which case a rise in income would lead to a smaller quantity and a fall in income to an increase in the quantity, then the YED coefficient will be negative, indicating the good in question is inferior.

Income elasticity of demand can be applied to measure the change in an individual's consumption of particular goods following a change in the individual's income, or it can be applied to analyse the effects of changes in national income on the demand for particular goods and services in a nation as a whole.

For instance, it was found in 2008 that while incomes in the US were falling due to the nationwide recession, the sale of bicycles began to increase. It turns out that bicycles may be inferior goods. When incomes are rising, car sales tend to increase, indicating that cars are normal goods. But as the US recession put downward pressure on average incomes, more people turned to bicycles since they present a more affordable option for getting around than fuel-consuming vehicles.

If bikes are an inferior good, demand should rise when incomes fall.

Interpreting the YED coefficient

As with the other types of elasticity covered in this chapter, YED can be elastic, inelastic or unit elastic.

If a good is income elastic, then a particular percentage change in income will lead to a larger percentage change in the quantity demanded for the good. For instance, if a rise in consumer income of 5% results in a 12% increase in the quantity demanded of hybrid cars, the YED for hybrid cars is 12/5 or 2.4. Demand for hybrids is said to be income elastic.

If a good is income inelastic, then a particular percentage change in income will lead to a smaller percentage change in the quantity demanded for the good. If a 5% rise in income leads to a 3% fall in the demand for fast food meals, the YED for fast food is 3/5 or −0.6. The negative sign indicates that fast food is an inferior good, and the fact that the absolute value of the YED coefficient is less than one is evidence that demand for fast food is income inelastic. Fast-food consumers are relatively unresponsive to changes in their income.

If a good is income unit elastic, then a particular percentage change in income will lead to an identical percentage change in the quantity demanded. If a 5% rise in consumer incomes leads to a 5% increase in the quantity of air travel demanded, then the YED coefficient is one and air travel (a normal good) is income unit elastic.

Fluctuations in bicycle sales are based on many variables. For consumers who view bikes as a means of transport, they are an inferior good. For consumers who view them as a recreational good, bikes may be a normal good. Bike sales also respond greatly to changes in the price of oil. Why do you think this is?

EXERCISES

14 Calculate the YED if an increase in income of 8% leads to an increase in the quantity demanded for good X of 12%. Identify an example of a product that good X could represent.

15 Assume the following levels of income and the quantities demanded of good A.
Y_{2010} = $40 000. Y_{2011} = $55 000. Q_{D2010} = 45 units. Q_{D2011} = 40 units.

  a From the information above, calculate the YED for good A and comment on your response.

  b Identify an example of a product that good A could represent.

16 For the following three products, comment on the elasticity values.

  a Gourmet ice cream: YED = 0.6

  b Fast food hamburgers: YED = −1.2

  c Air travel: YED = 1.8

Applications of income elasticity of demand

Understanding YED allows businesses and governments to analyse the effects of changing incomes among consumers and taxpayers on the level of demand for particular goods in an economy. A firm that must decide on production numbers for its product may wish to determine whether the incomes of its consumers are likely to rise or fall in the future. If a firm produces a good considered inferior, then a recession could be good for business and it will increase its output in order to meet the rising demand among consumers whose incomes are harmed by the recession. Producers of normal goods, on the other hand, may scale back production as incomes decline. Understanding the responsiveness of consumers of their products to changes in income better enables firms to produce at a more efficient level of output over time.

Governments also must recognize the effects of varying income elasticities of demand for different goods produced by their nation's economy. The largest source of tax revenue for most governments is a direct tax on income. A government's decision to raise or lower income tax on households will directly affect disposable income and therefore demand for goods and services in a nation. A tax increase that decreases disposable income will reduce demand for normal goods across the nation's economy and increase demand for inferior goods. A government must consider these effects in order to make informed decisions regarding tax policy.

The economic term 'inferior good' has a very specific and technical definition. What evidence is needed to determine if a particular good is inferior or normal from an economic standpoint? What about from a non-economic perspective? What might make a particular good 'inferior'?

Price elasticity of supply (PES) is a measure of the responsiveness of a producer of a particular good to a change in the price of that good.

4.6 Price elasticity of supply (PES)

Learning outcomes

- Explain the concept of price elasticity of supply, understanding that it involves responsiveness of quantity supplied to a change in price along a given supply curve.
- Calculate PES using the following equation.

$$PES = \frac{\text{percentage change in quantity supplied}}{\text{percentage change in price}}$$

- Explain, using diagrams and PES values, the concepts of elastic supply, inelastic supply, unit elastic supply, perfectly elastic supply and perfectly inelastic supply.
- Explain the determinants of PES, including time, mobility of factors of production, unused capacity and ability to store stocks.
- Explain why the PES for primary commodities is relatively low and the PES for manufactured products is relatively high.

PES measures the responsiveness of producers of a particular good to a change in the price of that good. The law of supply tells us that, *ceteris paribus*, there is a direct relationship between the price of a particular product and the quantity supplied in the marketplace. The sensitivity of producers to changes in price may be very low or very great, depending on the type of good produced, the availability of inputs, and the amount of time following the change in price.

The PES coefficient

Like PED, PES can be inelastic, unit elastic or elastic; it can range from zero to infinity. The formula for determining the PES coefficient is similar to that for PED, except that we measure movements along the supply curve rather than movements along the demand curve:

$$PES = \frac{\%\Delta Q_S}{\%\Delta P}$$

Where:

$\%\Delta Q_S$ is the percentage change in quantity supplied

$\%\Delta P$ is the percentage change in price

As in the case of the other elasticities, if the percentage changes in price and quantity are not known, then PES can be calculated using the simple elasticity formula:

$$PES = \frac{(Q_{S2} - Q_{S1}) \div Q_{S1}}{(P_2 - P_1) \div P_1}$$

Where:

Q_{S2} is the quantity supplied following the price change

Q_{S1} is the original quantity supplied

P_2 is the new price

P_1 is the original price

As with PED, PES can be highly elastic, highly inelastic, or somewhere in between (Figure 4.6). Take two goods, for instance: croissants and fighter jets. The market for croissants is highly competitive; any bakery can make a greater or lesser quantity of croissants day after day depending on the demand. If the demand for croissants grows, putting upward pressure on the price, bakeries can respond quickly and easily to the higher price, increasing the quantity supplied almost instantly to meet the higher demand.

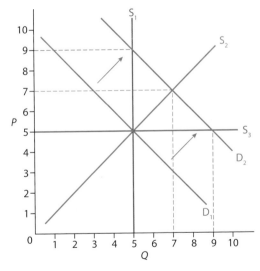

◀ **Figure 4.6**
The extremes of PES.

The supply of croissants is therefore nearly perfectly elastic. An increase in price of 10% will be met by a much larger increase in the quantity supplied since the inputs needed are easily acquired and the numerous producers can respond instantly and easily to changes in price. The end result of an increase in demand for croissants, therefore, will be almost no increase in the price but a large increase in the quantity supplied, as indicated by S_3 in Figure 4.6, showing a perfectly elastic supply curve.

On the other had, the supply of fighter jets is highly, if not perfectly, inelastic – especially in the short run. If the demand for fighter jets grows from D_1 to D_2, the producers of these jets will be unable to respond quickly to the change in price, and the quantity of fighter jets produced will remain nearly constant in the short run. A large increase in price will lead to almost no increase in the quantity of fighter jets sold, indicating that in the period immediately following an increase in demand, the supply of fighter jets is nearly perfectly inelastic, illustrated by S_1 in the diagram above.

Over time, as weapon and airplane manufacturers are able to acquire the scarce inputs needed for jet production and allocate more resources towards increasing their production of fighter jets, producers will become more responsive to the higher demand.

Croissants and fighter jets represent two extreme examples of price elasticity of supply. For the former, producers are extremely responsive to changes in demand but for the latter, producers are extremely unresponsive, particularly in the short run. In between these two extremes, supply can be relatively inelastic (PES < 1), relatively elastic (PES >1) or unit elastic (PES = 1). S_2 above, which originates at the origin, represents a unit elastic supply curve, indicating that a particular percentage increase in the price will lead to an identical increase in the quantity supplied.

In the real world, examples of goods for which supply is either perfectly inelastic or perfectly elastic are rare, but not nearly as rare as are goods for which demand is perfectly elastic or inelastic. Any good that is completely fixed in its supply due to its physical scarcity is perfectly inelastic in supply. Gold, for instance, is mined in only a few places in the world. Therefore, even a small increase in the demand for gold leads to a large increase in its price since gold producers have only limited capacity to increase their output of gold in the short run. Certain antiques or artwork will exhibit perfectly inelastic supply as well. Picasso's paintings, for instance, only exist in a limited number, and no matter how much demand rises or falls, the number of Picassos in the world will remain totally constant.

Supply can be perfectly elastic for a good if large inventories exist for that good. Inventories are the amount of a good held in stock by a firm. If demand for a good rises and large inventories exist, producers can respond to the increase in price instantly by releasing their inventories on the market to meet the increase in consumer demand. Even in the short run, supply can be perfectly elastic in markets in which firms have substantial quantities of inventory.

The determinants of price elasticity of supply

A good's PES depends on:

- the amount of time following a change in price
- the mobility of factors of production
- the ability to store stocks
- the amount of unused capacity.

Time following a change in price

Another important determinant of PES is the amount of time following a change in price over which producers are able to adjust their output. Figure 4.7 shows three supply curves for the same product: corn. Suppose a nation's government announces that by the end of the current decade, 20% of automobiles must be able to run on ethanol manufactured from corn. Thereafter, the demand for corn increases and the price rises from $5 per bushel to $6 per bushel as ethanol producers begin ramping up their production of fuel made from corn. In the days, weeks, months and years following an increase in the price of corn, we would expect to see the price elasticity of supply change as producers have time to adjust their output to the higher demand and price in the corn market.

Figure 4.7
PES changes over time.

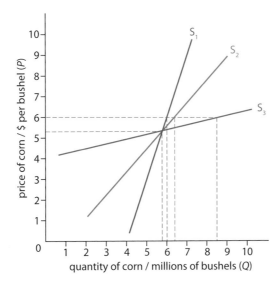

S_1: the market period

The period immediately following a change in price is known as the market period, and during this time supply would be highly inelastic, corresponding with S_1. In the market period, producers do not have the time to adjust their output to changes in price. Corn producers can release the little inventory they have and can perhaps harvest their crop earlier than planned, but the amount of land, labour and capital allocated to growing corn is fixed in the market period. In the market period, supply is highly inelastic and output can increase from 5.7 million bushels to around only 5.9 million bushels of corn following an increase in price from \$5 to \$6 per bushel.

S_2: the short run

Within a few months of the increase in the corn price, growers will be able to increase the intensity with which they use their fixed capital and land resources for growing corn. More labour and better or more fertilizer and pesticides can be applied to the existing crop in an attempt to increase the yield in order to meet the rising demand. The short run is the period of time over which land and capital are fixed, but labour is variable and therefore the intensity with which land and capital are used can increase, resulting in more elastic supply than was possible in the market period. S_2 represents the supply curve in the short run following an increase in the price of corn. In the short run, output can be increased from 5.5 million bushels to about 6.5 million bushels.

S_3: the long run

In the long run, supply is highly elastic. The long run is defined as the period of time over which all factors of production are variable. In the case of corn, the long run may be one or two years, a period of time over which farmers can switch land that was being used for other crops to corn production and bring idle land into production of corn as well. In addition, farmers can allocate more capital and labour towards growing corn, allowing them to be much more responsive to the increase in price. In the long run, following an increase in the price of corn from \$5 to \$6, output can be increased from 5.5 million bushels to around 8.6 million bushels.

Over time, producers are much more responsive to changes in the price of a good. In the period immediately following a change in price, all factors of production are fixed and therefore firms are unable to change their output to much extent. In the short run, capital and land are fixed but firms can hire more workers to meet increasing demand or lay workers off to adapt to falling demand, thereby using existing land and capital more or less intensively. In the long run, all factors of production are variable, so firms can be highly responsive to changes in demand in the marketplace.

Mobility of the factors of production

The more mobile the factors of production (the labour, land and capital resources needed for the production of a good), the more responsive a firm can be to changes in price. Whether a good is land intensive in its production or labour-and-capital intensive makes a significant difference to producers' ability to quickly shift resources into or out of production following a change in price.

Relatively elastic supply: manufactured goods and low-skilled services

Low-tech manufactured goods (e.g. clothes, toys and simple electronics) and low-skilled services (e.g. haircuts, laundry services, housekeeping) tend to have relatively elastic supply. Producers can easily hire more workers and acquire more raw materials and capital resources to meet increases in demand for such goods, thus they are highly responsive to increases in the price. When demand falls, producers of these goods find it quick and easy to lay off workers, take capital out of production, and cancel orders for raw materials, thus they can respond quickly to decreases in demand as well. The easy mobility of resources for manufactured goods and low-skilled services allows for supply of these items to be relatively responsive to changes in price.

The supply of corn and other commodities is highly inelastic.

Relatively inelastic supply: primary commodities and heavy industrial goods

The harder it is to shift factors of production into or out of the production of a good, the more inelastic the good's supply will be. The markets for airplanes, residential and commercial construction, automobiles, high-tech goods and highly skilled services (e.g. doctors, financial experts or university professors) tend to exhibit highly inelastic supply. Additionally, primary commodities that are land-intensive in production, such as coffee, rice, corn, wheat, coal, oil, gas and minerals also exhibit immobility of the factors of production. It is extremely time-consuming and costly to bring into production new plants for heavy industrial goods and primary commodities to meet rising demand, or to take them out of production in response to falling prices. Thus, the supply of such goods tends to be relatively inelastic.

The ability to store stocks

If large inventories of a good can easily be stored in warehouses or kept on hand by producers, then supply of the good can be highly responsive to changes in the price. Items such as video games, software, low-tech manufactured goods and certain non-perishable commodities can be produced in large quantities that aren't necessarily sold but added to inventories to be stored and used to meet future demand.

If, in the future, demand for such goods rises, the producers can quickly and easily release stored inventory on to the market to meet the increase in demand and prevent rapid rises in the price, responding to price rises with larger proportional increases in the quantity supplied. Likewise, when the demand for non-perishable commodities falls, producers can respond by putting supply into inventory and quickly reducing the quantity available in the market.

But not all goods can be easily stored. When demand for such perishable goods as milk, fruit, some grains and large-scale industrial goods such as airplanes and ships rises, producers have a very limited stock to dip into to meet rising demand. Likewise, inventories cannot be added to when demand falls; producers are not very responsive and must accept a lower price to sell the current output that would otherwise go bad or be very costly for the firm to store.

The amount of unused capacity

Excess capacity refers to the amount a firm is able to produce in the short run without having to expand its plant size and the amount of capital and land employed in production. If an industry is operating at a level of output at which it has large amounts of unused capacity, then producers are able to quickly and easily respond to changes in the demand for the good in question. If, however, an industry is operating at or near full capacity, supply will be highly inelastic in the short run, as in order to meet any increase in demand firms must first acquire new capital equipment and open new factories to meet the rising demand for their output. Such expansion takes time and means that supply will be relatively inelastic following an increase in demand.

 Excess capacity is the amount of output an industry can produce in the short run beyond its current level without having to expand its plant size. If large amounts of excess capacity exist, producers can be highly responsive to changes in the price. With little excess capacity, producers cannot respond quickly to changes in price.

EXERCISES

17 Calculate the PES if a price increase of 9% causes the quantity supplied to increase by 3%.

18 Assume the price of good A is \$4 and the quantity supplied is 400 units. With a PES of 0.5, how will a fall in the price from \$4 to \$3 affect the quantity supplied of good A?

19 The supply for good B is expressed with the function $Q_S = 30 + 2.5P$. Calculate the PES for this good if:

  a the price increases from \$10 to \$11

  b the price decreases from \$5 to \$4

20 'The price elasticity of supply for a good changes the more time goes by following a change in the demand for the good'. Using an example, explain how this is so.

Applications of price elasticity of supply

Understanding price elasticity of supply allows firm managers and government policymakers to better evaluate the effects of their output decisions and economic policies.

Excise taxes and PES

A tax on a particular good, known as an excise tax, is paid by both the producers and the consumers of that good. When a government taxes a good for which supply is highly elastic, it is the consumer who ends up bearing the greatest burden of the tax, as producers are forced to pass the tax onto buyers in the form of a higher sales price. If the producer of a highly elastic good bears the tax burden itself, it may be forced to reduce output to such a degree that production of the good becomes no longer economically viable. A tax on a good for which supply is highly inelastic will be borne primarily by the producer of the good. The price paid by consumers will only increase slightly while the after-tax amount received by the producer will decrease significantly, but in the case of inelastic supply this will have a relatively small impact on output. A graphical representation of the effects of taxes on different goods is introduced in Chapter 5 (page 101).

Price controls and PES

A common policy in rich countries aimed at assisting farmers is the use of minimum prices for agricultural commodities. In the European Union (EU), the Common Agricultural Policy (CAP) involves a complex system of subsidies, import and export controls and price controls, the objective of which is to ensure a fair standard of living for Europe's agricultural community. The use of minimum prices in agricultural markets can have the unintended consequence of creating substantial surpluses of unsold output. Take the example of butter in the EU.

Prior to reform of the CAP in 2013, the EU used to purchase millions of tonnes of surplus dairy produce every year. It did so at stated guaranteed market prices, and stored the reserves in vast quantities in what became known as Europe's 'butter mountains' and 'milk lakes'.

These excess reserves were the subject of fierce criticism and although they were said to have been eradicated in 2007, in January 2009 fears of a butter mountain loomed large once again.

Following a sharp drop in demand for butter and milk the European Commission bought 30,000 tonnes of unsold butter and 109,000 tonnes of unwanted skimmed powder milk at above market prices, costing €255 million.

Commission officials said the measure was a temporary move to stop dairy farmers going out of business in the wake of a drastic slump in milk prices and a 33 per cent fall in butter exports.

The situation in the EU butter market can be attributed to underestimation by policymakers of the responsiveness of butter producers to the price controls established under the CAP. A minimum price scheme of any sort, if effective, will result in surplus output of the good in question, but the 30 000 tons of unsold butter in Europe appears to exceed the expected surplus considerably. Figure 4.8 illustrates why.

Figure 4.8
The effect of a price floor depends on the responsiveness of producers to the higher price.

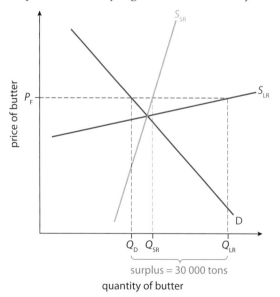

A price floor (P_F) is set above the equilibrium price of butter established by the free market. Butter producers in Europe are guaranteed a price of P_F euros, and any surplus not sold at this price will be bought by the European Commission (EC). Assuming a relatively inelastic supply, which corresponds with the short-run period (S_{SR}), the increase in butter production is relatively small (Q_{SR}), resulting in a relatively small surplus ($Q_{SR} - Q_D$).

In the short run, the amount of surplus butter the EU governments needed to purchase was minimal. But as you learned earlier, when producers of goods have time to adjust to the higher price (here, the price guaranteed by the EC), they become more responsive to the higher price and are able to increase their output by much more than in the short run. S_{LR} represents the supply of butter in Europe in the long run, after years of the minimum-price scheme. As demand fell due to the global economic slowdown, butter producers continued to produce at a level corresponding to the price floor, thus leading to ever-growing butter stocks and the need for the EC to spend 69 million euros on surplus butter.

Understanding the behaviour of producers in response to changes in prices, whether due to excise taxes or price controls, better allows both business managers and government policymakers to respond appropriately to conditions experienced by producers and consumers in the marketplace and thus to avoid inefficiencies resulting from various economic policies.

This chapter extended your analysis of the interactions of supply and demand for goods and services in the marketplace by focusing on the responsiveness of producers and consumers to changes in factors such as the price of the good, the price of related goods and the income of consumers.

The formulas for elasticities of demand, supply, income and cross-elasticity each measure the percentage change in quantity over the percentage change in another variable. Elasticity's applications are varied and wide; they affect consumers and producers of particular goods, as well as government policymakers who are trying to achieve various economic objectives while addressing the inefficiencies resulting from taxes and price controls.

In Chapter 5, you will explore in more depth the various forms of government intervention in free markets, expanding your understanding of the reasons for and effects of various government actions including indirect taxes, subsidies and price controls.

Government interference always reduces efficiency in the free market. Therefore, any attempt by government to help producers or consumers will make society worse off. What evidence would we need to support or refute this claim?

To access Worksheet 4.2 on price elasticity of supply, please visit www. pearsonbacconline.com and follow the onscreen instructions.

To learn more about elasticity, visit www. pearsonhotlinks.com, enter the title or ISBN of this book and select weblink 4.1.

To access Worksheet 4.3, a multiple-choice quiz on this chapter, please visit www.pearsonbacconline. com and follow the onscreen instructions.

PRACTICE QUESTIONS

1. a With the use of examples, explain why some products have a low price elasticity while others have a high elasticity. (10 marks) [AO2]

   b If you were employed as an economist by a business, discuss why a knowledge of the price elasticity of demand of your product would be useful. (15 marks) [AO3]

   © International Baccalaureate Organization 1999

2. a Carefully explain what it is that price, income and cross-elasticities of demand are meant to measure. (10 marks) [AO2]

   b Discuss the practical importance of the concept of price elasticity of demand for the government. (15 marks) [AO3]

   © International Baccalaureate Organization 1999

3. a Explain the factors which influence price elasticity of supply. Illustrate your answer with reference to the market for a commodity or raw material. (10 marks) [AO2]

   b Discuss the importance of price elasticity of supply and price elasticity of demand for producers of primary commodities in less developed countries. (15 marks) [AO3]

   © International Baccalaureate Organization 2002

5 GOVERNMENT INTERVENTION

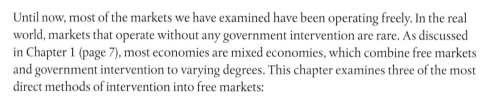

5.1 Indirect taxes

Learning outcomes

- Explain why governments impose indirect taxes.
- Distinguish between specific and *ad valorem* taxes.
- Draw diagrams to show specific and *ad valorem* taxes, and analyse their impacts on market outcomes.
- Discuss the consequences of imposing an indirect tax on the stakeholders in a market, including consumers, producers and the government.

They say nothing is certain except death and taxes.

Until now, most of the markets we have examined have been operating freely. In the real world, markets that operate without any government intervention are rare. As discussed in Chapter 1 (page 7), most economies are mixed economies, which combine free markets and government intervention to varying degrees. This chapter examines three of the most direct methods of intervention into free markets:

- taxes
- subsidies
- price controls.

The supply of government exceeds demand.

Lewis H Lapham

Indirect taxes are those taxes placed on goods and services. They are described as indirect because the government collects the revenues from the supplier after the supplier has collected them from the purchaser. Therefore, the government collects the money from the consumer *indirectly*. A sales tax is collected by the seller and delivered to the government: it is an indirect tax.

Indirect taxes can take either of two forms:

- a specific tax – the amount of the tax is an absolute value, such as $2 per pack of cigarettes
- an *ad valorem* tax – the amount of tax is a percentage of the sale, a value added tax (VAT) of 19% on the sales of most goods is an *ad valorem tax*.

 A tax is a charge, placed on a individual or firm, that is payable to the government under punishment of law.

The term 'excise tax' is used to refer to the taxing of one type of good, like cigarettes, alcohol, or hotel accommodation. Excise taxes can be either specific or *ad valorem*.

In contrast, income taxes are collected by the government *directly* from the individual or household.

As explained in Chapter 2 (page 45), firms generally view taxes as an increase in their operating costs because the tax is likely to erode the profitability of their product. For this reason, economists show the tax as a decrease in supply, a shift left of supply at all prices. This shift is shown differently, however, depending on whether the tax is specific tax or *ad valorem* tax.

Specific tax

Specific taxes charge a specific amount to be paid for every unit of a good sold. Also called a per-unit tax, typical examples of flat rate taxes include a tax on cigarettes or car tyres of $1 per unit. Figure 5.1 shows the initial effect of a per-unit tax. The supply curve shifts upward or left by exactly the amount of the tax, in this case $20, to S_1 (also known as S_{TAX}). This is a parallel shift because the amount of the per-unit tax is the same no matter the price or quantity of units.

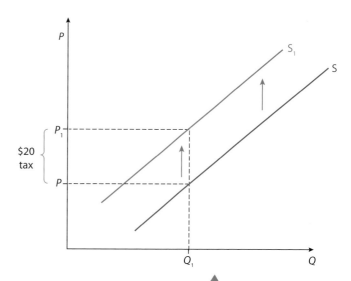

Ad valorem tax

In contrast, *ad valorem* taxes base the tax on a percentage of the purchase price. Therefore, the higher the price of the good, the overall amount of the tax will increase. A product whose price is $200 and has an *ad valorem* tax of 10% pays $20 tax. If the price of the good were $500, the total amount of the tax would rise to $50, but the percentage is still the same, 10%. Figure 5.2 shows the effect of an *ad valorem* tax. Supply still shifts upward or left by the amount of the tax, but the distance between S and S_1 grows as the price increases. This reflects the increased amount of tax charged as the price increases.

Figure 5.1
Specific or per unit tax.

Specific tax (also known as a flat rate or per-unit tax) is a set amount charged per unit of the product sold.

Figure 5.2
Ad valorem tax.

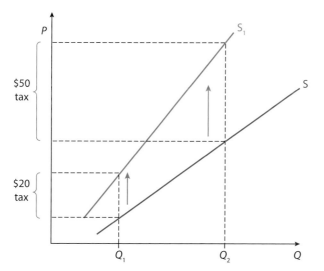

Ad valorem tax is a percentage tax on a good or a range of goods. In many countries it is known as value added tax (VAT) or general sales tax. (*Ad valorem* means 'according to value'.)

EXERCISES

1   Explain how specific and *ad valorem* taxes work.

2   List two examples each of per-unit tax and *ad valorem* tax.

The effect of taxes: stakeholder consequences

In either case, taxing the sales of a good has identifiable consequences. Some of the basic results are listed below.

• **Taxes raise prices**. Because taxes shift supply to the left, they inevitably raise the equilibrium price of the product.

- **Taxes reduce output**. Again, supply shifts left because of the increased costs. Reduced supply leads to smaller quantities offered for sale.
- **Market size shrinks**. Reduced output means a reduced market size.
- **Consumers suffer**. Consumers pay higher prices and receive less of the product.
- **Producers suffer**. Producers incur extra costs, produce less and are less likely to make profits.
- **Governments benefit**. The taxes collected will increase government revenues.

The extent of these effects is influenced by the size of the tax and the nature of the market. Some taxes might harm producers rather little, while consumers pay heavily. Other taxes might dramatically reduce market output, while some not at all.

The specific nature of these consequences is explored in the following HL section.

To access Worksheet 5.1 on taxing witchcraft, please visit www.pearsonbacconline.com and follow the onscreen instructions.

Tax incidence is a measure of the consequences of a tax on all the affected parties.

5.2   Tax incidence (HL only)

Learning outcomes

- Explain, using diagrams, how the incidence of indirect taxes on consumers and firms differs, depending on the price elasticity of demand and on the price elasticity of supply.
- Plot demand and supply curves for a product from linear functions and then illustrate and/or calculate the effects of the imposition of a specific tax on the market (on price, quantity, consumer expenditure, producer revenue, government revenue, consumer surplus and producer surplus).

Several important questions arise when a new tax is proposed. While it is true that a tax impacts the profitability of any product, the *degree* to which this is true varies considerably. When supply shifts backward by the amount of the tax, who really pays the majority of the tax can vary. Whoever pays the tax suffers the tax burden (or incidence) of the tax. Under most circumstances, the burden is shared by both consumer and producer, to different degrees.

Furthermore, questions arise over how powerful the tax will be. How much will the market shrink as a result of this tax? How badly will firms, and their employees, suffer as a result? Will the tax raise government revenue significantly or just a little?

We will examine these questions using the concepts of elasticity described in Chapter 4.

Tax incidence: PED similar to PES

Figure 5.3 shows a specific per-unit tax imposed on a market with a downward-sloping demand curve and an upward-sloping supply curve. There are a great many effects, even in this simple case. We might expect the price to rise by exactly the amount of the tax. If this were true, the price would shoot up from P_E to P_2, representing the full amount of the tax. However, because the demand curve slopes downwards, the producers cannot simply increase the price by the full amount. Consumers will decrease consumption as the price increases, so that the new equilibrium is at a point where the new S_{TAX} curve intersects the demand curve at P_{TAX}. Price has increased, but not by the full amount of the tax. The new equilibrium quantity is Q_{TAX}, which is a reduction from the original market quantity.

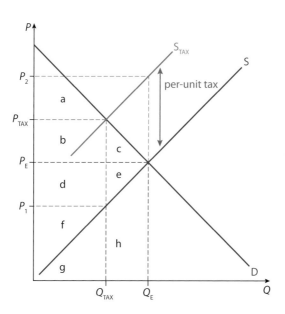

Figure 5.3
Tax incidence: PED similar to PES.

Who pays the largest share of the tax? In this case, the full tax area is represented by the boxes b and d. This is equivalent to the amount of the per-unit tax (P_1 to P_{TAX}) multiplied by the new equilibrium quantity, Q_{TAX}. Box b represents the difference between the old price and new tax price, and also lies in the consumer surplus area above the market price up to the demand curve. Therefore, this amount is paid by the consumer. Box d represents the rest of the tax, paid by the producer. This area falls in the producer surplus area, and represents a decreased producer revenue caused by the tax. In this case, the size of the two boxes is roughly equal, so we can say that consumers and producers share the burden of the tax equally.

More can be said of the effects on the market with this diagram. Consumers pay more and receive less output. Their previous consumer surplus area (areas a, b, and c) is now reduced to area a. Producer surplus is reduced as well. Previously, producers received areas d, e and f in surplus. Now they receive only area f.

The market size has clearly been reduced from Q_E to Q_{TAX}. This reduction in total quantity sold causes a welfare loss, a loss of benefit or utility to participants in the market. This kind of welfare loss is called a deadweight loss. It involves a complete loss of welfare from the market. Consumers have lost the area of consumer surplus shown by areas b and c. The loss of area b benefits the government in the form of tax revenues. However, area c is lost completely, since the quantity Q_{TAX} to Q_E is no longer consumed at all. In the same way, producer surplus areas e and d are taken by the tax: area d goes to the government and area e is lost completely.

Deadweight loss is the loss of welfare, utility or benefit to market participants, typically as a result of taxes, protectionist policies or externalities.

HL EXERCISES

3   'The power to tax is the power to destroy.' (US Supreme Court Justice John Marshall, 1819)

   a   To what extent do you agree with this statement?

   b   In what instances are taxes on specific products justified?

   c   List some examples of items that should not be taxed and justify your answer.

The simple case demonstrates the power of a tax to dramatically affect the market, but real-world examples in which producers and consumers of a taxed good share the burden of the tax equally are highly unusual. So, it is necessary to understand the effects of a tax on specific products where the price elasticities of demand and supply are different.

In each of the following cases, the type of tax applied is an excise tax: it is a tax applied to a type of good, like cigarettes or automobiles. In reality, most goods are taxed through larger categories of sales taxes, where most goods sold are included. This is called a value added tax (VAT). VAT taxes all goods in general, whereas excise taxes select specific categories for special taxation. Excise taxes can be charged on a per-unit or *ad valorem* basis, but for simplicity we will look at per-unit taxes exclusively. You should be aware that the analysis is similar overall, with some differences in the details of application for taxes.

Tax incidence: PED > PES

Figure 5.4 shows the impact of the same tax as in Figure 5.3 but applied when the price elasticity of demand is greater than the price elasticity of supply. Put simply, demand is more elastic than supply. Under these conditions, some distinctions are evident. With consumers more responsive to price changes, the same tax has led to a proportionally smaller increase in the price paid by consumers but the difference between Q_E and Q_{TAX} is proportionally much greater than in the previous case.

Figure 5.4

Tax incidence: PED > PES.

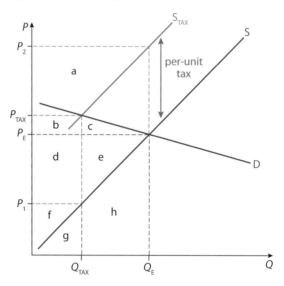

The price has increased, but by less than in the previous case. This is logical – consumers are more responsive to price, and therefore less tolerant of price increases. Correspondingly, the tax burden paid by consumers is less than half – area b is smaller than area d. Producers pay more of the burden of the tax. The relative size of the tax box is different too. It appears that with elastic demand, the government receives less revenue.

The market size decreases quite significantly, and therefore employment in the industry is more likely to decline. Finally, the amount of deadweight loss appears to be greater in this case. The areas c and e appear to be larger than in the original example. This, too, is logical. The size of the deadweight loss varies with decrease in the amount sold. The amount sold is determined mainly by the elasticity of demand. Highly responsive demand means larger decreases in quantity, and more deadweight loss.

Tax incidence: PED < PES

Figure 5.5 shows the case where the supply is more elastic than demand. In this case, demand is rigid as consumers are relatively indifferent to price changes. With demand less responsive to price changes, the quantity demanded has decreased very little, so the difference between Q_E and Q_{TAX} is less than in the previous two examples.

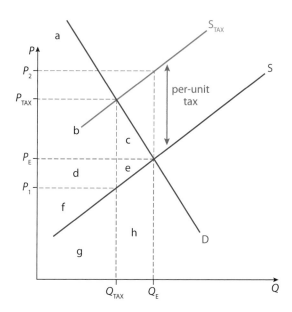

◀ **Figure 5.5**
Tax incidence: PED < PES.

The price has increased by much more than in the original case. This is logical – consumers are less responsive to price, and therefore more tolerant of price increases. Correspondingly, the tax burden paid by consumers is actually more than half – area b is much larger than area d. Producers pay less of the burden of the tax. Again, the relative size of the tax box is different. It appears that with inelastic demand, the government receives more revenue. Because consumers continue to buy the good in similar numbers, the tax is collected on a greater number of goods. Therefore, overall tax revenue is higher.

The market size decreases relatively little, and therefore employment in the industry is less affected. Finally, the amount of deadweight loss appears to be actually smaller in this case. The areas c and e appear to be smaller than in the original example. The unresponsive demand means smaller decreases in quantity, and less deadweight loss.

We can summarize these results as follows.

- The more elastic the demand relative to supply, the greater the burden paid by producers, the greater the deadweight loss, and the smaller the government revenue.
- The more inelastic the demand relative to supply, the greater the burden paid by consumers, (probably) the smaller the deadweight loss, and the greater the government revenue.

With this in mind, governments are very tempted to tax goods for which PED is relatively inelastic. Addictive goods like alcohol and cigarettes are frequent targets of excise taxes as a result. The government stands to gain more revenue and will harm industries less when demand is relatively inelastic.

It is also possible to calculate the value of the tax revenues and respective burdens on producers and consumers. In general:

- consumer tax burden: $b = (P_{TAX} - P_E) \times Q_{TAX}$
- producer tax burden: $d = (P_E - P_1) \times Q_{TAX}$
- total tax revenue to government: $b + d = (P_{TAX} - P_1) \times Q_{TAX}$

HL EXERCISES

4 When a tax is placed on a good, why does the price increase by less than the full amount of the tax?

5 Explain what determines whether producers or consumers pay the larger share of the tax.

6 Create an example of an *ad valorem* tax. Using an appropriate diagram, show the effects of the tax on consumer and producer expenditures, tax burdens, deadweight losses, and market size. Show one case with relatively elastic demand and another with relatively inelastic demand.

7 Create an example of a flat-rate or per-unit tax. Using an appropriate diagram, show the effects of the tax on consumer and producer expenditures, tax burdens, deadweight losses, and market size. Show one case with relatively elastic demand and another with relatively inelastic demand.

Tax incidence and linear functions

Chapters 2 and 3 explained how linear functions are used to express supply and demand. Linear functions can also be used for the analysis of tax incidence. This section reviews how to use linear functions to plot supply and demand and shows you how to calculate the effects of a tax on various stakeholders.

Worked example

Let's assume supply and demand functions for cigarettes as follows:

$$Q_D = 1600 - 200P$$
$$Q_S = 600 + 300P$$

Now solve for P.

Simplify by subtracting 600 from both sides.

$$1000 - 200P = 300P$$

Simplify again by adding 200P to both sides.

$$1000 = 500P$$

Now, divide both sides by 500.

$$1000/500 = 500P/500$$

Thus,

$$P = 2$$

Now that we have the equilibrium price, the equilibrium quantity can be determined by plugging the price into the demand and supply functions.

$$Q_D = 1600 - 200(2) = 1200$$
$$Q_S = 600 + 300(2) = 1200$$

Thus the equilibrium quantity is 1200 packs. The demand schedule is shown in Table 5.1.

TABLE 5.1 LINEAR MARKET SCHEDULE: CIGARETTES		
Price (P) / $	Quantity demanded (Q_D)	Quantity supplied (Q_S)
5	600	2100
4	800	1800
3	1000	1500
2	1200	1200
1	1400	900
0	1600	600

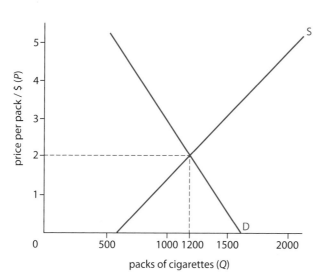

Figure 5.6
Linear functions market equilibrium: cigarettes.

Figure 5.6 (above) shows the points of demand and supply from the schedule in Table 5.1.

Now, let's assume that the local government placed a $1 tax on each pack of cigarettes. A tax is a cost imposed on the producers of cigarettes, so whatever price consumers pay, $1 must be given over to the government. Therefore, producers will receive $1 less than the new equilibrium price. The new supply function can be expressed as: $Q_S = 600 + 300(P-1)$. This can be simplified by multiplying 300 by $(P-1)$, so $Q_S = 600 + 300P - 300$. Simplify again by subtracting 300 from 600: $Q_S = 300 + 300P$.

To find the new equilibrium price, we make the new supply function equal to the demand function.

Worked example

$300 + 300P = 1600 - 200P$

Now solve for P.

Simplify by subtracting 300 from both sides.

$300P = 1300 - 200P$

Simplify again by adding $200P$ to both sides:

$500P = 1300$

Finally, divide both sides by 500 to solve for P.

$P = 2.6$

The new equilibrium price of cigarettes after the tax is $2.60. Knowing this, we can determine the equilibrium quantity of cigarettes sold after the tax by plugging the price into the demand function and the new supply function:

$Q_D = 1600 - 200(2.6) = 1600 - 520 = 1080$

$Q_S = 300 + 300(2.6) = 300 + 780 = 1080$

1080 packs of cigarettes will be sold after the tax (down from 1200 before the tax) at a price of $2.60 per pack. Of that price, producers must pay $1 to the government, so the effect on producer revenues is undoubtedly negative. The effect of the tax on the market is shown in Figure 5.7 (overleaf).

It is clear from Figure 5.7 that a $1 tax levied on cigarette sellers is borne not only by the sellers, but primarily by the consumers of cigarettes. Because demand for cigarettes is relatively inelastic, the larger burden of the tax can be passed on to buyers rather than being paid by producers. This is shown by the consumer tax box a + b being larger than the producer tax box e + f.

 Did you know that the taxation of cigarettes is an expected part of government policy? The World Bank offers a guide for government officials (*Design and Administer Tobacco Taxes* by Ayda Yurekli) to help officials struggling to create a proper tax. In it, the authors suggest a combination of per-unit and *ad valorem* taxes to get the 'best of both worlds' of taxation.

Figure 5.7
Linear functions and tax
incidence: cigarettes.

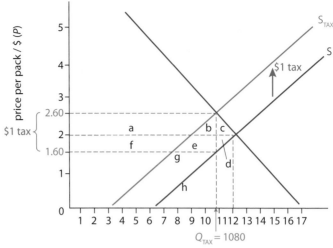

To learn more about
taxes, visit www.
pearsonhotlinks.com,
enter the title or ISBN
of this book and select
weblink 5.1.

- **Total tax revenue**. The total tax revenue, shown by the area a + b + e + f, is simple to calculate. At $1 per pack, with 1080 packs sold, the total tax revenue generated is $1080. Determining how much of the total tax was paid by consumers requires us to calculate the consumer tax burden (area a + b).

- **Consumer tax burden**. The consumer tax burden is represented by the area a + b. The price increased from $2 before the tax to $2.60 with the tax, indicating that consumers are paying $0.60 of the $1 tax. Multiplied by the quantity sold of 1080, the consumer tax burden is: $0.60 × 1080 packs = $648.

- **Producer tax burden**. Shown by the area f + e, the producer tax burden tells us the amount of tax paid by producers of cigarettes. Since consumers paid $0.60 of the $1 tax on each pack, producers paid the additional $0.40. Multiplied by the quantity sold of 1080, the producer tax burden is: $0.40 × 1080 = $432.

- **Effect on producer surplus**. The loss of producer surplus is represented by the area d + e + f. We already know the area of f + e = 432, so we can add the area d, which is 0.5((1200 − 1080) × 0.4) = 0.5(48) = 24. Total surplus lost = 432 + 24 = 456. $456 of producer surplus is lost due to the tax.

- **Effect on consumer surplus**. The loss of consumer surplus is represented by the area a + b + c. We have already determined that a + b = 648. The area of triangle c is 0.5((1200 − 1080) × 0.6) = 0.5(72) = 36. Total surplus lost = 648 + 36 = 684. $684 of consumer surplus is lost due to the tax.

- **Welfare loss from the tax**. Overall, the amount of both consumer and producer surplus in the cigarette market falls because of the tax. The total loss of consumer and producer surplus equals 684 + 456 = 1140. However, not all of this loss of welfare is lost to society, since $1080 goes to the government as tax revenue, this should not be considered welfare loss. Therefore, we can determine the net welfare loss by subtracting the increase in government tax revenue from the total loss of consumer and producer surplus.

net welfare loss = 1140 − 1080 = 60

To access Worksheet
5.2 on elasticity and tax
incidence, please visit
www.pearsonbacconline.
com and follow the
onscreen instructions.

The $1 tax on each pack of cigarettes creates $1080 of government revenue, but imposes a loss of $60 of welfare on society as a whole, since consumers and producers of cigarettes lose more welfare than society gains in tax revenue. The greater portion of the tax is paid by consumers, whose demand for cigarettes is relatively inelastic. Likewise, consumers suffer the larger loss of welfare because of the tax. In the end, fewer cigarettes are sold at a higher price.

8 Try solving for P and Q_D with the following linear supply and demand functions:

$Q_S = -8 + 6P$; $Q_D = 37 - 3P$

9 Create a supply and demand schedule for prices of $0, $1, $3, $5, $7 and $9.

10 Plot the points for each curve.

11 Show the market equilibrium price and quantity.

12 Place a specific tax of $2 per good. Plot the new supply curve that is the result of the tax, labelling it 'S_{TAX}.'

13 Identify the changes in equilibrium price and quantity.

14 Show and identify the change in producer and consumer surplus, deadweight loss, and the area of the tax.

15 Calculate the amount of tax paid by consumers and the amount of tax paid by producers.

16 Calculate the total amount spent by consumers (**a**) before the tax and (**b**) after the tax.

17 Calculate the total revenue earned by producers (**a**) before the tax and (**b**) after the tax.

18 **a** Explain the connection between the tax burdens you observe here and relative elasticities of supply and demand.

    b How would the value of b (for a linear demand function $Q_D = a - bP$) need to change for a more elastic demand? For a less elastic demand?

The bar chart opposite shows in which countries taxes make up the highest percentage of the purchase price of cigarettes, as well as some where the percentage is lowest.

- What do you think motivates governments to have high cigarette taxes?
- To what extent do you think the prices in these countries will reflect the higher taxes?

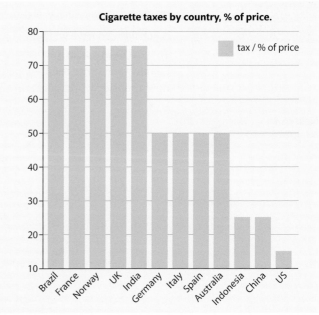

Cigarette taxes by country, % of price.

5.3 Subsidies

Learning outcomes

- Explain why governments provide subsidies, and describe examples of subsidies.
- Draw a diagram to show a subsidy, and analyse the impacts of a subsidy on market outcomes.
- Discuss the consequences of providing a subsidy on the stakeholders in a market, including consumers, producers and the government.
- (HL only) Plot demand and supply curves for a product from linear functions and then illustrate and/or calculate the effects of the provision of a subsidy on the market (on price, quantity, consumer expenditure, producer revenue, government expenditure, consumer surplus and producer surplus).

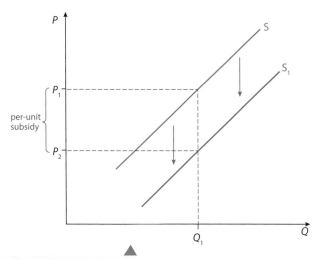

Figure 5.8
Per-unit subsidy.

A subsidy is a payment from the government to an individual or firm for the purpose of increasing the purchase or supply of a good.

As explained in Chapter 2 (page 46), a subsidy is a payment made by the government to a firm for the purpose of increasing the production of a good. Governments may have several different motivations to subsidize.

- To increase the consumption of some goods by lowering the price. This might address a positive externality such as the under-consumption of some healthcare services.
- To support a particular industry by helping with production costs. The industry might be considered critical for economic security – for example, steel – or might be one of political influence.
- To address a balance of payments deficit by increasing export revenue. Subsidies may lower costs enough to make a particular good more competitive on the world market.

Subsidizing a product will cause the supply curve to shift right or downwards by the amount of the subsidy. Firms find that their costs of production are lower at every price, making production at every price more profitable. Therefore, supply expands and more is produced at every price. Figure 5.8 (above) shows the supply shift for a per-unit subsidy.

A subsidy can have wide-ranging effects on consumers, producers, and even taxpayers. To what extent does a subsidy lower the price? As with taxes, the ultimate effect on price, quantity and other results depends on the relative elasticities of demand. Figure 5.9 shows how a subsidy works generally.

Figure 5.9
Subsidy: simple case.

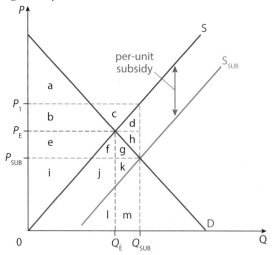

The supply curve shifts right or downwards by the amount of the subsidy. The price falls, but only by half of the subsidy amount from P_E to P_{SUB}, because the price elasticities of demand and supply are roughly equal. Quantity sold and consumed increases, from Q_E to Q_{SUB}. Consumers spend less (and get more) than before. Before the subsidy, spending was calculated by adding e + f + i + j + l. After the subsidy, spending is calculated by adding i + j + k + l + m, for more product.

The subsidy increases consumer surplus because it lowers the price paid. Consumer surplus increases from a + b to a + b + e + f + g. Producers benefit by receiving much more revenue. Previously, they received only e + f + i + j + l. When subsidized, the producers get b + c + d + e + f + g + h + i + j + k + l + m. However, the government pays significantly for the subsidy: b + c + d + e + f + g + h.

We can calculate the amount of government expenditure on the subsidy.

Total subsidy: $b + c + d + e + f + g + h = (P_1 - P_{SUB}) \times Q_{SUB}$

The split-the-cheque phenomenon

Sometimes, industries actively influence political decisions to subsidize their industry even when there is little benefit to the rest of society. In fact, they act in perfect accordance with economic theory of rational decision making in the process. Unfortunately, this can lead to bad outcomes, when unworthy industries win massive subsidies solely through shady political influence. Trying to reduce such subsidies is difficult, because although the benefit to producers can be enormous, the costs are spread among all citizens, and tend to be rather small. Economics writer Tim Harford has aptly characterized this type of poor incentive as the splitting-the-cheque problem.

- Why do you think Harford refers to this as the splitting-the-cheque problem?
- Explain the poor incentives at work with the type of subsidy described above.

Subsidy and linear functions (HL only)

As we did with taxes, let's now apply the theory of subsidies to linear supply and demand functions.

Worked example

Let's assume a supply and demand function for cotton, as follows:

$Q_D = 30 - 4P$
$Q_S = 6 + 2P$

Now solve for P and Q_S.

$6 + 2P = 30 - 4P$

Simplify by subtracting 6 from each side.

$2P = 24 - 4P$

Simplify further by adding $4P$ to each side.

$6P = 24$

Divide each side by 6.

$6P/6 = 24/6$

Thus,

$P = 4$

To calculate the equilibrium quantity, we can substitute the price ($4) into each function.

$Q_D = 30 - 4(4) = 14$
$Q_S = 6 + 2(4) = 14$

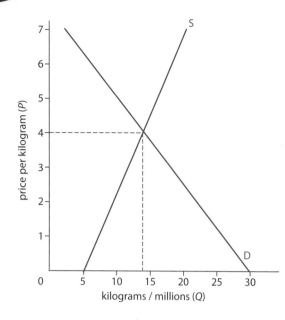

Figure 5.10
Linear functions and market
equilibrium: cotton.

TABLE 5.2 MARKET SCHEDULE, COTTON		
Price (P) / $	Quantity demanded (Q_D)/ millions kilos	Quantity supplied (Q_S)/ millions kilos
7	2	20
6	6	18
5	10	16
4	14	14
3	18	12
2	22	10
1	26	8
0	30	6

Table 5.2 shows possible prices and the corresponding quantities for both supply and demand, computed through the above functions. This clearly establishes a market-clearing price at $4, where 14 million kilograms are sold.

Figure 5.10 demonstrates the market equilibrium, using the supply and demand curves derived from the market schedule.

Let's assume the government chooses to subsidize cotton production, with the goal of making it cheap enough to export on global markets. The government wishes to pay cotton producers $3 per kilogram produced and sold, so effectively, the producers will now receive $3 more per kilogram produced than the price the consumers pay. The new supply function is therefore: $Q_S = 6 + 2(P + 3)$. This can be simplified by multiplying 2 by ($P + 3$), to get

$Q_S = 6 + 2P + 6$. Simplify again, to get the new supply function: $Q_S = 12 + 2P$.

To find the equilibrium price after the subsidy is granted, we can set the new supply function equal to the demand function and solve for P.

Worked example

$12 + 2P = 30 - 4P$

Simplify by subtracting 12 from both sides.

$2P = 18 - 4P$

Simplify again by adding $4P$ to both sides.

$6P = 18$

Now divide both sides by 6 to solve for P.

$P = 3$

The new equilibrium price paid by consumers for cottons is $3. To determine the equilibrium quantity of cotton produced, plug the new price into the supply and the demand functions:

$Q_D = 30 - 4(3) = 30 - 12 = 18$

$Q_S = 12 + 2(3) = 12 + 6 = 18$

18 million kilograms of cotton will be produced and sold after the subsidy, up from only 14 million before the subsidy. The price paid by consumers falls to $3, while the price received by producers is the consumers' price plus the $3 subsidy, $6.

The effect of the subsidy on market equilibrium price and quantity is shown in Figure 5.11.

As can be seen in Figure 5.11, the subsidy appears to benefit both producers and consumers of cotton. Consumers enjoy a lower price ($3) than before the subsidy ($4) and consume a greater quantity (18 million kg rather than 14 million kg). Likewise, producers are able to sell their output for $3, but receive an additional $3 subsidy, so the effective per unit price received by the sellers is $6.

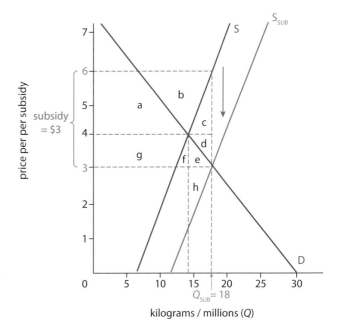

The increase in producer and consumer welfare can be determined by calculating the change in producer and consumer surplus resulting from the $3 subsidy.

- **Change in producer surplus**. The increase in producer surplus due to the subsidy is represented by the area a + b (the area below the new price and above the supply curve). To calculate the change in producer surplus, we can find the area of the rectangle a + b + c and subtract the area of the triangle c. The area of rectangle a + b + c = (6 – 4) × 18 = 2 × 18 = 36. The area of triangle c area is 0.5((18 – 14) × 2) = 0.5(4 × 2) = 4. The net change in producer surplus is therefore 36 – 4 = 32. Producer surplus increases by $32 million as a result of the subsidy.

- **Change in consumer surplus**. The increase in consumer surplus due to the subsidy is represented by the area e + f + g, since consumers now enjoy a lower price and a greater quantity. To calculate the change in consumer surplus, we can find the area of the rectangle d + e + f + g and subtract the area of the triangle d. The area of rectangle d + e + f + g = (4 – 3) × 18 = 1 × 18 = 18. The area of triangle d is 0.5((18 – 14) × 1) = 0.5(4) = 2. The net change in consumer surplus is therefore 18 – 2 = 16. Consumer surplus increases by $16 million as a result of the subsidy.

- **Increase in total consumer and producer welfare**. The subsidy increases cotton producers' and consumers' total welfare by a total of $32 million + $16 million = $48 million.

A subsidy appears to be a win–win situation. Both consumers and producers benefit. However, we have not yet taken into account the cost the subsidy imposes on society as a whole, which is the cost to taxpayers of subsidizing cotton growers. The total amount of the subsidy can be easily calculated by multiplying the per-unit subsidy times the quantity of output.

- **Total cost of the subsidy**. In Figure 5.11, the total cost of the subsidy is represented by the area a + b + c + d + e + f + g. This is a rectangle with a base of 18 million (the quantity of cotton sold) and a height of 3 (the per-unit subsidy). 18 × 3 = 54. The total cost to taxpayers of the subsidy is $54 million.

- **Net effect on welfare**. Now we can determine whether or not the subsidy had a greater benefit for cotton producers and consumers than its cost to taxpayers. The cost was $54 million, but the benefit was only $48 million, so the net loss of welfare for society was $6 million.

- **Deadweight (welfare) loss of the subsidy**. The deadweight or welfare loss is represented by the area of triangle c + d. If you were to calculate this area, it would come out as 6, representing the $6 million lost to society from subsidizing cotton producers.

Just like the tax on cigarettes, the subsidy for cotton growers creates a deadweight loss for society as a whole. In this case, the taxpayer money used to subsidize cotton growers exceeds the increase in cotton growers' and consumers' welfare by $6 million.

Agricultural subsidies

www.researchrecap.co

To access Worksheet 5.3 on letting markets work, please visit www.pearsonbacconline.com and follow the onscreen instructions.

This bar chart shows the percentage gross domestic product (GDP) given by various governments to subsidize agriculture in their country.

- Which countries subsidize their farms the most?
- On what basis did you answer question 1?
- What other information would you need to be sure of your answer?

HL EXERCISES

24 Try solving for P and Q_D with the following linear supply and demand functions:

$Q_S = -3 + 4P$; $Q_D = 21 - 2P$

25 Create a supply and demand schedule for prices of $0, $2, $4, $6, $8, and $10.

26 Plot the points for each curve.

27 Show the market equilibrium price and quantity.

28 Place a per-unit subsidy of $1 per good. Plot the new supply curve that is the result of the tax, labelling it 'S_{SUB}'.

29 Identify the changes in equilibrium price and quantity.

30 Show and identify the change in producer and consumer surplus, and the area of the subsidy.

31 Calculate the amount of the subsidy paid by the government.

32 Calculate the total amount spent by consumers before the subsidy and after the subsidy.

33 Calculate the total revenue earned by producers before the subsidy and after the subsidy.

34 With the given demand function, what would happen to the diagram if the value of d (the price coefficient) were greater, a number such as –5? How would this change the elasticity of demand? How would it change the amounts of subsidy and producer revenue?

5.4 Price controls: maximum price controls

Learning outcomes
- Explain why governments impose price ceilings, and describe examples of price ceilings, including food price controls and rent controls.
- Draw a diagram to show a price ceiling, and analyse the impacts of a price ceiling on market outcomes.
- Examine the possible consequences of a price ceiling, including shortages, inefficient resource allocation, welfare impacts, underground parallel markets and non-price rationing mechanisms.
- Discuss the consequences of imposing a price ceiling on the stakeholders in a market, including consumers, producers and the government.
- (HL only) Calculate possible effects from the price ceiling diagram, including the resulting shortage and the change in consumer expenditure (which is equal to the change in firm revenue).

While freely operating competitive markets have many virtues, there are situations where the outcomes are not optimal for all the participants. In some of these situations, the government enacts price controls to get different results.

Price ceilings

In this market situation, the government determines that there is great potential for high prices, and makes a goal of keeping prices low. Often governments take this step to make basic goods and services more affordable for poorer residents. Thus, by preventing an increase, the government places a 'ceiling' on the price of a good. Normally, the price would rise to P_E, and the market would clear. The price ceiling prevents this from happening. Figure 5.12 demonstrates a maximum price that has this effect. When the price ceiling prevents a price from rising to a higher equilibrium, we call it a binding or effective price ceiling.

Note: It is possible that some price ceilings are written into law but are not in effect because prices have already fallen below the maximum.

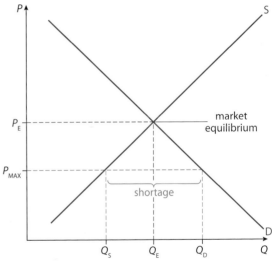

Figure 5.12
Price ceiling.

Effects of price ceilings

Shortages

In Figure 5.12, at P_{MAX}, the quantity supplied is much lower (Q_S), than the quantity demanded (Q_D). The artificially low price has caused more demand for the product, a movement from Q_E along the demand curve to Q_D. At the same time, producers cut production in response to the lower price, moving down along the supply curve from Q_E to Q_S. The distance between Q_D and Q_S reflects a shortage of the good. If the price is kept at P_{MAX}, there will be many left wanting the good who previously would have consumed it, as well as new entrants to the market who will not access the good.

A price ceiling (maximum price) is a maximum legally allowable price for a good, set by the government.

Rationing

Without price to guide the rationing of the good, consumers and producers will use other means to determine who receives the product. Some methods of rationing include government-created ration cards or vouchers, which may have their own system by which consumers receive the product (perhaps 'family size' if the product is a staple food). Waiting in line for a scarce good is common. Additionally, special barter deals may be arranged with the seller, which effectively increase the price of the good.

Decreased market size

At the low maximum price, the output will be limited to Q_S, a decrease from Q_E. This means less overall utility to consumers and producers, a decrease in overall market surplus.

Elimination of allocative efficiency

As described in Chapter 3 (page 69), allocative efficiency is achieved when marginal benefits (MB) equal marginal costs (MC), which is when supply meets demand in competitive markets. The price ceiling eliminates this efficiency. Now, the market price is set by the government, not where MB = MC. Society is not producing enough of the good with the price ceiling in place.

Informal (black) markets

The gap between Q_S and Q_D creates a tension in the market. At Q_S there are many consumers who would be willing to pay more than P_{MAX}, (some even more than P_E), if only Q_S is on the market. Figure 5.13 suggests what may happen as a result of the price ceiling.

Figure 5.13
Price ceiling, black market.

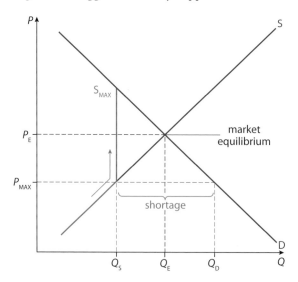

At Q_S, the demand curve rises high above P_{MAX} or P_E. This suggests that some consumers have a strong incentive to pay more, informally or on the black market, to acquire the good. With that in mind, it can be said that the supply curve shoots directly up at Q_S. This shows that the price could rise as high as that point on the demand curve. Thus, some price ceilings may actually drive the price higher than the original equilibrium.

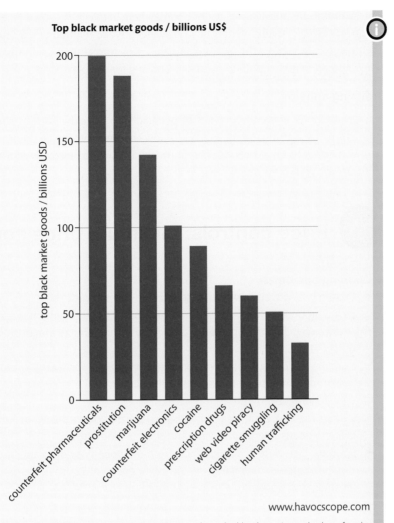

Top black market goods / billions US$

top black market goods / billions USD

(Bar chart values, approximately:)
- counterfeit pharmaceuticals: 200
- prostitution: 187
- marijuana: 142
- counterfeit electronics: 100
- cocaine: 88
- prescription drugs: 67
- web video piracy: 60
- cigarette smuggling: 51
- human trafficking: 32

www.havocscope.com

This bar chart shows a selection of the most-traded black market goods, ranked by the estimated value of trade.

- Which of these goods are black market goods because of artificial price floors and taxes?
- Which goods are simply banned or illegal?
- What accounts for the size of some other markets, such as counterfeit drugs or web piracy?
- Select three goods. Evaluate the free market view that each of these goods should be legal and/or traded without price restrictions/taxes/government intervention.

Examples of price ceilings

Rice, bread and other staple foods

Price ceilings on these products can cause many of the effects we've just discussed, including hoarding of basic food items. This can make black market prices actually exceed those shown in Figure 5.13 because the expectations of a shortage will shift the immediate demand curve outward.

Rent control

Some cities enact rent control laws to reduce the cost of housing for lower-income citizens. Though well intentioned, the limitations of this policy have a wide range of effects. Renters may bid the effective price higher by paying 'key money' or direct payments to the owner outside the rental agreement. Another problem is that the overall amount of housing drops, as a result of the policy, to Q_S. Renters in these apartments have an incentive to rent

In 2007, in the face of rising prices, President Mugabe of Zimbabwe enacted price ceilings on all food items. The controls were intended to help poor families but they almost immediately led to a huge shortage of food. News reports told of desperate citizens who went so far as to kill and eat a giraffe during the period of price controls.

out their units by 'sub-letting' at a rate somewhere between P_{MAX} and P_E, even though this practice is illegal. Finally, owners have little incentive to maintain their buildings. With their revenue limited by the price ceiling, they seek to maintain profits by reducing costs. This can lead to unsafe and poor-quality housing for the occupants.

Housing subsidy

To access Worksheet 5.4 on price controls and the free market, please visit www.pearsonbacconline.com and follow the onscreen instructions.

In rare situations, governments may be persuaded to solve the housing shortage caused by rent control by subsidizing the market for low-income housing. In theory, this would shift supply from Q_S to Q_E or beyond. This approach is likely to be costly, depending on the size of the shortage in housing.

5.5 Price controls: minimum price controls

Learning outcomes

- Explain why governments impose price floors, and describe examples of price floors, including price support for agricultural products and minimum wages.
- Draw a diagram of a price floor, and analyse the impacts of a price floor on market outcomes.
- Examine the possible consequences of a price floor, including surpluses and government measures to dispose of the surpluses, inefficient resource allocation and welfare impacts.
- Discuss the consequences of imposing a price floor on the stakeholders in a market, including consumers, producers and the government.
- (HL only) Calculate possible effects from the price floor diagram, including the resulting surplus, the change in consumer expenditure, the change in producer revenue, and government expenditure to purchase the surplus.

Price floors

A price floor is a minimum legally allowable price for a good, set by the government.

In some instances, governments may artificially increase the prices of some goods and resources. This form of price control is called a minimum price or price floor. The government may believe the good is important or necessary, or it may be supporting employment in a particular industry. The motivation and effects of a price floor more specifically depend on the good itself.

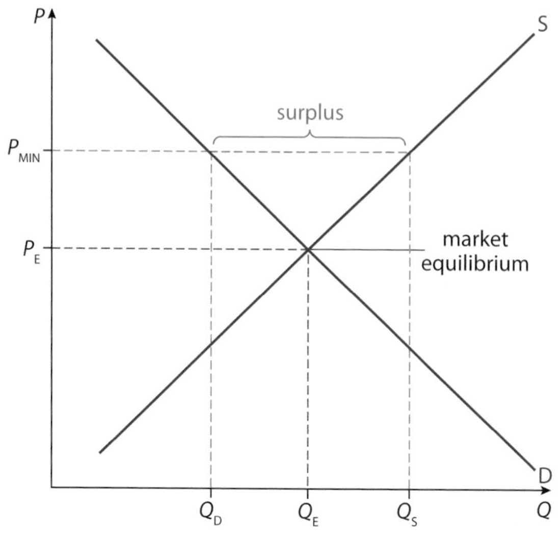

Figure 5.14
Price floor.

Figure 5.14 shows the effect of a price floor. Because the price established is artificially high (raised from P_E to P_{MIN}), the quantity supplied increases, a movement up along the supply curve to Q_S. Consumers also respond, by reducing the quantity demanded to Q_D. Normally, the price would drop to P_E, and the market would clear. The price floor prevents this from happening. The excess supply at P_{MIN} is called a surplus.

Some price floors may not be binding or effective if the market price is already above the equilibrium.

Effects of price floors

Surplus
As shown in Figure 5.14, at the original equilibrium price there is no surplus because the quantity demanded and supplied are equal. At P_{MIN}, however, the quantity supplied, Q_S, is far greater than the quantity demanded, Q_D, so there is a surplus in the market.

Reduced market size
Because only the amount Q_D will be purchased, the market size decreases. This reduces the amount of consumer and producer surplus compared to the free market price and quantity.

Cost inefficiency
The higher price increases production from Q_E to Q_S – a level above what could satisfy the market at the original equilibrium. Higher-cost production is inefficient, and uses resources that could be devoted to other things.

Allocative inefficiency
The high price inspires producers to produce at a quantity of output at which marginal cost is well above the marginal benefit, beyond where supply and demand meet. This means the market overproduces, beyond the optimal point where MB = MC.

Informal markets
Firms may choose to sell their surplus at prices below equilibrium. This practice is illegal, and will contradict the purpose of the price floor.

Examples of price floors

Agricultural price supports
Many countries want to ensure a stable domestic food supply and choose to subsidize their agricultural markets with price floors called price supports. Price supports can be applied to wide range of goods including corn, wheat, soybeans, milk, coffee, sugar and more. These price supports are an attempt to raise farmers' incomes by providing a better market price. Figure 5.15 illustrates the benefits and problems posed by price supports. The policy increases the per-unit price of sugar from P_E to P_{MIN}. However, in this example, the total revenue for producers has changed, going from d + e to d + b. Consumers pay more and receive less, as price has increased and the quantity consumed has decreased. Consumer surplus has decreased from a + b + c to merely a.

There also remains the problem of what to do with the surplus sugar. There are a variety of options. The government might purchase the extra supply. Depending on the negotiated price of that policy, it could be quite expensive, $(P_{MIN} \times (Q_S - Q_D))$. It cannot reintroduce the good back onto the market as that would destroy the minimum price. Instead, the government could arrange for the surplus to be sold to another country. However, countries that find their market flooded with cheap sugar may protest that the extra product is being 'dumped' on them. Some surplus can be distributed as a form of foreign aid, although the outlets for this kind of offering are irregular. The

Figure 5.15
Price supports: sugar.

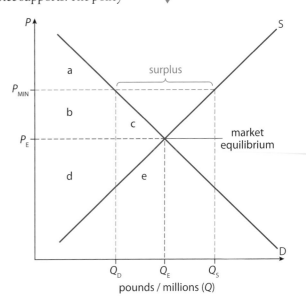

administrative cost of these policies can be high, especially if the goods require storage over a period of time. Much of the surplus output may be destroyed – a clear waste of resources.

Despite the market distortion that takes place and mindful of the high costs of such schemes, nearly all governments enact such policies with regard to agriculture. Countries with the largest combinations of subsidies and price supports are under intense pressure from poorer countries that cannot afford the lavish expenditure and waste involved. Poorer countries hope to trade their agricultural goods freely with the richer countries, a hope that has dim prospects with these policies in place.

> A minimum wage is a form of price floor, a legal minimum price for labour, set by the government.

Minimum wage

Reformers and poverty activists have long cherished the minimum wage as a tool to raise living standards among the poor. The idea is simple: raise the minimum pay for all workers, and those earning the worst wages will be able to get basic necessities. Figure 5.16 shows a minimum wage, where W_{MIN} is the minimum price for labour (a wage is the price of labour). This price floor also produces a surplus.

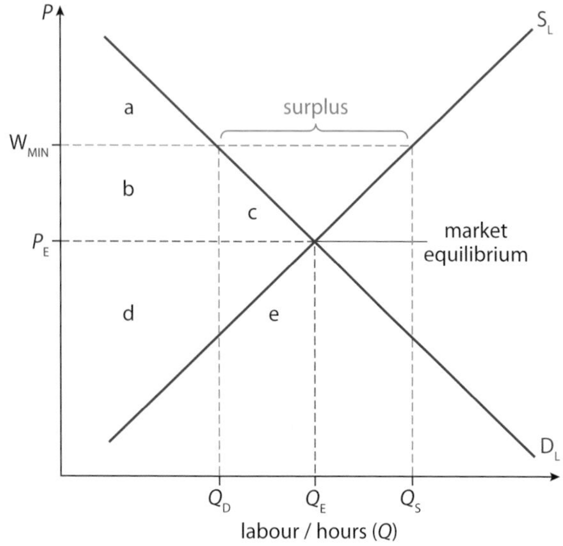

At W_{MIN} the price of labour is above the equilibrium, and the quantity of labour demanded by firms has decreased, moving up along the demand curve from Q_E to Q_D. At the same time the higher wage has brought new entrants into the labour market, the quantity from Q_E to Q_S, who did not seek jobs at P_E. The entire group, from Q_S to Q_D, will be unemployed. Those still employed, the quantity Q_D, do enjoy the higher wages, although at the cost of what appear to be significant trade-offs in the form of unemployment for the other workers.

An additional effect of the minimum wage may be to increase the incentive for firms to illegally hire workers below the minimum wage. Firms may resort to hiring illegal workers, typically migrants, for their cheapest jobs.

Fixed prices

Legal price controls are kept in place by the force of law and government. In other instances, firms may set a fixed price on their own, by agreement or custom. Depending on the specific good being sold, the price may be fixed below or above equilibrium. Price fixing is most commonly seen in tickets for sporting events, movies, plays and concerts. The amount supplied by the seating capacity is fixed, so supply is completely inelastic. Demand, however, can vary significantly. The appetite for one movie compared to another or one concert compared to another can be so different as to cause a shortage of tickets in some cases and a surplus in others.

Figure 5.17 shows what happens when the price is set too high. At P_{FIX}, the surplus of tickets (Q_D to Q_E) will not be sold. What will happen next? Where possible, the extra seats will be sold on the informal market to buyers willing to pay a price in line with demand. Figure 5.18 shows the result of pricing too low. More tickets than are available are demanded at P_{FIX}. The

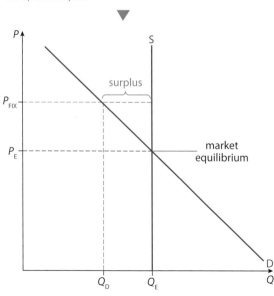

Figure 5.16
Minimum wage.

Figure 5.17
Fixed prices: surplus.

shortage between Q_E and Q_D is likely to be satisfied through the informal market. Buyers along the demand curve between Q_E and Q_D are willing to pay above P_{FIX}, and will bid the price higher by making online offers or buying the tickets more expensively outside the event itself.

Events like movies, which tend to have a single price, often suffer these effects. Cinemas (movie houses) make up for this by having multi-screen buildings, showing a variety of films. Should the audience for one movie shrink, they can move showings to a smaller venue inside the building, freeing up the larger venue for the next big blockbuster.

In contrast, sporting venues, theatres and concert venues are able to charge different prices for different seats, effectively discriminating between those at different points (high and low) on the demand curve. To some degree, these events can avoid the problem by having several prices. However, if the demand is simply too low compared to the supply, it's time to move to a smaller stadium or concert hall.

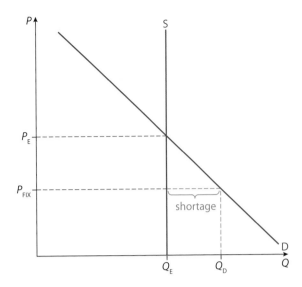

Figure 5.18
Fixed prices: shortage.

Quantifying the effects of price controls (HL only)

HL students need to be able to quantify the results of price floors and ceilings.

Price ceilings

Let's start with a ceiling on the price of rice. This might be done to prevent starvation among low-income groups in some countries. Figure 5.19 shows the effects of maximum price set for rice at $1 per kilogram. The equilibrium price is $2.00, at which price 9000 kilograms of rice are sold. The price ceiling reduces the price to $1, which increases the quantity demanded to 13 000 kilos. But at the same time it reduces the quantity supplied to 5000 kilos. Thus at the price-ceiling price, there is excess demand of 8000 kilos.

Figure 5.19
Price ceiling for rice.

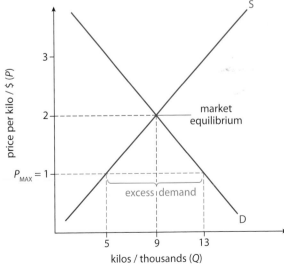

Consumer expenditure and producer revenue (the same amount in this case) before the price ceiling was $2 × 9000 = $18 000. With the price ceiling, consumer expenditure/producer revenue will be $1 × 5000 = $5000. Thus, consumer expenditure/producer revenue has fallen by $13 000. There is also considerably less rice sold on the market.

To fill the gap in demand, the government could pay a subsidy to producers. This subsidy must shift supply far enough to the right to meet the quantity demanded at $1, which is 13 000 kilos. It must, therefore, make up the gap of 8000 kilos. Figure 5.20 (overleaf) demonstrates the shift.

To find the per-unit amount necessary to fill the gap, calculate the distance between the old supply curve S, and the new supply curve S_{SUB} at 13 000 units. In this case, the per-unit amount would be $2.75 – $1 = $1.75 per unit. The total amount of the subsidy is calculated by multiplying the per-unit amount by the number of units to be subsidized (here, 13 000): $1.75 × 13 000 = $22 750.

Figure 5.20
Price ceiling and subsidy for rice.

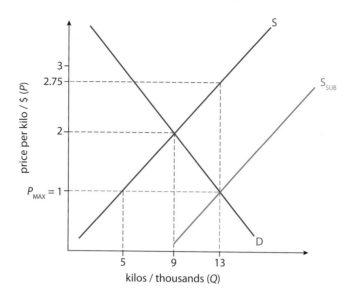

If this option seems too costly, the government could directly provide the good. In this case, the government would have to establish its own rice-growing farms. In either case, it is reasonable to consider the significant opportunity cost of allocating government resources in such a manner.

Price floors

Now let's assume that the government has set a price floor for milk. This might be done to protect the income and employment of the country's dairy farmers. Figure 5.21 shows the effects of a minimum price for milk set at $3 per litre. The equilibrium price is normally $2, at which price 18 000 litres of milk are sold. The price floor raises the price to $3, which increases the quantity supplied to 24 000 kilos. But at the same time it reduces the quantity demanded to 16 000 kilos. At the price-floor price, there is an excess supply of 8000 litres.

Figure 5.21
Price floor for milk.

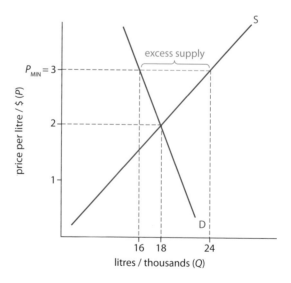

Producer revenue and consumer expenditure are the same here. In this case, producer revenue/consumer expenditure before the price floor was $2 × 18 000 = $36 000. Now it is $3 × 16 = $48 000. Milk producer revenue has increased by $12 000, which explains the popularity of price support schemes for the favoured producers.

The excess supply can be managed in several ways.

- The government could throw out the excess milk. However, the waste might be politically and ethically objectionable, and producers would still be losing revenue.
- The government might dump the excess product onto foreign markets. A product like milk spoils easily, so this is not so easy to do, and is a better solution for storable commodities like corn or wheat. But even if it were possible, the price would probably be very low, and the dumping might harm trade relations.
- The government might buy up the surplus. In this case, the government must pay the $3 price-floor price, and buy the difference between quantity demanded (16 000 litres) and the new quantity supplied with the price floor (24 000 litres). Thus the cost would be $3 × 8000 = $24 000. Like any decision to intervene in the market, the government must weigh the opportunity cost of such expenditure. The decision to support one industry will limit the government's ability to provide other services such as education and healthcare.

To access Worksheet 5.5 on price controls, please visit www. pearsonbacconline.com and follow the onscreen instructions.

To learn more about price controls, visit www. pearsonhotlinks.com, enter the title or ISBN of this book and select weblink 5.2.

HL EXERCISES

35 Select a product and create a market supply and demand diagram.

   a Show the equilibrium price and quantity, and set a binding price ceiling.

   b Calculate the change in consumer expenditure/producer revenue.

   c Identify and calculate the government subsidy expenditure needed to eliminate the shortage.

36 Select a product and create a market supply and demand diagram.

   a Show the equilibrium price and quantity, and set a binding price floor.

   b Calculate the change in consumer expenditure/producer revenue.

   c Identify and calculate the government expenditure needed to eliminate the surplus.

37 Explain how a maximum price policy gives rise to a shortage.

38 Using an appropriate diagram, explain the effect of a maximum price on goods with highly elastic demand and supply.

39 Using an appropriate diagram, explain the effect of a maximum price on goods with relatively inelastic demand and supply.

40 Explain how a minimum price policy gives rise to a surplus.

41 Using an appropriate diagram, explain the effect of a maximum price on goods with highly elastic demand and supply.

42 Using an appropriate diagram, explain the effect of a maximum price on goods with relatively inelastic demand and supply.

43 How does the price system 'go around' the policy goals of price controls through informal markets?

44 What is the effect of price controls on allocative efficiency?

45 Evaluate the effectiveness of price supports.

46 Evaluate the effectiveness of rent control.

To access Quiz 5, an interactive, multiple-choice quiz on this chapter, please visit www.pearsonbacconline.com and follow the onscreen instructions.

PRACTICE QUESTIONS

1 Explain, using a diagram, the effect of a specific tax on various stakeholders.
(10 marks) [AO2], [AO4]

2 Explain, using a diagram, the effects of a per-unit subsidy on various stakeholders.
(10 marks) [AO2], [AO4]

3 **a** Explain the concepts of maximum and minimum price controls. (10 marks) [AO2], [AO4]

   b Evaluate the idea that government intervention in the form of price ceilings and price floors is well intentioned, but often leads to undesirable side effects. (15 marks) [AO4]
   © International Baccalaureate Organization 2004

4 **a** Using an appropriate diagram, explain the likely effects of an decrease in the maximum price set for petrol (gasoline), which is already set below the market price.
(10 marks) [AO2], [AO4]

   b Evaluate the effects of this kind of government intervention into the market for petrol.
(15 marks) [AO3]

5 **a** Using a diagram explain the effect on various stakeholders of a high specific tax on alcohol.
(10 marks) [AO2], [AO4]

   b Evaluate the effectiveness of a policy that would impose substantially higher levels of taxation on the sale of alcohol.
(15 marks) [AO3]
   © International Baccalaureate Organization 2004 (part **b** only)

6 MARKET FAILURE

6.1 The meaning of market failure and externalities

Learning outcomes

- Analyse the concept of market failure as a failure of the market to achieve allocative efficiency, resulting in an over-allocation of resources (over-provision of a good) or an under-allocation of resources (under-provision of a good).
- Describe the concepts of marginal private benefits (MPB), marginal social benefits (MSB), marginal private costs (MPC) and marginal social costs (MSC).
- Describe the meaning of externalities as the failure of the market to achieve a social optimum where MSB = MSC.

◀ Who pays for industrial pollution like this? In a way, everyone does, which is a clear case of market failure.

Meaning of market failure

We have so far looked at how effective markets can be in bringing society what it wants with efficiency. However, the strict conditions that apply for the theory to work may not always be in effect. When real-world conditions cause markets to function inefficiently, market failure has occurred. Market failure is any situation where the allocation of resources by a free market is not efficient. These situations, from society's viewpoint, could be improved on if resources were allocated differently. Market failure is most often associated with market power, asymmetric information and externalities.

First, it is important to remember that markets function quite well if left free and competitive. Consumers enjoy allocative efficiency, and large amounts of producer and consumer surplus are produced. You will recall that the supply and demand curves explained in Chapter 2 also represent the marginal cost (MC) and marginal benefit (MB)

 Market failure is any situation where the allocation of resources by a free market is not efficient.

curves. Furthermore, allocative efficiency is achieved where marginal benefits equal marginal costs: MB = MC. Normally, this is where supply meets demand. We can now expand the idea of marginal analysis to include society's benefits and costs, and so MB becomes MSB (marginal social benefit) and MC becomes MSC (marginal social cost).

Figure 6.1 shows the supply (MSC) and demand (MSB) curves at market equilibrium. At P_E and Q_E, to produce any greater quantity would cause costs to exceed benefits. Any less output, a quantity to the left of Q_E, and some portion of consumer/producer surplus is left unenjoyed. Therefore, the equilibrium point results in what economists call a maximum of community surplus, where community surplus is the combination of producer and consumer surplus.

Figure 6.1
Community surplus.

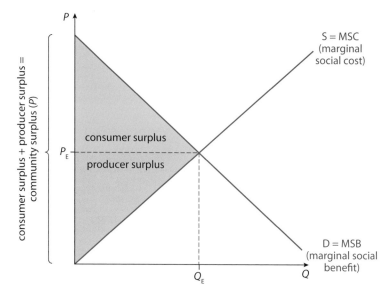

At this normally functioning competitive market equilibrium, economists argue that there exists a state of Pareto optimality. 'Pareto optimal' refers to a market situation where no one can be made better off without making someone else worse off. Look again at Figure 6.1. There are no other possible combinations of price and quantity that can improve one group's situation without hurting the other. If the price were higher than P_E, consumers would be worse off. If price were below P_E, producers would be worse off. If the quantity produced were greater than Q_E, society's costs (MSC) would be greater than its benefits (MSB), so everyone would be worse off. If the quantity were less than Q_E, some amount of community surplus would be lost. Thus, maximization of community surplus achieved at P_E and Q_E, where MSB = MSC, is synonymous with Pareto optimality, and is also called social efficiency.

Competitive markets provide Pareto optimality by maximizing community surplus. These markets also tend to be allocatively efficient, delivering the goods society wants by matching MSB and MSC. However, markets often do not meet the conditions of free competition, and we admit that markets can fail. When resources are not allocated in an optimal or socially efficient manner, this is called market failure. When this occurs, it is left to governments to address the problem to help society get the most from its resources.

To learn more about market failure, visit www.pearsonhotlinks.com, enter the title or ISBN of this book and select weblink 6.1.

This chapter considers various forms of market failure and evaluates the solutions most often proposed to deal with them.

Types of market failure:

- negative externalities (of production and consumption)
- positive externalities (of production and consumption)

- lack of public goods
- common access to resources and threat to sustainability
- asymmetric information
- abuse of monopoly power.

Meaning of externalities

We have made the assumption that marginal benefit and marginal cost can now be viewed more broadly, going beyond the individual and incorporating all the costs and benefits to society. When true, it is said that the marginal social costs and marginal social benefits are taken into account. For example, consider the purchase of a simple good like a pencil. If the buyer enjoys all the benefits of the pencil, we can assume that his or her private enjoyment represents all of society's enjoyment. And if the producer of the pencil pays all the costs associated with making the pencil, his or her cost is the same as society's cost.

However, there are many instances where someone outside of a transaction, a third party, may suffer the costs or enjoy the benefits of someone else's transactions. When this occurs, it is called an externality. Someone outside the original transaction is being affected by it, either positively (enjoying benefits) or negatively (suffering costs).

When the side-effects are good, it is called a positive externality. When the side-effects are bad, it is called a negative externality. Another term for externality is 'spillover,' which suggests that costs or benefits have gone beyond the initial actors in the transaction. Thus, someone suffering the effects of a negative externality may be paying some of the spillover costs. Someone feeling the effects of a positive externality is enjoying spillover benefits.

An externality is a transaction where someone other than the buyer or seller (a third party), experiences a benefit or loss as a result of the transaction.

When an externality occurs, there is a difference between society's experience and that of the individual firm or consumer. No longer can we assume that the private benefit is equal to society's benefit. For example, in the case of a positive externality, the utility experienced by someone is only part of the overall benefit to society. Others share in the enjoyment of the good as well. Therefore it is possible to say that marginal social benefits of the good are equal to the private benefit *plus* the additional amount of beneficial externality. Figure 6.2 demonstrates the idea of externalities in terms of spillover costs and benefits.

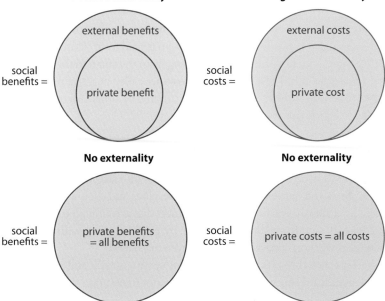

◀ **Figure 6.2**
Social benefits and social costs.

We can also summarize the concept mathematically.

Where there are externalities:
- social benefits = private benefit + external benefit
- social costs = private cost + external costs.

Where no externalities exist:
- social benefits = private benefits
- social costs = private costs.

Furthermore, externalities of both types can occur in the course of the production or consumption of a good. This makes four types of externality:

- negative externality of consumption – use of a product creates spillover costs to others
- negative externality of production – making of a product creates spillover costs to others
- positive externality of consumption – use of a product creates spillover benefits to others
- positive externality of production – making of a product creates spillover benefits to others.

6.2 Negative externalities

Learning outcomes
- Explain, using diagrams and examples, the concepts of negative externalities of production and consumption, and the welfare loss associated with the production or consumption of a good or service.
- Explain that demerit goods are goods whose consumption creates external costs.
- Evaluate, using diagrams, the use of policy responses, including market-based policies (taxation and tradable permits), and government regulations, to the problem of negative externalities of production and consumption.

Negative production externalities

Sometimes, the most innocuous products cause problems for other people. Not for the consumer, who enjoys using it, nor for the producer, who is paid for it. Third parties, who had no part in the transaction, suffer costs ranging from the small to the very large, from lost money to poor health. These production costs are called negative production externalities. Beyond private costs, the external costs suffered by others increase the overall social costs, as seen in Figure 6.2 above.

There are many examples of negative production externalities.

- Nearly all school and office furniture contains wood particle board. This board is made from large amounts of processed pieces of wood, pressed into shape and held there by strong chemical glues and hardeners. The use of these glues and chemicals may cause workers' health to diminish, and create waste products that are difficult to eliminate.
- Coal is produced with significant air pollution as a by-product, along with the deaths of hundreds of miners working in dangerous conditions every year.
- Oil production appears to be getting more and more costly, as spills and refinery pollution cause significant external losses worldwide, not to mention the depletion of reserves.

Using supply and demand with marginal analysis, it is possible to represent negative production externalities using a typical market diagram (Figure 6.3). Note that the supply curve has been split. Marginal private cost (MPC) is another name for the supply curve representing the costs paid by the firm to produce. However, making particle board incurs costs suffered by others, so the cost to society, marginal social cost (MSC), is higher than the private cost.

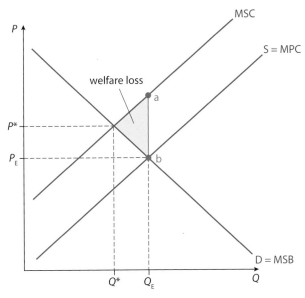

◀ **Figure 6.3**
Negative externality of production.

At the free market equilibrium of P_E, quantity Q_E is produced. At that quantity, the external costs to society are quite high, represented by the distance between points a and b. This implies that if the good were priced to cover all of the relevant costs, the price would be much higher. In fact, the entire MSC curve lies above the MPC curve, showing that the private costs of production are less than the costs to all of society at every price.

This is *not* a shift to the left of the supply curve, merely a more accurate representation of the full costs of production. You could refer to the MSC curve as the 'true' supply curve because it shows all the costs to society.

Moreover, if the marginal social costs are the accurate costs to society, the intersection of MSC with the MSB curve should provide the optimal equilibrium point, the best allocation of resources, at the point where MSC = MSB. The socially efficient price and output would be P^* and Q^*. When all the costs are added into the process, it appears that the optimal amount of production is Q^*, significantly less than Q_E. We can also conclude that the equilibrium price would be higher, at P^*, than the current free market price of P_E.

This implies that goods whose production creates a negative externality are overproduced, and are sold at prices that are too low, or below what the market would show if all costs were added in. Furthermore, because production is not where marginal costs are equal to marginal benefits, resources are being misallocated. The distance between MSC and MPC at Q_E represents the marginal negative externality at that point. If the optimal output and price are Q^*P^*, then the production beyond that amount produces the negative externality, shown by the area of the shaded triangle. Economists refer to this area as a welfare loss.

Potential solutions

Taxes

Some governments choose to tax the product that produces the externality. A tax of this sort will shift the MPC curve to the left. Figure 6.4 (overleaf) shows the possible effects of a tax on particle board. Supply shifts to the left, raising the price to P_{TAX}, and reducing the amount consumed to Q_{TAX}. This tax covers only a portion of the externality costs. The welfare loss triangle is still present, though significantly reduced. In sum, prices have increased to nearly the optimal market price, and quantity has decreased to nearly the optimal quantity.

Figure 6.4
Tax applied to negative externality.

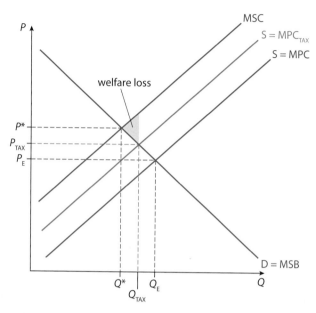

Debate over carbon tax has raged in many developed economies for the last 20 years. Since it became clear that industry's emissions of carbon dioxide were contributing to global warming, governments have tried to develop tax schemes to reduce these emissions. Not surprisingly, industry's response has been overwhelmingly negative. As a result, comprehensive agreements across the EU and especially for the US have yet to happen.

Some advantages of this approach are that it:
- reduces the size of the externality (shaded triangle box)
- 'internalizes the externality,' by compelling producers and consumers to pay the costs of their transaction
- brings output down towards the optimal level, Q^*.

Disadvantages of the approach are that:
- assessing the magnitude of the externality is extremely difficult; governments and firms normally hire cost–benefit analysts to determine this
- determining the appropriate tax amount is a challenge
- taxing the good may not deter pollution, only reduce it.

Legislation and regulation

Governments can enact laws to deter production of products or services that cause harm to others. It may force cleaner production with improved technology or order the firms to reduce the amount of the good actually produced. In any case, the effect would be to reduce the size of spillover costs, likely moving MSC closer to MPC. It may also move the MPC to the left, decreasing supply because the new technology will increase costs of production. This can be very costly to implement. To enforce their regulations, the government must then create an agency or office to monitor and enforce compliance with the rules. Again, determining the value of pollution losses can be very difficult. The complexity of such lawmaking and enforcement is very challenging.

Furthermore, there is a cost to government resources, as well as the cost firms will spend on meeting the regulation requirements. Disputes between governments and firms often incur extra costs in legal expenses as well. The extreme course is an outright ban on the good. This would eliminate the externality. But this extraordinary measure is likely to destroy the market completely, as well as all previous community surplus in the process. Bans incur major opportunity costs in terms of lost market benefit.

Tradable permits

As a special category relating to sustainable development, tradable permits are discussed in detail later in this chapter (page 141).

Negative consumption externalities

Spillover costs can occur on the consumption side as well. In these cases, a person's use of a product affects others adversely. A surprising number of products create obvious third-party costs:

- smoking
- alcohol consumption
- gambling
- automobile use.

Recently, some have argued that the consumption of high-fat diets, which contribute to heart disease, constitutes the same kind of consumer spillover cost. In the case of a negative externality of consumption, the costs are seen on the marginal benefit curve.

While this may seem counter-intuitive, remember that this is a consumption externality and, therefore, it is the demand (or consumption) side where the costs occur. For negative externalities of consumption, the marginal social benefits are less than the benefits enjoyed by the private consumer. In other words, the benefit of a cigarette that is enjoyed by the smoker is greater than society's benefit. This is because the smoker is a part of society, so their enjoyment is part of the total. But others will eventually pay some of the costs of this smoking (in higher insurance premiums or taxes for government health programmes). This cost to others actually reduces the overall benefit to society. Figure 6.5 shows the negative externality where marginal social benefit falls below or behind the marginal private benefit.

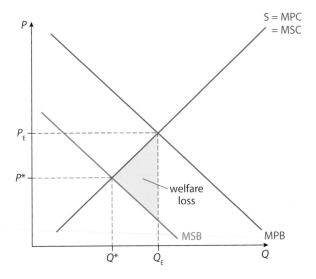

Figure 6.5
Negative externality of consumption.

Automobile use creates negative externalities of consumption with noise pollution, air pollution, and car accidents. In fact, in the developed world, death in traffic accidents is consistently ranked in the top 10 causes of death. At the same time, cars tend to be one of the most income-elastic goods (Chapter 4, page 87). As people's income rises a little, their propensity to buy cars rockets upwards. So, as the ranks of developed countries grow, we can expect the size of this externality, in global terms, to grow as well. Figure 6.5 shows the actual price and quantity at P_E and Q_E, and the optimum price and quantity at P^* and

Q^*, where marginal costs and benefits to society are equal. If the market were able to incorporate all the associated costs of car consumption, it would demand fewer cars at Q^* and would value them less, at only P^* per car.

In reality, marginal private benefit is greater than (and to the right of) marginal social benefit, reflecting the greater benefit enjoyed by private car users than the benefit enjoyed by society overall. With all of the respective costs and benefits in mind, we can say that there are too many cars produced and too many consumed. The shaded triangular area shows the area of welfare loss, resulting from problems that third parties will pay for eventually.

Worldwide, car crashes kill more people than war. How far will society go to address the problem?

According to a World Health Organization/World Bank report The Global Burden of Disease, *deaths from non-communicable diseases (or other social problems) are expected to climb from 28.1 million a year in 1990 to 49.7 million by 2020 – an increase in absolute numbers of 77%. Traffic accidents are the main cause of this rise. Road traffic injuries are expected to take third place in the rank order of 'disease burden' by the year 2020.*

RANKING OF CAUSES OF DEATH		
Cause of death	**Position in rank order (1990)**	**Position in rank order 2020 (projected)**
road traffic accidents	9	3
war	16	8
self-inflicted injury	17	14
violence	19	12

- Interpret the citation of an increase of 77% in traffic deaths. To what extent is this statistic worrisome?
- Is there more or other types of information that could be useful in understanding the issue? Explain.
- Evaluate some of the possible solutions to this growing problem.
- As poorer countries race to catch up with richer ones in terms of car consumption, to what extent is it ethical to limit car consumption in poor countries?
- Consider the way we have come to understand this issue. How does our perception of it change based on way of knowing about it? How would our perception change based on whether we have:
  a   seen the statistics cited above?
  b   suffered from a traffic accident ourselves?
  c   lost someone close to us in a car accident?

Potential solutions

Legislation and regulation

Governments can ban the consumption of goods with high spillover costs to society. And many governments do indeed deem certain activities illegal for just this reason. They may limit behaviours such as consumption of alcohol or use of phones while driving, or require new residential buildings to have garages and car parks. Children are banned from smoking in most countries, and the consumption of many drugs is heavily regulated. Drug use, prostitution, gambling and other activities with the potential to harm others are widely banned in many societies.

Goods that have a long cultural history of acceptable use may be limited or restricted by legislation, rather than being banned completely. Bans on alcohol, especially in countries where its use is common, have typically failed dramatically. Strict enforcement of drinking laws (in relation to driving and underage consumption) reflects a more modest limit on alcohol use, and an attempt to reduce the costs specifically.

It is difficult to imagine a ban on, say, car use because the good seems so vitally important to modern life. However, in several congested major cities, governments allow car use only on alternate days of the week, in effect banning use half of the time. As you might expect, this kind of restriction is subject to major deception by drivers who find ways around it. More likely, governments will attempt to reduce the externalities by limiting emissions, encouraging alternative methods of transport, limiting sound pollution, and so on. It goes without saying that the greater legal restrictions on the production of a good, the greater the costs of production, as well as the more bureaucracy required to enforce the laws.

Taxation

In an attempt to 'internalize the externality,' governments may also choose to tax the good. This should compel the market actors involved to pay the costs to society instead of the third parties. A tax would increase the MPC and shift private supply to the left. This has the beneficial effect of reducing consumption, perhaps to some point close to the optimum level of Q^*. This result would, of course, depend on an accurate assessment of the external costs and an equally accurate application of the tax. In this desirable but somewhat unlikely case, MPC shifts back to intersect exactly at Q^*, decreasing the amount sold and raising the market price to P_{TAX}. Figure 6.6 shows the supply curve shifting backwards by the amount of the per-unit tax, from S to S_{TAX}. This brings the market to P_{TAX} and Q_{TAX}, in line with the optimal amount of output at Q^*.

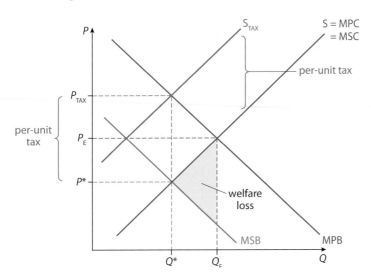

Figure 6.6
Taxing a negative consumption externality.

131

Advertising and persuasion

Governments can also attempt to persuade consumers to change their behaviour. Most often and most expensively, this is done through advertising the negative effects of the product to discourage further use. This method has been used to discourage smoking, drinking and driving, littering, the sale of endangered species, and to encourage recycling, among many other examples. In combination with activism and legal changes, advertising can be effective at changing the value that consumers place on a good. And, in turn, they may switch to other products that serve the same ends (e.g. public transport in the case of automobiles) or merely reduce their consumption, shifting demand left in either case.

Figure 6.7 shows the effect of a decrease in demand on the negative externality. The government has advertised the virtues of public transport compared to driving your own car. Advertising shifts private demand (MPB) to the left as consumers find the product less desirable. This brings the equilibrium price and quantity closer to the socially optimal P^* and Q^*.

Figure 6.7
Advertising and negative consumption externalities.

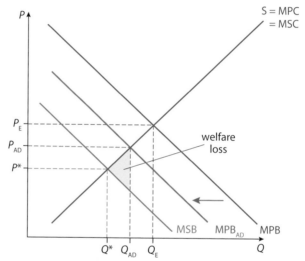

The price decreases, as does quantity consumed, with perhaps less direct market interference than a specific tax. The area of the welfare loss has shrunk as a result. However, changing attitudes through advertising can be expensive, especially in an age of fragmented and narrowly cast media messages. For example, how does advertising reach smokers? The media available include television, billboards, web advertising, social networking, radio, and so on. Officials must weigh the opportunity cost of such expensive campaigns against the social good that can be achieved.

An externality challenge: food or fuel

Maize is usually a food crop ...

... but some farmers grow it for biofuel.

The negative externalities associated with car emissions are well known: carbon dioxide gas and carbon monoxide gas are the primary pollutants from cars. Carbon monoxide is very poisonous because it prevents the blood from carrying oxygen round the body (without oxygen, you die). The American Lung Association says that in 1998, 30 000 people in the US died as a result of car emissions. With this in mind, scientists and business leaders have sought cleaner-burning car fuels.

One category of these fuels is called biofuels because their primary source is some form of biomass, as liquid, solid or gas. One such plant fuel, ethanol, is an alcohol added to normal gasoline by government requirements. In the US, up to 10% of gasoline bought at the pump is ethanol. In Brazil, 25% of all gasoline is ethanol. But ethanol may be more expensive to produce than gasoline. Recent debate has focused on the environmental costs of the extra corn production used in the production of ethanol. Often these crops are subsidized as well, adding to their overall costs.

Increasingly, environmentalists point out that the use of fertilizers and degradation of soil resources may outweigh the benefits of the cleaner fuel.

The food price crisis of 2007 and 2008 revealed another problem with ethanol: it reduces the amount of food available for human consumption. Ethanol can be made from corn, sugar cane, potatoes and other common foods, and ethanol markets may pay more for such crops than the food markets. The amount of land available for growing food crops is also reduced.

As prices for food rose during this period, nutrition levels reached critical levels in some countries. This has led some economists to note the conflict between food and fuel needs. If current trends continue, it is possible that the world will go from producing a net surplus of food to a net deficit. Experts worry these policies will result in a humanitarian disaster.

> The world's largest producer of ethanol is Brazil, where the large sugar cane harvest is used to produce a cheap, clean substitute for petrol. In the US, most ethanol comes from maize, which is far less clean and more inefficient as a fuel source. Despite Brazil's clear comparative advantage in ethanol production, the US imports little or none from Brazil. This is due to protectionism (Chapter 21).

EXERCISES

1   Using an appropriate diagram, explain the externality associated with car emissions.
2   Using an appropriate diagram, explain the externality associated with food production.
3   Evaluate the dilemma and solutions posed by ethanol use for biofuels.

 To access Worksheet 6.1 on the market and pollution reduction, please visit www.pearsonbacconline.com and follow the onscreen instructions.

6.3 Positive externalities

Learning outcomes

- Explain, using diagrams and examples, the concepts of positive externalities of production and consumption, and the welfare loss associated with the production or consumption of a good or service.
- Explain that merit goods are goods whose consumption creates external benefits.
- Evaluate, using diagrams, the use of government responses, including subsidies, legislation, advertising to influence behaviour, and direct provision of goods and services.

Positive externalities of production

The production of some goods creates positive spillover effects, creating benefits for third parties. At first glance, these may appear to be rather rare compared to the other types of externality.

- Tree farms created for the production of wood oxygenate the atmosphere to everyone's benefit.

- A school placed in a neighbourhood may improve the property values of families with no children in school.
- Workers trained by one company can be hired by another which enjoys the benefits of the training.
- Research and development by one firm can be used by another to make further advances in a particular field.
- Software companies create new technologies that may not succeed on their own but inspire others to create valuable new products by imitation.

In all of these cases, the company, in producing one good, benefits others beyond itself and the customer.

In Figure 6.8, the positive externality of production is shown as a gap between social costs and private costs on the supply side of the transaction. Marginal social cost, the true cost to society, is lower at every point than the private cost experienced by firms. Thus, at the market equilibrium of P_E, there appears to be too little being produced. At P_E, the MPC indicates private costs at point a, where the MSC indicates costs to be much lower at point b. This suggests that more could be produced, and society would enjoy the extra benefits of that production, shown by the blue triangle as 'potential welfare gain.' As production continues beyond Q_E, the gap between private costs and social costs narrows, to the point of P^* and Q^*, where MSC = MSB, and output is at its optimal point.

Figure 6.8

Positive externality of production.

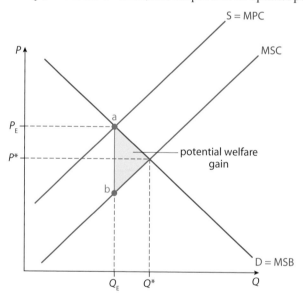

Potential solutions

Subsidies

The government can actively encourage extra production by the payment of subsidies. This may occur in the form of a lump-sum payment to the industry, or more commonly as a per-unit subsidy (Chapter 5, page 108). The goal would be to push MPC outwards towards the production of the socially optimal Q^* units of output. The subsidy, however, is paid by tax revenue, and is drawn from other areas of the government budget. So again the opportunity cost of using these resources must be considered. Subsidies of this kind can be very expensive.

In Figure 6.9, the subsidy shifts MPC to the right by exactly the amount sufficient to encourage production to the optimal point, Q^*. This lowers the price to P^* and allows more consumers to enjoy the product. This example is dependent on an accurate assessment of the value of the positive externality, as well as the expert designation of the subsidy amount. Furthermore, the granting of such subsidies can create a political problem. Other firms may see an opportunity to be subsidized, which may lead to a barrage of appeals to government for subsidies on the basis of the external benefits their product creates.

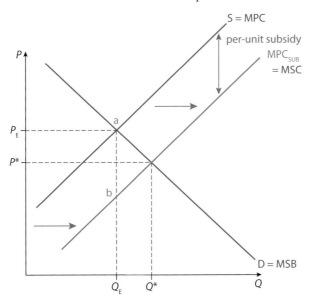

Figure 6.9
Subsidy solution to positive production externality.

State provision of the article

In the case of worker training or tree farming, the government may decide to provide directly the good creating the positive externality. For example, states can build and staff worker-training centres to provide the same training experience that private firms offer. However, this can be costly and depends on government accurately predicting the needed training shortage areas. Governments can devote large areas of public land to oxygen production through tree farming or the protection of national forests or national parks, but these decisions are subject to the same questions about the true value of the externality, and the opportunity cost of using resources in such a fashion.

Positive externality of consumption

Figure 6.10
Positive consumption externality.

The consumption of some goods can create benefits to third parties. Additional years of education, it is said, create strong spillover benefits for the rest of society. With more education, a person is more likely to be a skilled and productive member of the workforce. Their income will provide tax revenue, and they are relatively less likely to engage in criminal activity. Since these are benefits potentially enjoyed by the whole of society, we can say that the social benefits of education exceed the private benefits. In other words, MSB will be greater than MPB. This is shown in Figure 6.10.

Left alone, the market will produce Q_E worth of education at a price of P_E. The optimal production, however, appears to be at Q^* with a price of P^*, where social costs and benefits are equal. Thus, the free market will not produce enough education by itself. And, if society's true value for education were included, if demand were reflected in the MSB curve, the demand

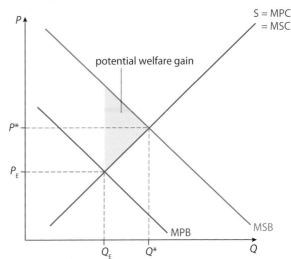

and, therefore, the price would be higher than it is. Society would gain considerably by consuming more education. The amount of the potential gain in welfare is shown by the shaded triangle.

Potential solutions

Subsidies

Governments might subsidize the good to make it more affordable. They can and often do subsidize education. Public education of children to a certain age is common in many countries. In this case, government directly provides the good. A less extreme approach encourages education by paying for the majority of costs, leaving extra costs to be paid for by families. In any case, the effect of this government intervention is to subsidize education, shifting the private supply curve (MPC) to the right. Figure 6.11 demonstrates the effect of a subsidy on private consumption externalities. If we assume the subsidy is paid to schools on a per-unit basis, MPC shifts right by the amount of the subsidy, lowering the price of education and increasing its availability.

Figure 6.11
Subsidy of education.

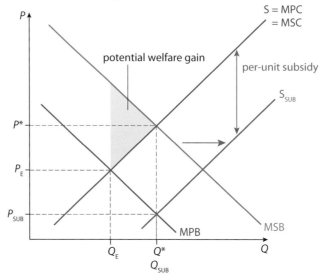

The new equilibrium is at the socially efficient quantity of students, Q^*. Schools receive revenue equal to what would be received at P^*, but the difference between P_{SUB} and P^* is provided by the per-student subsidy. Subsidies to education are popular. Their expense is considerable, however. Political debates over education often revolve around the amount of the subsidy rather than whether or not to subsidize at all. Thus, the opportunity costs of such subsidies must be weighed against the relative merit of the good.

Education subsidies can also be delivered to consumers in the form of tuition 'vouchers' that allow families to spend their subsidy on the school of their choice, private or public. In this case, demand (MPB) would shift to the right, encouraging more consumption of education.

Advertising

To encourage consumption, governments can advertise the benefits of positive consumption externality goods. For instance, the consumption of most healthcare goods tends to benefit the rest of society. This is most acutely true in the area of communicable disease and illness, but society also benefits from increased overall general health levels by raising productivity. More specifically, vaccinations against diseases such as polio offer dramatic benefits to third parties by reducing the spread of disease even to those who are not vaccinated. On a more routine daily basis, the use of condoms reduces the spread of sexually transmitted infections and prevents unplanned pregnancy.

In many such instances, governments attempt to persuade the public to use such goods through advertising and public campaigns. The effect would be to change consumer tastes, shifting MPB to the right, with the goal of pushing it nearer to the socially efficient quantity (Figure 6.12). With private demand increasing, society reduces the size of the externality, in effect absorbing or enjoying at least part of the potential welfare gain. The effects of such advertising vary considerably, depending on the type of good being advocated, as well as the strength of cultural attitudes. Condom use, for example, is more difficult to encourage in countries where public discussion of sexual behaviour is considered offensive.

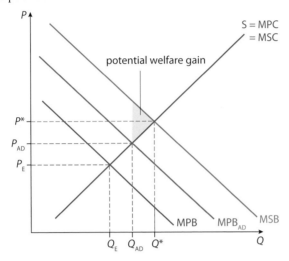

 Figure 6.12
Advertising solution to positive consumption externality.

Legal requirements

Governments can legally mandate behaviour that it deems to the public benefit. It can require children go to school to a certain age, or to get vaccinations. However, unless the good is publicly provided, full compliance is unlikely. Furthermore, mandates without reasonable government support will foster resentment of government policy.

A critical consideration when formulating such policy is the size of potential benefits. In other words, government intervention is most likely in areas where the benefits are large, as they are with education and healthcare. The measures enacted for less demonstrably 'positive' behaviour are lighter. While governments may sponsor libraries in recognition of the benefits derived from them, for example, they are less likely to require their adult population to read the books contained inside.

W To learn more about externalities, visit www. pearsonhotlinks.com, enter the title or ISBN of this book and select weblink 6.2.

6.4 Lack of merit goods and public goods

Learning outcomes
- Using the concepts of rivalry and excludability, and providing examples, distinguish between public goods (non-rivalrous and non-excludable) and private goods (rivalrous and excludable).
- Explain, with reference to the free-rider problem, how the lack of public goods indicates market failure.
- Discuss the implications of the direct provision of public goods by government.

Under-supply of merit goods

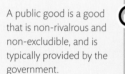
Merit goods or services are those that create positive spillover benefits, and are under-produced by the free market. Economists and governments advocate policies that encourage the consumption of these goods to capture potential welfare gain that would not be enjoyed without such intervention.

Governments encourage the consumption of lesser merit goods with a combination of persuasion and incentives. Advertising and public opinion campaigns may encourage consumption. Governments can subsidize merit goods, either by direct payment or reduced taxation. Religious schools, for example, may be actively subsidized, as they are in many countries, or implicitly subsidized by reducing or eliminating taxes for religious organizations themselves. The degree of government provision or encouragement is directly related to the amount of spillover benefits provided by the good.

Under-supply of public goods

Public goods are extreme examples of merit goods, and are typically provided entirely by the government. Typical examples include roads, prisons, streetlights, and public theatre and arts. Public goods are both non-rivalrous and non-excludable.

- **Non-rivalrous**. A good is non-rivalrous if one person's consumption of it does not prevent others from enjoying it. National defence is provided by a nation's military, and the security it offers is enjoyed by every individual in the country. One person's consumption does not infringe on any other individual's, so national defence is non-rivalrous. On the other hand, when one person is eating an ice cream, others are prevented from enjoying its benefits (Table 6.1).
- **Non-excludable**. A good is non-excludable if the producer cannot prevent particular individuals from enjoying its benefits. Streetlights are non-excludable because once installed and turned on, it is impossible to prevent particular people from benefiting from them. In contrast, an ice cream is completely excludable by its producer. If you don't pay for it, you don't get to benefit from it (Table 6.1).

Only goods that are both non-rivalrous and non-excludable are declared public goods. Streetlights can be enjoyed by one and all without rivalry, and even those who do not pay (children, tourists) will enjoy the good.

TABLE 6.1 TYPES OF GOOD		
	Excludable	**Non-excludable**
Rivalrous	Private goods: clothing, food, electronics	Common goods: fish, seafood, coral, timber, air
Non-rivalrous	Collective/club goods: movie theatre, internet websites	Public goods: national defence, police and fire departments, lighthouses

Oversupply of demerit goods

Demerit goods are those that create negative spillover costs to third parties. Negative externality goods are generally considered to be demerit goods. Because of their extra costs to society, they are considered to be over-produced and over-consumed. An optimal allocation of society's resources would reduce their use. Goods like cigarettes, alcohol, gambling, and addictive drugs are examples of such goods, and governments often attempt to reduce the consumption of them.

Public persuasion, taxation, regulation, and banning of the good can all be employed, depending on the perceived severity of the problems associated with the good. Cigarettes are heavily taxed and are often labelled with large warnings and photographs to discourage consumption. Normally, alcohol and cigarettes are restricted to adult use by law. Bans against the consumption of demerit goods rarely destroy the market. Instead, bans drive the market underground to the black market. Demerit goods are most often associated with personal health habits, but the term can arguably be applied to any good with accompanying spillover costs, including automobiles, golf courses (environmental costs) and the consumption of meat (environmental and healthcare costs).

To learn more about public goods, visit www.pearsonhotlinks.com, enter the title or ISBN of this book and select weblink 6.3.

6.5 Common access resources and the threat to sustainability

Learning outcomes
- Describe, using examples, common access resources.
- Describe sustainability.
- Explain that the lack of a pricing mechanism for common access resources means that these goods may be overused/depleted/degraded as a result of activities of producers and consumers who do not pay for the resources that they use, and that this poses a threat to sustainability.
- Explain, using negative externalities diagrams, that economic activity requiring the use of fossil fuels to satisfy demand poses a threat to sustainability.
- Explain that the existence of poverty in economically less developed countries creates negative externalities through over-exploitation of land for agriculture, and that this poses a threat to sustainability.
- Evaluate, using diagrams, possible government responses to threats to sustainability, including legislation, carbon taxes, cap and trade schemes, and funding for clean technologies.
- Explain, using examples, that government responses to threats to sustainability are limited by the global nature of the problems and the lack of ownership of common access resources, and that effective responses require international cooperation.

Common access resources such as fisheries often result in over-exploitation, due to their non-excludability. Recent attempts to 'privatize the commons' have helped achieve a more sustainable level of fish harvest in certain countries.

The tragedy of the commons

The tragedy of the commons is a dilemma posed when common resources are used or degraded rapidly by private individuals who enjoy the short-term benefits of the resource, but who are ignorant or neglectful of its long-term depletion. The most common example is that of a herd of cows using a common pasture. Each cow owner has a strong private incentive to place his or her cow in the pasture for feeding. The cumulative effect of this, however, is the long-term destruction of a once lush resource, as more and more cows eat up the field. All users will eventually suffer this loss. Economists and environmental scientists have also applied the idea to the world's common fishing waters, citing the dwindling of fish stocks everywhere.

The critical problem is that common access resources are essentially 'free' to the user, but use of them depletes the availability of the resource to everyone else. Economists and scientists call these subtractable resources. Because users do not pay a market price for use of the good, they have little incentive to ration it wisely. Economists call this behaviour the free-rider problem: those who benefit and draw from a resource but do not have to pay for it. Examples are abundant.

- Water sources in nearly every country are receivers of toxic waste, thus diminishing ecosystems.
- Forests are slashed for wood and to make way for farming, which reduces oxygen production and erodes the soil.
- The atmosphere is infused with pollutants generated from industry, cars, and the methane output of animals that are kept for meat production.

Originally articulated by Garrett Hardin in the journal *Science* in 1968, the tragedy of the commons points to the likelihood of ruin in a world of common access resources such as fisheries, forests and pastures: 'Ruin is the destination toward which all men rush, each pursuing his own best interest in a society that believes in the freedom of the commons. Freedom in a commons brings ruin to all.'

The goal of sustainable development is to avoid resource depletion and encourage environmentally benign forms of economic progress. Recognizing the obstacles to sustainability posed by the tragedy of the commons allows us to better assess the ability of society to grow and develop in a sustainable manner.

EXERCISES
4 List two other commonly held resources that may be subject to this dilemma.
5 To what extent does each situation fit the category of the tragedy of the commons?
6 Speculate on some ways that better management of the resource may be possible.

Fossil fuel consumption

One of the most acute problems of sustainability is the consumption of fossil fuels. The production and burning of natural gas, petroleum and coal emits the largest share of greenhouse gas emissions. It also produces many air pollutants, such as volatile organic compounds, nitrogen oxides, sulfur dioxide, and heavy metals. It is blamed for acid rain, as well as for threatening water and vegetation habitats in many parts of the world.

Clearly, fossil fuel use is creating significant negative externalities (Figures 6.3 and 6.5, pages 127 and 129). Among the more challenging questions is exactly how severe the problem is – that is, how large the external costs are (how large is the externality triangle?). This knowledge problem is typical of market failure, and of externalities in particular. But in the case of fossil fuel consumption, the scale of the problem is global. This makes estimates of the damage imprecise, but it is generally agreed that the problem is widespread, with potentially extraordinary consequences.

Debate about global warming continues between political leaders, but most scientists and economists acknowledge the role fossil fuel consumption plays in climate change. Several economic schemes for mitigating the effects of industrial activity on the environment have been proposed, and most rejected. It can be argued that the atmosphere is a common access resource, and that until a value can be placed on its protection, human industrial activity will continue to exploit it unsustainably.

Poverty in less developed countries

Less developed countries (LDCs) are more desperate than others for income. Most LDCs sell goods for which the demand is not increasing especially fast (Chapter 25). As global incomes rise, the demand for advanced goods, which these countries must import, is rising much faster. This is worsening the terms by which poorer countries trade with richer ones. In simple terms, incomes in poor countries are rising more slowly than in rich ones.

One result of this is that LDCs must sell more of their agricultural or primary goods to keep up. This puts pressure on their resource base. For agriculture-based economies, it means more intensive cultivation and the potential to deplete the soil of its nutrients. It could also mean the widespread slashing of forests to make way for farms and livestock. For extractable resources, it might result in mining and drilling operations without regard for the effect on the landscape, or on soil and water resources.

The pressure on resources in an LDC is intensified if the country carries a significant international debt burden, as many do. Among the first requirements of foreign lenders is for debtor countries to maximize their export earnings. It is for this reason that lending institutions like the World Bank and International Monetary Fund are blamed for indirectly encouraging environmentally unsustainable development policies.

Potential solutions to sustainability problems

Extension of property rights

In the case of common access resources, the lack of a price mechanism leads to a depletion of resources. Economists have proposed that these cases call for an extension of property rights to encourage the protection and management of the scarce resource. The idea is that if the users of the resource had a long-term interest in survival of the resource, their incentives would be balanced between short- and long-term goals. Some success has been achieved on limited, smaller projects. In practice, the extension of property rights depends on a number of factors, and the concept has proven difficult for policymakers to enact effectively on large-scale projects.

Carbon taxes

A carbon tax is a charge levied by government on firms burning fossil fuels in their production processes. It is the burning of carbon in all fossil fuels that creates carbon dioxide. One approach proposes to tax fuel by carbon level, thus 'internalizing the externality' with the consumer and producer. This is done with a specific tax, the effects of which are shown in Figures 6.4 and 6.6. Ideally, the tax would decrease the amount consumed or produced to be in line with the allocatively efficient level of output, where MSC = MSB. The tax acts as a disincentive to use fossil fuels, and encourages the demand for (and development of) non-carbon-emitting substitutes.

Of the largest carbon dioxide producers, none have comprehensive or 'harmonized' carbon tax systems. The US and China, in particular, have failed to enact such policies, primarily on the grounds that they would harm economic growth. Many EU countries have independently enacted such schemes, to varying levels. However, an EU-wide policy has been stalled because of the reluctance of former Eastern Bloc countries. They have argued that they will be unduly penalized for 'starting late' to modernize and re-equip the technologically dated energy systems of the communist years: they need more time to catch up with the West.

Policies such as carbon taxes and tradable permits are meant to internalize the external costs of burning fossil fuels.

▼

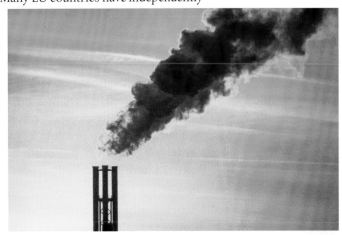

Tradable permits

The rules for tradable permits seek to avoid the adversarial relationship seen with tax and regulation policies. They aim to do so by using market forces

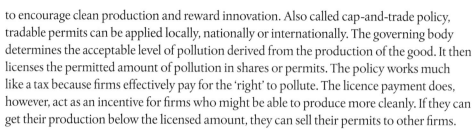

to encourage clean production and reward innovation. Also called cap-and-trade policy, tradable permits can be applied locally, nationally or internationally. The governing body determines the acceptable level of pollution derived from the production of the good. It then licenses the permitted amount of pollution in shares or permits. The policy works much like a tax because firms effectively pay for the 'right' to pollute. The licence payment does, however, act as an incentive for firms who might be able to produce more cleanly. If they can get their production below the licensed amount, they can sell their permits to other firms.

Alternatively, if a firm expects to exceed the licensed pollution amount, they can try to buy up extra permits from other firms. This creates a market for such permits, where high demand makes polluting expensive. This would further encourage firms to take another approach, to innovate and reduce their own pollution levels. Economists favour these schemes because they create incentives to reduce pollution, but also compel polluters to pay more as they pollute more.

Figure 6.13 shows how a tradable permit scheme may look. Q represents the total licensed amount of pollution, and is perfectly inelastic because it is established by the government. This quantity of allowed pollution is then sub-divided into smaller quantities for which permits can be issued. Companies buy the permits to pollute up to the level allowed by the permits. An increase in production might increase the demand for such licences to D_1, and cause the market price to increase. This would give relatively clean firms an incentive to further innovate and reduce their pollution levels and sell their permit to the high polluters. Over time, to reduce the overall level of pollution, the government could gradually reduce the allowable Q, or quantity of pollution, moving the supply curve to the left. This would increase the price of permits and compel firms to seek out cleaner technology or pay the higher permit fees. Critics argue that such an approach relies heavily on enforcement and heavy fines to reinforce the policy, and that it does not sufficiently discourage polluting.

Figure 6.13

The market for tradable pollution permits.

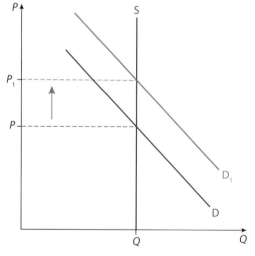

The most famous tradable permit scheme has been the United Nations Kyoto Protocol, developed and ratified by several dozen countries in the year 2000. This agreement placed limits and agreed reductions in the amount of greenhouse gas (GHG) emissions on the basis of regions, development categories, and country-specific factors. Under the scheme, countries would pay penalties for missing their targets, and countries that beat their reduction goals might potentially receive credits. Developed countries may buy carbon permits from lesser developed ones, which have little or no emissions restrictions.

Significant conflict arose over the strictness of emission levels, the difference between the tougher restrictions on rich countries and the more lax ones on poor countries, and the severity of enforcement penalties. In effect, since 2005, over 160 countries participate in the system. The US, the largest *per capita* emitter of GHGs, participated in negotiations and signed the treaty, but has not ratified it and operates outside Kyoto rules (Table 6.2).

TABLE 6.2 TOP 10 GREENHOUSE GAS EMITTERS BY COUNTRY, 2005		
Country	% share of global GHG emission	Tons of GHG *per capita*
China	17	5.8
US	16	24.1
EU	11	10.6
Indonesia	6	12.9
India	5	2.1
Russia	5	14.9
Brazil	4	10
Japan	3	10.6
Canada	2	23.2
Mexico	2	6.4

Problems of cooperation

A common difficulty with solutions to sustainability problems is the difficulty of enforcement of policies to encourage sustainable growth. In the case of polluting industries, nothing is solved when companies can move from place to place, in search of lax rules and enforcement. In the case of carbon taxes and tradable permits, countries which move first towards implementation are at a competitive disadvantage when attempting to lure industry and encourage business growth. All of which suggests that the critical ingredient in solutions to sustainability is international cooperation. Whatever the details of the specific policies, only with common agreement and coordinated enforcement can these environmental issues be addressed effectively.

EXERCISES

7   What might the government do if it wanted to raise the price of pollution?

8   If the scheme works and firms do innovate for cleaner production, what could happen to the market?

9   Why do you think the Kyoto protocol excluded poor countries from its pollution limits? Evaluate.

10   Review the list of top GHG emitters. What accounts for the differences in the percentage rankings and *per capita* numbers?

 To learn more about economics and the environment, visit www.pearsonhotlinks.com, enter the title or ISBN of this book and select weblink 6.4.

6.6 Additional forms of market failure

Factor immobility

Market theory operates on the assumption that factors of production gravitate to the places where they are most needed. Capital, for example, moves to where the rates of return are highest. In theory, workers (labour), should do the same, and move to where real wages are greatest. In reality, however, factor resources can be immobile. Workers stay in places where opportunities are slim and wages weak. Family connections and housing commitments, among other factors, can prevent the idealized free movement of workers. Land or natural resources are in many cases quite locally fixed. For example, space is in demand in Tokyo (where rents are among the highest in the world) but there's little prospect of actually adding more land. Thus, when factors are immobile, market theory becomes more complicated and less easily applicable in all situations.

Inequality

Inequality in income may be a market failure itself. Does the free market allocate enough resources towards improving the lives of the world's poor? These children are working in the Stung Meanchey Dump in Cambodia.

While free markets reward the qualities of risk-taking, innovation, and entrepreneurship, they can also reward anti-competitive behaviour. Furthermore, the rewards vary dramatically depending on the nature of the opportunities being exploited. Because free markets can lead to significant inequality, some economists regard the problems associated with this as a market failure. The inequality created by free markets exists on the current income level as jobs are paid very differently. It also exists at the future opportunity level, where income disparities can lead (in purely free markets) to a block on educational and life opportunities for the youngest members of society, whose situations are dependent on the actions of their families. Governments can act to mitigate the effects of this inequality by redistribution of income through progressive taxes, the creation of welfare insurance for the unemployed, and government support for public and subsidized education.

Government failure or policy failure

Policy failure exists when government action to correct some form of market failure actually creates a worse set of negative outcomes. These outcomes may be a result of policies that have poorly designed incentives or unforeseen consequences, or may be a result of self-interested politics on the part of lawmakers. Examples of policy failure include 'logrolling', where lawmakers trade votes on policy rather than voting from conscience. Also included is 'crowding-out', where short-term expansionary fiscal policy leads to a reduction in the availability of future capital. Crowding-out is discussed in Chapter 17.

Short-termism

Short-termism is how the pursuit of rational short-term objectives can create long-term problems. Short-termism can exist in both the private and public sphere. For example, when corporate chief executive officers (CEOs) are rewarded on stock valuations, they are encouraged to push for short-term results and perhaps distort those results at the expense of the long-term health of the firm. In similar fashion, politicians may be drawn to create policies for the purpose of election results. For example, the 'political business cycle' of fiscal policy occurs when governments spend and cut taxes for an immediate surge in economic activity and to encourage re-election voting. Over the long term, however, these results have opportunity costs in terms of foregone services or increased debt.

 ## 6.7 Asymmetric information and abuse of monopoly power (HL only)

Learning outcomes
- Explain, using examples, that market failure may occur when one party in an economic transaction (either the buyer or the seller) possesses more information than the other party.
- Evaluate possible government responses, including legislation, regulation and provision of information.
- Explain how monopoly power can create a welfare loss and is therefore a type of market failure.
- Discuss possible government responses, including legislation, regulation, nationalization and trade liberalization.

Asymmetric information

Market theory presupposes that all actors are in possession of the same, perfect levels of information regarding market transactions. All consumers, for instance, will know the variety of prices and quality levels available for a particular good. Of course, this is highly unlikely, as consumers are constrained by time and access to such information. Even in the digital information age, when far more information on any product is widely available, consumers make a decision about the opportunity cost of absorbing all the alternatives, and rarely possess anything close to perfect information. With this reality in mind, it is more than likely for consumers to make 'mistakes' regarding purchases, in pure market theory terms.

Today, consumers are also more likely to be subjected to sophisticated marketing techniques that aim to limit information and choice. Another variety of asymmetric information has one party in a transaction holding more information than the other party. For example, the seller of a plot of land might know that neighbouring land will be used for a chemical plant, while the buyer is ignorant of this information. The buyer will pay too much for the land – an example of market failure.

One particular form of information asymmetry occurs when individuals neglect to take full responsibility for their actions. Economists call this phenomenon a moral hazard, and have applied the term to a variety of unethical and criminal behaviours. When polluters dump waste into common resources like rivers, they shun their responsibility for the problems this may cause. In this way, a firm may be acting legally, but is using the absence of specific rules or lax enforcement to offload costs to innocent parties. The term has come back into use recently, during the crisis of 2008 and 2009, when describing the negligent actions of banks, bank regulators, investment bankers and the borrowing public.

 The financial crisis of 2008–09 may have been the result of market failure rooted in information asymmetry. The investment banks which created and sold the complex financial instruments at the heart of the crisis were careful not to convey all the information about the assets from which those instruments were assembled. For example, many of the bonds purchased by investors were rated as AAA (very safe), yet contained loans made to very-low-income households, whose lack of ability to repay should have been conveyed to the investors.

 To access Worksheet 6.2 on market failure, please visit www.pearsonbacconline.com and follow the onscreen instructions.

 To access Worksheet 6.3 on Wall Street and market failure, please visit www.pearsonbacconline.com and follow the onscreen instructions.

Potential solutions to asymmetric information

Legislation to punish 'insider' information use

Laws like this are difficult to enforce as they require proof of insider knowledge.

Active dissemination of information

Monopoly power is the power of a firm to raise the price above the prices of competitors.

The promotion of information attempts to fill the market gap and create more efficient outcomes. Some believe that the internet is the best means to address this gap in information and, with this in mind, the United Nations has proposed that internet access be considered a human right. In July 2010, Finland made broadband access a human right.

Monopoly power

Monopoly power exists where a firm is able to influence or increase the price they receive to a price above the competitive-market equilibrium. Monopolists and other imperfect competitors will restrict output to increase prices. As a result, they no longer produce where the market is socially efficient. Figure 6.14 demonstrates the effect of a monopolist's output decisions, compared to that of the competitive market.

Figure 6.14
Monopoly power may lead to less output and higher prices.

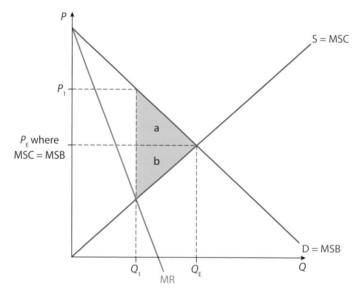

The monopolist produces less and charges a higher price. If the market were competitive, it would produce where supply and demand intersect, at Q_E and P_E, respectively. However, by producing at Q_1, the monopolist does not produce the allocatively efficient output. It produces where the firm's marginal revenue (MR) equals marginal cost. Marginal revenue represents the benefit the firm receives from each additional unit of output. From the monopolist's perspective, this is a rational, profit-maximizing decision. Monopolies are discussed in more detail in Chapter 9.

But this is not where society's marginal benefit (MSB) is equal to marginal cost. This is not Pareto optimal, a problem which is demonstrated by the decreased community surplus represented by areas a and b. The decreased production from Q_E to Q_1, compared to competitive market outcome of Q_1, means that while the producer gains at the expense of the consumer, the overall community surplus decreases.

Potential solutions

Legislation

Governments can pass 'anti-trust' legislation aimed at preventing the market power from becoming concentrated in relatively few firms' hands. These laws specify the maximum percentages of the market to be controlled by one or a few firms. The legislation is enforced by preventing monopolistic mergers or by breaking up companies that the courts deem too dominant.

Regulation

Governments may choose to monitor and control monopolies with regulatory agencies. Such government agencies track the pricing and production decisions of the firm. For the public interest, the agencies may have some power to enact or recommend changes in the firm's behaviour – for example, by setting prices for the firm.

Natural monopolies

Natural monopolies are granted in some industries because they keep costs lower than a competitive market would. Public utilities of water and power are two examples. However, the market may still under-produce the good for the profit maximization reasons. Governments can address this with a subsidy to increase production, and move output to a more optimal quantity. Remember that the purpose of such monopolies is to provide a necessity good to the public, so a subsidy to encourage production is a logical choice.

PRACTICE QUESTIONS

1 **a** Using an appropriate diagram, explain how negative externalities are a type of market failure. [10 marks] [AO2], [AO4]

   b Evaluate the measures that a government might adopt to correct market failure arising from negative externalities. [15 marks] [AO3]

   © International Baccalaureate Organization 2009

2 **a** What are positive externalities and how do they arise? Illustrate your answer with examples. (10 marks) [AO2], [AO4]

   b To what extent should governments attempt to influence markets where positive externalities exist? (15 marks) [AO3]

   © International Baccalaureate Organization 2002

3 'National policies and international agreements must be implemented in order to reduce global environmental problems.'

   a Using the concept of market failure, explain the statement above from an economist's point of view. (10 marks) [AO2], [AO4]

   b With reference to both national policies and international agreements, discuss three solutions that could be recommended by economists. (15 marks) [AO3]

   © International Baccalaureate Organization 2003

 To access Quiz 6, an interactive, multiple-choice quiz on this chapter, please visit www.pearsonbacconline.com and follow the onscreen instructions.

COSTS, REVENUES AND PROFIT (HL ONLY)

7.1 Costs of production: economic costs

Learning outcomes
- Explain the meaning of economic costs as the opportunity cost of all resources employed by the firm (including entrepreneurship).
- Distinguish between explicit costs and implicit costs as the two components of economic costs.

In their effort to minimize costs, firms often cut corners, as BP may have done on its oil rig *Deepwater Horizon*, seen here after an explosion in summer 2010.

On 20 April 2010, *Deepwater Horizon*, an oil rig in the Gulf of Mexico, burst into flames following the failure of a pressure-release valve on the seabed 5000 feet below the surface. The rig sank and the deep-sea well proceeded to spew between 10 000 and 20 000 barrels of oil per day into the Gulf. By the time the well was sealed months later, over 100 million gallons of oil had leaked into the Gulf of Mexico, making this the largest oil spill and one o the worst environmental catastrophes in American history.

About two months after the rig's failure, evidence emerged that, when building the well, B may have made cost-cutting decisions that contributed to its eventual failure.

The company made a series of money-saving shortcuts and blunders that dramatically increased the danger of a destructive oil spill in a well that an engineer ominously described as a 'nightmare' just six days before the blowout, according to documents … that provide new insight into the causes of the disaster.

'Time after time, it appears that BP made decisions that increased the risk of a blowout to save the company time or expense. If this is what happened, BP's carelessness and complacency have inflicted a heavy toll on the Gulf, its inhabitants, and the workers on the rig', said Democratic Representatives Henr A Waxman and Bart Stupak …

In the design of the well, the company apparently chose a riskier option among two possibilities to provid a barrier to the flow of gas in space surrounding steel tubes in the well, documents and internal emails show. The decision saved BP $7 million to $10 million; the original cost estimate for the well was about $96 million.

Mathew Daly and Ray Henry, Associated Press writers

BP's decision to minimize costs in the construction of its oil well seems foolish in retrospect. The current estimate of monetary damages BP will have to pay to victims of the oil spill is in the range of $40 billion, 4000 times more than the company saved by choosing the lower-cost option when building the well. So why did BP do it? What drives firms to reduce costs at every opportunity, even if it may lead to a lower-quality product or the risk of future engineering failures as with BP's oil well? This chapter and the three that follow examine the theories surrounding the behaviour of firms in market economies.

Businesses, like individuals, respond to incentives in the pursuit of their economic objectives. The goal of individual consumers in a market economy is to maximize their utility or happiness which, in the economic realm, is achieved through increased consumption of goods and services made possible through increased income. Individuals, therefore, seek to maximize their incomes by selling their productive resources (land, labour and capital) to those firms which demand them in the resource market.

Firms, on the other hand, seek to maximize their profits through the production and sale of their various goods and services in the product market. The interaction of firms and individuals in the resource and product markets is the defining activity of the market economic system. In the pursuit of their goal of profit maximization, firms must accomplish two distinct objectives: *reducing costs* and *increasing revenues* until the difference between the two (the *profit*) is maximized.

Costs in economics are those things that must be given up in order to have something else. Costs can be explicit or implicit. Explicit costs are the monetary payments that firms make to the owners of land, labour and capital in the resource market (i.e. rent, wages and interest, respectively). Implicit costs include the opportunity costs of entrepreneurs who decide to allocate their time and energy to one enterprise over other possible economic activities (in economics, the implicit cost of an entrepreneur is called normal profit).

Revenue is the income earned from a firm's sale of its good or service to consumers in the product market.

A firm's *profit* is the difference between its total revenue (TR) earned in product market and its total cost (TC) in the resource market, as shown in the following equation:

Profit = TR − TC

A key concept we must understand as we begin our study of firm behaviour is that most firms are profit maximizers, which requires them to be cost minimizers. This is because the difference between a firm's revenues and its costs are its profit.

To return to our question: Why would BP choose the cheaper and inferior component for its oil well rather than the more costly yet superior part? The answer is that BP made the decision in the best interests of its shareholders at the time. Corporations like BP are actually legally bound to maximize profits, which requires them to minimize their costs whenever the opportunity arises.

The late Nobel Prize-winning economist Milton Friedman reflected on the responsibilities of corporations:

There is one and only one social responsibility of business – to use its resources and engage in activities designed to increase its profits so long as it stays within the rules of the game.

…

And further:

The only entities who can have responsibilities are individuals … A business cannot have responsibilities. So the question is, do corporate executives, provided they stay within the law, have responsibilities in their

 Revenues are the income earned from a firm's sale of its good or service to consumers in the product market.

 Profit is the difference between a firm's total revenues and its total costs.

business activities other than to make as much money for their stockholders as possible? And my answer to that is, no, they do not.

Milton Friedman, *Business & Society Review*

BP did not act out of greed or disregard for the well-being of others when it saved $10 million while building its well. It acted in the best interests of the members of the public who held shares in the company, as it is legally bound to do, by minimizing costs in order to maximize profits.

In this chapter, you will consider the various costs, both short run and long run, explicit and implicit that firms face in their effort to maximize profits. You will examine normal profit and economic profit, and consider the 'rule' that firms must follow in determining their profit-maximizing level of output and price. In the chapters that follow, you will examine different market structures (ranging from highly competitive to monopolistic) and the behaviours of firms in each type of market.

> The short run is the period of time during which the number of firms in an industry and the amount of land and capital employed by existing firms towards the production of a good are fixed in quantity.
>
> In the long run, the number of firms and the amount of capital used in production by existing firms are variable. This means that as demand grows, firms increase capital and new firms enter a market in the long run. If demand falls for a particular good, in the long run, the amount of capital used by firms and the number of firms in a market may be reduced.

Explicit and implicit costs of production

We've already distinguished between two distinct microeconomic time periods, the short run and the long run. The short run is defined as the period of time over which firms cannot acquire land or capital resources to increase production or take land or capital out of production, but within which labour can be applied to a greater or lesser degree in order to change output. The only variable resource in the short run is labour. In the long run, firms are able to acquire and put into production all factors of production – labour, land, capital and other resources – to produce output. In the long run, all resources are variable.

The short run is also known as the fixed-plant period, since the amount of capital a firm employs (otherwise known as its plant size) is fixed. The long run is also known as the variable-plant period, since the amount of all resources, including capital, can be adjusted in the long run.

In understanding the cost-minimizing behaviour of firms, we need to distinguish short-run costs of production from long-run costs of production. In the short run, a firm may alter the amount of labour and raw materials it employs towards its production of output, but not the amount of capital or land. The short-run costs faced by firms can be either explicit or implicit.

Explicit costs

Explicit costs are the monetary payments a firm makes to the owners of the resources it employs in the production of its output. Wages for workers, raw material costs, energy and transport costs, rent payments for factory or retail space and interest payments to banks are all explicit costs a firm may face.

Implicit costs

Implicit costs refer to the opportunity costs faced by the entrepreneur who undertakes a business venture and who could otherwise have earned money by hiring his self-owned resources out to another employer. The founders of all business enterprises face implicit costs that represent the foregone wages of the entrepreneur who chose to start a business as opposed to earning a wage working for someone else. Also considered an implicit cost is the normal profit an entrepreneur expects to earn above and beyond all his or her explicit costs. Normal profit is the entrepreneur's implied value of his or her own talent; it is the cost to do business, and if a firm's revenues do not cover the normal profit, the firm owner may choose to shut down and direct his or her efforts towards another industry or area of employment.

The difference between implicit and explicit costs

To demonstrate the difference between explicit and implicit costs, imagine a PhD chemist who chooses to leave her job paying €100 000 at a pharmaceutical company to start her own research firm. Her explicit costs as a new business owner are the wages she must pay herself and her five researchers, the rent she pays for her lab space, and the interest she pays the bank for the loans she took out to acquire equipment for her laboratory.

The chemist's implicit cost is her perceived value of her entrepreneurial talent, represented by the profit she expects to earn above and beyond her old salary to compensate her for the risk she took when starting her own business. Assume the chemist expects to earn the €100 000 she sacrificed when she left her old job, plus an additional €50 000 to compensate her for the risk she took by starting her own lab. The €50 000 is her normal profit, which she must earn in order for her to consider the venture worth her while.

A mnemonic for implicit and explicit costs: WIRP

- **W** – Wages are the monetary payments a firm faces as it pays its workers for their labour. Wages are an explicit short-run variable cost, since the quantity of labour employed by a firm can vary in the short run.
- **I** – Interest is the explicit cost faced by a firm for its use of capital. Interest must be paid on the loans firms take out to acquire capital. Additionally, by investing the revenues it earns in new capital, a firm forgoes the interest payments it could have received by investing its revenues in other assets such as bonds or savings accounts. Interest payments are typically a fixed cost in the short run, since capital is fixed in the short run, but variable in the long run as a firm is able to employ more or less capital in the long run.
- **R** – Rent is the explicit cost of land resources. A business owner who employs his own land resources forgoes the rent he could have earned by leasing his land to another tenant, and businesses that do not own their own land must rent space on which to produce their goods or services. Rent is a fixed cost in the short run, since land is a fixed resource, but variable in the long run as a firm is able to vary the amount of land it uses in the production of its output over time.
- **P** – Profit, or normal profit, is the implicit cost an entrepreneur must cover in order to remain in business. The level of normal profit may vary from entrepreneur to entrepreneur. For instance, a mechanic who leaves an auto garage to start his own oil-changing business may have a level of normal profit that is much lower than the chemist who leaves a lucrative job at a pharmaceutical company. The chemist expects to earn a much greater return beyond her explicit costs than the mechanic whose skills and talents are less scarce and are deemed to be of lower monetary value in the marketplace.

Implicit costs are the opportunity costs faced by a business owner who chooses to use his skills and resources to operate his own enterprise rather than seek employment by someone else. A business's implicit cost is also known as its normal profit.

Explicit costs are the monetary payments a firm makes to the owners of the resources it employs in its production.

To learn more about costs of production, visit www.pearsonhotlinks.com, enter the title or ISBN of this book and select weblink 7.1.

To access Worksheet 7.1 on the intelligence of economics students, please visit www.pearsonbacconline.com and follow the onscreen instructions.

7.2   Production in the short run: law of diminishing marginal returns

Learning outcomes

- Distinguish between the short run and long run in the context of production.
- Define total product, average product and marginal product, and construct diagrams to show their relationship.
- Explain the law of diminishing returns.
- Calculate total, average and marginal product from a set of data and/or diagrams.
- Explain the distinction between the short run and the long run, with reference to fixed costs and variable costs.
- Distinguish between total costs, marginal costs and average costs.
- Draw diagrams illustrating the relationship between marginal costs and average costs, and explain the connection with production in the short run.
- Explain the relationship between the product curves (average product and marginal product) and the cost curves (average variable cost and marginal cost) with reference to the law of diminishing returns.

At its peak in the mid-2000s, Krispy Kreme Doughnuts had stores in 18 countries.

Krispy Kreme started out as a single shop in North Carolina in the 1930s, employing only a few workers and providing doughnuts to hundreds of happy customers.

As the business's popularity grew, it did not begin opening new shops right away. In the short run, Krispy Kreme simply hired more workers and asked its existing employees to work longer hours. Doughnut makers who worked part time were given full-time jobs, and the shop extended its hours so it was open longer each day. Thus, in the short run, Krispy Kreme varied only the quantity of labour it employed in doughnut production, not the quantity of capital or land. In other words, until Krispy Kreme had time to open a second doughnut shop and fill it with new deep fryers and ovens, the company could only respond to the rising demand of its customers by varying the quantity of labour employed on its fixed capital and land.

Krispy Kreme's short-run costs of production included only those that changed in the period of time before the business opened its second doughnut shop, specifically the costs of its raw materials and the labour it had to employ to meet the rising demand for its doughnuts.

A firm's labour cost (the wages it pays its workers) is the primary variable cost a firm faces in the short run. To understand how a firm's variable costs change in the short run, we must understand how the productivity of the short-run variable resource, labour, changes as workers are added to or taken away from a fixed quantity of capital and land.

Productivity is defined as the amount of output attributable to a unit of input. Highly productive resources result in lower costs for firms, while low productivity means firms' costs will be higher. Naturally, a firm wishes to maximize the productivity of its resources in order to minimize its costs. In the case of Krispy Kreme, all new employees had to undergo several days of training to learn how to use the equipment in the kitchen. This meant that when an employee began making doughnuts, he was highly productive and made as many doughnuts as possible during each hour of his labour, thus keeping Krispy Kreme's per-unit costs low and its profit margin high.

The law of diminishing returns

To determine how a firm's costs change as it varies its level of production in the short run, let's examine the effect that a change in the quantity of labour has on a firm's output given that land and capital resources remain fixed in quantity.

Imagine a doughnut shop with one oven and two fryers. These machines are the firm's capital. Its land is the shop itself. In order to increase production of doughnuts in the short run, the firm can hire more workers and use more doughnut ingredients, but it cannot open a new shop or employ more capital. How will the output of doughnuts (the total product) change as more workers are employed, and why? Table 7.1 represents the output of one doughnut shop with three machines as it goes from employing zero workers to eight workers.

TABLE 7.1 SHORT-RUN PRODUCTION RELATIONSHIPS				
Number of workers (Q_L)	Number of machines (Q_K)	Total product (TP)	Marginal product (MP = ΔTP/ΔQ_L)	Average product (AP = TP/Q_L)
0	3	0	–	–
1	3	4	4	4
2	3	9	5	4.5
3	3	15	6	5
4	3	20	5	5
5	3	24	4	4.8
6	3	26	2	4.33
7	3	26	0	3.7
8	3	24	-2	3

Table 7.1 tells us how the doughnut shop's total product (TP, the output of doughnuts per hour) changes as workers are added to a fixed amount of capital. It also shows us the firm's marginal product (MP), which is the change in the total product attributable to the last worker hired, and its average product (AP), which is the output per worker.

$$MP = \frac{\Delta TP}{\Delta Q_L}$$

$$AP = \frac{TP}{Q_L}$$

HL EXERCISES

Using Table 7.1, answer the following questions.

1 What is the firm's total product when Q_L = 0? Why is this the case?

2 a What happens to total product as the firm hires its first, second and third workers?

   b What about when it hires the sixth, seventh and eighth workers?

   c Why does the growth in total product decline when the last three workers are hired compared to the first three workers?

3 What is the relationship between the marginal product of labour and the total product?

4 At what point does the marginal product of labour stop increasing and begin declining? Why does marginal product eventually decline?

How did you get on? Let's examine what happens as the first, second and third workers are added to the one oven and two fryers in the doughnut shop.

- Without any workers, when Q_L is zero, the business won't make any doughnuts because, well, the machines can't operate themselves.
- When one worker is added, total output is four doughnuts per hour.
- The second and third workers cause output to increase to 9 and 15 doughnuts, respectively.
- The change in total product for the second and third workers, which is the marginal product, increased with each worker added. The second and third workers resulted in increasing marginal returns.

Increasing marginal returns in the doughnut shop are explained by understanding that with fewer than three workers, the existing capital was not being used efficiently nor to its full capacity. With three workers, the machines are used efficiently, so from one to three workers, the marginal returns to labour are increasing, meaning that the output attributable to each additional worker is greater than the output attributable to the previous worker hired.

Now let's observe what happens as the fourth, fifth, sixth, seventh and eighth workers are added to the business.

- Beyond three workers, additional workers hired continue to increase total product for a while, but at a decreasing rate. In other words, the marginal product of labour decreases beyond three workers. The doughnut shop begins to experience diminishing marginal returns.
- With only three machines, the fourth, fifth and sixth workers are able to contribute less and less additional output to the doughnut shop's production. The kitchen is literally getting too crowded to allow for continued increases in productivity.
- Beyond six workers, additional labour adds nothing to total output. The eighth worker actually causes the total output of doughnuts to fall, indicating that his presence simply interferes with, rather than contributes to, the production of doughnuts.

Graphically, our doughnut shop's production data is shown in Figure 7.1.

Figure 7.1
Total, average and marginal production relationships in the short run.

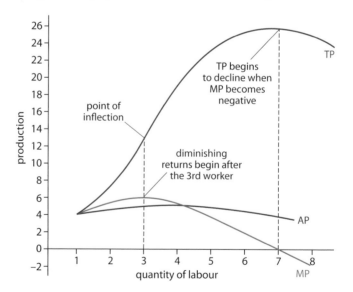

Marginal returns to labour begin to diminish beyond the third worker, becoming negative with the eighth worker. The law of diminishing returns states that as additional units of a variable resource (in this case, labour) are added to fixed resources (land and capital), beyond a certain point the marginal product of the variable resource will decline.

When a firm wishes to expand in the short run, it can hire more workers and ask its existing employees to work longer hours. But if a firm wishes to grow in the long run, it can only do so by adding more capital. The law of diminishing returns explains the shapes of the total, marginal and average product curves in Figure 7.1.

The relationship between marginal and total product

Figure 7.1 shows that the value of MP at any level of employment is given by the slope of the TP curve at that point. As long as the MP is positive, additional workers are adding to TP and output continues to increase. Beyond the seventh worker, MP becomes negative as additional workers lead to a fall in TP. While MP is increasing, between the first and third worker, the doughnut shop experiences increasing marginal returns to labour and the slope of TP becomes steeper. But beyond the third worker, the doughnut shop experiences diminishing marginal returns because the productivity of labour declines as it is added to the fixed capital and the slope of TP changes as it rises less steeply prior to levelling out.

The relationship between marginal and average product

The AP curve shows us the output per worker at each level of employment. There is a clear relationship between marginal product and average product. Whenever MP is greater than AP, AP increases. If MP is less than AP, AP falls. This is shown in Figure 7.2 and Table 7.2.

Look closely at the selection of the shop's production table below to understand the relationship between marginal and average product.

The law of diminishing returns shows that as more and more of a variable resource (typically labour) is added to fixed resources (capital and land), beyond a certain point the productivity of additional units of the variable resource declines. Because the amount of capital is fixed, more workers find it harder to continually add to the firm's output, so they become less productive as they are added in the short run. The law of diminishing returns explains the shapes of a firm's short-run labour productivity curves (and its short-run cost curves, page 158).

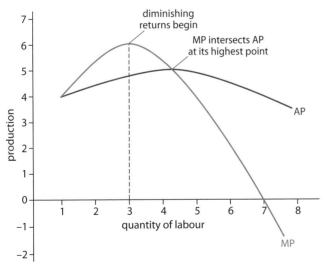

◀ **Figure 7.2**
Marginal and average product in the short run.

TABLE 7.2 MARGINAL AND AVERAGE PRODUCT IN THE SHORT RUN		
Number of workers (Q_L)	Marginal product (MP)	Average product (AP)
1	4	4
2	5	4.5
3	6	5
4	5	5
5	4	4.8

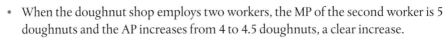

● **Examiner's hint**

One way to understand the relationship between MP and AP is to imagine a non-economic scenario in which a change on the margin affects the average. For instance, you may be at a school that uses percentages to determine grades on tests, quizzes and other assignments. Imagine that up until now your average percentage grade on tests is 80%. If, on the next test you take, your grade were 90%, how would this affect your average? The obvious answer is that your average would increase.

If, on the other hand, you earn 70% on your next test, your average will decrease. The score you earn on your next test is your marginal score. If your score on the margin is higher than your average score, your average will increase; if it is lower than your average score, your average will decrease. This is precisely the relationship that exists between marginal product and average product, and it also holds true for marginal and average cost.

Figure 7.3 ▶

Total, average and marginal product relationships in the short run.

To learn more about the law of diminishing returns, visit www.pearsonhotlinks.com, enter the title or ISBN of this book and select weblink 7.2.

To access Worksheet 7.2 on the law of diminishing returns, please visit www.pearsonbacconline.com and follow the onscreen instructions.

- When the doughnut shop employs two workers, the MP of the second worker is 5 doughnuts and the AP increases from 4 to 4.5 doughnuts, a clear increase.
- The additional output attributable to the third worker is 6 doughnuts and the average output subsequently increases from 4.5 to 5 doughnuts. When an additional worker adds more to output than the average worker, the average must increase.
- When the fourth worker is hired, he adds only 5 additional doughnuts, and since this is the same as the average output with three workers, the average does not change.
- With the fifth worker, however, the marginal product has decreased to 4 doughnuts and the average output therefore begins to decline, to 4.8 doughnuts. The fifth worker hired produces less than the average so the average falls.

Whenever MP is greater than AP, the average will increase. When MP is the same as AP, the average stays the same, and when MP is less than the AP, the average declines. Notice that graphically, the MP curve intersects the AP curve at the latter's highest point. Later in this chapter, you will notice that the same relationship holds true for marginal cost and average cost (page 160).

There are some important points to notice on Figure 7.3.

Figure 7.3a plots TP and Figure 7.3b shows MP and AP. The graphs include some important points to understand about the relationships between these three productivity measures.

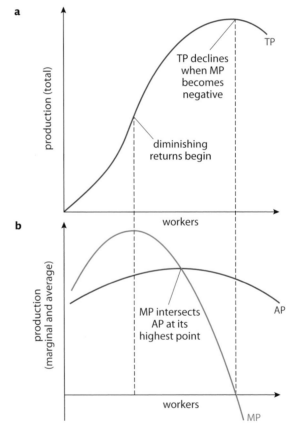

The dotted line on the left indicates the point at which the MP of new workers stops increasing and begins to decline. On the TP curve, this is called the point of inflection, where the slope of the curve changes (prior to levelling out) as MP falls. The dotted line on the right indicates the point at which TP begins to decrease because the MP of labour has become negative. A firm employing workers beyond this point is definitely not a cost-minimizer and should lay off workers until MP becomes positive and TP increases again.

From short-run productivity to long-run costs of production

Learning outcomes
- Calculate total fixed costs, total variable costs, total costs, average fixed costs, average total costs and marginal costs from a set of data and/or drawings.
- Distinguish between increasing returns to scale, decreasing returns to scale and constant returns to scale.
- Outline the relationship between short-run average costs and long-run average costs.
- Explain, using a diagram, the reason for the shape of the long-run average total cost curve.
- Describe factors giving rise to economies of scale, including specialization, efficiency, marketing and indivisibilities.
- Describe factors giving rise to diseconomies of scale, including problems of coordination and communication.

So: a firm's short-run costs of production are determined by the productivity of its short-run variable resources, most importantly labour. When worker productivity rises, the firm's per-unit costs of production fall. More-productive workers mean fewer inputs to produce a certain amount of output or more output with a certain number of workers. Less-productive workers mean firms must employ more inputs to produce a certain amount of output or that a certain number of workers will produce less output; either way the firm's per-unit costs of production rise with falling productivity and fall with rising productivity. A firm's short-run costs of production and labour productivity are therefore inversely related.

In the short-run cost table below (Table 7.3), assume the firm employs labour, land and capital to produce its output, a popular toy called the robotron. In the short run, labour is the only variable resource and therefore the total variable cost represents the wages paid to the firm's workers. The total fixed cost of $100 represents the interest the firm pays for the use of its capital and the rent it pays for the use of the factory space in which it produces robotrons.

In order to increase its output in the short run, the firm must hire additional workers. Assume the wage rate is $5 per worker, so as the firm hires more workers its total variable cost increases. Fixed costs, on the other hand, remain at $100 since the quantity of land and capital does not change in the short run (the fixed-plant period).

TABLE 7.3 SHORT-RUN COSTS OF PRODUCING ROBOTRONS

Total output per hour (Q)	Number of workers (Q_L)	Total fixed cost (TFC)	Total variable cost (TVC)	Total cost (TC = TFC + TVC)	Average fixed cost (AFC = TFC ÷ Q)	Average variable cost (AVC = TVC ÷ Q)	Average total cost (ATC = TC ÷ Q)	Marginal cost (MC = ΔTC ÷ ΔQ)
0	0	100	0	100	–	–	–	–
1	6	100	30		100	30	130	30
2	10	100		150	50		75	
3	13	100	65	165		21.7		
4	17	100	85			21.3	46.3	20
5	23	100		215	20		43	30
6	32	100		260	16.7		43.4	
7	44	100	220	320	14.3	31.4		60
8	62	100	310			38.8		90

Use Table 7.3 to answer the following questions.

5 Complete the table by filling in the empty cells.

6 Why does total variable cost increase as output increases in the short run?

7 Why does total fixed cost remain constant regardless of the level of output?

8 Explain the relationship between total cost, total variable cost and total fixed cost.

9 Which column tells us the per-unit cost of robotrons at each level of output?

10 What is the relationship between the marginal cost and the total cost?

11 How do the Q and Q_L columns demonstrate the law of diminishing returns?

Total costs: fixed and variable

Figure 7.4 shows the graphical representations of the total cost data in Table 7.3.

Figure 7.4

Total costs in the short run.

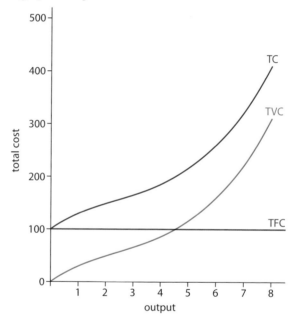

First, let's examine some the relationships between the total fixed cost (TFC), total variable cost (TVC) and total cost (TC) curves.

- When output is zero, the firm's TC equals its TFC. When producing zero output, the firm does not need to employ any workers, so TVC equals zero. However, the firm must pay its interest on capital and rent on land regardless of its level of output, so fixed costs must be covered whether output is zero units, five, eight, or more.
- As the firm begins to produce output, it must hire workers. This causes its TVC to increase. The rate at which TVC increases varies with the changing productivity of labour, reflected by the S shape of the TVC curve.
- TFC remains at $100 in the short run because the firm is not increasing its land and capital inputs, only its labour.
- TC increases at the same rate as TVC and is a parallel line $100 above TVC. At each level of output, the firm's TC equals the sum of its TFC and its TVC:

    TC = TFC + TVC

The shapes of the TC and TVC curves are important. Notice that while TC and TVC increase as output increases, the slopes vary across the range of output. At first, between one and three units of output, the slopes of TC and TVC become flatter and flatter, but beyond three units, the curves become steeper and steeper. This is because as workers are hired, the marginal returns on labour at first increase as existing capital is used more efficiently. Then, beyond a certain point, the marginal returns on labour begin to diminish as more and more labour is added to a fixed amount of capital.

TVC increases at a decreasing rate while marginal returns to labour are increasing, and at an increasing rate while labour experiences diminishing marginal returns. A firm's TVC curve is therefore the mirror image of its total product curve.

As can be seen in Figure 7.5, the shapes of and relationship between a firm's total productivity (TP) and its TVC reflect the law of diminishing marginal returns and the two curves therefore display an inverse relationship. Over the range of increasing marginal returns, TP increases at an increasing rate and TVC increases at a decreasing rate because output rises with each additional unit of input. Beyond the dotted line, TP increases at a decreasing rate and TVC at an increasing rate, since each additional worker adds less and less to the firm's output.

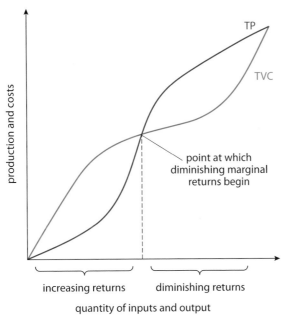

Figure 7.5
Total product and total variable cost.

Figure 7.6
Average variable, average fixed, average total and marginal costs in the short run.

Per-unit costs: average and marginal costs

Figure 7.6 shows the average variable cost (AVC), average fixed cost (AFC), average total cost (ATC) and marginal costs (MC) for the robotron producer.

Let's consider some important observations about the average and marginal cost curves.

- AFC decreases as output increases. Since TFC is constant at $100, AFC continually decreases at higher levels of output. This fall in AFC at higher level of output is known as 'spreading the overhead'.
- MC decreases and then increases as output increases. From one to three units, MC falls because of increasing marginal returns to labour. Beyond three units, MC

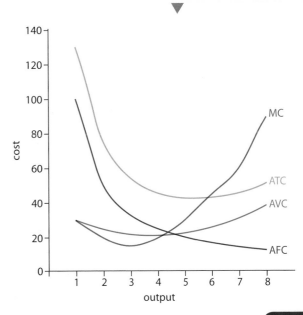

increases due to the law of diminishing returns and the declining productivity of labour as it is added to a fixed amount of land and capital. The increase in MC corresponds with the increase in slope of total cost.

- ATC lies above AVC. Just as a firm's TC is equal to the sum of its variable and fixed costs, the firm's ATC is equal to the sum of its AVC and AFC. At any level of output, the distance between the ATC curve and the AVC curve equals the firm's AFC.
- MC intersects ATC and AVC at their lowest points. The same relationship that held for marginal product (MP) and average product (AP) holds for MC and AC. If the last unit produced costs the firm less than the average per-unit cost then the average cost falls. If the last unit produced costs more than the average cost, then the average rises.

AVC, AFC, ATC and MC can be found using the following formulas.

$$AVC = \frac{TVC}{Q}$$

$$AFC = \frac{TFC}{Q}$$

$$ATC = AFC + AVC$$

$$MC = \frac{\Delta TC}{\Delta Q}$$

Figure 7.7 shows a firm's short-run per-unit costs of production.

Figure 7.7
Short run costs of production relationships.

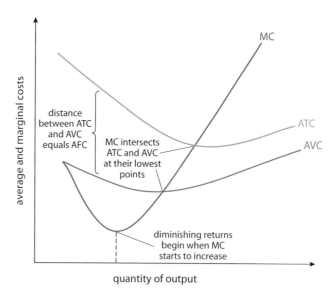

You will notice that AFC is not shown in Figure 7.7. It is not necessary to show AFC separately because its presence is inferred from the distance between ATC and AVC at any level of output. Several important characteristics of a firm's short-run cost curves are noted on the graph.

The shapes and relationships between the three curves above are very important. A firm that alters its output in the short run (fixed-plant period) faces costs similar to those shown in Figure 7.7. In deciding at which level it should produce in order to maximize its profits in the short run, a firm must take its marginal and average costs into consideration, because its total profits equal its total revenues minus its total costs (page 149). Another way to state this is in terms of per-unit profits:

average profit (profit per unit of output) = average revenue – average total cost

Later, you will learn the rule to produce at the profit maximizing level of output.

Costs of production in the long run

By the late 1930s, the first Krispy Kreme doughnut shop in North Carolina had reached its full capacity of production and the company had to make a decision: stay small and make our customers at our one shop as happy as possible, or expand and meet the demands of new customers all over the US? Of course, opening a second or third doughnut shop would not immediately allow Krispy Kreme to serve customers all over the country, but beginning in the late 1930s, the firm did begin to expand its operations around the American South, and now, nearly 80 years later, the firm operates in thousands of locations in over a dozen countries.

Economies of scale and diseconomies of scale

As Krispy Kreme's operations expanded from the short run to the long run, it was able to open more locations, thus adding more capital, land and labour to its production of delicious, glazed, doughy rings. The long run in economics, it should be remembered, is defined as the variable-plant period. In the long run, a firm may vary all of its factors of production. The law of diminishing marginal returns no longer applies in the long run since the quantity of capital workers have at their disposal is no longer fixed. To understand how a firm's costs change in the long run, we must examine with new eyes the ATC curve (Figure 7.8).

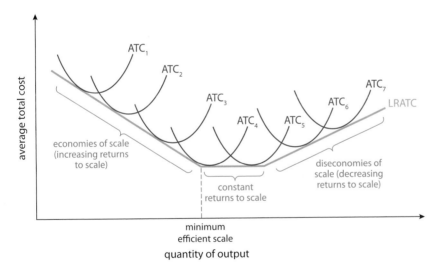

To access Worksheet 7.3 on costs of production, please visit www.pearsonbacconline.com and follow the onscreen instructions.

To access Worksheet 7.4 on economies of scale, please visit www.pearsonbacconline.com and follow the onscreen instructions.

Figure 7.8
Long-run average total cost (LRATC) – consisting of several short-run periods over which a firm can open or shut plants.

To understand a firm's long-run costs of production, it helps to imagine the long run as a period of time over which a firm can open several new plants. (The term 'plant' may refer to factories, offices, shops, etc. depending on the type of firm in question.) The long-run variable-plant period is, therefore, made up of several short-run, fixed-plant periods.

Figure 7.8 shows our firm producing robotrons expanding to a level of output that is far beyond what it could have achieved with only one factory. ATC_1 shows the firm's average total costs if it operates only one factory. As you can see, beyond a certain level of output, diminishing returns would cause the single factory's average costs to rise rapidly, making it worthwhile for the firm to open a second factory, represented by ATC_2, in order to keep its costs low. Notice, however, that when it opens the second factory, the entire ATC_2 curve is at a lower average cost of production than when the firm operated only one plant. The same reduction in average costs occurs when the firm opens its third (ATC_3) and fourth (ATC_4) robotron factories.

Economies of scale help us understand why certain products produced and sold by global corporations are cheap and ubiquitous in our world. Nike trainers are inexpensive because of Nike's economies of scale. iPhones are relatively inexpensive because Apple has achieved economies of scale. Even airplanes are built at relatively low average cost because Boeing and Airbus achieve economies of scale.

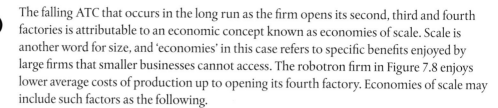

There are examples throughout history of empires experiencing diseconomies of scale: the Romans and the Mongols are just two. 'The sun never sets on the British Empire' was a popular saying about the vastness of the colonies under British control. How might getting so big create challenges that may lead to the collapse of extremely large organizations such as General Motors or the Mongol Empire?

The falling ATC that occurs in the long run as the firm opens its second, third and fourth factories is attributable to an economic concept known as economies of scale. Scale is another word for size, and 'economies' in this case refers to specific benefits enjoyed by large firms that smaller businesses cannot access. The robotron firm in Figure 7.8 enjoys lower average costs of production up to opening its fourth factory. Economies of scale may include such factors as the following.

- Better prices for raw materials such as plastic and rubber parts for the robotrons due to larger bulk orders made by the firm as it grows.
- Lower costs due to higher quality and more technologically advanced machinery operating in larger factories.
- Lower average shipping and transportation costs as the firm produces and ships larger quantities of toys to the market when operating four factories than when operating only one.
- More favourable interest rates from banks for new capital as the firm becomes larger and therefore more credit-worthy.
- More bargaining power with labour unions for lower wages as the firm employs larger numbers of factory workers.
- Improved manufacturing techniques and more highly specialized labour, capital and managerial expertise.

Increasing returns to scale means that an increase in inputs leads to a larger proportional increase in output. For example, if a firm doubles the number of workers and capital and its output triples, the firm is experiencing increasing returns to scale.

The basic idea is behind the concept of economies of scale is that the larger a firm becomes, the cheaper it is to produce one unit of output because of the cost advantages that a firm experiences as it expands. Throughout the range of long-run ATC over which the firm enjoys economies of scale, it experiences increasing returns to scale. This means that each additional unit of input produces increasing amounts of output.

At a certain point, further reductions in average cost become difficult or impossible, and a firm eventually achieves minimum efficient scale (MES). MES is the size at which a firm achieves its lowest possible per-unit cost of production. Beyond this size, no further cost advantages accrue as the firm continues to expand.

Constant returns to scale occur when an increase in inputs leads to a proportionally identical increase in output. For instance, if a firm adds 20% more capital, land and labour to its production and output increases by 20%, the firm is experiencing constant returns to scale. Graphically, this is the range of output over which ATC does not change with the level of output.

Over the range of output during which ATC remains constant, the firm experiences constant returns to scale – that is, a particular increase in inputs leads to a proportionally identical increase in output.

It is possible for a firm to become 'too big for its own good'. This may occur if a very large firm begins experiencing inefficiencies that cause its average costs to rise as the firm grows. This may seem counter-intuitive, as conventional wisdom would suggest that the larger a firm becomes, the better it gets at producing its output and the lower its ATC should be. However, several examples exist in the real world of firms that have experienced diseconomies of scale that have led to rising average costs and decreased competitiveness as the firms have grown larger and larger.

Long before it sought a bailout from the US government in 2008, America's largest automobile manufacturer, General Motors, struggled with the challenges related to its massive size, which actually made the firm less competitive in the auto market. Diseconomies of scale may include the following.

Decreasing returns to scale means that an increase in the quantity of inputs leads to a proportionally smaller increase in the quantity of output. A firm of this size may be 'too big for its own good'.

- Communication inefficiencies – a firm with multiple levels of management located around the world may experience increasing costs associated with communication across divisions and plant facilities. As a result, many processes may be unnecessarily duplicated throughout the company, adding to the firm's costs of production but not to its revenues.
- Office politics – managers in a mega-corporation may focus more on achieving their personal goals than on promoting the best interest of the firm itself. To this end, managers

may promote incompetent or inefficient workers in order to make themselves look better and to increase their own chances of earning a promotion to the higher ranks.

- Increased regulation – the larger a firm gets, the more likely it is to be regulated by government agencies. A firm that grows to become a dominant market force may face anti-monopoly regulations that add to the costs of production, or may be subject to anti-competitive lawsuits that lead to significant legal costs. An example here is Microsoft, which has faced several government lawsuits relating to its alleged anti-competitive behaviour.

A firm facing diseconomies of scale may be forced to deal with its rising costs by breaking up into multiple smaller firms to compete at a smaller scale against one another. Over the years, General Motors has been forced to sell or shut down several of its divisions to keep its costs down and remain competitive in the auto industry: in the early 1990s, the company shut down 21 plants and, in 2004, it folded one of its major brands, Oldsmobile.

You have now learned how a firm's costs of production are influenced by the law of diminishing marginal returns (which determines a firm's short-run costs of production) and by economies and diseconomies of scale (which explain the shape of the long-run ATC curve). However, we are not yet in a position to understand how firms can achieve their economic objective of profit maximization. A firm's total profit is a function of both its total cost and its total revenue. Thus, we must now examine what determines a firm's revenues.

7.4 Revenues: total, average and marginal revenue

Learning outcomes

- Distinguish between total revenue, average revenue and marginal revenue.
- Illustrate, using diagrams, the relationship between total revenue, average revenue and marginal revenue.
- Calculate total revenue, average revenue and marginal revenue from a set of data and/or diagrams.

Revenue is the income a firm receives from the sale of its output. Whether producing petroleum, doughnuts or children's toys, a firm will always attempt to maximize the difference between its total revenues and its total costs in order to earn the greatest amount of profit possible. Most firms seek to maximize profit, not revenue. To understand how they do this, we must look at how a firm's revenues are earned and how they change as the quantity of output changes.

Let's examine the revenue tables for two different types of firm: a perfectly competitive firm and an imperfectly competitive firm.

Revenues for a perfectly competitive firm

You will recall from Chapter 2 (page 23) that a perfectly competitive firm is one that competes in a market with a very large number of firms each producing an identical product, and each firm's output making up a tiny fraction of the total market supply. This makes it impossible for a single firm to affect the market price by increasing or decreasing

To learn more about economies of scale, visit www.pearsonhotlinks.com, enter the title or ISBN of this book and select weblink 7.3.

Economies of scale are the cost-reducing advantages that allow a firm to produce at ATC as it expands its production in the long run, adding new labour, land and capital.

Diseconomies of scale are the factors that cause a firm to experience rising ATC as it grows in size. If a firm adds a factory and ATC rises across all its factories, it is experiencing diseconomies of scale.

Minimum efficient scale (MES) is the size a firm must achieve in order to produce its output at the lowest possible per-unit (or average) total cost. Before this level of output, the firm experiences increasing returns to scale; beyond, returns to scale are constant or decreasing.

its output unilaterally. Firms in perfectly competitive markets are known as price-takers. The price at which such a firm sells its output remains unchanged regardless of the firm's output.

Table 7.4 shows the revenues for a perfectly competitive firm – the robotron manufacturer – assuming the market price of robotrons is $50.

	TABLE 7.4 REVENUES FOR A PERFECT COMPETITOR	
Quantity of output (Q)	**Price (P) = average revenue (AR) = marginal revenue (MR) / $**	**Total revenue (TR) / $**
1	50	50
2	50	100
3	50	150
4	50	200
5	50	250
6	50	300
7	50	350
8	50	400

Notice that the price of $50 also equals the firm's average revenue (AR) and its marginal revenue (MR). The definitions of AR and MR explain why this is the case. AR is the revenue per unit of output, which is the price at which each unit is sold. MR is the amount by which total revenue (TR) changes with each additional unit of output sold, which again is the price at which each unit is sold. AR is equal to the price (P), which in the case of a price-taking perfect competitor, is equal to MR, since the firm will always sell additional units of output for the market price.

$$TR = P \times Q$$

$$AR = \frac{TR}{Q}$$

$$MR = \frac{\Delta TR}{\Delta Q}$$

$$MR = AR = P$$

Figure 7.9
Total, average and marginal revenue for a perfectly competitive firm.

TR is equal to the price times the quantity of output sold. Since the price is constant at all levels of output, the firm's TR increases at a constant rate as it produces and sells greater quantities of output. Therefore, MR equals P and AR.

Graphically, the TR curve is an upward-sloping line with a constant slope equal to the price (Figure 7.9). MR and AR are the horizontal line equal to the price of the firm's output, which itself is determined in the market for robotrons, in which this firm is only one of hundreds of identical competitors.

Determining the MR and AR for a perfectly competitive firm is easy once you know the market price of the output. Market price, of course, is determined not by each individual firm, but in the market itself. Figure 7.10 represents the market for robotrons, which includes 1000 identical firms, and the revenue data for an individual robotron producer.

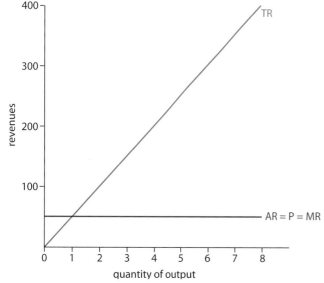

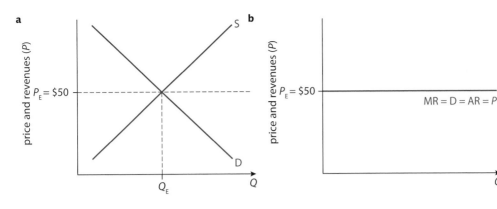

a

price and revenues (P)

P_E = $50

S

D

Q_E

Q

b

price and revenues (P)

P_E = $50

MR = D = AR = P

Q

◀ **Figure 7.10**
a A perfectly competitive
market; **b** a single firm in the
market, for which demand
is determined by the market
equilibrium price.

The price of robotrons, P_E, is determined by the market supply and the market demand for the toy. Supply in the market represents the total output of 1000 robotron producers and how those firms respond to a change in the price. Demand represents responsiveness of robotron consumers to changes in the price. The intersection of market demand and market supply determines the equilibrium price of robotrons.

In Figure 7.10b, the price of $50, established by the market, is used to derive an individual robotron producer's MR and AR curve and to represent the demand for an individual firm's output. Notice that when viewed as a demand curve, the MR = AR = P line is perfectly elastic at the market price of $50.

A price taker faces perfectly elastic demand from its consumers for a very simple reason: it is one of hundreds of firms selling an identical product, all charging the same price. If a single firm should lower its price even by a few cents the quantity demanded by the market would increase dramatically. In fact, every rational consumer aware of this price decrease would wish to buy robotrons from the one firm charging a price lower than market equilibrium. On the other hand, if one firm raises its price at all, rational consumers will demand zero output from that firm since there are hundreds of others selling the same product at the lower equilibrium price.

The responsiveness of consumers to changes in the price of an individual firm in a perfectly competitive market is perfectly elastic. Demand as seen by the perfectly competitive firm is, therefore, horizontal at the equilibrium price established by the market.

● **Examiner's hint**

A trick to remember what
to label the demand curve
in a perfectly competitive
firm's diagram is to give
the horizontal line a name.
Demand is actually known as
Mr Darp. Mr Darp is a useful
way to remember how to
label demand for a perfectly
competitive firm, because the
name is made up of the four
identities of this curve:
MR = D = AR = P.

Revenues for an imperfectly competitive firm

In Chapter 2 (page 23), you met the four market structures:

- perfect competition
- monopolistic competition
- oligopoly
- monopoly.

The latter three of these are considered imperfectly competitive, and firms within such markets share certain important characteristics that affect their revenues.

- There are fewer firms in imperfectly competitive markets than in perfectly competitive markets, which means that a change in the output of an individual firm will have at least some effect on the market price of its output.
- Firms in imperfectly competitive markets differentiate their products from one another. This adds to their price-making power. A firm with a unique product can raise its price without fear of losing all its customers, as would happen if a perfect competitor raised its price.

- Imperfect competitors are price-makers, which means that in order to sell additional units of output, such a firm must lower the price it charges consumers.

An imperfectly competitive firm, regardless of whether it's in a monopolistically competitive market or is a pure monopoly, faces a downward-sloping demand curve, as opposed to the perfectly elastic demand curve faced by perfect competitors. Table 7.5 shows the demand schedule, and the TR, AR and MR of a purely monopolistic robotron producer.

TABLE 7.5 REVENUES FOR AN IMPERFECT COMPETITOR			
Quantity of output (Q)	**Price (P) = average revenue (AR)**	**Total revenue (TR)**	**Marginal revenue (MR)**
0	450	0	–
1	400	400	400
2	350	700	300
3	300	900	200
4	250	1000	100
5	200	1000	0
6	150	900	−100
7	100	700	−200
8	50	400	−300

Unlike the purely competitive robotron producer, the monopolist must lower the price it charges for its output in order to sell greater quantities. There are no longer hundreds of identical firms for customers to choose from, so consumers are less responsive to higher prices, thus the quantity demanded does not immediately fall to zero when the firm raises its price, nor does every consumer in the market wish to buy from this firm when its price decreases. There is an inverse relationship between the price the imperfect competitor charges and the quantity demanded of its output.

Additionally, unlike the perfect competitor, the monopolist's MR is no longer equal to its price and AR. You will recall that MR measures the change in the firm's TR when it increases its output by one unit. Since a perfect competitor can sell all of its output for the market price, the MR equals the price at all levels of output. An imperfect competitor, however, must lower the price of all of its output to increase the quantity it sells to consumers. When it does so, it must accept a lower price for the additional unit it sells, and for *all* of its output (assuming the firm does not price discriminate, which is discussed in Chapter 9).

Table 7.6 shows what happens to TR, AR and MR when this firm increases its output from three to four robotrons.

TABLE 7.6 AS PRICE FALLS, MR FALLS MORE QUICKLY FOR AN IMPERFECT COMPETITOR			
Q	**P = AR**	**TR**	**MR**
3	300	900	200
4	250	1000	100

The marginal revenue of the fourth unit ($100) is less than the price it sold the fourth unit for ($250). Since the firm is a single-price seller, meaning all customers will pay the same price as all others, the firm must sacrifice some of the revenue it was earning by selling three units at a price of $300 in order to sell four units at the price of $250. The marginal revenue is not, therefore simply the price of the fourth unit, since in order to sell the additional unit, the firm had to accept $50 less for the three units it could have sold at a price of $300. While the AR at four units is $250, the MR must account for the lost revenue ($3 \times \$50$) the firm experiences when it lowers its price to $250 to sell the fourth unit. Therefore, MR is $250 (the price at which four units are sold) minus $150 (the revenue sacrificed when lowering the price to sell one more unit), equalling $100.

All this is a complicated way of saying that a single-price monopolistically competitive, oligopolistic or monopolistic firm must lower the price of all of its output in order to sell an additional unit, hence its MR declines faster than its AR and price. Only for the first unit of output will price, AR and MR be the same (Table 7.5).

Graphically, the TR, AR and MR curves for the robotron producer discussed above will look like Figure 7.11.

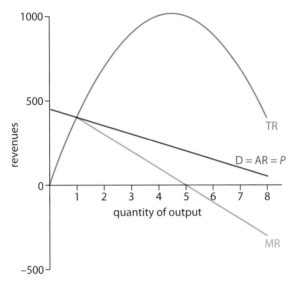

Figure 7.11
Total, average and marginal revenue for an imperfect competitor.

TR is maximized when MR = 0

The relationship between TR and MR reflects the same relationship described between TP and MP and costs (page 154). MR is given by the slope of TR, since marginal revenue measures the rate of change in total revenue.

As long as MR is positive, TR will increase. Since MR decreases as output increases, the slope of the TR curve levels out until MR equals zero, at which point the firm's TR is maximized. When MR falls below zero, the firm's TR begins to decrease. If the robotron producer above were producing beyond five units, it would certainly do better by decreasing its output, which would increase its TR while lowering its total costs, thus increasing the firm's profits.

Let's take a closer look at the relationship between marginal revenue and the D = AR = P line. Figure 7.12 shows demand, AR and MR for an imperfect competitor.

The blue curve in Figure 7.12 represents this firm's AR and price, and also demand as seen by the firm. The imperfect competitor is a differentiating price-maker facing a downward-sloping demand curve. The AR = P line is also the firm's demand curve. We no longer have a single MR = D = AR = P

Figure 7.12
Demand, average revenue and marginal revenue for an imperfect competitor.

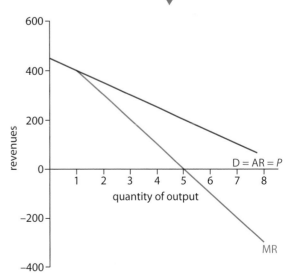

line, because the MR curve lies below the D = AR = P line at every level of output beyond one unit. The slope of a single-price imperfectly competitive firm's MR curve will be twice that of its demand curve, since MR falls at a greater rate than price because the firm must lower all of its prices in order to sell more output.

HL EXERCISES

Use Figure 7.12 to answer the following questions.

12 Identify the revenue-maximizing level of output for the monopolistic firm represented.

13 Explain why the firm's marginal revenue curve is equal to the price at an output of one unit, but is less than price at every quantity beyond one.

14 Why would the firm never wish to produce a level of output beyond five units?

The total revenue test revisited

You may recall from Chapter 4 (page 81) that one way to determine whether demand is elastic or inelastic is to determine how TR changes following a change in price. The total revenue test tells us that if a fall in price leads to an increase in TR, demand is elastic, but that if TR falls following a price decrease, demand is inelastic. Figure 7.13 applies the total revenue test for elasticity to an imperfectly competitive firm's demand, MR and TR curves.

Figure 7.13

The relationship between demand, MR and TR for an imperfect competitor.

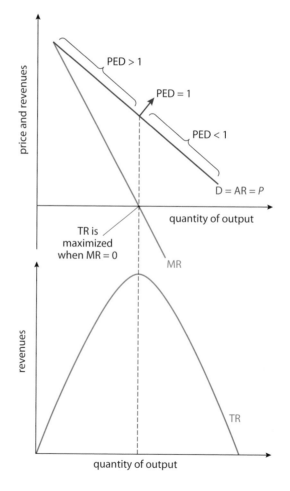

An imperfect competitor will never wish to produce at a point beyond the unit elastic point (PED = 1) on its demand curve, and for a very good reason. As the firm increases its output beyond this point, its total costs continue to rise, but as you can see above, its total revenue decreases. Recall that profit equals total revenue minus total cost. An increase in TC accompanied by a fall in TR will definitely lead to a decline in a firm's profits, thus we know that a profit-maximizing firm will never produce in the inelastic range of its demand curve.

To learn more about cost minimization, visit www.pearsonhotlinks.com, enter the title or ISBN of this book and select weblink 7.4.

7.5 The short-run profit-maximization rule

Learning outcomes
- Describe economic profit as the case where total revenue exceeds economic cost.
- Describe normal profit as the amount of revenue needed to cover the costs of employing self-owned resources (implicit costs, including entrepreneurship) or the amount of revenue needed to just keep the firm in business.
- Explain that economic profit is profit over and above normal profit, and that the firm earns normal profit when economic profit is zero.
- Explain why a firm will continue to operate even when it earns zero economic profit.
- Explain the meaning of loss as negative economic profit arising when total revenue is less than total cost.
- Calculate different profit levels from a set of data and/or diagrams.
- Explain the goal of profit maximization where the difference between total revenue and total cost is maximized or where marginal revenue equals marginal cost.

Why did BP begin drilling for oil in the Gulf of Mexico? Why did Krispy Kreme start making doughnuts in North Carolina? And why did our imaginary robotron companies start making children's toys? One goal of any entrepreneur who embarks on a new business venture is undoubtedly to earn a profit beyond his or her costs, both explicit and implicit.

We have identified these costs, including wages for labour, interest for capital, rent for land and what we defined as normal profit for the entrepreneur. Normal profit is a cost to firms since an entrepreneur who does not earn this base level of profit will shut the business down and seek to employ his or her self-owned resources in a market in which the possibility for greater profits exist.

Economic profits occur when a firm earns revenues in excess of all of its costs, both explicit and implicit, including a normal profit for the entrepreneur. Economic profits are, therefore, also known as supernormal or abnormal profits, since they are above and beyond the normal profit required to keep the firm in operation.

Any business manager must decide in the production process just how much output to produce in order to maximize the firm's profits, or in a less desirable scenario, minimize its losses. The profit-maximization rule of output helps firms decide just what this golden level of output is.

An economic profit is earned when a firm's total revenues exceed all its explicit and implicit costs of production, including a normal profit. Economic profits are greater than normal profits, and are, therefore, sometimes referred to as abnormal profits or supernormal profits.

The total revenue/total cost approach

We know that total profits are found by subtracting TC from TR, so one way a producer can maximize profits is by producing at the quantity where the difference between TR and TC is the greatest. When we combine the revenue and cost data for our perfectly competitive robotron producer, we can determine at what level of output the profits are maximized (Table 7.7, overleaf).

TABLE 7.7 TOTAL REVENUES AND COSTS FOR A PERFECT COMPETITOR

Total output (Q)	Price (perfect competitor) (P)	Total revenue (TR)	Total cost (TC)	Total profit = TR – TC
0	50	0	100	–100
1	50	50	130	–80
2	50	100	150	–50
3	50	150	165	–15
4	50	200	185	15
5	50	250	215	35
6	50	300	260	40
7	50	350	320	30
8	50	400	410	10

At six units of output, the difference between the firm's TR and TC is maximized. Graphically, this is the quantity at which the distance between the TR and TC curve is maximized (Figure 7.14).

Figure 7.14

Total revenue and total cost approach to profit maximization for a perfectly competitive firm.

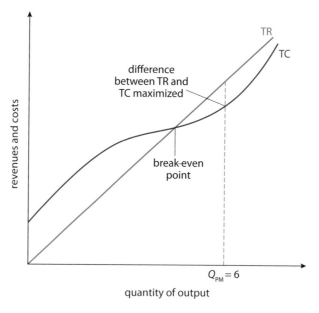

Figure 7.14 shows the TR and TC curves of a perfectly competitive firm in order to determine the quantity of output at which the difference between TR and TC is maximized and its economic profits are maximized, in this case at six units of output. Of course, the firm wants to produce at a quantity at which TR is greater than TC so that its economic profits are positive. At the break-even point, the firm is covering all its economic costs and earning a normal profit, but it is not earning any economic profits. At any point below the break-even point, the firm is earning economic losses since its total costs exceed its total revenues.

An imperfectly competitive firm trying to maximize profits should choose a level of output following the same approach as the perfect competitor, producing where the difference between the TR and TC curves is maximized. Table 7.8 combines the revenue and cost data for our imperfect competitor robotron producer.

TABLE 7.8 TOTAL REVENUE AND TOTAL COST FOR AN IMPERFECT COMPETITOR				
Total output (Q)	Price (imperfect competitor) (P)	Total revenue (TR)	Total cost (TC)	Total profit = TR – TC
0	450	0	100	–100
1	400	400	130	270
2	350	700	150	550
3	300	900	165	735
4	250	1000	185	815
5	200	1000	215	785
6	150	900	260	640
7	100	700	320	380
8	50	400	410	–10

Figure 7.15 shows a price-making, imperfectly competitive firm's TR and TC curves and the level of output at which the distance between the two is maximized.

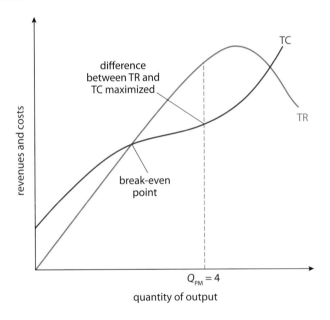

Figure 7.15
Total revenue and total cost approach to profit maximization for an imperfect competitor.

While the TR/TC approach can be used to determine the level of output at which firms should produce to maximize their economic profits, a more common approach requires firms to examine their MR and MC.

The marginal revenue/marginal cost approach

Firms, like individuals, think on the margin. In economics, marginal thinking is a key characteristic of self-interested, utility-maximizing individuals and firms. Consumers think on the margin when they decide whether the marginal benefit of a decision or a purchase is greater than or less than the marginal cost. For instance, if the benefit of one more ride on a roller coaster at an amusement park outweighs the few dollars it costs, then you take that additional ride.

Likewise, a firm weighs the benefits and costs of additional units of output when deciding at what level of output it should stop producing more units. For a firm, however, it is not marginal utility that is weighed against marginal cost, it's marginal revenue. If

The profit-maximization rule of production states that to maximize its total profits, a firm in any market structure should produce as close as possible to the point at which its marginal revenue equals its marginal cost of production, where MR = MC.

the additional revenue a firm earns by producing one more unit of output exceeds the marginal cost of production, then it is always in the profit-maximizing firm's interest to produce additional units. However, if one more unit of output costs more than the revenue it brings in, then it should not be produced.

At what level should a firm target its production in order to maximize economic profits? It should follow the marginal revenue/marginal cost rule of profit maximization, which states that in order to maximize its total economic profit, a firm should produce up to the level of output at which its marginal revenue equals its marginal cost.

Table 7.9 shows marginal cost and marginal revenue data for our perfectly competitive robotron producer.

TABLE 7.9 MARGINAL COST AND MARGINAL REVENUE FOR A PERFECT COMPETITOR

Total output (Q)	Price (perfect competitor) (P)	Total cost (TC)	Marginal cost (MC)	Total revenue (TR)	Marginal revenue (MR)
0	50	100	–	0	–
1	50	130	30	50	50
2	50	150	20	100	50
3	50	165	15	150	50
4	50	185	20	200	50
5	50	215	30	250	50
6	50	260	45	300	50
7	50	320	60	350	50
8	50	410	90	400	50

HL EXERCISES

Use Table 7.9 to answer the following questions.

15 Identify the following from the data in the table:

a the profit-maximizing level of output and price

b the level of economic profit earned when producing at this level of output

c the level of output below which this firm would earn economic losses

d the level of output beyond which the firm would earn economic losses.

16 Why does the price seen by the perfect competitor remain constant as the firm's output increases?

17 Why does the firm's marginal revenue equal its price at every level of output?

At six units of output, the marginal cost of $45 is just below the marginal revenue of $50. To maximize its profits, the firm should produce up to, but no more than, 6 robotrons. To see why six units maximizes profits, examine what happens if the firm produces less than or more than this number.

- At five units of output, the last unit produced cost the firm only $30 and earned the firm $50 of revenue. The profit on the last unit was $20.
- The sixth unit of output cost the firm $45 and earned the firm $50 of revenue. The profit on the sixth unit was only $5, less than on the fifth unit, but still positive, adding to the firm's total profits.
- The seventh robotron costs the firm $60 and only brings $50 of revenue. The firm would lose $10 on the seventh unit of output.

Clearly, at every level of output up to and including the sixth unit, this firm can earn profits on each unit produced and sold. The goal of firms is to maximize total profits, so even if the marginal cost of the sixth unit were $49.99, the firm would still wish to produce it even though the profit is only $0.01. Profits are profits, and as long as there is any profit at all to be earned, firms should produce additional output. But as soon as an additional unit costs the firm more than it can be sold for, the firm should stop producing more output and maintain its profit-maximizing level at which MR =MC.

The seventh robotron imposes a loss on this firm, so it should not be produced. Profit maximization on the margin requires a firm to produce as close as possible to the point at which it is breaking even on the margin (i.e. on the last unit of output it produces, it earns zero economic profit). At this point, the firm's total profit is maximized.

An imperfect competitor can follow the same short-run profit-maximization rule as a perfect competitor. Table 7.10 shows the costs and revenues for an imperfect competitor.

TABLE 7.10 MARGINAL COST AND MARGINAL REVENUE FOR AN IMPERFECT COMPETITOR					
Total output (Q)	Price (imperfect competitor) (P)	Total cost (TC)	Marginal cost (MC)	Total revenue (TR)	Marginal revenue (MR)
0	450	100	–	0	–
1	400	130	30	400	400
2	350	150	20	700	300
3	300	165	15	900	200
4	250	185	20	1000	100
5	200	215	30	1000	0
6	150	260	45	900	–100
7	100	320	60	700	–200
8	50	410	90	400	–300

HL EXERCISES

18 Use Table 7.10 to answer the following questions.
   Identify the following from the data in the table:
   a the profit-maximizing level of output and price
   b the level of economic profit earned by the firm at this quantity
   c the revenue-maximizing level of output and price
   d the level of output beyond which this firm would earn economic losses.

19 How does this firm's profit-maximizing level of output and price differ from those of the perfectly competitive firm with the same costs of production?

20 Why does the imperfect competitor's price decrease as its output increases?

21 Why does MR fall faster than price?

For the imperfectly competitive firm whose costs and revenues are shown in Table 7.10, there is no single level of output at which MR = MC. However, following the same rationale as the perfect competitor shown in Table 7.9, this firm will produce up to, but not beyond, the level at which the last unit produced cost as much as to produce as it added to the firm's revenue.

- The third unit cost the firm $15 to produce and added $200 to the firm's revenue. Clearly it was a good idea to produce the third unit.
- The fourth unit cost the firm only $20 yet added $100 of revenue. The firm earned a profit of $80 on the fourth unit.

- The fifth robotron costs this firm $30 to produce yet adds nothing to its revenues. The firm in fact loses $30 in the production and sale of the fifth unit.

Following the profit-maximization rule, this firm should produce only four units of output. Any quantity less than that and the firm is missing out on potential profits, anything beyond that and the firm is incurring unwanted economic losses.

Graphically, the MR = MC rule for profit maximization can be shown by plotting a firm's MC and MR curves on the same axes. MC and MR curves for the perfectly competitive firm in Table 7.9 are shown in Figure 7.16.

Figure 7.16
Profit-maximization rule (perfectly competitive firm): produce at the quantity at which marginal revenue equals marginal cost.

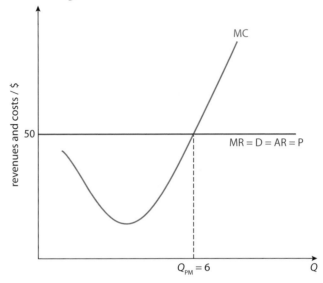

This profit-maximizing firm will produce up to, but not beyond six units of output. Anything beyond six units and the additional cost to the firm exceeds the additional revenue, incurring economic losses. Any quantity below six units and the firm is missing out on potential additional profits.

Figure 7.17 shows an imperfectly competitive firm, evidenced by the downward-sloping demand curve showing that this firm has price-making power. The MR curve lies below the demand, AR and price line. The firm will produce four units, the level of output at which the next unit produced will cost more than it adds to the firm's revenue.

Figure 7.17
Profit-maximization rule (imperfectly competitive firm): produce at the quantity at which marginal revenue equals marginal cost.

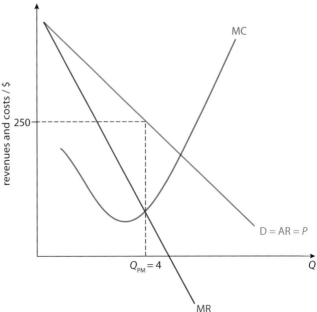

Notice that the equilibrium price in the perfectly competitive market is less than that in the single-price imperfectly competitive market. This and other characteristics of the different market structures are explained in more depth in the next few chapters. We will add average cost curves to our graphical analyses to illustrate areas of economic profit and loss and to understand how the existence of profits and losses affects different markets in the short run and the long run.

This chapter has introduced the theory of the firm and identified the various costs, both implicit and explicit, faced by firms in the short run and in the long run. Two important economic principles were introduced which explain the shapes of firms' short- and long-run cost curves, the law of diminishing returns and economies/diseconomies of scale.

You now know why BP made the decision to save $10 million in the construction of its *Deepwater Horizon* well in the Gulf of Mexico, and you also learned why Krispy Kreme chose to begin its long period of expansion from its one doughnut shop in North Carolina way back in the 1930s to its thousands of outlets around the world today. You learned why General Motors, once the largest auto manufacturer in the world, was forced to downsize in the 1990s to combat diseconomies of scale and remain competitive. Additionally, you have learned the difference between normal profit and economic profit and the two approaches firms in all market structures may take to maximize their economic profits.

In the coming chapters, you will explore in more depth the competitive behaviours and profit-maximizing decisions of firms in markets from the highly efficient, yet mostly theoretical, perfectly competitive markets to the allegedly evil empires of near monopolistic firms.

To learn more about profit maximization, visit www.pearsonhotlinks.com, enter the title or ISBN of this book and select weblink 7.5.

Evaluate the claim that the ultimate goal of all firms should be to maximize their profits. What are the moral or ethical outcomes that may result from firms pursuing maximum profits over all other possible ends?

To access Quiz 7, an interactive, multiple-choice quiz on this chapter, please visit www.pearsonbacconline.com and follow the onscreen instructions.

PRACTICE QUESTIONS

1   **a**   Explain the relationship in the short run between the marginal costs of a firm and its average total costs.   (10 marks) [AO2]

    b   Define the law of diminishing returns and assess the likelihood that it will be experienced by a firm producing a product in a consumer good market.   (15 marks) [AO3]
    © International Baccalaureate Organization 2005 (part **a** only)

2   **a**   What are the distinctions between decreasing returns to scale and diminishing marginal returns?   (10 marks) [AO2]

    b   Evaluate the options available to a firm experiencing decreasing returns to scale to reduce its costs and remain competitive, using an example to guide your response.
                                                                                                 (15 marks) [AO3]
    © International Baccalaureate Organization 2000 (part **a** only)

3   **a**   At what level of output should a firm produce to maximize its total profits? Use a diagram to help explain your response.   (10 marks) [AO2], [AO4]

    b   'Whatever the type of market structure, profit maximization will always be the only goal of firms.' Discuss.   (15 marks) [AO3]
    © International Baccalaureate Organization 2005 (part **b** only)

8 PERFECT COMPETITION (HL ONLY)

8.1 Perfect competition: assumptions of the model

Learning outcomes
- Describe, using examples, the assumed characteristics of perfect competition: a large number of firms; a homogeneous product; freedom of entry and exit; perfect information; perfect resource mobility.

Watermelon trucks line the streets of Shanghai, an example of a perfectly competitive market.

Every October, a funny thing happens along the streets leading out of Shanghai, China. This city of 19 million people, China's largest, has a centre of glass skyscrapers, a perimeter of smoke-belching factories, and a hinterland of fertile agricultural fields. It is from these fields that, for two or three weeks every autumn, blue trucks come rumbling in to line up on practically every street corner on the way into downtown Shanghai. The trucks flood into the city by the hundreds, maybe even the thousands, each one loaded down with freshly harvested watermelons.

You can buy watermelons in Shanghai at any time of year, but for 11 months the price of watermelons is higher than the typical Chinese consumer is willing to pay because the watermelons have been transported great distances from the warmer climates to the south or even from abroad. Yet for two or three weeks, during the watermelon harvest in the fields just beyond Shanghai, watermelons are abundant and cheap. For this sweet and juicy period in Shanghai, the watermelon market briefly becomes perfectly competitive.

If you were to hop on a bicycle in Shanghai's factory district and ride 20 kilometres into the city centre during the watermelon harvest, this is what you would see. Every 500 metres or so along the road, there would be a large blue flatbed truck pulled up to the kerb with its tailgate down. In the back of the truck would be hundreds of watermelons, probably picked the day before in a field not far away. If you were to stop and ask the man standing beside the truck the price of a watermelon, chances are he would tell you something in the range of 12 RMB (around $1.50). If you continued to cycle down the road another 500 metres you'd come to another, very similar, truck also selling watermelons. Ask the price here, and you'd probably be told the same amount. As you continue your journey into the city and stop at another dozen or so blue trucks, chances are you'd find the price of watermelons to be the same at every stop.

The watermelon market in Shanghai during October displays many of the characteristics of a perfectly competitive market: the product on sale is homogeneous and identical from seller to seller. The price the melons sell for, if you do a little bargaining, is nearly the same everywhere, and the barriers to entry into this market are extremely low. Anyone with a flatbed truck and a few hours on their hands could drive out to the countryside and load their truck with melons to sell in the city.

This is one real-world example of a perfectly competitive market, but other examples are hard to find. The model is mostly theoretical but, as you will see, it provides economists with a valuable tool for evaluating the efficiency of more realistic market models – the imperfectly competitive markets discussed in Chapters 9 and 10.

The perfectly competitive model

As you learned in Chapter 2 (page 23), perfectly competitive markets are those in which individual firms produce such a small proportion of the overall supply of the product that altering their own output has no influence over the market price of the product. In this regard, firms in such an industry are price-takers; this means that they find it impossible to charge a price higher than that charged by their competitors, nor can they successfully offer their output at a lower price since competition forces the price down to the producers' lowest average total cost.

In addition to perfectly competitive markets consisting of a large number of identical, price-taking firms, the model also assumes that the firms:

- produce completely identical products; the goods are not differentiated and act as perfect substitutes for each other
- can enter or exit the market very easily, with effectively no barriers to entry or exit.

While perfectly competitive industries are rare in the real world, examples of markets with some of these characteristics do exist in certain industries, including certain agricultural commodities, low-tech manufactured goods, certain types of low-skilled labour, markets in which there are many firms producing nearly identical products or millions of households supplying an identical resource (such as labour). Despite being rare, perfectly competitive markets are worth studying for what they teach us about resource allocation and the efficiency resulting from high levels of competition between firms.

Assuming there are no spillover benefits or costs (externalities) in the production or consumption of the product, perfectly competitive markets result in the most socially optimal level of output and price of any of the four market structures, and are therefore considered allocatively efficient. Shortages and surpluses are non-existent in perfectly competitive markets, wherein the high level of competition ensures that the marginal social benefit of a particular product will align with the marginal social cost and neither too much nor too little will be produced. The perfectly competitive model can be held up as an example of perfect efficiency when compared to less competitive market models in which the price-making market power of individual firms results in a level of output that is lower than and a price that is higher than that achieved under perfect competition. This provides evidence that efficiency decreases as markets become less competitive.

 A market is perfectly competitive if there are a large number of firms producing identical products facing identical production costs and in which there are no barriers to entry or exit.

With the assumptions above to guide our analysis, we can begin to examine the behaviour of firms in perfectly competitive industries to determine how such a market adjusts to changes in demand and supply and how output and price are determined in both the short run and the long run.

8.2 Cost and revenue curves in a PC market

Learning outcomes

- Explain, using a diagram, the shape of the perfectly competitive firm's average revenue and marginal revenue curves, indicating that the assumptions of perfect competition imply that each firm is a price-taker.
- Explain, using a diagram, that the perfectly competitive firm's average revenue and marginal revenue curves are derived from market equilibrium for the industry.

In Chapter 6, you learned about short-run costs and revenue curves of firms in different market structures, distinctions between the fixed and variable costs firms face in the short run (the fixed-plant period), and the law of diminishing returns and its influence on the shape of a firm's marginal cost curve. You will recall that a firm increasing its output in the short run may alter its variable resources (labour and raw materials) while keeping its land and capital inputs constant. As more labour and raw materials are added to production while the amount of capital and land are fixed, the output attributable to additional labour beyond a certain point begins to decline. This explains why a firm's short-run marginal cost (MC) curve slopes upward beyond the point at which diminishing marginal returns begins (Figure 8.1). If you need to refresh your memory of terms such as ATC and AVC, as well as MR DARP, now is a good time to do so.

Figure 8.1
A firm's short-run costs of production.

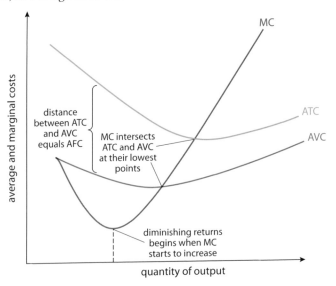

A perfectly competitive firm seeking maximum profits must examine both its short-run costs and revenues. The revenue a firm earns depends on two factors: the price it can sell its output for and the quantity of output it sells. Since perfect competitors are price-takers, the price a firm sells its output for is determined by the market supply and market demand for the product it makes.

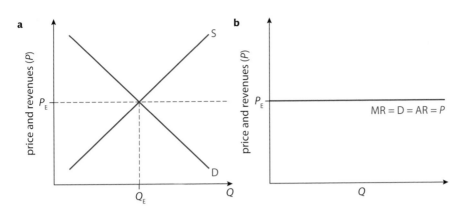

a

b

You will recall that the demand seen by an individual firm in a perfectly competitive market is perfectly elastic, illustrated graphically as a line horizontal at the equilibrium market price (Figure 8.2, above). Consumers are perfectly responsive to a change in the price by an individual seller. Any change in price by one firm in a market consisting of hundreds of identical firms selling identical products will grab the attention of all the buyers in the market; a price increase will lead to a loss of all customers, while a price decrease will lead all buyers to want to buy from the one firm that lowered its price.

 To learn more about perfect competition, visit www.pearsonhotlinks.com, enter the title or ISBN of this book and select weblink 8.1.

8.3 Profit maximization in the short run

Learning outcomes
- Explain, using diagrams, that it is possible for a perfectly competitive firm to make economic profit (supernormal profit), normal profit or negative economic profit in the short run based on the marginal cost and marginal revenue profit-maximization rule.

A profit-maximizing firm will produce at the level of output in the short run at which its marginal revenue (MR) equals its marginal cost (MC), following the profit-maximization rule (page 171). To illustrate a firm maximizing its profits, we simply draw a firm diagram with its costs and revenues, with the firm producing at the quantity that corresponds with the intersection of its MC and MR curves (Figure 8.3).

The firm in Figure 8.3b maximizes its profits when producing at the quantity Q_F. At any level of output below Q_F, MR (the revenue earned when selling the next unit produced which, in the case of a perfectly competitive firm, is the equilibrium price, P_E) would exceed MC and the firm's total profits would increase if it produced one more unit. Beyond Q_F, the last unit

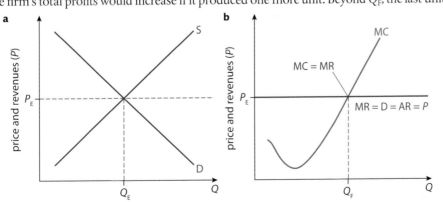

a

b

Figure 8.3
A profit-maximizing firm in a perfectly competitive market.
a Perfectly competitive industry; **b** perfectly competitive firm.

produced costs the firm more than it adds to revenue (MC is greater than MR). The firm is earning losses on the margin and would reduce its losses by reducing its output back to Q_F.

Following the profit-maximization rule does not guarantee a firm will earn economic profits. If, at the MC = MR quantity, a firm's average total cost (ATC) of production is less than its average revenue (AR, the price), then the firm will experience economic profits. If, however, ATC is greater than the price, then the firm may be in a loss-minimizing position, where it cannot possibly earn profits and instead is producing at the quantity at which its losses are minimized. On the other hand, it is also possible that a firm is simply breaking even. If, at the MC = MR quantity, the ATC equals the price, then the firm is earning zero economic profits, and is simply covering its costs of production (and is earning only a normal profit).

To determine whether or not a firm is actually earning profits at its profit-maximizing level of output, we must examine its AR and ATC at that level of output. If ATC is less than AR at the profit-maximizing quantity, then the firm is earning economic profits, meaning it is covering all its explicit and implicit costs, including a normal profit, and earning additional profit beyond all these costs (Figure 8.4).

Figure 8.4
A firm earning economic profits in a perfectly competitive market.
a Perfectly competitive industry; **b** perfectly competitive firm.

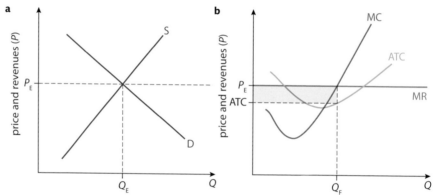

The firm in Figure 8.4b is producing at the level of output at which MR = MC, at a quantity of Q_F. At this level of output, the firm's average total cost (determined by where the dotted line above Q_F intersects the ATC curve) is less than its average revenue (the MR = D = AR = P line). For its average unit of output, the firm is able to sell for more than its cost of production, indicating that the firm is earning a profit equal to $P_E - $ ATC on each unit it produces.

Since the firm's total output is Q_F, the total amount of profit earned by the firm can be calculated as $(P_E - $ ATC$) \times Q_F$. The area indicated by the blue rectangle in the graph represents the firm's total profits.

Figure 8.5 puts some numerical values into this situation.

Figure 8.5
Economic profits: when price is greater than average total cost.

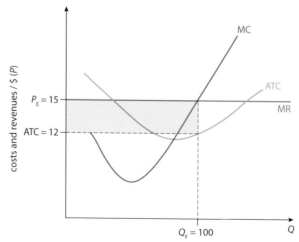

Study Figure 8.5 and answer the following questions.

1   Why does the firm wish to produce at a level of output equal to 100 units?

2   What is the firm's total revenue when producing 100 units?

3   What is the firm's total cost?

4   Calculate the firm's level of economic profits.

5   Assuming there are no barriers to entry to this perfectly competitive market, how do you think the existence of economic profits will affect the number of firms producing this good in the long run?

Figure 8.5 shows a perfectly competitive firm maximizing its profits by producing at its MC = MR level of output. The price of $15 is determined by market supply and demand (the market diagram is not shown). The firm's average total cost is $12 and its output is 100 units. To determine the firm's total economic profit, calculate its total revenue (TR) and subtract its total cost (TC).

- $TR = P \times Q = \$15 \times 100 = \$1500$
- $TC = ATC \times Q = \$12 \times 100 = \$1200$
- Economic profit $= TR - TC = \$1500 - \$1200 = \$300$

The economic profit of $300 represents the firm's economic, or abnormal profits; the revenue earned above and beyond the firm's explicit and implicit costs of production, including the normal profit needed to keep the firm in business. As stated above, not all firms earn economic profits at all times. Sometimes, a firm producing at its profit-maximizing level of output faces a situation in which it is still earning economic losses.

The loss-minimizing firm

Economic profits, while desired, are not always guaranteed. Competitive firms often find themselves in situations in which economic losses are being earned, even when producing at their profit-maximizing level of output. In other words, a firm doing as well as it can do may still be losing money (Figure 8.6).

The firm in Figure 8.6 is producing at the level of output at which MR = MC, which is the profit-maximizing level. However, its costs appear to be much higher than the firm in Figure 8.4. Therefore; despite doing as well as it can, the firm is earning economic losses equal to the shaded rectangle. The firm's ATC is greater than its AR at the MC = MR point, meaning that it is earning losses on each unit of output it produces and sells. This firm cannot possibly earn economic profits unless one of two things happens: either the price of the product must rise or the firm must reduce its costs.

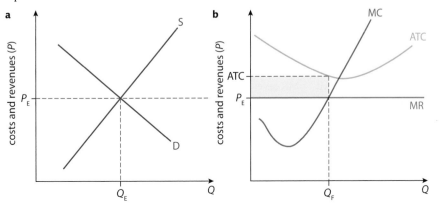

Figure 8.6
A firm minimizing losses in a perfectly competitive market. **a** Perfectly competitive industry; **b** perfectly competitive firm.

Figure 8.7

Economic losses: when price is less than average total cost.

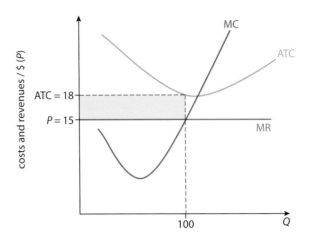

Figure 8.7 puts some numerical values into this situation.

HL EXERCISES
Study Figure 8.7 and answer the following questions.
6 Calculate the firm's total revenues when producing 100 units.
7 What is the firm's total cost at this output level?
8 Calculate the level of economic losses being earned by this firm.
9 Identify two things that could have caused a profit-earning firm like that in Figure 8.5, to go to earning economic losses.
10 Assuming no barriers to exit in this market, what will the existence of economic losses cause to happen to the number of firms in the long run?

The firm in Figure 8.7 is producing at its profit-maximizing level of output where MR = MC but at this quantity, it is earning economic profits of negative $300, meaning the firm is earning economic losses of $300. Total losses are found by subtracting the firm's total cost (TC) from its total revenue (TR).

- $TR = P \times Q = \$15 \times 100 = \$1500$
- $TC = ATC \times Q = \$18 \times 100 = \$1800$
- Total profit $= TR - TC = \$1500 - \$1800 = -\$300$

Producing at the quantity at which MR = MC allows firms to earn the greatest level of economic profit; but a profit is not guaranteed. A firm may also experience economic losses if its costs of production are too high or the equilibrium price in the market is too low. A firm may also break even, which occurs when the firm's ATC = AR.

The break-even firm

A firm producing at the MC = MR level of output may simply be breaking even, which means that its total revenues are equal to its total costs. The break-even firm is earning only a normal profit, which is the minimum profit needed to keep the owner of the firm producing in the market (Figure 8.8).

The firm in Figure 8.8 is producing at its profit-maximizing level of output, Q_F. At this quantity, the firm's ATC = AR. Per-unit economic profits are zero, meaning total profits are zero. The firm is breaking even.

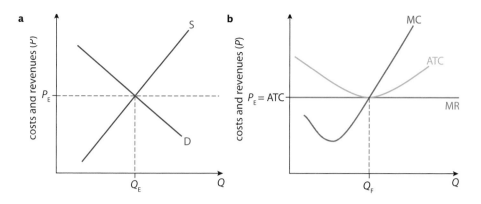

Figure 8.8
A perfectly competitive firm in a perfectly competitive market which is in long-run equilibrium: the firm is breaking even. **a** Perfectly competitive industry; **b** perfectly competitive firm.

Remember that firms in a perfectly competitive market are identical in every way. In addition to producing exactly the same product, perfectly competitive firms also face identical costs of production. Therefore, a diagram illustrating the profits or losses of one firm represents the situation faced by all firms. To understand the behaviour of firms in a perfectly competitive industry, therefore, we can examine the behaviour of a typical firm in response to one of the three scenarios illustrated above (the profit-maximizing firm, the loss-minimizing firm and the break-even firm).

Only when firms in a perfectly competitive market are breaking even is the market said to be in equilibrium. If firms are earning economic profits in the short run, then the market will adjust to a new long-run equilibrium level at which firms are breaking even. Likewise, if the typical firm is earning economic losses, the market will adjust to eliminate those losses until firms are once again breaking even.

8.4 Profit maximization in the long run

Learning outcomes
- Explain, using a diagram, why, in the long run, a perfectly competitive firm will make normal profit.
- Explain, using a diagram, how a perfectly competitive market will move from short-run equilibrium to long-run equilibrium.

Let's now consider how a perfectly competitive market adjusts in the long run to the existence of economic profits or economic losses among firms in the market.

In the short run, you will recall, the amount of capital employed by firms in an industry is fixed. The short run is the fixed-plant period, in which firms are neither able to increase nor decrease the amount of capital or land resources employed in the production of their output. In the short run, labour is the only variable resource to increase or decrease output. A firm can hire more workers or ask existing workers to work longer hours in response to an increase in price, or lay off workers and cut back on hours in response to a fall in price. This explains why firms' output is only able to vary by small amounts in response to changes in the market price.

In the long run, however, firms are able to vary their output by much more in response to changes in price. In addition, the number of firms in an industry can vary in the long run in response to the existence of economic profits and losses. When the market price rises, some firms will build new plants and employ more resources in their production, and new firms will enter the industry, attracted by the prospect of economic profits. When the demand for a product and its equilibrium price fall in a perfectly competitive industry, some of the existing firms will reduce their plant sizes and others will exit the industry altogether to avoid earning economic losses.

No barriers to entry

To understand how perfectly competitive industries adjust from a short-run equilibrium in which firms may be earning economic profits or losses to the long-run condition in which all firms are breaking even, we must remember one of the main characteristics of perfectly competitive markets: the lack of barriers to entry or exit. Because it is easy to enter or exit a perfectly competitive industry, the existence of economic profits or losses acts as a powerful incentive to attract new firms or repel existing ones.

The lack of barriers to entry in perfectly competitive markets allows for the easy entry and exit of firms in response to the existence of profits or losses. If firms in a particular industry are earning profits, other firms will wish to enter the market to enjoy the profits to be had. Entry is easy and cheap, allowing entrepreneurs to produce the product with relative ease. Likewise, if firms in a perfectly competitive industry are facing losses, some of those firms will leave the market. Firms can reduce their output or shut down altogether and face no barriers to exit.

Entry eliminates profits

To illustrate the long-run adjustment that takes place in a perfectly competitive industry in which economic profits are being earned, let's imagine a market for brownies in which a large number of identical firms are each producing an identical quantity of the same brownies. There are 100 producers, each producing 200 dozen brownies per week. The market for brownies and the costs and revenues of a typical producer are shown in Figure 8.9.

Figure 8.9
If perfectly competitive firms are earning economic profits, new firms will be attracted to the market. **a** Market for brownies; **b** single firm in the brownie market.

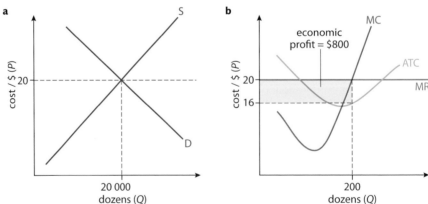

The 20 000 dozen brownies produced each week in the entire industry is the sum of all 100 producers' individual outputs of 200 dozen each. Total output equals the individual output of each firm multiplied by the number of firms: $200 \times 100 = 20\,000$.

As you can see in Figure 8.9, brownie producers are doing rather well. The typical producer earns a profit of $4 per dozen produced and sold at the market price of $20. Each week, the typical producer earns an economic profit of $800. These profits, however, will only be enjoyed in the short run. In the short run, the number of brownie producers and the plant size of those producers are fixed. So how will the market and the costs and revenues of the firms in the market change in the long run?

The long run is the variable-plant period, meaning that the profit-earning brownie producers have time to expand their operations in response to the high profits being earned. Additionally, since barriers to entry in the brownie market are practically non-existent, the number of firms in the market will increase. As new firms enter, we see the situation in Figure 8.10 occur.

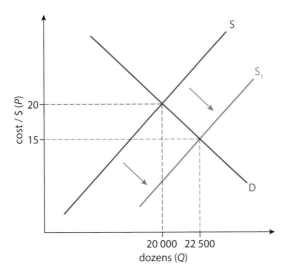

Figure 8.10
The entry of new firms increases the market supply.

The economic profits earned by brownie producers attract new firms to the industry, causing the market supply curve to shift to the right, the equilibrium price to fall and the total output of brownies to increase.

Since firms are price-takers, the marginal revenue faced by brownie producers decreases and, in response, the existing firms reduce their output to the level at which marginal. cost equals the new marginal revenue of $15 (Figure 8.11).

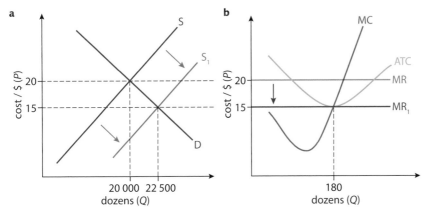

Figure 8.11
The entry of new firms reduces the MR and demand as seen by the existing firms, eliminating economic profits.
a Market for brownies;
b single firm in the brownie market.

Total output of brownies increases because of the existence of economic profits and the entrance of new firms. Meanwhile, the increased competition gives the existing firms a smaller share of the total brownie market and their individual output falls correspondingly, to 180 dozen. The market is now made up of 125 firms, up from the original 100, each producing 180 dozen brownies for a total output of 22 500 dozen.

In Chapter 2 you learned about the role that prices play in allocating resources in a market economy. The above illustration is a perfect example of the allocating power of prices. The price of $20 in the brownie market meant firms were earning profits, a signal to other entrepreneurs that society values brownies and would be better off with more of them. Resources are correspondingly re-allocated from other sectors of the economy (perhaps from bagels or croissants or cookies) into the production of brownies, meeting the demands of consumers and reducing the profits of brownie producers to the 'normal' level, where price equals average total cost. The brownie market moves to its long-run equilibrium level of output and price, at which individual firms are only breaking even. At this point, there is neither an incentive for firms to enter nor exit the market, hence equilibrium is achieved.

Exit eliminates losses

In the same way that the existence of profits sends the signal to entrepreneurs that more of a good is demanded and therefore leads to a re-allocation of resources towards the production of that good, the existence of economic losses sends the opposite message. In Figure 8.12, the demand for brownies is low and the equilibrium price is just $12 per dozen. The typical profit-maximizing firm (Figure 8.12b) is earning economic losses because its average total cost is greater than the price of $12.

Figure 8.12
If perfectly competitive firms are earning economic losses, some firms will wish to leave the market. **a** Market for brownies; **b** single firm in the brownie market.

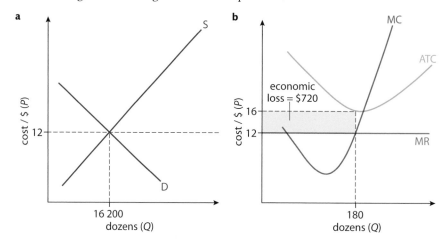

The total losses of the typical firm in the brownie market are equal to the per-unit loss ($12 − $16 = −$4) multiplied by the firm's output (−$4 × 180 = −$720). There are 90 firms in the market producing a total output of 16 200 dozen brownies per week.

As firms earn economic losses, some will decide that the costs of remaining in this industry outweigh the benefits and will choose to leave the market to seek profits in another industry. As firms exit the industry, the market supply curve shifts to the left and the equilibrium price of brownies rises once again (Figure 8.13).

Figure 8.13
The exit of some firms reduces the market supply and increases the equilibrium price.

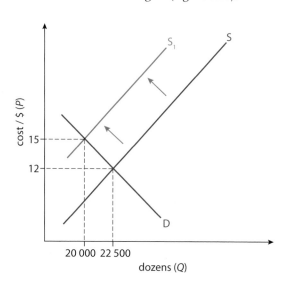

The economic losses experienced by brownie producers leads some firms to shut down and exit the brownie market, causing the supply curve to shift to the left, increasing the equilibrium price of brownies. The firms that remained in the brownie market now see their losses eliminated because of the higher price of brownies (Figure 8.14).

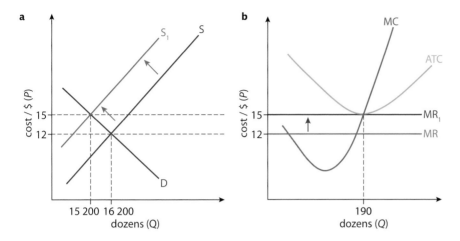

◀ **Figure 8.14**
The exit of some firms raises the MR and demand of remaining firms, eliminating the economic losses. **a** Market for brownies; **b** single firm in the brownie market.

The exit of firms from the brownie market shifts supply to the left and causes the equilibrium price of brownies to rise. Firms that remained in the market increase their output since they suddenly face a larger share of the total market demand than previously. The higher price allows remaining firms to increase their output until the point at which MR = MC which, in this case, is at 190 dozen brownies. Each firm now produces 10 more brownies than before but there are fewer firms in the market.

Before firms exited to avoid losses, there were 90 firms producing 180 dozen brownies each, for a total market output of 16 200 dozen. Following the exit of firms fleeing losses, there are 80 firms remaining, each producing 190 dozen for a total market output of 15 200 dozen.

The weak demand for brownies caused firms to earn economic losses, which created the incentive to leave the market. Some firm-owners sought to allocate their resources towards other industries in which the prospects of economic profits were greater. Others chose to remain in the market, which ultimately meant they would break even once the long-run adjustments took place and the price rose to a level where it equalled the firms' minimum average total cost (the break-even level).

Once again, we have demonstrated the allocating power of prices in a free market economy. The equilibrium price of brownies sends a message from the buyers to the sellers regarding how much output is truly demanded. When firms were earning profits, the incentive among entrepreneurs was to enter the market, satisfy the demands of consumers, earn economic profits in the short run until those profits are eliminated and the allocation of resources towards brownies is efficient once again. Weak demand forced the price down, which caused firms to earn losses. This encouraged some firms to leave the market, leading to a fall in supply and a decrease in the total output of brownies. Eventually, long-run equilibrium is restored at a level of output that is allocatively efficient, meaning the right amount of resources are allocated towards brownies where the marginal cost of producing brownies is exactly equal to their price.

To access Worksheet 8.1 on economic concepts, please visit www.pearsonbacconline.com and follow the onscreen instructions.

Entry eliminates profits and exit eliminates losses. Because of the ease of entry and exit in a perfectly competitive market, any economic profits will be eliminated in the long run as new firms attracted to the profits enter the industry, forcing the price down until all firms break even. If losses are being earned, firms will exit the market, reducing supply of the good until the price increases to the break-even level.

To access Worksheet 8.2 on profit maximization, please visit www.pearsonbacconline.com and follow the onscreen instructions.

● **Examiner's hint**

Breaking even does not mean a firm is doing poorly. Remember, a break-even firm is still earning normal profits, so the business owner is earning a level of profit high enough to remain in business. If normal profits are not being earned, then a firm is earning economic losses and may very well shut down and leave the market.

To learn more about profit maximization, visit www.pearsonhotlinks.com, enter the title or ISBN of this book and select weblink 8.2.

8.5 The shut-down rule

Learning outcomes

- Distinguish between the short-run shut-down price and the break-even price.
- Explain, using a diagram, when a loss-making firm would shut down in the short run.
- Explain, using a diagram, when a loss-making firm would shut down and exit the market in the long run.
- Calculate the short-run shut-down price and the break-even price from a set of data.

Our analysis so far of the brownie industry in which firms were experiencing losses fails to explain which firms will choose to exit the industry and which firms will stay. To determine if it should shut down or not when faced with economic losses, a firm must compare its total losses to its total fixed costs. If total losses exceed total fixed costs, then losses would be minimized by shutting down. In this case, the firm will lose its fixed costs (those costs which must be paid regardless of the level of output) but the amount lost will be less than if the firm continues to operate.

To illustrate the shut-down scenario, we must imagine a situation in which the equilibrium price of a product is so low that the typical firm cannot cover its average variable costs of production when producing at the MR = MC point (Figure 8.15).

As you can see in Figure 8.15, the price of brownies is so low that the typical firm is not even able to cover its AVC of production. Recall that variable costs include the wages for workers and the costs of other variable inputs such as raw materials (in this case, ingredients

Figure 8.15
If the firm's total loss is greater than its total fixed cost, the firm should shut down to minimize losses. **a** Market for brownies; **b** single firm in the brownie market.

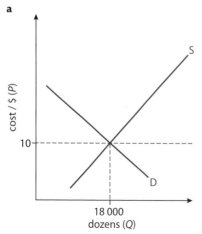

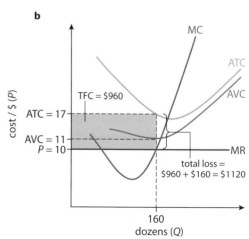

for brownies). With the price this low, the brownie producer cannot afford to continue producing brownies. Its costs of production are simply too high and the price is too low.

Another way to look at the firm's situation is to look at its total loss and its total fixed costs (TFC). The area of total loss (the red and green rectangles; $(ATC - AR) \times Q$)) is greater than its TFC (the red rectangle; $(ATC - AVC \times Q)$)). Recall that the distance between a firm's ATC curve and its AVC curve represents the firm's AFC. Therefore, the red rectangle shows the firm's TFC $(ATC - AVC) \times Q)$). This firm will minimize its total losses by shutting down and sacrificing the costs already sunk into capital and land, rather than by continuing to operate and experiencing losses exceeding its fixed costs.

Why doesn't a firm shut down as soon as $P <$ ATC?

It may seem strange that a firm earning economic losses would continue to operate at all. To understand why a firm will only shut down when $P <$ AVC, we must look at the options facing a firm earning a small economic loss (one that is less than the firm's fixed costs).

Basically, business owners are always trying to do one of two things: maximize profits or minimize losses. When price falls below the average cost of production, a firm goes into loss-minimizing mode. At any point, losses will be minimized by producing at the MC = MR quantity, unless at that level of output the total loss exceeds the TFC.

Remember, fixed costs must be paid whether the firm produces zero units or a million units. For this reason, a firm will actually minimize its losses by producing at a loss as long as that loss is less than TFC. Only when the losses experienced while operating at the MC = MR quantity become larger than the TFC should a firm close its doors and shut down.

 A firm will minimize its total losses by shutting down if the price of its output is less than its average variable cost of production. In other words, if the firm's total losses exceed its total fixed costs, the firm will minimize its losses by shutting down.

Different levels of normal profit and the shut-down rule

The analysis so far presents a puzzle: if our assumptions about firms in a perfectly competitive market are true, and all firms face identical costs of production as the model suggests, then won't all firms begin experiencing losses that exceed their fixed costs simultaneously and thus choose to shut down all at once? This is a very good question, and the answer requires us to step outside our rigid assumptions of the perfectly competitive model and discuss this issue in a more real-world context.

In reality, firms in a perfectly competitive market do not face identical costs of production. Even if all firms pay the same hourly wages for workers, face the same costs for raw materials, rents and interest on land and capital, there is still one cost that will vary between any one producer and all others: the opportunity cost of the entrepreneur who runs the business. In economics, the opportunity cost of running a business is known as the normal profit. Some owners of brownie businesses will incorporate a higher expected level of normal profit into their costs of production than others. For this reason, firms that expect to earn higher normal returns in a particular market are more likely to shut down when earning losses than firms with a lower level of normal profit.

The firms whose owners value their time, energy and skills more than others will be the firms that exit an industry first in the face of economic losses. Firm-owners who believe their skills and energy would be less likely to earn profits in other industries are those most likely to ride out the storm of weak demand in the hope that, in the long run, the equilibrium price of their product returns to a level at which a normal profit can be earned.

HL EXERCISES

15 Assume a firm in a perfectly competitive market is currently producing at a level of output at which it experiences the following costs and revenues:

- MC = 16
- P = 20
- ATC = 22
- AVC = 18
- Q = 50

At its current level of output, calculate this firm's economic profit or loss.

16 The firm is considering its options. For each of the following possibilities, explain whether the firm should or should not do it and why:

- **a** keep output constant
- **b** reduce output
- **c** shut down
- **d** increase output.

17 Assume that, at the profit-maximizing quantity, this firm's ATC = 21. Is the market in long-run equilibrium? Why or why not?

8.6 Efficiency in the perfectly competitive market

Learning outcomes
- Explain the meaning of the term allocative efficiency.
- Explain that the condition for allocative efficiency is $P = MC$ (or, with externalities, $MSB = MSC$).
- Explain, using a diagram, why a perfectly competitive market leads to allocative efficiency in both the short run and the long run.
- Explain the meaning of the term productive/technical efficiency.
- Explain that the condition for productive efficiency is that production takes place at minimum average total cost.
- Explain, using a diagram, why a perfectly competitive firm will be productively efficient in the long run, though not necessarily in the short run.

Efficiency in economics is defined in two ways.

- **Productive efficiency**. This requires that the resources used to produce a good or service are used in the least-cost manner. A firm is productively efficient when it produces at its minimum ATC. Any level of output that corresponds with an ATC of production that is greater than the minimum ATC is indication that a firm is not achieving productive efficiency, since it is not producing in the least-cost manner.

  Productive efficiency is achieved when P = minimum ATC

- **Allocative efficiency**. This requires that the MC of production is equal to the price of the output. Prices, you will recall, are signals from consumers of the marginal benefit they derive from goods to the producers of those goods. If the price of a good is higher than the MC of firms producing it, the message is that society benefits more from the product than it costs firms to produce it. A greater quantity is demanded by the market when price exceeds MC. If the price of a product is less than the firms' MC of production, the message being sent by the market is that less output is desired. Only when a product's price is equal to the MC of producers is a market said to be allocatively efficient, meaning that the right amount of the good or service and the marginal benefit enjoyed by society are equal to the marginal cost incurred in its production.

  Allocative efficiency is achieved when $P = MC$

Productive efficiency in perfectly competitive markets

Firms in perfectly competitive markets are productively efficient when the market is in its long-run equilibrium state. This is due to the nature of competitive markets – competition forces price down to the firms' minimum ATC. Firms that are not productively efficient face one of two choices:

- produce in a manner that reduces the average cost of production to the lowest level possible (i.e. improve efficiency of production)
- experience economic losses and eventually be forced to shut down.

For illustration, let's examine a perfectly competitive industry and a firm in that industry when economic profits are being earned (Figure 8.16).

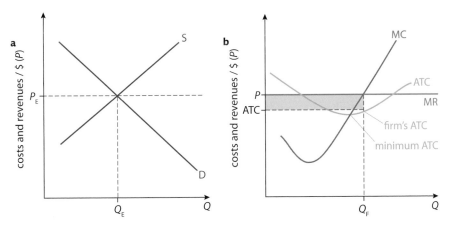

Figure 8.16
If profits are being earned, the firms are not productively efficient because price is greater than minimum ATC. **a** Perfectly competitive industry; **b** perfectly competitive firm.

The typical firm in Figure 8.16 is earning economic profits represented by the green rectangle. The firm is maximizing its profits by producing at the quantity at which its MC = MR. At Q_F this firm is *not* producing at maximum efficiency, since its ATC is greater than the minimum ATC of production. The high price and the existence of economic profits allow this firm to produce at a level greater than that required for productive efficiency, where its costs are minimized.

The industry is not in its long-run equilibrium, however, because economic profits are being earned. In the short run, firms in this industry can get away with producing at a productively inefficient level of output (Q_F). In the long run, however, the existence of profits will attract new firms, and due to the easy entry in this market, the market supply eventually increases and the equilibrium price falls. Figure 8.17 (overleaf) shows the effect on total market output and the output and profits for an individual firm.

Figure 8.17
When firms are breaking
even, they achieve productive
efficiency because the price
equals the minimum ATC. **a**
perfectly competitive industry;
b perfectly competitive firm.

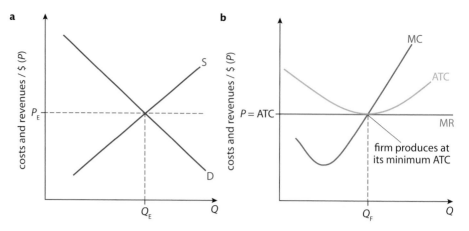

Competition forces the price in the market down to the firm's minimum ATC. As MR and price fall, the firm reduces its output to maintain the profit-maximizing quantity where MR = MC. Once the market achieves its long-run equilibrium, at which individual firms are breaking even, the average total cost of the typical firm is minimized. The result is that due to the ease of entry and the existence of economic profits, perfect competition forces the price down to firms' minimum ATC, ensuring that, in the long run, firms in perfectly competitive markets are productively efficient.

If the firms were to continue to enter the market, the supply would increase again and price would fall below the firms' minimum ATC. In this case, economic losses would force some firms to exit until the price increased back to the break-even level. Only when economic profits are zero and the price of the product is equal to the typical firm's minimum ATC is a perfectly competitive industry in equilibrium.

Allocative efficiency in perfectly competitive markets

Efficiency means more than just producing in the least-cost manner. To be efficient, a market must also allocate the right amount of resources towards the production of the good or service it provides. Allocative efficiency occurs when land, labour and capital are allocated towards the production of goods and services in combinations that are socially optimal. In other words, the right amount of output of various products is being produced given the demands of consumers in the economy and the costs faced by firms.

Because of firms' profit-maximizing behaviour, perfectly competitive markets allocate resources efficiently, neither over nor under-producing the goods consumers demand.

Under the conditions of perfect competition, a market will be allocatively efficient as long as the firms in that market produce at the P = MC level of output. Price is a signal from buyers to sellers, and the price seen by firms signals the marginal benefit of consumers in the market. If the price consumers pay for a product is greater than the marginal cost to firms of producing it, then the message sent to producers is that more output is demanded. In the pursuit of profits, more resources will be allocated towards the production of the product until the MC and the price are equal. At the P = MC point, firms maximize their profits and resources are said to be efficiently allocated (Figure 8.18).

Assume that the firm in Figure 8.18b represents the typical firm in a perfectly competitive market. When firms produce at Q_1 level of output, resources are under-allocated towards this good, since the price consumers are willing to pay (P_E, determined by market supply

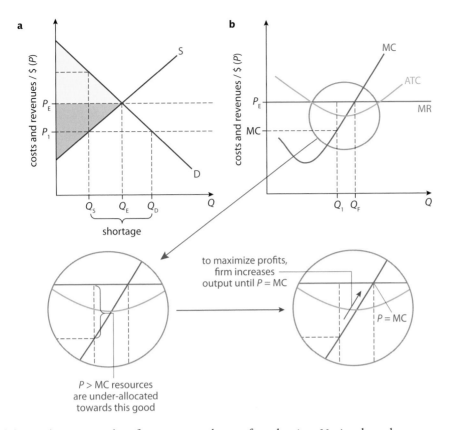

and demand) is greater than firms' marginal cost of production. Notice that when individual firms produce Q_1 units, the market supply of Q_S is less than the market demand of Q_D; there is a shortage in the industry as long as firms produce only Q_1 units.

However, firms are unlikely to produce at this socially undesirable level for long because in their pursuit of profits they will increase their output to the quantity at which marginal cost equals the price. When they increase their output to Q_F, firms maximize their profits and as a result the shortage in the market that existed when firms produced at Q_1 is eliminated, improving social welfare and maximizing the total amount of consumer and producer surplus (the combined areas of the yellow and green triangles in Figure 18.18a).

Because of the profit-maximizing behaviour of self-interested business managers in the competitive market above, resources are more efficiently allocated than they would be otherwise. The price determined by supply and demand in the market signals the benefit society derives from this good, and as long as the price is greater than the marginal cost, the message sent from buyers to seller is 'we want more!' On the other hand, if at a given level of output marginal cost exceeds the price, resources are over-allocated towards the good. The message sent in such a market is that consumers value the product less than it costs firms to produce, so firms will reduce their output to maximize profits, correcting the over-allocation of resources and restoring a socially optimal level of output.

Allocative efficiency is achieved in a perfectly competitive market precisely because firms will always wish to maximize their profits by producing the quantity of goods at which their marginal cost equals the price.

To be efficient, the market price of a good must be equal to firms' marginal cost (allocative efficiency) and the minimum average total cost (productive efficiency). If price is greater than either of these, then firms in the market do not have the incentive to produce the socially optimal quantity of output nor to produce at the level at which their average total costs are minimized, thus resources will be under-allocated towards the good and resources will be used inefficiently by producers.

 To learn more about efficiency, visit www.pearsonhotlinks.com, enter the title or ISBN of this book and select weblink 8.3.

 In their pursuit of economic profits, firms in a competitive market will, through their collective pursuit of self-interest, inadvertently achieve an allocation of society's scarce resources that is socially optimal. Discuss the view that allocative efficiency as defined in this chapter is a socially desirable outcome. Is it accurate to say that goodness can be achieved through greediness in a market economic system?

CASE STUDY

Crops left to rot due to labour shortage

Thousands of acres of farm crops are being left to rot in fields due to a shortage of immigrant labour, forcing some farmers to consider switching crops.

From asparagus to berries and nuts, crops are going unpicked across the United States as tough anti-immigration laws have kept immigrant workers away.

Farmers across the country are turning away from growing fruit and vegetables to produce far less labour-intensive crops such as corn that is ripe for industrial farming.

Besides the crackdown on immigrant workers in states from Arizona to Alabama and South Carolina, the labour shortage appears to be systemic. Mexico has long been the primary provider of low-wage agricultural workers in the US, supplying nearly 70 per cent of the workforce. But, for a host of economic and educational reasons, many rural Mexicans are turning their backs on farm work.

The American Farm Bureau Federation (AFBF) blames the strict anti-immigration laws for multi-billion dollar losses to the agricultural industry each year. Fruit growers in particular are bearing the brunt of the labour shortage and are increasingly having to face up to a stark realisation: go out of business or switch from a berry harvest to an industrial crop such as corn that can be harvested by machine.

According to the California Farm Bureau, 71 per cent of tree fruit growers and nearly 80 per cent of raisin and berry growers were unable to find enough employees in 2014 to prune trees and vines or pick crops.

"The time is long overdue for our nation to have a comprehensive agricultural labour plan that works for all sectors of agriculture and across all regions of our nation," AFBF President Bob Stallman said.

To access Worksheet 8.3 on competition and farmers, please visit www. pearsonbacconline.com and follow the onscreen instructions.

HL EXERCISES

18 Assuming the market for berries is perfectly competitive, illustrate the effects of the shortage of immigrant workers on the short-run production costs and profits of berry growers in the American Southwest.

19 Based on your answer to question 1, explain how the berry market will change in the long run in response to the shortage of immigrant workers. How will the market for corn and other capital-intensive agricultural commodities be affected?

20 Assume the US berry market reaches a new long-run equilibrium following the shortage of immigrant labour. Now demand for berries increases. Use a diagram to illustrate how the profit-maximizing behaviour of berry grower farmers assures that there will not be a shortage of berries following the increase in consumers' demand.

As you learned at the beginning of this chapter, the existence of perfectly competitive markets in the real world is rare. Only certain industries fit the characteristics of the model, which requires a very large number of firms selling an identical commodity with easy entry and exit. The value in studying perfect competition lies in the lessons the model teaches us about the impact that competition has on efficiency in product markets. Although rare, perfectly competitive markets represent the most efficient models of competition. Because easy entry and exit allows for the number of firms, supply, and equilibrium price to adjust in the long run (based on the existence of economic profits or losses), perfect competition will always result in both allocative and productive efficiency.

In Chapters 9 and 10, you will examine the three remaining market structures: monopoly, monopolistic competition and oligopoly. Each of these has characteristics that differ from perfect competition, most significantly the number of firms is fewer and the barriers to entry are greater. These two characteristics mean that the less competitive markets are also less efficient, both productively and allocatively. Without the ease of entry and exit that characterizes perfectly competitive markets, the existence of economic profits will not necessarily lead to an increase in the output of the product in imperfectly competitive markets. This means that an under-allocation of resources towards such goods will not automatically be corrected. Furthermore, without the incentive to produce in the least-cost manner that the large number of firms in perfect competition creates, imperfectly competitive firms may find it in their best interest to produce at a level of output where the average total cost is not minimized, which means they are not productively efficient.

PRACTICE QUESTIONS

1   a   Using a suitable diagram, explain the difference between short-run equilibrium and long-run equilibrium in perfect competition.   (10 marks) [AO2]

    b   To what extent is the perfectly competitive market likely to exist in the real world?
                                                                                (15 marks) [AO3]

2   a   Using a diagram, explain how allocative and productive efficiency will be achieved in long-run equilibrium in perfect competition.   (10 marks) [AO2], [AO4]

    b   Evaluate the view that consumers, not producers, are the main beneficiaries of perfectly competitive market structures.   (15 marks) [AO3]

                © International Baccalaureate Organization 2003 (part **a** only)

3   a   A firm in perfect competition is producing at the profit-maximizing output, but making a loss. Using diagrammatic analysis, explain how this is possible.

                                                                          (10 marks) [AO2], [AO4]

    b   Discuss the claim that all costs are identical among different firms in a perfectly competitive market. If this claim is correct, then why do some firms shut down before others when earning economic losses?   (15 marks) [AO3]

To access Quiz 8, an interactive, multiple-choice quiz on this chapter, please visit www.pearsonbacconline.com and follow the onscreen instructions.

9 MONOPOLY (HL ONLY)

 9.1 Monopoly: assumptions of the model

Learning outcomes
- Describe, using examples, the assumed characteristics of a monopoly: a single or dominant firm in the market; no close substitutes; significant barriers to entry.

Three famous monopolists: John D Rockefeller, Bill Gates and Carlos 'Slim' Helu. ▶

A monopoly is a market where one firm dominates the market for a good that has no substitutes and where significant barriers to entry exist. To most people, monopoly might seem akin to autocracy, where one company makes the rules, sets the prices and controls its destiny. As you will see, monopolies can occur in different types of market and take many forms.

> A monopoly is a market where one firm dominates the market for a good that has no substitutes and where significant barriers to entry exist.

A traditional view of monopoly is of a company whose power has been forged through the personality of its chief. John D Rockefeller, of Standard Oil, once famously sought to control the entire world market for the refining of oil. At its peak, Standard Oil processed 80% of global crude oil. Public sentiment against this control led to restrictions on this kind of market power.

Eventually Standard Oil was broken into smaller companies by the US government. But for decades, Rockefeller was the world's richest man. More recently, Bill Gates's company Microsoft has widely been considered a monopolist in the market for operating systems. This, too, drew significant government interest, as Microsoft lost major anti-trust cases in the US and Europe. Courts ruled that Microsoft engaged in predatory and anti-competitive behaviour, and ordered the company to change many of its practices. The EU courts threatened to break the company apart. Those rulings were eventually softened, especially as the technology sector changed, but Gates emerged one of the wealthiest men in the world.

Meanwhile, in Mexico one man's companies control 80% of the cellphones and 90% of the landlines. Carlos 'Slim' Helu is now generally regarded as the world's wealthiest man, with assets of over $60 billion. These examples suggest that monopoly ownership is synonymous with profit-making. Why is this so?

This chapter explores the market structure of monopoly: its characteristics, advantages and disadvantages, as well as government policy towards monopolies. The following are some of the characteristics of a monopoly.

- **Single seller**. When a firm controls the market entirely and is the only producer of the good, it is called a pure monopoly. The term 'monopoly' is derived from the Greek *mono* (single) and *polein* (to sell). However, the case where a single firm controls a dominant share of the market is much more common than a pure single seller.
- **No close substitutes**. Being the single seller of a good would hold little value if that good were easily replaceable with something else. Therefore, for true monopoly power, a firm must be selling something that has no substitutes.
- **Price-maker**. As the single seller of a good without substitutes, the firm will have some power to set the price of the good. The extent of that power is limited by the overall demand for the good, but this power can be considerable. In contrast to the perfect competitor, which must accept whatever price is set in the larger market, the monopolist has significant price-making power.
- **Barriers to entry**. A monopolist keeps the dominant position because there are significant barriers to other firms' entry into the market. In the absence of competition, the firm can maintain its price-making power, and will continue to make abnormal profits.

 To learn more about monopoly, visit www.pearsonhotlinks.com, enter the title or ISBN of this book and select weblink 9.1.

9.2 Barriers to entry

Learning outcomes
- Describe, using examples, barriers to entry, including economies of scale, branding and legal barriers.

Market power

Market power (also known as monopoly power) is the ability to set the price of the good. Monopolies, although still limited by the market demand, have considerable power to set their prices.

Barriers to entry are defined as the characteristics of a market that make it difficult for firms to join the industry, such as:

- economies of scale
- legal barriers
- ownership of essential resources
- aggressive tactics.

 Barriers to entry are the technical, competitive or cost-related impediments to joining a market and competing against the existing firms.

Economies of scale

Economies of scale were explained in Chapter 7 (page 161). If economies of scale occur over a large amount of output, it is possible that the total market demand may be too low to warrant the existence of more than one firm in the industry. The established firm may have achieved a size that has lowered their long-run average costs of production. New entrants would not produce enough to reach the same level of cost reduction. As a result, potential new competitors are deterred from entering because they would be 'too small to compete' with established firms.

Figure 9.1 shows the long-run average total cost (LRATC) decreasing as the individual firm grows larger and larger, moving from ATC_1 (having one factory) to ATC_4 (having four factories). At this monopolist's current level of output (Q_M), it is achieving a low average total cost of C_1, made possible by its multiple plants and the economies of scale it has already achieved while becoming as large as it is. Were another firm to enter the market it would, at best, split the market between the two firms and each would produce smaller quantities, operating fewer factories and having a higher average cost. If each of the two firms shared the market and produced at C_2, the costs would be much higher than only one firm producing at C_1. The ability of one firm to produce the total output at a lower average cost creates a barrier to entry to any new competitors thinking of entering this market.

Industries such as airplane building, shipbuilding and other major manufacturing businesses are relatively uncompetitive, because the total demand for such products is insufficient to attract more than a handful of extremely large-scale firms. In each of these industries, the existence of significant economies of scale poses a major barrier to entry for potential new firms, because in order to compete with existing firms, they would have to produce at a level of output that is simply unachievable over any reasonable period of time and at a reasonable cost.

Figure 9.1
Economies of scale.

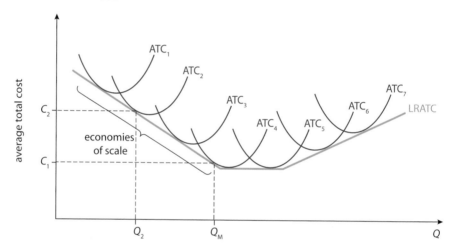

Legal barriers

Patents, copyrights and government licences present barriers to entry in certain markets. For example, Microsoft's patent on its Windows operating system and Apple's patent on the 'click wheel' on its early iPods presented barriers to entry to other firms which may have wanted to compete in these markets. This keeps competition out, and makes the industries less competitive. In another instance, government-granted licences on radio and television bands have limited competition in the past. Tariffs, quotas and other trade barriers can also effectively achieve barriers to foreign entry into the market as well.

Ownership of essential resources

Industries in which certain firms own access to the resources essential to their goods' production tend to be less competitive than those in which resources are readily available to any firm wishing to compete. A few large firms control most of the richest mines for many important mineral resources, making it hard for new mining companies to enter the industry. Professional football and basketball teams have contracts with the top athletes in those sports, making it nearly impossible for a new club to form and compete at the highest levels.

I think it's wrong that only one company makes the game *Monopoly*.

Steven Wright, Comedian

Aggressive tactics

Faced with competition, a monopolist can buy out a rival firm. Indeed, if the expected profits without competition exceed the reduced profits and the amount of the purchase price, it would be prudent to do so. The monopolist can also engage in a price war, cutting prices to cost or below-cost levels. This might hurt profits in the short run, but the monopolist has large reserves of profit. The new competitor is not likely to survive by charging the same low prices, and so will be driven out of the business.

To learn more about barriers to entry, visit www. pearsonhotlinks.com, enter the title or ISBN of this book and select weblink 9.2.

9.3 Demand and revenue curves under monopoly

Learning outcomes

- Explain that the average revenue curve for a monopolist is the market demand curve, which will be downward sloping.
- Explain, using a diagram, the relationship between demand, average revenue and marginal revenue in a monopoly.
- Explain why a monopolist will never choose to operate on the inelastic portion of its average revenue curve.

The demand curve facing the monopolist is quite different from that facing the perfectly competitive firm. Figures 9.2b and 9.2c show the contrast between the two. You will recall that the perfect competitor is one of very many firms and the proportion of the market it sees is quite small. This, in part, explains the perfectly elastic demand curve in 9.2b. Such firms are price-takers, they receive a price set in the overall market at P_E. The monopolist in Figure 9.2c, however, faces the entire market alone, selling to all types of customer. The monopolist therefore faces a downsloping demand curve that looks rather like that facing the whole industry for the perfect competitor. For the monopolist, the firm is the industry, and so it faces a downsloping market demand curve.

This has important implications for price and quantity for the monopolist. For the perfectly competitive firm, any price above the market price will be rejected by buyers. For the monopolist, an increase in price will reduce the quantity demanded. However, this may still be desirable for the monopolist, if revenue increases as a result. Also, the perfect competitor can seemingly sell whatever it can produce at the market demand price. The monopolist is constrained from increasing quantity. It is limited by the demand curve, and must reduce the price from P_1 to P_E to increase quantity demanded from Q_1 to Q_E.

Figure 9.2
a Perfectly competitive industry demand; **b** perfectly competitive firm demand; **c** monopolist demand.

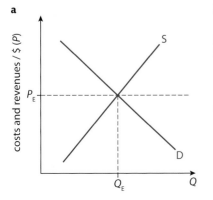
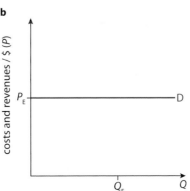
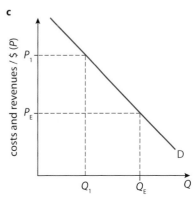

The shape of the demand curve also has implications for the revenue earned by the monopolist.

Table 9.1 lists a downsloping demand curve's revenues.

Output (Q)	Price (P)/$	Total revenue (TR = P × Q)/$	Marginal revenue (MR = ΔTR/ΔQ/$	Average revenue (AR = TR/Q)/$
0	–			
1	10	10	10	10
2	9	18	8	9
3	8	24	6	8
4	7	28	4	7
5	6	30	2	6
6	5	30	0	5
7	4	28	-2	4
8	3	24	-4	3
9	2	18	-6	2
10	1	10	-8	1

TABLE 9.1 MARGINAL AND AVERAGE REVENUE FOR DOWNSLOPING DEMAND CURVE

Note the following points about Table 9.1.

- As price (P) decreases, the quantity demanded (Q) increases. Thus, demand is downsloping as we would expect for a monopolist.
- Average revenue (AR, column 5) is consistent with P because we are assuming that the monopolist is charging the same price to all customers. As a single-price monopolist, if P is lowered for one it is lowered for all. For this reason P = AR.
- Total revenue (TR = P × Q) initially rises as P is lowered and more Q is consumed. It stops rising at the 5th and 6th unit, and then drops consistently afterwards.
- TR decreases at exactly the point where marginal revenue (MR) is 0. This suggests that further production adds nothing to revenue and may reduce it.
- MR is the amount earned from the next group of units sold. In column 4, you can see that MR decreases as P decreases. Moving from a price of $10 to a price of $9 means that two units are now sold at $9 each. TR at a price of $10 was $10. TR at a price of $9 is $18. The difference between TR before and after the decrease in price is $8. This pattern holds true for a single-price monopolist: as P decreases, MR decreases at twice the rate of the price change. In Table 9.1, each time P drops by $1, the MR drops by $2. Thus, the MR curve will fall below the demand curve as price decreases.

Figure 9.3 demonstrates the relationship between total revenue (TR) and marginal revenue (MR) and demand for the monopolist. As price drops, the demand curve slopes down to the right. MR falls below it at a faster rate, eventually dropping to zero at the price of $5.

In Table 9.1, as P drops from $6 to $5, TR stalls at $30, meaning that no additional revenue has been added, so MR = 0. In Figure 9.3, this is shown as MR crossing the x-axis at the point that corresponds to $5 on the demand curve.

Again in Table 9.1, as price drops from $10 down to $5, TR is increasing. This tells us something about the elasticity of demand over this range of prices. You will recall that the total revenue test states that as price decreases and total revenue increases, demand must be elastic (PED > 1). We can therefore conclude that demand is elastic in the upper portion of the demand curve, as price drops from $10 to $5 (Figure 9.3). When the price drops below $5, total revenue decreases (as marginal revenue actually becomes negative). The

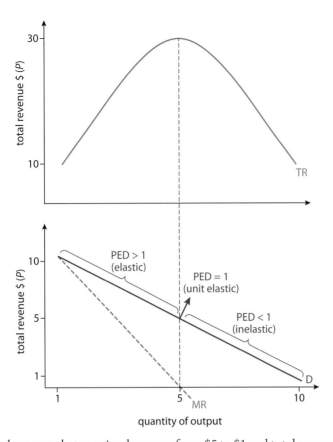

Figure 9.3
Monopolist total revenue and
price elasticity of demand.

total revenue test here says that as price decreases from $5 to $1 and total revenue drops,
demand must be price inelastic (PED < 1) (Figure 9.3, above).

Why is this important? One conclusion we can draw from this concept is that a monopolist
will not produce where marginal revenue is negative. This would violate the basic
assumption that producers are rational. Therefore, we can assume that the monopolist will
produce in the elastic portion of the demand curve, where marginal revenue is positive.
In Figure 9.3, the monopolist will not produce any more than five units. Any more output
would lower TR, as MR becomes negative.

 ## Profit maximization for the monopolist

Learning outcomes
* Explain, using a diagram, the short- and long-run equilibrium output and pricing
  decision of a profit-maximizing (loss-minimizing) monopolist, identifying the firm's
  economic profit (or losses).
* Explain the role of barriers to entry in permitting the firm to earn economic profit.

The monopolist firm determines output and profit maximization the same way perfect
competitors do, by producing where marginal costs are equal to marginal revenue
(MC = MR). However, for the monopolist or any other imperfect competitor, the
MR = MC point is reached at a different quantity from the perfect competitor because of
the different demand and MR curves they face. (It is also possible to determine the profit-
maximization level using TC and TR. This is covered in detail in Chapter 7.)

In the short run, firms can experience abnormal profits, losses, or normal profits. The firm uses the same approach to production in any case, because MR = MC will either maximize any profits or minimize whatever losses may be occurring. Whether profits or losses are occurring depends on the amount of demand and corresponding level of revenue received.

Short-run profits for the monopolist

To understand these cases more clearly, let's examine Figure 9.4. You will recall from Chapter 7, the nature of the average cost (AC) and marginal cost (MC) curves. Marginal costs decrease initially, but as the law of diminishing marginal returns sets in, marginal costs rise. Also note that as a mathematical imperative, MC will intersect average total cost (ATC) at the minimum of ATC. Remember that the firm will produce where MR = MC to maximize its profits. Producing any quantity beyond that will increase MC above MR, and will reduce the profit of the firm. The monopolist sets the price at P_E, the point on the demand curve that corresponds with Q_E. Why this price? Because the monopolist will charge the highest price it can, as a good profit maximizer.

Figure 9.4
Profit maximization for the monopolist.

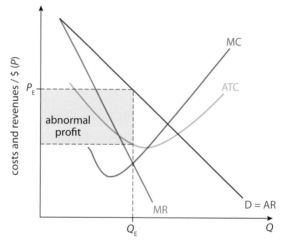

Thus, the price a monopolist charges is set by the demand curve at the profit-maximizing level of output, in this case P_E. As shown in Figure 9.4, price (AR) is above average cost (ATC), which means there is profit being made. The distance between AR and ATC at Q_E shows the per-unit profit. That amount, multiplied by the quantity, will give us the value of the shaded rectangle, or total abnormal profit.

Short-run losses for the monopolist

However, even a monopolist can suffer losses. This can occur when either (a) costs rise to a point at which they are no longer covered by the amount of demand and revenue or (b) demand shrinks thus lowering revenues to a point below costs. In either case, the firm still applies the same rule of profit maximization for the purpose of minimizing losses. By producing at MR = MC, the firm will lose less than it would if it produced at any other point.

In Figure 9.5, demand for the monopolist's product is lower, relative to the costs, than in Figure 9.4. The firm still produces at MR = MC, producing Q_E, and selling at a price P_E set by the demand curve. Above the demand curve at that output level is the ATC, telling us that the firm is losing money. The amount of the per-unit loss is shown by the distance between ATC and the demand curve, and the total loss is shown by the pink rectangle.

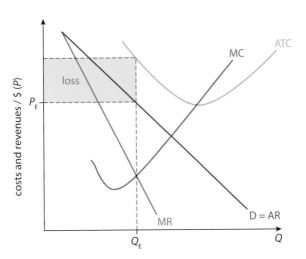

Figure 9.5
Loss minimization for the monopolist.

A monopoly firm can continue to produce while making losses, just as the perfectly competitive firm can, as long as variable costs are covered. However, in the long run, the monopolist is much more likely to continue earning profits because barriers to entry prevent any competitors from entering the market.

HL EXERCISES

1 a Create a diagram showing a profit-maximizing monopolist earning short-run profits.

   b From the diagram, describe two possible events that might eliminate these profits.

2 a Create a diagram showing a profit-maximizing monopolist making short-run losses.

   b From the diagram, describe two possible events that might eliminate these losses.

 9.5 # Revenue maximization

Learning outcomes

- Explain, using a diagram, the output and pricing decision of a revenue-maximizing monopoly firm.
- Compare and contrast, using a diagram, the equilibrium positions of a profit-maximizing monopoly firm and a revenue-maximizing monopoly firm.
- Calculate from a set of data and/or diagrams the revenue-maximizing level of output.

While economists traditionally assume that firms seek to maximize profits, there are other views of the market that emphasize revenues rather than profits. If the monopolist were to produce for the sake of maximizing revenues, the resulting levels of output may be quite different. Figure 9.6 (overleaf) shows the monopolist maximizing revenues rather than profits. Under the rules of profit maximization, the monopolist would produce at $Q_{PROFMAX}$, setting a price at $P_{PROFMAX}$. If the monopolist were maximizing revenues, it would be producing where marginal revenue intersects the lower axis, where $MR = 0$ and TR is at its highest. Producing less than this level of output would be to miss out on extra revenue, since MR is still positive up to this point. Producing beyond Q_{REVMAX} would be to produce where marginal revenue is negative, reducing revenues. (This corresponds to producing at five units in Figure 9.3 (page 201), as this is where TR is at its peak, and just as $MR = 0$.)

Figure 9.6
Monopoly revenue
maximization.

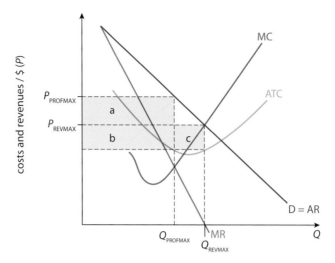

In contrast, the profit-maximizing monopolist would produce at $Q_{PROFMAX}$, where MC = MR, and would charge $P_{PROFMAX}$. The profit maximizer charges more and produces less. To become a revenue maximizer, this firm would lower the corresponding price to P_{REVMAX}, and expand output to Q_{REVMAX}. From Figure 9.6, we can see that the revenue-maximizing firm earns less profit, going from shaded area a + b to the area b + c. Thus, we can conclude that monopolists who seek to maximize revenues will sell at lower prices and produce more output, but also earn less profit than monopoly firms seeking to maximize profits.

HL EXERCISES

3   Assume a monopolist faces a demand curve with prices and quantities of $8 and 3 units, $7 and 4 units, $6 and 5 units, $5 and 6 units, $4 and 7 units, $3 and 8 units. With this information, create a table showing prices, quantities demanded, total revenue and marginal revenue.

4   **a**   Plot these points on a graph showing the demand (AR) curve, and marginal revenue (MR) curve.

     b   Show the point at which marginal revenue equals zero.

     c   Add an MC curve to your diagram and identify the profit-maximizing price and output level.

     d   Identify the revenue-maximizing price and output level.

 Natural monopoly

Learning outcomes
- With reference to economies of scale, and using examples, explain the meaning of the term 'natural monopoly'.
- Draw a diagram illustrating a natural monopoly.

When a single large firm can produce more cheaply than two or more smaller firms, it is called a natural monopoly. More specifically, a natural monopoly typically occurs when production of a good or service requires significant fixed costs. Because the fixed costs are so large, the average costs decrease only after very large runs of output (in a way very similar to the existence of economies of scale). Long-run average total costs (LRATC) decrease only with exceptionally large quantities. Figure 9.7 demonstrates this occurrence. One firm, producing 2000 units for the entire market, lowered short-run average total costs to $SRATC_{1FIRM}$. If the market were split between two firms, with each firm producing 1000 units, the cost at $SRATC_{2FIRMS}$ is much higher. Thus, it is more efficient for a single firm to produce in this market.

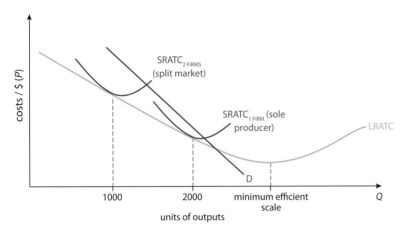

◀ **Figure 9.7**
Natural monopoly.

Typical natural monopolies are public utilities such as power, sewage, and water production. These firms have enormous infrastructure costs, including the cost of running pipes and power lines from the production facility into each home. To have more than one firm, for the sake of consumer choice, could mean having several sets of pipes and power lines. The high fixed cost of infrastructure was the rationale behind creating (state-run) power and utility monopolies. In the UK, the National Grid carries all electrical power, and functions as a kind of regulated monopoly. But there are several companies providing energy to households. Why do these companies not have their own power grids? Because the high fixed cost of infrastructure would make them inefficient.

 A natural monopoly occurs in a market where the lowest costs can be achieved when only one firm sells to the market. It is typically associated with large fixed start-up costs.

9.7 Disadvantages and advantages of monopoly

Learning outcomes

- Draw diagrams and use them to compare and contrast a monopoly market with a perfectly competitive market, with reference to factors including efficiency, price and output, research and development (R & D) and economies of scale.
- Explain why, despite inefficiencies, a monopoly may be considered desirable for a variety of reasons, including the ability to finance research and development (R & D) from economic profits, the need to innovate to maintain economic profit, and the possibility of economies of scale.

Disadvantages
Higher prices and lower quantity produced

Compared to industry output for the competitive firm, monopolies produce less and charge higher prices (this is an industry-wide comparisons, not firm-to-firm). Figure 9.8 (overleaf)

Figure 9.8
Perfect competition *vs*
monopoly prices and
quantities. **a** Perfectly
competitive industry;
b monopoly.

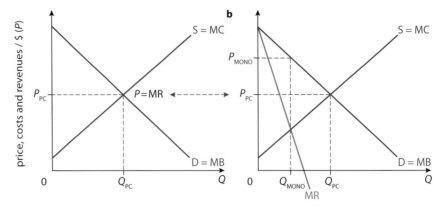

compares production by the competitive firm to that of the monopolist. The competitive market produces at Q_{PC} at a price P_{PC}, where supply and demand intersect. Recall that this sets the price for all firms, and thus their marginal revenue. Therefore, P = MR for the competitive industry.

If those firms produced as a single firm, that firm would follow the same rules for profit maximization, but would be operating under different revenue conditions. For the monopolist, marginal revenue is far below the demand curve, pulling production back to Q_{MONO}, and raising price to P_{MONO}. This reduces the amount made available to the market, compared to competitive markets, as well as increasing the price.

This obviously benefits producers and hurts consumers. More specifically, it can harm relatively poor consumers the most. Where the good is a necessity, low-income consumers will not be able to purchase the good in sufficient quantities.

Producer welfare gains at the expense of consumers

The degree to which producers gain at the expense of consumers can be understood using the concept of consumer and producer surplus. Figure 9.9a shows consumer and producer surplus for the competitive market, producing where supply and demand intersect at Q_{PC} and charging P_{PC}. Consumer surplus is shown by triangle A and producer surplus by triangle B. In Figure 9.9b, as the monopolist marginal revenue falls below demand, the intersection point with marginal cost is further back, and output is at Q_{MONO} with price at P_{MONO}.

Figure 9.9
Perfect competition *vs*
monopoly consumer and
producer surplus. **a** Perfectly
competitive industry;
b monopoly.

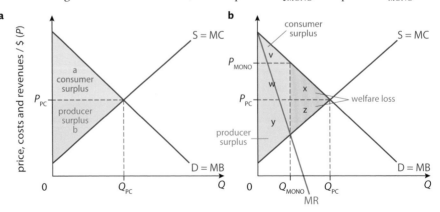

As a result, consumer surplus shrinks from a to the smaller triangle v for consumers in the monopoly. Producer surplus expands from b in perfect competition to the larger w + y under the monopoly. Finally, the decreased quantity results in a loss to both producers and consumers. These welfare losses are shown by triangles x and z, respectively. Triangle x is consumer surplus that is not enjoyed under monopoly, whereas triangle z represents the loss of surplus for producers. In sum, production under monopoly clearly benefits the welfare of the single producer at the expense of consumers and the multiple producers that would exist in a more competitive market.

Incentive problems

The monopolization of a particular industry may result in a loss of the incentives that make markets efficient in the first place.

Lack of innovation

Because the monopolist is insulated from competition, monopolies are likely to be complacent. Research and development can be costly, which will reduce profits, and the monopolist may conclude that it is not worth the cost when profits are guaranteed. As a result, monopoly firms are unlikely to innovate to improve product quality or to reduce costs. As costs will not decrease through innovation, the quantities produced on the market will not increase.

Incentive to avoid competition

Monopolies may choose to preserve their market power by using the aggressive tactics described earlier, rather than by innovating or lowering costs. In particular, where such monopolies are granted by government licence, there is significant incentive for the firm to persuade lawmakers to preserve the monopoly. With their profits at stake, they can spend money on advertising and influencing the process, rather than improving their production.

Advantages of monopoly
Economies of scale

Among the more serious advantages to monopoly is the reduction in costs through economies of scale. In some cases, the high fixed costs of production mean that lower costs can only be achieved through massive runs of output. As shown in Figures 9.1 and 9.7, the average costs can be lowered as production expands to greater and greater levels by the single firm. If the firm is able to reduce costs sufficiently, it may be able to lower prices to a point that is more competitive than that of the perfect competitor. This is especially true of a natural monopoly, and in the specific case of public utilities (Figure 9.10). Here, the monopoly price and output are shown with those of perfect competition. Again, because the marginal revenue curve of the monopolist falls below demand, it intersects MC at a smaller level of output than that of the perfect competitor.

Firms like Facebook, Google and Apple currently dominate the market for online activities, suggesting we may be entering a new era of monopoly power. Many industrial monopolies of the past failed to innovate their products, but some online superpowers provide endless innovation. Do consumers benefit from the market power of firms like Facebook and Google in ways which might not be possible if more firms participated in the market for online products such as search engines and social networks?

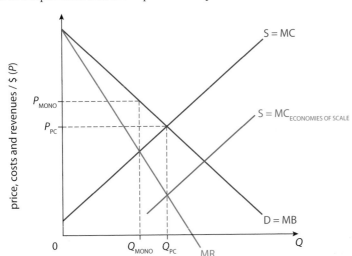

◀ **Figure 9.10**
Economies of scale.

To achieve the same level of output and to lower price to P_{PC}, the marginal costs of the typical monopolist must be lowered through economies of scale. This would shift MC to the right, hypothetically to the point where it sets a quantity and price equal to that of the competitive firm.

Higher profits enable greater research and development

To learn more about economies of scale, visit www.pearsonhotlinks. com, enter the title or ISBN of this book and select weblink 9.3.

Perfectly competitive firms achieve profits only in the short run. Therefore, they have fewer resources available to improve efficiency. In contrast, while the monopolist may have little incentive to invest in research and development, they have much greater capacity to do so because of their long-run profits. If they do invest wisely, these firms may yield even greater profits with new products and services, or may be able to entrench their position with even more significant barriers to entry.

9.8 Monopolies and efficiency

Learning outcomes
- Explain, using diagrams, why the profit-maximizing choices of a monopoly firm lead to allocative inefficiency (welfare loss) and productive inefficiency.

So far, our comparisons of perfect competitors and monopolists have been at the industry level. Our analysis of efficiency will consider the individual firm. This is because the firm-view level allows us to consider the cost and revenue curves that are relevant to discussions of productive and allocative efficiency.

Figure 9.11
Perfect competition *vs* monopoly, allocative and productive efficiency.
a Perfectly competitive firm;
b monopoly.

Figure 9.11 shows each type of firm in long-run equilibrium. For the perfectly competitive firm, this means a condition of normal profits because of the ease of entry and exit. For the monopolist, this most likely means a condition of economic profits because barriers to entry prevent other firms from competing and causing a reduction in profits.

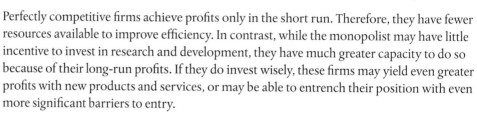

$$P_{MONO} > MC$$
$$P_{MONO} > \text{minimum ATC}$$

Recall that allocative efficiency is achieved by having $P(AR) = MC$ at the profit-maximizing level of output. For the competitive firm, price is equal to marginal cost in the long run, so allocative efficiency is achieved. For the monopolist, at the profit-maximizing level of output, price at Q_{MONO} is considerably higher than marginal cost. This suggests that the monopolist under-produces the good, and would need to produce more to achieve allocative efficiency, but does not in order to maximize profits.

Productive efficiency is achieved when the price at the profit-maximizing level of output is equal to the minimum average costs (P = minimum ATC). For the competitive firm, in the long run, price is at the lowest point of the ATC, and so productive efficiency is achieved. For the monopolist, the marginal revenue curve intersects marginal cost at a quantity less than that needed for the firm to achieve its minimum average total cost. This suggests that the monopoly does not produce enough of the good to achieve productive efficiency.

 ## 9.9 Policies to regulate monopoly power

Learning outcomes
- Evaluate the role of legislation and regulation in reducing monopoly power.

Natural monopoly

Governments will grant exclusive production rights to single firms where a natural monopoly is likely to yield lower costs and more output for consumers. However, even the natural monopolist still has the incentive to set a price above and a quantity below that of a perfect competitor. And, in the case of public utilities, there are likely to be significant extra welfare benefits to all of society to having water, sewage and power enough for all citizens. As a result, most governments subsidize these public monopolies, paying them to provide more services at lower prices.

While perhaps initially counter-intuitive, the policy of subsidizing natural monopolies is widely accepted as a necessary method to achieve greater social good. With this in mind, public monopolies are usually subject to regulation and government oversight.

We don't have a monopoly. We have market share. There's a difference.

Steve Ballmer, CEO of Microsoft

Anti-trust legislation

Economists and governments are highly suspicious of monopolies that occur in the private sphere. As a result, most countries have some degree of anti-trust legislation to protect consumers against anti-competitive behaviour. While the firms prosecuted under these laws rarely qualify as pure monopolies, all of them are seeking a degree of monopoly power by seeking to act as a single firm. They collude and set prices or agree to stay out of each other's markets in ways that drive up profits at consumer expense.

Many mergers between large firms are investigated under these laws (e.g. when major IT companies or airlines want to combine). The laws seek to preserve open competition to keep markets working efficiently. When firms are found to have flouted these laws, punishments are usually in the form of corporate fines, but bosses can sometimes be held accountable. In 2009, the US jailed 35 corporate officers for an average of two years each.

 To access Worksheet 9.1 on regulation of monopoly prices, please visit www. pearsonbacconline.com and follow the onscreen instructions.

9.10 Price discrimination

Learning outcomes
- Describe price discrimination as the practice of charging different prices to different consumer groups for the same product, where the price difference is not justified by differences in cost.

Price discrimination occurs when different people are charged different prices for the same good. There are many examples:

- air travel ticket prices in the same section of a flight can vary tremendously
- movie tickets are cheaper for older people and students
- shoppers willing to spend time cutting out 'coupons' from newspapers enjoy lower prices than those who do not bother.

Whether it agrees with our sensibilities or not, such pricing inequities are rather common. This section examines the conditions necessary for price discrimination, how it works in practice, and evaluates the effects of this pervasive business practice.

Price discrimination occurs when different prices are charged to different consumers for the same good by the same provider.

Necessary conditions for price discrimination
Price-setting ability

The firm must be able to charge different prices to different customers, so it must have some market power. Thus, it cannot be a perfectly competitive firm, which can only charge the market price. As a kind of imperfect competitor, the firm will have a downsloping demand curve, suggesting that it sees a large portion of the market, with customers of many types.

Varied consumer elasticities

There should be a variety of price elasticities of demand among customers. If demand is more rigid among some customers, the price discriminator can, in theory, compel them to pay more than those who are more sensitive about the price. In other words, high-elasticity customers and low-elasticity customers can be charged differently according to their sensitivity to the price.

Where, how, and when you buy airplane tickets makes a difference to the price. Book your tickets the week before a flight, and you will pay more than the traveller who booked months in advance. But if you wait until just hours before the flight, you may get the cheapest ticket of all. If you use a travel agent, the price will differ from what you pay online or over the phone. What accounts for the variety of prices paid by different passengers on the same flight?

Ability to separate consumers

People who were aware of the difference between their higher price and the lower one could take steps to avoid the extra charges. For price discrimination to work, it must be difficult or impossible for those able to buy at the cheaper price to resell at a discount to high-price customers. Firms seek to separate customers in the following ways.

- **Time**. Demand for a service can peak at different times. Christmas is often a high-travel time and the prices of air tickets and hotel rooms rise accordingly. Train and taxi services are often higher at peak travel hours. Taxi service can also be more expensive late at night, when other transport options are unavailable.
- **Age**. A popular form of discount for theatre or movie tickets is that given to children, students and older people. Older people can also receive lower rates on meals, hotels, and a variety of goods. This may be in recognition of the belief that seniors have less money to spend and more time to shop around for the best deals.

- **Income**. Professional services often charge more to high-income clients. Dentists, for example, might charge the children of a low-income customer a fraction of the price charged to rich families. Lawyers perform *pro bono* work (i.e. for low fees or for free) which is subsidized by their wealthier customers.
- **Taste**. A subtle form of price discrimination: producers can market products with only the slightest amount of differentiation and charge significantly higher prices to a willing segment of consumers. This happens in the car market (e.g. cars with special 'sport' styling) or in your local coffee shop (e.g. espresso being much cheaper than a fancy latte).
- **Gender**. Firms sometimes charge different prices for men and women. In some countries, bars are banned from staging 'ladies' nights' where women pay no admission or reduced prices, on the grounds of gender discrimination. Dry-cleaners in America are known to charge men less than women for cleaning shirts. Conversely, Austrian beauty salons have stopped a long-standing practice of charging men more than women for manicures and pedicures. In the EU, insurance companies have recently been told they must stop charging men more than women for car insurance.
- **Location**. Distance between markets means that firms in one market may charge a higher price, based on greater inelasticity of demand. Transport costs make it too costly to ship and resell those goods priced more cheaply into the high-price area.
- **Consumer type**. Airlines are able to discriminate between leisure travellers and business travellers. Leisure travellers are not limited to specific times, so these customers probably have a higher elasticity of demand. Business travellers have less choice about travel times and often pay higher prices as a result. Large industry can be charged lower rates for power than residential customers. This is a form of a volume discount, and could be done to encourage industrial production in the area.

Types of price discrimination
First degree: by customer

First-degree price discrimination occurs when firms are able to charge exactly the maximum price that each customer is willing to pay. This presumes some insight by firms into the precise elasticity of demand for the good. It also presumes the ability of the firm to separate customers individually and charge the exact reservation price for each customer. This type of price discrimination is called perfect price discrimination. Because of the extremity of these assumptions, it may seem an improbable occurrence. It is difficult to imagine that a firm would have the kind of specific insight into the desires of its customers. Being able to separate so distinctly (down to the individual level) also seems unlikely.

Nevertheless, some real-world situations approximate first-degree price discrimination. In the US, car salesmen often have significant discretion over the specific price of any single car on the lot. Effective salesmen talk to buyers and assess their knowledge of the car market, their enthusiasm for the specific car, their income based on their appearance and education level, as well as a number of other visual and verbal cues. This is all geared towards estimating the buyer's price elasticity of demand for the car, so the salesman can charge the maximum price possible.

In theory, the perfect sales force would be able to discriminate the market perfectly, and negotiate the maximum price for each customer. If so, the result would appear as shown in Figure 9.12 (overleaf). This compares the community surplus and revenue differences between perfectly competitive markets and a perfect price discriminator. In a perfectly competitive market, the consumers retain some surplus (triangle a), because firms in the

Figure 9.12
Perfect price discrimination.
a Perfect competition
industry level; **b** perfect price
discrimination industry level.

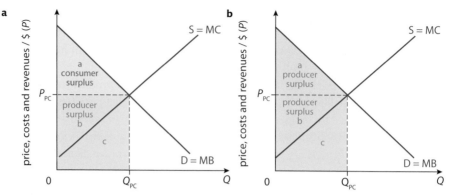

market can only charge a single price. Some consumers will gain extra utility as a result. And total revenue is confined to the area of b + c. However, as a perfect price discriminator, all consumer surplus disappears and goes to the producers, who now gain surplus of a + b. Total revenue is defined by all three shaded areas, a, b, and c. Thus, the firm enjoys significantly higher revenue (and mostly likely higher profits), than if it were charging a single price.

Figure 9.13 demonstrates the advantage to a monopolist who is able to discriminate perfectly. Figure 9.13a shows the profit and surplus levels for the single-price monopolist. The green shaded area represents the consumer surplus and the yellow area the abnormal or economic profits earned by the firm. Figure 9.13b shows the perfectly price-discriminating monopolist. There is no single price for the market on the diagram. Also, here demand is equal to marginal revenue because the firm is not charging a single price for each good, it is charging a different price for each customer. Therefore, the marginal revenue is equal to whatever the next price will be (MR = D).

Figure 9.13
a Single-price monopolist;
b perfectly discriminating
monopolist.

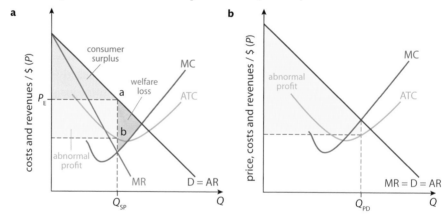

● **Examiner's hint**

First-degree price
discrimination may be rare
in the real world, but it
should be emphasized that
such practice may increase
overall welfare in society.
While there are certainly
losers (e.g. those who end
up paying higher prices
for the product), society
benefits overall as output
approaches a more socially
optimal level, and consumers
who otherwise would be
excluded from a market can
better afford goods that may
improve their welfare.

Several conclusions are evident here.

* Consumer surplus is completely eliminated.
* Profits are greatly expanded.
* Output is greater (Q_{PD} compared to Q_{SP}).
* The area of welfare loss is also eliminated. This suggests that there may be some benefit to price discrimination. The ability to discriminate has allowed the firm to charge the maximum to all its customers, but it will also serve some customers who would not have afforded the product before – quantity Q_{SP} to quantity Q_{PD}.
* Allocative efficiency is achieved with price discrimination when final price = MC.

Examples of this kind of price discrimination include the perfect car salesmen above. Real estate agents, as well as the hagglers in open markets, may also have a similar degree of price-discriminating power.

Second degree: by quantity

Second-degree price discrimination acknowledges the observation that consumers may choose to buy additional amounts of a good if the price decreases. Thus, firms may offer lower prices with the purchase of successively larger quantities: the first batch sold will be at the highest price, the second at a lower price, and so on. Instances of this kind of price discrimination by quantity include:

- 'buy two, get one free' offers in retail markets of food and consumer items (here, buying items in threes reduces the average price, while technically preserving the higher price of the first two units)
- frequent-flyer programmes that award free or reduced rate flights to good customers
- season tickets for concerts or sports team events
- public utility companies charging less for extra units of power or water
- bulk buying on behalf of a company (a manufacturer of large family cars probably pays less per unit for auto-quality steel than does a much smaller sports car company)
- rewards programmes of all kinds, offered by many retail stores, which offer special deals and discounts to loyal buyers.

Figure 9.14 shows the likely results of second-degree price discrimination. Compared to the perfectly discriminating firm, the second-degree discriminator earns extra revenue in distinct blocks. These blocks correspond to the discounted price levels.

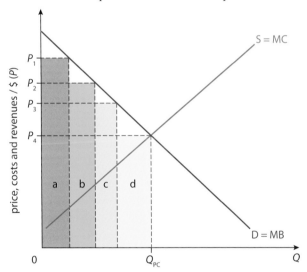

◀ **Figure 9.14**
Second-degree price discrimination.

When compared to first-degree price discrimination, some results are evident. Total revenue increases over the single-price firm. The shaded areas a, b, c and d represent increases in total revenue as the price is lowered for larger quantities. The firm may approach, but not achieve, allocative efficiency ($P = MC$). Further more, it is likely to earn greater economic profits than the single-price firm.

Third degree: by consumer groups

Third-degree price discrimination acknowledges and takes advantage of the fact that different consumer groups have differing price elasticities. It moves to separate the groups and charge them the highest price possible. This type of price discrimination is quite prevalent, and can be seen in:

- bars offering 'happy hours' when drink prices are lower to draw customers in at unusual or off-peak times

- women being charged more for dry cleaning than men
- phone companies offering lower prices at off-peak times (weekends and evenings)
- airlines charging more to customers who book closer to flight date
- restaurants and cinemas charging less to children, elderly people and students.

In each instance, the consumer group being charged differently has different price elasticities. Students and elderly people are more price-sensitive than 30-year-olds. Businesses require phone services during office hours, and so are compelled to pay higher prices than those who are making social calls later in the day or at the weekend. Someone looking to book flights for tomorrow will not have very many options (possible substitutes), and so will pay a higher price than those who shopped for fares weeks earlier.

Figure 9.15
Third-degree price discrimination. **a** Market A; **b** market B; **c** market A + B.

To maximize profits, the firm must take the differing demand elasticities into account. In Figure 9.15, the markets are separated into the inelastic demand group (market A), the elastic demand group (market B), and the combined markets (market A + B).

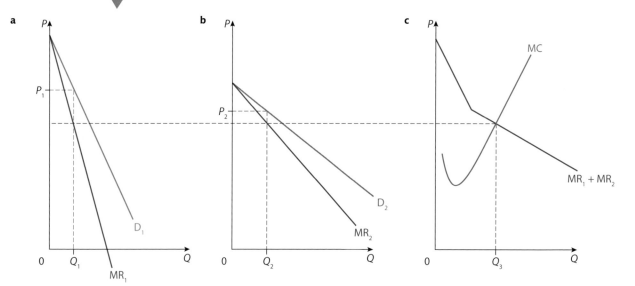

In Figures 9.15a and 9.15b, the marginal revenue curves are shown for each market. In Figure 9.15c, marginal revenues for markets A and B are added together to get the kinked MR curve. Figure 9.15c also shows the firm's marginal cost. Starting with Figure 9.15c, the firm produces the output where $MR_1 + MR_2 = MC$ which equals an output of Q_3. Then, the firm calculates the point where $MR = MC$ for the separate markets, MR_1 and MR_2.

- For Market A, the dotted line shows where MC intersects MR_1, determining an output of Q_1 and a price determined by the demand at Q_1, which is P_1.
- For Market B, the dotted line shows where MC intersects MR_2 at Q_2. At Q_2, the demand determines the price to be P_2. They will influence the price charged through the demand curve and the amount produced through the intersection of marginal revenue and marginal cost.
- P_1 in market A is higher than P_2, reflecting the lower price elasticity of these consumers.
- P_2 in market B is lower than P_1, reflecting the higher price elasticity of demand there.

To access Worksheet 9.2 on everyday price discrimination, please visit www.pearsonbacconline.com and follow the onscreen instructions.

As a result, it appears that profits and total revenue are likely to increase over those of the firm that does not price-discriminate. Allocative efficiency will not be reached, as P will not equal MC in either market. Prices may increase for some groups and decrease for others. As with other forms of price discrimination, this may result in some being drawn into the market who would not otherwise afford it, such as students, children and elderly people.

Evaluation of price discrimination

The results of price discrimination resist simple summary as the effects depend on the type of discrimination practised. Nevertheless, some generalizations can be made.

- **For firms**. Profits and total revenues will increase. It is possible that price discrimination will enhance monopoly power over consumers. Deadweight losses may be reduced or eliminated.
- **For consumers**. Total output increases in first-degree and second-degree price discrimination, and may also increase for third-degree price discrimination. This probably extends the market to consumers who would otherwise miss out, typically those who couldn't pay the single price-equilibrium price. Consumers generally will pay higher prices overall, however, as firms take advantage of their ability to separate the market. Consumer surplus is reduced, sometimes completely.

Overall, it is possible that society benefits from some degree of price discrimination as firms extend output to lower-income groups and welfare loss is reduced. Greater allocative efficiency is sometimes achieved as well. And it is possible that the greater levels of output may inspire the firm to reduce costs and achieve economies of scale.

To access Worksheet 9.3 on price discrimination 101, please visit www.pearsonbacconline.com and follow the onscreen instructions.

CASE STUDY

Market insight

The costs of most of Starbucks coffee drinks are very similar, from the small cappuccino to the largest café latte, costs vary by only a few cents. However, the prices are dramatically different, as the largest latte can be nearly $5.00, with the smallest cappuccino being around $2.50. What's going on? Starbucks is trying to separate the market between price-conscious customers and those who are 'price blind.' By setting distinct prices for slightly different products, Starbucks allows some customers to reveal themselves as having lower price elasticities than others.

Tim Harford, author of *The Undercover Economist* books and columns, sees Starbucks as practising a particularly subtle form of price discrimination.

To learn more about price discrimination, visit www.pearsonhotlinks.com, enter the title or ISBN of this book and select weblink 9.4.

HL EXERCISES

5 **a** Does charging coffee drinkers widely different prices for very similar products qualify as price discrimination?

  b If so, what degree of price discrimination applies here?

PRACTICE QUESTIONS

1 **a** Explain, using an appropriate diagram, why price and marginal revenue are not equal for the monopolist. (10 marks) [AO2], [AO4]

  b Evaluate a government's decision to use anti-trust legislation to break a large technology company up into dozens of smaller companies. (15 marks) [AO3]

2 **a** Explain, using an appropriate diagram, how the monopolist determines the profit-maximizing level of output and price. (10 marks) [AO2], [AO4]

  b Discuss the view that competitive markets are always more efficient than monopolies.

  (15 marks) [AO3]

To access Quiz 9, an interactive, multiple-choice quiz on this chapter, please visit www.pearsonbacconline.com and follow the onscreen instructions.

3 **a** Explain, using an appropriate diagram, why the monopolist would choose to operate in the elastic portion of their demand curve.   (10 marks) [AO2], [AO4]

   b Compare and contrast the different objectives a monopoly may pursue in its price and output decisions.   (15 marks) [AO3]

4 **a** Explain, using examples and an appropriate diagram, the concept of a natural monopoly.   (10 marks) [AO2], [AO4]

   b To what extent do natural monopolies act against the best interest of society?   (15 marks) [AO3]

5 **a** Explain how a third-degree price discriminator will determine price and output.   (10 marks) [AO2], [AO4]

   b Price discrimination of any kind only brings harm to consumers. Discuss.   (15 marks) [AO3]

6 With the aid of at least one diagram, explain one way a consumer might gain from the behaviour of a monopolist and one way a consumer might lose from the behaviour of a monopolist.   (10 marks) AO2], [AO4]

   © International Baccalaureate Organization 2010

7 **a** Explain how a monopolist may earn economic profits in the long run.   (10 marks) [AO2], [AO4]

   b Evaluate the view that, compared to competitive markets, monopolies will always harm the consumer.   (15 marks) [AO3]

8 'Monopoly price is higher and output smaller than is socially ideal. The public is the victim.' (JK Galbraith, 1974)

   a Explain the economic reasoning behind the statement that 'monopoly price is higher and output smaller than is socially ideal'.   (10 marks) [AO2], [AO4]

   b Do you agree that the public is always the 'victim' of monopoly? Justify your answer.   (15 marks) [AO3]

   © International Baccalaureate Organization 2000

10 MONOPOLISTIC COMPETITION AND OLIGOPOLY (HL ONLY)

10.1 Monopolistic competition: assumptions of the model

Learning outcomes

- Describe, using examples, the assumed characteristics of a monopolistic competition: a large number of firms; differentiated products; absence of barriers to entry and exit.

◀ Shoes: they're not all alike, but they all serve essentially the same purpose.

We have so far looked at two extremes in the market: monopoly and perfect competition. Monopoly sits at one end of the spectrum of competition, with the most market power. Monopolies may be inevitable, but they have significant limitations to output and efficiency. Perfect competitors, at the other end of the spectrum, have no real market power, and offer significant efficiency of production and allocation. But they have little capacity for innovation or research because they earn no real long-run profits.

In this chapter, you are going to examine two models that are more commonly found in the real world: monopolistic competition and oligopoly. Our guiding principle of distinction, relative market power, is still in effect here. With that in mind, monopolistic competition can be seen as a step up from perfect competition in terms of market power whereas oligopoly is a step closer to the ultimate market power of a monopoly firm.

Monopolistic competition is a market where there are many firms producing differentiated products and in which there are no barriers to entry or exit.

 A market is monopolistically competitive if there are many firms producing differentiated products and there are no barriers to entry or exit.

Sometimes markets move very quickly from monopolistic to monopolistically competitive. Just a few years ago there was one dominant maker of touch-screen smartphones, Apple. Today over 40 companies produce similar products, each with slightly different features (operating system, type of camera, size of screen). How does such product differentiation give firms like Apple, Samsung, Sony and HTC the power to set their own prices?

Monopolistic competition is based on the following assumptions.

- **Large number of relatively small firms**.
  This trait is shared with perfect competition, without being quite as extreme. The number of firms is high enough that it is unlikely, but not impossible, for one firm to influence the market. Cooperation between firms is not possible as there are too many firms for this to take place.
- **Relatively free entry and exit**. Like perfect competition, there are few barriers to entry and exit. It is rather easy to get into or out of the business.
- **Product differentiation**. This marks the most significant departure from perfect competition, where products are completely identical. Monopolistic competitors strive to differentiate their products in the hopes of deriving some market power (price-setting ability). Product differentiation occurs when consumers perceive a product as being different in some way from other substitute products. Firms differentiate products in a number of ways:
  - *appearance*: shape, colouring, materials, 'look and feel', as well as packaging can influence perceptions of a product
  - *service*: firms can be faster with assistance and sales, or offer additional help with home delivery, product guarantees, and more
  - *design*: products having the same function can be designed for more ease of use or with more fashionable styling
  - *quality*: variations in quality can bring higher or lower market power, depending on the good
  - *expertise/skill*: especially in service industries, the perceived level of skill can significantly differentiate one firm from another
  - *location*: some firms will benefit from location, such as the last gas station for one hundred kilometres, or exchange bureaus and convenience stores in airports
  - *brand reputation/image*: many firms spend advertising money persuading and reminding customers how their products are superior or priced well (creating a brand image can also differentiate one firm from another).

Examples of monopolistically competitive industries include nail salons, jewellers, car mechanics, plumbers, book publishing, clothing, shoes, gas stations, restaurants.

To learn more about monopolistic competition, visit www.pearsonhotlinks.com, enter the title or ISBN of this book and select weblink 10.1.

HL EXERCISES
1   Apply the assumptions of monopolistic competition to three of the industries noted as monopolistically competitive .
2   List three more of your own examples, and note the ways in which these firms attempt to differentiate themselves from their competitors.

10.2   Demand and revenue curves for monopolistic competition

Learning outcomes
- Explain that product differentiation leads to a small degree of monopoly power and therefore to a negatively sloping demand curve for the product.

Monopolistic competition has a combination of the attributes of monopoly and perfect competition. However, the single distinguishing feature of monopolistic competition, when compared with monopoly, is product differentiation. The degree to which a firm can 'create' demand for its goods is the degree to which it can create market power, or price-setting ability. Figure 10.1a shows a perfectly competitive firm with no such power. It is a small firm in a massive market, and the price and demand curve for the firm is set in the overall market. Its demand curve is, therefore, perfectly elastic. Because goods in perfect competition are exact substitutes, any attempt to get a higher price will fail; none of the higher-price goods will sell.

In contrast, firms in the monopoly market face a downward-sloping demand curve (Figure 10.1b). This curve is relatively steep, suggesting a generally inelastic demand for the good. This comes from the fact that the monopolist is the only provider of the good, so no substitutes are available. Thus, demand is relatively more inelastic or rigid.

The firm showing monopolistic competition (Figure 10.1c) is viewed as a hybrid of the previous two. It is relatively elastic; consumers are price-sensitive because there are similar goods available from many producers. However, the firm that successfully differentiates its product may have inspired a belief that its goods are not exactly the same as other goods, and may be somewhat better.

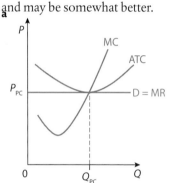
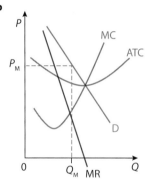
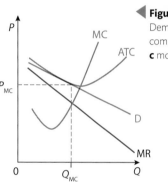

Figure 10.1
Demand for: **a** perfect competition; **b** monopoly; **c** monopolistic competition.

This gives us insight into the behaviour of the monopolistic competitor. A more steeply sloping demand curve, where demand is more inelastic, means more market power. It means more power to set higher prices and earn higher profits. A more inelastic demand for your good, it is logical to conclude, is highly desirable for your bottom line. Firms often advertise to persuade consumers of the uniqueness of a particular brand. By differentiation and advertising, a firm can make its product appear essential or necessary, and thus inspire brand loyalty and inelasticity of demand. Thus, firms can move demand for their product outwards, and make it steeper at the same time.

10.3 Profit maximization in monopolistic competition

Learning outcomes

- Explain, using a diagram, the short-run equilibrium output and pricing decisions of a profit-maximizing (loss-minimizing) firm in monopolistic competition, identifying the firm's economic profit (or loss).
- Explain, using diagrams, why in the long run a firm in monopolistic competition will make normal profit.

The monopolistic competitive firm operates under the same demand, revenue and costs situation as the monopolist, except for their much more elastic demand curve.

Profit and loss scenarios for the monopolistic competitor

- Short-run profits
- Adjustment to long-run normal profits
- Short-run losses
- Adjustment to long-run normal losses

Short-run profits

In the short run, a monopolistic competitor can earn economic profits. Figure 10.2 shows the monopolistic competitor producing quantity Q_E where marginal cost (MC) and marginal revenue (MR) are equal. Like the monopolist, the monopolistic competitor sets the price at that quantity by charging as much as the demand at that quantity will allow, P_E. At Q_E, average total costs (ATC) are below the price P_E, therefore economic profits are being earned. The area of the shaded box gives the total economic profit. In a numerical example, this could be calculated using the formula: total economic profit = $(AR - ATC) \times Q_E$.

Figure 10.2
Monopolistic competition, short-run profits.

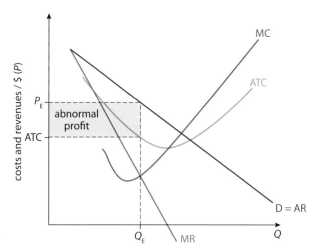

Adjustment to long-run normal profits

Because it is relatively easy to enter and exit the industry, the profit-making industry will get attention and new entrants rather immediately. When this occurs, the demand experienced by each individual firm will decrease, shifting demand to the left. This will cause MR to intersect MC at a smaller quantity, reducing output and profitability for the firms in the industry.

If economic profits are still present, this process of new entrants to the market will continue until all the economic profits have been eliminated. The long-run result is normal profits, as shown in Figure 10.3. Here, demand for the individual firms has shifted to the left so that it is only touching a portion of the ATC curve. Thus, only normal profits, which include all operational costs plus the opportunity costs of having the firm, are earned.

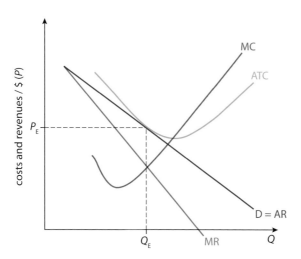

Figure 10.3
Monopolistic competition,
normal profit.

Short-run losses

The monopolistic competitor may also experience losses in the short run. Figure 10.4 shows the firm producing at the profit-maximizing/loss-minimizing point where MR = MC, and so producing Q_E output. The firm sets the price as high as demand will allow at P_E, but this still falls below the ATC experienced by the firm at this level of output. As a result, the firm is clearly making losses, shown by the area of the shaded rectangle.

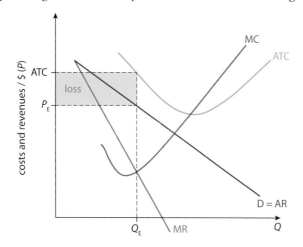

Figure 10.4
Monopolistic competition,
short-run losses.

Adjustment to long-run normal profits

Where firms are losing money, some will be forced to shut down. As firms shut down, the remaining demand is divided between fewer firms; thus the demand curve faced by each firm shifts to the right. This increases output because the new MR = MC quantity will occur at a point to the right of the previous equilibrium. Also, because demand shifts upwards and outwards, the firms remaining in the market will experience a decrease in losses. This process will continue, with particularly weak firms shutting down, and demand increasing for the remaining firms, until a minimum of normal profits are attained. This would describe the long-run equilibrium, shown in Figure. 10.3.

● **Examiner's hint**
Since the long run is basically a series of short runs and monopolistic competitors can earn profits in the short run by differentiating their products, continual differentiation may enable them to earn abnormal profits, even in the long run.

10.4 Price and non-price competition

Learning outcomes
- Distinguish between price competition and non-price competition.
- Describe examples of non-price competition, including advertising, packaging, product development and quality of service.

Firms compete on price when they lower their price in hopes of increasing the demand at the expense of another firm. Firms will also engage in non-price competition when they engage in differentiation and advertising to encourage the purchase of their products.

Generally, the greater the level of differentiation, the more inelastic the demand for the good and the less a firm needs to compete on price. Firms that have trouble differentiating have more elastic demand, and will emphasize lower prices to attract customers.

10.5 Monopolistic competition and efficiency

Learning outcomes
- Explain, using a diagram, why neither allocative efficiency nor productive efficiency are achieved by monopolistically competitive firms.

As with monopoly and perfect competition, we assess the efficiency of monopolistic competition based on whether the firm achieves allocative and productive efficiency. As detailed previously, allocative efficiency is achieved where P or (AR) = MC, and productive efficiency is achieved where P = minimum ATC. When viewed in terms of the long-run equilibrium, it seems clear that neither form of efficiency is achieved in monopolistic competition.

Figure 10.5 shows long-run equilibrium for the monopolistic competitor. The firm produces at a price P_E that is far higher than MC, thus allocative efficiency is not achieved. It also produces a quantity far to the left of where price is equal to the minimum ATC.

Figure 10.5
Monopolistic competition and efficiency.

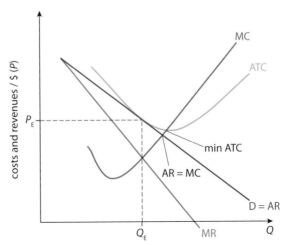

Thus, productive efficiency is not met either. For the monopolistic competitor to achieve either type of efficiency it would need to produce more quantity. Because it produces the amount that maximizes profits, it will not do so.

Excess capacity

For both types of efficiency, the monopolistic competitor produces too little output. It is often said of such firms that they have excess capacity. This excess capacity is derived from the downsloping demand curve, which drops MR far below AR, and shifts the equilibrium quantity backwards. Thus, the greater the differentiation, the steeper the slope of the demand curve and the greater the excess capacity of the firm. Thus, the firm has greater inefficiency. Excess capacity is observable throughout monopolistically competitive industries.

 Monopolistic competition _vs_ perfect competition and monopoly

Examples of excess capacity: nail salons may only have a few customers at a time, hotels are often partially occupied, retail clothing stores have spacious showrooms.

Learning outcomes
- Compare and contrast, using diagrams, monopolistic competition with perfect competition, and monopolistic competition with monopoly, with reference to factors including short run, long run, market power, allocative and productive efficiency, number of producers, economies of scale, ease of entry and exit, size of firms and product differentiation.

Monopolistic competition _vs_ perfect competition

Perfect competition is the closest market structure to the monopolistically competitive one, especially in the number of firms and the ease of entry. How do they compare overall?

- In the long run, both industries achieve only normal profits. Because it is easy to enter and exit, profits are consistently 'competed away' while attrition reduces losses over the long run.
- Perfect competition is more efficient. While the perfect competitor achieves both types of efficiency, the monopolistic competitor achieves neither.
- Choice and variety are greater among monopolistic competitors. Product differentiation provides consumers with a wider range of choices than perfectly competitive firms. This expanded choice is consistent with the free market idea of allowing consumers and producers to act based on price information and the profit incentive.

Monopolistic competition *vs* monopoly

- Monopolists can earn long-run profits because they have barriers to entry. The monopolistic competitor will see profits competed away by new entrants.
- Neither industry is efficient. Their downsloping demand curves restrict output and price goods higher than in perfect competition, lowering efficiency on both allocative and productive grounds.
- The monopolist faces no real competition. Monopolistic competitors do, and so have an incentive to keep costs down and to differentiate.
- Cost-savings of economies of scale are far more likely under monopoly, whereas the monopolistic competitor is unlikely to grow large enough to see these benefits. Meanwhile, the monopoly will have greater capacity to innovate through research and development investment.

10.7 Oligopoly

Learning outcomes
- Describe, using examples, the assumed characteristics of an oligopoly: the dominance of the industry by a small number of firms; the importance of interdependence; differentiated or homogeneous products; high barriers to entry.
- Explain why interdependence is responsible for the dilemma faced by oligopolistic firms – whether to compete or to collude.
- Explain how a concentration ratio may be used to identify an oligopoly.

Oligopolies exist all around us. Any time a few large firms dominate a market, there may be an oligopoly.

One step further up in the realm of market power lies oligopoly. From the Greek for 'few sellers' the oligopoly model represents a significant concentration of market power within a few firms. Oligopoly is defined as an instance where a few sellers dominate the industry. There may be more than a few in the entire market, but a small group exert significant market power.

Oligopoly and monopolistic competition are grouped together in this chapter because it is sometimes difficult to discern a clear difference between the two in the real world. As more areas of local and national economies expand to a global scale, the frequency of oligopoly has increased.

Defining oligopoly: concentration ratios

An oligopoly is a market where a few sellers dominate the market for an identical or differentiated good, and where there are significant barriers to entry.

Oligopoly may have just a few firms in the industry, or it may have several more. A common method of determining whether or not an industry operates under oligopoly conditions is called the concentration ratio. A concentration ratio attempts to quantify the density of market power held by a certain number of firms. It is expressed as CR_X, where X is the number of firms controlling a certain percentage of the market. A value for CR_{10} would tell us how much of the market is controlled by the top 10 firms. The higher the

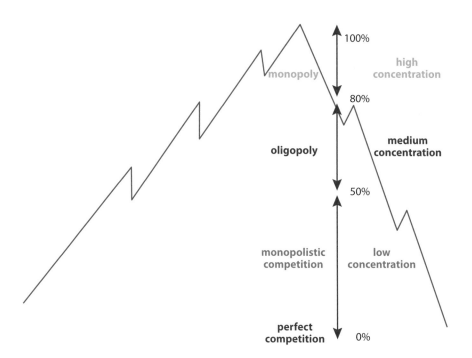

Figure 10.6
Concentration ratio, four
largest firms (CR₄).

percentage, the greater the market power. Typically, the CR_4 is the guideline measure for determining the type of industry. Figure 10.6 (above) shows the CR_4 percentage criteria for classifying a firm as a particular type of industry.

In the UK, one measure of CR_5 data revealed that the top five firm concentration ratios were in the market for sugar and tobacco (99%), gas distribution, oils and fats, and confectionery. This means that 99% of the market for sugar and tobacco is served by the top five firms, a situation that approaches monopoly status. Among the industries with the lowest concentration ratios were metal forging (4%), plastic products, and furniture and construction. This suggests that these industries are rather close to being perfectly competitive.

Assumptions of the model

Oligopolies can be very different. What follows is an attempt to summarize some key points of similarity and comparison.

A few large firms

Concentration ratios can mislead one into thinking that all the firms share their concentration equally. This may be the case. However, it is also possible that one firm is significantly larger than the other three or four. What can be said is that the market is dominated by a small group of firms that are relatively large compared to the others.

Barriers to entry

Oligopolies are characterized by high barriers to entry. These barriers may be the same types as those enjoyed by monopoly firms: high initial fixed costs, access to resources, economies of scale, legal barriers such as licences and patents, and the employment of aggressive anti-competitive tactics.

Differentiated or non-differentiated (homogeneous) goods

Oligopolies may produce differentiated goods, like the monopolistic competitor. Oligopoly industries like soaps, soft drinks and sodas, breakfast cereals, and automobiles all strive

 How can a market with 100 firms be oligopolistic? There are many industries in which a few large firms compete against dozens or even hundreds of small firms. Computer software is an example. The giants Microsoft, Oracle, Adobe, and Google compete for the lion's share of customer demand, but thousands or hundreds of thousands of small firms and individuals develop and sell software to consumers for all sorts of devices, from smartphones to tablets and desktop computers.

mightily to differentiate their products in hopes of drawing customers away from their competitors. Other oligopolies, typically in the provision of raw materials like timber (wood), oil, and aluminium, produce essentially the same good.

Interdependence

An especially distinct feature of oligopolies is that there being relatively few firms in the industry creates a tendency towards especially interdependent relationships between firms. In other words, a firm's actions in the market are watched by its competitors, which may react with actions of their own. Recall that in more competitive markets, the actions of one firm had no effect on the overall market. With an oligopoly, the single firm is large enough, relative to the market, to affect the market by its actions.

Strategic thinking

One result of interdependence is that firms are thereby inclined to think strategically, considering the possible reactions of other firms to any particular initiative. As they do so, the firms have relatively few other firms to monitor, and this leads to a choice between following the strategies employed by most of the other firms, or to compete with them. With oligopoly, firms are regularly tempted to cut prices to win customers away from competitors. This type of price competition can reduce profits throughout the industry, especially if it leads to a protracted 'price war.' An alternative approach would be to keep prices high, either passively or in active coordination with other firms. This is only possible because the collective firms have enormous market power. The strategy can yield extra profits as a result. Thus the oligopoly must choose between opposite strategies, to compete or to collude. This is explored in the remaining sections of this chapter.

10.8 Game theory

Learning outcomes
- Explain how game theory (the simple prisoner's dilemma) can illustrate strategic interdependence and the options available to oligopolies.

One area of economics helps to explain the 'collude or compete' dilemma more clearly. Game theory uses applied mathematics to understand how individuals act strategically, where their success depends on the choices made by others in the so-called 'game.' This simplest form of game theory can illustrate the quandary posed to the oligopolist. Called the prisoner's dilemma, this form of a game has two players, in effect a duopoly.

In this game, Bonnie and Clyde (a famous pair of criminals) are arrested for robbery. They have agreed beforehand that if caught, both will keep quiet in the hopes of reducing their prison sentence. Now both are being interrogated separately, and they face conflicting incentives. Figure 10.7 shows the rewards (in this case, punishments) for the choices each can make paired with the possible choices of their partner.

As they decide what to do, both Bonnie and Clyde face competing incentives. If they hold to their original agreement, to keep quiet and deny all the charges, each will get a small sentence of three years related to their possession of unlawful guns and other weapons. However, each will be tempted to confess, knowing that if they do so while their partner

To access Worksheet 10.1 on oligopolistic scuba operators, please visit www.pearsonbacconline.com and follow the onscreen instructions.

To learn more about oligopoly, visit www.pearsonhotlinks.com, enter the title or ISBN of this book and select weblink 10.2.

Game theory is a branch of mathematics and social sciences that tries to capture behaviour in strategic situations (games).

To access Worksheet 10.2 on game theory and oligopoly, please visit www.pearsonbacconline.com and follow the onscreen instructions.

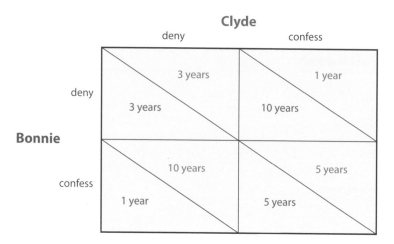

Clyde

	deny	confess
Bonnie deny	3 years / 3 years	1 year / 10 years
confess	10 years / 1 year	5 years / 5 years

Figure 10.7
Prisoner's dilemma payoff matrix.

During the Cold War, game theory was employed by the US and the USSR to try and understand the strategies the other side would use in making decisions regarding use of their nuclear arsenals. The 'delicate balance of terror' reached between the two superpowers, often on the brink of a nuclear attack, demonstrated the same type of interdependence two firms face when competing in an oligopolistic market.

continues to loyally deny the charges, the confessor will have their sentence reduced to one year as a reward for their cooperation. The loyal partner, however, will be locked up for 10 years. If both Bonnie and Clyde act on this incentive and confess, both will be jailed for five years. In this case, since both confessed, the evidence will be quite solid but each will get a reduced sentence for cooperation. There is a powerful incentive at work here. At best, confessing will reduce the sentence to the absolute minimum; at worst, confessing will help to avoid the worst-case scenario of a 10-year sentence. It is likely, but not certain, that both Bonnie and Clyde will confess, as it offers the best payoff given the possible actions by their partner.

The above dilemma can be applied to market duopoly, where firms are deciding whether or not to advertise, a common dilemma for markets with products that are differentiated. In Figure 10.8, two cola companies, Company C and Company P, are assessing their incentives. If the firms split the market 50% each, and neither advertises, then their profits will be $5 billion each.

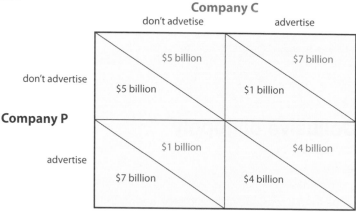

Company C

	don't advetise	advertise
Company P don't advertise	$5 billion / $5 billion	$7 billion / $1 billion
advertise	$1 billion / $7 billion	$4 billion / $4 billion

Figure 10.8
Duopoly payoff matrix, advertising.
Gregory Mankiw, *Principles of Economics*

However, if Company C advertises and Company P does not, it will win over vast numbers of new customers and earn $7 billion, mostly at the expense of Company P, who will earn only $1 billion. (This might be enough profit to allow Company C to buy Company P and become a monopoly.) Of course the reverse is true, as Company P will dramatically out-earn Company C if it advertises and Company C does not. Thus both firms have a strong incentive to compete (advertise) rather than to collude. The dilemma still exists, however, because collusion could bring more overall profit, $10 billion total, than any combination that includes advertising.

Table 10.1 (overleaf) shows the top 10 advertisers (in terms of spending) in the US in 2006.

To learn more about game theory, visit www. pearsonhotlinks.com, enter the title or ISBN of this book and select weblink 10.3.

TABLE 10.1 TOP 10 ADVERTISING SPENDERS, US, 2006

Company (type of product most advertised)	Advertising spending in billions USD
Proctor and Gamble (soap, toothpaste, health and beauty)	4.09
AT&T (cellular network)	3.34
General motors	3.3
Time-Warner (news, television, movies, media)	3.09
Verizon (cellular network)	2.84
Ford (automobiles)	2.58
GlaxoSmithKline (prescription drugs)	2.44
Walt Disney (movies, theme parks)	2.34
Johnson and Johnson (non-prescription drugs, soap, beauty)	2.33
Unilever (soap, tea, diet drinks)	2.10

HL EXERCISES

Examine Table 10.1 and answer the following questions.

3 Which of the firms above do you think fit the criteria for an oligopoly?

4 Select three companies and explain why differentiation is so important to them.

5 What does this suggest about the degree of interdependence in these industries? To what degree to they compete, or collude?

 Collusive oligopoly

Learning outcomes

- Explain the term 'collusion', give examples, and state that it is usually (in most countries) illegal.
- Explain the term 'cartel'.
- Explain that the primary goal of a cartel is to limit competition between member firms and to maximize joint profits as if the firms were collectively a monopoly.
- Explain the incentive of cartel members to cheat.
- Analyse the conditions that make cartel structures difficult to maintain.

This section explores in further detail the distinction between firms that actively cooperate to fix prices and restrict output (i.e. collusive oligopolies) with firms that do not (i.e. non-collusive oligopolies). Collusion need not be explicit, it can be tacit and happen without

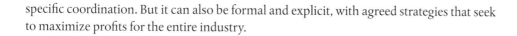

specific coordination. But it can also be formal and explicit, with agreed strategies that seek to maximize profits for the entire industry.

Formal collusion: cartel formation

When oligopolists agree to take specific market action in a coordinated and sustained effort to enhance profits, a cartel is at work. Cartels differ from occasional acts of market coordination by being continuous business arrangements. Firms can coordinate a variety of market behaviours together. They can restrict output to drive up prices. They can fix prices within a specified range. They can decide to restrict innovation and avoid extra costs of research and development. They can agree not to advertise or in any way compete with each other.

When the firms agree to fix the market price and output level, they are essentially acting as one industry. Figure 10.9 shows the collusive oligopoly in action. It functions just as a monopoly would, with firms producing at the profit maximization output where MR = MC, setting price at the demand curve at P_E, and enjoying whatever profits are produced, shown by the shaded area of the diagram.

 Collusion is an agreement, whether formal or informal, between competitive parties to limit competition and raise prices.

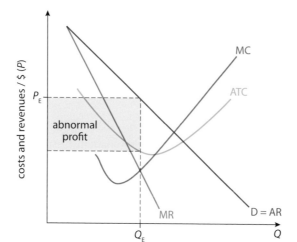

◀ **Figure 10.9**
Collusive oligopoly.

Relatively few industries have been able to obviously and provably achieve this level of market power. Food conglomerates in the 1990s were accused of this kind of price fixing in the market for a particular chemical. Most price fixing is done among firms that could not constitute a full-scale monopoly – for example, British Airways was convicted of price fixing certain charges with Virgin Atlantic in 2007. In the same year, a more conclusive act of near-monopoly price fixing occurred when Heineken, Grolsch, and Bavaria (together serving 95% of the Dutch beer market) were convicted in the EU courts of price fixing.

The most famous and overt cartel is the Organization of Petroleum Exporting Countries (OPEC), a group of 12 oil-producing countries founded in 1965. OPEC regularly meets to set production quotas in the hope of establishing the 'right price' for oil in world markets. OPEC countries possess two-thirds of latent oil reserves, and currently produce one-third of all oil. Thus, they have considerable

OPEC headquarters in Vienna.
▼

229

influence on world oil markets. In fact, OPEC is a useful example to keep in mind when observing the dual tendencies to collude or compete. After agreeing to production quotas with a target oil price in mind, countries are tempted to produce and sell secretly. This, of course, would lower world prices and reduce profits for all.

Difficulties in cartel formation

The paucity of outright collusive cartels provides a clue to the difficulties oligopolists face when attempting to work together in a sophisticated fashion. Price and production fixing is specifically illegal in the EU, the US and the UK, which drives the practice underground, if it is practised at all, in those areas. Also, there is the strong incentive to cheat other firms in the industry. Firms, it should also be noted, are not all alike in their demand and costs situations. Some firms could compete on cost, where other firms need higher prices to survive. Furthermore, if firms successfully coordinate, some industries can draw competition if they are earning dramatic economic profits.

To learn more about collusion, visit www.pearsonhotlinks.com, enter the title or ISBN of this book and select weblink 10.4.

 10.10 ## Tacit or informal collusion

Learning outcomes
- Describe the term 'tacit collusion', including reference to price leadership by a dominant firm.

Informal or tacit collusion occurs when a single dominant firm establishes price leadership. The leading firm sets general price levels, and smaller firms follow with comparable prices. While no specific agreement exists, the informal understanding can endure because the smaller firms resist the urge to cut prices as the dominant firm would be able to survive any price wars. This does not prevent all forms of competition. Firms may still compete on service or brand power, or on another basis of non-price competition. Industries that have seen instances of price leadership include rental cars and breakfast cereals.

Informal collusion, while perhaps more common than the formal kind, is still somewhat difficult to achieve. Cost and demand differences among firms cause each firm to have their own incentives. Firms are still tempted to cheat. And this kind of price fixing may also be illegal.

Avis is one of the major players in the world of international car hire.

10.11 Non-collusive oligopoly

Price competition

Non-collusive oligopoly occurs when firms do not cooperate and, therefore, exist in a strategic environment where one must consider the actions and reactions of other firms at all times. When firms do not actively collude, the dual tendencies to compete and collude are in force. Firms face the choice described in the prisoner's dilemma. However, it is also possible to show this situation in a diagram (Figure 10.10).

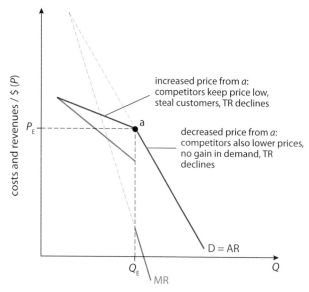

increased price from *a*:
competitors keep price low,
steal customers, TR declines

decreased price from *a*:
competitors also lower prices,
no gain in demand, TR
declines

Figure 10.10
The kinked demand curve.

Here the oligopolist faces a dilemma regarding price and output. We should assume that the firm is itself a price leader or that price leadership has already been established at P_E (point a on the demand curve). The firm faces two new possible options with regard to price. It could increase the price from point a (P_E). Note that the demand curve is then flatter from this point, suggesting that the firm will face more elastic demand. Why? Because the other firms in a non-collusive oligopoly would not necessarily follow this lead and increase prices also. Instead, they would stay at the lower price position, and the price-increasing firm would see its market share, as well as total revenue (TR), decrease. Therefore, increasing the price seems like a bad idea to the non-collusive oligopolist.

If the firm tried to decrease the price from point a, they would be lowering price in hopes of stealing market share from other firms. This would be borne out as more TR and probably more profit. However, the demand curve below point a is quite steep. The steeper slope is not good news for the firm. In response to the decreased price (which appears to

 Think about your favourite fast-food restaurant. When was the last time you remember the prices changing? Why do fast-food chains have little incentive to raise their prices? Why do they have little incentive to lower their prices? How does the kinked demand curve model of non-collusive oligopolies help explain the fact that fast-food prices rarely change?

be an aggressive action to the other oligopolists), competitors also lower their prices. The result of this is a price war, which lowers TR for each firm, as firms find they are lowering prices without earning any new customers.

So, if an oligopolist tries to show price leadership and increase prices, no competitors will follow. If the firm decides to cheat and lower prices, other firms will follow with price cuts and reduce everyone's revenue. Thus, the firms in the non-collusive oligopoly still have a tremendous incentive to keep prices stable, to do nothing that will upset this delicate balance. Firms in this situation are left primarily to compete on a basis other than price.

Figure 10.10 has no specified cost curves. Presumably, the firm will only operate if it is earning at least normal profit in the long run. But if firms have little control over their pricing, this is where firms may be able to increase profits – by lowering their costs. Thus, it is possible that such oligopolies will focus on non-price competition as well as cost-efficiency as their primary means of competing.

Non-price competition

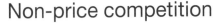

Oligopoly firms often seek ways other than price to maximize profits (non-price competition as for the monopolistic competitor, page 222). Service, design and appearance, quality, and brand power are among the most typical aspects of non-price competition. Evidence of non-price competition among oligopolists occurred in the early decades of commercial flight, when most airlines were heavily regulated on the prices they could charge customers. As a result, airlines competed in every other way possible, including offering lavish meals, with beverages. Only after deregulation did 'budget' airlines offer an alternative, with no meals and reduced services, to attract price-conscious customers.

Furthermore, as with monopolistic competition, actual differences in product are only important insofar as they are perceived to be different by consumers. This is where advertising plays a pivotal role in oligopoly as well as monopolistic competition. Firms spend lavishly with the purpose of convincing the public of sometimes rather small differences in products. Recall that they do so in the hope of yielding some extra economic profit (at least temporarily, until the competitor copies or counters the innovation), or of preventing a loss of market share (the fate of firms that choose not to compete).

That said, the impulse to differentiate can be defended on the basis of consumer choice. In short, society may not need several dozen breakfast cereals, nor a plethora of shaving creams, but consumers do apparently enjoy having the variety.

Advantages and disadvantages of oligopoly

While oligopoly tends to have the most complicated and elusive type of firm, it is possible to establish some areas of criticism and possible benefit.

Disadvantages

Disadvantages to oligopoly are the apparent lack of allocative and productive efficiency. Like monopoly and monopolistic competition, the downward-sloping demand curve of the oligopolist (kinked though it may be) has the same effect. It raises price above marginal cost ($P > MC$), and so allocative efficiency is not achieved. It also brings the profit-maximizing level of output to the left of where ATC is at its minimum. Thus, productive efficiency is also not achieved. The other major problems with oligopoly involve the tremendous incentives to coordinate and collude. These incentives seek merely to take

New examples of product differentiation are popping out at us all the time. You may have a new flat-screen TV. But if it's up to the TV manufacturers, you'll be dropping it off at the dump soon and buying a new 3D TV. The battle for consumers in the electronics market may take place in the third dimension in the near future, as more and more devices come equipped with 3D screens.

To learn more about non-price competition, visit www.pearsonhotlinks.com, enter the title or ISBN of this book and select weblink 10.05.

To access Worksheet 10.3 on creative destruction, please visit www.pearsonbacconline.com and follow the onscreen instructions.

advantage of the firm's market size, and to discourage the competition that could yield innovation and efficiency.

Advantages

Oligopoly, like the monopolist, may earn continuous economic profits as a result of the barriers to entry. Thus, firms do have the economic resources to conduct research and development. It is, therefore, possible that firms that do invest in innovation may yield some economies of scale that could ultimately yield lower prices for consumers.

PRACTICE QUESTIONS

1 Analyse to what degree monopolistically competitive firms are considered allocatively and productively efficient. (10 marks) [AO2], [AO4]

2 Using a game theory payoff matrix, explain how firms in an oligopoly face strategic choices. (10 marks) [AO2], [AO4]

3 Why do some oligopolistic firms engage in non-price rather than price competition? (10 marks) [AO2], [AO4]

© International Baccalaureate Organization 2002

4 **a** Explain the difference between short-run equilibrium and long-run equilibrium in monopolistic competition. [10 marks] [AO2], [AO4]

   b 'Perfect competition is a more desirable market form than monopolistic competition.' Discuss. [15 marks] AO3

© International Baccalaureate Organization 2007

5 **a** Explain the differences between monopolistic competition and oligopoly as market structures. (10 marks) [AO2], [AO4]

   b Discuss the differences between a collusive and a non-collusive oligopoly. (15 marks) [AO3]

© International Baccalaureate Organization 2005

To access Quiz 10, an interactive, multiple-choice quiz on this chapter, please visit www.pearsonbacconline.com and follow the onscreen instructions.

11 MEASURING NATIONAL ECONOMIC PERFORMANCE

 11.1 ## The circular flow model of income

Learning outcomes
- Describe, using a diagram, the circular flow of income between households and firms in a closed economy with no government.
- Identify the four factors of production and their respective payments (rent, wages, interest and profit) and explain that these constitute the income flow in the model.
- Outline that the income flow is numerically equivalent to the expenditure flow and the value of output flow.
- Describe, using a diagram, the circular flow of income in an open economy with government and financial markets, referring to leakages/withdrawals (savings, taxes and import expenditure) and injections (investment, government expenditure and export revenue).
- Explain how the size of the circular flow will change depending on the relative size of injections and leakages.

Three Gorges Dam – as this model shows, it is a project of enormous scale. Consequently, it is a symbol of great national achievement for China.

Every year, the US business magazine *Forbes* publishes a list of the world's richest individuals. In 2010, the list was headed by Carlos Helu of Mexico, Bill Gates and Warren Buffett of the US, then Murkesh and Lakshmi Ambani of Mittal of India. In creating the list, *Forbes* has a methodology for assessing the net worth of the world's billionaires and ranking them accordingly.

There are many organizations that attempt to make similar assessments about countries. The OECD, World Bank, IMF, and other groups have all developed and published their assessments of each country's economic performance. Even the Central Intelligence Agency (CIA) gathers its own statistics and (paradoxically) publishes this information openly for all to use.

The matter is not trivial. In a modern society, improving the overall level of economic performance is perhaps the single most important job of every government. All governments attempt to 'keep score,' in other words, to assess their performance against measurements of the well-being of their people. Many governments, especially democratic ones, rise and fall on the fortunes told by economic data.

In this chapter you will look at some methods of keeping score and evaluate the values and limitations of such data.

In Chapter 1, you looked at the circular flow model of the economy showing the movement of resources and money through the economy. In that simplified model, the economy was roughly divided into two types of market, with two types of economic agents interacting (households and firms). In the goods and services market, households bought goods and services, and in exchange paid money to the firms. In the market for factors of production, firms buy land, labour, capital and entrepreneurship from households. Households, in a free market economy, own these factors, and thus earn income in the form of rent, wages, interest and profits, respectively. Money flows in one direction while goods, services and factors of production flow in the other.

The model helps to reinforce a few critical ideas about the nature of a modern economy. First, that for every transaction, a payment for one side is income to the other. It also follows that interruptions to the factor market will affect the demand for goods and services. For example, a decrease in profits will reduce incomes to households, who will then spend less in the product market.

The basic concepts of the circular flow model are as follows.

- In the product market, households are exchanging money payments for the goods and services provided by companies.
- In turn, firms are buying the factors of production (land, labour, capital, and entrepreneurship) from households. When they do so, they make factor payments in the form of rent, wages, interest and profits, respectively.

Additional elements

We can now introduce additional elements into the model to make it more realistic.

The previous model was self-contained but the new model will acknowledge that there are other actors in the system and that money exits and enters the system in a variety of ways. Money that exits the system is referred to as 'leakages,' while money that enters the system is called 'injections.'

The government sector: taxes and spending

Probably the single largest actor not included in the old model is the government. The government has a profound impact on even the most avidly free market economies. Governments draw tax money from the population, a leakage of income out of the model. However, that money should eventually re-enter the model as government spending on everything from salaries to infrastructure. (Even if we assume that some of the money is lost through corruption, it may also eventually re-enter as consumer spending.) This idea, that the flow of money never truly escapes the model, is one that holds true with the other new actors in the model.

The foreign sector: imports and exports

The previous model assumed a closed economy, hardly a realistic notion in a world of increasingly globalized trade. If we assume that some of the money spent in either the factor or product market is spent on imported goods, then that income will leak from the system. However, roughly the same amount of money should enter in the form of exports sold to other countries. This tendency towards a balance of import and export flows is explained in more detail in Chapter 23. For now, it is sufficient to acknowledge the leakage and injection that takes place with the addition of the foreign sector to the model.

The financial sector: savings and investment

Some consumers save a portion of their money, rather than spend it. Savings would slow down the flow of expenditure and eventually income. However, money that is saved in banks is made available to borrowers. These borrowers then inject the savings back into the economy in the form of investment, whether as capital goods or by the purchase of housing by households. Thus the leakages of savings re-enter the system through loans made by the financial sector.

Figure 11.1 illustrates the new, more complicated circular flow model, one that includes injections and leakages via three sectors: the government, foreign and banking sectors. Injections are insertions of money into the circular flow and include government spending, export purchases, and investments. Leakages are the diversions of money outside the circular flow and occur when the government collects taxes, imports are purchased, or when people save money. Figure 11.1 shows the government sector taking taxes away from firms and households, then injecting the money into the flow again. It shows imports leaking money out of the economy, while exports inject it back in. It shows savings leaking out of the economy, while investment from the savings inject it back in.

To access Worksheet 11.1 on the circular flow model, please visit www. pearsonbacconline.com and follow the onscreen instructions.

Figure 11.1
Circular flow model with leakages and injections.

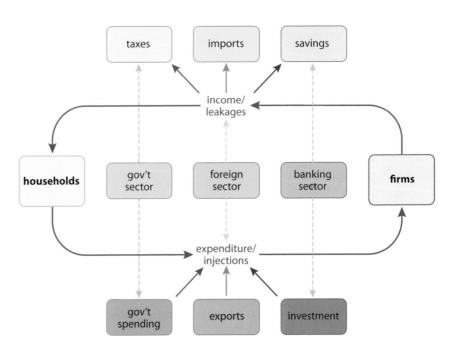

While the new model is still a simplified one, it makes an allowance for some realities. If one sector leaks more than it injects, the flow merely becomes smaller. For example, if imports are greater than exports, the flow may be reduced. If government spending, an injection, is greater than taxes in any given year, the flow will increase. Of course, in that event, most governments will borrow money to do the spending. So it is likely that, in some future year, taxes will be more than spending to pay off the debt. Although there is a tendency for the leakages and injections to be equal, in the real world it is unlikely that they will be at any particular time.

 To learn more about the circular flow model, visit www.pearsonhotlinks.com, enter the title or ISBN of this book and select weblink 11.1.

 # 11.2 The measurement of economic activity: GDP, GNP and GNI

Learning outcomes

- Distinguish between GDP and GNP/GNI as measures of economic activity.
- Distinguish between the nominal value of GDP and GNP/GNI and the real value of GDP and GNP/GNI.
- Distinguish between total GDP and GNP/GNI and per capita GDP and GNP/GNI.
- Examine the output approach, the income approach and the expenditure approach when measuring national income.
- Evaluate the use of national income statistics, including their use for making comparisons over time, their use for making comparisons between countries and their use for making conclusions about standards of living.
- Explain the meaning and significance of 'green GDP', a measure of GDP that accounts for environmental destruction.
- (HL only) Calculate nominal GDP from sets of national income data, using the expenditure approach.
- (HL only) Calculate GNP/GNI from data.
- (HL only) Calculate real GDP using a price deflator.

The circular flow model illustrates the essential idea that all the spending in the economy will roughly equal all the income received. The identity of output as equivalent to the value of income may at first seem odd, or an overly tidy result. However, when viewed at the level of an individual transaction, the identity becomes clearer. Consider the purchase of an apple from your local market for $1. This price represents the value of the output to you, the consumer. To the seller, it represents income. Some portion of that $1 goes to the grower, transporter, wholesaler and final market. This income may go to pay wages, to profits, even to rent. Thus, we can say that spending on output must, at the same time, represent income to the factors of production.

 National income accounting is a term that describes a set of principles and standards used by countries to measure their production and income.

When economists set out to add up the value of a country's economic output, they have an enormous task. The equivalence of expenditure to income guides them as they seek to check the validity of their conclusions. With this in mind, economists have three main methods of counting national income:

- the spending (expenditure) approach
- the income approach
- the output approach.

Gross domestic product (GDP) is the value of all final goods and services produced in a country within a given time period.

Each of these seeks to ascertain the value of output or income in a given year, in the hopes of quantifying the level of activity in the economy. Each approach seeks to measure the country's gross domestic product (GDP) – the total value of all final economic production in a country in a given year.

The expenditure approach

The expenditure (spending) method counts the total spending on final new goods and services in a given year. Final goods are ready for consumption; this category does not include goods that will be input goods or are raw materials for other production. Apples bought at the grocery store count as final goods, apples sold to a baker for apple pie are not counted until they are sold in their final form. This approach places such spending into four broad categories:

- **Consumption (C)**. Consumption includes the durable and non-durable goods and services purchased by private individuals and households.
  - *Durable goods*: these are generally defined as goods that last more than one year. Large appliances like refrigerators and televisions, as well as automobiles, are considered durable goods.
  - *Non-durable goods*: goods that do not last as long as a year are considered non-durable goods. Rapidly consumed goods like food, magazines, health and beauty products, soaps and detergents, are all examples of non-durable goods.
  - *Services*: services are actions performed by a firm. Legal services, insurance, sales firms, healthcare and education are all examples of services counted in GDP statistics.

- **Investment (I)**. Investment refers to spending by firms and households.
  - *By firms*: on capital goods like equipment, buildings, machinery.
  - *By households*: on housing and new construction. This is included because housing has resale value, unlike most other private consumption, so buyers view it more in terms of personal investment.

- **Government spending (G)**. Government spending is all spending on government purchases, which includes salaries for workers as well as capital goods spending. Not included are transfer payments. Transfer payments (tax revenue redistributed to pensioners, veterans and the unemployed) do not represent any new production and are thus excluded.

- **Net Exports (X – M)**. Net exports count all exports as an inflow and thus an increase in GDP while subtracting imports as an outflow and a decrease in GDP. Therefore, it can be expressed as:

Net exports = export revenues (X) – import payments (M)

The expenditure approach can be expressed as:

$$GDP = C + I + G + (X - M)$$

An example of the expenditure method is shown in Table 11.1. This shows the spending totals for each sector in the US economy for 2009. For the US, a free market economy, the largest spending sector is consumption. This is typical of free market economies. Next is government spending, then private investment, and net exports. Net exports is expressed as a negative number (–386 billion USD), which means that the US imported that much more than it exported in that year.

TABLE 11.1 EXPENDITURE APPROACH: US, 2009

Expenditure category	Billions USD
personal consumption expenditure (C)	10 001
gross private domestic investment (I)	· 1 590
government expenditures (G)	2 914
net export goods and services (X – M)	–386
gross domestic product	14 119

US Bureau of Economic Analysis, 2010

EXERCISES

1   Identify the percentage values that each sector contributes to the GDP total.

2   Research your own country's spending approach GDP.

3   Calculate the percentage values for each sector. Are they different from the one above? Why do you think this is true?

The income approach

The income approach to national income accounting attempts to count GDP through the market view of the circular flow of income. In other words, if all spending on goods and services must be income to the firms and individuals receiving payment, it must be possible to arrive at an accurate GDP number by counting the income received in a given year.

The income approach roughly approximates to the returns for factors of production described in Chapter 1. Wages, interest, rent and profits are the factor payments made for labour, capital, land and entrepreneurship, respectively. Table 11.2 shows the income approach to national income accounting for the US in 2009. These numbers give us a net national income of $10 993 billion. Added to this total are business taxes (since they represent production) and fixed capital consumption (another term for depreciation – an accounting term that reflects the drop in value for assets as they become used or worn). Capital is consumed so some spending goes to the replacement of that capital. Some minor statistical adjustment is also made. The total is equivalent to the GDP number arrived at by the expenditure method in Table 11.1. This confirms the equivalence that enables GDP to be counted via the expenditure approach because, for each transaction, the expenditure is income to the factors of production.

TABLE 11.2 INCOME APPROACH: US, 2009

Income category	Billions USD
compensation of employees (i.e. wages) (W)	7 819
rents (R)	274
interest (I)	982
proprietors' income (P)	1 012
corporate income taxes	255
dividends	612
undistributed corporate profits	39
national income	10 993
indirect business taxes	1 081
consumption of fixed capital	1 861
net foreign factor income	5
statistical discrepancy	179
gross domestic product	14 119

US Bureau of Economic Analysis, 2010

The output approach

The output approach takes a completely different view when adding the overall level of economic activity. Like the other approaches, the output approach seeks to ascertain the total value of all final goods and services produced in a year. When adding production, however, it would be easy to double count by counting goods that are intermediate goods and then counting the final product. To avoid this, economists attempt to identify the value added at each stage of the production process.

For a simple example, let's consider the production of a car, for which an astonishing number of small parts and components are required. Starting from the beginning, raw materials of metals and plastics are created. Many auto parts suppliers take the raw form of these goods and shape them into something useful. This is the value added by that producer. The car-maker then assembles all the parts into a finished car, adding significant value along the way. Table 11.3 shows how double counting could lead to inflated GDP results.

TABLE 11.3 OUTPUT APPROACH *VS* DOUBLE COUNTING	
Output approach: value added/euros	**Addition of all expenditures: double counting/euros**
(a) labour 900	(a) labour 900
(b) parts 6500	(b) parts 6500
(c) engineering and research 3000	(c) engineering and research 3000
(d) marketing and advertising 1200	(d) marketing and advertising 1200
(e) value added by car company 1400	(e) final selling price 13 000
total = a + b + c + d + value added = 13 000	total = a + b + c + d + final price = 24 600

Using the output approach, the contribution at each level of production is counted. With the approach shown on the right, each level is counted but then the final selling price is counted rather than just including the value added. The result is nearly double that found using the output approach.

Economists seek to assess the value added at each level and add that to GDP. Table 11.4 shows the output approach to national accounting for the US in the year 2009. Here the totals reflect the final new production by industry. The final total approximates the totals for the other approaches, after some adjustment for statistical discrepancy.

TABLE 11.4 OUTPUT APPROACH: US, 2009	
Output category	**Billions USD**
agriculture, forestry, fishing, hunting	99.6
mining	196.1
utilities	184.3
construction	518.6
manufacturing	1 215.2
transportation, warehousing	337.9
wholesale trade	706.1
retail trade	812.4
information	423.2
professional and business services	1 684.8
finance. insurance, real estate, rental and leasing	1 901.5
educational, healthcare, social assistance	1 244.8

Output category	Billions USD
arts, entertainment, recreation, accommodation, food services	453
other services	352
government	1 897.2
rest of world	146.3
national income	*12 173*
capital consumption	1 861
statistical adjustment	85
gross domestic product	*14 119*

US Bureau of Economic Analysis

EXERCISES

4   Find the top five industries, by level of production, and calculate their percentage of total GDP.

5   Research the output approach for your home country.

6   Calculate the same top five industries and their percentage contributions to total GDP.

7   How are they similar to those above? How are they different?

Why measure economic performance?

The compilation of good economic data is not easy. It requires enormous administrative work, as well as persistent and rigorous mathematical analysis. It can also be quite expensive. The US government's primary agency for national income accounting, the Bureau of Economic Analysis, spends nearly $100 million dollars a year to do this job. A logical question is whether this kind of information is worth that kind of money or, as an economist would say, is the opportunity cost too high? There are three main reasons for measuring economic performance.

- **Information is political power**. Accurate data gives people the ability to understand or interpret their own experience of the economy. This kind of information may help people understand fiscal policies that affect their lives. It also empowers voters in democratic countries to assess the effectiveness of their leaders and make more informed voting choices. In a year when it seems as though everyone knows someone who has lost their job, it is useful to know that unemployment is statistically much higher than usual. And voters can make judgements based on this information.
- **Evaluation of economic performance**. Policymakers and economists of all kinds can use the data to evaluate the overall performance of the economy. Making good policy to affect the economy depends on good information as the basis for those decisions. This is a dimension of positive (rather than normative) economics that everyone agrees on – the need for accurate data. Furthermore, when agencies openly publish the methods used to obtain the data, it allows experts to determine the full value of the information.
- **Making policy adjustments**. Politicians regularly refer to this kind of economic data in order to craft effective legislation. For example, lawmakers who want to soften the impact of major job losses will want to know the areas of greatest loss, the types of worker affected most often, and other relevant data that a good information-gathering bureau can provide. With strong data, policymakers can better predict the effectiveness of a given policy proposal.

Gross national product (GNP) is the market value of all the products and services produced in a time period by the labour and capital supplied by the residents of a country.

GNP *vs* GDP

We defined GDP as the total value of all final economic production in a country in a given year. But we haven't yet explored what is actually meant by 'country'. GDP measures production within the borders of a country, regardless of who owns the factors of production. Thus, Ireland's GDP may count the production of many English-owned firms that have factories or outlets in Ireland. And Irish firms operating in England add their production to English GDP.

Gross national product (GNP) attempts to measure the flow of income based on actual ownership of the factors of production. GNP statistics do this by subtracting from GDP any payments to foreign factors of production. At the same time, it adds any factor payments from domestically owned factors of production located in other countries. In our Irish example, Irish production in England would be subtracted from English GDP and added to Irish GDP to help arrive at Irish GNP. The term for this is 'net property income' from abroad, which takes the sum of income from domestically owned assets abroad, minus the income from foreign-owned assets within the country. It is possible to summarize the method of accounting for GNP as:

GNP = GDP + net property income from abroad

Table 11.5 illustrates the calculation necessary to arrive at GNP totals. In this case, income receipts are a net positive (in other words, they add to the overall income of the US).

TABLE 11.5 GROSS NATIONAL PRODUCT: US, 2009	
Category	**Billions USD**
gross domestic product	14 119.0
plus: income receipts from US firms in the rest of the world	629.8
minus: income receipts from foreign-owed assets in the US	–483.6
gross national product	14 265.3

US Bureau of Economic Analysis

The data above can be shown as a flow of income across borders. For GNP, the ownership of production factors is paramount, and receipts of income are measured to gain an accurate understanding of the income flows experienced by a country. Figure 11.2 shows how US income earned in the rest of the world (ROW) flows back to the US. At the same time, to get the net effect, US GNP figures must subtract the income receipts of firms in the US but owned by the rest of the world.

Gross domestic product refers to all production *domestically*, or within the geographical area. Gross national product suggests that *nationality of ownership* is paramount for this measure. Countries that have a much higher GNP than GDP are likely to have workers or firms overseas who send income back to home country accounts. Correspondingly, the presence of foreign workers and firms, and the profits and income they repatriate, is

Figure 11.2
GDP – net income = GNP.

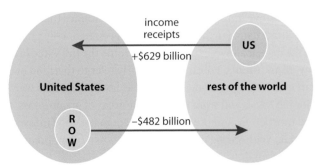

lower by comparison. Countries with higher GDP than GNP may have significant foreign presence, in either workers or companies. Therefore, they suffer a net income loss when GDP is compared to their GNP. Net income is reduced by the outflow of foreign-earned income on the country's soil.

Net national product (NNP)

Economists also manipulate the data to better understand the quality of a country's economic performance. In reality, part of a country's production goes to the replacement of capital goods that have been used or are wearing down. This does not actually count as a contribution towards new production, and so may overestimate the magnitude or impact of the GNP numbers.

 Net national product (NNP) is the market value of production supplied by labour and capital supplied by the residents of a country, minus the depreciated value of capital goods.

For example, the reinforcement of a major river dam may be counted as the provision of goods and services. The effect, however, is to maintain a level of service that already existed. The wearing down of capital goods is called depreciation. Economists have complicated methods of determining the degree to which a sector of the economy may be paying to repair or replace old capital goods. This measure appears in Tables 11.2 and 11.4 as 'consumption of fixed capital' or 'capital consumption.' When economists subtract these numbers from the overall output, they are trying to assess the level of truly new production.

Net national product can therefore be calculated by deducting the capital consumption from the gross national product.

net national product = gross national product – capital consumption

So, for the US in 2009,

US net national product (2009) = 14 265 billion – 1861 billion = 12 404 billion

Thus, when spending on the replacement of old goods and services is factored out, the total level of truly new goods and services spending is revealed. Why is this important? In some years, spending on depreciation can be quite high. In those years, it's possible that new investment is comparatively low. It is new investment, in particular, that creates new productive capacity. Therefore, the net numbers for both GNP and investment give economists a notion of how strong this economy will be in future years, not just the current one.

HL EXERCISES

8 **a** Using the table below, calculate GDP using the expenditure approach.

CATEGORY	BILLIONS USD
government spending on goods and services	900
transfer payments	320
gross private domestic investment	410
income from foreign employment	750
taxation	340
consumption	950
imports	330
exports	150
net property income from abroad	–270
saving	60

  b Now calculate GNP/GNI.

Nominal *vs* real GDP

Economists hope to determine the actual level of output of cars, houses, clothing, medical services and everything else produced in a year. Because we count this output by tabulating the transaction prices charged at the time, price changes can distort attempts to measure actual output. Economists seek to distinguish between the nominal value of output as it is shown in current prices (which may be inflated or deflated), with 'real' output. Real GDP refers to measures of output that factor out price changes and should show a more accurate measure of the true output from one year to the next.

For example, consider a car manufactured and sold for $20 000 in a given year. One year later, exactly the same car is manufactured and sold for $25 000. Simple mathematics tells us that the price has increased by 25%, but nothing about the car is actually 25% greater than in the previous year. So a nominal measure of GDP for the second year would count this 25% increase in price as a contribution to national income, when really it is only an increase in the price of the good. This is how price increases from inflation could cause GDP to be overestimated, causing us to think the economy is doing better than it is in reality.

Nominal GDP is the value, in current prices, of all final goods and services produced in a country within a given time period.

When taking account of goods and services in their current prices, economists use the term 'nominal.' Nominal GDP is simply the value of goods and services produced in a country in a given year, expressed in the value of the prices charged for that year. In the example above, the new car would have added $25 000 to nominal GDP, providing an artificially high estimate of how much output actually grew.

Real GDP is the value, in constant prices, of all final goods and services produced in a country within a given time period, usually measured against prices of predetermined base year.

- Price level increases (inflation): nominal GDP exaggerates value of output compared to real output.
- Price level decreases (deflation): nominal GDP underestimates value of real output compared to actual output.

Per capita GDP

While real GDP adjusts for price changes, economists use another measure to adjust for population size. After all, we would expect countries with large populations to have large economies: their supply of labour resources and human capital can be a tremendous advantage. At the same time, it is important for a country to be growing enough economically to keep pace with the growth of its population. Table 11.6 shows the GDP rankings of the top five economies by sheer size for 2009.

TABLE. 11.6 GDP COUNTRY RANKING, 2009	
Country	**Total GDP/trillions USD**
US	14.2
Japan	5.0
China	4.9
Germany	3.3
France	2.6

***Per capita* GDP** is an average based on the national income of the country divided by the country's population.

Note that the Japanese and Chinese economies are approximately equal in size at about $5 trillion per year (2009 was the last year that China was ranked behind Japan). We could thus mistakenly infer that the Japanese and Chinese have roughly the equivalent material standard of living. This conclusion would ignore the fact that China divides that income between 1.2 billion more people than Japan does.

A simple mathematical adjustment provides a more accurate picture. By dividing GDP by the population size, we arrive at a *per capita* (per head) income for the country. *Per capita* GDP is the amount of national income divided by the population size. It gives us a better sense of the approximate standard of living in a country than total GDP does (Table 11.7).

	Country (*per capita* rank)	Total GDP/trillions USD		Country (total rank)	Per capita GDP/USD
	TABLE 11.7 A CROSS-COMPARISON OF SOME OF THE LEADERS IN TOTAL GDP AND *PER CAPITA* GDP, 2009				
1	US (6)	14.2	1	Luxembourg (68)	105 350
2	Japan (14)	5.0	2	Norway (24)	79 089
3	China (86)	4.9	3	Denmark (29)	55 992
4	Germany (13)	3.3	4	Ireland (37)	51 049
5	France (12)	2.6	5	Netherlands (16)	47 917

The World Bank

You can see that among the leaders in total GDP, none rank in the top five in *per capita* GDP and only the US is in the top 10. China ranks 86th in the *per capita* GDP list, suggesting that its enormous GDP is averaged out among an equally enormous population. Among this group, only China ranks as a developing country. You should note that among the *per capita* leaders, all are relatively small countries and all are in Europe.

Clearly, real GDP *per capita* gives us a better picture of how productive a country is on a per person basis. However, an average measure like *per capita* GDP can hide as much as it reveals. Income is actually distributed unequally, sometimes dramatically so. In many countries, a far-above-average level of income among a small elite is the norm, while the vast majority of the population live on much less than the average. In far too many places, people live on less than $1 per day. So, while *per capita* information provides us with more information about a country's economic performance, and allows us to better compare one country to another, it tells us little about the income distribution within the country itself.

Country groups by income

International aid and development agencies such as the World Bank have attempted to categorize the world's countries by income level. The World Bank has set benchmark levels of income to distinguish between high-, upper-middle-, lower-middle-, and low-income countries. The stated aim of the World Bank is to promote the economic development of countries in the bottom three categories to increase their standards of living and to further other development goals (economic development is covered in more detail in Chapters 26–29). Briefly put, development refers to the standard of living that is typical in a country, and includes income, education levels, health and life expectancy.

As one might expect, income level and development status are highly correlated: most of the richest countries tend to have the highest development levels. But the correlation is not perfect. Many countries have incomes that suggest a development level far greater than has actually been achieved. And some countries have done well enough in the categories of education and health to supersede the disadvantage of a low income level.

Tables 11.8a–d (overleaf) show the World Bank grouping of countries according to *per capita* income levels (GNI *per capita*). The criteria for the four levels are:

- low-income economies – GNI *per capita* $995 per year or less
- lower-middle-income economies – GNI *per capita* $996 to $3945
- upper-middle-income economies – GNI *per capita* $3946 to $12 195
- high-income economies – GNI *per capita* $12 196 or more.

Some of the richest countries in the world are among the nations with the most unequal distribution of income. China, the US and Brazil have very large economies producing vast amounts of output, but with massive inequalities in income distribution. At the other extreme, some of the poorest countries have the highest levels of income equality. Pakistan, Bosnia and Bulgaria are all in this bracket (income equality is explored in Chapter 16).

TABLE 11.8a WORLD BANK COUNTRY INCOME: LOW-INCOME COUNTRIES (GNI < 995 USD)		
Afghanistan	Guinea	Nepal
Bangladesh	Guinea-Bissau	Niger
Benin	Haiti	Rwanda
Burkina Faso	Kenya	Sierra Leone
Burundi	Korea, Dem Rep.	Solomon Islands
Cambodia	Kyrgyz Republic	Somalia
Central African Republic	Lao PDR	Tajikistan
Chad	Liberia	Tanzania
Comoros	Madagascar	Togo
Congo, Dem. Rep	Malawi	Uganda
Eritrea	Mali	Zambia
Ethiopia	Mauritania	Zimbabwe
Gambia, The	Mozambique	
Ghana	Myanmar	

The World Bank

TABLE 11.8b WORLD BANK COUNTRY INCOME: LOWER-MIDDLE-INCOME ECONOMIES (996 TO 3945 USD)		
Angola	India	São Tomé and Principe
Armenia	Iraq	Senegal
Belize	Jordan	Sri Lanka
Bhutan	Kiribati	Sudan
Bolivia	Kosovo	Swaziland
Cameroon	Lesotho	Syrian Arab Republic
Cape Verde	Maldives	Thailand
China	Marshall Islands	Timor-Leste
Congo, Rep.	Micronesia, Fed. Sts.	Tonga
Côte d'Ivoire	Moldova	Tunisia
Djibouti	Mongolia	Turkmenistan
Ecuador	Morocco	Tuvalu
Egypt, Arab Rep.	Nicaragua	Ukraine
El Salvador	Nigeria	Uzbekistan
Georgia	Pakistan	Vanuatu
Guatemala	Papua New Guinea	Vietnam
Guyana	Paraguay	West Bank and Gaza
Honduras	Philippines	Yemen, Rep.
Indonesia	Samoa	

The World Bank

TABLE 11.8c WORLD BANK COUNTRY INCOME: UPPER-MIDDLE-INCOME ECONOMIES (3946 TO 12 195 USD)		
Albania	Dominican Republic	Namibia
Algeria	Fiji	Palau
American Samoa	Gabon	Panama
Antigua and Barbuda	Grenada	Peru
Argentina	Iran, Islamic Rep.	Romania
Azerbaijan	Jamaica	Russian Federation
Belarus	Kazakhstan	Serbia
Bosnia and Herzegovina	Lebanon	Seychelles
Botswana	Libya	South Africa
Brazil	Lithuania	St. Kitts and Nevis
Bulgaria	Macedonia, FYR	St. Lucia
Chile	Malaysia	St. Vincent and the Grenadines
Colombia	Mauritius	Suriname
Costa Rica	Mayotte	Turkey
Cuba	Mexico	Uruguay
Dominica	Montenegro	Venezuela, RB

The World Bank

TABLE 11.8d WORLD BANK COUNTRY INCOME: HIGH-INCOME ECONOMIES (> 12 196 USD)		
Andorra	Germany	New Caledonia
Aruba	Gibraltar	New Zealand
Australia	Greece	Northern Mariana Islands
Austria	Greenland	Norway
Bahamas, The	Guam	Oman
Bahrain	Hong Kong SAR, China	Poland
Barbados	Hungary	Portugal
Belgium	Iceland	Puerto Rico
Bermuda	Ireland	Qatar
Brunei Darussalam	Isle of Man	San Marino
Canada	Israel	Saudi Arabia
Cayman Islands	Italy	Singapore
Channel Islands	Japan	Slovak Republic
Croatia	Korea, Rep.	Slovenia
Cyprus	Kuwait	Spain
Czech Republic	Latvia	Sweden
Denmark	Liechtenstein	Switzerland
Estonia	Luxembourg	Trinidad and Tobago
Equatorial Guinea	Macao SAR, China	Turks and Caicos Islands
Faeroe Islands	Malta	United Arab Emirates
Finland	Monaco	UK
France	Netherlands	US
French Polynesia	Netherlands Antilles	Virgin Islands (US)

The World Bank

The usefulness and accuracy of GDP data

Does wealth make one happy? This age-old question arises quite appropriately when the question of GDP and well-being is raised. In other words, to what degree does a higher GDP *per capita* mean a better quality of life? Economists use the term 'welfare' to describe a way of speaking about the quality of life. We would assume that, *ceteris paribus*, more income is better than less income. And so we could easily conclude that countries ranked according to *per capita* income levels could be ranked in the same order for welfare.

However, it is possible to argue that GDP masks our view of a country's true welfare. Some have contended that GDP has little relevance for the everyday person. Economists have noted that national income accounting sometimes exaggerates well-being, and sometimes underestimates it. And sometimes, it misleads in unpredictable ways.

GDP overestimates well-being

GDP exaggerates well-being in the following ways.

- **Adding clearly negative social behaviours and transactions as net positives for GDP**. These include the environmental damage from many kinds of production. Furthermore, the money spent to jail criminals, fight wars, and consume unhealthy products all add to GDP figures, without contributing much to overall welfare.
- **Under-reporting the loss of natural resources**. The degradation of rainforests is more likely to count as increased production than the despoiling of potentially valuable resource bases and watersheds. Strip mining of metals, the destruction of endangered species, and other environmentally harmful endeavours count as adding to GDP, though their long-term consequences may be devastating.

Green GDP

One interesting and potentially groundbreaking benchmark for measuring the performance of an economy is the concept of 'Green GDP'. Green GDP seeks to estimate a country's aggregate output while factoring in any output losses created by environmental degradation. The approach seeks to establish a monetary value to soil erosion, water pollution, loss of biodiversity, and contributions to climate change. The approach is controversial because losses from environmental damage are very difficult to estimate accurately (Chapter 6). The concept received a large publicity boost when Wen Jiabao, China's premier, announced in 2004 that Green GDP would replace traditional GDP measures. However, a few years later China's government dropped the focus on Green GDP due to arguments among Chinese officials over the estimated losses. Despite this change of focus, it is expected that attempts to frame economic growth in terms of sustainability (of which Green GDP is an example) will continue as pressure on global resources continues to grow.

GDP underestimates well-being

GDP underestimates well-being in the following ways.

- **The fact that people are living longer is not included**. Longer life-expectancy is a universal goal among all countries. Most countries have seen their life expectancies climb. GDP does not tell this story.
- **Black and underground market activity is not included**. For some countries, the estimated value of black market or parallel market activity is quite high. The income generated in these markets is not counted in final GDP numbers.

What can a tiny kingdom high in the Himalaya teach us about economic well-being? The Kingdom of Bhutan, under its revered King Jigme Dorji Wangchuk, began measuring gross national happiness (GNH) in 1976. The country focused its government growth and development policies on various areas of wellness, instead of on the output of goods and services. The areas of wellness measured under GNH include environmental, physical, mental, workplace, social, political and economic wellness.

HOW BIG IS THE BLACK MARKET?	
Country	**Estimated shadow economy/%GDP, average 1990–93**
Developing economies	
Africa	
Nigeria and Egypt	68–76
Tunisia and Morocco	39–45
Central and South America	
Guatemala, Mexico, Peru and Panama	40–60
Chile, Costa Rica, Venezuela, Brazil, Paraguay and Colombia	25–35
Asia	
Thailand	70
Philippines, Sri Lanka and Malaysia	38–50
Hong Kong and Singapore	13
Transition economies	
Central Europe	
Hungary, Bulgaria and Poland	20–28
Romania, Slovakia and Czech Republic	7–16
Former Soviet Union	
Georgia, Azerbaijan, Ukraine and Belarus	28–43
Russia, Lithuania, Latvia and Estonia	20–27
Developed economies	
Greece, Italy, Spain, Portugal and Belgium	24–30
Sweden, Norway, Denmark, Ireland, France, the Netherlands, Germany and UK	13–23
Japan, US, Austria and Switzerland	8–10

International Monetary Fund

Can a natural disaster be good for a country's GDP? In March 2011, a massive earthquake struck off the coast of Japan, triggering a tsunami that wiped out dozens of communities along Japan's northeast coast. There are now estimates that the disaster may lead to an increase in Japan's GDP of hundreds of billions of dollars. Does such destruction really create economic welfare? Or is there something flawed about how we measure it?

- **Unpaid output is not counted**. In other words, GDP only counts paid work. Volunteer efforts, which can be considerable in some countries, are not counted. Housework and childcare done by mothers or fathers, while clearly desirable socially, are not counted. Furthermore, the work of poor farmers in subsistence economies is not counted, since these families will eat the product of their labour, rather than sell it. GDP figures show countries with subsistence economies to be poorer than perhaps they really are.
- **GDP adds market transactions, regardless of the quality of output**. Technological and managerial techniques are expected to improve the choice, quality and safety of most of our material goods and services. These improvements are unseen by GDP figures, which merely report the type of output and the purchase price value of the product. For example, consider the calculators that many students use in their maths classes. To replicate the collective computing power of these small, inexpensive machines in a single computer would require a machine the size of a room, costing thousands of dollars.

GDP lacks information

GDP does not provide enough information. Below are examples of why not.

- **The composition of the output is a mystery**. Does the economy produce large amounts of demerit goods, such as weapons or cigarettes, or spend money controlling the damage of natural disasters and criminal activity? Or instead does the economy have more hospitals and doctors than average, with greater access to education? Raw GDP numbers do not communicate the types of production, or their value to society.

- **GDP does not measure many aspects of quality of life**. Community activity that includes participation in groups beyond the family (e.g. social clubs, volunteer participation, church groups, sports or outdoor activities) have been linked to greater life satisfaction. Faith in government, trust in the law and the courts, a sense of mutual responsibility among citizens, all these are desirable qualities for any country, but are unreported by national income data.

- **GDP provides no information about the distribution of income**. In other words, GDP cannot tell us who gets what. Income distribution can be very divergent, with a large gap between rich and poor. Furthermore, there is no guarantee that those at low income levels are experiencing growth along with growth in GDP. While GDP may grow, individuals at the lowest levels of income may experience decreased standards of living.

- **GDP, as commonly reported in the news, does not account for purchasing power**. This caveat is explained in detail below.

In 1984, the newly launched Apple IIC computer sold for $1295. In today's money, that would be over $3000. For $3000 today, you can buy a top-of-the-range Mac desktop or high-end Macbook. Of course, you'd get a machine with millions of times the computing power of the 1984 model. How do GDP figures account for the change in the quality of computers over the decades? Or do they?

Robert Kennedy, a US Senator, ran for President and made the following protest about the over-importance of national income accounting numbers.

Too much and too long, we seem to have surrendered community excellence and community values in the mere accumulation of material things. Our gross national product ... if we should judge America by that – counts air pollution and cigarette advertising, and ambulances to clear our highways of carnage. It counts special locks for our doors and the jails for those who break them. It counts the destruction of our redwoods and the loss of our natural wonder in chaotic sprawl. It counts napalm and the cost of a nuclear warhead, and armoured cars for police who fight riots in our streets. It counts Whitman's rifle and Speck's knife, and the television programs which glorify violence in order to sell toys to our children.

Yet the gross national product does not allow for the health of our children, the quality of their education, or the joy of their play. It does not include the beauty of our poetry or the strength of our marriages; the intelligence of our public debate or the integrity of our public officials. It measures neither our wit nor our courage; neither our wisdom nor our learning; neither our compassion nor our devotion to our country; it measures everything, in short, except that which makes life worthwhile. And it tells us everything about America except why we are proud that we are Americans.

Speech at the University of Kansas, 1968

- List some of the ways Kennedy argues that GDP overestimates the national welfare.

- List some of the ways that social welfare is not measured by GDP at all, according to Kennedy.

- What kind of argument is Kennedy making?

- Do you agree with this argument? Why?

- Would your parents agree with this argument? Why?

- Which of our ways of knowing (sense perception, reason, emotion and language/symbols) do GDP statistics appeal to?

- Which ways of knowing does Kennedy's assertion appeal to?

Purchasing power parity comparisons

Of course, when doing any national income accounting, the statisticians involved tabulate output and incomes in the local currency. But comparisons between Norwegian kroner and Thai baht would be meaningless; the figures need to be translated into a single currency – the US dollar.

While this translation makes comparisons more useful, the spending power of money in Norway may be very different from that in Thailand. Resources, goods and services may be more expensive in Norway than in Thailand, which means that more income may be needed to enjoy the same standard of living as in Thailand.

Purchasing power parity (PPP) is the theory that, in the long run, identical products and services that are sold in different countries should cost the same.

To more accurately reflect the buying power of any amount of income, and so to better assess the standard of living in a country, economists use a comparison called purchasing power parity (PPP). PPP is based on the law of one price, which states that an identical good in one country should cost the same in another country, and that the exchange rate should reflect that price. (The implications this has for the way we look at exchange rates are covered in Chapter 22.) For our purposes here, PPP is a tool to assess more accurately the standard of living available for a given amount of income in a country.

For example, the Norwegian equivalent of $100 (Nk588) may buy a certain amount of food, perhaps three pizzas. The Thai baht equivalent of $100 (THB2994) may buy six pizzas, because staple goods are cheaper in Thailand. This means that every $100 of income earned in Norway will buy less in goods and services than the same amount in Thailand. Therefore, Norway's high GDP *per capita* (Table 11.7) may overrate the standard of living there.

When the purchasing power is factored into national income measures, it produces a refined view of the GDP data. Table 11.9 shows how the *per capita* GDP leaders in Table 11.7 are adjusted for purchasing power in their countries. In each case, PPP adjustments reduced the *per capita* GDP. All of these are West European countries, where the cost of living tends to be higher.

TABLE 11.9 MORE DEVELOPED COUNTRIES: *PER CAPITA* GDP ADJUSTED DOWNWARDS WITH PPP ACCOUNTING			
Country	**GDP *per capita*/thousands USD**	**GDP *per capita* PPP/thousands USD**	**Rank**
Luxembourg	105 350	84 003	1
Norway	79 089	55 672	3
Denmark	55 992	36 762	13
Ireland	51 049	41 278	6
Netherlands	47 917	40 715	7

Table 11.10 shows examples of several countries whose *per capita* GDP is revised upwards when purchasing power is taken into account.

TABLE 11.10 LESS DEVELOPED COUNTRIES: *PER CAPITA* GDP ADJUSTED UPWARDS WITH PPP ACCOUNTING		
Country	**GDP *per capita*/thousands USD**	**GDP *per capita* PPP/thousands USD**
China	3744	6 838
Romania	7500	14 198
India	1134	3 275
Ethiopia	345	936
Russia	8800	18 945

In the case of less developed countries, many are shown as having GDP *per capita* PPP greater than their nominal GDP values. This suggests that when ranked against other countries nominally, their potential standard of living is underestimated. What these countries also share is some level of underdevelopment. In some, like Ethiopia and perhaps India, the vast majority of people live in conditions of absolute poverty. In others, like Romania and Russia, portions of the country are underdeveloped, although the country itself is considered a lower-middle-income country.

To learn more about gross domestic product, visit www. pearsonhotlinks.com, enter the title or ISBN of this book and select weblink 11.2.

Economists pay attention to PPP-adjusted GDP levels to better understand the attainable quality of life, and to compare one country with another in this regard.

Calculations (HL only)

Using price indices to determine real GDP

To solve the problem created by nominal GDP accounting (nominal *vs* real GDP, page 244), economists have developed methods to adjust the numbers to reflect real output. This is done by factoring out the changes in price levels for any given year, whether they are increases or decreases. To get a clear sense of how prices have changed over a given period, a price index is constructed for a set of goods. This index tracks changes in the prices of the same goods, every month, year by year. When prices rise, the index number increases; as prices decrease, it falls. A full explanation of how price indices are created is given in Chapter 14, page 302.

Briefly put, the 'basket' of goods depends on the type of price changes being monitored. Most countries track consumer prices. A consumer price index follows prices for the goods typically consumed by an urban household. It includes spending on rent/mortgage, transport, food, clothing, medical care, and entertainment, among many other things. Another type of index, often called the GDP deflator, watches price changes across all goods in the economy.

Because prices are relative measures, economists arbitrarily pick one year as a starting point. This is called the base year. Changes in price for all goods and services are measured against the benchmarks established in the base year. When the basket prices are compiled again, the final numbers are expressed as a change in percentage compared to the base year.

For example, the year 1 (base year) index is established as 100. If prices in year 2, the year after the base year, have increased overall by 5%, the year 2 index number will be 105. If prices were to increase further and the year 3 index was 107, it would mean that prices increased by 7%, compared to the base year. Again, index numbers reflect changes in prices measured against base year prices.

The GDP deflator and real GDP

To accurately measure real output, it is necessary to use a price index to factor out any changes in prices hidden by nominal GDP, price changes that might distort our picture of the nation's production. The GDP deflator, because it measures prices across the economy, is the index created to accomplish this.

It is called a deflator because the more common experience of most economies is some type of price inflation. So, normally, this index will deflate nominal GDP to a smaller number that reflects the actual output. This price-adjusted number is called real GDP, because inflation (or deflation) has been factored out, and the number better reflects the true measure of goods and services produced that year. The formula for calculating real GDP is:

$$\text{real GDP} = \frac{\text{nominal GDP}}{\text{GDP deflator}} \times 100$$

So, assume, for example, that in year 1, nominal GDP is $500 billion and the GDP deflator is 100. In year 2, nominal GDP is $560 billion and the GDP deflator is 103 (reflecting a 3% increase in prices over year 1), how much would GDP have really increased?

$$\text{real GDP year 2} = \frac{560}{103} \times 100 = \$543.6 \text{ billion}$$

So, the nominal GDP of $560 billion in year 2 has been deflated to the real GDP of $543.6 billion. Similarly, nominal GDP for every year is either deflated or inflated using the GDP deflator. Figure 11.3 (overleaf) shows how this might be visualized.

Figure 11.3
Nominal GDP to real GDP.

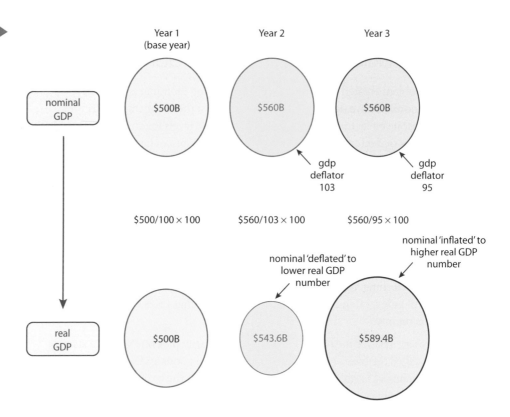

- The green bubbles represent the base year situation. Nominal GDP is divided by the base year index number (100) and multiplied by 100, leaving it unchanged.

- The orange bubbles represent year 2. In year 2, the nominal GDP is $560 billion. The price index of that year (103) shows some price inflation, so the nominal GDP requires deflating. The formula calculations reveal that the real GDP is $543.6 billion.

- The purple bubbles represent year 3. In year 3, nominal GDP is the same as in year 2, $560 billion. However, it appears that the price level of the economy has decreased significantly compared to years 1 and 2. As a result, the real GDP is inflated by the GDP deflator index, revealing a rather higher real GDP of $589.4 billion.

Real GDP growth rate

Using only nominal numbers, a relatively small amount of inflation or deflation can alter the way we view the economy. A rise of nominal GDP by 2% could, in reality, be a recessionary decrease of GDP when inflation is running at 3%. In real terms, the economy would have actually shrunk by 1%. With this in mind, economists are likely to use real GDP or real GNP numbers when comparing one economy to another, or the performance of a single economy from year to year.

EXERCISES
Calculate real GDP for the following examples.
9   Nominal GDP: $431 billion; index (GDP deflator): 115
10   Nominal GDP: $1.5 trillion; index (GDP deflator): 106.5
11   Nominal GDP: $900 million: index (GDP deflator): 97

Calculating rates of growth or decline

How well is your country's economy actually doing? To answer that question, most people will compare recent performance to the previous year or the past few years. However GDP is counted, what matters most is that there is progress, or economic 'growth.' Growth is defined as an increase in real GDP from one year to the next. It is found by using a rate of change equation.

The rate of change in anything can be calculated by dividing the change in a value by the original value and multiplying the result by 100. Take for instance, the rate of change in your height over the last year. If last year, you were 175 cm tall, and this year you are 180 cm tall, the rate of change in your height is simply the change in height from last year to this year, divided by your height last year, multiplied by 100. So, to find the rate of change in your height, you would solve the equation:

$$\text{Rate of change in height} = \frac{180 - 175}{175} = 0.028 \times 100 = 2.8\%$$

Your height increased by 2.8% over the last year.

The same formula can be used to calculate the rate of change in anything. We used a similar calculation to determine elasticities, since the formula for elasticities requires that we compare the percentage changes in prices and the percentage changes in quantities. To review, percentage change of a variable (x) is always found using the following equation:

$$\text{Percentage change in } x = \frac{\text{New value of } x - \text{initial value of } x}{\text{initial value of } x} \times 100$$

Using this simple equation, we can find the percentage changes in important macroeconomic indicators, such as real gross domestic product (Chapter 15) and the price level (Chapter 14). Thereby, we can determine the economic growth rate of a country between one period of time and another, or we can calculate the rate of inflation by measuring the percentage change in a price index over time.

Use the equation above for measuring percentage changes to complete the following exercise.

EXERCISES

12 Calculate the values for the yearly GDP growth rate and yearly inflation rates for years 2–5 in the table below.

YEAR	REAL GDP/ BILLIONS	GDP GROWTH RATE	PRICE INDEX	INFLATION RATE/%
1	543	–	100	–
2	560		105	5
3	551		109	
4	559		123	
5	615		104	

Economic growth is deemed important enough to be a macroeconomic policy goal for most governments. But not all countries are equal when it comes to growth. A study by Columbia professor Jeffery Sachs has found that there is an inverse relationship between the *per capita* income level of a country and the rate of growth, meaning poor countries grow more rapidly than rich ones. Why do you think this might be?

11.3 The business cycle

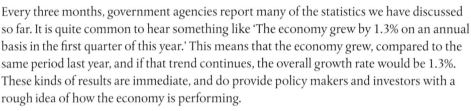

Learning outcomes

- Explain, using a business cycle diagram, that economies typically tend to go through a cyclical pattern characterized by the phases of the business cycle.
- Explain the long-term growth trend in the business cycle diagram as the potential output of the economy.
- Distinguish between a decrease in GDP and a decrease in GDP growth.

Short-term results

The business cycle is a term used to describe the fluctuations of national income from expansion to contraction to recovery. It can also be associated with changes in price levels.

Every three months, government agencies report many of the statistics we have discussed so far. It is quite common to hear something like 'The economy grew by 1.3% on an annual basis in the first quarter of this year.' This means that the economy grew, compared to the same period last year, and if that trend continues, the overall growth rate would be 1.3%. These kinds of results are immediate, and do provide policy makers and investors with a rough idea of how the economy is performing.

Economies tend to rise and fall, sometimes with warning and at other times rather suddenly. The fluctuations of GDP, and the important changes in employment that go with it, are often called the business cycle because there sometimes appears to be a pattern of increase and decrease, followed by another increase and then decrease. However, as Figure 11.4 shows, a more appropriate term might be the business roller-coaster.

Figure 11.4
The business cycle.

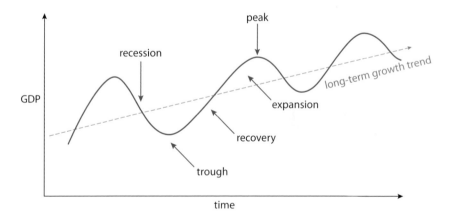

Economic growth, as you now know, is an increase in the GDP from one year to the next. But sometimes, the economy shrinks. A recession is defined as two consecutive quarters of declining national output. In other words, if the economy contracts over a six-month period, it is classified as a recession.

The casual reader of news may fail to make an important distinction between a recession (a decrease in the *size of the economy*) and decrease in the *rate of growth*. For example, when the economy grows at 4% one year and at 2.5% the next, the economy has still grown, just at a decreased rate. To qualify as a recession, the 'growth' rate must be negative (e.g. −1%) over six months.

Why is this distinction important? The term 'recession' carries significant power over consumer and market confidence. When there is danger that the economy is going to slip into recession and actually shrink, the news is met with concern by businesses and governments. Less economic activity means there will be fewer workers required to produce because less output requires fewer workers. This raises the fear of unemployment and workers losing their jobs because there's not enough activity in the economy. It is at these points that policymakers usually try to change policy and attempt to help the economy in some way.

The lowest point of a recession is called the recessionary trough. Nobody really knows exactly when this point is reached until output has begun to recover and growth has resumed. Hopefully, the economy will quickly enter a recovery period. Recovery is defined as an increase in GDP from a recessionary level to match the level of output produced before the recession. The economy is getting back to where it was before the contraction.

Should the economy grow beyond its previous level of output, it is called expansion. For most countries, expansion happens in short bursts, rather than a steady level of growth. When these bursts hit an apex (just before a recession) it is called the peak. Again, no one really knows (until afterwards) when a peak has been reached, and economists speculate about the length of any given economic boom period.

The specific ways an economy can go from recession to recovery, and from recovery to expansion to recession again, are covered in detail in the chapters that follow. What is important to note here is that short-term fluctuations, the highs and lows of the roller-coaster, can be quite dramatic. Many believe that it is the job of policymakers to 'smooth out' the peaks and troughs, to allow for more economic stability whenever this is possible.

Just as important, however, is that the roller-coaster moves generally upwards. Look again at Figure 11.4 and note the trend line that runs through the peaks and troughs. The trend line suggests that, over the long term, the economy is growing. This may mean an improvement in the standard of living. Or it may not, if the growth in population is faster than the growth of GDP, or if the income is going to only the richest few. However, whatever the distribution or the population, for the population of a country to improve its quality of life, growth is a necessary ingredient. As you will discover later in our discussion of economic development, growth is a necessary, but not sufficient, condition for a better life.

To learn more about the business cycle, visit www.pearsonhotlinks.com, enter the title or ISBN of this book and select weblink 11.3.

What is the empirical evidence for the existence of the business cycle? How do we decide whether this evidence is sufficient?

To access Quiz 11, an interactive, multiple-choice quiz on this chapter, please visit www.pearsonbacconline.com and follow the onscreen instructions.

PRACTICE QUESTIONS

1. Distinguish between GDP and GNP/GNI as measures of economic activity. (10 marks) [AO2]

2. Explain how the circular flow of income functions as a system with leakages and injections. (10 marks) [AO2]

3. a Explain the process by which nominal GDP is calculated and distinguish it from real GDP. (10 marks) [AO2], [AO4]

   b To what extent do measures of GDP accurately estimate national well-being? (15 marks) [AO3]

4. a Analyse the use of GNP *per capita* to compare living standards in different countries. (10 marks) [AO2]

   b Assess the value of two other measures which might be used to compare living standards. (15 marks) [AO3]

   © International Baccalaureate Organization 2001

AGGREGATE DEMAND AND AGGREGATE SUPPLY

12.1 ## Aggregate demand

Learning outcomes
- Distinguish between the microeconomic concept of demand for a product and the macroeconomic concept of aggregate demand.
- Construct an aggregate demand curve.
- Explain why the AD curve has a negative slope.

In April of 2010, US president Barack Obama's chief economic advisor, Dr Christina Romer, delivered a speech at Princeton University about the causes of the deep recession the US was in the midst of at the time, when unemployment was at 10%, its highest level in decades.

This rise in long-term unemployment is readily explained by the prolonged collapse of aggregate demand. When hiring rates are very depressed, workers who lose their jobs are unlikely to find work quickly, and thus face a substantial chance of becoming long-term unemployed ... Thus, the rise in long-term unemployment is the almost inevitable consequence of the severe recession ... There is every reason to expect that long-term unemployment will come back down when aggregate demand recovers.

Dr Christina Romer, Princeton University 2010

Christina Romer knows the importance of aggregate demand to the US economy.

This is just a short passage from her speech at Princeton, in which Dr Romer uses the phrase 'aggregate demand' 11 times. What is this all-powerful aggregate demand, and how can its collapse lead to the deepest economic crisis in much of the world since the Great Depression?

Aggregate demand (AD) is the total demand for the goods and services of a nation at a given price level and at a given period of time. Unlike demand, which represents the willingness and ability of consumers to buy a particular good or service, aggregate demand collects together the demands of *all* consumers for *all* the goods and services produced in a nation *in a given time period at different price levels*. AD measures the demand for a nation's output of goods and services in a year or its gross domestic product (GDP). There is an inverse relationship between AD and the price level: at lower price levels there is greater amount of output demanded and at higher price levels the amount of output demanded decreases.

Demand for a nation's output includes the demand for consumer goods and services by households *and* the spending of all other stakeholders, domestic and foreign, on a nation's goods and services. To better understand how AD can change in a nation we need to examine each of its components separately.

12.2 The components of AD

Learning outcomes
- Describe consumption, investment, government spending and net exports as the components of aggregate demand.

Demand for a particular nation's goods and services comes from households, but also from firms, the government and from foreign consumers of domestically produced goods, services and resources. There are four components that make up a country's aggregate demand.

- **Consumption (C)**. Consumption measures all spending by domestic households on goods and services during a particular period of time. Consumption is a function of household income and the marginal propensity to consume (MPC).
- **Investment (I)**. Investment is short for gross domestic private investment, and measures the total spending by firms on capital equipment. The level of investment in a nation is a function of the national output and the interest rate.
- **Government spending (G)**. Government spending is short for gross government investment and spending and measures a country's government's expenditures on goods and services.
- **Net exports (X – M)**. Net exports measures the total income earned from the sale of exports (X) to foreigners minus the total amount spent by a nation's households, firms and government on goods and services imported (M) from other countries. Net exports can be negative or positive, depending on whether a nation spends more on imports than it earns from the sale of its exports.

AD can therefore be expressed using the following formula:

$$AD = C + I + G + (X - M)$$

 Aggregate demand (AD) is the total demand for a nation's goods and services from domestic households, firms, the government and foreigners.

The AD curve

As shown in Figure 12.1, AD is a downward-sloping curve reflecting an inverse relationship with the average price level in a nation.

At lower average price levels, more of a nation's output is demanded by households, firms, the government and foreigners; at higher price levels, less is demanded. In Figure 12.1 at a price level of PL_1, the quantity of national output demanded by households, firms,

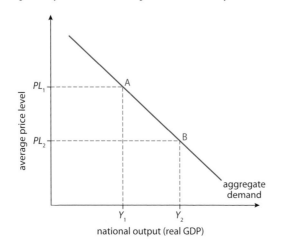

◀ **Figure 12.1**
The aggregate demand curve.

foreigners and the government corresponds with a level of national output of Y_1. At a lower price level of PL_2, the quantity of output demanded is greater, at Y_2. In this regard, the AD curve is similar to the demand curve studied in microeconomics. But demand slopes downwards because of the income effect, the substitution effect and diminishing marginal utility (Chapter 2); AD slopes downwards for the three different reasons discussed below.

The wealth effect

Higher price levels reduce the purchasing power or the real value of the nation's households' wealth and savings. The public feels poorer at higher price levels and thus demands a lower quantity of the nation's output when price levels are high. At lower price levels, people feel wealthier and thus demand more of a nation's goods and services. (This is similar to the income effect, which explains the downward-sloping demand curve.)

The interest rate effect

In response to a rise in the price level, banks raise the interest rates on loans to households and firms who wish to consume or invest. At higher interest rates, the quantity demanded of products and capital for which households and firms must borrow decreases, as borrowers find higher interest rates less attractive. The opposite results from a fall in the price level and the decline in interest rates, which makes borrowing more attractive and thus increases the quantity of output demanded.

The net export effect

As the price level in a particular country falls, *ceteris paribus*, goods and services produced in that country become more attractive to foreign consumers. Likewise, domestic consumers find imports less attractive as they now appear relatively more expensive, so the net expenditure on exports rises as price level falls. The opposite results from an increase in the price level, which makes domestic output less attractive to foreigners and foreign products more attractive to domestic consumers. (This is similar to the substitution effect, which explains the downward-sloping demand curve.)

The above effects explain the inverse relationship between the average price level of a nation's output and the quantity demanded by households, firms, the government and foreign consumers.

 12.3 Determinants of AD or shifts in the AD curve

Learning outcomes
- Explain how the AD curve can be shifted by changes in consumption due to factors including changes in consumer confidence, interest rates, wealth, personal income taxes (and hence disposable income) and level of household indebtedness.
- Explain how the AD curve can be shifted by changes in investment due to factors including interest rates, business confidence, technology, business taxes and the level of corporate indebtedness.
- Explain how the AD curve can be shifted by changes in government spending due to factors including political and economic priorities.
- Explain how the AD curve can be shifted by changes in net exports due to factors including the income of trading partners, exchange rates and changes in the level of protectionism.

Just as with demand for a product (for which a change in the price leads to a movement along demand and a change in the quantity demanded), a change in the price level leads to a movement along a nation's AD curve and a change in the national output demanded. But AD will shift if any of its four components changes: any change in consumption (C), investment (I), government spending (G) or net exports (X – M) will shift the AD curve. Each of these four components has its own determinants that may cause it to increase or decrease.

Determinants of consumption (C)

Households demand goods and services in a nation's product market (picture the circular flow from Chapter 1). The level of consumption in a nation depends on several factors. In many countries, household consumption makes up the single largest component of aggregate demand. Figure 12.2 shows the makeup of several countries total demand for goods and services, organized from the countries in which consumption makes up the least to those in which consumption makes up the most as a percentage of total demand.

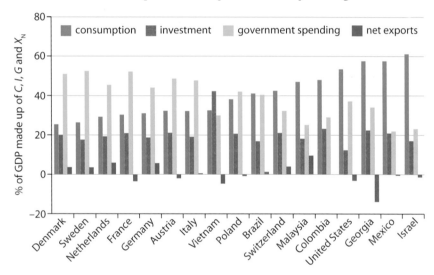

◄ **Figure 12.2**
Aggregate demand around the world.

As you can see, the countries in which consumption is the smallest component of total demand are mostly Western and Northern European nations in which tax rates are high and government spending on public goods and services make up a much more substantial proportion of total demand. In Denmark, for instance, tax rates are over 50% for most households, which leaves little disposable income for personal consumption. The Danish government, however, provides goods and services such as education, healthcare and transfer payments such as unemployment benefits, job training and welfare at a level that results in government spending making up over 50% of the total country's total economic activity.

On the other end of the table are countries such as the US, Mexico and Israel, where income taxes are low compared to Europe, leaving more disposable income for households to consume with, which explains why consumption makes up much larger proportions of total spending.

 How do the different consumption patterns of different countries reflect the cultural differences between countries? Are there cultural differences between a country like Sweden and the US that allow the vast consumption gap between such countries to be maintained?

Level of national income

The level of national income is the primary determinant of consumption in a nation. As national income rises, the level of consumption of a nation's households rises, and as national income falls, consumption falls. A nation's income does not equal its consumption, but consumption is a function of national income. In addition to consuming goods and services, a nation's households will also pay taxes, save, or buy imports with the income earned in a year.

Consumption

The percentage of national income that goes towards consumption is determined by the nation's average propensity to consume (APC). APC is found by dividing the level of consumption (C) by the level of national income (Y).

$$APC = \frac{C}{Y}$$

Savings

At lower levels of income, households tend to consume with a greater proportion of their income than at higher incomes levels. This means that the amount of income saved is less at lower income levels. The average propensity to save (APS), is savings (S) divided by national income (Y); this tells us the percentage of a nation's income that is saved.

$$APS = \frac{S}{Y}$$

Taxes

All governments collect taxes. The percentage of the nation's income collected in taxes tells us the average rate of taxation (ART). The ART is found by dividing the total taxes collected in a country (T) by the national income (Y).

$$ART = \frac{T}{Y}$$

Imports

Finally, households may consume goods or services produced abroad, which counts as imports to a nation and is thus not included as a part of the nation's aggregate demand and is subtracted from GDP. The average propensity to import (APM) is the percentage of national income spent on imports (M).

$$APM = \frac{M}{Y}$$

All of a nation's income goes towards consumption, savings, paying taxes or buying imports. Therefore:

$$APC + APS + ART + APM = 1$$

Consumption increases at a decreasing rate with income. The higher the nation's income of households, the lower the average propensity to consume.

The Keynesian consumption function

This is a schedule showing the relationship between household consumption and income (Figure 12.3). The direct relationship between national income (Y) and consumption (C) is clearly visible.

The 45-degree dotted line in Figure 12.3 shows where consumption plus import spending equals income. When the blue consumption curve is above the dotted line at low income levels, consumption and import spending exceed national income. When income falls near to zero, consumption is sustained by dipping into savings or by going into debt. When a nation's consumption is greater than its income, the nation is experiencing dis-savings.

At higher levels of income, both consumption and savings are higher, but households consume with a smaller *proportion* of their income. Thus, as income rises, the average

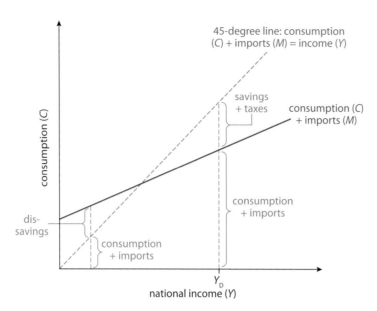

Figure 12.3

The consumption curve: household spending increases as national income rises.

propensity to consume falls, but total consumption increases with income. Savings also increase as income rises. Households that can afford to save tend to save at higher rates than those whose incomes are lower and who must use more of their incomes to consume, so the APS increases as income rises.

Figure 12.4 shows the levels of consumption and savings for two income levels.

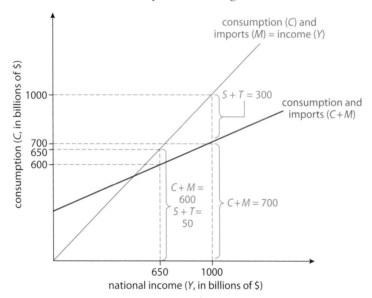

Figure 12.4

The consumption curve: proportion of income used for consumption decreases as income rises.

From Figure 12.4 we can observe the following points.

- When national income equals $650 billion, consumption and import spending total $600 billion. Assume consumption of domestically produced goods is $500 billion and import spending equals $100 billion
  - APC is 500/650 = 0.77
  - APM is 100/650 = 0.153
- Savings and taxes total only $50 billion when national income is $650 billion. Assume that $30 billion is taxes and $20 billion is savings.
  - ART is 30/650 = 0.046
  - APS is 20/650 = 0.031

- APC + APM + ART + APS = 1:
  - 0.77 + 0.153 + 0.046 + 0.031 = 1
- When national income rises to $1000 billion, consumption and import spending increase from $650 billion to $700 billion, while savings and taxes increase to $300 billion.
  - APC + APM = 700/1000 = 0.7
  - ART + APS = 300/1000 = 0.3

Savings, taxes, consumption and import spending all increase as national income rises. Notice, however, that the change in consumption and imports (from $600 billion to $700 billion) is less than the change in national income (from $650 billion to $1000 billion), while the change in savings and taxes ($50 billion to $300 billion) is greater than the change in consumption and import spending.

In this example, as national income rises from $650 billion to $1000 billion, consumption and imports increase by a smaller amount, from $600 billion to $700 billion. Assume that of this $100 billion increase, $20 billion went towards the purchase of imports and $80 billion towards the purchase of domestic output. Knowing the changes in consumption and imports resulting from a change in national income, we can determine the marginal propensity to consume (MPC) and the marginal propensity to import (MPM).

$$MPC = \frac{\Delta C}{\Delta Y} = \frac{80}{350} = 0.23$$

23% of the $350 billion increase in national income went towards the consumption of domestically produced goods and services. The MPM is the change in import spending divided by the change in income, so:

$$MPM = \frac{\Delta M}{\Delta Y} = \frac{20}{350} = 0.057$$

5.7% of the $350 billion increase in income went towards the purchase of imported goods and services.

Next, we can determine the marginal propensity to save (MPS) and the marginal propensity to tax (MPT).

Assume that of the $250 billion increase in savings and taxes, $100 billion went towards taxes, and savings increased by $150 billion. Now we can determine the proportion of the change in national income of $350 billion that went towards paying taxes and savings.

The MPS is the change in savings divided by the change in income, so:

$$MPS = \frac{\Delta S}{\Delta Y} = \frac{150}{350} = 0.429$$

42.9% of the increase in national income from $650 billion to $1000 billion went towards increased savings among the nations households. Taxes also increased.

The MPT is the change in taxes divided by the change in income, so:

$$MPT = \frac{\Delta T}{\Delta Y} = \frac{100}{350} = 0.286$$

28.6% of the increase in national income went towards taxes collected by the government. Notice that at higher income levels, the level of savings and taxes increases as a percentage of total income, while the level of household consumption actually decreases as a percentage of total income. Saving, it could be argued, is a luxury enjoyed more by nations with high incomes than those at low incomes. Simply put, high-income households are inclined to save more of their income than low-income households.

Economic theory suggests that savings should increase as a proportion of income as income rises. However, recent data from some developed nations have suggested otherwise. Throughout the 1990s and early 2000s, for instance, US national income grew at an average rate of 3.5% per year (a healthy growth rate) but during the same period, savings rates fell to historic lows. In the face of rising incomes, households may become overly optimistic about the future and consumers spend beyond their means by accumulating large debts. On a nationwide level, this can result in negative savings rates.

Since consumption, saving, paying taxes and purchasing imports are the only things a nation's households can do with an increase in national income, then the sum of MPC, MPS, MPT and MPM must equal one.

MPC + MPS + MPT + MPM = 1

In our example: 0.23 + 0.057 + 0.429 + 0.286 = 1.

You will recall from Chapter 11 that in the circular flow model, taxes, savings and the purchase of imports are considered leakages since these activities do not contribute to the creation of jobs or growth in the domestic economy. The MPS, MPT and MPM together are therefore sometimes referred to as the marginal rate of leakage (MRL).

MRL = MPS + MPT + MPM

Although the level of income of the nation's households is the primary determinant of consumption in a nation, it is not the only one. The level of consumption in a nation can increase or decrease depending on other, non-income determinants of consumption.

Non-income determinants of consumption

These include the wealth of households, real interest rates, the level of household debt, household expectations and consumer confidence.

Wealth

In addition to income, the level of wealth among households determines the level of consumption. Wealth is defined as the net worth of an individual or a household including the value of all its assets minus all its liabilities. A household's assets may include real assets (such as the value of a house or stock in companies) or financial assets (such as the value of money in savings or retirement accounts). When either real wealth or perceived wealth increases, household consumption tends to increase. Households perceive themselves as being richer when the value of the home rises or stock prices rise, leading to a higher level of consumption even if disposable income remains constant. This is why wealth is a non-income determinant of consumption.

Figure 12.5 shows the relationship between house prices and consumption in the UK from 1975 to 2004. The dotted red line shows the percentage change in household spending on goods and services year on year (left-hand scale) and the solid blue line shows the percentage change in house prices year on year (right-hand scale).

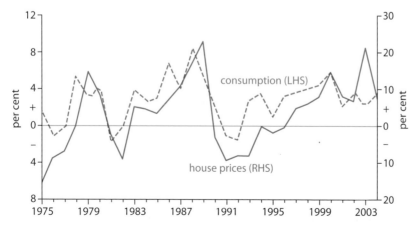

O Attanasio, L Blow, R Hamilton, A Leicester, *Consumption, house prices and expectations.* September 2005, Bank of England

Marginal propensities to consume, save, tax and import (MPC, MPS, MPT and MPM) measure the proportion of a change in household income that is used to consume domestic output, saved by households, paid in taxes and used to purchase imports, respectively.

To learn more about savings, visit www.pearsonhotlinks.com, enter the title or ISBN of this book and select weblink 12.1.

Wealth is the total value of the accumulated assets owned by an individual, household, community or country, minus all its liabilities. The wealthier a nation's households, the greater level of consumption. Wealth differs from income, because it does not measure the money flowing to households from their provision of land, labour and capital in the resource market; it measures the value of assets accumulated over time.

◀ **Figure 12.5**
Household wealth is an important determinant of consumption.

There is a strong correlation between the two curves in Figure 12.5. In years in which house prices increased, consumption almost always increased with it. In years in which house prices fell, so did consumption. Homes are a physical asset that make up a large proportion of many households' wealth, therefore an increase in house prices makes households feel wealthier and leads to more consumption at every level of income. Graphically, this would be illustrated as an upward shift of the consumption curve.

Besides house prices, changes in the values of other assets such as stocks and bonds affect household consumption. A slump in the stock market is likely to decrease consumption and increase savings even as incomes remain unchanged. Likewise, a rise in stock prices makes households feel richer and results in greater consumption at all levels of income.

Real interest rates

Consumption of durable goods is interest sensitive, since households sometimes finance the purchase of 'big-ticket items' (automobiles, household appliances, computers, televisions, etc.) through borrowing. Households respond to higher real interest rates by decreasing their consumption of these non-essential items since it becomes more costly to borrow when interest rates rise.

Real interest rates are determined by taking the nominal interest rate (i.e. the actual percentage charged by banks for a loan) and subtracting the rate of inflation. For instance, a nominal interest rate of 5% in a situation where unanticipated inflation is 2% equates to a real interest rate of 3%. Households consider the real rate of interest when deciding to purchase durable goods requiring financing.

If inflation is anticipated, banks will charge higher nominal interest rates to borrowers. Therefore, anticipated inflation has little or no effect on the real interest rate and consumption. Nominal interest rates rise with anticipated inflation as banks must charge higher nominal rates to maintain their profits, since inflation erodes the value of money and a borrower would be paying back money worth less than the money borrowed if nominal rates were not increased. However, if there is unanticipated inflation or inflation greater than that anticipated by banks and incorporated into the rate charged to borrowers, then the real interest rate will be reduced and households induced to spend on durable goods. This is because the opportunity cost of holding money (inflation rate) increases while the opportunity cost of spending money (nominal interest rate) remains the same.

During periods of unanticipated inflation, the real interest rate falls and households are more likely to consume more at every level of income. If there is unanticipated deflation (a decrease in the price level), then the real interest rate rises and, since households would now have to repay loans with money worth more than that borrowed, the incentive is to save more and decrease consumption. A rise in real interest rates caused by a decrease in the price level results in less consumption at each level of household income.

Household debt and expectations of future income

The level of household debt can shift the consumption curve upwards or downwards. Household debt is the amount of money owed by a household to lenders, including consumer debt accrued through the use of credit cards or by borrowing from a bank to finance consumption of durable goods. In the short run, an increase in consumer debt allows households to increase consumption at each level of household income. But in the long run, debts must be paid back, which is only achieved through reductions in future consumption as household income must go towards repaying past debts.

Increases in household debt allow households to consume beyond their income limit but ultimately require a decrease in consumption when debts must be paid back. The degree to which access to credit and the corresponding increase in household debt actually affects consumption depends on the expectations among households of future income. When expectation of future household income is raised, households are more willing to take on debt to finance current consumption, increasing consumption at all levels of current income. If, on the other hand, households expect future incomes to fall, the willingness to incur debts to finance current consumption declines and households shift their focus to paying off past debts in anticipation of harder economic times ahead.

National debt refers to the debts held by government. Increasing the national debt by deficit spending allows a government to spend more on goods and services than it collects in tax revenue. Government spending is a separate component of AD, but the concept of national debt and household debt are similar in that they both allow for spending beyond the level of current income.

Consumer confidence

John Maynard Keynes used the term 'animal spirits' to describe the confidence (or lack of confidence) among households and firms in an economy. Consumer confidence is an economic indicator that measures the degree of optimism that consumers feel about the overall state of the economy, and is therefore an important determinant of overall household consumption. During periods of economic growth with low unemployment and stable prices, confidence tends to be high and consumer spending strong. In periods of macroeconomic uncertainty, when overall output is falling, unemployment is rising and prices are declining, consumer confidence can collapse and households will reduce their consumption and increase savings in expectation of future economic hardships.

A change in any of the determinants of consumption above will increase or decrease consumption at all levels of income (Figure 12.6).

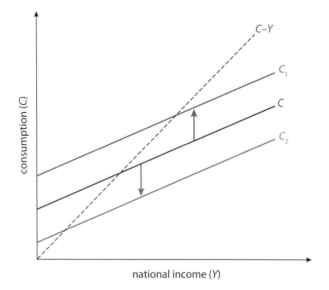

Figure 12.6
A change in the determinants of consumption will shift the consumption curve up or down.

The line C in Figure 12.6 represents consumption. An increase in household wealth, a decrease in real interest rates, an increase in indebtedness or an improvement in consumer confidence will all shift the consumption curve from C to C_1. On the other hand, if wealth declines, real interest rates rise, households begin to pay off past debts or consumer confidence falls, consumption will decrease from C to C_2. The determinants of

You will probably soon receive your first credit card offer in the mail. While the temptation to spend this 'plastic money' is often strong in the present, any spending you do now must be repaid in the future. A credit card allows you to spend *more than* your income level now, but ultimately you'll have to consume far less in the future, as you begin to pay off the debt.

To learn more about consumption, visit www.pearsonhotlinks.com, enter the title or ISBN of this book and select weblink 12.2.

consumption are the non-income factors that can shift the overall level of consumption among a nation's households.

Determinants of investment (*I*)

Investment is the second component of a nation's AD. Investment is defined as spending by firms on capital equipment or technology and by households on newly built homes.

Look again at Figure 12.2, which shows the components of AD in several countries. It can be seen that in most of the countries represented, investment made up approximately 20% of the nation's total demand. The one exception is Vietnam, where investment made up around 45% of the country's total spending on goods and services. It is not uncharacteristic for less developed countries such as Vietnam to have high levels of private investment relative to other components of aggregate demand.

In 2009, 45.9% of China's total spending was investment by firms. Countries such as China and Vietnam (in which economic growth is based on manufacturing) are more likely to experience higher levels of investment (as their private sectors expand to meet the growing demands of both domestic and foreign consumers) than the more developed, industrialized countries in which capital is already relatively abundant.

Interest rates

The level of investment by firms in an economy is determined primarily by the real interest rate. The interest rate is the opportunity cost of spending money.

At higher interest rates, the amount of investment in the economy declines for the following reasons.

- Firms have an incentive to save earnings from the sale of their output, as the returns on savings are higher. Firms, always the profit-maximizers, will be less likely to invest in capital when returns are greater on investments in interest-earning assets such as savings accounts and government bonds.
- Higher interest rates mean greater returns on household savings, so households prefer to keep their money in banks or other interest-bearing assets rather than investing in capital or new homes.
- At higher interest rates, the cost of borrowing to finance capital investments is greater. Since interest payments add to a firm's costs, higher interest rates mean higher costs and smaller profits.
- There are fewer investments in capital with an expected rate of return equal to or greater than the rate of interest.

At lower real interest rates, the amount of investment in the economy increases for the following reasons.

- The opportunity cost of buying new capital falls and firms are more likely to invest revenues earned from their sales in new capital equipment in order to expand their output or simply to replace deteriorating capital stocks.
- The returns on interest-bearing assets such as savings accounts and government bonds fall when interest rates are low, so there is less incentive to save earnings. Households are less willing to save and more willing to borrow to invest in new homes when interest rates are low.
- The cost of borrowing to finance investments in new capital or technology is lower.
- More capital investments have an expected rate of return equal to or greater than a lower interest rate than when interest rates are high.

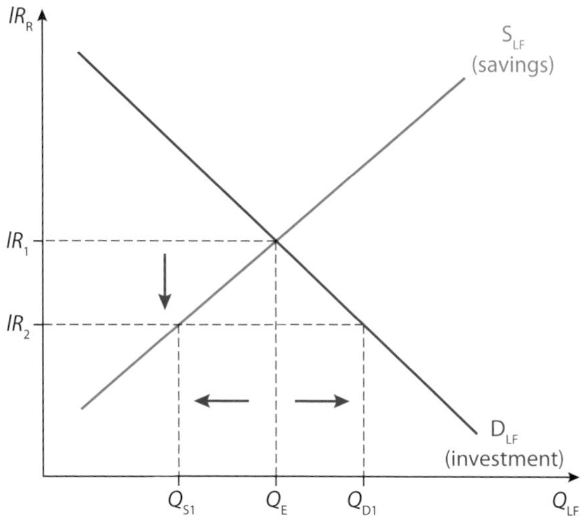

Figure 12.7
The loanable funds market
diagram.

There is an inverse relationship between the real interest rate in the economy and the demand for funds for private investment and a direct relationship between real interest rate and the supply of loanable funds. This relationship can be illustrated in a diagram known as the loanable funds market diagram (Figure 12.7 above).

At the higher interest rate of IR_1 the supply of funds provided by households is equal to the demand from firms and households for investment; the loanable funds market is in equilibrium. However, if the interest rate were lower, at IR_2, the quantity of funds demanded for investment would increase, since there are far more investments in capital and technology with an expected rate of return high enough to cover the interest payments. Notice, however, that at a lower interest rate, households are willing to save less money in banks, and the quantity supplied is less than the quantity demanded (a shortage of loanable funds). At IR_2 the loanable funds market is in disequilibrium, since there is a greater demand for investment than there is a supply of funds available.

Assume that IR_1 is 8%. A firm willing and able to borrow at 8% must expect to make a return on that investment of at least 8%. Otherwise, with an expected rate of return of less than 8%, borrowing and investing would add more to the firm's costs than to its revenues and lead to economic losses.

Assume IR_2 is 4%. At this lower interest rate, there are far more investments in capital and technology with an expected rate of return high enough to cover the interest payments of 4%. Since more investments are likely to pay a return greater than 4% than 8%, the quantity of funds demanded for private investment increases as the real interest rate decreases.

Lower interest rates will lead to greater investment as long as firms are responsive to changes in the interest rate. This fact will play an important role in later chapters when we examine the policy options available to governments and central banks for managing the level of AD in a country. Monetary policy involves the manipulation of a nation's money supply by its central bank with the goal of affecting interest rates and stimulating or contracting private investment in capital, thus affecting the overall level of demand in an economy.

If firms are relatively unresponsive to changes in the interest rate, then policies that raise or lower the interest rate will have little effect on the demand for funds for investment. In other words, the demand for loanable funds for investment can be relatively elastic or it can be relatively inelastic (Figure 12.8, overleaf).

In Figure 12.8, when demand for loanable funds is D_1, a decrease in the interest rate from

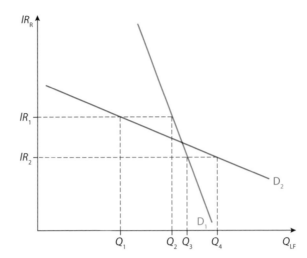

Figure 12.8
The demand for loanable funds can be relatively elastic or inelastic.

The loanable funds market is a hypothetical market that shows the relationship between the real interest rate in a country and the supply of and demand for money from households and firms for private investment. In equilibrium, the quantity supplied by households (who save money in commercial banks) and demanded by firms (who borrow from banks to finance capital spending) are equal.

IR_1 to IR_2 leads to a very small increase in the demand for funds for investment, from Q_2 to Q_3. Demand for investment funds is highly inelastic (i.e. unresponsive to changes in the interest rate). With an investment demand of D_2, however, a fall in the interest rate from IR_1 to IR_2 leads to a proportionally larger increase in the quantity of funds demanded by firms for investment in new capital, from Q_1 to Q_4.

Business confidence

In addition to the real interest rate, investment in the private sector also depends on the expectations of firms, or Keynes's animal spirits. If firms are feeling confident, both about their future sales outlook and that the price of their output will be higher in the future, then they are more likely to invest now.

Investor confidence is directly influenced by consumer confidence. As we learned from the circular flow model (page 236), firms and households in a market economy are totally interdependent. The well-being of firms depends on the demand for their output among consumers. If consumption is falling, investment will fall as well. Less investment reduces firms' demand for capital and labour, leading to higher unemployment and further declines in disposable income and consumption. Such a slump in AD is the most common cause of a recession, a macroeconomic condition in which total output of a nation declines, unemployment rises and price levels fall.

In addition to their expectations of future consumer demand for their products, firms must also consider other factors when deciding whether or not to invest.

Future prices

If there is deflation in a nation (decrease in the average price of goods and services), firms are more likely to save their revenues and postpone investments until prices start to rise again. If prices are rising, however, firms will wish to invest now to take advantage of the higher prices they will be able to sell their output for in the future.

Technology

New technologies often lead to periods of increased investment by firms adopting the technology or providing goods and services to consumers that incorporate the new technology. One of the best examples of this is the period following the invention of the world wide web in the mid-1990s when households began to gain wide access to the internet. The dot-com boom of the late 90s saw trillions of dollars in new investments in companies which were formed to meet the growing demands of households connected to the internet. Consumer technologies such as smartphones, tablet computers and mobile global positioning systems (GPS) have triggered new markets for firms to invest in. Additionally, technologies that increase productivity in production of traditional consumer goods (e.g. robots that make automobiles; chemical fertilizers and pesticides that increase agricultural productivity; other mechanical and industrial techniques of production) may induce periods of investment by firms.

Business taxes

An increase in tax on profits or on investment reduces demand for funds for investment at all interest rates because firms have less incentive to acquire new capital when the government takes a larger share of the returns. Even the expectations of higher taxes in the future affect firms' behaviour in the present. When a government builds up a large national debt by spending more than it collects in tax revenues, business owners may be hesitant to invest if they suspect the government may increase taxes down the road to reduce the deficit and pay off the national debt.

Inventories

When businesses are unable to sell all the output they produced in a given period of time, their inventories grow and this reduces the need to invest in new capital. Inventory investment is the difference between what is produced in a year and what is sold in the same year. If firms expect there to be a greater need for inventories in a given year (in other words, if they expect past inventories to dwindle because of strong demand), then they invest in new capital to add to their inventories to meet the expected demand from consumers. However, if inventories are growing and expected to continue to grow, firms reduce investment now in the hope of selling off existing inventories before contributing to their already growing stock of unsold output.

The degree of excess capacity

If firms can easily increase output because they are producing below their full capacity, they are less likely to invest in new capital now. However, if a nation's firms are using existing capital resources at or near their full capacity, the need for investment to replace old capital or expand existing capital is greater.

The expectations that firms hold of future business conditions are of great importance in determining firms' willingness to invest. During the recession of 2008–09 in Europe and the US, interest rates fell to almost 0% in many countries yet private sector investment seemed completely unresponsive to the low costs of borrowing. The lack of confidence among households and firms around the world helps explain why the low interest rates failed to spur new investment and jump-start the stagnant economies of the world during these difficult years.

When business confidence is low, it is extremely difficult to turn things around in a struggling economy. In later chapters, we examine the policy tools a government or central bank might implement to stimulate AD when a nation's households' and firms' confidence about the future prevents the private sector from sufficiently contributing to the nation's AD to keep employment and output strong.

Determinants of government spending (G)

Government spending includes a broad range of expenditure: public schools and universities, national defence, highways and roads, parks and hospitals. Governments may

As it turned out, the dot-com boom of the 1990s ended in a bust as the value of internet-based companies plunged by $5 trillion between 2000 and 2002. The dot-com bubble, as it has become known, was the result of a huge over-investment in a sector of the economy that would ultimately be much less lucrative than investors originally thought it would.

Business confidence is a contributing factor to the level of AD. What knowledge issues arise in attempting to measure business confidence?

To learn more about investment, visit www. pearsonhotlinks.com, enter the title or ISBN of this book and select weblink 12.3.

spend directly on the provision of goods and services or may subsidize their provision by the private sector. Government spending makes up a huge range of total AD across nations. As you saw in Figure 12.2, government spending makes up the largest proportion of the economies of Northern and Western European nations such as Denmark, Sweden, the Netherlands, France and Germany. In these countries, government provides services such as healthcare and education to all citizens, paid for almost entirely by taxpayers.

In countries with large government sectors, taxes on households and firms tend to be much higher than in those where government spending makes up a smaller proportion of AD. This makes sense since ultimately all government spending on goods and services must be financed by the nation's taxpayers.

The level of government spending in a nation in a particular year depends on the government's fiscal policy, which refers to the government's use of taxes and spending to stimulate or contract the overall level of AD in an economy. Fiscal policy is explained in detail in Chapter 17, but what you need to know here is that its use can raise or lower the level of government spending in a given period to help meet the macroeconomic objectives of full employment, price stability and economic growth.

Determinants of net exports ($X - M$)

Expenditure on a nation's output includes spending by domestic households (C) and domestic firms (I), but also foreign households and firms. In a global economy, nearly every nation depends to some degree on foreign demand for its output as a component of its GDP. Net exports measures the spending by foreigners on a nation's goods and services minus the amount spent by domestic households and firms on imports from other countries. Net exports is, therefore, the only component of AD that can be negative, which occurs when a nation spends more on imports than it earns from the sale of its exports.

Of the countries whose components of AD are shown in Figure 12.2 (page 259), eight (most prominently Georgia) had negative net exports, meaning they spent more on imports from the rest of the world than the rest of the world spent on their goods and services. In 2009, the total GDP in the US was around $14 trillion; Americans spent $450 billion more on other countries' output than foreigners spent on theirs. America's net exports of −$450 billion contributed −3% to America's GDP. In contrast, Germany's net exports were around $200 billion in 2009, meaning German firms sold $200 billion more to the rest of the world than German households consumed of foreign goods and services. Net exports accounted for 4.8% of Germany's total output in 2009.

Incomes abroad

The macroeconomic health and households' incomes of a nation's trading partners determine demand for the nation's exports. For example, Canada's largest trading partner is the US (75% of Canada's trade takes place with the US). As incomes in the US fell during the recession of 2008–09, Canada's exports fell from $460 billion in 2008 to $323 billion in 2009, a decline of 30%. However, during the same period, Canada's imports from the rest of the world also declined, from $415 billion to $327 billion, a decline of 21%. Canada's net exports in 2008 were $44 billion but in 2009 fell to −$4 billion, a decline of $48 billion in one year. Falling incomes in the US are the most likely explanation for this massive decline in Canada's net exports, supporting the fact that household income in trading nations is a major determinant of a nation's net exports.

● **Examiner's hint**

The key thing to remember about net exports is the *net* part of the term. Exports may be a huge part of a nation's economy, but account for only a tiny percentage of its GDP. Switzerland, for example, exports goods and services with a value of roughly 70% of Swiss GDP. But since it also imports vast amounts, Switzerland's *net* exports account for only about 5% of its GDP. Switzerland still earns more from its exports than it spends on imports, but the large value of its exports is offset by the nearly equally large expenditure on imports.

Tastes and preferences of consumers

Some countries just do it better. German cars are known around the world for craftsmanship and quality. Among discerning consumers, Swiss watches will always be preferred over cheap ones made in China. The Japanese always seem to be on the cutting edge of home entertainment technologies (e.g. the PlayStation and Sony's 3D TVs). The taste of consumers is a major determinant of a country's exports. Once a country's producers have developed a strong reputation in the global marketplace, that country can count on steady demand from abroad for its output. Creating demand abroad for a nation's goods and services is an important objective of any government's diplomatic missions and the marketing departments of countless multinational corporations.

Exchange rates

An exchange rate is simply the price of a currency expressed in units of another currency. While a strong currency may sound desirable, in fact a weak currency is more likely to contribute to a country's net exports. A weaker currency makes the output of a country's producers cheaper to consumers abroad, whose own currency is relatively strong. Governments often take measures to intervene in foreign exchange markets to devalue or depreciate their currencies relative to others in order to help their domestic producers compete in the global market and to stimulate AD by shifting the balance of the country's net exports towards the positive. A weaker currency also makes foreign products less desirable to domestic consumers and may also lead to a growth in domestic household consumption. In contrast, a strong currency reduces demand for a country's output abroad and increases the attractiveness of foreign products among domestic households, shifting a country's net exports towards the negative. Exchange rates are discussed in Chapter 22.

Protectionism

The degree to which a nation and its trading partners practise protectionism affects what percentage of its GDP is made up of net exports. If a nation chooses to erect high barriers to trade such as tariffs, quotas, or subsidies to domestic producers, it may experience retaliatory protectionism from countries with which it trades and, over time, the percentage of its AD accounted for by net exports will decline. Protectionism is discussed in Chapter 22.

 To learn more about exports, visit www.pearsonhotlinks.com, enter the title or ISBN of this book and select weblink 12.4.

Causes of shifts in the AD curve

A change in any of the components of AD leads to a shift in the AD curve, meaning that, at a given price level, either a larger or a smaller amount of total output in a nation is demanded (Figure 12.9, overleaf).

An increase in either consumption, investment, net exports or government spending in a nation shifts the AD curve in Figure 12.9 from AD_1 to AD_2, increasing the output of the nation demanded at PL_1 to Y_2. A fall in consumption, investment, net exports or government spending shifts AD from AD_1 to AD_3, reducing the amount of output demanded at PL_1 from Y_1 to Y_3.

A nation's aggregate demand increases whenever households, firms, foreigners or the government increase their spending, and falls when spending falls. In this regard, the aggregate demand of a nation is the sum of the total expenditures by the private and public sectors on the nation's output. This method of measuring is called the expenditures method for measuring AD:

$$AD = C + I + G + (X - M)$$

 To access Worksheet 12.1 on America in the recession, please visit www.pearsonbacconline.com and follow the onscreen instructions.

Figure 12.9
AD shifts when any of the components of AD change.
▶

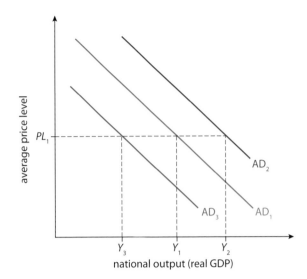

12.4 The Keynesian spending multiplier

Learning outcomes

- Explain, with reference to the concepts of leakages (withdrawals) and injections, the nature and importance of the Keynesian multiplier.
- Calculate the multiplier using either of the following formulae.

$$\frac{1}{(1 - \text{MPC})}$$

or

$$\frac{1}{(\text{MPS} + \text{MPT} + \text{MPM})}$$

- Use the multiplier to calculate the effect on GDP of a change in an injection in investment, government spending or exports.

The existence of the Keynesian spending multiplier has been the topic of fierce debate in recent years. Following America's Reinvestment and Recovery Act (the 'Obama stimulus') of 2009, economists attempted to measure the multiplier effect of an $800 billion increase in government spending. Their findings were widely varied, and some economists determined that the multiplier could be negative (i.e. an $800 billion increase in government spending could lead to an increase in national income of *less than* $800 billion).

Understanding how a particular injection of national income will ultimately affect a nation's GDP requires us to examine the proportion of the injection that is leaked from the circular flow relative to the amount that continues to circulate in the economy, creating additional income and employment for the nation's households.

One tool of fiscal policy is the use of government spending (G, a component of a nation's AD) to promote the macroeconomic objectives of full employment and economic growth. If the government increases its spending, or if any of the other external components (I, investment or ($X - M$), net exports) of AD increase, it is possible to estimate the ultimate effect on national income if we know the value of the Keynesian spending multiplier.

The Keynesian spending multiplier tells us the amount by which a particular injection of government spending, investment, or export spending will ultimately increase the nation's total GDP. The larger the proportion of the initial change in income that goes towards consumption, the larger the ultimate change in GDP will be following an initial increase in aggregate demand. Therefore, the spending multiplier (k) is a function of the marginal propensity to consume, and is determined using the following formula:

$$k = \frac{1}{(1 - \text{MPC})} \text{ or } k = \frac{1}{\text{MRL}}$$

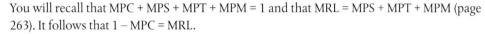

You will recall that MPC + MPS + MPT + MPM = 1 and that MRL = MPS + MPT + MPM (page 263). It follows that 1 − MPC = MRL.

The larger the marginal propensity to consume in a nation, the larger the spending multiplier, and the greater the ultimate effect of initial increase in spending on total GDP.

Let's consider two examples.

Worked example

- In country A, 50% of a change in income goes towards consumption of domestic goods and services. Country A's MPC is 0.5.
- In country B, 80% of any increase in income goes towards consumption. Country B's MPC is 0.8.

To determine the effect of an increase in spending of $10 billion in these two countries, we must determine the spending multiplier (k) in both countries.

In country A, the spending multiplier is:

$$k_A = \frac{1}{(1 - 0.5)} = 2$$

In country B, the spending multiplier is:

$$k_B = \frac{1}{(1 - 0.8)} = 5$$

With these figures, we can now estimate the effect of an increase in investment, government spending or exports of $10 billion. The ultimate change in GDP resulting from an initial change in expenditures (E) is:

$$\Delta GDP = k \times \Delta E$$

Assume for example, the governments of both countries are considering a fiscal policy involving an increase in government spending of $10 billion. With the spending multipliers known, we can determine the effect such a fiscal policy will have in both countries.

- In country A, $10 billion new income will ultimately result in an increase in GDP of $20 billion (10 billion × 2), since the initial change in income is multiplied through successive increases of consumption spending.
- In country B, where the MPC is greater (0.8), the same increase in government spending results in an ultimate increase in GDP of $50 billion (10 billion × 5).

Since country B's households spend a greater proportion of a change in income than country A's, the $10 billion fiscal policy will have a greater impact on country B's GDP than country A's. The larger the marginal propensity to consume, the greater impact a change in government spending, investment or exports will have on the level of national income in the country.

The concept of the Keynesian spending multiplier is explored in more depth in Chapter 17.

EXERCISES

1 Between 2009 and 2010, Germany's national income increased by $100 billion. As a result:
- taxes increased by $20 billion
- household spending (on all goods, including imports) increased by $70 billion
- savings increased by $10 billion
- imports increased by $10 billion.

a Calculate the marginal propensities to consume, tax, save and import.

b Calculate the marginal rate of leakage.

c Calculate the value of the government spending multiplier.

d Calculate the ultimate effect on Germany's GDP of an increase in investment spending of $50 billion.

12.5 Aggregate supply and equilibrium national output

Learning outcomes

- Describe the term aggregate supply.
- Explain, using a diagram, why the short-run aggregate supply curve (SRAS curve) is upward sloping.
- Explain, using a diagram, how the AS curve in the short run (SRAS) can shift due to factors including changes in resource prices, changes in business taxes and subsidies and supply shocks.
- Explain, using a diagram, that the monetarist/new classical model of the long-run aggregate supply curve (LRAS) is vertical at the level of potential output (full employment output) because aggregate supply in the long run is independent of the price level.
- Explain, using a diagram, that the Keynesian model of the aggregate supply curve has three sections because of 'wage/price' downward inflexibility and different levels of spare capacity in the economy.

A nation's aggregate supply (AS) is the total amount of goods and services that all the firms in all the industries in a country will produce at every price level in a given period of time. The AS curve illustrates the relationship between the average price level in a nation and the total output of the nation's producers. There are competing theories on the possible response of a nation's producers to changes in the price level, depending on how prices and wages in an economy change following a change in AD. Therefore, we will examine two models of AS: the Keynesian AS curve, and the neo-classical AS curve (Figure 12.10).

Figure 12.10
a The Keynesian aggregate supply curve; **b** the neo-classical aggregate supply curve.

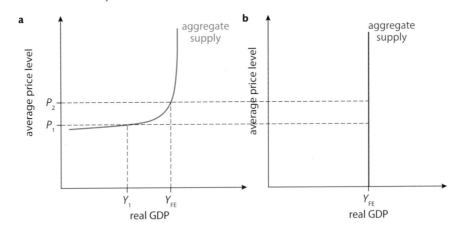

The two aggregate supply curves in Figure 12.10 illustrate two different views of the responsiveness of a nation's producers to changes in the price level. Assume, for example, that the nation's price level starts at P_1. On the Keynesian AS curve, when the price level rises to P_2, producers are responsive to the higher price and increase their output from Y_1 to Y_{FE} (i.e. full-employment output); in other words, AS is *relatively elastic* when the nation is producing at a relatively low level of output.

In the neo-classical model of aggregate supply, a change in the average price level of the nation's goods from P_1 to P_2 has no effect on the level of output. The neo-classical model assumes that regardless of the price level in a nation, the nation's producers will always produce at the level of output at which all the nation's resources are fully employed. Aggregate supply is *perfectly inelastic* at the nation's full employment level of output.

For our purposes, we will use both the Keynesian and the neo-classical AS curves in our analysis. But rather than referring to them by these names, we will instead identify the Keynesian model as the short-run aggregate supply (SRAS) curve and the neo-classical model as the long-run aggregate supply (LRAS) curve. The two models can be combined with an AD curve to illustrate the changes in the equilibrium level of national output resulting (in both the short run and the long run) from a change in AD.

Full employment national output

In the AS/AD model, Y_{FE} refers the nation's full employment level of output, which is the level of output of goods and services achieved when a nation is producing at or near its potential by employing all available land, labour and capital. A nation achieving Y_{FE} is producing either on or near its production possibilities curve, enjoys a low rate of unemployment and a stable price level and is, therefore, an economy that can be considered strong and healthy.

The LRAS curve is vertical at the full employment level of output, while the SRAS curve slopes upwards, but is highly elastic below full employment and becomes highly inelastic beyond full employment output.

To understand the theories of SRAS *vs* LRAS, two somewhat contradictory theories of how workers, producers and consumers respond to changes in the overall demand in an economy must be explained.

The Keynesian and neo-classical positions differ on the shape of the AS curve. What is needed to settle this question: empirical evidence (if so, what should be measured), strength of theoretical argument, or factors external to economics such as political conviction?

 12.6 ## Short-run equilibrium in the AD/AS model: the Keynesian, sticky wage model

Learning outcomes
- Explain, using a diagram, the determination of short-run equilibrium, using the SRAS curve.
- Examine, using diagrams, the impacts of changes in short-run equilibrium.
- Explain, using the Keynesian AD/AS diagram, that the economy may be in equilibrium at any level of real output where AD intersects AS.
- Explain, using a diagram, that if the economy is in equilibrium at a level of real output below the full-employment level of output, then there is a deflationary (recessionary) gap.
- Discuss why, in contrast to the monetarist/new classical model, the economy can remain stuck in a deflationary (recessionary) gap in the Keynesian model.
- Explain, using a diagram, that if AD increases in the vertical section of the AS curve, then there is an inflationary gap.
- Discuss why, in contrast to the monetarist/new classical model, increases in aggregate demand in the Keynesian AD/AS model need not be inflationary, unless the economy is operating close to, or at, the level of full employment.

The SRAS curve is based on the theories of the early 20th-century economist John Maynard Keynes, whose work during the Great Depression forms the basis for many of our modern macroeconomic theories. SRAS is generally upward-sloping, but the SRAS curve demonstrates two important characteristics that require further explanation:

- SRAS curve is horizontal (relatively elastic) at levels of output below full employment
- SRAS curve is vertical (relatively inelastic) at levels of output beyond full employment .

Both of these points reflect an important component of Keynesian macroeconomic theory.

SRAS is horizontal at levels of output below full employment

In the short run, firms are very responsive to a decrease in the demand for national output. SRAS is relatively elastic when AD declines and the price level falls. A fall in AD will lead to a small decrease in the price level, but a relatively large decrease in total output (Figure 12.11).

Figure 12.11
SRAS is highly elastic below the full-employment level of output.

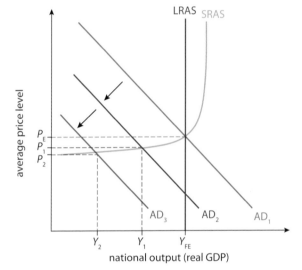

Equilibrium national output is defined as the total output of goods and services by firms in a nation at a particular period of time at a particular price level. Equilibrium output is determined by the intersection of a nation's AD and AS. In Figure 12.1, there are three short-run equilibrium levels of output corresponding to three different levels of AD. They are as follows.

- Y_{FE}. When AD (i.e. $C + I + G + (X - M)$) is at AD_1, the equilibrium quantity of output is the full-employment level of output. At Y_{FE} the nation experiences very low unemployment, stable prices (meaning low inflation), and the nation's resources are generally being used efficiently and near their full capacity towards the production of goods and services.
- Y_1. A decrease in AD from AD_1 to AD_2 (caused by a decrease in any of the components of AD) causes a fall in the price level from P_E to P_1. As the average price level of goods in this economy fall, firms respond by reducing their output and laying off workers. In the short run, the decrease in the price level is proportionally smaller than the decrease in the equilibrium output.
- Y_2. If AD continues to fall to AD_3, firms must again reduce their employment and output. The result of a decrease in AD in the short run is, therefore, a fall in the price level and a fall in output. However, due to the highly elastic nature of SRAS below the full-employment level, the decline in output is proportionally greater than the decline in the price level.

The decline in the short-un equilibrium output and employment resulting from a fall in AD is explained by the fact that in the short run, wages and prices are downwardly inflexible. In macroeconomics, the short run is referred to as the fixed-wage period. Firms find it difficult or impossible to adjust workers' wages in the short run, due to several rigidities that exist in many countries' labour markets. Labour market rigidities that make wages inflexible in the short run include the following.

- **Worker contracts**. Workers in most industrialized nations sign contracts for periods of months or longer with their employers. A contract may include a guaranteed wage over the contract period; such legally binding agreements make it difficult for firms to simply slash wages in the face of falling demand for their products.
- **Minimum wage laws**. A minimum wage set by the government may make it difficult for employers of low-skilled workers or those in the service sector to reduce costs without laying off workers when demand falls. The existence of a minimum wage prevents the price level from adjusting downwards in times of weak AD and may cause unemployment to increase more than it otherwise would during periods of weak demand.
- **Wage agreements with labour unions**. Labour unions pose an obstacle to firms seeking to reduce costs as demand for their output falls. The threat of walk-outs or strikes by their unionized workforces prevents firms from slashing wages or benefits, in some cases forcing firms to shut down and lay off their entire workforce when overall demand is weak in the economy.
- **Government regulations**. Regulations mandating fair pay and fair treatment in the workplace make it difficult for firms to easily cut costs by slashing wages when demand is low.

Because of the inflexible nature of wages in the short run, firms find it difficult to lower their prices quickly, and therefore must reduce output and lay off workers in response to falling demand.

Keynes's observations of the Great Depression included the fact that as total demand began to decline in the US and Europe in the early 1930s, the typical response of firms was to reduce employment and output, rather than slash wages and maintain their output at pre-depression levels. This observation actually makes sense to someone who has studied microeconomics, as in a market for a particular good or service a fall in demand leads firms to respond by reducing the quantity they supply and lowering their prices. In a nation as a whole, however, prices are slow to adjust in the short run due to the rigidities in a nation's labour market that make it difficult for firms to cut their costs quickly in response to falling demand. Therefore, a fall in AD leads to a fall in national output and only a small decrease in the price level in the short-run, fixed-wage period.

The SRAS curve, which shows the response of a nation's firms to a change in the price level during the fixed-wage period, is sometimes referred to as the sticky wage, sticky price model of AS. Since wages are relatively inflexible over a period of months following a change in AD, firms must respond to a decline in demand by reducing their output and laying off workers to reduce their costs and avoid having to shut down. In later chapters, we will apply the sticky wage, sticky price AS model to help us understand why unemployment reached its highest levels in decades in Europe and the US during the recession of 2008–09. Keynes's analysis of the rising unemployment experienced during the Great Depression of the 1930s seemed to help explain the doubling of unemployment in many countries over the last few years as well. For instance, while US unemployment increased from around 5% in 2007 to 10% by 2009, changes in the average price level over the same period were much less dramatic, as the US experienced inflation rates of between 0% and −2%.

Many of the institutions meant to protect workers (minimum wages, labour unions, contracts and government regulations) may harm workers, in that the rigidities they create could mean firms have to lay workers off during times of falling demand. Should such a claim be evidence enough to support the dismantling of such institutions? What other evidence is necessary before you can know whether worker protections are harmful to workers or not?

Sticky wage / sticky price model is another name for the Keynesian, short-run aggregate supply curve. Because firms find it difficult to cut workers' wages in the short run, they must lay workers off to reduce costs, hence output and employment fall when AD falls in the short run.

SRAS is vertical at levels of output beyond full employment

The inflexibility of wages in the short run also helps explain what happens following an increase in AD beyond the full-employment equilibrium level of output. In Figure 12.12, increases in either consumption, investment, government spending or net exports cause the AD curve to shift from AD_1 to AD_2 and then to AD_3, resulting in short-run equilibrium levels of output beyond the full-employment level (Y_{FE}).

Figure 12.12
SRAS is highly inelastic beyond the full employment level of output.

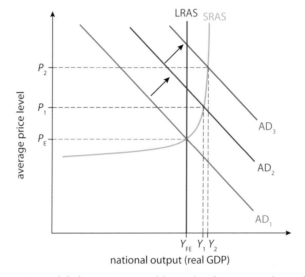

According to the SRAS model above, it is possible, in the short run at least, for a nation to produce beyond its full-employment level of output. Notice, however, that relatively small increases in output (from Y_{FE} to Y_1 and then to Y_2) come at the cost of increasing inflation, as rising AD is met with an increase in the price level first from P_E to P_1 and then from P_1 to P_2.

The inflexibility of wages in the short run helps explain the decreasing elasticity of SRAS beyond the full employment level of output. However, we must first address a point of confusion that students often express: how can a nation possibly produce beyond its full-employment level of output?

The full-employment level of output (Y_{FE}), represents the national output and income achieved by a nation when its resources are fully employed. This means that nearly all the nation's land, labour and capital are engaged in the production of goods and services. A nation achieving Y_{FE} is producing on, or at least very close to, its PPC. However, producing at full employment does not mean that the nation has zero unemployment. In fact, a nation is said to be producing at full employment when the level of unemployment in the nation is low and stable, and the people who are unable to find work are generally in between jobs or have lost their jobs because of a mismatch of their skills with those that are in demand in the labour market. In other words, even when a nation is producing at full employment, there are still workers willing and able to work who are unemployed.

When AD increases from AD_1 to AD_2, firms wish to respond to the higher demand and the higher prices it brings by increasing their production. You will recall that in the short run, wages in the economy are fixed, therefore firms find it a bargain to hire more workers at the constant wage rate, since the rising prices promise greater profits for producers. However, as output grows, the number of workers available to hire begins to decrease and firms find they must compete for the increasingly limited supply of labour available. Therefore, output begins to increase at a decreasing rate when AD rises beyond the full-employment level.

As AD continues to increase to AD_3, further increases in output become almost impossible, as the economy is now producing beyond full employment, at nearly its full capacity level. Unemployment in the economy falls as AD increases, causing a tight labour market as firms find it harder to meet the rising demand from their customers. The result is a SRAS curve that is increasingly inelastic beyond the full-employment level of output, meaning that small increases in GDP are met with proportionally larger increases in the price level and inflation in the economy.

Keynes's view of the AS curve reflects the theory of sticky wages and prices in the short run. When AD falls, firms must reduce output and lay off workers since the existence of rigidities in the labour market makes it difficult to simply slash workers' wages in response to falling demand. Subsequently, when the total demand falls, output falls and unemployment rises in the short run, leading to a recession.

When AD rises, increases in output are proportionally smaller than the rise in the price level due to the rising demand for workers whose wages have yet to increase in response to higher demand for output. But because even a healthy nation producing at full employment has some unemployment, it is possible in the short run for a nation to achieve a level of output beyond full employment.

The Keynesian SRAS curve reflects the stickiness or inflexibility of wages in the short run by showing how a fall in demand leads to recession and high unemployment but only a slight deflation, while an increase in demand can lead to economic growth, reductions and unemployment, and ultimately inflation when output increases beyond the full-employment level.

 Sometimes too much aggregate demand is a bad thing. China's economy grew at an annual rate averaging 10% between 2000 and 2010, fuelled mainly by high levels of investment and net exports. In 2011, in its most recent Five Year Plan, the Chinese Communist Party announced that it would attempt to lower the growth rate over the next five years to 7%. The inelastic nature of the SRAS curve beyond full employment helps explain why China wishes to slow the growth of its AD; too much demand leads to inflation, which would harm the Chinese people (Chapter 14).

 ## 12.7 Long-run equilibrium in the AD/AS model: the neo-classical, flexible wage model

Learning outcomes
- Explain, using a diagram, the determination of long-run equilibrium, indicating that long-run equilibrium occurs at the full-employment level of output.
- Explain why, in the monetarist/new classical approach, while there may be short-term fluctuations in output, the economy will always return to the full-employment level of output in the long run.
- Examine, using diagrams, the impacts of changes in the long-run equilibrium.

In stark contrast to Keynes's interpretation of AS, the curve we identify as long-run aggregate supply (LRAS) illustrates a very different view of the macroeconomy. In the century leading up to the Great Depression, the prevailing view among economists known as the neo-classical school was that there was no relationship between the level of demand in an economy and the level of output. Rather, it was assumed that regardless of the total demand in a nation, the level of output would typically return to a level corresponding with the nation's production possibilities; in other words, output would always be at the full-employment level (Figure 12.13, overleaf).

The fundamental assumption behind the neo-classical view of AS is that wages and prices are perfectly flexible and will, therefore, adjust to the level of demand to ensure that output always remains at its full-employment level. There can be no involuntary unemployment, according to the neo-classical view, because workers who might lose their jobs as demand

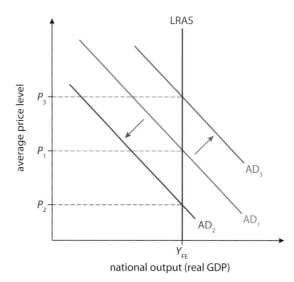

Figure 12.13
LRAS is perfectly inelastic at the full employment level of output.

for the goods or services they produce declines will simply accept lower wages, which allows firms to maintain their output and employment while lowering their prices in response to declining demand.

While demand in an economy falls, the quantity of output remains steady because prices will adjust downwards to maintain the full-employment quantity. If workers are unwilling to work at the prevailing wage rates, then they are voluntarily unemployed, which in the neo-classical view is natural in an economy at any level of AD and, therefore, not of concern.

The neo-classical view of AS is highly unlikely to be realized in the short run because wages tend to be highly inflexible in the short run. However, over a period of months, or more likely years, the wages of workers in an economy are more likely to adjust in response to changes in AD. For this reason, we will generally apply the neo-classical, flexible-wage model of AS to our analysis of the long-run effects of a shift in AD, and use the model to illustrate LRAS.

For instance, in Figure 12.13 as AD falls from AD_1 to AD_2, in the short run, we would expect unemployment to rise, output to fall, and only a slight decrease in the price level (as in Figure 12.11, page 276). In the long run, as unemployment rises and demand remains weak, workers begin to accept the lower wages offered by firms in order to get back to work. Consequently, employment and output return to the full-employment level, while prices in the economy simply adjust downwards. When AD rises to AD_3, firms scramble to hire workers to increase their profits, but as labour markets tighten and workers become more scarce, there is upward pressure on wages. This means that firms must cut employment and reduce their output in response to the rising costs of production that higher wages cause. In the long run, therefore, output and employment return to Y_{FE}, and only the price level increases following a rise in AD.

The neo-classical, flexible-wage model of AS demonstrates that in the long run, there is no trade-off between the level of demand in an economy and the level of output. Changes in demand lead only to changes in the wage rate and the price level, as workers and consumers adjust their expectations and behaviour to the macroeconomic conditions in the nation.

To access Worksheet 12.2 on Hayek, Keynes and AS, please visit www. pearsonbacconline.com and follow the onscreen instructions.

Recessions, or periods during which a nation's output contracts and unemployment rises, are only likely if wages and prices are inflexible, in other words, in the short run. Assuming wages are flexible over time, then in the long run, the economy is able to self-correct from a recession as wages and prices adjust downwards and firms hire workers and increase their output until the economy is producing at full employment once more. Likewise, long-run economic growth cannot be achieved by an increase in AD beyond the full-employment level because, over time, wages and prices adjust upwards increasing firms' costs and forcing them to reduce output and employment until the economy returns to its full-employment level of output.

 To learn more about the AD/AS model, visit www. pearsonhotlinks.com, enter the title or ISBN of this book and select weblink 12.5.

 ## 12.8 Shifts in aggregate supply

Learning outcomes

- Explain, using the two models above, how factors leading to changes in the quantity and/or quality of factors of production (including improvements in efficiency, new technology, reductions in unemployment, and institutional changes) can shift the aggregate supply curve over the long term.

Causes of an increase in AS

A change in the price level in a country resulting from a shift in AD causes a movement along the nation's AS curve. In the short run, a fall in AD causes a fall in output and a small decrease in the price level. In the long run, when wages have adjusted to the lower AD, the SRAS curve shifts to the right and output is restored at the full-employment level and at a lower price level (Figure 12.14).

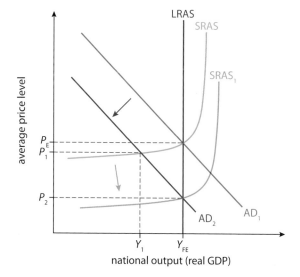

Figure 12.14
SRAS shifts out when wages have had time to fall following a demand-deficient recession.

The SRAS curve shifts to the right only after the wage rate in the economy falls because of low demand for output and labour. Besides a change in the wage rate, other factors that can lead to an increase in SRAS include:

- lower resource costs (e.g. oil, minerals and other raw materials)
- improvement in the productivity of land or capital
- reduction in the minimum wage
- government subsidies to producers
- investment tax credits (encouraging firms to invest in capital)
- reduction in trade union power
- better infrastructure

- better educated or more skilled workforce (increases productivity of labour)
- stronger currency (makes imported resources cheaper).

An improvement in any of the above determinants of AS shifts the SRAS curve to the right, increasing the equilibrium level of output and putting downward pressure on prices in the economy. For an economy in a demand-deficient recession (Figure 12.14) an increase in SRAS does not necessarily increase LRAS, as the economy must return to full employment before its long-run level of output can expand.

If an economy is already producing at its full-employment level and any of the above determinants of SRAS improve, both the nation's SRAS and LRAS curves shift to the right, increasing the nation's full-employment level of output (Figure 12.15).

Figure 12.15
Increase in productivity or the quantity of a nation's resources shifts both SRAS and LRAS outwards.

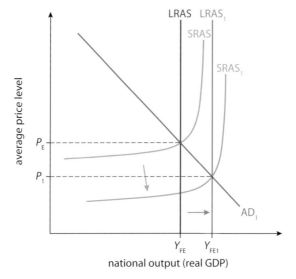

Lower production costs for firms allow them to produce more goods and services and sell their product for lower prices, increasing the full-employment level of output and reducing long-term unemployment in the economy. Figure 12.15 illustrates economic growth resulting from more productive use of resources and lower production costs and an outward shift of AS.

Causes of a decrease in SRAS

An increase in AD when an economy is already producing at full employment will result in inflation as the nation's output increases in the short run. In the long run, however, wages adjust upwards and the SRAS curve shifts to the left, restoring output at its full-employment level with more inflation in the economy (Figure 12.16).

SRAS shifts to the left in Figure 12.16 because wages increased in the economy following the demand-pull inflation resulting from an increase in AD from AD_1 to AD_2. In the long run (flexible-wage period), the economy returned to its full-employment level. Other factors that can reduce SRAS in a nation include:

- increase in resource costs (oil shocks, energy shortages, higher food prices)
- increase in trade union power
- increase in the minimum wage
- higher business taxes
- weaker currency (makes imported raw materials more expensive).

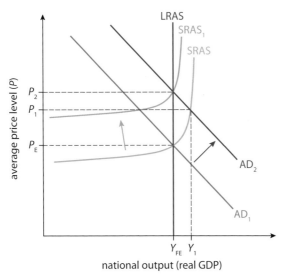

Figure 12.16
SRAS shifts inwards if wages
and other resource costs rise
during a period of demand-
pull inflation.

If any of the above occur, a nation's SRAS curve shifts to the left, causing an increase
in the price level and a fall in output (Figure 12.17). If the economy is producing at full
employment and any of the above change, it will result in both a recession (a fall in national
output) and inflation (caused by higher costs of production for firms).

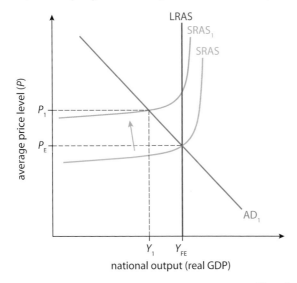

Figure 12.17
A supply shock causes SRAS
to shift to the left, resulting in
cost-push inflation.

In later chapters, we explore the policies governments can use to affect the overall supply
of goods and services in a country. As we've seen, the willingness and ability of firms
to produce goods and services at any given price level depends primarily on the costs
of production. Factors that increase firms' production costs shift the SRAS to the left,
reducing output and causing inflation, while lower costs of production or more productive
resources shift AS to the right, with economic growth, and price stability or even deflation.

The controversy over AS

Our use of two AS curves recognizes the validity of both the Keynesian view of the
macroeconomy (wages and prices are relatively inflexible in the short run) and the neo-
classical view (over time, wages adjust downwards or upwards in response to changes in
demand and total output returns to the full-employment level). The implication, therefore,
is that an economy in which AD falls will experience rising unemployment and a fall in

To access Worksheet 12.3, an exercise on aggregate demand and aggregate supply, please visit www. pearsonbacconline.com and follow the onscreen instructions.

output in the short run. However, if left alone, it will self-correct and output will return to the full-employment level in the long run. According to the neo-classical model, there is little need for a government to manage AD to maintain full employment, because an economy will always achieve full employment if the market is left to itself.

The debate over the shape of the AS curve has been going on for decades, and will likely continue long into the future. The reality is, whether AS is vertical, upward-sloping or horizontal depends on what nation is being discussed, the characteristics of that country's labour markets and the extent to which government is involved in the nation's economy. In the chapters that follow, the role of government in managing AD and AS is explored in more detail. In addition, the unprecedented shocks to the overall level of AD in the world's economies during the recession of 2008–09 is put into context and their effects on peoples' lives and the well-being of nations is explored.

Understanding the interactions of AD and AS in a nation's economy helps governments, households and firms to respond better to fluctuations in the level of economic activity, and gives all stakeholders involved the ability to understand the appropriate responses to periods of macroeconomic uncertainty or prosperity.

To access Quiz 12, an interactive, multiple-choice quiz on this chapter, please visit www.pearsonbacconline. com and follow the onscreen instructions.

PRACTICE QUESTIONS

1

a Use an AD/AS diagram to analyse the likely effects of an increase in interest rates.
(10 marks) [AO2], [AO4]

b To what extent is the level of interest rates in an economy the primary factor businesses consider when making investment decisions? (15 marks) [AO3]
© International Baccalaureate Organization 2002 (part **a** only)

2

a Use an AD/AS diagram to analyse the likely effects of an increase in income tax.
(10 marks) [AO2], [AO4]

b Compare and contrast the levels of household consumption relative to total aggregate demand in countries with relatively high income taxes to those with relatively low income taxes. (15 marks) [AO3]
© International Baccalaureate Organization 2002 (part **a** only)

3

a Using AD/AS diagrams, analyse the likely impact on an economy of the following:

i a general rise in wage costs

ii the discovery of new raw material sources

iii capital stock increases. (10 marks) [AO2], [AO4]

b Examine the likely effect of one of the events above on a nation's economy in the short run and in the long run. (15 marks) [AO3]
© International Baccalaureate Organization 2006 (part **a** only)

4

a Identify the components of aggregate demand and briefly explain two factors which might determine each of these components. (10 marks) [AO2]

b Evaluate the likely impact on an economy of a substantial rise in the level of savings among the nation's households. (15 marks) [AO3]
© International Baccalaureate Organization 2006 (part **a** only)

13 MACROECONOMIC OBJECTIVE: UNEMPLOYMENT

13.1 Introduction to the four macroeconomic objectives

During the Great Depression, queues for jobs and queues for food were a common sight.

Throughout your study of microeconomics, a prevailing theme was the inefficiency resulting from the intervention of government in free markets. It was observed that a government's role in the microeconomy should generally be limited to intervening to promote a more socially optimal level of output when markets fail to allocate resources efficiently. Whenever the market can achieve efficiency on its own, the goal of government should be to not interfere, lest it run the risk of misallocating society's scarce resources. Microeconomics focuses mainly on the objectives of private firms and individuals in their efforts to maximize profits and utility, and on the impacts on efficiency of the free market interactions of individual consumers and producers.

Macroeconomics, on the other hand, is rooted in the formulation of economic policies on a national and international level. You will examine the impact of various interventions by government and central banks, analyse the effects of government policies on various macroeconomic indicators, and evaluate the various policy options available to governments and central banks based on competing theories of the macroeconomy.

Macroeconomic policies are aimed at the following four objectives:

- **Full employment**. Most of the people who are willing and able to work in a nation should be able to find work. High unemployment creates social and economic challenges for a nation and should be avoided through macroeconomic policies wherever possible.

- **Low inflation**. The average price level of goods and services in a nation should increase slowly over time. Unanticipated fluctuations in the price level in a nation are undesirable and should be avoided through macroeconomic policies.

- **Economic growth**. The nation's output of goods and services should increase year after year, so as to ensure constant improvement in the standard of living of the nation's people. Avoiding recession (i.e. negative growth) should be a goal of macroeconomic policies.

- **Income distribution**. The nation's income should be distributed relatively equally across the various levels or classes of society, so as to ensure economic opportunity to all the nation's citizens. A grossly unequal distribution of income is an obstacle to economic development and may lead to social, political or economic unrest in a country. Therefore, promoting some degree of equality in income distribution is a goal of macroeconomic policies.

Economists and policymakers encounter numerous obstacles in the pursuit of these macroeconomic objectives. Deciding on an appropriate policy for achieving them is a

What criteria can be used to order macroeconomic objectives in terms of priority? Are such criteria external to economics (that is, normative)?

contentious and often lengthy process. The competing theories of the Keynesian and neo-classical schools of economic thought form the basis for economic policies that offer governments various methods of achieving these goals. However, the effectiveness of these policies is often questionable and difficult to determine without implementing the policies in a real economy.

This chapter examines the first of the four macroeconomic objectives: low unemployment.

13.2   The meaning of unemployment

Learning outcomes
- Define the term unemployment.
- Explain how the unemployment rate is calculated.
- (HL only) Calculate the unemployment rate from a set of data.
- Explain the difficulties in measuring unemployment, including the existence of hidden unemployment, the existence of underemployment, and the fact that it is an average and therefore ignores regional, ethnic, age and gender disparities.

Defining unemployment

From an economic perspective, to be unemployed means that you are actively seeking but unable to find work. A person who is not working is not necessarily unemployed, to be considered unemployed in an economic sense, a person must:

be out of work and willing to accept a suitable job or start an enterprise if the opportunity arises, and actively looking for ways to obtain a job or start an enterprise.

International Labour Organization (ILO)

The International Labour Organization monitors and measures employment data around the world and promotes fair and equal employment through its development of labour standards which are adopted by member states.

How unemployment rate is calculated

Governments monitor the level of unemployment in the nation by calculating the unemployment rate (UR), which is found by dividing the number of unemployed by the labour force.

$$UR = \frac{\text{number of unemployed}}{\text{labour force}} \times 100$$

According to the World Bank, a country's labour force is the sum of employed and unemployed persons aged 15–64 (age range may vary from nation to nation). Persons who are neither employed nor seeking employment are not in the labour force; this includes retired persons, students, those taking care of children or other family members, and others who are neither working nor seeking work.

Unemployment is the condition of someone of working age (16–64) who is willing and able to work, actively seeking employment, but unable to find a job.

Examples of people who *are* part of the labour force:

- A part-time retail sales clerk who is also going to college is part of the labour force because she is employed.
- A full-time nurse is part of the labour force because he is employed.
- A factory worker whose plant closed and who is applying for jobs at other firms is part of the labour force because he is unemployed.

Unemployment rate is the percentage of the total labour force in a nation that is unemployed.

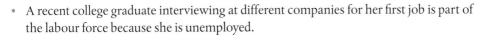

- A recent college graduate interviewing at different companies for her first job is part of the labour force because she is unemployed.

Examples of people who *are not* part of the labour force:

- A stay-at-home mother is not part of the labour force because she is not employed nor seeking employment.
- A college graduate who volunteers in a community centre is not part of the labour force because although he is working, he is not formally employed nor is he seeking employment.
- A discouraged worker who has been looking for a job for 18 months but has given up the job search is not part of the labour force because he is no longer seeking employment.
- An engineer who goes back to school to earn a teaching degree is not part of the labour force because he is not currently seeking employment.

Figure 13.1 shows average unemployment rates over the years 2005–07 for 19 developed and developing countries. National governments employ their own means of collecting unemployment data, but the Organization for Economic Cooperation and Development (OECD) uses the method devised by the ILO. Therefore, the figures in the bar chart can be compared with confidence despite the fact that the figures reported by each individual nation may vary due to different methods of collection.

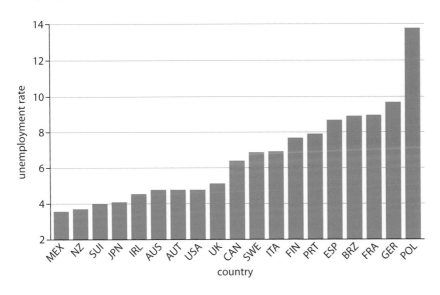

Figure 13.1
Unemployment rates in the OECD countries (2005–07).

Unemployment rates vary across countries depending on the current macroeconomic conditions and institutional factors such as the existence of social safety nets, the education levels of the workforce, and the evolving structures of the economy, among others. Figure 13.2 (overleaf) shows the unemployment rates across Europe in 2008.

Calculating the unemployment rate (HL only)

The unemployment rate is found by dividing the number of unemployed by the total labour force.

$$UR = \frac{\text{number of unemployed}}{\text{labour force}} \times 100$$

Figure 13.2
Unemployment rates in
Europe (2008).

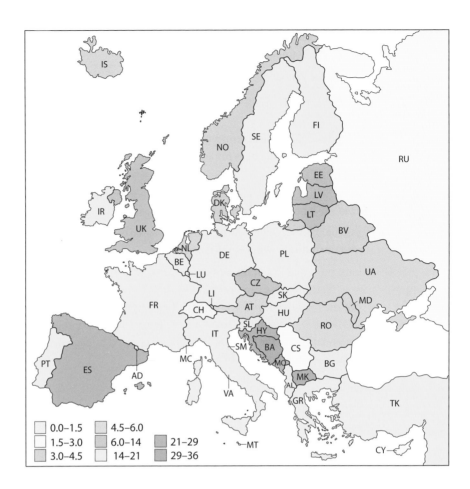

What evidence would
we need to determine
the underlying causes
for the different levels of
unemployment across
geographically similar
countries such as those in
Europe?

Legend:
- 0.0–1.5
- 1.5–3.0
- 3.0–4.5
- 4.5–6.0
- 6.0–14
- 14–21
- 21–29
- 29–36

Worked example

In 2007, Brazil's labour force totalled approximately 100 million people. The number of
people of working age who were actively seeking but unable to find work (the unemployed)
in Brazil totalled 8.9 million. What is Brazil's unemployment rate (UR)?

UR = number of unemployed/labour force × 100

 = 8.9 million/100 million × 100

 = 8.9%

HL EXERCISES

1   In country X, there are 60 million people of working age. Of these, 70% are available for
work, while 39 million are currently employed.

    a   Calculate the number of people in country X's labour force.

    b   Calculate country X's unemployment rate.

2   Assume immigration increases the number of people of working age in country X to
65 million, while the labour force increases to 44 million.

    a   Calculate the new labour force participation rate (percentage of working-age
population in the labour force) in country X.

    b   Assume unemployment is now 9%. How many unemployed people are there in
country X?

Labour force participation rate

The labour force participation rate (LFPR) is the ratio of the number of people in the labour force to the entire working-age population of a nation. LFPRs vary from country to country as well as over time.

Throughout the second half of the 20th century and into this century, LFPRs rose across much of the western world, primarily because of the large numbers of women entering the workforce during those years.

Along with labour productivity, a country's LFPR is an important determinant of its potential for economic growth (another of the four macroeconomic objectives). The greater the proportion of the working-age population that is in the labour force, the greater a nation's production possibilities, since the main factor that can increase a nation's production possibilities curve (PPC) is the quantity of resources. A greater LFPR means a larger number of workers available for employment in a nation and, therefore, it increases the nation's production possibilities.

A government may promote a growth in the LFPR by enacting supply-side policies such as:

- reduction in unemployment and social security benefits
- improved access to public education and job training for all members of society including women, minorities and immigrants
- other policies that encourage and enable people of working age to enter the labour force and become productive members of society.

Shortcomings of the unemployment rate as a measure of economic health

Changes in the labour force participation rate make the unemployment rate appear lower than it really is

During recessions, the LFPR tends to decline as discouraged workers give up on their job search and leave the labour force. One of the major shortcomings of using the UR as an indicator of the well-being of a nation's citizens is that it does not account for the workers who have left the labour force due to low expectations for employment. Figure 13.3 shows the LFPR in the US during the recession of 2008–09.

During the recession in the United States, the LFPR declined by 2%, indicating that several million people left the labour force. Many of these were discouraged workers who, while they were unable to find work, were not counted among the unemployed since they

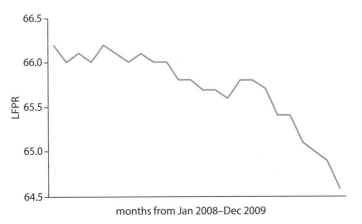

months from Jan 2008–Dec 2009

Figure 13.3
LFPR declines during a recession.

were no longer seeking employment. At the same time, the unemployment rate doubled from 5% to 10%, representing millions of new unemployed Americans looking for but unable to find jobs (Figure 13.4).

Figure 13.4
Unemployment rate rises during a recession.

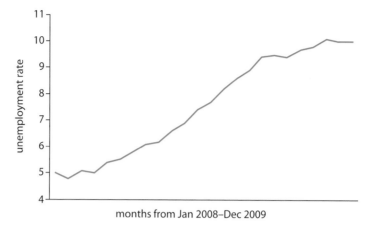

months from Jan 2008–Dec 2009

> The labour force participation rate (LFPR) is the proportion of the working-age population that is either unemployed or employed. If the LFPR drops, it may be because people have chosen to give up searching for jobs or they have decided to retire early or go back to school. A decline in the LFPR can cause the unemployment rate to understate the true number of people out of work in a nation.

Notice, however, that during the last few months of the period, the LFPR dropped dramatically from around 66% to 64.5%. The sudden drop in LFPR caused the increase in unemployment of the previous two years to slow and eventually level out at 10%. Does the levelling out of the unemployment rate mean Americans stopped losing their jobs? Probably not; rather, the unemployment rate stopped rising because the number of people who continued to lose their jobs roughly equalled the number of people dropping out of the labour force because they had given up on the job search.

The fact that unemployment stopped increasing at 10% around the end of 2009 could be interpreted as a sign that the economic slowdown in America was coming to an end. On the other hand, the drop in the LFPR at the same time is evidence that millions of American workers were giving up the job search due to low expectations of finding work, a fact which can be interpreted as a sign that America's economy was doing worse than the unemployment rate might suggest.

To better understand how the unemployment rate may understate the number of people out of work during a recession, let's consider a scenario based on Figures 13.3 and 13.4.

Worked example

In 2008, the size of the US working-age population was approximately 225 million people.

- In January 2008, LFPR = 66.2%. This tells us that 66.2% of the working-age population were either employed or unemployed, so the size of the labour force was 149 million.
- With unemployment at 5%, 7.5 million Americans would have been considered unemployed in January 2008.
- By December 2009, LFPR = 64.6%, putting the labour force at 145.3 million people. In other words, about 3.7 million people had left the labour force since January 2008.
- Unemployment, meanwhile, had climbed to 10% by January 2009, meaning 14.5 million people were unemployed (10% of the labour force):
  - labour force at the beginning of 2008 = 149 million
  - labour force at the end of 2009 = 145.3 million
  - number of people who left the labour force between January 2008 and December 2009 = 149 – 145.3 = 3.7 million.
- The 2% decline in LFPR is most likely explained by the decision of unemployed Americans to give up searching for work and drop out of the labour force. If these

individuals had persisted and continued to fail in their pursuit of a job, then an additional 3.7 million Americans would have been counted as unemployed.

The 3.7 million discouraged workers are not considered unemployed since they left the labour force. In addition to the 14.5 million unemployed Americans at the end of 2009, there were nearly 4 million more who had given up on the job hunt and left the labour force. If these individuals had been accounted for, then there would have been over 18 million unemployed Americans by the end of 2009, which would have put the unemployment rate at roughly 13%. Because discouraged workers are not included in the unemployment measure, unemployment understates the hardships of a nation's workers during economic downturns.

This example over-simplifies a far more complex situation. For instance, as the LFPR declined between 2008 and 2009, America's working-age population actually grew due to normal population growth and immigration, therefore the total number of unemployed and discouraged workers would have been even larger than our calculations indicate. In addition, millions of Americans became *underemployed* as employers cut back on hours to reduce costs during the slowdown in aggregate demand.

Underemployment *vs* unemployment

Another reality not reflected in unemployment data is that an individual's status as 'employed' does not take into account the number of hours or the type of employment the individual is experiencing. Part-time workers who would rather be working full-time are considered employed, despite the fact that from their perspective they are underemployed. Additionally, people stuck in jobs for which they are over-qualified (e.g. an engineer waiting tables because of the lack of engineering jobs) are also considered employed. Such workers' dissatisfaction with their level of employment or their type of employment is not reflected in the nation's unemployment figures – another shortcoming of the unemployment rate as a measure of well-being of the nation's workforce.

In March 2010, when the US unemployment rate was 9.7%, a poll (by the Gallup organization) of 20 000 American households determined that underemployment in the US stood at 20.3%. This figure included the 9.7% of Americans counted as unemployed, but also counted those who were working part-time but wanting full-time work. According to Gallup:

> As unemployed Americans find part-time, temporary, and seasonal work, the official unemployment rate could decline. However, this does not necessarily mean more Americans are working at their desired capacity. It will continue to be important to track underemployment – to shed light on the true state of the U.S. workforce, and the millions of Americans who are searching for full-time employment.

Underemployment is the condition of a worker who is technically employed, but is either over-qualified for the type of work he or she is doing or is working part-time when full-time work is desired. Underemployment is not accounted for in unemployment figures, this helps explain why the unemployment rate is an imperfect measure of a nation's macroeconomic reality.

	EXERCISES	

3 (HL only) Study the employment data below and answer the questions that follow.

	SWITZERLAND	SPAIN
Population aged 15–64 (total)	5 175 054	31 141 200
Unemployed persons (total)	153 518	1 821 917
Labour force (total)	4 264 435.1	21 950 810.9

Data from The World Bank

a   Calculate Switzerland's labour force participation rate (LFPR).

b   Calculate Switzerland's unemployment rate (UR).

c   Calculate Spain's labour force participation rate (LFPR).

d   Calculate Spain's unemployment rate (UR).

4   What macroeconomic factors might explain the differences in the unemployment rates in Spain and Switzerland?

5   What political, institutional and social factors might explain the different labour force participation rates in Spain and Switzerland?

6   Evaluate the unemployment rate as an accurate measure of the well-being of a nation's workforce.

Graphing unemployment: the labour market diagram

A nation's labour market consists of the aggregate supply of labour (ASL) of and aggregate demand for labour (ADL) in all sectors of the nation's economy. An economy in which national output is at its full-employment level has achieved equilibrium in the labour market, meaning at the equilibrium wage rate (the price of labour) almost everyone who wants a job has a job.

A labour market being in equilibrium does not mean that there is no unemployment, rather that the unemployment which exists is natural unemployment, consisting only of those workers who are in between jobs, those whose skills no longer match up with the demand for workers in the economy and those who are voluntarily unemployed. Voluntary unemployment describes workers who would be able to work if they were willing to accept the wages offered, but choose to remain unemployed in the hope of attaining a better-paid job down the road.

In Figure 13.5 a and b, the national economy is producing at its full-employment level of real output (Y_{FE}). The price level (P_E) in the economy is stable and corresponds with the equilibrium wage level (W_E) at which the labour market is cleared (everyone who wishes to work at the market wage rate is employed, with the exception of those members of the labour force mentioned above).

Figure 13.5
The national labour market: at full employment output, unemployment is equal to the natural rate.

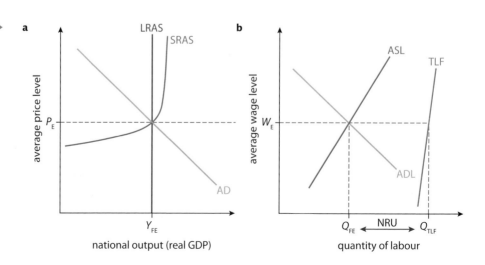

The total labour force (TLF) is greater than the ASL, since at any given time there will exist a certain level of 'natural' unemployment in the economy. TLF is upward-sloping because as wage rates in the economy rise, members of the working-age population who are not part of the labour force may be incentivized to enter the labour force. At lower wage rates, members of the labour force may decide to leave and pursue opportunities other than formal employment (e.g. continued education or early retirement).

At the full-employment level of national output, the unemployment that prevails is known as the natural rate of unemployment, and is represented by the difference between Q_{FE} and Q_{TLF} (Figure 13.5b).

13.3 Consequences of unemployment

Learning outcomes
- Discuss possible personal and social consequences of unemployment, including increased crime rates, increased stress levels, increased indebtedness, homelessness and family breakdown.
- Discuss possible economic consequences of unemployment, including a loss of GDP, loss of tax revenue, increased cost of unemployment benefits, loss of income for individuals, and greater disparities in the distribution of income.

Unemployment is certainly one of the most unfortunate and uncomfortable situations an individual can find him- or herself in. The individual, social and economic consequences of unemployment can be severe and long-lasting, which explains why maintaining a low level of unemployment is an important macroeconomic objective.

Individual consequences of unemployment

- **Decreased household income and purchasing power**. An obvious consequence of unemployment is a decline in a household's ability to provide the standard of living to which it may have grown accustomed when one or more members of the household were employed. The decline in personal income could result in foreclosure on or eviction from a home, or worse, inability to meet the nutritional needs of the household.
- **Increased levels of psychological and physical illness, including stress and depression**. A less obvious consequence of unemployment is the psychological and even physical toll it imposes on the unemployed. Some studies have shown that higher unemployment rates are correlated with higher rates of cardiovascular disease, suicides, and psychiatric hospital admittances.

You might expect the unemployment rate and the suicide rate to be related. It is true that during the Great Depression, suicide rates in the US increased dramatically. However, recessions that have been studied since then (including Sweden's in the 1990s) have not shown such a clear correlation.

Social consequences of unemployment

- **Downward pressure on wages for the employed**. High unemployment means the supply of available labour has increased in the nation. Since wages are determined by supply and demand, an increase in the labour supply can lower the equilibrium wage rate for those who still have jobs, forcing them to accept pay cuts and reducing the real incomes of all workers.
- **Increased poverty and crime**. Regions or cities in which unemployment occurs

To appreciate how large a migration this movement of Chinese people is, imagine nearly all the people of Eastern Europe migrating to the French, Portuguese and Spanish coasts after the collapse of Communism in the 1990s.

may become depressed and therefore less attractive to new investment by businesses. The low income levels of the largely unemployed population deter businesses from opening, further contributing to the unemployment and poverty problem. Crime and unemployment are also closely linked.

- **Transformation of traditional societies**. Unemployment in particular regions or sectors of the economy can lead to social upheaval and large-scale migrations of human populations. High unemployment in rural areas of China (resulting from the replacement of farm labour with capital during the last three decades) has resulted in the largest migration in human history as nearly 300 million Chinese have left their ancestral homes to relocate to the coastal cities looking for employment opportunities in the growing manufacturing sector.

Economic consequences of unemployment

- **Lower level of AD**. Consumption, a major component of AD, is primarily determined by disposable incomes. Unemployment lowers households' disposable income and consumption, reducing the level of demand and output in the nation as a whole. This leads to more unemployment and can pull an economy into a recession.
- **Under-utilization of the nation's resources**. Unemployment means a nation is not fully utilizing its productive resources, therefore a nation with high unemployment is producing within its PPC at a level below that which is most beneficial to an economy trying to improve the standards of living of its people.
- **Brain-drain**. Skilled workers may choose to leave a country with high unemployment if job opportunities are more abundant elsewhere. This further leads to a fall in the production possibilities of the nation with high unemployment.
- **A turn towards protectionism and isolationist policies**. Rising unemployment is often blamed by politicians and policymakers on competition from cheap foreign producers. This can lead to the rise of protective tariffs and quotas or increased government spending on subsidies for domestic producers. Such policies lead to a misallocation of society's scarce resources and in the long run will make the nation less competitive in global markets.
- **Increased budget deficits**. Unemployed workers do not pay income taxes, yet often receive monthly payments from the government to assist them until they find work. High unemployment reduces tax revenues flowing to a government while increasing public expenditures on financial support for the unemployed. This necessitates either a decrease in government spending on public goods such as infrastructure, education, defence and healthcare, or an increase in government borrowing to finance its budget deficit. As you will see (Chapter 17) large government budget deficits bring their own set of problems to a nation's economy.

The individual, social and economic consequences of unemployment are not limited to those outlined above, but it should be clear that the costs of unemployment are wide-ranging, thus making low unemployment a worthy and important goal for macroeconomic policymakers.

To access Worksheet 13.1 on Chinese workers, please visit www.pearsonbacconline.com and follow the onscreen instructions.

Could unemployment lead to terrorism? There may actually be a correlation between the level of unemployment in a country and the likelihood of terrorism occurring there. The highest unemployment rate in the world is thought to be in the Palestinian territory of the Gaza Strip. In 2010, 45.2% of the workforce in Gaza was unemployed. Israel's long-term blockade of the territory is thought to be the main cause of the unemployment, which helps explain why, over the years, so many Gazans have turned to violence to express their outrage at their desperate economic plight, which many blame on Israel.

13.4 Types of unemployment and their causes

Learning outcomes
- Describe, using examples, the meaning of frictional, structural, seasonal and cyclical (demand-deficient) unemployment.
- Distinguish between the causes of frictional, structural, seasonal and cyclical (demand-deficient) unemployment.
- Explain, using a diagram, that cyclical unemployment is caused by a fall in aggregate demand.
- Explain, using a diagram, that structural unemployment is caused by changes in the demand for particular labour skills, changes in the geographical location of industries, and labour market rigidities.
- Evaluate government policies to deal with the different types of unemployment.

Unemployment comes in different forms that have different causes. There are three basic categories of unemployment:

- frictional and seasonal unemployment
- structural unemployment
- cyclical unemployment.

The first two of these are considered to be part of the natural rate of unemployment (NRU).

Frictional and seasonal unemployment

Workers who are in between jobs or just entering the labour force for the first time are referred to as frictionally unemployed. For example, an accountant in Bristol may wish to start a new career as a mathematics teacher in Nottingham. The accountant will quit his job and move to Nottingham to seek employment as a teacher. During the period of time between his old job and his new job, which he is fairly certain he will be able to acquire rather quickly, he is frictionally unemployed. Frictional unemployment is generally short-term (three months or less) and is often voluntary in nature, meaning the unemployed person has chosen to seek employment in a different location or industry. In addition to workers in between jobs, first-time job-seekers who are fresh out of high school or university are also considered frictionally unemployed. The key characteristic among the frictionally unemployed is that such individuals possess skills that are demanded by the nation's employers, thus their prospects for employment are generally positive.

Workers who do seasonal labour (e.g. golf course employees, migrant farmers, ski-lift operators or summer-camp instructors) may be unemployed between seasons. Seasonal unemployment is also considered a type of voluntary unemployment as many such workers choose their jobs for the freedom and other benefits such employment offers.

The level of frictional and seasonal unemployment can be influenced by government policies that affect incentives among the labour force. For instance, if unemployment benefits can be collected for an entire 12 months as long as a worker is actively seeking employment, the individual has little incentive to rush the job search process and take the first decent job offered to him; such a worker is likely to remain unemployed for longer than one who can only collect benefits for three months before being cut off by the government. Additionally, if information about employment opportunities around the country is readily available and means exist to quickly match frictionally unemployed workers with employers through job centres or online employment services, then the duration of frictional unemployment and its prevalence in the economy may be reduced.

Structural unemployment

Joseph Schumpeter, an Austrian–American economist, famously reworked the Marxist view of the phrase 'creative destruction' to stand for the innovation and progress that destroys old methods of production. Structural unemployment is considered one of the necessary evils of this process.

When a worker loses his job due to the changing structure of the nation's economy, the individual becomes structurally unemployed. Such a situation may at first seem incredibly undesirable, as those who have been 'made redundant' because of automation through technology, cheaper foreign labour, or the decline of an entire industry in a nation are the unfortunate victims of economic change. However, structural unemployment is considered a 'natural' form of joblessness as it is only natural that as a nation grows and becomes incorporated into the global economy, the makeup of its GDP will change.

Structural unemployment occurs when a developing country moves from an agricultural base to a manufacturing base and farming techniques become less labour intensive and more capital intensive. Farmers whose skills were passed down through generations find themselves unemployed as their old techniques for tilling the land are replaced by new technology. Likewise, as a more developed nation transitions from a manufacturing base to a larger service sector, factory workers' skills may no longer be in demand, while the demand for highly educated and highly skilled 'knowledge workers' increases. In both of these examples, the nation as a whole is getting richer as productivity in the primary, secondary and tertiary sectors grows and national output rises, but the victims of such growth are those workers whose skills are no longer in demand in the new economy.

Structural unemployment is likely to endure much longer than frictional unemployment. Strategies for reducing structural unemployment lie primarily in the realm of increased worker training and improved education. Unfortunately, there are few short-term fixes to help the structurally unemployed that do not involve protectionist policies such as tariffs and subsidies that would only prolong the decline of the industries in which such workers are employed. To reduce structural unemployment over the long term, a nation must invest heavily in public education and training for adult workers in the skills that will be needed for the future economy, rather than those that were needed for the economy of the past or even the present.

The natural rate of unemployment (NRU)

A nation producing at its full-employment level of output still experiences some unemployment. This can be a confusing concept because the term 'full employment' makes it sound as if everyone has a job. In fact, an economy producing at full employment still experiences frictional, seasonal and structural unemployment. These combined are known as the natural rate of unemployment.

Labour markets clear when the total demand for labour equals the total supply of labour at the equilibrium wage rate. The caveat here is that the aggregate supply of labour represents those members of the working-age population who are willing and able to work. The existence of some workers whose skills are mismatched with the demand for labour given the structure of the nation's economy (the structurally unemployed) is expected in a nation producing at full employment; such unemployment is, therefore, natural. Additionally, members of the labour force who are voluntarily in between jobs or just out of school and seeking their first job (the frictionally unemployed) are also considered part of the natural rate of unemployment.

CASE STUDY

Help wanted: why that sign's bad

The nation has 3 million jobs going begging. And without retraining, US workers may not be able to fill them.

Surprising statistic: in the midst of the worst recession in a generation or more, with 13 million people unemployed, there are approximately 3 million jobs that employers are actively recruiting for but so far have been unable to fill. That's more job openings than the entire population of Mississippi.

Sound like good news? It's not. Instead, it's evidence of an emerging structural shift in the US economy that has created serious mismatches between workers and employers. People thrown out of shrinking sectors such as construction, finance, and retail lack the skills and training for openings in growing fields including education, accounting, healthcare, and government. At the same time, the worst housing bust in decades has left the unemployed frozen in place. They can't move to get work because they can't sell their homes.

As bad as it is now, the mismatch will create bigger problems when the economy begins to expand again. First, the unemployment rate is likely to remain distressingly high because many people who want jobs will lack the appropriate qualifications. Second, inflation could pick up sooner than expected if employers are forced into bidding wars to recruit the few people who are qualified for the work. Third, if unemployment stays high, it will put additional political pressure on Congress and the Obama Administration to push through fixes that could make matters worse in the long run, such as insulating workers from the cost of long-term unemployment to the point where they lose their appetite for work.

Business Week, 30 April 2009

Something that is bad for an individual could be good for society. To what extent is the existence of structural and frictional unemployment in an economy a sign of economic health *vs* economic hardship? What evidence would we need to evaluate the existence of these types of unemployment?

To access Worksheet 13.2 on 3 million job openings, please visit www.pearsonbacconline.com and follow the onscreen instructions.

EXERCISES

7 In what way may structural unemployment be a sign of a healthy economy, rather than a sick one?

8 How might government's extension of benefits to the unemployed actually prolong America's unemployment problem?

9 Historically, the natural rate of unemployment in Western European economies has been higher than that of the US. What types of government policy might help explain this?

Cyclical unemployment

Without question, the type of unemployment that poses the greatest obstacle and, therefore, the one which policymakers attempt to avoid at all costs is cyclical unemployment. Workers whose skills are in demand given the structure of the nation's economy but who nonetheless lose their jobs due to a fall in total demand for the nation's goods and services are cyclically unemployed. Cyclical unemployment arises due to fluctuations in the nation's business cycle; it is also referred to as demand-deficient unemployment. Cyclical unemployment occurs when a contraction in private or public spending (consumption, investment, government spending or net exports) reduces AD and leads to a fall in national output. As output of goods and services falls the demand for labour falls and there is downward pressure on wages and prices.

Weak AD explains the doubling of the unemployment rate in the US between 2008 and 2009. In early 2008, as the value of American assets (primarily real estate and stocks) declined, consumer spending fell as well as investment by firms now wary about future business conditions. Soon after America's largest trading partners (the EU, Canada, Japan and China) experienced declines in income and, therefore, demand for US exports fell as well. The result was a contraction of overall output and an increase in the unemployment rate. Cyclically unemployed workers would typically be able to find work relatively quickly in an economy producing at or close to its full-employment level; but in the environment of low confidence and weak expectations for the future, firms hesitate to employ more workers, leaving highly skilled and educated members of the workforce without job prospects.

In Figure 13.6, a fall in consumption, investment or net exports leads to a fall in AD and a decline in national output and employment. Due the inflexible nature of wages in the short run, the labour market experiences a disequilibrium wherein the total demand for labour falls as demand for goods and services declines, but the wage rate remains high (at W_E). There is a surplus of labour, known in this case as cyclical unemployment of $Q_1 - Q_{FE}$. The sticky wage rate acts similarly to a minimum wage in the labour market, whereby during a recession the quantity supplied of labour (those seeking employment) exceeds the quantity demanded (the opportunities for employment). As national output falls during a demand-deficient recession, cyclical unemployment occurs in the labour market. As demand for their goods and services falls, firms must lower costs to remain in operation. Since workers are unwilling to accept lower wages in the short run, the only way firms can cut costs is to reduce the number of workers they employ.

Figure 13.6

Cyclical unemployment arises from a fall in aggregate demand.

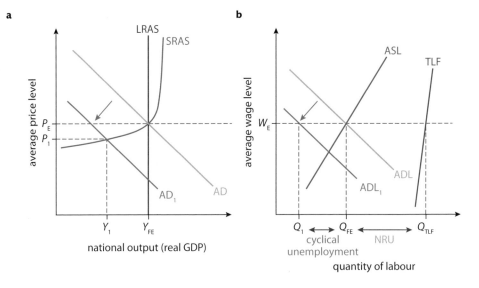

In addition to the frictional, seasonal and structural unemployment that prevailed when the economy was producing at its full-employment level, there exists during a recession a level of unemployment greater than the NRU. $Q_1 - Q_{FE}$ represents the number of cyclically unemployed workers caused by a decrease in demand for the nation's output. Demand-deficient unemployment is best addressed using demand-side policies aimed at stimulating the level of expenditure in an economy during a recession. Government and central bank policies that affect AD are discussed in Chapters 14 and 15.

To access Worksheet 13.3 on unemployment in Denmark, please visit www.pearsonbacconline.com and follow the onscreen instructions.

If someone is structurally unemployed, you could argue that the economy no longer demands that person's skills. Cyclical unemployment, however, is strictly a function of the business cycle. Should governments pay more attention and intervene more forcefully to stop cyclical unemployment? Should the cause of unemployment influence our decision to help the unemployed?

Types of unemployment summarized

Table 13.1 summarizes the four types of unemployment along with possible causes and solutions.

Type of unemployment	Description	Causes	Possible solution
TABLE 13.1 TYPES OF UNEMPLOYMENT SUMMARIZED			
Frictional unemployment	People who are in between jobs or looking for their first job; generally very short-term; part of NRU.	Young workers entering the labour force for the first time; workers who voluntarily quit to seek better job opportunities.	Improve information symmetry between employers and job seekers; reduce unemployment benefits.
Seasonal unemployment	Seasonal workers who need to seek other work between seasons; part of NRU.	Workers choosing jobs that allow for flexibility of time and location; such unemployment is considered voluntary.	Improve information symmetry between employers and job seekers; reduce unemployment benefits.
Structural unemployment	Workers unable to find work because their skills do not match those demanded by firms; part of NRU.	Globalization; outsourcing of secondary and tertiary sector jobs; new technologies that automate processes which used to require labour.	Improve training, education and mobility of labour force to encourage relocation as demands for labour change in regional areas.
Cyclical (demand-deficient) unemployment	Workers unable to find work because a reduction in private and public spending reduces AD.	Fall in consumption, investment or net exports reduces demand for labour; employment falls as the nation's output falls.	Implementation of fiscal or monetary stimulus aimed at increasing the level of AD and raising the nation's output and employment.
Natural rate of unemployment (NRU)	Unemployment occurring when an economy is producing at full-employment output level; structural plus seasonal plus frictional unemployment.	NRU is caused by the natural changes and shifting of resources in the economy and is considered a healthy and desirable level of unemployment.	A nation's NRU can be reduced via government policy aiming to increase productivity of the labour force and create incentives to accept work.

In this chapter you have learned about the concepts of unemployment and underemployment, seen how countries calculate their unemployment rates, and examined the various types of unemployment a nation's labour force might experience. Low unemployment is a macroeconomic objective that governments and central banks direct their policies towards in order to avoid the harsh realities of high unemployment that are imposed on individuals, society and the national economy.

 To learn more about unemployment, visit www.pearsonhotlinks.com, enter the title or ISBN of this book and select weblink 13.1.

 To access Quiz 13, an interactive, multiple-choice quiz on this chapter, please visit www.pearsonbacconline.com and follow the onscreen instructions.

PRACTICE QUESTIONS

1　**a** Distinguish between structural unemployment, frictional unemployment and seasonal unemployment. (10 marks) [AO2]

　　b To what extent is the existence of structural unemployment in a nation a sign of economic weakness? (15 marks) [AO3]

2　**a** Using an AD/AS model and a national labour market diagram, illustrate and explain the causes of cyclical unemployment. (10 marks) [AO2], [AO4]

　　b Examine the various costs of a persistently high level of cyclical unemployment. (15 marks) [AO3]

3　**a** Explain the concept of the natural rate of unemployment. (10 marks) [AO2]

　　b Justify the claim that the unemployment rate may understate the true number of people out of work in a nation. (15 marks) [AO3]

MACROECONOMIC OBJECTIVE: LOW INFLATION

14.1 ## The meaning of inflation, disinflation and deflation

Learning outcomes

- Distinguish between inflation, disinflation and deflation.
- Explain that inflation and deflation are typically measured by calculating a consumer price index (CPI), which measures the change in prices of a basket of goods and services consumed by the average household.
- Explain that different income earners may experience a different rate of inflation when their pattern of consumption is not accurately reflected by the CPI.
- Explain that inflation figures may not accurately reflect changes in consumption patterns and the quality of the products purchased.
- Explain that economists measure a core/underlying rate of inflation to eliminate the effect of sudden swings in the prices of food and oil, for example.
- Explain that a producer price index measuring changes in the prices of factors of production may be useful in predicting future inflation.
- (HL only) Construct a weighted price index, using a set of data provided.
- (HL only) Calculate the inflation rate from a set of data.

Definitions

Inflation erodes the value of money.

In addition to maintaining a low level of unemployment, national governments and central banks also focus their policies on the average price level of goods and services in a nation. Maintaining price level stability is considered a fundamental objective of macroeconomic policy, since price level instability can have negative effects on a nation's economic health.

Inflation is defined as an increase in the average price level of goods and services in a nation over time (Figure 14.1). Deflation, on the other hand, occurs when the average price level of goods and services decreases over time. The key word in these definitions is *average* since inflation does not measure changes in the relative prices of particular goods. For instance, certain types of technology (e.g. MP3 players, cellphones and laptop computers) have come down in price considerably since their widespread adoption in the early 2000s. The fall in prices of these particular goods does not mean that nations have experienced deflation, since only certain types of good have become cheaper. Even as certain technologies have fallen in price, the overall price levels of most developed countries have risen over the last decade.

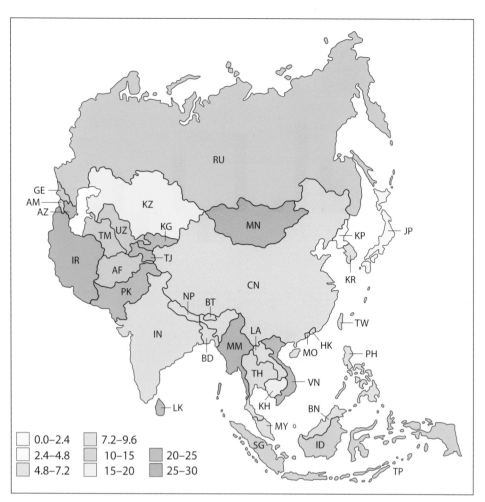

Figure 14.1
Inflation rates in Asia (2008).
www.indexmundi.com

Another way of understanding inflation is that it causes the value of money to decrease. An increase in the price level essentially makes money less valuable and reduces its purchasing power. In an environment of inflation, a particular amount of money will buy less in the future than it does in the present; thus inflation encourages households and firms to spend now rather than postponing spending until the future when prices are higher. The anticipation of future inflation can trigger a positive feedback loop in which households increase their spending now, thereby causing inflation and encouraging further increases in spending.

Deflation occurs when the average price level decreases over time. A fall in prices results in an increase in the value of money, since its purchasing power increases. A particular amount of money will buy more in the future than it does in the present when deflation occurs. Anticipated deflation incentivizes savings over current consumption and investment, since households and firms will wish to postpone purchases until the future when prices are expected to decline. Much as anticipated inflation can trigger an inflationary spiral, anticipated deflation can create a deflationary spiral in which spending falls, driving prices down, encouraging even less consumption and investment.

Disinflation refers to a decrease in the *rate of inflation*. You may find this term confusing at first, but its use should be clearer after you've done the exercises below.

Deflation is a decrease in the average price level of a nation's output.

Disinflation is a decrease in the rate at which the average price level is rising (a decrease in the inflation rate).

 Inflation is a sustained increase in the average price level of goods and services in a nation.

EXERCISES

1   Examine this graph which shows inflation in selected OECD countries, and answer the questions that follow.

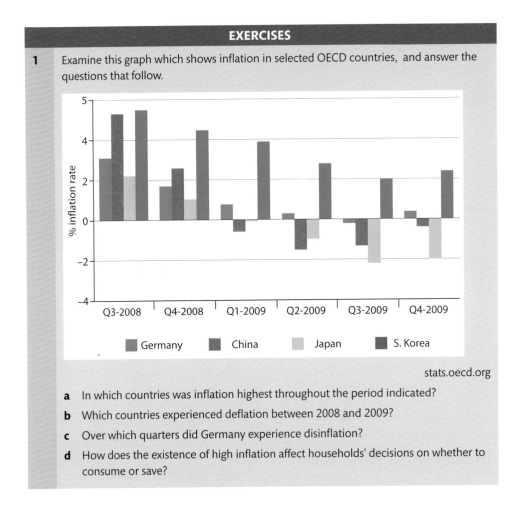

stats.oecd.org

a   In which countries was inflation highest throughout the period indicated?

b   Which countries experienced deflation between 2008 and 2009?

c   Over which quarters did Germany experience disinflation?

d   How does the existence of high inflation affect households' decisions on whether to consume or save?

Measuring inflation using a price index

Changes in price levels in nations are monitored on a monthly or quarterly basis in all 30 OECD nations. The methods for collecting inflation data are similar across countries, and employ a tool known as a price index. A price index is a relatively straightforward measure estimating the average price of goods and services purchased by households and firms within a region or nation. Calculating a price index involves the government conducting a regular survey of the prices of hundreds or even thousands of different consumer and producer goods.

The consumer price index (CPI) measures the prices of consumer goods and services and is widely used by governments to measure changes in the price level of the products that the typical household may buy in a particular time period. The metaphorical basket of goods measured for the CPI may include items such as clothing, food, fuel, electricity, rents, DVDs, airline tickets, bus fares, laptop computers, mobile phone service and so on. It also includes services, and its composition may be updated annually or bi-annually as new types of product become fashionable among consumers. For instance, the CPI in the mid-90s would probably have included the price of musical CDs. Today's CPI may instead include the price of digital music downloads.

A price index is found by dividing the price of a basket of goods in one period by the price of the identical basket of goods in a base period and multiplying by 100. To determine the price index, first a base period index must be established. For instance, assume the

A price index is an average of prices for a selection of goods and services in a particular nation during a given interval of time. A price index can be used to measure the changes in the price level of goods between one period of time and another.

government wishes to determine how much prices have risen between July and August. The index for the base period of July (CPI_J) is determined by the formula:

$$CPI_J = \frac{P_{bJ}}{P_{bJ}} \times 100$$

where P_{bJ} is the price of a particular basket of goods in July.

Since P_{bJ} divided by P_{bJ} is 1, the index for the base period (July) is $1 \times 100 = 100$. Now the price of the same basket of goods can be measured in August, and using this information we can determine the consumer price index for August (CPI_A).

$$CPI_A = \frac{P_{bA}}{P_{bJ}} \times 100$$

As a simple demonstration, let's revisit Country I and imagine that this country measures only three goods in its CPI: pizza, haircuts and wine (Table 14.1).

TABLE 14.1 CALCULATING A PRICE INDEX			
Good or service	**Price in July/euro**	**Price in August/euro**	**Price in September/euro**
pizza	10	10.50	10.50
haircuts	20	19	18
wine	8	10	10
total basket price	38	39.50	38.50

Assume July is the base period. To calculate Country I's CPI for August, we take the price of the basket of goods in August and divide it by the price of the same basket of goods in July and multiply the result by 100.

$$CPI_A = \frac{39.5}{38} \times 100 = 104$$

A real consumer price index, of course, includes hundreds of goods and services of various types, not just three. But the interpretation of the results is the same regardless of how many products make up the basket of goods. In our example, an increase in the price index from 100 to 104 indicates that a basket of goods that would have cost €100 in July would cost €104 in August. The purchasing power of the euro in Country I decreased and the country's economy experienced inflation between July and August.

Next, we can determine the price index for September (CPI_S) with the base period remaining July:

$$CPI_S = \frac{38.5}{38} \times 100 = 101.3$$

The price index in September indicates that the average price level decreased from August, but was still higher than in July. The economy experienced deflation between August and September. But, using July as the base period, Country I experienced inflation. A basket of goods that would have cost €104 in August costs only €101.3 in September. The purchasing power of the euro in Country I increased between August and September, but the euro still buys less in September than it did in July, since the basket of goods costing €100 in July cost €101.3 in September.

 Is there such a thing as a typical household in a nation? What issues arise with fairness and equality when choosing the contents of a nation's CPI?

Weighting of categories in the CPI (HL only)

To account for the different proportions of a typical household's disposable income that goes towards the purchase of different types of goods, governments assign weights (% total income spent) to categories of goods measured in the CPI. The weight of any individual category reflects its relative importance to the purchasing households and the total weight of all categories must add up to 100%.

The purpose of weighting categories in a CPI is to ensure that when a particular category of good experiences large fluctuations in price over time, the overall CPI does not fluctuate wildly. It simply adjusts in a manner that reflects the relative impact that price changes in that category have on the typical consumer's cost of living.

For instance, the US CPI divides the thousands of goods it measures into eight major categories, each assigned a weight reflecting its relative importance to the typical consumer (Table 14.2). The weight reflects the percentage of income spent on each good.

Category (examples of goods and services included)	Weight – reflecting relative importance/%
food and beverages (breakfast cereal, milk, coffee, chicken, wine, full service meals, snacks)	14.795
housing (rent of primary residence, owners' equivalent rent, fuel oil, bedroom furniture)	41.96
apparel (men's shirts and sweaters, women's dresses, jewellery)	3.695
transport (new vehicles, airline fares, gasoline, motor vehicle insurance)	16.685
medical care (prescription drugs and medical supplies, physicians' services, eyeglasses and eye care, hospital services)	6.513
recreation (televisions, toys, pets and pet products, sports equipment, admissions)	6.437
education and communication (college tuition, postage, telephone services, computer software and accessories)	6.434
other goods and services (tobacco and smoking products, haircuts and other personal services, funeral expenses)	3.483
total	100

TABLE 14.2 WEIGHTED CATEGORIES IN THE US CONSUMER PRICE INDEX

Worked example

To establish a weighted price index, we first determine the weighted price of a basket of goods by adding together the average price (P) of each category multiplied by the category weight expressed in hundredths.

Assuming a price index has three categories, A, B and C, the weighted price of the basket of goods is:

$(P_A \times$ weight in hundredths$) + (P_B \times$ weight in hundredths$) + (P_C \times$ weight in hundredths$)$

Examine Table 14.3.

Good	Average price in 2009 ($)	Average price in 2010 ($)	Percentage of income spent on each good (weight)/%
banana	2	1.50	25
haircut	11	10	30
taxi ride	8	10	45

TABLE 14.3 ESTABLISHING A SIMPLE WEIGHTED PRICE INDEX

To establish a price index with 2009 as the base year, we calculate the weighted price of the basket of goods for 2009. To do this, we multiply the average price of each good by its weight, expressed in hundredths:

- average price banana = $2 \times 0.25 = 0.5$
- average price haircut = $11 \times 0.3 = 3.3$
- average price taxi ride = $8 \times 0.45 = 3.6$

So, the weighted price of this basket of goods in 2009 = 7.4

Since we want 2009 to be our base year, we can establish the price index for 2009.

Price index for 2009 = $\frac{7.4}{7.4} \times 100 = 100$

The price of both bananas and haircuts falls in 2010. You might think, therefore, that the average price level falls in total. However, the price of taxi rides increases and, because taxi rides are weighted more heavily than the other two goods, it is likely that this increase in price increases the average price level for a consumer in this country. To find out, we calculate the weighted price of the basket of goods for 2010:

- average price banana = $1.5 \times 0.25 = 0.375$
- average price haircut = $10 \times 0.3 = 3$
- average price taxi ride = $12 \times 0.45 = 5.4$

So, the weighted price of this basket of goods in 2010 = 8.775

To determine the price index for 2010, we divide the 2010 weighted price by the 2009 weighted price then multiply by 100:

- price index for 2010 = $\frac{8.775}{7.4} \times 100 = 118.58$

Based on the category weights, we can estimate the effect a change in the price of one good will have on the overall CPI and therefore the official inflation figure.

For instance, assume the price of bananas rises 15% between 2010 and 2011, but the price of haircuts and taxi rides remains unchanged. This 15% increase should be reflected in the inflation figure for that year, but the relatively small importance of banana expenditures for the typical household means that the total CPI and therefore inflation will rise by something less than 15%.

Worked example

If bananas account for 25% of the total CPI, determine how much a 15% increase in price in this category will affect inflation.

Multiply change in category price (P_C) by the category weight expressed in hundredths.

$\%\Delta CPI = \%\Delta P_C \, (\text{weight} \times 0.01)$

In the case of a 15% increase in banana prices, the effect on the CPI is:

$\%\Delta CPI = 15 \times 0.25 = 3.75\%$

If the price of bananas increases by 15% and the prices of all other categories remain constant, the effect on the overall CPI will be an increase of 3.75%.

If there is an increase in the price of goods in a category of greater relative importance to households (e.g. taxi rides), the impact on the overall CPI will be greater.

If the average price of taxi rides rises by 15% and all other categories remain unchanged, determine the impact on the CPI .

$$\%\Delta CPI = 15 \times 0.45 = 6.75\%$$

A 15% increase in the price of taxi ride will cause the overall CPI to increase by 6.75%, whereas an equal increase in the price of a relatively less important category of goods leads to a smaller increase in the overall CPI.

Through the weighting of categories based on relative importance to the typical households, a government attempts to make the consumer price index as accurate as possible a reflection of the actual effect of changing prices of different goods and services on the typical household.

Calculating the inflation rate using a CPI (HL only)

A price index such as the CPI can be used to determine the *rate of inflation* between two periods of time. The inflation rate (IR) is determined using the following formula:

$$IR = \frac{CPI_2 - CPI_1}{CPI_1} \times 100$$

CPI_2 refers to the consumer price index for the second time period, CPI_1 for the time period *from which* the inflation rate is being determined. Dividing the change in the CPI by the original CPI will give a decimal, which when multiplied by 100 will give a percentage.

Referring back to Table 14.1, to calculate Country I's inflation rate between July and August, the percentage change in the price index must be found.

$$IR = \frac{CPI_A - CPI_J}{CPI_J} \times 100 = \frac{104 - 100}{100} \times 100 = 4\%$$

Between July and August, Country I experienced 4% inflation. The average price of the three consumer goods in the CPI increased by 4%; alternatively, the purchasing power of Country I's currency decreased by 4%. To determine the inflation rate between August and September, make the following calculation:

$$IR = \frac{CPI_S - CPI_A}{CPI_A} \times 100 = \frac{101.3 - 104}{104} \times 100 = -2.6\%$$

Between August and September, Country I experienced inflation of −2.6%. The average price level decreased. The economic term for negative inflation is deflation. Another way to interpret deflation is that the purchasing power of Country I's currency increased between August and September, since what would have cost €104 in August cost €101.3 in September.

> The inflation rate is the percentage change in a price index between one period of time and another. It measures the change in the average price of goods and services in a nation over time. The inflation rate can be either positive, negative, or zero.

HL EXERCISES

2 Use the table below to answer the questions that follow.

CPI date for Country I; Q3 = third quarter (i.e. July–September); Q4 = fourth quarter (i.e. October–December) etc.

	Q3 2008	Q4 2008	Q1 2009	Q2 2009	Q3 2009	Q4 2009	Q1 2010
Country I's CPI	108.4	107.9	107.7	108.3	108.5	108.6	109.1

a Calculate Country I's inflation rates between each of the seven quarters.

b Between which quarters was the inflation rate highest? Lowest?

c Between which quarters did Country I experience disinflation?

d Between which quarters did Country I experience deflation?

3 Use the bar chart below to answer the questions that follow.

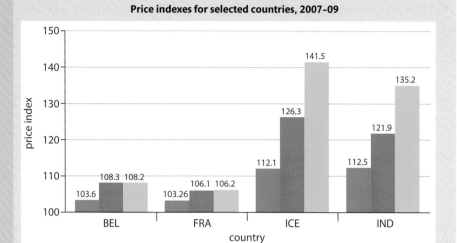

Price indexes for selected countries, 2007–09

a In which country was the inflation rate greatest between 2007 and 2008? Calculate the inflation rate.

b Which country or countries experienced deflation between 2007 and 2009? Calculate the deflation rate.

c Was inflation greater in Iceland between 2007 and 2008 or between 2008 and 2009? How do you know?

4 The table below shows the average prices of the goods purchased by a typical consumer in country Y in 2010 and 2011, as well as the percentage of a typical household's income spent on each item.

Good	Average price (2010)/$	Average price (2011)/$	Percentage of income spent on each item/%
hamburger	5.00	5.50	15
DVD	12.50	10	10
rent	90	105	40
book	8	6.50	15
petrol	15	18	20
weighted total	_____	_____	

a Use the table to construct a weighted price index for country Y for 2010 and 2011, using 2010 as the base year (= 100).

b Use your results to calculate the rate of inflation in country Y from 2010 to 2011.

c Assume the price of books increases by 10% from 2011 to 2012, but the price of all other goods remains constant. What would be the effect on the inflation rate?

d Now assume the price of rent increases by 10% instead, and all other prices remain constant. What would be the effect on the rate of inflation?

e Why does an increase in the price of some goods have a greater effect on inflation than identical percentage changes in the prices of other goods?

To access Worksheet 14.1 on inflation measures, please visit www. pearsonbacconline.com and follow the onscreen instructions.

Shortcomings of the CPI as a measure of inflation

The CPI is used in most nations to measure changes in the average price of goods and services purchased by the typical household in the nation between one time period and another. While the CPI provides an inflation rate that is meaningful to most households, the figure does have some shortcomings that must be acknowledged.

CPI does not reflect the purchases of all households in a nation

Not all of a nation's households are typical in that the income of a nation is not evenly distributed across all households. Some consumers will typically purchase a very different basket of goods than is measured to determine the CPI and inflation. If a large percentage of a consumer's income goes towards a small selection of the goods measured by the CPI, then the CPI as a whole may over or understate inflation depending on how the prices of those particular goods have changed relative to the rest of the goods measured.

CPI does not reflect changes in the quality of the products produced and consumed in a nation

The CPI only looks at one characteristic of the consumer goods it records: the price. What is not accounted for is the quality or the technology behind the products. For instance, the price of televisions may be measured in the CPI. Over the last several years, television technology has evolved rapidly from the bulky cathode-ray tube TVs of a decade ago to sleek, flat-screen HD TVs today. Soon, 3D televisions will become available and, at first, the prices of these models will be much higher than older models, which will make the CPI figure higher than it would be otherwise. What is not captured by this measure, however, is the improvement in consumer happiness resulting from improved quality and technology of newer and better televisions and other products that increase in both price and quantity.

Inflation calculated using the CPI may not measure changes in prices of important products like food and oil

In many countries, what is reported most often to households by the government is what's known as the core CPI. This price index does not include changes in the price of food and fuel, which economists ignore because of the frequent dramatic swings in price from one period to the next. However, for many households food and fuel make up a significant proportion of their total expenditures. A CPI that does not account for these goods may not accurately reflect the effect that inflation is having on the typical household.

What information would be needed to develop a more accurate measure of the impact of rising prices in a nation on the various households within that nation? Could technology be better employed by governments or individuals to determine more accurate personal price indexes?

CPI does not reflect price changes that affect producers

A nation's inflation rate is typically reported based on a *consumer* price index. For business firms, however, a more useful measure of inflation is the *producer* price index (PPI). A PPI measures a basket of goods made up primarily of intermediate products such as capital, raw materials, minerals and energy. An increase in the PPI from one period of time to the next affects costs of production for a nation's firms, and is more useful than the CPI in determining the extent to which AS will be affected by changes in the price of goods and services.

14.2 Types of inflation and their causes

Inflation is an increase in the average price level of a nation's goods and services over time. The AS/AD diagram shows the average price level of a nation on its y-axis; therefore, any factor that changes the equilibrium price level in a nation causes inflation or deflation. The price level can change due to a shift in either a nation's AD or its AS.

Demand-pull inflation

An increase in any of the components of a nation's AD will lead to an increase in the nation's price level. Demand-pull inflation is defined as an increase in prices arising from the increased overall demand for a nation's output when consumption, investment, government spending or net exports rise without a corresponding increase in the level of AS (Figure 14.2). Demand-pull inflation is the macro equivalent of an increase in the price of a particular good arising from an increase in the demand for that good.

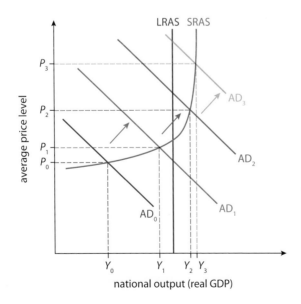

◀ **Figure 14.2**
Demand-pull inflation in the AD/AS model.

The degree to which inflation will rise following an increase in AD depends on equilibrium level of output in the nation before AD began to rise. If a nation producing close to or at its full-employment level of national output (at AD_1 and Y_1 in Figure 14.2) experiences an increase in demand for its goods and services, either because of a rise in consumption, investment, government spending or export sales, then the competition among buyers for the economy's limited output will put upward pressure on prices and increase the price level from P_1 to P_2 and national output from Y_1 to Y_2.

SRAS is relatively inelastic around the full-employment level of output, because the nation's resources (land, labour and capital) are already nearly fully employed. This explains why an increase in AD will lead to a large increase in the price level (P_1 to P_2) but a relatively small increase in the level of output (Y_1 to Y_2).

As can be seen, if AD were to continue to increase beyond AD_2, little or no growth in output will result and inflation will rise even more as the price level increases to P_3. High levels of demand-pull inflation correspond with an economy producing beyond its full-employment level of national output in which resources are nearly all employed in the output of goods and services. Such an economy is said to be over-heating and in the long run, the competition for scarce resources will drive up nominal wages, rents and other costs to firms, shifting the SRAS to the left and returning the economy to its full-employment level of output, at a much higher price level.

Next observe what happens if this nation were to begin at AD_0, a level of demand at which this economy experiences a rather low price level (P_0) and a level of output far below its full-employment level (Y_0). The economy is in a recession, meaning that resources are underemployed and there are large quantities of land, labour and capital sitting idle. An increase in AD from AD_0 to AD_1 will, therefore, result in a relatively small increase in the price level (P_0 to P_1) and a larger proportional increase in national output (Y_0 to Y_1). Producers in this economy find it cheap and easy to hire workers and invest in capital since there is an excess capacity of labour and capital in the country. SRAS is highly elastic below full employment, indicating that an increase in AD can lead to relatively large increases in output without causing significant inflation.

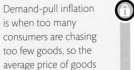

What evidence would be needed to determine whether the level of inflation in an economy is good or bad?

The implication of this analysis is that policymakers need to be conscious of the existence of demand-pull inflation, but must also be able to evaluate its likelihood given the current equilibrium level of national output. Policies aimed at increasing AD can be very effective at stimulating economic growth (increasing real GDP) when an economy is producing far below its full-employment level (Y_0 in Figure 14.2) without the threat of inflation arising. However, if an economy is producing near or at its full-employment level of GDP (Y_1 and Y_2 in Figure 14.2), then policies aimed at stimulating AD will do little to achieve increases in output but will likely lead to higher and higher rates of inflation as the spending on goods and services rises but the nation's AS remains unchanged.

Demand-pull inflation is when too many consumers are chasing too few goods, so the average price of goods and services in a nation rises. Demand-pull inflation is illustrated by an outward shift of AD when a nation is at or near its full-employment level of output.

Cost-push inflation

A second type of inflation arises when the costs of production to a nation's firms increases. The primary determinants of SRAS are the productivity of the nation's resources and the costs of production of the nation's firms. Anything that decreases productivity or increases costs of production will shift a nation's SRAS to the left and drive up costs of production (Figure 14.3). An unexpected decrease in AS is known as a negative supply shock and may arise as a result of the following.

- **An increase in oil prices**. Oil is used in the production or transportation of nearly everything. An increase in the price of oil drives up costs of production across all sectors of a nation's economy and will shift AS to the left, increase inflation and reduce national output.
- **An increase in the nominal wage rate**. In some countries, labour unions have the power to force large increases in nominal wages. Also, minimum wage laws may raise labour costs to firms, forcing them to pass higher costs on to consumers as higher prices. If wages increase across industries, national output will decrease as inflation increases.

- **Depreciation of the nation's currency**. If a country's currency suddenly decreases in value relative to other currencies, imported raw materials become more costly to firms and their costs of production rise, reducing SRAS.
- **Natural disaster or war**. Events such as hurricanes, droughts, earthquakes and other natural disasters can destroy a nation's infrastructure and lead to higher costs of production for firms. Likewise, a devastating war may reduce the labour force and nation's capital stock, leading to higher costs and a fall in national output.
- **Higher taxes on firms**. Corporate taxes raise firms' costs of production and may force businesses to reduce employment and raise their prices.

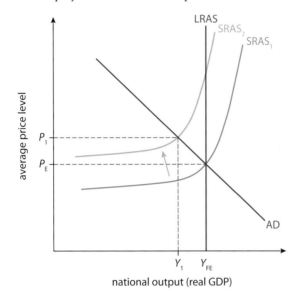

◀ **Figure 14.3**
Cost-push inflation in the AD/AS model.

Cost-push inflation poses a particular challenge to policymakers, since it leads to an increase in both inflation and unemployment. In the short-run, macroeconomic policies are rather ineffective at resolving both of these problems. The only way a nation experiencing cost-push inflation can bring price levels down without driving up unemployment rates is by increasing its SRAS through policies that lower costs to firms that have experienced unexpected cost increases due to one of the reasons above. Supply-side policies are discussed in more depth in Chapter 19.

> ⓘ Cost-push inflation is when the costs of production faced by a nation's producers rise (due to higher energy costs, wages for workers, business taxes, etc.) so the nation's SRAS curve shifts to the left and the average price level of the nation's output rises. Cost-push inflation is sometimes accompanied by stagflation – a term that means the economy is stagnating, experiencing either zero or negative economic growth.

 14.3 ## Consequences of inflation

Learning outcomes
- Discuss the possible consequences of a high inflation rate, including greater uncertainty, redistributive effects, less saving, and the damage to export competitiveness.

Maintaining a stable price level

Maintaining a stable price level by keeping inflation low is a major goal of macroeconomic policies. Governments and central banks regularly use monetary, fiscal and supply-side policies (Chapters 17, 18 and 19) to target an inflation rate of 2–3%. An inflation rate of below 2% may send a signal to a nation's households and firms that disinflation may continue and lead to deflation, which itself poses a major threat to an economy's health. Inflation of greater than 3%, on the other hand, can have its own detrimental effect on a nation's economy, including:

- loss of purchasing power
- lower real interest rates for savers
- higher nominal interest rates for borrowers
- reduction of international competitiveness.

Loss of purchasing power

As prices rise and household incomes remain constant or rise at a slower rate than inflation, people become poorer in real terms. Even if a household's income rises in nominal terms, if the inflation rate rises by more than the household's does, then real income is actually falling. A change in a household's real income is found by subtracting the inflation rate from the change in nominal income. As a nation's price level rises, households' real incomes decrease.

As an example of inflation's effect on income, let's examine a hypothetical Indian worker using the price index data shown earlier in the chapter.

Worked example

A worker earning a nominal income (Y_N) of 100 000 rupees in 2008 gets a pay rise and earns 110 000 rupees in 2009. The worker's nominal wage has increased by 10%. In order to determine the effect on the worker's real income (Y_R), we must first calculate his real income in 2008 and his real income in 2009. Real income is found by dividing nominal income by the year's price index expressed in hundredths.

$$Y_R = \frac{Y_N}{CPI \times 0.01}$$

Using the CPI data for India in 2008 and 2009, we can calculate the worker's real income for both years.

$CPI_{2008} = 121.9$

To find the worker's real income in 2008, we divide his nominal income by the CPI for 2008 expressed in hundredths.

Real income in 2008 = 100 000/1.219 = 82 034 rupees

$CPI_{2009} = 135.2$

The worker's real income in 2009 is his nominal income divided by the price index expressed in hundredths.

Real income in 2009 = 110 000/1.352 = 81 361 rupees

To find the inflation rate between 2008 and 2009, divide CPI_{2009} by CPI_{2008} and multiply by 100.

Inflation between 2008 and 2009 = (135.2 − 121.9)/121.9 × 100 = 10.9%

The worker's nominal income increased by 10%, but inflation was 10.9%. Therefore, the worker's real income, once inflation has been accounted for, fell.

Change in real income = (81 361 − 82 034)/82 034 × 100 = −0.82%

Despite his nominal pay increase of 10%, the worker in our example actually became poorer in real terms, since the average price of goods and services increased by 10.9%. His real income actually declined by 0.82% due to the higher prices in 2009.

Lower real interest rates for savers

Savers in fixed-interest assets (such as most government bonds and savings accounts) are negatively affected by inflation since the real interest rate earned on savings falls as the inflation rate rises.

For example, if a household places $1000 in the bank today at a fixed annual interest rate of 5%, and there is inflation of 7% over the next year, then the real value of the savings decreases by 2%. While the saver will have $1050 (5% more) in dollar terms, $1070 (7% more) would be needed to consume the same amount of output as the $1000 a year earlier. The real interest (IR_R) on savings is the nominal interest rate (IR_N) minus the rate of inflation. Therefore, investments with a fixed interest rate are harmed by inflation.

$$IR_R = IR_N - \text{inflation}$$

Higher nominal interest rates for borrowers

In times of high inflation, banks raise the nominal interest rates they charge borrowers. A lender who intends to earn a real return of 4% on loans will charge a higher interest rate if inflation is expected in the near future. The nominal rates borrowers pay rise with the expected inflation rate, making it more costly for firms and households to borrow. The nominal interest rate (IR_N) borrowers pay equals the real interest rate (IR_R) plus an inflation premium (IP) added to offset the decrease in the value of money repaid by the borrower caused by inflation.

$$IR_N = IR_R + IP$$

Reduction of international competitiveness

High inflation at home makes domestic output less attractive to foreigners, and imports more attractive to domestic consumers. The resulting fall in demand for exports and increase in demand for relatively cheaper imports will move a country's trade balance towards a deficit, reducing AD and leading to a loss of jobs in export industries.

The inflationary spiral

In a situation in which demand-pull inflation exists, an economy can produce beyond its full-employment level of output in the short run. It could be argued that such inflation is desirable because it leads to increases in output and lower unemployment. Such gains are only experienced in the short run, however, since in the long run, the expectation of further inflation forces workers to demand higher nominal wages to offset the decline in real wages caused by higher prices. Wage hikes and the rise in other input costs due to the increasing scarcity of productive resources force firms to reduce employment and raise their prices. In other words, demand-pull inflation, if it persists, leads to cost-push inflation. This is known as an inflationary spiral and it poses a major threat to an economy (Figures 14.4 and 14.5, overleaf).

Figure 14.4
The inflationary spiral.

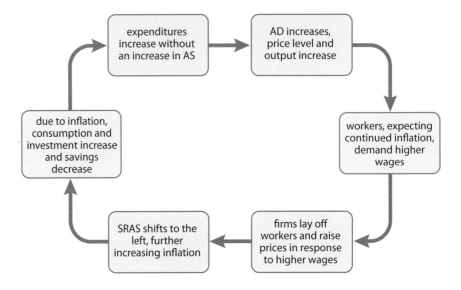

Figure 14.5
An inflationary spiral in the
AD/AS diagram.

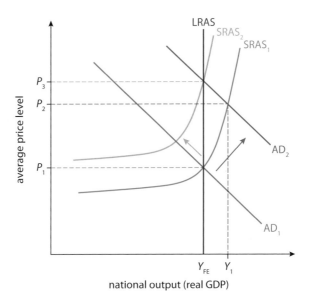

Inflation's costs to the many (fixed-income earners, savers and lenders and exporters) generally outweigh its benefits to the few (borrowers with a fixed-interest rate) (Table 14.4). Macroeconomic fiscal and monetary policies, therefore, aim to maintain a low and stable rate of inflation in the nation so that households and firms can anticipate price level

TABLE 14.4 WHO IS HELPED AND HURT BY INFLATION?			
Helped/not affected by inflation	**Explanation**	**Hurt by inflation**	**Explanation**
Borrowers	Inflation lowers the real interest rate paid by borrowers, so money paid back from a loan is worth less than the money borrowed.	Lenders	Inflation lowers the real interest rate earned on loans, so the money paid back by borrowers is worth less than the money lent.
Flexible-income earners	Wages are indexed to inflation, so any increase in the price level is matched by an income increase.	Fixed-income earners	Inflation reduces real income, making fixed-income earners poorer in real terms as inflation rises.
Importers	Imports appear relatively cheaper when the price of domestic output rises.	Savers	Inflation lowers the real interest rate earned on savings, so money saved is eroded by inflation.
		Exporters	Domestic inflation makes products to be exported less attractive to foreign buyers.

changes and make confident economic decisions based on the expectation of future price level stability. Low inflation gives firms confidence that their products will continue to rise in price in the future and makes investment in new plant and technology a profitable prospect. Deflation, on the other hand, poses a much more serious threat than mild inflation to a nation's economy.

To learn more about inflation, visit www. pearsonhotlinks.com, enter the title or ISBN of this book and select weblink 14.1.

Deflation and its consequences

Learning outcomes

- Discuss the possible consequences of deflation, including high levels of cyclical unemployment and bankruptcies.

Despite the negative effects of inflation outlined above, mild inflation is desirable and evidence of a healthy, growing economy. Deflation, a decrease in the average price level (or an increase in the value of money) is a major threat to a nation's economy and can plunge an economy into a steadily worsening recession in which firms faced with continuously falling prices lay off increasing numbers of workers, lowering disposable incomes and further worsening the deflationary pressure in the economy.

There are two basic causes of deflation; one is extremely undesirable while the other is actually desirable. Deflation due to a fall in AD (demand-deficient deflation) is a dangerous threat to an economy (Figure 14.6a). However, generally speaking, lower prices of goods and services can be a good thing for a nation, as long as they are not accompanied by increasing unemployment and falls in consumption and investment. If deflation is caused by increase in productivity of the nation's resources or lower costs of production to firms, it is considered desirable (supply-side deflation) (Figure 14.6b). An outward shift of a nation's AS curve increases employment, output, and the real incomes of households who find their nominal incomes able to purchase more output as prices fall in the economy.

a
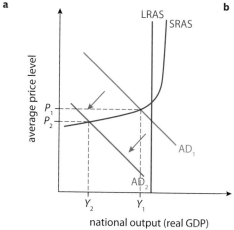

b
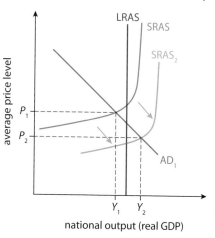

◀ **Figure 14.6**
Deflation in the AD/AS model. **a** Demand-deficient deflation; **b** supply-side deflation.

Supply-side deflation

Causes of supply-side deflation:

- lower oil prices
- more productive labour force
- appreciation of the nation's currency

- lower minimum wage
- better infrastructure
- lower corporate taxes.

An increase in AS can lead to a lower level of unemployment, greater output, and higher real incomes as the price level decreases while nominal incomes stay the same. Such outcomes are certainly desirable, and certain macroeconomic policies may be used to help promote increases in AS. These supply-side policies are discussed in depth in Chapter 19.

Deflation due to fall in AD

The more dangerous form of deflation is that caused by a fall in AD in a nation. A demand-deficient recession leads to rising unemployment and puts downward pressure on the price level. Following a decrease in expenditures, prices tend to be inflexible in the short run as AD moves along the horizontal portion of the AS curve. The longer a recession lasts, the greater the downward pressure on prices becomes. Firms are forced to lay off workers in response to falling demand, which reduces households' disposable incomes leading to further falls in consumption.

The expectation of future falling prices creates an incentive for firms to postpone new investments in capital since they can reasonably expect lower returns on such investments as prices are falling. Less capital means less demand for workers, further adding to unemployment. Households faced with the prospect of falling prices and wages also have an incentive to reduce consumption and increase savings in anticipation of lower incomes and prices in the future. Deflation increases the value of savings since the real interest rate rises when prices are falling (remember, the real interest rate equals the nominal interest rate minus the inflation rate; therefore if inflation is negative then the real interest rate is greater than the nominal interest rate, increasing the incentive to save).

Furthermore, deflation increases the real amount of debt owed by borrowers, so households with credit card or other consumer debts will face a greater real debt burden which, combined with falling incomes, reduces their ability to consume even more. Therefore, AD continues to fall and deflationary pressures build as an economy plunges further into recession (Figure 14.7). The deflationary spiral is perpetuated as firms and households face the uncertainty of future economic conditions and adjust their behaviours based on the reality and future prospects of deflation.

Figure 14.7
The deflationary spiral.

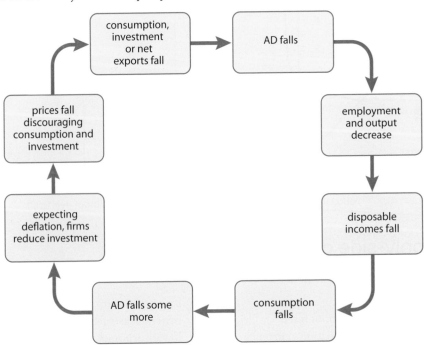

The costs of deflation can be summarized as follows:

- rising unemployment
- falling investment
- falling consumption and increased savings
- increased debt burden on households.

If left unchecked, deflation in an economy may lead in a downward spiral towards recession and unemployment. It is, therefore, important that policymakers in government and central banks take measures to maintain a stable price level with a low and predictable rate of inflation. Avoiding demand-deficient deflation is of the utmost importance; on the other hand, policies that promote an increase in SRAS and thereby lead to supply-side deflation may prove effective at promoting economic growth and full employment. The distinction between demand-side and supply-side policies is explored in depth in Chapters 17–19.

The concepts of inflationary and deflationary spirals highlight the fact that individuals in society do not always act in a purely rational way. Why don't workers simply accept lower wages and allow firms to maintain full employment in periods of deflation? Is human nature so selfish that we would rather see those around us become unemployed and risk becoming unemployed ourselves than accept a lower wage?

CASE STUDY

Deflation may post a greater threat than inflation

The US economy is at its lowest point since 1982. And this situation is likely to worsen in the coming months. Downward pressure on wages and prices is strengthening due to declining house prices and an unemployment rate of 9% leading to intense worker competition for scarce jobs. The deflationary environment is exacerbated by energy prices dropping 4.4% in a month and firms undercutting each other for sales.

With the Fed's (central bank's) latest monetary stimulus, fear of inflation is widespread, but the evidence points to deflation being the greater threat. Pay freezes and wage cuts indicate that prices may fall before they rise. Nearly a third of US households report a cut in pay or a cut in working hours in the last year.

It is economic progress if prices fall because worker productivity improves (as when industrial progress mechanized production). But current deflation is due to falling demand not rising productivity. Falling household incomes and high debt levels reduce the ability of Americans to consume, and this contributes to falling demand for labour. Lower incomes and declining sales increase the burden of debt on households and firms; this causes borrowers to further reduce spending to service their debts and deepens the recession.

In the first four years of the Great Depression (1929–33), prices in the US fell by 27%. Today, central banks are taking action: in the US, Britain, Japan and Switzerland interest rates have been pushed close to zero.

Inflation is a threat to any economy, but deflation must not be under-estimated. Inflation may be easier to correct than deflation: interest rates can be raised as high as a central bank wishes, but they can be lowered only to zero. Falling incomes and rising unemployment will continue to depress growth, deepen deflation and reduce incentives for firms to invest and hire workers. The Fed and other central banks should now undertake policies that err on the side of inflation, a little of which would be less catastrophic than the deflation looming today.

EXERCISES

5   When is deflation desirable? What is the difference between the deflation of the late 19th century and the deflation of today? What are some the threats posed by deflation?

6   Using an AD/AS diagram and evidence from the case study above, illustrate what you believe represents the US current equilibrium level of output and prices.

7   Explain why the expectation of future deflation can have as equally devastating an effect as actual deflation.

8   Why does deflation pose a particular threat to households with high levels of debt?

9   In what ways does deflation present a bigger challenge to macroeconomic policymakers than inflation?

To learn more about deflation, visit www.pearsonhotlinks.com, enter the title or ISBN of this book and select weblink 14.2.

14.5 Relationships between unemployment and inflation: the Phillips curve (HL only)

Learning outcomes

- Discuss, using a short-run Phillips curve diagram, the view that there is a possible trade-off between the unemployment rate and the inflation rate in the short run.
- Explain, using a diagram, that the short-run Phillips curve may shift outwards, resulting in stagflation (caused by a decrease in SRAS due to factors including supply shocks).
- Discuss, using a diagram, the view that there is a long-run Phillips curve that is vertical at the natural rate of unemployment and, therefore, there is no trade-off between the unemployment rate and the inflation rate in the long run.
- Explain that the natural rate of unemployment is the rate of unemployment that exists when the economy is producing at the full-employment level of output.

You will have noticed in our analysis of inflation and deflation that in some cases, there is a short-run trade-off between unemployment and inflation. If AD increases in a nation producing at or near its full-employment level of output, firms will hire more workers to meet the increase in demand and the nation's unemployment rate falls. Additionally, since there is more demand for the same level of AS, increases in AD beyond the full-employment level lead to an increase in the average price level. A change in AD, therefore, leads to a short-run trade-off between inflation and unemployment.

This relationship was first observed by New Zealand economist William Phillips in a 1958 paper 'The relationship between unemployment and the rate of change of money wages in the United Kingdom 1861–1957', published in *Economica*. In his paper, Phillips observed historical data comparing unemployment rates and the rate of change in money wages, in other words, how much the average wage rate increased or decreased compared to the change in the unemployment rate (Figure 14.8).

Phillips observed that in years in which UK unemployment was relatively low (for instance,

Figure 14.8
The original Phillips curve.

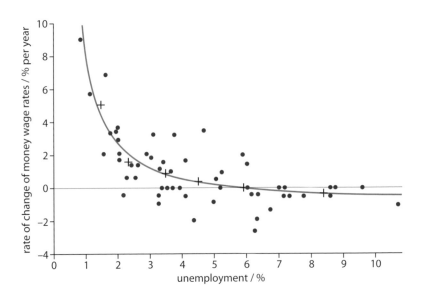

below 3%), there tended to be upward pressure on the average wage rate (with wage increases in excess of 2%). As can be seen, in the years when unemployment was at its lowest (below 2%), money wage rates grew most rapidly (by 6% or more).

On the other hand, when unemployment was high (greater than 6%) money wages tended not to increase or they would even decrease. The explanation for this trade-off is rooted in simple supply and demand analysis. High unemployment means a greater supply of labour, which puts downward pressure on the price of labour, the nominal wage. Conversely, when unemployment is low, the supply of labour available to firms falls and the price of labour increases.

The short-run Phillips curve

Modern economists have modified Phillips's analysis slightly, and replaced the rate of change in money wages with the rate of change in the average price level, or inflation. The modern Phillips curve, therefore, compares the unemployment rate with the inflation rate. In addition, the Phillips curve which reflects an inverse relationship between inflation and unemployment is now known as the short-run Phillips curve because, in the long-run, there is no clear trade-off between the two variables (Figure 14.9).

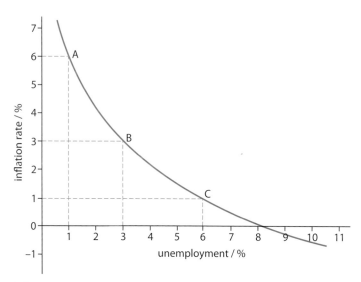

◀ **Figure 14.9**
The short-run Phillips curve.

A short-run Phillips curve (SRPC) looks almost identical to the original Phillips curve. The only difference is that the y-axis shows the inflation rate as opposed to the percentage change in money wages. The modification is easily justified when we consider that one of the primary determinants of a nation's price level is the nominal wage rate in the economy. In most developed countries, the cost of labour makes up the largest component of firms' costs of production. Therefore, when the money wage rate increases in an economy, this tends to correspond with an increase in the price level. Likewise, at lower wage rates, there is downward pressure on prices.

Shifts in AD and movements along the SRPC

According to the SRPC model, high levels of unemployment correspond with low levels of inflation (point C in Figure 14.9), while low unemployment is accompanied by high inflation (point A in Figure 14.9). To understand the reason for this trade-off, it is useful to think of the SRPC in relation to a nation's short-run SRAS.

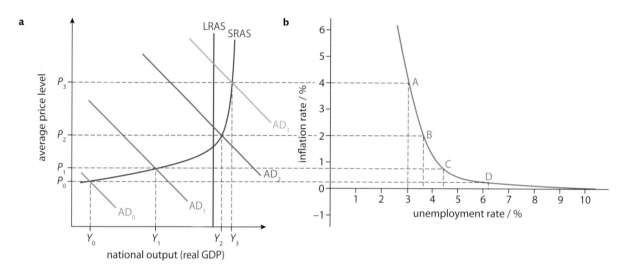

Figure 14.10
Mirror images: **a** SRAS;
b SRPC.

The y-axis of the AD/AS diagram shows the nation's average price level (PL) and the same axis in the SRPC diagram shows the change in the average price level (inflation). Anything that leads to a change in PL is naturally leading to change in inflation.

Similarly, the x-axis in the AD/AS model shows national output, which is directly related to the level of employment in the nation (since higher output leads to more employment). The x-axis in the SRPC model shows unemployment; therefore anything that increases employment and output in the AD/AS diagram will lead to a decrease in unemployment in the SRPC model.

The two curves are mirror images, as you can see in Figure 14.10 (above). Therefore, anything that causes a movement along a nation's SRAS will cause a movement along its SRPC.

In Figure 14.10, observe what happens when the nation's AD increases from AD_0 to AD_1. The increase in demand for the nation's output leads to an increase in employment of workers, which reduces unemployment in the economy from 6.2% to 4.4% as seen in the SRPC diagram. As resources become more scarce due to increased demand from producers, there is a slight increase in the price level from P_0 to P_1, which is reflected by an increase in inflation from around 0.2% to around 0.8% as seen in the SRPC diagram. The increase in AD causes a movement up and to the right along the nation's SRAS, and a movement up and to the left along the SRPC (from point D to point C). Increased demand for the nation's output causes a fall in unemployment and an increase in inflation.

As AD continues to increase from AD_1 to AD_2 and then from AD_2 to AD_3, output and employment continue to increase, albeit at a decreasing rate as the economy moves beyond its full-employment level of national output. Unemployment continues to fall, but at a slower rate, in the SRPC diagram, while inflation begins to accelerate. You will recall that when an economy approaches its full-employment level of output, the threat of demand-pull inflation becomes imminent. This is reflected in the inelastic range of the SRAS and the steep section of the SRPC when unemployment falls below the natural rate of unemployment (NRU) and inflation begins to accelerate. At AD_3, the economy experiences an inflation rate of 4% while unemployment falls to around 3%, indicating that firms faced with rising demand have had to raise the price of their output to avoid shortages.

A movement of AD along the SRAS curve will cause a change in employment and the price level, which corresponds with changes in unemployment and inflation in the SRPC model. The short-run trade-off between unemployment and inflation is therefore observed when the level of AD changes but SRAS remains the same.

Supply shocks and shifts of the SRPC

Just as a movement along the SRAS corresponds with a movement along the SRPC, a shift of a nation's SRAS causes a shift of its SRPC. An increase in the nominal wage rate or any other cost of production across a nation's primary, secondary and tertiary sectors will shift SRAS to the left, causing an increase in both inflation and unemployment.

The term coined by economists to describe the effects of such a negative supply shock is stagflation; a combination of the words stagnant and inflation. In the case of an increase in costs of production to firms, growth in output will become stagnant or even negative and both inflation and unemployment will increase. Stagflation results from any of the factors that cause cost-push inflation in a nation. The effects of a supply shock on the SRPC are illustrated in Figure 14.11.

Figure 14.11
Supply shock shifts the SRPC outwards.

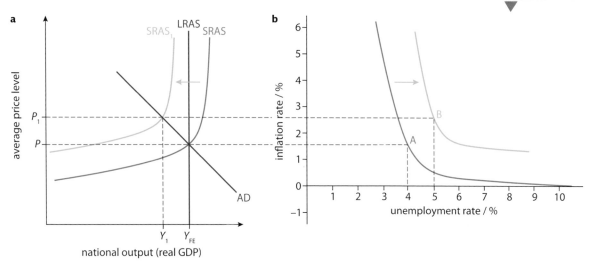

The economy in Figure 14.11 has experienced an increase in both unemployment and inflation (stagflation) due to a negative supply shock. The shift to the left of the SRAS (Figure 14.11a) and the resulting shift to the right of the SRPC (Figure 14.11b) could have resulted from an increase in the nominal wage rate, and increase in energy prices, an increase in business taxes or a non-economic event such as a natural disaster that destroyed the nation's infrastructure and made doing business more costly for firms.

An increase in SRAS would have the opposite effect on the SRPC, shifting it to the left, reducing unemployment and inflation. Any factor that leads to lower costs to firms or greater productivity of resources could lead to a lower rate of inflation and lower unemployment, as firms are able to hire more workers and sell their output for lower prices.

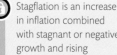
Stagflation is an increase in inflation combined with stagnant or negative growth and rising unemployment, caused by a negative supply shock. Stagflation is the result of a decrease in short-run aggregate supply.

The long-run Phillips curve

To understand why the downward-sloping Phillips curve first posited by William Phillips and later adapted by modern economists only represents the short-run relationship between unemployment and inflation, it is useful to continue our analysis of the scenarios depicted in Figure 14.11.

Assume an economy is producing at its full-employment level of output and AD increases. Inflation is now higher than desired by policymakers, and unemployment is at a rate that is below the nation's NRU. Labour markets are tight (firms find it harder and harder to hire new employees since pretty much everyone who wants a job is already employed).

In the long run (the flexible-wage period) workers begin to calculate the higher price levels into their salary negotiations, and therefore the tight labour markets will force firms who wish to hire more workers to offer higher nominal wages than their competitors in order to attract talent away from other firms. The effect of demand-pull inflation, in the long run, is an increase in the nominal wage rate, which will ultimately force firms to reduce employment and raise prices even further.

And herein lies a problem with the Phillips curve model. According to the SRPC, anything that leads to an increase in unemployment should cause a fall in inflation. However, as we have just seen, anything that increases costs to firms will lead to both an increase in inflation and unemployment, apparently contradicting the Phillips curve model. In the long run, once wages have adjusted upwards in response to demand-pull inflation, the unemployment rate will return to its natural level and inflation will return to a stable rate higher than before the initial increase in AD.

In other words, in the long run, there is no trade-off between unemployment and inflation; unemployment will return to the natural rate regardless of the rate of inflation. Figure 14.12 illustrates the transition from the SRPC to the LRPC.

Figure 14.12
The long-run Phillips curve following an increase in AD.

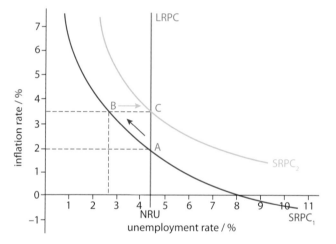

In Figure 14.12, the economy began at point A when the equilibrium level of output is at the full-employment level. The unemployment rate that prevails at full-employment output is considered the nation's NRU (here, at around 4.5%). An increase in AD beyond the full-employment level leads to a fall in unemployment and a rise in inflation and a move up and to the left along SRPC$_1$ to point B.

In the long run, higher inflation forces workers (who anticipate a decline in their real wages due to the inflation ahead) to demand higher wages; a demand to which firms respond by laying off some of their now more costly workers. The increase in AD and higher nominal wages lead to a higher level of inflation, but ultimately the same level of unemployment as before AD increased. Once wages have adjusted upwards in response to demand-pull inflation, unemployment returns to its natural rate and inflation in the economy rises (from 2% to 3.5%).

In the long run, it is observed, there is no trade-off between unemployment and inflation. Just as the nation's output will always return to its full-employment level in the AD/AS model due to the flexibility of wages in the long run, unemployment will always return to the NRU in the LRPC model. Any time unemployment falls below the natural rate, inflation forces workers to demand higher wages, which leads firms to cut back on hiring until unemployment has once again increased to the natural rate.

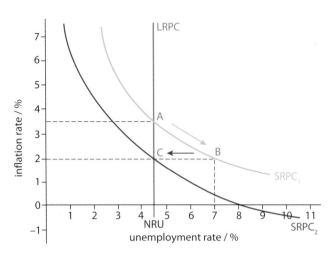

Figure 14.13
The long-run Phillips curve
following a decline in AD.

On the other hand, if unemployment increases above the natural rate, the surplus of labour in the economy causes wages to fall in the long run, leading firms to hire more workers and lower their prices until unemployment returns to the natural rate at a new, lower level of inflation. The LRPC demonstrates that there is no trade-off between unemployment and inflation following a decrease in AD (Figure 14.13, above).

A demand-deficient recession puts downward pressure on prices as AD moves left and downwards along the SRAS, which leads to an unemployment rate greater than the NRU and a move right and downwards along $SRPC_1$. In the long run, in an economy with high unemployment and low inflation, unemployed workers begin accepting lower nominal wages, which encourages firms to once again hire workers, increasing output and reducing unemployment until it returns to its natural rate. In the long run, the economy self-corrects, returning output to its full-employment level due to the flexibility of wages and prices.

The theory of the LRPC aligns nicely with the neo-classical theory of AS, which is believed to be vertical at the full-employment level of national output. According to the neo-classical school of economic thought, the real output of a nation is independent of the price level, and returns to the full-employment level once wages and prices have adjusted to fluctuations in AD; therefore AS is perfectly inelastic at the full-employment level of output. Since the rate of unemployment which prevails at Y_{FE} is the natural rate or NRU, the unemployment rate in the economy returns to the NRU in the long run regardless of the level of AD and inflation. Therefore, the LRPC is vertical at the NRU.

Another name for the NRU is the non-accelerating inflation rate of unemployment (NAIRU). Since an economy producing at its full-employment level should experience a stable rate of inflation, maintaining the NAIRU ensures that inflation neither rises nor falls. If unemployment falls below the NAIRU, inflation is expected to accelerate in the short run and, as the economy returns to its NAIRU, once again to stabilize, possibly at a higher rate. If unemployment increases above the NAIRU, disinflation or even deflation result until, in the long run, wages and prices adjust so unemployment returns to the NAIRU and the inflation rate stabilizes once again at a lower rate. An economy achieving its NAIRU feels neither upward nor downward pressure on the inflation rate as long as AD does not fluctuate too much beyond or below the full-employment level.

The reflective nature of LRPC and LRAS indicates that it may be possible to reduce a nation's NRU in the long run. Anything that reduces the level of structural and frictional unemployment may result in a lower NRU. Supply-side policies such as fewer unemployment benefits for those looking for jobs, better education and training, and lower income taxes may promote an increase in the LRAS and a corresponding shift left of the LRPC (Figure 14.14, overleaf).

 Non-accelerating inflation rate of unemployment (NAIRU) is the level of unemployment that prevails when a nation is producing at its full-employment level of output. The phrase 'non-accelerating inflation' refers to the fact that at this unemployment rate, there is very little upward pressure on the price level in the economy, since firms are able to employ more workers without the wage rate being driven up, causing cost-push inflation.

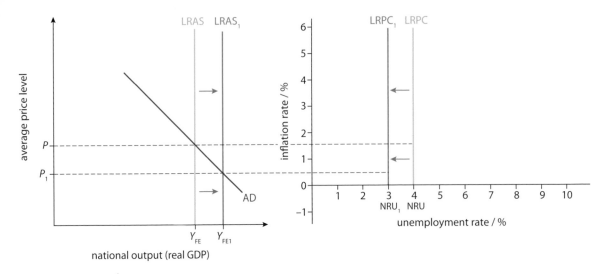

Figure 14.14
LRAS and LRPC.

Real-world evidence of the Phillips curve relationship

It should be noted that the original Phillips curve theory did not distinguish between the short run and the long run. In fact, the original Phillips curve itself was a long-run model demonstrating a trade-off between unemployment and changes in the wage rate over a span of 52 years in the UK. Up until the early 1970s, the Phillips curve was treated as a generally accurate demonstration of the relationship between two important macroeconomic indicators. Throughout the 1960s, data for the US showed in most cases that increases in unemployment corresponded with lower inflation rates, and *vice versa* (Figure 14.15 and Table 14.5).

Figure 14.15
America's Phillips curve, 1960–69.

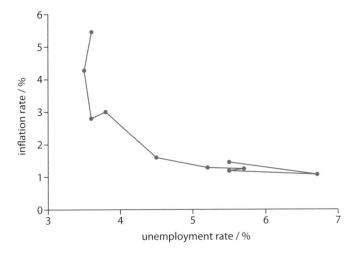

TABLE 14.5 DATA FOR AMERICA'S PHILLIPS CURVE, 1960–69									
Year	1960	1961	1962	1963	1964	1965	1966	1967	1968	1969
UR	5.5	6.7	5.5	5.7	5.3	4.5	3.8	3.6	3.5	3.7
IR	1.46	1.07	1.2	1.24	1.28	1.59	3.01	2.78	4.27	5.46

As can be seen above, between almost every year of the decade a fall in the inflation rate corresponded with a rise in unemployment. The only exceptions were between 1962 and 1963, when both unemployment and inflation increased slightly, and between 1968 and 1969, when again both variables increased. Phillips's theory of the trade-off between unemployment and inflation was generally supported throughout most of the decade, as the downward slope of the curve in Figure 14.15 shows.

To access Worksheet 14.2 on the Phillips curve trade-off , please visit www. pearsonbacconline.com and follow the onscreen instructions.

Beginning in 1970, however, data for the US began to point to a flaw in the Phillips curve theory. Throughout the decade, both unemployment and inflation rose in the US, as oil exporters in the Middle East, united under the Organization of Petroleum Exporting Countries (OPEC) cartel, placed embargoes on oil exports to the US in retaliation for America's support of Israel in a war against its Arab neighbours. The resulting supply shock in the US led to energy and petrol shortages and rising costs for US firms, forcing businesses to reduce costs by laying off workers, while simultaneously raising output prices. Several other macroeconomic variables contributed to rising unemployment and inflation in the late 1970s, including the return of tens of thousands of troops from the Vietnam War who entered the labour market and found themselves unemployed as firms reduced output in the face of rising energy costs. The Phillips curve for the 1970s told a somewhat different story about inflation and unemployment than that of the 1960s (Figure 14.16 and Table 14.6).

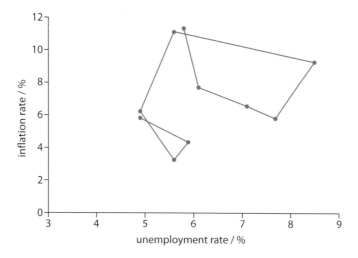

Figure 14.16
America's Phillips curve, 1970–79.

TABLE 14.6 DATA FOR AMERICA'S PHILLIPS CURVE, 1970–769									
Year	1970	1971	1972	1973	1974	1975	1976	1977	1978	1979
UR	4.9	5.9	5.6	4.9	5.6	8.5	7.7	7.1	6.1	5.8
IR	5.84	4.3	3.27	6.16	11.03	9.2	5.75	6.5	7.62	11.22

Between 1973 and 1974, both the unemployment rate and the inflation rate increased significantly, and even as unemployment increased by almost 3% between 1974 and 1975, the inflation rate fell by less than 2% but still remained at nearly 10%. Unlike the 1960s, the 1970s was a decade of both high unemployment *and* high inflation. By the end of the decade, unemployment was at approximately the same level as it was in 1963 (5.8%) but inflation was nearly 10 times higher (11.22% in 1979; 1.24% in 1963). The Phillips curve theory was apparently busted, as the seemingly random scattering of data in Figure 14.16 points to no discernible trade-off between unemployment and inflation throughout the 1970s.

Milton Friedman, 1912–2006.

The LRPC and the rise of monetarism

Several prominent economists in the 1970s, including Nobel Laureate Milton Friedman, revived the classical view of the macroeconomy which held that policies aimed at managing AD would ultimately be unsuccessful at decreasing unemployment in the long run, since a nation's output and employment would always return to the full-employment level regardless of the level of demand in the economy. Friedman, whose theory of the macroeconomy would come to be known as monetarism, believed that changes in the money supply would lead to inflation or deflation, but no change in unemployment in the long run.

Monetary policy and its effects on AD and AS are explored in depth in Chapter 18. The basic premise of the monetarists, however, was that in order to maintain stable prices and low unemployment, the nation's money supply should be permitted to grow at a steady and predictable rate, corresponding with the desired level of economic growth. Any increase in the money supply aimed at stimulating spending and AD would result in an increase in inflationary expectations, an increase in nominal wages, and a shift to the left of AS, resulting only in higher inflation and no change in real output and employment. Therefore, monetary rules were needed to ensure that policymakers would not manipulate the supply of money to try and stimulate or contract the level of AD in the economy.

By the late 1970s, the current interpretation of the Phillips theory as including both a short-run and a long-run model was widely adopted. The short-run Phillips curve may accurately illustrate the trade-off between unemployment and inflation observed in the period of time over which wages and prices are relatively inflexible in a nation's economy. For instance, during the 12-month period between July 2008 and June 2009, the level of consumption and investment in the US fell as the economy slipped into recession. Unemployment rose and inflation decreased and eventually became negative in the final three months of the period. Figure 14.17 shows the relationship between unemployment and inflation during the onset of the recession in 2008–09.

Monetarism is the school of economic thought promoted by American economist Milton Friedman. It argues that changes in the money supply aimed at affecting aggregate demand will only cause inflation or deflation, but no change in the level of employment in the economy. Monetarism supports the view that the Phillips curve is vertical at the natural rate of unemployment, which is further supported by the neo-classical view of aggregate supply, which shows that regardless of the level of demand in an economy, output always returns to the full-employment level in the long run.

Figure 14.17
America's Phillips curve, July 2008 to June 2009.

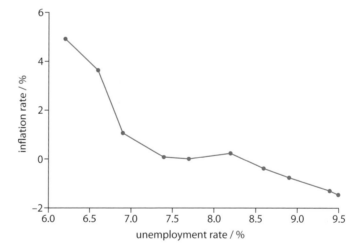

A clear trade-off appears to have existed in the 12-month period covered by Figure 14.17. It is yet to be seen whether the unemployment rate returns to its pre-recession level in the US. Although in the short run it seems likely that the downward-sloping Phillips curve holds some truth, a look at a longer period of time for the same country tells a different story. Figure 14.18 shows the relationship between unemployment and inflation during the 12 years leading up to the onset of recession in 2008.

To access Worksheet 14.3 on politics and the Phillips curve, please visit www.pearsonbacconline.com and follow the onscreen instructions.

Looking at data for a longer period of time shows that even as inflation fluctuated between 0.5% and 4%, US unemployment remained in a relatively narrow range of between 4% and 6%. Year-on-year unemployment and inflation often increased together but at other times showed an inverse relationship as Phillips's theory predicts it should. The narrow range of unemployment portrayed in the data above is evidence that the LRPC for the US between 1997 and 2008 was more like a vertical line than a downward-sloping one. During that

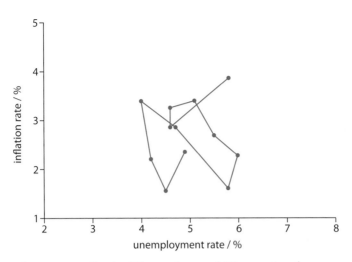

Figure 14.18
America's long-run Phillips curve, 1997–2008.

period, the unemployment rate for the US stayed around 5%; meaning that even as AD increased and decreased in the short run, the level of unemployment remained relatively steady around the natural rate of 5% in the long run.

The 1970s represented a turning point in the mainstream economic analysis of the relationship between inflation and unemployment. Demand-management policies by governments may be effective at fine-tuning an economy's employment level and price level in the short run, but as data from the 1970s and early 2000s shows, in the long run a nation's level of unemployment tends to be independent of the inflation rate, and is likely to remain around the NRU once wages and prices have adjusted to fluctuations in AD. In response to supply shocks such as the oil shortages of the 1970s, both inflation and unemployment may increase at the same time, calling into question the validity of the original Phillips curve relationship. Despite the breakdown in the relationship between unemployment and inflation in the long run, the evidence from the recession of 2008 and 2009 seems to support the theory that an economy in which AD is falling experiences a short-run trade-off between the rate of inflation and the rate of unemployment.

 To learn more about the Phillips curve, visit www.pearsonhotlinks.com, enter the title or ISBN of this book and select weblink 14.3.

PRACTICE QUESTIONS

1 **a** Use an AD/AS diagram to explain two possible causes of demand-pull inflation.
(10 marks) [AO2], [AO4]

b Assuming a government takes no action to control demand-pull inflation, examine the likely effect it will have on a nation's economy in the long run.   (15 marks) [AO3]

2 **a** What are the costs of a high rate of inflation?   (10 marks) [AO1]

b 'What is wanted is not inflation or deflation but price stability.' Discuss. (15 marks) [AO3]
© International Baccalaureate Organization 2001 (part **b** only)

3 **a** Use an AD/AS diagram to explain how cost-push inflation may occur.(10 marks) [AO2]

b Compare and contrast the effects of inflation in an economy on different stakeholders.
(15 marks) [AO4]
© International Baccalaureate Organization 2004 (part **a** only)

4 **a** Explain how the theory of the Phillips curve can be used to explain why it is often thought that a low level of unemployment makes an inflationary outburst inevitable.
(10 marks) [AO2], [AO4]

b Examine the view that each country has a natural rate of unemployment that it will always return to in the long run. Can a nation's NRU change? If so, how?
(15 marks) [AO3]

 To access Quiz 14, an interactive, multiple-choice quiz on this chapter, please visit www.pearsonbacconline.com and follow the onscreen instructions.

15 MACROECONOMIC OBJECTIVE: ECONOMIC GROWTH

15.1 The meaning of economic growth

Learning outcomes
- Define economic growth as an increase in real GDP.

Economic growth is enjoyed by different countries to different degrees.

Microeconomics and macroeconomics differ in numerous ways, as you have seen in Chapters 13 and 14, which have emphasized aggregate measures of a nation's economic health, from changes in the average price level to the unemployment rate.

The use of aggregates in macroeconomics sets it apart from microeconomics, which focuses on individual markets producing and selling particular goods and services. An increase in production of a particular good or service may result from an increase in its demand or its supply. But an increase in the output of an entire national economy is achieved through the increase in the nation's aggregate demand (AD) and/or its aggregate supply (AS). Economic growth is defined as a sustained upward trend in the total output of goods and services in a nation.

Growth is good. This, at least, is the established consensus among macroeconomic policymakers. As a nation's output increases over time, the quantity and quality of goods and services available to the people of the nation increases.

It is a basic tenet of economics that the standard of living of people improves when they are able to produce and consume more goods and services. However, a nation with a large GDP is not necessarily a rich nation. What matters is not the total output of goods and services, but the *average output per person*. A nation with a large population may have a higher GDP than a much smaller nation, but the large nation is not necessarily richer. To compare GDP across nations in a way that tells us something about the living standards of the people of those nations, GDP *per capita*, or the average GDP per person, is measured (Table 15.1).

Economic growth is an increase in the total output of goods and services (GDP) in a nation over time.

TABLE 15.1 GDP *VS* GDP *PER CAPITA*			
	GDP (2008)/billions of $	**Population (2008)**	**GDP *per capita*/$**
Germany	2816	82329758	34204
India	2816	1166079217	2415
Singapore	218	4657542	46806
Algeria	218	34178188	6378

As you can see, the German and Indian economies are the same size – the total value of Germany's output was the same in 2008 as the total value of India's output. But Germany is the richer country on a *per capita* basis, since the population of Germany is less than 10% of the population of India. The average income of a person in Germany is, therefore, more than 10 times greater than the average income of an Indian citizen. The same analysis applies to Singapore (a rich country) and Algeria (a middle-income country). Again the figures for GDP are the same, but because the size of the populations differ substantially, GDP *per capita* is vastly different.

Any increase in a nation's GDP while its population is held constant will by definition increase the *per capita* GDP of the nation and the average output and income of the people of the nation. Economic growth is therefore a goal of macroeconomic policies, since a GDP growth rate that is greater than the population growth rate will make the average income of the nation rise.

However, it is not certain that an economy will experience growth over time. Population growth in much of the world is greater than GDP growth, meaning that, over time, the average income in such nations falls. This is the reality for many countries in the world, particularly the 40 countries of sub-Saharan Africa and around 20 countries in Central and South Asia and Latin America, yet the global trend over the last 50 years has been a vast increase in *per capita* income. In particular, this is notably true in the US (Figure 15.1).

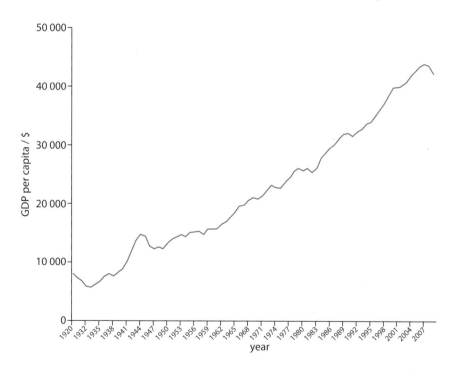

◀ **Figure 15.1**
Per capita GDP in the US since the Great Depression.

The global population has more than doubled since 1960, from 3 billion to almost 7 billion people. Over the same period, the word's nominal GDP has grown from $1.35 trillion to over $60 trillion, a 45-fold increase. The world's *per capita* nominal income today is therefore more than 20 times what it was in 1960. The phenomenal increase in the total value of the world's output is evidence of a massive improvement in the standard of living of the average world citizen from 50 years ago. Of course, this increase in nominal income does not account for the effect inflation has had on the value of people's income over the years but, nonetheless, the output of goods and services in the world has far outpaced the growth in population, pointing to an increase in the average income and standard of living of the world's people due to economic growth.

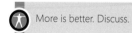
More is better. Discuss.

Illustrating economic growth

Several macroeconomic models can be used to illustrate economic growth. As you learned in Chapter 1, the most basic method for showing growth is with a production possibilities curve (PPC).

Economic growth in the PPC model

The PPC model (Figure 15.2) can be used to illustrate growth in a number of ways.

Figure 15.2
Economic growth is shown as an outward shift in the PPC.

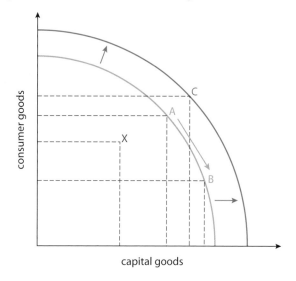

Movement from point X to point A or B

Point X is inside the nation's PPC, indicating that the economy's resources are underemployed or not being used to their greatest efficiency. If the nation were to move from point X to points A or B (both on the PPC), then the nation would experience an overall increase in the total output of goods and services, achieving economic growth. This would correspond with a movement from below full employment in the AD/AS model to a level of output at which the AD curve intersects the long-run aggregate supply (LRAS) curve at the full-employment level of output.

Movement from points A or B to point C

An outward shift of a nation's PPC shows that the nation is able to produce and consume more of everything. A movement from point A or B to point C in Figure 15.2 is only possible through an increase in the quality or quantity of the nation's productive resources. More capital, land or labour, or better capital, land or labour could lead to economic growth shown by an outward shift of a nation's PPC.

Movement from point A to point B

At points A and B, the nation is producing at its full-employment level of national income. A movement from point A to point B is not considered economic growth in the short term, since the total output of the nation does not increase. The nation's output of capital goods does increase, but at the expense of fewer consumer goods. Aggregate output remains the same, but a movement from A to B may actually lead to an eventual outward shift from the orange PPC to the red PPC.

How can a movement along the PPC lead to an outward shift of the PPC? The answer requires an understanding of sources of long-run economic growth in a country. One such source is an increase in the quantity of resources. Capital goods are inputs, or factors of production, whereas consumer goods are outputs, or goods and services. A nation that moves from point A to B on the PPC is sacrificing current consumption of goods and services for current production of capital goods.

The production of capital goods leads to future economic growth and ability of this country to produce and consume at a level beyond its current full-employment level. The opportunity cost of producing more capital goods today is the current consumption of consumer goods, but the benefit is the increased future output, consumption, and income of both consumer and capital goods. The various sources of economic growth are discussed in more depth later in this chapter.

Economic growth in the business cycle

A second model that shows economic growth is the business cycle (Figure 15.3). The business cycle illustrates both short-run economic growth and long-run economic growth. Due to the short-term fluctuations in consumption, investment, government spending and net exports experienced as a normal part of a nation's business cycle, an economy may experience periods of rapid expansion followed by sudden contractions in output and employment.

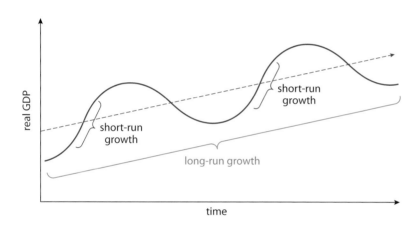

Figure 15.3
The business cycle illustrates both short-run and long-run economic growth.

The upward-sloping sections of the business cycle represent periods of rapid short-run economic growth. When the level of demand for a nation's output grows more rapidly than the level of AS, output may increase beyond the full-employment level in the short run, but as wages and prices adjust to higher levels of demand, output will eventually fall and the period of rapid growth is followed by a contraction or recession.

A nation's business cycle reflects periods of unsustainable short-run growth fuelled by fluctuations in AD, but also a long-run upward trend in output resulting from increases in the quantity and the quality of the nation's resources over time. Despite short-run fluctuation of the business cycle, most developed countries have experienced long-run economic growth over the last 50 years (Figure 15.4, overleaf).

Each of the countries whose GDP is shown in Figure 15.4 experienced periods of stagnant or even negative growth over the last 50 years. Generally, however, the lines are upward sloping, showing that the long-run trend line of these nations' business cycles is one of economic growth.

Economic growth in the AD/AS model

The most useful and detailed model for illustrating economic growth in both the long run and the short run is the AD/AS diagram (Figure 15.5, overleaf). Economic growth occurs any

Humans are rational beings, therefore our economic interactions with one another are driven by rational behaviour. Yet the business cycle demonstrates that despite our rational, self-interested behaviour, the economy still experiences periods of instability and volatility. Why do the collective actions of rational beings result in a seemingly irrational outcome? Are humans as rational as economists assume?

Figure 15.4
GDP in selected countries –
1960–2008.

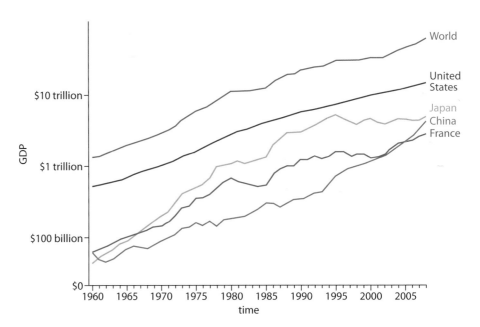

time a nation's GDP increases. An increase in GDP occurs any time AD increases when an economy is below its full-employment level of output. An economy in a recession that begins to recover is, therefore, technically growing as output returns to its full-employment level.

Figure 15.5
Economic growth in the
AD/AS model. **a** Short-run
economic growth; **b** long-run
economic growth.

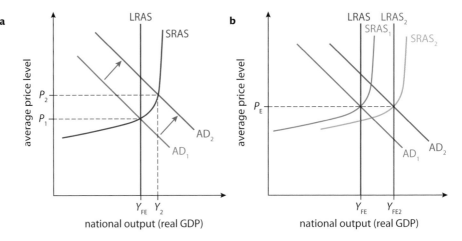

In the short run, as shown in Figure 15.5, if an economy producing at its full-employment level experiences a rise in AD, it produces at a level of output beyond its full-employment level, although at the cost of higher inflation. In the long run, however, an increase in AD alone does not result in economic growth since the wage rate increases and AS will shift left until output returns to its full-employment level.

This suggests that, in the long run, an economy cannot expect to increase its output beyond its full-employment level by stimulating AD alone. Long-run economic growth is achieved only when the nation's full-employment level of output increases, in other words, when LRAS shifts outwards.

Figure 15.5b shows an economy experiencing long-run economic growth – all three curves, LRAS, SRAS and AD, have shifted to the right. Increases in consumption, investment, government spending and exports may account for the shift in AD, but the increases in SRAS and LRAS are what allow this economy to achieve a greater level of output in the long run. Without increases in AS, this economy's ability to grow is restrained to the full-employment level by its limited supply of land, labour and capital.

In this regard, a nation's LRAS reflects its production possibilities given its existing stock of resources. That brings us to the sources of economic growth: factors that increase either the quantity or the quality of a nation's productive resources.

To access Worksheet 15.1 on macroeconomic indicators, please visit www.pearsonbacconline.com and follow the onscreen instructions.

 15.2

Causes of economic growth

Learning outcomes

- Describe, using a production possibilities curve (PPC) diagram, economic growth as an increase in actual output caused by factors including a reduction in unemployment and increases in productive efficiency, leading to a movement of a point inside the PPC to a point closer to the PPC.
- Describe, using a PPC diagram, economic growth as an increase in production possibilities caused by factors including increases in the quantity and quality of resources, leading to outward PPC shifts.
- Describe, using an LRAS diagram, economic growth as an increase in potential output caused by factors including increases in the quantity and quality of resources, leading to a rightward shift of the LRAS curve.
- Explain the importance of investment for economic growth, referring to investment in physical capital, human capital and natural capital.
- Explain the importance of improved productivity for economic growth.

Productivity growth

An outward shift of a nation's PPC is made possible only by an increase in the quantity or the quality of productive resources in the nation. But just how do more and better resources lead to economic growth? The answer is rooted in a very important concept that must be explored in some depth: worker productivity.

Economists define productivity as the amount of output per unit of input. Worker productivity is measured in output per hour, and indicates the value of the average worker's output attributable to one hour of work. Increases in productivity allow for a nation's economy to grow, but more importantly lead to growth in *per capita* income.

Growth in national output can also result from increases in the number of workers, but since the size of the labour force usually only grows when the entire population increases, this type of growth in GDP is unlikely to lead to increases in the average income of a nation. Therefore, productivity growth is the primary prerequisite for long-run economic growth of a nation and improvement in *per capita* income and the average standard of living of a nation's people.

Since 1947, output per hour of labour has increased at an average annual rate of 2.27% in the US. At this rate, the amount of output attributable to each American worker doubles every 30 years. If productivity gains continue at this rate, an American born today can expect to be twice as productive (and therefore earn twice the income) when he enters the labour force as his parents were.

Sources of productivity growth: physical capital

So why does productivity matter? Simple: if the output per worker doubles every 30 years, then the income of the average worker also doubles. Twice as much stuff per worker corresponds with a higher standard of living.

Productivity refers to the amount of output attributable to each unit of input. Productivity is an important source of economic growth, as the more productive a nation's resources (land, labour and capital), the more output and income can be generated on a *per capita* basis.

A major source of increases in worker productivity is the increase in the quantity and the quality of the physical capital available to each worker in a nation. Physical capital refers to the human-made resources employed in the production of goods or services. Factories, robots, computers, buildings, tools and other such equipment are all considered physical capital.

Higher national levels of private investment increase the quantity and the quality of physical capital, which makes workers more productive and leads to long-run economic growth. To demonstrate why more capital increases productivity, imagine for a moment that a nation's whole economy is a single bakery.

- A bakery with one oven and three bakers cannot produce as much per hour of labour as a bakery with three ovens and three bakers.
- More ovens allow each baker to produce more bread per hour, increasing the productivity of labour.
- Economies with greater quantities of capital per worker experience a greater level of output per hour of labour and, therefore, a higher level of economic growth.
- Increases in capital stock result from high levels of private investment, as firms replace old capital and expand existing factories to meet rising AD over time.

Perhaps more important than the *quantity* of capital available to workers, is the *quality* of capital in a nation. Increases in the quality of capital and technology lead to vast improvements in worker productivity and, therefore, higher rates of growth. Let's consider a single sector of an economy – farming.

- A farmer with a buffalo and an iron plough is far more productive than a farmer with a bamboo rake.
- A farmer with a John Deere tractor is even more productive than the farmer with the buffalo.
- The quality of capital in an economy matters as much if not more than its quantity in determining the overall growth rate.

Improvements and innovations in primary, secondary and tertiary sector technologies have transformed the structures of economies from the time of the agricultural revolution 10 000 years ago to the industrial revolution 200 years ago and the internet revolution 20 years ago. Each of these waves of technological innovation plunged human societies and economies into new eras of productivity growth and increased income and welfare: first in food production when farming was invented, second in the manufacture of consumer goods when assembly lines and modern factories transformed the secondary sector, and most recently in services when high-speed internet and computer technologies allowed instantaneous exchange of knowledge, information, and highly skilled services around the world.

Without high levels of private investment by entrepreneurs and their capitalist backers, improvements in technology would be slow to come to the market and economic growth would be hindered because economies would lack access to cutting-edge, productivity-improving methods of production.

Sources of productivity growth: human capital

Increases in the quantity or the quality of physical capital increase labour productivity and promote economic growth. But a tool is only as useful as the worker operating it – which brings us to the ultimate resource and driver of economic growth, human capital.

Human capital refers to the value of labour created through education, training, knowledge and health. Just as better technologies improve the quality of physical capital, better

> The average American worker today is backed up by around $110 000 worth of physical capital – far more than a US worker had 100 years ago and far more than the average worker in most countries has today.
>
> Paul Krugman,
> *Macroeconomics*, 2006

human capital is achieved through improvements in the education and health of a nation's workforce.

Resources are scarce: this is the basic problem of economics, which addresses questions surrounding the allocation of earth's scarce resources. The planet's natural capital (minerals, fossil fuels, forests and fisheries) will eventually be depleted if our industrial economy continues to exploit them at an unsustainable rate. Physical capital (machines and tools employed in production) depends on inputs of natural resources for production – this means that physical capital is also limited by the scarcity of natural capital.

Human capital, on the other hand, is effectively limitless, to the extent that it can be improved through education. Economist Julian Simon considered human ingenuity and creativity the 'ultimate resource' that would allow human societies to overcome the physical scarcity of natural resources and thereby achieve long-run economic growth even in the face of resource depletion.

Adding more people to any community causes problems, but people are also the means to solve these problems. The main fuel to speed the world's progress is our stock of knowledge, and the brake is our lack of imagination. The ultimate resource is people – skilled, spirited, hopeful people.

Julian Simon, *The Ultimate Resource*, 1998

The infinite nature of human capital, argued Simon, is the key to overcoming the physical scarcity of natural capital. More and better education is the key to improving human capital and achieving long-run economic growth among all nations.

Governments that recognize the importance of human capital will promote policies that contribute to the education and training of the nation's population. Such policies lead to greater productivity and output per worker and ultimately promote long-run economic growth.

Figure 15.6 shows the correlation between literacy and output per worker for six developing nations – a simple example of the importance of education for a nation's economic health. Literacy is one measure of the education level of a nation's people. It may seem obvious, but the better educated a nation, the richer the people of that nation tend to be.

Socially optimal levels of education and healthcare are not likely to be provided if they are left entirely to the free market. Such merit goods will be under-provided by the private sector due to the non-rivalrous nature of their benefits to society as a whole. Without government provision of education, job-training, and healthcare, a nation's labour force

 Julian Simon argued that humans were the ultimate resource, and that all other scarce resources could be overcome by human ingenuity. To what extent is population growth an obstacle to or a contributor to economic growth?

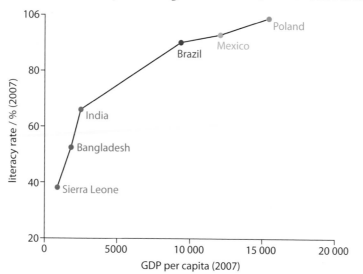

◀ **Figure 15.6**
A better-educated workforce correlates with higher *per capita* income.

Which comes first, high education levels or high incomes? What kind of information would you seek out to test your hypothesis?

To access Worksheet 15.2 on jobless growth, please visit www.pearsonbacconline.com and follow the onscreen instructions.

will become relatively unproductive in the competitive global economy. Therefore, long-run economic growth will be severely restricted and, over time, the standard of living of the nation's people will decline if the government fails to provide the people with an education system that prepares people to be productive members of the economy.

Much as private sector investment is needed to replace and expand a nation's stock of physical capital, government investment is required to improve and equip a nation's stock of human capital with the skills and knowledge necessary to promote economic growth and increases in income and quality of life for the average worker.

Productivity's effect on unemployment: Ironically, the effect of increased productivity on unemployment is not always a positive one. Recent studies have actually shown that as productivity increases, greater unemployment could result.

CASE STUDY

Okun's law and the unemployment surprise of 2009

In 2009, strong growth in productivity allowed firms to lay off large numbers of workers while holding output relatively steady. This behaviour threw a wrench into the long-standing relationship between changes in GDP and changes in the unemployment rate, known as Okun's law. If Okun's law had held in 2009, the unemployment rate would have risen by about half as much as it did over the course of the year.

Economists have long known that the overall performance of the economy as measured by GDP has a direct bearing on unemployment. But the relationship between changes in output and changes in the unemployment rate deviated from expectations in 2009. Over the course of the year, unemployment rose rapidly, while GDP remained relatively flat, or near zero growth. This pattern was surprising because it departed substantially from a long-standing forecasters' rule of thumb known as Okun's law. Named for Yale University economist Arthur Okun (1962), the law describes the empirical relationship between changes in output and changes in the unemployment rate. Okun's law tells us that, for every 2% that real GDP falls below its trend, we will see a 1% increase in the unemployment rate. Since real GDP was almost flat in 2009 while the corresponding trend level increased by 3%, the unemployment rate under Okun's law should have increased by 1½ percentage points. Instead it rose by 3 percentage points, more than twice the predicted increase.

Human beings are of economic value insofar as they can contribute to the economic growth of a nation. Therefore, the greatest argument for improving a nation's education system is the positive effect a more productive workforce will have on economic growth. Discuss this view with your class.

The factor that turns out to be the main driver of the recent departure from Okun's law is average labour productivity, measured as GDP per non-farm hour worked. The deviation in average labour productivity relative to the GDP gap is far outside the range plotted over time and is consistent with the rapid productivity growth recorded in 2009. The surge in labour productivity allowed employers to keep output steady while shedding workers and reducing hours of work in the economy. As such, it allowed unemployment to rise much more than expected given the change in GDP, breaking the normal pattern between the two measures observed over the past 60 years … If productivity keeps on growing at an above-average pace, then unemployment forecasts based on Okun's law could continue to be overly optimistic.

Mary Daly and Bart Hobijn, Federal Reserve Bank of San Francisco Economic Letter, 8 March 2010

EXERCISES

1 Explain how increases in productivity may allow a nation to increase its level of output without increasing employment.

2 Would America be better off today if productivity had not increased during the recession of 2009? Why or why not?

3 If productivity gains continue, how will this affect the rate of unemployment in the economy as the US economy emerges from the recession of 2009?

Calculating economic growth (HL only)

Learning outcome
- (HL only) Calculate the rate of economic growth from a set of data.

Economists measure the rate of economic growth in a nation by comparing the total value of the output of one year to the output of the previous year. The growth rate (GR) in nominal GDP is found by the formula:

$$GR = \frac{GDP_2 - GDP_1}{GDP_1} \times 100$$

Economic growth rates vary from country to country for year after year based on the macroeconomic conditions within each country (Figures 15.7 and 15.8). A positive growth rate indicates the total output of goods and services has increased from one year to the next. Negative growth is evidence of a recession, caused by either a decrease in AD or a decrease in AS. However, a fall in the rate of growth does not necessarily mean an economy is experiencing a recession, rather that the level of output is increasing at a slower rate.

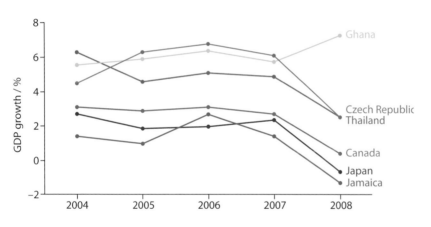

◀ **Figure 15.7**
Economic growth in different countries, 2004–08.

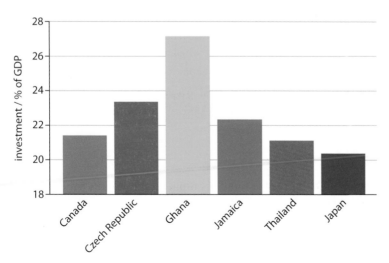

◀ **Figure 15.8**
Greater levels of investment correspond with higher economic growth, 2004–08.

To calculate the growth rate for an economy, information on the prices and the quantities of the nation's output of goods and services is needed. As an illustration, Let's go back to Country I and consider its production of only two goods: calzones and robots. Using price and output data for Country I's output in 2010 and 2011, we can determine the rate of increase in nominal GDP between the two years (Table 15.2).

TABLE 15.2 CALCULATING NOMINAL GDP AND ECONOMIC GROWTH IN A SIMPLE ECONOMY

Goods and their prices	Quantity and price of output in 2010	Quantity and price of output in 2011
quantity of calzones	4000	3500
price of calzones	€10	€15
quantity of robots	500	550
price of robots	€200	€250
nominal GDP (total value of output)	40 000 + 100 000 = €140 000	52 500 + 137 500 = €190 000
nominal GDP growth rate: $\dfrac{(\text{GDP}_{2011} - \text{GDP}_{2010})}{\text{GDP}_{2010}} \times 100$	–	$\dfrac{(190\,000 - 140\,000)}{140\,000} = 0.357 \times 100 = 35.7\%$

The total euro value of Country I's output in 2011 increased by 35.7% over 2010. A large increase in nominal GDP tells us one of two things; either the quantity of the nation's output increased or the price of the nation's output increased, or both. In fact, both output and prices increased in Country I.

In order to measure the *real economic growth* (the change in the total value of the goods produced calculated as if prices had stayed at the level they were in the base year) we must adjust the change in nominal GDP for the change in the price level over the same period.

Changes in the price level are determined using a price index (Chapter 14). The real GDP (GDP_R) equals the nominal GDP (GDP_N) divided by the consumer price index expressed in hundredths ($\text{CPI} \times 0.01$):

$$\text{GDP}_R = \frac{\text{GDP}_N}{\text{CPI} \times 0.01}$$

The real GDP in 2011 tells us the amount of output for the year once the change in the price level has been accounted for. Country I's real GDP increased by much less than its nominal GDP because the effect of higher prices is cancelled out (Table 15.3).

Using nominal GDP to compare the output of a nation year to year can be misleading since growth can be overstated if the average price level rises. Adjusting the change in output for inflation gives us the ability to focus on changes in the quantity of output by cancelling out changes in the price level.

As you can see, a nominal GDP growth rate of 35.7% is deflated by the CPI; once the change in the price level is accounted for, Country I's real GDP growth rate is a more modest 7.7%.

TABLE 15.3 CONVERTING NOMINAL GDP TO REAL GDP REQUIRES A PRICE INDEX		
Price index (2010 base year): $\left(\dfrac{P_{B2}}{P_{B1}}\right) \times 100$	$\dfrac{210}{210} = 1 \times 100 = 100$	$\dfrac{265}{210} = 1.26 \times 100 = 126$
Real GDP (2010 euros): $\dfrac{\text{nominal GDP}}{\text{price index in hundredths}}$	$\dfrac{140\,000}{1} = €140\,000$	$\dfrac{190\,000}{1.26} = €150\,793$
Real GDP growth rate: $\dfrac{(\text{real GDP}_{2011} - \text{real GDP}_{2010})}{\text{real GDP}_{2010}} \times 100$	–	$\dfrac{(150\,793 - 140\,000)}{140\,000} = 0.077 \times 100 = 7.7\%$

To determine whether or not Country I's real GDP growth of 7.7% led to an increase in the *per capita* GDP we would simply compare the change in real GDP to the change in the population. If population grew by less than 7.7%, it could be stated that the average worker in Country I earned a higher income and enjoyed a higher level of consumption in 2011 than in 2010. This reminds us that economic growth, or an increase in the real value of a nation's output year on year, is an objective of macroeconomic policy due to the impact that a positive growth rate has on people's well-being.

For example, the US has successfully achieved its goal of economic growth for most of the last 80 years. Since the Great Depression, when GDP shrank for several consecutive years, most of the rest of the century has seen positive growth.

In Figure 15.9, recessions are easy to spot, because a recession is defined as a decrease in the output of a nation over two consecutive quarters. While some recessions may not appear as negative growth (because the growth rates in Figure 15.9 are annual), the major recessions of the last 80 years are starkly visible.

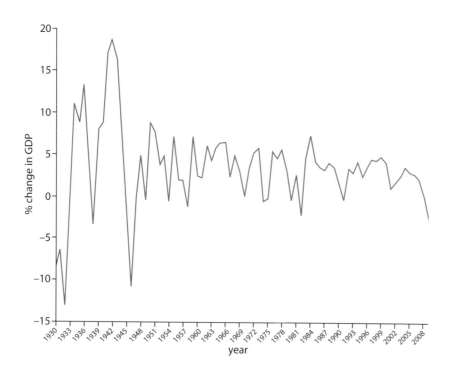

Figure 15.9
Economic growth in the US since the Great Depression.

HL EXERCISES

8 In which years did the US experience recessions?

9 Explain why the highest growth rates tend to occur in the years following the lowest growth rates.

10 In general, what has happened to the fluctuations in growth rates in the US since the late 1970s? What does this tell us about the effectiveness of macroeconomic policy in the US?

11 **a** Using the table below, calculate the nominal growth rate between each of the years:

- 2004, 2005
- 2005, 2006
- 2006, 2007
- 2007, 2008

YEAR	2004	2005	2006	2007	2008
Australia's nominal GDP/$	631 302 000 000	669 699 000 000	710 288 000 000	760 212 000 000	798 320 000 000
Australia's population	20 127 400	20 394 800	20 697 900	21 072 500	21 431 800
Price index Australia	145.2	149.075	154.35	157.95	164.825

b Between which years did Australia's nominal GDP grow most rapidly?

c Calculate the inflation rate in each of the years from 2005 to 2008.

d Calculate the real GDP growth rate between each of the years.

e Between which years did Australia's real GDP grow most rapidly?

15.4 Consequences of economic growth

Learning outcomes

- Discuss the possible consequences of economic growth, including the possible impacts on living standards, unemployment, inflation, the distribution of income, the current account of the balance of payments, and sustainability.

Measuring economic growth tells economists whether the value of a nation's output of goods and services increases or decreases year after year. Changes in nominal GDP alone do not tell us whether an economy is actually producing a greater quantity of output since increases in nominal GDP may result from inflation *or* an increase in actual output. Therefore, changes in real GDP (determines whether or not output has increased regardless of the inflation rate) are a more accurate measure of the size of the economy.

But even real GDP growth has its shortcomings as an indicator of an increase in the well-being of a nation's people. If population grows more rapidly than output, then the average person may have a lower income even as real GDP grows; for this reason *per capita* real GDP is a superior measure of the standard of living of a nation's people.

Economic consequence of growth

The economic consequence of growth in *per capita* GDP is an increase in the average level of income and consumption in a nation.

Non-economic consequences of growth

There are several non-economic consequences of growth that should be considered when evaluating growth as a goal of macroeconomic policymakers.

Externalities

Increases in a nation's output often lead to decreases in environmental and physical health. Firms that externalize their production costs by polluting air and water keep their costs low and are thereby able to sell their products at lower prices and produce greater quantities of output. The real GDP of the nation may grow, increasing *per capita* income, but the environmental and physical health of the nation may simultaneously diminish due to the externalizing behaviour of growth-focused firms.

Inflation

Growth achieved primarily through increases in AD can result in greater output per worker but also inflation. It was recently reported that China's real GDP growth rate for 2010 reached an astonishing 10.3%, a rate which made China the second largest economy in the world by early 2011, surpassing both Japan and Germany. If both China and the US continue to grow at their 2010 rates, China will become the largest economy in the world in less than 20 years.

On the downside, official inflation in China was around 5% in 2010; but this rate does not reflect the real impact of growth on the average Chinese household because it excludes both food and fuel price rises. The negative effect of China's rapid growth is an ever-increasing cost of living for the Chinese household, a hardship ignored by official growth and inflation figures.

Resource depletion

Sustainability is not reflected in a nation's growth figures. In its pursuit of greater output, a nation's non-renewable resource base may be depleted at an unsustainable rate.

For instance, Brazil's GDP may increase as the Amazon rainforest is converted into sugar and soy plantations and land for grazing cattle because these commodities are counted in the national output. However, the economic value of the standing forest is not subtracted from Brazil's growth figures, nor is the depletion of soil fertility and the decline in biodiversity resulting from environmentally harmful economic behaviour. A nation in pursuit of more and more rapid economic growth may reduce its potential for achieving long-run sustainable economic development.

Structural unemployment

Growing economies experience structural changes as productivity gains in the secondary and tertiary sectors lead to an ever-shifting demand for skills in the labour force. Unemployment results among workers whose skills are no longer needed as an economy grows and the composition of output evolves from primary commodities to manufactured goods to high-skilled services.

Composition of output (capital *vs* consumer goods)

Growth may be the result of high levels of investment by firms in capital rather than high levels of consumption by households. In the case of China, for most of the last decade private investment has made up roughly 50% of the country's GDP. Capital investment, while contributing to the nation's stock of productive resources, does not directly benefit households, for whom production of goods and services for domestic consumption is desirable.

Additionally, a nation with a large export sector may experience rapid growth as foreign demand for its products grows, but domestic consumers will benefit little from such growth if it is accompanied by large trade surpluses resulting from the country exporting more of its output than it consumes in imports from abroad.

Composition of output (military *vs* civilian goods)

An economy which invests heavily in military equipment or weapons technology may achieve rapid economic growth, but such production does little to improve the material well-being of the average person in that country, for whom production of consumer goods and services is more beneficial. Military spending may help a nation expand its industrial and political agenda abroad and create employment at home, but the trade-off is a decreased quantity and variety of consumer goods for the nation's households to enjoy.

Unequal income distribution

The benefits of economic growth may be enjoyed by an elite minority within the nation's economy or even among foreign owners of capital in the country. The gains in income often accrue among the capital owners, shareholders in large corporations, corrupt political leaders or the educated classes, while the working class, lower-skilled workers in the secondary sector or the rural poor may be left out of the gains from growth. Governments must ensure through progressive taxation and transfer payments that the benefits of growth are enjoyed by all citizens.

The chance that growth will lead to less equal income distribution presents policymakers with a final macroeconomic objective, equity in the distribution of income. Chapter 16 explores the meaning of equity in income distribution, measures for determining income equality and the role of taxation and government spending in re-allocating national income to achieve a more balanced distribution across a nation's people.

To learn more about economic growth, visit www.pearsonhotlinks. com, enter the title or ISBN of this book and select weblink 15.1.

Effect on the balance of payments

In Chapter 23, we will learn about the composition of a nation's balance of payments, which measures all the flows of money, income, goods, services and resources between one nation and the rest of the world. A nation with a high rate of income growth is likely to demand more of the rest of the world's output than the rest of the world demands of its output. Rising domestic incomes generally lead to a net inflow of goods from the rest of the world, shifting a nation towards a deficit in its trade balance with other countries.

Is economic growth always beneficial? What could be meant by the word 'beneficial'? Is there always a cost to economic growth?

When this is the case, the deficit is necessarily accompanied by an inflow of funds from investors abroad seeking to purchase domestic assets, such as factories, real estate and government debt. While such trade imbalances are not necessarily a bad thing, they do lead to several other challenges for government that are explored in more depth in Chapter 23.

1 **a** Outline three strategies which governments may use to increase their economic growth rates.   (10 marks) [AO1]

   b Discuss whether increasing the rate of economic growth should be the major policy objective of government.   (15 marks) [AO3]

   © International Baccalaureate Organization 2003

2 **a** Why might the goal of full employment conflict with the goal of economic growth?   (10 marks) [AO2]

   b Examine the possible impact economic growth may have on the distribution of income among a nation's households.   (15 marks) [AO3]

   © International Baccalaureate Organization 2003 (part **a** only)

3 **a** Using an AD/AS model, distinguish between short-run economic growth and long-run economic growth.   (10 marks) [AO2], [AO4]

   b Discuss the importance of investment for economic growth.   (15 marks) [AO3]

To access Quiz 15, an interactive, multiple-choice quiz on this chapter, please visit www.pearsonbacconline.com and follow the onscreen instructions.

16 MACROECONOMIC OBJECTIVE: EQUITY IN INCOME DISTRIBUTION

16.1 Equality *vs* efficiency in market economies

Learning outcomes

- Explain the difference between equity in the distribution of income and equality in the distribution of income.
- Explain that due to unequal ownership of factors of production, the market system may not result in an equitable distribution of income.

Inequality exists in every society, and to an extent is a by-product of the free market system. ▶

Market economies are good at several things:

- allocating resources efficiently in the absence of spillover benefits and costs
- encouraging innovation and creativity when property rights exist to protect the inventions brought to market by entrepreneurs
- achieving increases in total output and average standards of living through the pursuit of self-interest and profits in labour, capital and product markets.

These and myriad other characteristics make market economies more efficient and successful in achieving macroeconomic objectives than the alternative economic systems available to nations.

Command economies, in which society's scarce resources are allocated not by the forces of supply and demand, rather by the very visible hand of the state, failed throughout the 20th century to achieve long-run growth and improvements in the overall living standards of people of the nations in which such economic systems were implemented. What command economies did manage to achieve to some extent, however, was relative equality in the distribution of the nation's income and output across the nation's people. However, critics of the socialist system pointed out that while such economies may have strived to achieve equality, by the time everyone was equal, they were .

Modern market economies, on the other hand, allow for the creation of vast personal wealth and unfathomably high incomes among the most skilled and most well-capitalized members of society. A household's income is not determined by central planners employing complex formulas, but by the productivity of the labour provided by each household to the market. Households with high levels of human capital (in other words, whose skills and education set them apart from other households) enjoy high levels of income. Households whose human capital is of a low level (those whose access to education and skill levels are low) earn lower incomes and experience a lower standard of living. In a truly free market system, higher incomes act as an incentive for households to improve their human capital and work harder to increase their standard of living.

Equality and efficiency: the big trade-off

The gains market economies promote in efficiency, however, are often accompanied by a reduction in equality. There is nothing inherent in a market economy that promotes equality in the distribution of income and output. In fact, much of history has shown quite the opposite to be true. Throughout the late 20th century, as one economy after another emerged from decades of communist economic policies under the Soviet Union (including Russia itself), the gaps between rich and poor grew wider and wider. While average incomes in most emerging market economies have risen, the distribution of income has become increasingly unequal with rising gross domestic product (GDP).

According to economist Arthur Okun, the free market system presents a fundamental challenge at achieving both efficiency and equality because of the system of incentives lying at its core.

In many countries, inequality is growing. In 1970, the salary of the average CEO was 70 times the wage of the average worker. In 1988, the figure was 191 times. And by 2010, the average American CEO earned 1039 times the wage of the average worker.

The contrast among families [in capitalist societies] in living standards and in material wealth reflects a system of rewards and penalties that is intended to encourage effort and channel it into socially productive activity. To the extent that the system succeeds, it generates an efficient economy. But that pursuit of efficiency necessarily creates inequalities. And hence society faces a trade-off between equality and efficiency.

Arthur Okun, *Equality and Efficiency, the Big Trade-off*, 1975

The trade-off between equality and efficiency must be considered when analysing the impact of many macroeconomic policies and the consequences of economic growth.

Inequality exists in the market system. There is no denying this fact. When relative incomes are based on the relative value of the labour provided by different households, it is inevitable that some households will earn higher incomes than others. There will be rich people whose incomes far exceed those whose skill levels and education levels are lower. The inequality that results from the market system is considered by many to be unfair, and evidence that market economies are a failure.

Equality and efficiency are major themes in the IB Economics course. Efficiency means getting the most out of a given input, while equality means smaller disparities among a nation's households in their maintainable living standards and in the distribution of income and wealth.

However, inequality may arise due to the success of the market system at lifting large numbers of people out of the poverty that they may have experienced under a more 'fair' and 'equal' economic system. Even as the gap between the rich and the poor in an economy grows under the market system, the average household can still become richer.

Nonetheless, inequality in the distribution of income may pose several problems for a nation, which is why in the distribution of income is the fourth and final objective of macroeconomic policies. In this chapter you will examine how governments use taxation and government spending to promote a more equitable distribution of income than would otherwise result from a market economy.

Equality *vs* equity

Whereas the market system may fail to promote due to the very system of incentives aimed at encouraging efficiency, is not an unachievable goal for economic policymakers. While no economic policy can ever create equality in a market economy due to the conflict such a policy would create with the aim of efficiency, equity is a slightly different concept in economics. Equity refers to in economics.

What is fair is not necessarily equal. For instance, a taxation system rooted in the idea that those who can afford to pay the highest tax rates should pay the highest tax rates, while those whose incomes are lowest should pay lower rates does not create equality, but it is equitable.

A market system can be equitable even if it cannot create total equality. To a certain extent, a free market economy is in fact more equitable than a command system, in that every individual is free to improve him- or herself through education and professional growth, and then make his or her labour available to the market. In the pursuit of self-interest, however, there are sometimes those who are left behind. In this regard, it is the responsibility of government to promote equity through policies that give every citizen in society a fair shot at achieving economic success in the free market.

Equity refers to fairness in economics, while equality means minimizing the disparities in income and wealth among a nation's households. Equity requires a level playing field on which individuals in society can all have a fair shot at achieving economic success. Equity ultimately promotes greater equality in income distribution.

To learn more about income distribution, visit www.pearsonhotlinks.com, enter the title or ISBN of this book and select weblink 16.1.

Fairness and equity *vs* efficiency and competition. Equity is a difficult concept to define because every individual is likely to have his or her own opinion of what is fair and what is unfair. A market economy is not guided by concepts of fairness and equity, but by the pursuit of profits and self-interest. Therefore, it is up to students of economics to impose on the field their own values in order to create a market system that accounts for more than just the well-being of rich resource owners. The well-being of the lower and middle classes must also be accounted for while protecting property rights and promoting the pursuit of efficiency achieved in a competitive market system.

Indicators of income equality/inequality

Learning outcomes
- Analyse data on relative income shares of given percentages of the population, including deciles and quintiles.
- Draw a Lorenz curve and explain its significance.
- Explain how the Gini coefficient is derived and interpreted.

Relative income shares

In order to determine the equality or inequality of income distribution across a nation's population, economists first determine how much of a nation's total income is earned by the richest and the poorest groups of households. Table 16.1 divides five nations' households into five quintiles representing the richest 20% of households down to the poorest 20% and then indicates what percentage of total income is earned by each quintile.

TABLE 16.1 INCOME DISTRIBUTION FOR SELECTED DEVELOPING COUNTRIES						
Country	Percentage of total income earned by:					Gini index
	first quintile (lowest 20%)	second quintile (next to last 20%)	third quintile (middle 20%)	fourth quintile next to top 20%	fifth quintile (top 20%)	
Cambodia	6.5	9.7	12.9	18.9	52.0	43
Indonesia	7.4	11.0	14.9	21.3	45.5	39.4
Brazil	3.0	6.9	11.8	19.6	58.7	56.7
Vietnam	7.1	10.8	15.2	21.6	45.4	37
Turkey	5.4	10.3	15.2	22.0	47.1	41

From Table 16.1 you can see that the highest concentration of income among the top 20% of households exists in Brazil, where the richest fifth of the population earns 58.7% of the income. The poorest fifth of Brazilian households, on the other hand, earn only 3% of the nation's income. Indonesia, another large developing country with a population roughly the size of Brazil's, displays a more even distribution of income; its richest 20% of households account for 45.5% of the income while the poorest earn 7.4%. Both Brazil and Indonesia have large numbers of poor people, but the poorest 20% of people in Brazil are much poorer relative to the richest 20% in Brazil than are the poorest group in Indonesia. Brazil's poor have a much smaller 'slice of the GDP pie' than do Indonesia's poor. Income is distributed less equally in Brazil than in Indonesia.

The Lorenz curve

The Lorenz curve is a graphical representation of a country's income distribution. It plots the cumulative percentage of the nation's income across the cumulative percentage of the population (Figure 16.1). The shape of a country's Lorenz curve tells us much about the country's income distribution.

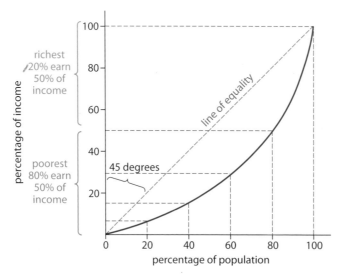

Figure 16.1
The Lorenz curve represents the distribution of income across a nation's population.

The line of equality is the 45-degree line, representing a country in which each quintile (20%) of the population earns exactly the same income as each other quintile. No country has perfectly equal income distribution, therefore the line of equality is only used for comparison. The Lorenz curve in Figure 16.1 represents the data for Cambodia, where the bottom 20% of the population earn 6.5% of the income. On the graph, this is reflected between 0 and 20 on the -axis and 0 and 6.5 on the-axis. The second 20% of Cambodians

To learn more about the
Lorenz curve, visit www.
pearsonhotlinks.com,
enter the title or ISBN
of this book and select
weblink 16.2.

earn 9.7% of the income, which is seen between 20 and 40 on the -axis and 6.5 and 16.2 (i.e. 6.5 + 9.7) on the -axis. Finally, the top 20% of income earners in Cambodia account for around 50% of the national income, as can be seen between 80 and 100 on the -axis and 50 and 100 on the -axis.

The Gini coefficient

Rather than draw Lorenz curves for every country to illustrate the level of income inequality, economists use a tool called the Gini coefficient to quantify the degree of income inequality in a nation. The Gini coefficient is the ratio of the area above a country's Lorenz curve and below the line of equality to the total area below the line of equality. In Figure 16.2, the Gini coefficient is the ratio of area A to the area A + B. The further away the Lorenz curve is from the line of equality, the greater the proportion of area A to the total area below the 45-degree line. Therefore, the higher the value of A/(A + B), the greater the Gini coefficient and the more inequality exists in income distribution in the nation. On Cambodia's Lorenz curve, the ratio of area A to area A + B is 0.43, indicating that the area between the line of equality and the Lorenz curve makes up 43% of the total area below the line of equality. Cambodia's Gini coefficient is 0.43.

Figure 16.2
The Gini coefficient measures the ratio of area A to the area A + B. The higher the ratio, the greater the inequality in a country.

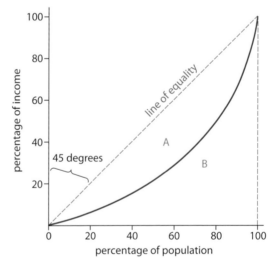

The Gini index

Economists more commonly refer to the Gini index. This is the Gini coefficient multiplied by 100. A Gini index of 100 would indicate perfect inequality of income distribution in the nation. The top 1% of the population earns 100% of the income. This represents an extreme example and is not technically possible, since even in a nation in which poverty is extremely widespread the large number of poor require some income just to survive.

On the other extreme, a Gini index of zero would indicate perfect equality of income distribution. The Lorenz curve would lie along the line of equality, meaning every household in the nation would enjoy an identical share of the national income. There would be neither rich nor poor citizens since everyone's income would be the same. Just as a Gini index of 100 is impossible, so is an index of zero. Even in the world's communist countries of the Soviet bloc and Asia during the mid-20th century there existed a rich elite whose share of the national income was larger than others. This was because of their control of essential resources or political connections or corruption.

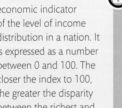
The Gini index is an economic indicator of the level of income distribution in a nation. It is expressed as a number between 0 and 100. The closer the index to 100, the greater the disparity between the richest and poorest households in a nation. The closer to zero, the more equally income is distributed across the nation's households.

Today, the countries with the highest Gini index are mostly sub-Saharan African nations and other extremely poor developing countries. The existence of a small group of extremely rich people and a large majority of extremely poor people makes for a high Gini index and vast income inequalities. The nations with the lowest Gini indexes and the greatest equality in income distribution are mainly Northern and Western European countries in which the government plays an active role in the redistribution of income through taxes and government spending. Figure 16.3 shows the Lorenz curve and the Gini indexes for four major world economies.

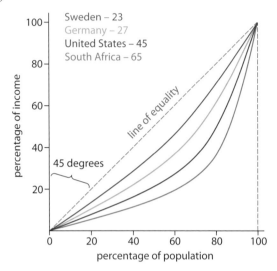

◀ **Figure 16.3**
The Lorenz curves for a selection of countries, some more equal than others.

 The notion of fairness can be approached from a number of perspectives – equality of opportunity, maximizing the income of the least well-off group, and absolute equality of income.
- Which of these notions seems to be most attractive? Why?
- Examine what each of these perspectives suggests is a fair distribution of income.

Sweden has the world's most equal distribution of income, while South Africa is among the world's most unequal countries. The US falls right in the middle of the 130 countries for which data exists, with a Gini index roughly equal to that of Cambodia. It should be emphasized that the Gini index and Lorenz curve do not tell us anything about the of a nation, only the of people within the nation. America's poorest 20% earn far less than its richest 20%, but they are still much richer than even the richest 20% in Cambodia. Many of the richest countries in the world have highly unequal income distribution, with Gini indexes as high or higher than many of the world's poorest countries. Some examples include:

- Hong Kong, Gini index = 53.3; Honduras, Gini index = 53.3
- Singapore, Gini index = 48.1; Ecuador, Gini index = 47.9
- USA, Gini index = 45; Cameroon, Gini index = 44.6
- Japan, Gini index = 38.1; Guinea, Gini index = 38.1

Each of the countries on the left is considered a high-income country, those on the right are extremely poor countries; yet they are roughly identical when it comes to equality of income distribution.

Figure 16.4 (overleaf) shows a selection of national Gini indexes, from the world's most equal (Sweden) to the least equal (Namibia).

Figure 16.5 (overleaf) shows the Gini coefficients for the 130 countries for which data is available.

Figure 16.4
The most and least equal
income distributions.

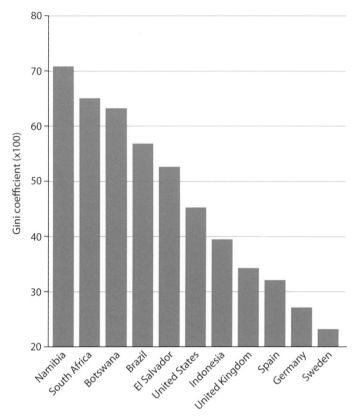

Figure 16.5
Gini coefficients worldwide.
World CIA Report, 2009

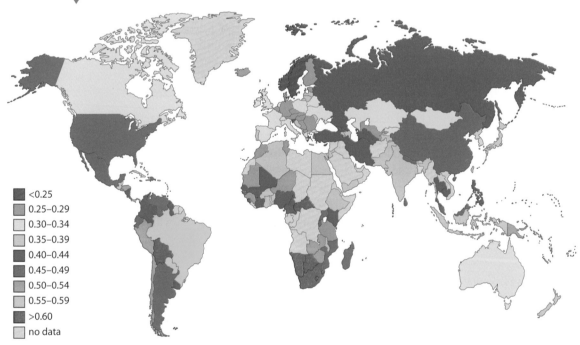

<0.25
0.25–0.29
0.30–0.34
0.35–0.39
0.40–0.44
0.45–0.49
0.50–0.54
0.55–0.59
>0.60
no data

EXERCISES

1   Study Figure 16.5. Generally speaking, are there regions of the world in which income inequality is greater than other regions? What regions appear to have the most equal distribution of income? The least?

2   Why do you think certain countries have more equal income distribution than others?

3   Are rich countries necessarily more equal than poor countries?

16.3 Indicators of poverty

Learning outcomes
- Distinguish between absolute poverty and relative poverty.
- Explain possible causes of poverty, including low incomes, unemployment and lack of human capital.
- Explain possible consequences of poverty, including low living standards, and lack of access to healthcare and education.

What does it mean to be poor? Despite the popular belief that there are rich countries and poor countries, in reality there is poverty in every country in the world. There are also incredibly rich people even in the world's poorest countries. So it is an over-simplification to say that one country is rich while another is poor. Poverty exists everywhere; but in higher-income countries, the poverty is typically while in the poorest countries, we are looking at .

Relative *vs* absolute poverty

Relative poverty is the condition experienced by people in a country whose incomes are considerably lower than the higher income groups in the same country. To be considered poor in America, for instance, an individual must earn less than $10 830 per year, or a family of four must live on less than $22 050 per year. In India, on the other hand, a person living in a city is considered poor if he or she earns less than 500 rupees per month, which equates to roughly $140 per year. An individual with an annual income of $10 000 lives in poverty in America, but would be among the richest 20% of Indians, while an Indian earning $1000 a year is among the middle class in India but would be likely to starve to death in the US.

Relative poverty exists even in the world's richest countries, but absolute poverty is, for the most part, limited to the world's poorest countries with the lowest incomes. To be relatively poor in a country where the average income is already very low may mean you live in absolute poverty.

Absolute poverty is the condition experienced by individuals who cannot afford to acquire the basic necessities for a healthy and safe existence. Such necessities are sanitation, shelter, clean water, nutrition and healthcare. Absolute poverty does not exist everywhere; it is primarily concentrated across the 60 poorest countries of the world – among the people whom Cambridge economist Paul Collier calls the 'bottom billion'.

If the average income of a nation rises and the income distribution remains the same, the level of relative poverty will stay the same, while the number of people in absolute poverty will decrease. It is important to keep this distinction in mind as we examine the efforts of policymakers to eradicate poverty. While absolute poverty may be reduced through international economic development strategies (Chapters 26–29), relative poverty persists and could lead to macroeconomic instability unless policies aimed at redistributing the nation's income are enacted on a national level.

Definitions of poverty vary between nations (and even individuals). To what extent does the definition of poverty we use dictate how we view poverty in the world around us?

Possible causes of poverty

The definition of poverty is a topic of debate among economists, politicians, sociologists, historians, the media, and pretty much anyone else who is asked to define it. It is not an exaggeration, however, that regardless of each person's definition, around half of the world's population lives in either relative or absolute poverty. A mainstream view is that approximately 1 billion people, or around 15% of the world's population, live in absolute poverty, subsisting on less than $2 per day.

The causes of poverty are myriad and warrant a whole book to themselves. In Chapters 26–29, the causes and consequences of poverty are explored in detail. In the meantime, here are some of the obvious causes of poverty that people in all countries, rich and poor, must deal with.

- **Low income.** By the most basic definition, means 'being poor'. Households with low incomes are more likely to live in poverty than those with high incomes, because they cannot afford to buy the necessities required to maintain a healthy, comfortable standard of living.
- **Unemployment.** The lack of a job reduces a household's ability to meet its material needs and wants. A country with high rates of unemployment will experience greater poverty than one with low unemployment, unless that country has a well-funded, reliable set of social safety nets that provide public support to individuals who have lost their jobs.
- **Lack of human capital.** The ultimate cause of poverty is lack of human capital among individuals in society. Without education, skills, and access to healthcare, individuals will be less productive; they will produce and consume at a reduced level of income.

CASE STUDY

Wealth gap in China continues to widen

The gap between the rich and poor in China continues to widen as labourer wages make up a lesser proportion of gross domestic product (GDP), an official at the country's only umbrella union said Wednesday.

Zhang Jianguo, an official at the All-China Federation of Trade Unions (ACFTU) claimed that worker wages accounted for just 36.7 percent of China's GDP in 2005, down sharply from 56.5 percent in 1983.

'It is urgent to reform the current income distribution system in China. The key is to raise the wages of workers,' Zhang said in an interview with Beijing-based daily Xinjingbao, South Korea's Yonhap news agency reported Wednesday.

The ACFTU is the sole national trade union federation in China and the largest trade union in the world with 134 million members.

Zhang said the steady rise in the gap between rich and poor has caused labour-management disputes.

Su Hainan, director of the Institute for Labour and Wages Studies of the Ministry of Human Resources and Social Security, expressed a similar view, noting that the income of urban residents is 3.3 times that of people in the countryside.

'Senior managers at listed state-owned enterprises receive incomes that are 18 times higher than those of their employees,' Su said.

'On average, a senior manager's income is 128 times higher than the average wage in the whole country.'

According to the most recent World Bank figures, China's Gini index comes to 47 – considered an 'alarming' level.

Malaysian National News Agency (Bernama), 12 May 2010

In 2010, China experienced a wave of large-scale public strikes in the electronics and auto industries. After a string of suicides committed by workers at a Foxconn factory in Shenzen, China's workers became emboldened. Their strikes are symptomatic of major worker unrest as income gaps continue to widen in China.

EXERCISES

4 Based on information in the above news article, what has most likely happened to China's Gini index between 1983 and 2010? Justify your answer.

5 Why should the increasing gap between the rich and the poor in China be a concern to the Chinese government?

6 Identify the reasons that may explain why 'the income of urban residents is 3.3 times that of people in the countryside.'

Consequences of poverty

Inequality in the distribution of income is an inevitable result of an economic system that rewards the households with the highest skills, best education and most access to capital with higher wages and incomes in the marketplace.

Poverty, both relative and absolute, poses several obstacles to improvements in well-being for a nation's people. Social unrest among the poorest members of society can lead to political and economic instability for a nation as a whole. The hardships experienced by society's poorest members are ultimately felt by the rest of society because the needs of the poor must be met in one way or another and, in extreme circumstances, may lead to a violent struggle between economic classes.

The existence of absolute poverty is a major problem for a nation. Those who experience it are unlikely to contribute to national output and economic growth because of their low levels of health, education and productivity.

Without promoting some degree of equity in the distribution of income, governments run the risk of undermining their accomplishment of other social and economic objectives. So how do governments achieve more equal income distribution? Before we look at the modern mechanisms by which this objective is achieved, it is important to examine the historical ideology that frames modern economic policy.

The role of taxation in income distribution

Learning outcomes

- Distinguish between direct and indirect taxes, providing examples of each, and explain that direct taxes may be used as a mechanism to redistribute income.
- Distinguish between progressive, regressive and proportional taxation, providing examples of each.
- (HL only) Calculate the marginal rate of tax and the average rate of tax from a set of data.

For centuries the role of government has been debated among economists. The extent to which it is the government's job to ensure equity in the distribution of income has never been fully agreed on by policymakers; opinions differ depending on the school of economic ideology to which they subscribe.

The Marxist view

On the far left of the economic spectrum is Marxist/socialist ideology, which believes that households' money incomes should be made obsolete and each household's level of consumption should instead be based on the use-value of the output which it produces. In a purely Marxist/socialist economy, money incomes do not matter since the output of the nation will be shared equally among all those who contribute to its production. Private ownership of resources and the output those resources produce are wholly abolished in a socialist economy. The ownership and allocation of resources, goods and services are in the hands of the state. Production and consumption are undertaken based on the principle of equality.

The slogan 'from each according to his ability, to each according to his need', made popular by Karl Marx, summarized the view that a household's consumption should be based on its level of need, rather than the amount of capital it owns and the income it can earn from that capital. The logical conclusion of this idea is that all households in a nation have essentially the same basic needs, therefore household incomes and consumption should be equal across the nation.

The *laissez-faire* view

On the other extreme of the economic spectrum is the , free market model which argues that the only role the government should play in the market economy is in the protection of private property rights, ensuring that the private owners of resources are able to pursue their own self-interest in an unregulated marketplace where their money incomes are determined by the exchange-value of the resources they own, including capital, land and labour.

In a market economy, the level of income and consumption of households vary greatly across society because the exchange-value of the resources owned by households is what determines income, not the principle of equality, which drives a socialist economy. Each individual in society is free to pursue his monetary objectives through the improvement of his human capital and the accumulation of physical capital and land and the resulting increase in exchange-value in the resource market.

The modern, mixed economy

In today's world, there exists neither a purely socialist economy nor a purely free market economy. In reality, all modern economies are mixed economies in which governments do much more than simply protect property rights, but do not go so far as to own and allocate all factors of production. The role of government in the distribution of income in today's economies is relegated to the collection of taxes and the provision of public goods and services and transfer payments.

The role of government: taxes

A tax is simply a fee charged by a government on a person's income, property or consumption of goods and services. Taxes can be divided into two main categories: direct and indirect.

Direct taxes

These are taxes paid directly to the government by those on whom they are imposed. An income tax is a direct tax because it is taken directly out of a worker's earned income. Corporate and business taxes are also direct taxes based on the revenues or profits of firms.

Direct taxes cannot be legally avoided since they are based on the earned income of each individual. The burden of direct taxes is borne entirely by the households or firms paying them.

Indirect taxes

These are the taxes paid by households through an intermediary such as a retail store. The consumer pays the tax at the time of his purchase of a good or service and the amount of the tax is usually calculated by adding a percentage rate to the price of the item being purchased.

Indirect taxes include sales taxes, value added taxes (VAT), goods and services tax (GST) as well as taxes (excise taxes) which are placed on specific goods such as cigarettes, alcohol or petrol. Indirect taxes can be avoided simply by not consuming certain products or by consuming less of all products. The burden of indirect taxes is borne by both households and firms, the proportion borne by each is determined by the price elasticities of demand and supply (Chapter 4).

Different taxes result in different burdens

Taxes can be proportional, regressive or progressive in nature. This means that different taxes place different burdens on the rich and the poor.

Proportional tax

A tax for which the percentage remains constant as income increases is a proportional tax. The rich will pay more tax than the poor in absolute terms, but the burden of the tax will be no greater on the rich than it is on the poor.

A household earning 20 000 euros may pay 10% tax to the government, totalling 2000 euros. A rich household in the same country pays 10% on its income of 200 000 euros, totalling 20 000 euros in taxes. There is a difference in total value but the proportional burden is the same on the rich household as it is on the poor household.

Proportional taxes are uncommon in advanced economies, although some payroll taxes (i.e. those collected to support social security or welfare programmes) are based on a percentage of employees' incomes up to a certain level. For instance, the US social security tax is 6.2% of gross income up to $108 000. Regardless of a person's income below $108 000, he or she will pay 6.2% to the government to support the country's social security programme.

Regressive tax

A tax that decreases in percentage as income increases is said to be regressive. Such a tax places a larger burden on lower income households than it does on higher income earners since a greater percentage of a poor household's income is used to pay the tax than a rich household's.

You may be wondering why a government would ever levy a tax that harms the poor more than it does the rich, but in fact almost every national government uses regressive taxes to raise a significant portion of its tax revenues. Most indirect taxes are actually regressive, which may not make sense at first, since a sales tax is a percentage of the price of products consumed. The regressiveness becomes apparent when the amount of the tax is compared to the income of the consumer.

Direct taxes are taxes paid directly to the government by those on whom they are imposed.

Indirect taxes are paid by households through an intermediary such as a retail store. The intermediary then pays the government.

State and national lotteries are often criticized as regressive taxes. Putting aside the voluntary aspect of lottery playing, is the effect regressive? Economist Emily Oster examined lottery sales by postal code; her study suggests that when jackpots are low, the poor bought a larger share of tickets. But when the jackpot grows, high-income groups buy more.

To demonstrate how a sales tax is regressive, imagine three different consumers who purchase an identical laptop computer for €1000 in a country with a value added tax of 10% added to the price of the computer (Table 16.2).

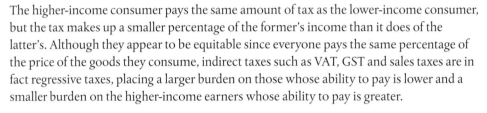

Income of buyer/€	Amount of tax paid/€	% of income taxed
10 000	100	1
50 000	100	0.2
100 000	100	0.1

TABLE 16.2 INDIRECT TAXES ARE REGRESSIVE BECAUSE THE TAX PAID IS A SMALLER PROPORTION OF THE INCOME OF A RICH PERSON THAN THE INCOME OF A POOR PERSON

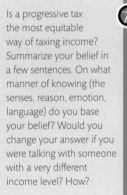

Are lotteries a tax at all? Would your answer change if we learned more about human behaviour patterns from economics and psychology?

The higher-income consumer pays the same amount of tax as the lower-income consumer, but the tax makes up a smaller percentage of the former's income than it does of the latter's. Although they appear to be equitable since everyone pays the same percentage of the price of the goods they consume, indirect taxes such as VAT, GST and sales taxes are in fact regressive taxes, placing a larger burden on those whose ability to pay is lower and a smaller burden on the higher-income earners whose ability to pay is greater.

Progressive tax

This is a tax for which the percentage paid in tax increases as income increases. The principle underlying a progressive tax is that those with the ability to pay the most tax (the rich) should bear a larger burden of the nation's total tax receipts than those whose ability to pay is less. In this way, a progressive tax is the most equitable of the three types of taxes a government collects.

Is a progressive tax the most equitable way of taxing income? Summarize your belief in a few sentences. On what manner of knowing (the senses, reason, emotion, language) do you base your belief? Would you change your answer if you were talking with someone with a very different income level? How?

Lower-income households not only pay less tax, but they pay a smaller percentage of their income in tax as well. Most nations' income tax systems are progressive, the most progressive being those in the Northern European countries which, not surprisingly, also demonstrate the most equal distributions of income. Of the various types of taxes, a progressive income tax aligns most with the macroeconomic objective of equity in the distribution of income.

Comparing income tax systems

Figure 16.6 shows the relationship between an individual's income and the amount of tax the individual will pay under each of the three tax systems. Assuming a proportional tax,

Figure 16.6
The amount of tax paid relative to income under progressive, regressive and proportional taxes.

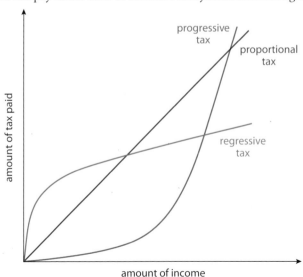

for instance, each household will pay an identical proportion of its income in tax, so as income rises, the amount of tax paid rises at a constant rate.

Under a regressive system, on the other hand, lower-income households pay a larger percentage of their income in taxes. Regressive taxes are mostly indirect, consumption taxes, so higher-income households still pay more in tax (since they consume more), but the amount paid increases at a decreasing rate because at higher incomes the marginal propensity to consume becomes less and more income goes towards savings instead (thus left untaxed).

A progressive tax places very little burden on low income households, since under most progressive income tax systems, the lowest income earners actually pay no tax at all. At higher-income levels, a greater percentage of income is paid as tax, so the amount paid increases at an increasing rate as household income rises. The highest income earners in the economy pay the most tax in all three systems. However, only under a progressive tax system do the richest households also bear the greatest tax burden, meaning that they pay a higher proportion of their income in taxes than lower-income households.

Arguments for a progressive income tax

The main argument against progressive income taxes is that taxing higher incomes at higher rates creates a disincentive to work, in effect punishing any increase in productivity or effort among the nation's workers. However, the fact that higher rates only apply to marginal income, rather than total income, ensures that a worker's after-tax income is always an increasing function of gross income. Therefore, there is always an incentive to increase income by working harder, longer, or more efficiently because the increase in taxes will always be less than the increase in income.

A progressive income tax system provides governments with an effective means of re-distributing the nation's income because those with the greatest ability to pay (the rich) provide the nation with far more of its tax revenue than those with the least ability to pay (the poor). Figure 16.7 shows the total amount of tax revenue generated by each of the five quintiles of income earners in the US in 2006. While the lowest 20% of income earners accounted for around 1% of total tax receipts, the top quintile contributed nearly 70% to America's tax revenues.

In other Western economies, progressive income taxes typically account for the largest proportion of total tax receipts by the government. Canada has an even higher top marginal tax rate than the US and, rather than applying to people earning above $370 000, as it does in the US, Canada's top tax rate kicks in for workers earning just $100 000 per year. In Canada, personal income taxes account for around 50% of total federal tax

A regressive tax is one in which the percentage decreases as the taxpayer's income rises. Lower-income earners pay a larger percentage of their income in tax than higher-income earners.

A proportional tax is one in which the proportion of income paid in tax is constant at all income levels. A low-income household pays the same percentage in tax as a higher-income household.

A progressive tax is the most equitable of the three types of tax, because it places the largest burden on high-income earners. The percentage paid in tax increases as income rises, allowing for those with the greatest ability to pay to pay the greatest proportion of a nation's tax.

To access Worksheet 16.1 on tax progressivity, please visit www.pearsonbacconline.com and follow the onscreen instructions.

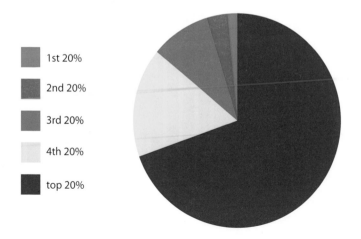

Figure 16.7
Progressive income tax burden.

- 1st 20%
- 2nd 20%
- 3rd 20%
- 4th 20%
- top 20%

Figure 16.8
Sources of Canada's tax revenues.

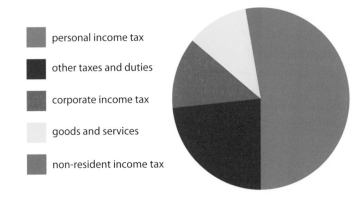

- personal income tax
- other taxes and duties
- corporate income tax
- goods and services
- non-resident income tax

revenues, while the corporate tax and the national goods and services tax make up the next largest portions (Figure 16.8, above).

The highest marginal tax rates tend to exist in the social democratic nations of Northern and Western Europe (Figures 16.9 and 16.10). Denmark, a country with a Gini index of 29, has the highest tax rate on top income earners. More significant than the high rate, however, is the fact that it kicks in at such a low income level, around $50000 per year. This means that a large number of Danish workers are paying a high marginal and average tax rate. The burden of the income tax in Denmark is not just borne by the rich, but by the middle class

Figure 16.9
Marginal tax rates in OECD countries.

Figure 16.10
Income levels at which highest marginal tax rate applies.

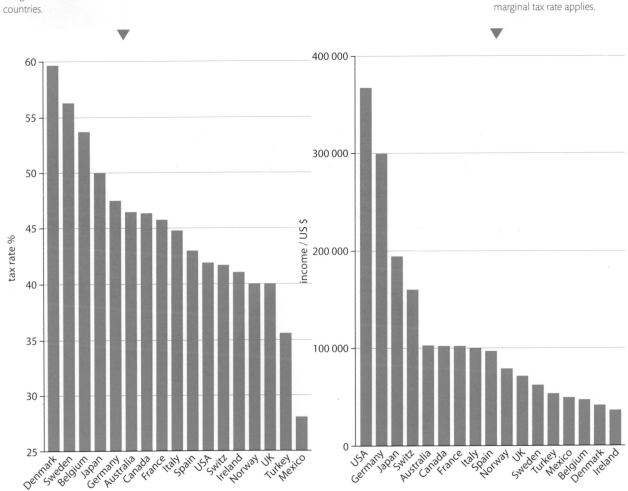

as well. In contrast, Germany's top marginal tax rate of 47% is reached only when a worker's gross income exceeds $300 000 per year, meaning the income tax burden in Germany is borne more by the rich than those earning lower incomes, as is the case in the US.

The effects of a progressive tax on income distribution

Referring to the Lorenz curve model for showing the distribution of a nation's income, it can be argued that the more progressive a nation's income tax, the closer the Lorenz curve is to the line of equality. It is no coincidence that some of the countries with the lowest Gini indexes (Sweden, Germany, Belgium) also have some of the highest marginal tax rates in the world, while those with the lowest marginal tax rates (Mexico, Turkey) have a higher Gini index and a Lorenz curve further from the line of equality (Figure 16.11).

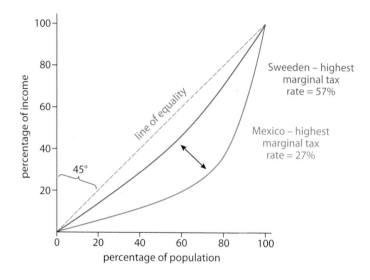

Figure 16.11
A more progressive income tax typically corresponds with more equal income distribution.

Taxes collected from higher-income earners in a high marginal tax country like Sweden are used to provide goods, services and transfer payments to those whose incomes would otherwise be much lower. The equity of such a progressive tax system is derived from the fairness behind making rich households bear a larger burden of the nation's tax system. Equity in the tax system leads to greater equality in the income distribution, as seen in the two Lorenz curves for Sweden and Mexico.

Arguments against progressive income taxes

The primary argument against the use of progressive income taxes as a means to redistribute national income comes from the supply-side school of macroeconomic thought. Supply-siders, whose views are formed by the classical theory of macroeconomics, base their perspective on the belief that a free market economy without government interference always maximizes a country's efficiency, production, and standard of living. They therefore believe that there is a certain level of taxation at which a nation's total tax receipts are maximized. Beyond this point, further increases in the tax rate are believed to lead to a decline in the amount of taxable income due to the disincentive created by the higher tax rate. The Laffer curve demonstrates the relationship between tax rate and tax revenue graphically (Figure 16.12, overleaf).

At a tax rate of 0%, households and firms keep 100% of their gross income and there is no tax revenue for the government. However, at a tax rate of 100%, there is also no tax revenue since no rational individual would choose to work if the government were to take everything he or she earned. The supply of labour falls as the tax rate increases because fewer individuals are willing to work as the government collects higher and

Figure 16.12
The Laffer curve shows the hypothetical relationship between the tax rate in a country and the amount of tax revenue generated.

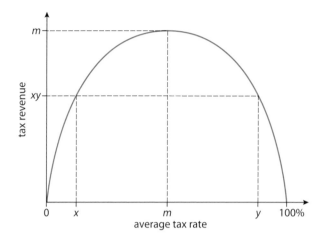

higher percentages of their earned income. Therefore, there would be no income for the government to tax at a tax rate of 100%.

Since tax rates of both 0% and 100% create zero tax revenue, the Laffer curve theory holds that at some tax rate () in between 0% and 100% the government's total tax receipts are maximized. The Laffer curve is often cited by supply-side advocates as an argument for reducing marginal income tax rates on the top income earners. If, for instance, the tax rate is at , it is possible that a lower tax rate could lead to higher tax revenue if the falling taxes incentivize individuals to join the labour force and existing workers to work harder and longer hours, creating more taxable income. In addition, entrepreneurs may be more inclined to start businesses and firms to increase their investments in physical and human capital, both activities contributing further to increases in national output and taxable income. At lower tax rates, argue the supply-siders, the level of taxable income may increase leading to higher tax revenues for the government.

It is not clear from the Laffer curve at what precise level of taxation tax revenues are maximized. The model is most commonly employed by supply-siders to justify their desire for lower income and corporate taxes and a general reduction in the interference of the government in the functioning of the free market. The supply-side argument holds that lower taxes lead to an increase in the supply of labour and capital as households and firms are incentivized to become more economically active, leading to increases in the nation's aggregate supply (AS) and thereby promoting the accomplishment of the macroeconomic goals of full employment and economic growth.

To access Worksheet 16.2 on tax choices, please visit www.pearsonbacconline.com and follow the onscreen instructions.

To learn more about taxes, visit www.pearsonhotlinks.com, enter the title or ISBN of this book and select weblink 16.3.

To learn more about the Laffer curve, visit www.pearsonhotlinks.com, enter the title or ISBN of this book and select weblink 16.4.

EXERCISES

7   The table below shows tax rates calculating marginal and average rates of taxation in France (2010).

FRANCE'S MARGINAL TAX RATES				
Marginal income brackets/€	Marginal rate of taxation/%	Worker's gross income/€	Tax paid/€	Average rate of taxation/%
0–6 000	0	5 000	0	0
6 000–12 000	5.5	10 000	–	–
12 001–26 000	14.0	20 000	1 450	7.25
26 001–70 000	30.0	50 000	–	19.0
70 000+	40.0	100 000	27 490	–

a Calculate the total amount of tax paid by a French worker earning €10 000 per year.

b Calculate the average rate of taxation the same worker pays. Which is greater, the marginal rate of taxation or the average rate of taxation? Explain.

c What does a French worker earning €50 000 pay in taxes?

d Calculate the average rate of taxation for a French worker earning €100 000 per year.

Calculate marginal rate and average rate of tax (HL only)

A progressive income tax typically consists of a marginal tax bracket in which the increasing tax rates apply to marginal income, rather than to total income. In such a system, the average tax a household pays increases less rapidly than the marginal tax because the higher marginal rate only applies to additional income beyond the upper range of the previous bracket. In other words, each successively higher tax rate is only charged on the income in excess of that already taxed at the previous level. Table 16.3 shows the marginal tax rates in the US in 2009. The third column shows the cumulative tax rate paid when tax on all the income in a given bracket has been calculated.

TABLE 16.3 US MARGINAL TAX RATES, 2009			
Income range/$	**Marginal tax rate/%**	**Tax paid by someone at top of bracket/$**	**Average tax rate/%**
0–8 375	10	837.50	10.00
8 376–34 000	15	4 681.25	13.77
34 001–82 400	25	16 781.25	20.37
82 401–171 850	28	41 827.25	24.34
171 851–373 650	33	108 421.25	29.02
373 851–500 000 (and above)	35	152 643.75 (on 500 000)	30.53

An American worker earning $8000, for instance, will pay $800 in income tax. But if his income increases to $10 000 he will pay 15% of the full $10 000 ($1500). He will pay 15% on the income earned above $8375. Such a worker would therefore pay 10% of his first $8375 ($837.50) plus 15% on the additional $1625 he earned, which is another $243.75.

The marginal rate of taxation (MRT) is the change in tax (Δ) divided by the change in gross income (Δ_G). His total tax would therefore equal $1081.25.

$$\text{MRT} = \frac{\Delta t}{\Delta Y_G}$$

The average rate of taxation (ART) at a particular level of income is found by dividing the amount of tax paid by the individual's gross income (Y_G).

$$\text{ART} = \frac{\text{tax}}{Y_G}$$

For workers in each of the income brackets above, the average rate of taxation is always lower than the marginal rate of taxation, since tax increases only apply to additional income earned beyond the previous bracket.

8 The following table shows annual income and marginal income tax rates for a country.

Annual income/$	Marginal income tax rate/%
0–20 000	15
20 001–50 000	25
50 001–100 000	40
100 000+	50

Calculate the annual tax paid by individuals earning

a $40 000

b $80 000

c $120 000

9 Calculate the average tax rate for each of the individuals above.

10 In the same country, the indirect tax (the tax on consumption) is set at 20%.

a If individual **a** above spends $50 000 a year, how much of this is indirect tax?

b Assume individual **c** spends $60 000 a year. How much of this is indirect tax?

11 Which system is more effective at redistributing the nation's income from high-income earners to low-income earners: the direct tax based on the marginal rates above or an indirect tax of 20%. Explain your answer.

16.5 Other measures to promote equality

Learning outcomes
- Explain that governments undertake expenditures to provide directly or to subsidize a variety of socially desirable goods and services (including healthcare services, education, and infrastructure that includes sanitation and clean water supplies), thereby making them available to those on low incomes.
- Explain the term transfer payments, and provide examples, including old age pensions, unemployment benefits and child allowances.

Collecting money from the private sector through direct and indirect taxation is only half of the task undertaken by a government in its efforts to achieve a more equitable distribution of income in the nation. The next step is the redistribution of the tax revenues collected through government expenditures on public goods and services and transfer payments.

The lower the income a household earns, the less its ability to enjoy a good quality of life. Not only will the luxuries enjoyed by the rich be out of reach of low-income households, but many of the necessities required for a healthy and safe existence may also be beyond the means of the lowest income earners, even in rich countries like the US, Australia or Germany. To avoid the vast disparities in standards of living that result from the unfettered workings of a market economy, governments use revenues from direct and indirect taxes to provide public goods and services to the nation's people and to redistribute the nation's income from the rich to the poor through transfer payments, such as welfare, social security and subsidies to the poor.

Role of government: provision of public goods

As you learned in Chapter 5, public goods are those items consumed by households that produce spillover benefits for society as a whole, yet they are often not provided by the free market because of their non-rivalrous nature. Goods such as education and health insurance are provided by private firms that are able to charge high tuition fees and high insurance premiums to those who are willing and able to pay for these services in the marketplace. But for many households, education and health insurance are viewed as optional expenditures that are less important than straightforward material needs such as food and shelter. A poor household, even in a rich country, is less likely to receive adequate education and healthcare if the provision of these necessities were left entirely to the free market, whereas the rich would find these services affordable and would be likely to consume them to a much greater extent.

The gap in consumption of education and healthcare between the rich and poor in a market economy leads to a poverty cycle and the perpetuation of the income gap. Poor households find it harder and harder to escape poverty due to their low levels of human capital. Upper-income households, on the other hand, have a competitive advantage in the marketplace, not due to their innate intelligence or skills, but due to the fact that they can afford better and more education and healthcare in the marketplace. By providing universal education and healthcare to all members of society, a government can help the poor escape poverty (Figure 16.13).

Figure 16.13
The poverty cycle can be turned into a prosperity cycle through government provision of public goods.

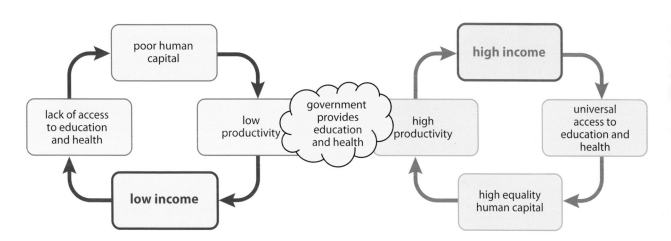

The provision of public education and public healthcare should, therefore, be of the utmost priority to a national government that wishes to reduce income inequality within the nation. Educating the poor increases the likelihood that they will escape poverty without infringing on the prosperity of the rich. Better access to healthcare also increases the chance that a low-income household will become more productive and achieve higher incomes in the future.

The provision of public goods benefits low-income earners but also leads to gains for society as a whole. High-income earners are often the business owners or managers in an economy, whose businesses will find it easier to hire highly skilled, better educated, healthier and more productive workers in a nation with national healthcare and public education. While the provision of these goods requires the collection of taxes from the private sector, which could have negative effects on aggregate supply in the nation, it also makes for a more productive workforce, which could have positive effects on aggregate supply.

Role of government: transfer payments

Another means by which government redistributes the nation's income is through the provision of transfer payments from high-income groups to low-income groups. A transfer payment is a payment from the government to an individual for which no good or service is exchanged. Transfer payments come in many forms, but one characteristic of all transfer payments is that in order to be eligible to receive them, an individual has to fall below a certain income threshold or to be experiencing economic hardship.

Transfer payments are not counted in the GDP of a nation because they are considered non-production transactions; income is transferred from one group (higher-income earners) to another group (lower-income earners) but no new income or output results from the transaction.

Transfer payments existing in most developed countries include:

- unemployment benefits
- social security benefits
- nutritional subsidies
- higher education grants and tuition subsidies
- welfare benefits.

> A transfer payment is a payment from the government to an individual for which no good or service is exchanged. Income is redistributed from one group to another.

Unemployment benefits

When a worker loses his or her job and is unable to find a new one, he or she may become eligible for unemployment compensation. The level of compensation and the length of time over which it can be collected vary from country to country. The intention of such benefits is to allow the unemployed worker to maintain during his period of unemployment a standard of living somewhat equal to that which he enjoyed before losing his job. Such benefits also help keep aggregate demand afloat during a time of recession and rising unemployment, because they prevent the disposable income and consumption of households from declining too much and thereby help offset the fall in total spending in the economy.

> Where is the best place to lose your job? Scandinavian countries offer unemployment payments that add up to 80% of your previous income, for a time period of 10 months up to four years.

Social security benefits

Social security benefits include retirement income and disability income for workers in a nation. Income is redistributed from current workers through their income or payroll taxes to currently retired individuals or those who are unable to work due to a disability. In many countries, social security taxes are collected separately from the normal income tax, and apply up to a limit determined by the government. In the US, a social security tax of 6.2% is deducted from workers' income up to $108 000. A further 6.2% must be contributed to social security by the employer. Income beyond $108 000 is not taxed. Social security is a transfer payment funded by a proportional tax on income up to a certain threshold, beyond which the tax becomes regressive since very high-income earners end up paying a smaller percentage of their total income to social security.

Nutritional subsidies

Low-income households often lack access to healthy food, a reality which leads to higher rates of diabetes, malnutrition, obesity and other food-related illnesses. This subsequently makes low-income households less productive members of the workforce and contributes to their continued poverty. Subsidized nutrition is a form of transfer payment by which low-income households receive coupons from the government to be used to purchase certain nutritional food items. This lowers the burden on poor households of feeding children, allows for their limited disposable income to be spent on other goods and services, and narrows the gap between the rich and the poor. Healthier households are also more productive and likely to earn higher incomes, further reducing the income inequality in the nation.

Higher education grants and tuition subsidies

In addition to providing universal primary and secondary education to all households in a nation, most developed nations also support or provide post-secondary education to citizens. In many European nations, a university education is available to all citizens at reduced tuition fees, which are supported by government subsidies. In the US, higher education is supported by state governments and the federal government. In addition, low-income students are eligible for subsidized loans and government grants based on financial need. Educational grants and subsidies from the government to low-income households represent a type of transfer payment aimed at reducing the education and income gaps explained above.

Welfare benefits

Finally, households whose income is below the official poverty line established by the government may be eligible for welfare benefits. These money payments represent income transfers by the government from high-income earners to low-income households and are intended to subsidize the income of the poor and allow them to enjoy a standard of living beyond that their incomes would allow.

Government expenditures on public goods such as health and education and transfer payments such as welfare and unemployment benefits help governments achieve a more equal distribution of income within their nations. Income inequality is an unavoidable reality of market economies; but it is a reality that should be addressed and offset through responsible fiscal policies involving various types of tax, both direct and indirect, regressive, progressive or proportional in nature.

The extent to which a government attempts to redistribute a nation's income depends on many factors, not the least of which is the political and economic preferences of voters within the nation. European nations such as Denmark and Sweden demonstrate a more socialist lean in their tax and spending policies, the outcome of which is a highly equal distribution of income across society. Some of the most unequal nations, including sub-Saharan African countries such as Botswana, South Africa and Namibia, in which weak political structures and corrupt governments result in the inability to effectively impose taxes on the rich and redistribute them to the poor, remain poor partially due to the inequality in income distribution.

 Equality of opportunity implies correcting for social advantage (for example, government might devote more resources to the education of a child brought up in less prosperous circumstances than one brought up in a comfortable home whose parents are university lecturers).
- How far should the state go in making such corrections?

- Should all parents be forced to read to their children so that no child would be at a disadvantage?

- Should the state attempt to correct for the uneven distribution of natural abilities such as IQ (intelligence quotient) by devoting proportionally more resources to children of less than average IQ?

16.6 The relationship between equity and efficiency

Learning outcomes
- Evaluate government policies to promote equity (taxation, government expenditure and transfer payments) in terms of their potential positive or negative effects on efficiency in the allocation of resources.

To access Worksheet 16.3 on Switzerland, please visit www.pearsonbacconline.com and follow the onscreen instructions.

A nation that successfully employs an equitable system of taxes and government spending is likely to achieve a more equal distribution of its income, reduce poverty, increase productivity, and thereby promote the achievement of its other macroeconomic objectives in the process.

A tax system that punishes innovation, productivity and hard work is clearly undesirable and should therefore be avoided. However, a tax system including progressive marginal income taxes combined with regressive indirect taxes ensures that both the rich and the poor share a portion of the nation's tax burden. Yet it also ensures that those with the greatest ability to pay bear the largest burden while those whose ability to pay is lowest benefit from the public goods and transfer payments that the government provides. This reduces the inequality of income distribution and corrects for the market failures that result in a free market system. Equity, efficiency, and increased equality in the distribution of income can all be achieved if a tax system is designed with the ideas outlined in this chapter in mind.

To access Quiz 16, an interactive, multiple-choice quiz on this chapter, please visit www.pearsonbacconline.com and follow the onscreen instructions.

PRACTICE QUESTIONS

1 a Using a Lorenz curve diagram and examples, distinguish between a country with a high level of income equality and one with a low level of income equality. (10 marks) [AO2], [AO4]

   b Justify the claim that poverty's consequences make its elimination the most important objective of economic policy. (15 marks) [AO3]

2 a In what ways might a more equal distribution of income contribute to greater economic growth? (10 marks) [AO2]

   b To what extent does greater growth lead to greater income equality? (15 marks) [AO3]

3 a Distinguish between progressive, regressive and proportional taxation, providing examples of each. (10 marks) [AO2]

   b Evaluate the effectiveness of a progressive income tax at bringing about a more equal distribution of a nation's income. (15 marks) [AO3]

17 FISCAL POLICY

17.1 The government budget

Learning outcomes
- Explain that the government earns revenue primarily from taxes (direct and indirect), as well as from the sale of goods and services and the sale of state-owned (government-owned) enterprises.
- Explain that government spending can be classified into current expenditures, capital expenditures and transfer payments, providing examples of each.
- Distinguish between a budget deficit, a budget surplus and a balanced budget.
- Explain the relationship between budget deficits/surpluses and the public (government) debt.

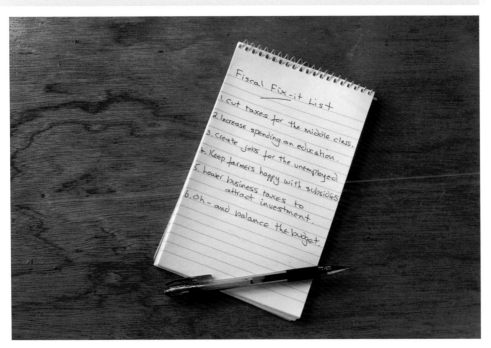

Every government has a fiscal fix-it list.

Governments and central banks in modern industrialized economies are charged with enacting policies to help an economy achieve the four objectives of macroeconomic policy (Chapters 13–16): a healthy economy is one in which employment levels are high, the price level is stable, output of goods and services increases over time, and national income is distributed in an equitable manner.

In their efforts to achieve their macroeconomic objectives, policymakers are equipped with three types of macroeconomic tool:

- fiscal policy
- monetary policy
- supply-side policies.

In this chapter, you will explore the tools of fiscal policy. Monetary policy and supply-side policies are the topics of Chapters 18 and 19 respectively.

Definition of fiscal policy

Fiscal policy is a government's manipulation of taxes and expenditures with the goal of increasing or decreasing the level of aggregate demand (AD) in an economy. As one of the four components of a nation's AD, government spending can have powerful effects on the level of economic activity in a nation. By increasing or decreasing the level of government spending on goods and services, overall demand can be directly influenced through fiscal policy. By changing the level of taxation on households and firms, the level of consumption and investment can be indirectly influenced through fiscal policy.

Whether aimed at reducing AD to reduce inflation or increasing AD to reduce unemployment, fiscal policy is used regularly by government to manage the overall level of economic activity of a nation.

Government budget concept

To understand the effect changes in government spending and taxes may have on a nation's economy, you need to grasp the concept of the government's budget. A nation's government must, in principle, finance its expenditures through the collection of taxes from households and firms, through borrowing from the public, or through the sale of state-owned enterprises to the private sector. The types of project that make up a government's expenditure depend on the country's public priorities. As an example, the projected expenditures and projected sources of government revenue of the UK in 2010 are shown in Figure 17.1.

These charts show that in 2010 the UK will spend £676 billion on public goods and services (e.g. infrastructure, health, education, defence), while it will collect only £498 billion in taxes (e.g. household income tax, corporate tax, indirect taxes such as value added tax (VAT), excise tax).

An increase in any of the expenditures or a decrease in any of the taxes would lead to an increase in AD and be considered expansionary fiscal policy. Such policies might be enacted to reduce unemployment and move the UK economy towards its full-employment level of output during a recession.

On the other hand, a decrease in any of the expenditures or an increase in any of the taxes would lead to a decrease in AD and therefore be considered contractionary fiscal policy. Such a policy could be used to reduce inflation and slow down an over-heating British economy.

Fiscal policy refers to the government's use of taxes and spending to influence the overall level of aggregate demand in the economy to promote the macroeconomic goals of full employment, stable prices and economic growth.

Figure 17.1
The UK government budget.

HM Treasury,
2009 Pre-budget Report

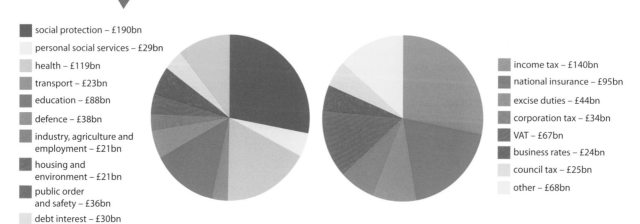

- social protection – £190bn
- personal social services – £29bn
- health – £119bn
- transport – £23bn
- education – £88bn
- defence – £38bn
- industry, agriculture and employment – £21bn
- housing and environment – £21bn
- public order and safety – £36bn
- debt interest – £30bn
- other – £72bn

- income tax – £140bn
- national insurance – £95bn
- excise duties – £44bn
- corporation tax – £34bn
- VAT – £67bn
- business rates – £24bn
- council tax – £25bn
- other – £68bn

Deficits, surpluses and debt

When a government's total expenditure exceeds its total tax revenue in a particular year (Figure 17.1), the government is running a budget deficit. The projected deficit for the UK in 2010 would be £178 billion (total expenditure minus total revenue = 676 billion – 498 billion = 178 billion). In order to pay for this deficit, the UK government must borrow from the public. The effects of government borrowing are examined later in this chapter.

Whenever a government borrows to finance a budget deficit (i.e. pay for the difference between its expenditure and its tax revenue), the government increases its national debt, which is the accumulation of the deficits from past years.

If, in a given year, a government's tax revenue exceeds its expenditure, the government's budget is in surplus. A budget surplus reduces the national debt, since surplus tax revenue can be used to pay down what the government owes the public from past deficits. If a government's expenditure exactly equals its tax revenue, the government has a balanced budget.

To learn more about the national debt, visit www.pearsonhotlinks.com, enter the title or ISBN of this book and select weblink 17.1.

A government's budget is in deficit if the total government expenditure in a given year exceeds the total revenue brought in from taxes in that year.

The national debt is the accumulation of all past years' deficits.

If a government's total spending in a year is less than the tax revenue collected, it experiences a budget surplus.

In a deficit year, the national debt grows by the amount of the budget deficit. In a surplus year, the size of the surplus is subtracted from the national debt.

EXERCISES

1 Examine the table below and answer the questions that follow.

Year	US national debt/billions of $
2000	5 674
2001	5 807
2002	6 228
2003	6 783
2004	7 379
2005	7 933
2006	7 933
2007	9 008
2008	10 025
2009	11 910
2010	13 562

based on data from US Dept of the Treasury, Bureau of the Public Debt, 2010

a In how many years between 2000 and 2010 did the US federal government run a budget surplus? Justify your answer.

b In which year was the US budget deficit the largest? Justify your answer.

c What must be true of the level of government spending relative to the total tax revenues collected in the United States during the period represented by this table?

d Discuss one possible explanation for the continuous growth in the US national debt between 2000 and 2010.

17.2 Automatic fiscal policy and the impact of automatic stabilizers

Learning outcomes
- Explain how factors including the progressive tax system and unemployment benefits, which are influenced by the level of economic activity and national income, automatically help stabilize short-term fluctuations.

Fiscal policy can be thought of as happening in two ways: automatically and at the discretion (i.e. based on the decisions) of policymakers.

Periods of economic growth

Automatic fiscal policy arises due to the nature of many of the expenditures made and tax revenues received by governments. An economy that is producing at or beyond its full-employment level of national output, in which unemployment is very low and household and firms' incomes and revenues are high, will experience an automatic decrease in the government's expenditures on certain items.

For example, if the UK economy were producing at a high level of gross domestic product (GDP) with very low unemployment, government spending on social protection, personal social services and health should automatically decrease. This is simply because when employment and incomes are high, fewer people will be collecting government benefits such as unemployment benefit, housing subsidies, welfare payments, subsidized food assistance, and so on.

In some countries, such as the US, where health insurance is provided by both the private and the public sector, low unemployment relieves the government's need to spend on healthcare for low-income or unemployed members of the workforce since more people receive health insurance from their employers. During periods of economic growth, when output and employment increase, government spending is automatically reduced.

With regard to tax revenues, a growth in a nation's GDP automatically leads to increases in tax revenues, which are based primarily on incomes and expenditures of households and firms. Since both incomes and expenditures rise during periods of economic growth, tax revenues automatically grow. The decrease in government spending and increase in tax revenues that occur during periods of expansion have the effect of automatically reducing AD and offsetting the inflationary pressures that often accompany expansions.

To learn more about government spending, visit www.pearsonhotlinks.com, enter the title or ISBN of this book and select weblink 17.2.

Periods of recession

During recessions and periods of high unemployment, the exact opposite occurs. If a nation's GDP falls, government spending on welfare, unemployment benefits, healthcare and subsidies for the victims of recession automatically increase as more of the nation's workforce receive social benefits from the government. At the same time, tax receipts decrease as incomes and expenditures by the nation's households and firms decline. The fall in AD is, therefore, counteracted through an automatic increase in government spending and decrease in taxes, keeping recession at bay. Figure 17.2 shows the effects of automatic fiscal stabilizers during growth and recession.

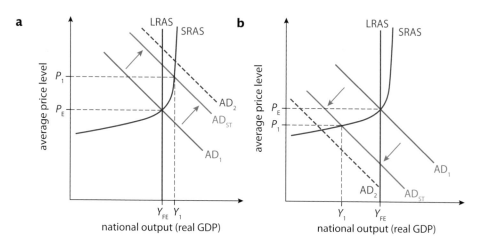

In Figure 17.2a, AD has risen beyond the full-employment level; at this high level of employment, the government's need to provide social benefits to the population falls so such government expenditures decline. In addition, businesses pay more in taxes to the government as their level of output rises. Therefore, an increase in AD that would normally increase demand from AD_1 to AD_2, causing significant inflation, is mitigated by the automatic stabilizers and grows only to AD_{ST}. Higher taxes and lower government spending have the effect of reducing the rate of growth in AD, moving the economy back towards its full-employment level (Y_{FE}).

In Figure 17.2b, the economy has entered a demand-deficient recession. Employment has fallen, so more workers are eligible to receive government benefits. Taxes on firms also automatically fall during a recession because firm revenues and profits decline. In this case, an AD decline that would normally result in AD_2 instead results in a recession that is less severe, to AD_{ST}. The increase in government benefit spending and the decrease in taxes paid have an expansionary effect on AD, moving the economy back towards full employment (or at the very least slowing the economy's decline into recession).

Built-in stability

Figure 17.3 shows the concept of built-in stability in fiscal policy. As GDP rises, tax revenues automatically increase and government spending falls. During a recession, when GDP declines, government spending on social benefits increases while tax revenues fall. In theory, there is a level of GDP at which a government could achieve a balanced budget where tax receipts equal government spending. This level of GDP is likely to be around the nation's full-employment level of output.

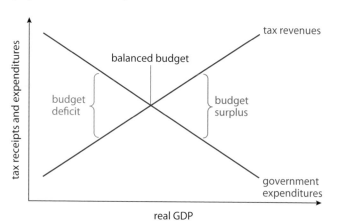

Figure 17.2
Automatic fiscal policy: changes to taxes and government spending happen automatically.
a During periods of growth;
b during periods of recession.

Automatic fiscal policy refers to the notion that, in most nations, tax and government spending systems have an element of built-in stability through which an increase in GDP is automatically accompanied by a decrease in government spending and an increase in taxes. A fall in total output and income, on the other hand, automatically results in an increase in government spending and a decrease in taxes.

The government is best which governs least. This aphorism is sometimes used to argue against the active role of government in an economy. Do you agree that society is better off with less government? Would we all be better off without any government in our lives? What do governments do that contributes to our well-being? What do they do that detracts from our well-being?

◄ **Figure 17.3**
Built-in stability in fiscal policy.

To learn more about fiscal policy, visit www.pearsonhotlinks.com, enter the title or ISBN of this book and select weblink 17.3.

17.3 Discretionary fiscal policy and its effect on potential output

Learning outcomes
- Explain how changes in the level of government expenditure and/or taxes can influence the level of aggregate demand in an economy.
- Describe the mechanism through which expansionary fiscal policy can help an economy close a deflationary (recessionary) gap.
- Construct a diagram to show the potential effects of expansionary fiscal policy, outlining the importance of the shape of the aggregate supply curve.
- Describe the mechanism through which contractionary fiscal policy can help an economy close an inflationary gap.
- Construct a diagram to show the potential effects of contractionary fiscal policy, outlining the importance of the shape of the aggregate supply curve.
- Explain that fiscal policy can be used to promote long-term economic growth (increases in potential output) indirectly by creating an economic environment that is favourable to private investment, and directly through government spending on physical capital goods and human capital formation, as well as provision of incentives for firms to invest.

The effects of the automatic adjustments in government spending and taxes that occur as a nation's GDP increases or decreases may be enhanced through a government's discretionary fiscal policies. During a deep recession, such as that which began in the US and Europe in early 2008 and lasted until mid-2009, governments may decide to increase expenditures on public goods and services such as roads, defence, education and health, while simultaneously reducing the level of taxation on households and firms in order to stimulate consumption and investment.

Such a fiscal stimulus package was implemented in 2009 under US President Barack Obama in the form of the American Recovery and Reinvestment Act (ARRA), which included over $200 billion in tax cuts and $500 billion in new government spending aimed at stimulating AD in the US.

Two of the goals of ARRA are to:

- *create new jobs and save existing ones*

- *spur economic activity and invest in long-term growth*

The Recovery Act intends to achieve these goals by:

- *providing $288 billion in tax cuts and benefits for millions of working families and businesses*

- *increasing federal funds for education and healthcare as well as entitlement programs (such as extending unemployment benefits) by $224 billion*

- *making $275 billion available for federal contracts, grants and loans*

Recovery.gov, the official website for data related to the Recovery Act

---

Discretionary fiscal policy is a change in taxes and spending undertaken by government with the explicit aim of either stimulating or contracting the overall level of demand in the economy to promote economic stability and full employment.

The ARRA is one example of discretionary fiscal policy. The difference between such a policy and the automatic stabilizers is that discretionary policies require action by government whereas automatic stabilizers do not.

Keynes, the demand-siders and fiscal policy

The regular use of discretionary fiscal policy to battle recessions was first advocated by John Maynard Keynes during the Great Depression of the 1930s when he argued that government's manipulation of taxes and spending could have powerful effects on AD in a nation, and thus move it towards full employment during recessions or periods of high inflation. Keynes's demand-side theories are rooted in the belief that economies will not necessarily self-correct (return to the full-employment level of output on their own) during periods of fluctuating AD, as the classical economic theory suggests.

Keynes's advocacy for an active role for government in promoting macroeconomic stability is based on his observations of the inflexible nature of wages and prices in an economy during recession. Since firms find it hard to lower the wages they pay their workers (due to long-term contracts and the influence of labour unions), they cannot simply lower their products' prices to keep demand high during recessions. As a result they must fire workers to keep their costs low, which leads to an increase in unemployment during periods of weak AD.

Keynes believed the government could make up for a decrease in private spending and reverse the corresponding rise in unemployment by cutting taxes and increasing government expenditures during recession, thereby shifting AD out towards its full-employment level. The automatic adjustments in spending and taxes, however, may not be enough to make up for the fall in private spending that often occurs during recessions, thus the need for fiscal stimulus packages such as the 2009 ARRA in the US.

The major argument against the use of expansionary fiscal policy during recession comes from the neo-classical supply-side school of economists and is based on the fact that an increase in spending accompanied by a decrease in taxes requires a government to run a budget deficit. Financing such a deficit requires the government to borrow from the public, which in turn could drive up interest rates and lead to a fall in consumption and investment, thus negating the intended expansionary effects of the fiscal policy. This concept is explained in depth later in this chapter.

John Maynard Keynes, a depression-era economist, argued that government should play an active role in managing the level of aggregate demand in a nation to help achieve the macroeconomic objectives.

 To learn more about the budget deficit, visit www.pearsonhotlinks.com, enter the title or ISBN of this book and select weblink 17.4.

 Keynes believed that private individuals are driven as much by their animal spirits as they are by rational thought. He therefore believed that free market theory was flawed because it assumed humans always act rationally.

Even apart from the instability due to speculation, there is the instability due to the characteristic of human nature that a large proportion of our positive activities depend on spontaneous optimism rather than mathematical expectations, whether moral or hedonistic or economic. Most, probably, of our decisions to do something positive, the full consequences of which will be drawn out over many days to come, can only be taken as the result of animal spirits – a spontaneous urge to action rather than inaction, and not as the outcome of a weighted average of quantitative benefits multiplied by quantitative probabilities.

John Maynard Keynes, *The General Theory of Employment, Interest and Money*, 1936

- Discuss with your class examples of decisions you or people you know have made that were decided more by emotion than by rationality.
- How can the actions of society as a whole, when driven by emotion and rationality, result in economic instability and ultimately recession and unemployment?

Demand-side policies are the macroeconomic policies of government aimed at stimulating or reducing the overall level of aggregate demand to promote the short-run achievement of the three macroeconomic objectives of full employment, price stability and economic growth. Fiscal policy is one tool for demand management, monetary policy is the other (Chapter 18).

Fiscal policy and short-term demand management
Closing a recessionary gap

During times of recession, a government may choose to implement an expansionary fiscal stimulus package, such as the $774 billion ARRA in the US or China's $585 billion fiscal stimulus launched in late 2008 to combat falling demand for its exports and slowing economic growth.

When private consumption, investment and export sales fall during a recession, an increase in government spending and a decrease in taxes can offset the fall in other spending and move AD and GDP back towards the full-employment level (Figure 17.4).

Figure 17.4
A recessionary gap: when AD intersects SRAS below the full-employment level of output.

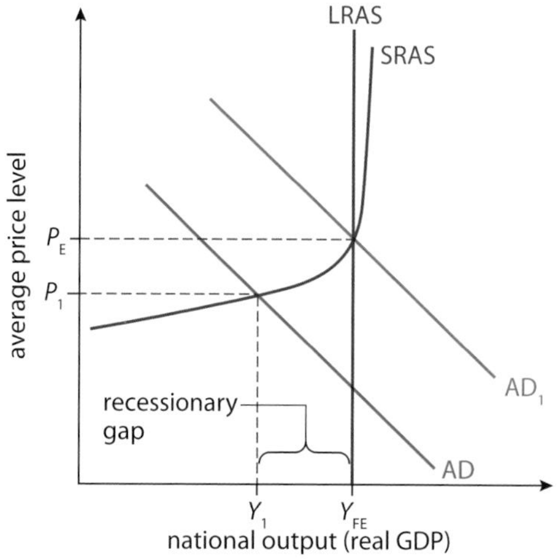

To learn more about the recession, visit www.pearsonhotlinks.com, enter the title or ISBN of this book and select weblink 17.5.

Expansionary fiscal policy is a decrease in taxes and/or an increase in government spending aimed at increasing the level of aggregate demand to close a recessionary gap and move an economy towards its full-employment level of output.

An appropriately sized tax cut and spending package could, in theory, increase the level of AD in the nation and fill the recessionary gap resulting from low private spending. To determine the amount of stimulus necessary to achieve a particular increase in AD and fill a recessionary gap, the government must consider the impact an increase in spending will have on total demand in the economy.

Closing an inflationary gap

Just as a fiscal stimulus package consisting of a decrease in taxes or an increase in government spending will have an expansionary effect on AD and help reduce the size of a recessionary gap, a contractionary fiscal policy consisting of higher taxes and less government spending can be used to reduce AD and thereby bring down inflation in an economy.

When private investment, consumption or net exports rise without a corresponding rise in aggregate supply (AS), the result is demand-pull inflation. As seen in Figure 17.5, demand-pull inflation results from a level of demand for a nation's output that exceeds the level of output achievable by the nation when producing at full employment. In the short run, GDP can grow beyond the full-employment level, but such growth is accompanied by high inflation and all the undesirable effects inflation brings (Chapter 14).

To reduce the level of AD in the economy in Figure 17.5, a government can employ a discretionary fiscal policy consisting of an increase in taxes and/or a decrease in government spending. Higher taxes will reduce households' disposable income and reduce the level of consumption and investment by firms. A decrease in government spending directly reduces the level of AD and puts downward pressure on the rate of inflation, moving the economy closer to its full-employment level of output.

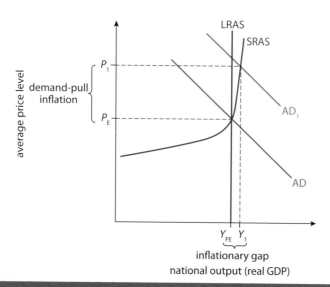

To learn more about Keynesian economics, visit www.pearsonhotlinks.com, enter the title or ISBN of this book and select weblink 17.6.

Contractionary fiscal policy is an increase in taxes and/or a decrease in government spending aimed at decreasing aggregate demand to close an inflationary gap and moving the economy to its full-employment level of output and price level stability.

EXERCISES

2   Study the table below and answer the questions that follow.

Year	Unemployment rate/%	Year	Inflation rate/%
1990	5.6	1978	7.6
1991	6.8	1979	11.3
1992	7.5	1980	13.5

US Bureau of Labor Statistics

a   Describe the macroeconomic conditions in the US during the two time periods represented above.

b   Identify a fiscal policy response to the macroeconomic conditions during the two time periods. Using an AD/AS diagram, illustrate the macroeconomic conditions in the US before the enactment of fiscal policy and after.

c   What risk does the use of fiscal policy to reduce inflation pose for policymakers? What risk does the use of fiscal policy to reduce unemployment pose for policymakers?

17.4 The Keynesian spending multiplier (HL only)

The size of the fiscal stimulus necessary to achieve a particular increase in total spending

Learning outcomes

- Explain, with reference to the concepts of leakages (withdrawals) and injections, the nature and importance of the Keynesian multiplier.
- Calculate the multiplier using either of the following formulae.

$$\frac{1}{(1 - MPC)} \quad \text{or} \quad \frac{1}{(MPS + MPT + MPM)}$$

- Use the multiplier to calculate the effect on GDP of a change in an injection in investment, government spending or exports.
- Draw a Keynesian AD/AS diagram to show the impact of the multiplier.

To learn more about the marginal propensity to consume, visit www.pearsonhotlinks.com, enter the title or ISBN of this book and select weblink 17.7.

To learn more about the marginal propensity to save, visit www.pearsonhotlinks.com, enter the title or ISBN of this book and select weblink 17.8.

in an economy depends on the size of the spending multiplier, which in turn depends on the public's marginal propensity to consume (MPC) and the marginal rate of leakage (MRL) (Chapter 12).

The multiplier effect of a change in government spending refers to the fact that any change in government spending affects household incomes in the nation, which thereby affects the amount of private spending among households and firms. Therefore, when government spending increases by a certain amount, say \$100 billion, the ultimate increase in the nation's GDP should be something greater than \$100 billion; just how much bigger depends on how much of the initial change in spending gets spent again by households and firms and how much gets saved or otherwise leaked from the circular flow.

The MPC is the proportion of a change in national income households use to purchase domestically produced goods and services. The MRL is the proportion of a change in income which gets taxed plus the proportion that households save and buy imports with (in other words, income that is leaked from the circular flow). MRL is the sum of the marginal propensity to save (MPS), the marginal propensity to tax (MRT) and the marginal propensity to import (MPM). Each of these is considered a leakage from the circular flow, so the larger proportion of a change in income that goes towards these, the lower the multiplier effect will be.

MPC + MRL = 1 since consumption, savings, taxes and buying imports are the only possible things a nation can do with a change in national income. The formulas below show how each of these propensities is calculated.

$$MPC = \frac{\Delta C}{\Delta Y} \qquad\qquad MPS = \frac{\Delta S}{\Delta Y}$$

$$MPT = \frac{\Delta T}{\Delta Y} \qquad\qquad MPM = \frac{\Delta M}{\Delta Y}$$

$$MRL = MPS + MPT + MPM \qquad MPC + MRL = 1$$

Any increase in government spending on public goods and services translates into an increase in income for someone in the country. For example, if the UK government were to increase its spending on the National Health Service (NHS), this may lead to higher incomes for healthcare professionals, contractors who build new hospitals and manufacturers of medical equipment. The increase in household income from the government's purchase of healthcare goods and services would enable British households to increase their private consumption, savings and import spending. The initial increase in government spending is thus multiplied through further increases in consumption by the recipients of the new government spending.

The government spending multiplier (k) indicates to policymakers the ultimate effect a particular increase in government spending will have on the level of AD in the economy. It is calculated using the following equation:

$$k = \frac{1}{(1 - MPC)}$$

or

$$k = \frac{1}{MRL}$$

The larger the proportion of new income that households spend on domestically produced goods and services (the MPC), the larger the multiplier effect of an increase in government spending.

The implication for policymakers, therefore, is that to achieve a particular increase in the nation's GDP, government spending must only increase by a proportion of the desired change in total spending. For example, if a government wishes to increase AD to a level that would result in a £200 billion increase in GDP, it would not have to increase government spending by the full £200 billion.

Let's assume that 60% of an increase in household income is used to consume domestic output by households and 40% is used to buy imports and put towards savings. The nation's MPC is therefore 0.6 and its MRL is 0.4. The spending multiplier and thus required increase in government spending can be determined using the formula above.

$$k = \frac{1}{1-0.6} = \frac{1}{0.4} = 2.5$$

With a marginal propensity to consume of 0.6, the spending multiplier equals 2.5. With this in mind, we can determine just how large an increase in government spending (ΔG) is needed to achieve a total increase in GDP of £200 billion.

$$\Delta G = \frac{desired\ \Delta GDP}{k} = \frac{200\ billion}{2.5} = 80\ billion$$

A desired change in GDP of £200 billion requires a change in government spending of only £80 billion. The £80 billion increase in national income of the nation will lead to an increase in AD that is 2.5 times as large. This is achieved through further rounds of consumption by households and investment by firms, which earn income from the government and then consume more British goods and services with a proportion of their increased income.

Through the multiplier effect, a fiscal policy involving an increase in government spending is multiplied throughout the economy, increasing the nation's total income beyond the initial increase in spending. Figure 17.6 shows the concept of the multiplier effect of an increase in government spending. The initial increase in spending of £80 billion results in an increase in aggregate GDP of £200 billion due to the multiplier effect.

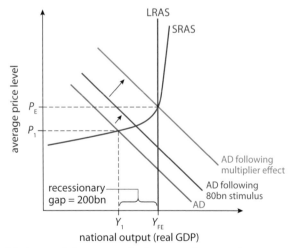

Figure 17.6
The multiplier effect: an increase in government spending leads to a larger increase in overall demand.

The multiplier could also work in reverse. In theory, a decrease in government spending by a particular amount also has a multiplier effect across the economy, also determined by the households MPC and the MRL. The decrease in household income resulting from a decrease in government expenditures will impact the level of consumption, savings, taxes and the amount of imports purchased. Therefore, a government spending cut ultimately impacts GDP by a greater amount than the reduction in government expenditures itself.

To access Worksheet 17.1 on the spending multiplier in the US, please visit www.pearsonbacconline.com and follow the onscreen instructions.

The multiplier effect is that any change in government spending will have a larger ultimate effect on the nation's GDP as the resulting change in household income leads to further changes in consumption and investment in the economy. The size of the multiplier effect depends on the government spending multiplier (k), which is a function of the nation's marginal propensity to consume.

$$k = \frac{1}{(1 - MPC)}$$

To learn more about the government spending multiplier, visit www.pearsonhotlinks.com, enter the title or ISBN of this book and select weblink 17.9.

3 In country X, at the current level of national income, the marginal propensity to consume is 0.6. The economy is currently experiencing a recessionary gap of $60 billion.

  a Calculate the size of the spending multiplier.

  b Calculate the amount of new government spending that would be needed to achieve an increase in income of $60 billion.

4 Would a cut in taxes of the same amount as you identified in 3b result in the same increase in national income as the increase in government spending of that amount? Why or why not?

5 Now assume the economy is producing at a level of output in which it is experiencing inflation of 10%. The inflationary gap is estimated at $20 billion. Assuming the same MPC, how much of a decrease in government spending is needed to stabilize inflation and return the economy to its full employment level?

 17.5 **Evaluation of fiscal policy**

Learning outcomes
- Evaluate the effectiveness of fiscal policy through consideration of factors including the ability to target sectors of the economy, the direct impact on aggregate demand, the effectiveness of promoting economic activity in a recession, time lags, political constraints, crowding-out, and the inability to deal with supply-side causes of instability.

Government spending *vs* tax cuts

A reduction in taxes of a particular amount is less effective at increasing national income than an increase in government spending of the same amount. To understand why, we must examine the process through which a tax cut affects the level of private spending in a nation.

If the UK government had responded to the £200 billion recessionary gap shown above by cutting taxes by £80 billion rather than by increasing government spending by that amount, then the increase in AD would have been less than £200 billion.

Here's why. An increase in government spending is a direct injection into the circular flow of income, whereas a tax cut is an indirect injection because households are able to determine precisely how much of it ends up being spent on domestic output, thereby contributing to national income, and how much is saved, used to buy imports or goes towards taxes.

Suppose the UK government had chosen to cut taxes by £80 billion and not changed the level of government spending. The tax cut would have increased household income by £80 billion. Based on an MPC of 0.6, only 60% of the £80 billion (£48 billion) would have turned into new spending in the economy; 40% would immediately have gone into savings or towards the purchase of imports – that is, would have leaked from the circular flow.

Essentially, the size of the actual stimulus is lower because it is not directly spent in the economy by the British government; it is indirectly injected through households who choose to save or buy imports with £32 billion of the government's £80 billion tax cut. The result is a smaller overall increase in GDP – only £120 billion (£48 billion of new spending multiplied by the multiplier of 2.5), leaving the recessionary gap of £200 billion only partially filled and the economy still in a recession.

Given the direct effect government spending has on AD, increasing government spending during a recession is more likely to stimulate economic activity than cutting taxes by the same amount. Both an increase in government spending and a decrease in taxes during a recession require the government to borrow money and increase its budget deficit. Therefore, increasing government spending is more desirable economically than decreasing taxes, since it requires the government to borrow a smaller amount to achieve the same increase in GDP.

The government will get a greater stimulus (more bang for its buck) by increasing spending than by cutting taxes to fill a recessionary gap and move the economy towards its full-employment level during a recession. However, in most cases (including America's ARRA fiscal stimulus package) both tax cuts and spending increases are used to fight recessions. Politically, of course, a tax cut is often a more desirable policy; the contradicting goals of politics and economics are explored later in this chapter.

Strengths and weaknesses of fiscal policy

The above analysis does not take into account the possible adverse effect that increased government borrowing might have on the level of private spending in the economy. It may be that a fiscal stimulus package financed by an increase in government borrowing could drive up the interest rates faced by households and firms in the private sector.

The crowding-out effect

To learn more about the loanable funds market, visit www.pearsonhotlinks. com, enter the title or ISBN of this book and select weblink 17.10.

The term 'crowding-out effect' refers to the effect on private consumption and investment of a deficit-financed increase in government spending that leads to an increase in interest rates. Any increase in AD intended through fiscal stimulus may be crowded out by a simultaneous decrease in consumption and investment.

To understand the effect that fiscal policy actions have on the level of private consumption, investment and net exports, it is useful to introduce a new diagram into our analysis. A nation's loanable funds market is a hypothetical market that represents the money in commercial banks that is available to be loaned out to firms and households to finance private investment and consumption. The price of loanable funds is the real interest rate; the loanable funds market therefore illustrates the relationships between real returns on savings and real price of borrowing and the private sector's willingness to save and invest. The supply curve represents savings and the demand curve represents investment (Figure 17.7).

Households respond to a higher real interest rate by increasing savings because the return on savings is greater; hence there exists a direct relationship between real interest rate and supply of loanable funds. At lower real interest rates, households and firms are less inclined to save and more inclined to borrow and spend, so the demand for loanable funds reflects an inverse relationship between

Figure 17.7
The loanable funds market.

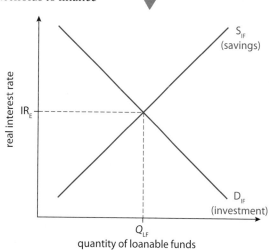

quantity demanded and the real interest rate. At higher interest rates, households prefer to delay their spending and increase their savings, since the opportunity cost of spending is higher.

A bond is a certificate of debt issued by a government (the borrower) to an investor (the lender) to provide the government with external funds to finance current expenditures. When a government borrows in order to finance a budget deficit, it must increase the interest rates on its bonds in order to attract more lenders. Investors respond to the higher rates of return on government bonds by taking money out of commercial banks (represented by the loanable funds market) and buying government bonds, thereby lending money to the government. Banks also lend out less of their excess reserves to private borrowers and instead purchase government bonds where their investment is relatively secure and now earns higher interest.

As households, firms and banks buy the newly issued government bonds, the supply of private loanable funds decreases. The decrease in money available to the private sector drives up interest rates as funds are directed towards the public sector. The government is able to finance its budget deficit, but reduced funds are now available to the private sector for consumption and investment. Private consumption and investment is thus crowded out by public-sector borrowing (Figure 17.8).

Figure 17.8
Crowding-out in the loanable funds market: higher interest rates on government bonds decreases the supply of funds available to the private sector, driving up interest rates.

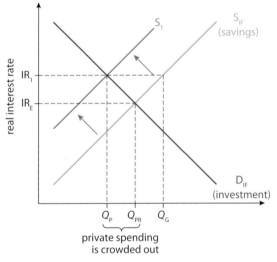

In Figure 17.8, before the government increased its deficit, private borrowing for investment and consumption was at Q_{PR}. As the interest rate on government bonds increases, individuals buy bonds and the supply of loanable funds decreases. At the higher real interest rates fewer funds are demanded by the private sector (Q_{PR}), but more are supplied (Q_G). The difference between Q_P and Q_G represents the increase in government borrowing. The decrease from Q_{PR} to Q_P represents the fall in private investment and consumption resulting from higher real interest rates in the economy.

Figure 17.9 shows the effect that crowding-out has on AD following a deficit-financed fiscal stimulus package. The economy started in recession at AD, Y_1 and P_1. The increase in government spending was intended to increase AD to AD_1 and return the economy to its full-employment level. However, due to crowding-out, private spending falls while public sector spending increases, resulting in a shift to the left back to AD_2. The end result is stronger AD than before, but the economy has not achieved its full-employment level of output.

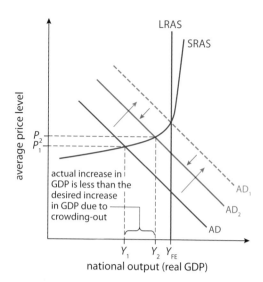

LRAS

SRAS

actual increase in
GDP is less than the
desired increase
in GDP due to —
crowding-out

AD₁

AD₂

AD

Y₁ Y₂ Y_FE

national output (real GDP)

average price level

Figure 17.9
Crowding-out in the AD/
AS model: The increase in
AD resulting from a deficit-
financed fiscal stimulus
may be smaller due to the
crowding-out of private
investment.

The crowding-out effect
refers to the possible
effect that a government's
deficit-financed fiscal
policy may have on
real interest faced by
the private sector. The
decrease in the supply
of private loanable funds
resulting from increased
government borrowing
may drive up private
interest rates and crowd
out private investment,
reducing the desired
expansionary effect of the
government's fiscal policy.

Another look at crowding-out: the recession of 2008–09

Neo-classical economists criticize the Keynesian argument for government deficit
spending during a recession by claiming that crowding-out will offset the expansionary
effects of a tax cut combined with an increase in government spending. The possible
fall in private investment resulting from higher interest rates may undermine a modern
economy's long-run growth potential. It is the private sector, argue the neo-classicals, not
the public sector that is the engine of growth in today's economies. Policy actions that
direct society's scarce financial, human and capital resources away from the private sector
and towards the public sector threaten to undermine the engine of economic growth in
market economies – free enterprise. The possibility of crowding-out points to a major
shortcoming in the use of expansionary fiscal policy to combat a recession.

Crowding-out may not occur in a nation during a deep recession such as that experienced
by the US, Europe and other countries between 2008 and 2009. Due primarily to President
Obama's ARRA fiscal stimulus package, the US federal budget deficit for 2009 reached an
unprecedented $1.4 trillion, increasing America's national debt from $11 trillion to over
$12.4 trillion in less than a year. The large increase in government borrowing needed to
finance this deficit, it might be expected, would necessitate substantial increases in the
interest rate on US government bonds and would therefore direct funds away from the
private sector and crowd out private consumption and investment. However, data seem to
show that crowding out did not occur during the recession of 2008–09 (Figure 17.10).

To access Worksheet 17.2
on the fiscal stimulus in
the US, please visit www.
pearsonbacconline.com
and follow the onscreen
instructions.

Figure 17.10 (overleaf) shows the US savings rate, the prime interest rate, and the interest
rate on US government bonds from January 2008 to January 1020. When examined
closely, these data refute the view that during a deep recession deficit-financed government
spending will drive up private interest rates and crowd out private spending in the economy.

Between early 2008 and late 2009, the US savings rate rose from as low as 0.8% to as high
as 6.4%. This represents a massive increase in the supply of loanable funds, as households'
willingness to provide capital to the private banking sector increased during the period of
economic uncertainty and low consumer confidence.

Prime interest rate is the
rate that commercial
banks charge their most
credit-worthy borrowers. It
is an indicator of the level
of interest rates charged to
all other borrowers in an
economy.

Over the same period, the prime interest rate in the US actually decreased from over 6%
to 3.25%. Even as the US budget deficit reached an all-time high and the national debt
ballooned to $12.4 trillion, interest rates on government bonds remained steady and even
decreased at times throughout the worst of the recession in the US. If the US stimulus
package had been causing crowding-out, as the neo-classical argument suggests it should,

Figure 17.10
US savings rates and interest rates 2008–10.

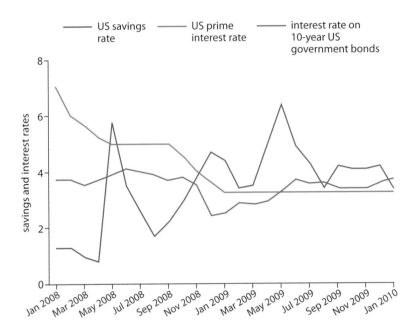

then both the interest on US government bonds and the prime interest rates charged to private borrowers would have risen throughout 2008 and 2009.

The fact that interest rates remained steady or fell indicates that there was actually a surplus of savings in the US during the worst of the 2008–09 recession. When the government increased its issuance of bonds, it was able to borrow from the public at extremely low interest rates. While funds were directed away from the private sector towards the government, there was little to no effect on the level of private spending, which was already depressed due to low consumer and investor confidence. In other words, there was such low demand for loanable funds and such a great supply before the ARRA stimulus package that there was no crowding-out of private spending as a result of the deficit-financed fiscal stimulus.

The US experiment with fiscal policy during the 2008–09 recession demonstrated that during a *deep* recession, crowding-out of private spending is unlikely. Policymakers should not, however, ignore the possibility of crowding-out when employing fiscal policy during a *mild* recession.

If an economy is producing at or near full employment, with resources employed and private demand for loanable funds high, it is more likely that a deficit-financed increase in government spending will drive up interest rates and crowd out interest-sensitive private spending. With this in mind, it can be argued that large fiscal expansions should be reserved for situations in which an economy is experiencing high levels of unemployment, deflation, and a general collapse of consumer and investor confidence.

To learn more about the crowding-out effect, visit www.pearsonhotlinks. com, enter the title or ISBN of this book and select weblink 17.11.

For an economy producing at or near full employment, supply-side policies such as lower corporate taxes, deregulation of the private sector, lower minimum wages and reducing the power of labour unions are likely to be more effective at reducing unemployment, as these policies lower firms' costs of production and encourage a greater level of output and employment (these policies are explored in Chapter 19).

The net export effect

During a period of rising unemployment and weak demand, a tax cut and increase in government spending financed by increased government borrowing may increase interest rates in the economy and make the country's currency more attractive to foreign investors who wish to buy the government's bonds. Demand for the currency rises, increasing the exchange rate against trading nations' currencies.

Furthermore, as AD grows in response to more domestic government spending, there is upward pressure on inflation as well as greater disposable incomes among households. Rising incomes and a stronger currency lead to an increase in demand for imports from abroad, and higher domestic prices and a higher exchange rate reduce demand for the country's goods among trading partners. Net exports may, therefore, fall following a deficit-financed increase in government spending. The net export effect of an expansionary fiscal policy counteracts the desired effect of the policy itself.

During a period of demand-pull inflation, a government may raise personal income taxes or cut back on its own expenditures to reduce overall demand and bring the economy closer to full employment. Such a policy reduces the government's need to borrow in the bond market, which brings down the interest rates on government debt. The nation's supply of loanable funds increases (this could be viewed as crowding-out in reverse). Interest rates in the economy fall, which in turn reduces foreign demand for the nation's currency, lowering the nation's exchange rate compared to that of trading partners.

Furthermore, a decrease in the rate of inflation resulting from less overall demand makes the nation's exports more attractive to the rest of the world. As imports fall and exports rise, the net export effect of contractionary fiscal policy counteracts the desired effect of the policy itself.

The net export effect presents another possible shortcoming in the use of fiscal policies. The increase in AD desired by a fiscal stimulus could be muted by the fall in net exports and rise in imports that result from higher interest rates and a stronger domestic currency. The increase in net exports resulting from a weaker currency and lower interest rates following a fiscal contraction will reduce the contractionary effects of the fiscal policy action.

The higher interest rates needed to attract lenders to finance an expansionary fiscal policy could lead to an appreciation of the nation's currency, reducing demand for its exports abroad. The fall in net exports may offset the desired expansionary effect of the fiscal policy.

During a contractionary fiscal policy, lower interest rates on domestic government bonds reduce demand for the currency, causing it to weaken and increasing demand for exports. The increase in net exports may offset the desired contractionary effect of the fiscal policy.

Time lags in fiscal policy

A change in a nation's discretionary fiscal policy often requires months of deliberation by those in government. The administrative lag of discretionary fiscal policy (the time between when the policy action is most needed and when it actually occurs) can be months or even years. Fiscal policies may also suffer from recognition lag (the time between the onset of an inflationary period or rising unemployment and the recognition by policymakers that it is actually happening).

Finally, the impact lag of fiscal policy may render it ineffective at promoting macroeconomic goals in the short run. Tax cuts and increases in government spending often take months or even years to actually begin contributing to the level of economic activity in a nation. An economy in recession may remain in recession long after government funds have been handed out and tax cuts implemented. The various lags explained here present possible shortcomings of Keynesian style demand-management through fiscal policy tools.

To access Worksheet 17.3 on stimulus and austerity, please visit www.pearsonbacconline.com and follow the onscreen instructions.

Political influence over fiscal policy

Another shortcoming of fiscal policy is the fact that policy decisions rest in the hands of politicians whose incentives may not lie entirely in the best interest of the nation's economy. Politicians may promote and push through fiscal policies that are popular among voters, even if they are economically irresponsible. Political hijacking of fiscal policies may lead to political business cycles in which total spending in the economy

Discuss the view that economic policy may be motivated more by the selfish political objectives of politicians than by the macroeconomic objectives of full employment, economic growth and price stability.

fluctuates depending on politicians' desire to enact popular tax breaks and government handouts even when an economy is close to or at full employment. The goal of such irresponsible policies, of course, is to maintain political support and earn votes in the next national election, while the effect is often prolonged periods of expansion and inflation.

On the other hand, despite the fact that government spending multipliers are known to be greater than tax multipliers, governments often turn to tax breaks during recessions before resorting to increases in government spending. For instance, during the last year of George W Bush's presidency (2008), the US officially entered its deepest recession since the 1930s. In response, President Bush enacted a fiscal stimulus package consisting entirely of a $168 billion tax rebate to the American people. By the end of the year, the US was deeper in recession. Bush's plan included no increases in government spending, a policy decision most likely rooted in the 'small government' political ideology of his Republican party rather than in basic economic theories.

In one sense, the imposition of taxes by government on individuals amounts to a restriction of individual freedom. How can we know when such government interference in individual freedom is justified?

Fiscal policy is not insulated from the political agendas of the individuals who form a nation's government. Policymakers must undertake implementation of fiscal policy cautiously and all possible effects should be considered.

Monetary policy, an entirely different category of macroeconomic policy, is explored in Chapter 18. Monetary policy is, in most nations, the responsibility of an independent central bank, and so is more insulated from political pressures. It presents macroeconomic policymakers with a powerful and nimble tool for affecting the level of output, prices and employment in a nation.

To access Quiz 17, an interactive, multiple-choice quiz on this chapter, please visit www.pearsonbacconline.com and follow the onscreen instructions.

PRACTICE QUESTIONS

1 **a** How might an accurate value for the spending multiplier aid a government in setting fiscal policy? (10 marks) [AO2]

    b Evaluate the view that a tax cut is more effective at stimulating aggregate demand than an increase in government spending. (15 marks) [AO3]

2 **a** What macroeconomic policies would a government adopt if it wished to reduce aggregate demand in an economy? (10 marks) [AO1]

    b Should a government attempt to manage the level of aggregate demand to influence unemployment and inflation rates? (15 marks) [AO3]

© International Baccalaureate Organization 2002

3 **a** Explain why an increase in government spending not accompanied by an increase in taxes may lead to a fall in private sector investment. (10 marks) [A02]

    b Evaluate the likelihood that this will happen during a demand-deficient recession. (15 marks) [A04]

4 **a** What are the main macroeconomic objectives of government? (10 marks) [A01]

    b Assume the government chooses to pursue one of these objectives. Evaluate the possible consequences for the other objectives. (15) [A03]

© International Baccalaureate Organization 2002

18 MONETARY POLICY

18.1 Interest rates and the role of a central bank

Learning outcomes
- Describe the role of central banks as regulators of commercial banks and bankers to governments.
- Explain that central banks are usually made responsible for interest rates and exchange rates in order to achieve macroeconomic objectives.
- Explain, using a demand and supply of money diagram, how equilibrium interest rates are determined, outlining the role of the central bank in influencing the supply of money.

It's hard to imagine a world without money. We take it so much for granted that we might overlook the magic it works in our daily lives.

Walk into a grocery store, pick out your food items for the week, and hand over a few pieces of paper, perhaps a couple of coins as well. To you, the benefits of such a transaction are obvious. You expect to eat the vegetables, meats, breads and chocolates. For the supermarket, there's a gamble. They take your paper and coins on faith, the trust that some other person or firm will accept the paper and coins in return for labour services or more goods to fill up the store. If the supermarket did not believe that, you would have to produce something else of value. Your car? A share of your house? A sack of gold? Clearly, money facilitates trade like nothing else, and it operates largely on faith. Money has value because we believe it does. When that faith declines, so does the value of the money.

While it may feel precarious to consider that the crucial ingredient of every market transaction relies on trust, it is a lesson that policymakers must always bear in mind. The amount and value of money is regularly manipulated to achieve macroeconomic goals. Economic growth and employment levels, as well as price stability, can be enormously influenced by the flow of money in the economy.

This chapter examines the means by which central banks and governments manage their money supplies, and evaluates the effectiveness of monetary policy as a tool in macroeconomics.

What money is and does

Money is any object or record that is widely accepted as payment for goods and services.

While we can acknowledge that some people are very wealthy, their wealth may not easily translate into having money. Money, as defined by economists, is a type of wealth that is widely accepted in exchange for goods and services. Steve Jobs, the owner of Apple, may be wealthy, but his shares in Apple are not necessarily easily transferable into goods and services as money in the way that economists define it.

For something to be considered money, it needs to fulfil three functions.

- **Money must be a medium of exchange**. Buyers and sellers must be willing to use money as a proxy for later use in other transactions. If you buy a bike from a store, the store owner accepts your money, knowing that he or she can later use the money in another transaction.
- **Money must serve as a unit of account**. Whatever items serve as money must be easily measurable so that everyone understands the value. When money serves as a unit of account, we can more easily post clear prices that are universally understood. In the absence of this feature, we would be left to price goods in terms of whatever we had available to barter. One bike would be equal to half of an electronic bike, perhaps a fifth of a motorbike, and so on.
- **Money must be a store of value**. For something to be used as money, you must be able to keep it and use it at a later date. It must hold value, independent of inflation or other changes in the economy. It must, therefore, be durable. When, in years past, communities used grain such as corn or wheat as money, they risked moulds or other deterioration of the crop, which would hurt their savings. Coins and durable paper, while hardly indestructible, now serve this purpose in most societies. Recently, many countries have moved to replace paper money with plastic money to improve durability and lower the cost of making it.

These stones are part of a collection of stone money used at Yap, Federated States of Micronesia.

Most money used today has little intrinsic value and is called fiat money. *Fiat*, a Latin word, means 'let it be done'. It is used to describe today's money because the materials used are practically worthless, but they are deemed to be money because the government declares it so. Money is money by government *fiat*. Less frequently in modern times, societies use *commodity money*. This type of money does possess some intrinsic value, and could be traded as a good in and of itself. A major challenge to the use of commodity money is that when the value of the commodity changes, the value of the money increases or decreases as well. Many items have been used as commodity money, including grains, conch shells, beads, gold, silver, copper, rice, special belts, and very large stones.

Modern money: M1 and M2

When the central bank of a country goes about the business of managing the supply of money, only a particular kind of money is in question. The first category of money, M1, includes all currency (paper and coin money), as well as demand deposits, traveller's cheques, and other checkable deposits. Demand deposits, as well as checkable deposits, are assets in banks that can easily be removed from the bank as currency. The second category, called M2, includes everything in M1, *plus* less accessible money such as savings deposits, which depositors can retrieve from the bank with a small penalty or loss of interest. These are timed deposits, which are kept for specified periods, and other similar deposit types (Figure 18.1).

While the details of these categories do not alter the fundamental analysis that follows, you should understand that money includes a wider array of deposits than is covered by our traditional understanding of money as cash and currency. Furthermore, when the central bank of a country acts to expand the money supply (page 391), its actions most directly affect these bank deposits, which are the dominant form of money in a modern economy.

(page 391)

Figure 18.1
2007 European Union eurozone M1 and M2.
European Central Bank

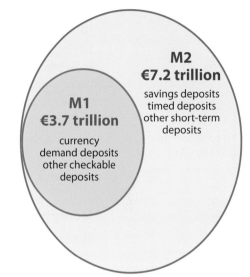

M2
€7.2 trillion
savings deposits
timed deposits
other short-term deposits

M1
€3.7 trillion
currency
demand deposits
other checkable deposits

The role of central banks

The two largest economies in the world, those of the European Union and the US, manage their money supply using a central bank system. The European Central Bank (ECB) has its headquarters in Frankfurt, Germany, and the US Federal Reserve (the Fed), is based in Washington DC. Both central banks are led by governing boards, made up of a combination of appointed economists and bankers. These and other central bank systems have the responsibility of managing monetary policy. Monetary policy is defined as the manipulation of the money supply to meet economic goals. Among the primary goals balanced by a central bank are economic growth, employment, and price stability. These goals sometimes conflict with each other.

Both the ECB and the Fed have enormous power to shape their respective economies. At the same time, both organizations have been vested with significant independence from politics. This conforms to a principle of organization that has become increasingly orthodox among developed economies, that of central bank independence. Like fiscal policy, monetary policy can be poorly made when the decisions are taken for purely political reasons. To avoid this pitfall, the heads and governors of the ECB and the Fed are appointed by politicians to fixed terms. This is designed to allow them to concentrate on policy without fear of unpopularity with voters.

Central banks and the money supply

Monetary policy is implemented by the central bank by managing interest rates primarily through manipulating the supply of money in the nation's banking system. The interest rate is the percentage charged above a loan by banks to the customers who borrow money. When a loan of €100 000 charges 5% per year, the interest paid by the borrower is €5000 each year. In addition, the borrower also has to pay back the initial €100 000 over the course of the loan period. The interest rate, then, is the 'price' of money, how much it costs to use someone else's money to buy a car or a house, or to invest in your business.

 A central bank is the monetary authority of a country, which performs the functions of issuing currency, managing the money supply, and controlling interest rates. Besides the Fed and the ECB, other central banks influencing the world's money supplies include the Bank of England, the Bank of Japan, the People's Bank of China and the Swiss National Bank.

 The money supply is the combined value of the currency and demand deposits of a country.

It's important to understand that individual interest rates vary. Credit card interest rates are usually higher than mortgage rates (the interest rate on a home loan). The rate charged to an established, profitable business is likely to be much less than that charged to a start-up firm. So, the type of loan and the amount of risk to the lender are factored into the specific rates. However, the general level of interest rates is heavily influenced by the supply of money available in the nation as a whole.

With a larger money supply, most interest rates throughout the economy will drop, and buying everything with borrowed money becomes cheaper. With a smaller money supply, most interest rates increase, and buying anything with borrowed money becomes more expensive. Ultimately, the overall level of interest paid is determined by the central bank and its monetary policy.

In its effort to influence interest rates, a nation's central bank plays an active role in the market for money. The market for money, like any market, is driven by the forces of supply and demand. When intervening in the money market, the central bank attempts to either increase or decrease the nominal interest rate that prevails in the economy.

Money demand

The demand for money is first determined by the desire to buy essential goods and services for daily living. This demand, called transaction demand, is relatively stable and autonomous to interest rate changes, although credit card rates may affect transaction spending to some degree. Transaction demand is, instead, positively influenced by increased real income and increased inflation. Higher incomes lead to more demand for transaction money, and higher inflation requires greater quantities of money to buy the same amount of a good as was previously purchased with less money.

Money demand includes the desire to hold money as an asset and the demand for money as a means to purchase goods and services. Money demand is inversely related to the interest rate and it increases or decreases with the overall level of national output.

Beyond transaction demand is the demand for money that is kept as an asset, called asset demand or speculative demand. Asset demand is inversely related to the interest rate. As interest rates rise, the opportunity cost of holding money as an asset increases. Fewer households hold onto cash; instead they deposit it in banks, which offer interest in return for savings. Households deposit money rather than hold onto it as an asset, reducing the quantity of money demanded at a higher interest rate. When rates fall, the opportunity cost of holding money as an asset decreases, thus the quantity of money demanded as an asset increases. More households hold onto cash as an asset since the returns offered by banks and on other investments are less attractive. Taken together, transaction and asset demand form the total demand for money and are shown as a downward-sloping curve, negatively related to nominal interest rates, in Figure 18.2.

Figure 18.2
The money market.

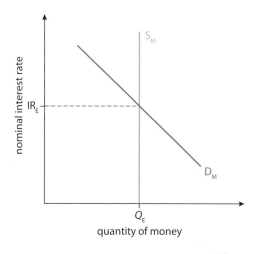

Money supply

The supply component of the money market, in contrast, is independent of changes to nominal interest rates; rather, money supply is determined by the actions of the central bank aimed at increasing or decreasing the overall supply of money available in a nation. As shown in Figure 18.2, the money supply curve is completely vertical, and not affected by changes in interest rates. This is because the central bank determines the supply of money through a variety of monetary policy tools. It does so with the specific goal of influencing nominal interest rates. By managing interest rates, the central bank can influence consumption spending and investment spending, as well as indirectly influence the international value of the country's currency.

So, the supply curve is perfectly inelastic because the central bank has the authority to set the level of the money supply. It operates independently of the interest rate, in an attempt to establish that rate and thereby either stimulate or contract the overall level of demand in the nation's economy. Note that this is a reversal of how we typically think of the relationship between supply and price. Normally, supply is upward sloping because price increases tend to increase the quantity of output supplied. In the money market, however, the central bank establishes the amount of money available. This supply is moved against the relative demand in order to change the interest rates charged in the market.

For example, Figure 18.3 shows how an increase or a decrease in the money supply can raise and lower the interest rate as the equilibrium moves up and down along the money demand curve. The original equilibrium is determined by the intersection of D_M and S_M, which sets the 'price' of money at IR_E and the quantity at Q_{ME}.

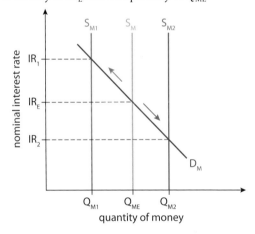

To learn more about the money market, visit www.pearsonhotlinks.com, enter the title or ISBN of this book and select weblink 18.2.

Figure 18.3
Shifts of the money supply.

Central banks and monetary policy

If the central bank were to undertake a contractionary monetary policy, decreasing the money supply and shifting the S_M to the left, the quantity of money demanded would decrease due to the increased scarcity of money in the economy and the corresponding higher interest rate of IR_1. At IR_1, all interest rates would be higher, which would discourage investment and consumption by charging households and firms more to borrow money at all levels.

If the central bank were to undertake an expansionary monetary policy and the supply of money were increased to S_{M2}, the new equilibrium interest rate IR_2 would be lower, making it cheaper to borrow money, which is now less scarce and in greater amounts in banks' reserves. This would encourage consumption and investment, and likely expand AD and output.

Contractionary monetary policy is the term for actions by the central bank to decrease the money supply and increase interest rates.

Expansionary monetary policy is the term for actions by the central bank to increase the money supply and reduce interest rates.

To grasp exactly how and why interest rates affect consumption and investment, let's return to the four major components of GDP, as determined by the consumption method:

- consumption (C)
- investment (I)
- government spending (G)
- net exports (X − M).

First, government spending is least likely to be affected because it is determined independently of interest rates. Net exports are affected in ways we will see later, but it is relatively much smaller than either consumption or investment. Of these two, interest rates most directly affect investment, because firms will choose to borrow if they can earn more than the interest they pay on the borrowed funds. While some consumption of high-priced goods (cars, appliances) can be influenced by interest rates, much more consumption is determined by income, expectations and other factors. Thus, private investment is the component most highly sensitive to the rate of interest.

Figure 18.4
Interest rates and investment demand.

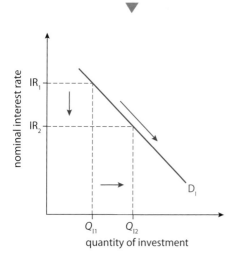

quantity of investment

With the effect of interest rates on investment in mind, Figure 18.4 shows the relationship between the interest rate and the demand by private firms for private investment. It is clearly an inverse relationship, as the demand for investment slopes downwards. This is because firms balance their borrowing decisions against the expected rate of return on the borrowed money. They can only afford to borrow at high interest if the returns are very great.

So, at high interest rates such as IR_1, less quantity of investment is demanded, Q_{I1}. At lower interest rates, more firms are confident they will be able to pay the interest and demand a greater quantity of investment, at Q_{I2}.

The effect on investment demand is one of the major concerns for the central bank. By indirectly influencing the amount of private investment (I) and consumption (C), the central bank is also encouraging and discouraging the amount of AD:

- limiting the money supply and increasing interest rates reduces private investment (as well as a little consumption) and decreases AD
- expanding the money supply and decreasing interest rates expands private investment and expands AD.

Figure 18.5 shows the desired effects of both lowering and increasing the money supply.

Figure 18.5
Changes in the money supply and effect on AD. **a** The money market; **b** AD/AS diagram.

a

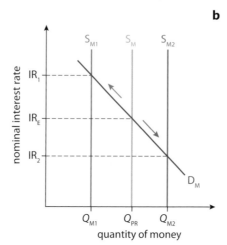

quantity of money

b

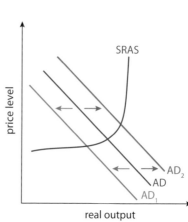

real output

In Figure 18.5a, a contraction of the money supply from S_M to S_{M1} results in a higher interest rate, IR_1. That higher interest rate reduces investment and consumption from AD, moving it back to AD_1 (Figure 18.5b). This process can work in the other direction, too. If the central bank expanded the money supply from S_M to S_{M2}, thus decreasing interest rate from IR_E to IR_2, consumption and investment would increase, pushing AD outwards to AD_2.

When the central bank actually implements these policy goals, it has a number of policy tools to choose from, each with different ways of contributing to the same effect on the money supply.

Tools for changing the money supply

Central banks manage the money supply with the following monetary policy tools:

- changing the discount rate
- buying or selling bonds
- changing the reserve requirement.

Changing the discount rate

The discount rate is the rate charged by central banks when they make loans to big commercial banks. The chief importance of changes to the discount rate is as a signal to the banking system that borrowing will become more or less expensive, respectively, at all levels. Changes to the discount rate may have only a minor effect on the money supply, since the central bank is typically the 'lender of last resort' to commercial banks. Generally, when banks need loans to meet the demand for funds from their customers, they prefer to borrow from other commercial banks. Only when the availability of credit in the commercial banking system is tight, in other words, in periods of strong investment demand, will commercial banks turn to the central bank for a loan. In such a scenario, a lower discount rate sends the signal to commercial banks that it is OK to increase their own lending activities. This allows banks to make lower interest loans to borrowers, increasing the money supply and lowering interest rates across the economy.

Buying or selling bonds

The central bank may also intervene directly in the open market for bonds. A bond is a certificate issued by a government that guarantees repayment of a principal amount charged with a stated rate of interest. Governments use bonds to raise money initially, and the bonds are then traded as a means of investing and saving. In addition to making loans to private firms and households, commercial banks also lend money to governments by purchasing and holding interest-bearing government bonds.

- **Expansionary monetary policy: central bank buys bonds**. When the central bank buys bonds from private banks, it puts cash into those banks' reserves, increasing the funds available for banks to make loans. This is a form of money creation. By buying up bonds, the central bank has turned a government bond into a demand deposit, which can be spent or withdrawn at any time. Thus, it adds to the nation's stock of M1 or M2 money. These excess reserves may be spent by their owners. Or, since they are not now earning interest for the banks, they are also likely to be loaned out to private borrowers who will pay interest to the banks for the privilege of borrowing. In other words, the central bank's open market purchase of government bonds from private banks expands the supply of banks' excess reserves, incentivizing them to lower the interest rates they charge private borrowers, thereby increasing the level of consumption and investment in the economy.

 Bank reserves are the money deposits held in banks. They are categorized as required reserves (legal minimums) and excess reserves (surplus reserves).

To learn more about banks, visit www.pearsonhotlinks.com, enter the title or ISBN of this book and select weblink 18.3.

- **Contractionary monetary policy: central bank sells bonds**. When the central bank sells government bonds on the open market, commercial banks' reserves are taken out of the private banking system. Private banks will, therefore, have less money available to loan, and will charge higher rates for what remains. A central bank's sale of bonds reduces the money supply, increasing interest rates and contracting the overall level of consumption and investment in the economy. This puts downward pressure on price levels, output and employment.

Changing the reserve requirement

The reserve requirement is the percentage of deposits that banks are required to have available at all times. Any amount held that is beyond the reserve requirement is called excess reserves. Banks loan out excess reserves on which they change interest to borrowers and thereby make profits. If the reserve requirement is raised, banks must keep a higher percentage of their deposits on reserve, and so must reduce the amount loaned out. This reduces the money supply and raises interest rates. If the reserve requirement is lowered, banks find they have excess reserves beyond the requirement, and can loan out the excess reserves. This increases the money supply and lowers the interest rate. Figure 18.6 shows changes to banking regulations in this area that have been made in response to the banking crisis of 2008–09.

Figure 18.6
Amount of capital banks must hold in reserve.

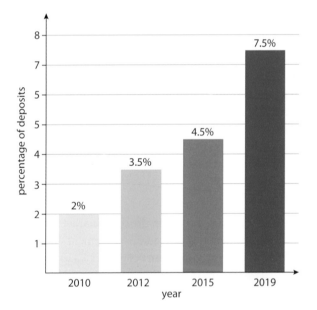

EXERCISES

1   Figure 18.6 is based on the Basel III international banking accords and reflects changes to banking regulations in response to the banking crisis of 2008–09.

   a   How will the changes in reserve requirements affect the money supply and aggregate demand?

   b   Why do you think the proposed changes will take place over nine years?

18.2 Monetary policy and short-term demand management

Learning outcomes

- Explain how changes in interest rates can influence the level of aggregate demand in an economy.
- Describe the mechanism through which easy (expansionary) monetary policy can help an economy close a deflationary (recessionary) gap.
- Construct a diagram to show the potential effects of easy (expansionary) monetary policy, outlining the importance of the shape of the aggregate supply curve.
- Describe the mechanism through which tight (contractionary) monetary policy can help an economy close an inflationary gap.
- Construct a diagram to show the potential effects of tight (contractionary) monetary policy, outlining the importance of the shape of the aggregate supply curve.

Expansionary monetary policy

Assume that the economy has fallen into a recession due to a lack of aggregate demand and the central bank decides to take action to expand AD and encourage a recovery. Figures 18.7a–c (overleaf) show the effect of an expansionary monetary policy by the central bank: (a) on the money market, (b) on the level of private investment and (c) on the overall AD in the economy. To stimulate AD and encourage a recovery, the central bank would employ one of the following methods:

- lower the discount rate
- buy bonds on the open market
- lower the reserve ratio.

Figure 18.7c shows us the initial problem. The short-run equilibrium at Y_E is below the full-employment level of income (Y_{FE}). This demand-side recession is often called a deflationary gap, because it results in lower prices as well as more unemployment. In theory, expansionary policy should address this by expanding AD and increasing employment.

- In Figure 18.7a, when the central bank increases the money supply, interest rates decline from IR_E to IR_2. The lower interest rate is carried over into the market for private investment (Figure 18.7b).
- In Figure 18.7b, the lower interest rate causes a movement down and to the right along the demand for investment curve, increasing the quantity of funds demanded for investment.
- In Figure 18.7c, the increased investment (along with likely growth of some consumption) shifts AD to the right to AD_2 leading to an increase in output from Y_E to Y_{FE}, an increase in the price level and an increase in the level of employment.

Figure 18.7
Expansionary monetary policy. **a** Effect on the money market; **b** effect on private investment; **c** Keynesian AD/AS diagram

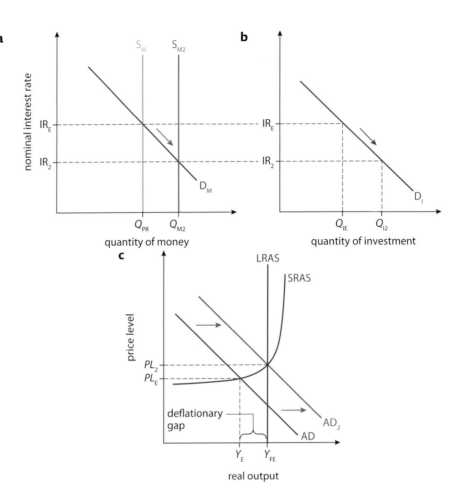

Contractionary monetary policy

Assume the economy is experiencing some inflation caused by excess aggregate demand, and the central bank wanted to contract AD and reduce the price level. Figures 18.8a–c show the effect of a contractionary monetary policy by the central bank: (a) on the money market, (b) on the level of private investment and (c) on the overall AD in the economy. To reduce AD, the central bank would employ one of the following tools:

- raise the discount rate
- sell bonds on the open market
- raise the reserve ratio.

Figure 18.8c shows us the initial problem. AD has expanded beyond the full employment level of output (Y_{FE}). This increase in AD spending has caused prices to rise from PL_1.

- In Figure 18.8a, when the central bank decreases the money supply from S_M to S_{M1}, the interest rate increases from IR_E to IR_1 due to the increased scarcity of money in commercial banks' reserves.
- In Figure 18.8b, the higher interest rate is carried over into the market for private investment, causing a movement up and left along the demand for investment from Q_{IE} to Q_{I1}, a decrease in the quantity of funds demanded for investment.
- In Figure 18.c, the decreased investment (along with likely decline of some consumption) shifts AD to the left to AD_1. Ultimately, the central bank's contractionary policy reduces the level of investment and consumption in the economy, putting downward pressure on the price level, reducing the level of national output from Y_E to Y_{FE}, and increasing the level of unemployment to a healthier rate closer to the nation's natural rate of unemployment.

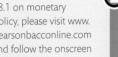

To access Worksheet 18.1 on monetary policy, please visit www.pearsonbacconline.com and follow the onscreen instructions.

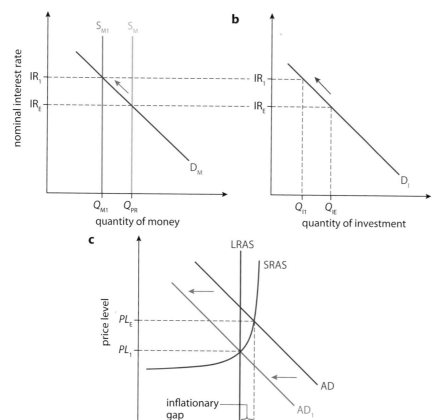

Figure 18.8
Contractionary monetary policy. **a** Effect on the money market; **b** effect on private investment; **c** Keynesian AD/AS diagram

EXERCISES

2   The central bank has just received news that inflation is higher than expected this quarter.

    a   List the policy tools available for the central bank to slow down inflation.

    b   Draw a three-part diagram that shows the ultimate effects of these policies on unemployment, output, and inflation.

18.3 **Evaluation of monetary policy**

Learning outcomes

• Evaluate the effectiveness of monetary policy through consideration of factors including the independence of the central bank, the ability to adjust interest rates incrementally, the ability to implement changes in interest rates relatively quickly, time lags, limited effectiveness in increasing aggregate demand if the economy is in deep recession and conflict among government economic objectives.

• Explain that central banks of certain countries, rather than focusing on the maintenance of both full employment and a low rate of inflation, are guided in their monetary policy by the objective to achieve an explicit or implicit inflation rate target.

While the maintenance of effective monetary policy is important for stability and general economic growth, it can also be assessed as a tool for managing macroeconomic problems such as recession or inflation.

Stimulating growth during recession

Strengths

If the demand for investment is highly unresponsive to changes in the interest rate, or if investment demand is extremely low, then expansionary monetary policy may be ineffective at stimulating aggregate demand. Japan had its 'lost decade' during the 1990s when 0% interest rates failed to stimulate investment. The US has experienced similar failures in monetary policy since the financial crisis began in 2008 and the US Federal Reserve began a period of massive monetary expansion. Despite interest rates close to 0% in the US, investment demand has been similarly slow to recover.

- **Speed**. Monetary policy can be enacted by the central bank as soon as the problem is recognized. The central bank skips the process by which legislators debate fiscal policy and create compromises in order to get the policy passed. For the central bank, policy decisions are relatively immediate, which improves the chances of a expansionary policy going into effect while the recession is still underway.
- **Control**. It is within the power of the central bank to adjust the money supply more discretely and finely than legislators can with fiscal policy. The central bank, for example, can buy bonds in the open market until it gets the target interest rate it desires. Monetary policy is thus more finely calibrated to solve the problem at hand.
- **No politics**. As mentioned above, the central banks of most countries are held to be independent of politics and not involved in election processes. This should prevent the desires of voters from influencing central bank policy. During a recovery, for example, the central bank may tighten monetary policy earlier than voters would like, in order to prevent inflation. Such a policy might be more difficult to enact if central bank governors were running for their offices in elections.
- **No crowding-out**. As explained in Chapter 17, expansionary fiscal policy typically requires the government to borrow money. Massive borrowing drives up interest rates, it is argued, and limits long-term growth. Monetary policy, by lowering interest rates, avoids this disadvantage.

Weaknesses

- **Investors reluctant to borrow**. In times of deep recession, consumer and investor confidence is at its lowest point. Consumers, fearful of losing their jobs and income, defer large purchases and cut back spending, instead saving 'for a rainy day.' Firms, knowing the reluctance of consumers, reduce their output, which thus reduces their demand for new investment funds. Few businesses aggressively expand during hard times. These crises of confidence render the reduction of interest rates rather meaningless. Money may be cheap, but consumers and investors lack the confidence that they will easily repay the loans. The impotence of expansionary monetary policy was most evident during Japan's 'lost decades' from 1991 to 2010. Interest rates during this time were held near to zero, making borrowing very easy. But firms and consumers refused the offer of low rates, and growth stagnated for year after year.
- **Time lags**. While monetary policy is quick to implement, it takes time to go into effect. Lower rates may spur borrowing in relatively good years, but not immediately. The speed at which interest rate changes have effect is influenced by elasticity of demand for investment.
- **Changes in elasticity of demand for investment**. In Figure 18.9a, an expansionary decrease of the interest rate from IR_1 to IR_2 increases investment demand from Q_{I1} to Q_{I2}. This might be a 'normal year' where demand is relatively elastic and businesses are keen to take advantage of the lower cost of borrowing. Figure 18.9b shows a relatively inelastic demand for investment, perhaps a typical recession period, where the same decrease in the interest rate, from IR_1 to IR_2, results in a far less encouraging increase in investment.

To learn more about recession, visit www. pearsonhotlinks.com, enter the title or ISBN of this book and select weblink 18.4.

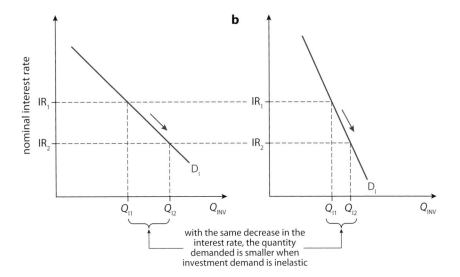

Figure 18.9
Interest rates and elasticity of
private investment demand.
a Elastic demand; **b** inelastic
demand

with the same decrease in the
interest rate, the quantity
demanded is smaller when
investment demand is inelastic

Inflation control

In last few decades, a sort of division of labour has taken place for most governments when it comes to macroeconomic management. The widespread inflation of the 1970s led many governments to conclude that fiscal policymakers were unlikely to enact possibly painful deflationary policies. This would leave inflation control in the hands of the central bank, where a certain amount of political independence would make deflationary policy possible. Thus, since then most governments delegate inflation control to the central bank as its most important priority.

Strengths

- **Direct action, speed and control**. Over the years, more central banks have taken the job of inflation control more seriously. Most, in fact, recognize that politicians rarely have the stomach to enact contractionary fiscal policies that might cost jobs and votes. And so, central banks accept that inflation control is almost exclusively their responsibility. Therefore most central banks monitor several price indices, including the consumer price index, the producer price index, the GDP deflator, and more. Decisions by the central bank board can be implemented as inflation begins to creep forwards. The central bank can intervene as much or as little as needed, so that the size of the price increases can be matched with commensurate interest rate increases.
- **Apolitical nature of the bank**. That central bank leaders and governors are not elected and not driven by the need to retain votes, enables them to act on the facts of the economy, even when such action would be unpopular. This is especially crucial during inflationary moments, as contractionary monetary policy can cause significant economic pain. If high interest rates are needed to drive down AD and limit inflation, the cost can be lower GDP and lost jobs. For example, the Federal Reserve under Paul Volker in 1979 pushed interest rates to nearly 20% in an attempt to dampen the double-digit inflation of the late 1970s. The recession that resulted was long and painful, with significant unemployment and political turmoil. It was, however, successful in slaying inflation, such that inflation rates have stayed below 5% for most of the 30 years that followed.

Weaknesses

- **Time lags during high inflation**. Although monetary policy can be enacted quickly, it can take several months of high interest rates for investors and consumers to change their behaviour.

 In the nearly 100 years since the US Federal Reserve Bank was established, 14 individuals have served in the role of Chairman, the person who makes the ultimate decisions over monetary policy in the US. Yet in the last 31 years, there have been only three Chairmen. During the same period, the US has had six presidents. The Fed Chairman, although appointed by the president, is not subject to political influence once in his role. This gives the bank relative autonomy to act in the interest of the nation's economy, rather than in the favour of special interest groups or potential voters.

- **Ineffective against cost-push inflation**. While it is agreed that monetary policy can be very effective at eliminating demand-induced inflation, it remains relatively powerless at stopping supply-side inflation. Often called 'cost-push' inflation, it is the result of higher input prices or other shocks to aggregate supply (AS). But the traditional tools of monetary management are effective at changing AD. So a move to shrink AD may reduce prices but deepen a recession. If the central bank chose to expand the money supply and increase AD, the result would not harm GDP, but could cause an inflationary spiral.

Exchange rate management

An exchange rate is the value of one country's currency expressed in terms of the amount of another country's currency needed to buy it (e.g. the number of euros you get for your dollars).

Depending on the type of exchange rate system a country follows, the central bank may play a role in the management of the currency's value. This subject is discussed extensively in Chapter 22, but the basics of the issue can be established here.

When a country raises or lowers its interest rates, it signals to potential depositors that domestic banks are now paying different rates of interest. Higher rates draw foreign depositors who must first exchange or buy the currency before making deposits locally. This new demand for the currency, called a capital inflow because it elicits an influx of money, pushes up the value of the currency. A lower interest rate, naturally, has the opposite result of driving demand for the currency down, and depreciating the exchange rate.

The central bank's role in exchange rate management tends to vary with the degree of control sought by the government over the currency value. As a result, fixed-rate regimes, which need to change interest rates more often to manage their currency, often find that they are torn between the objectives of managing economic growth, curbing inflation, and exchange rate control.

Conflicting goals

As with fiscal policy, monetary policymakers may find it difficult to achieve one macroeconomic goal without reducing the success of others (Figure 18.10).

Figure 18.10
Conflicting goals of monetary policy.

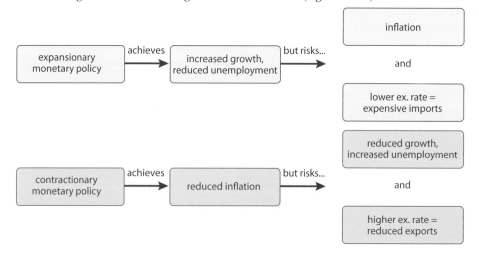

In Figure 18.10, the conflicting objectives of monetary policy are represented. Expansionary policies aimed at reducing unemployment may lead to inflation and a weaker currency, thus causing problems for the nation's trade balance. On the other hand, contractionary policies may succeed in bringing down inflation rates but, in the process, may increase unemployment and drive the value of the currency up, a result that may also have an undesired impact on the nation's trade balance.

Managing the conflicting outcomes of their policy decisions presents central bankers with an additional challenge when determining the nation's optimal interest rates.

Further debate on monetary policy

From the late 1940s until the 1970s, most developed economies were managed under the aegis of Keynesian demand-management policies (Chapter 17). After watching several inflationary spikes in the 60s and 70s, a critique of the Keynesian approach was beginning to gain ground among policymakers. This originated most prominently among the leaders of the Chicago school under Milton Friedman at the University of Chicago. Friedman and his colleagues had long advocated a more classical approach to the macroeconomy, and put a particular emphasis on the money supply. The monetarists, as they were later to be called, emphasized the critical role of the money supply with their quantity theory of money.

The quantity theory of money can be expressed as the following equation:

$$MV = PQ$$

Where:

M = money supply
V = velocity of money
P = price level
Q = real output

This theory holds that V, the velocity of money, represents the number of times an average item of money (say, 1 euro) changes hands. This, they argue, tends to be relatively constant. At the same time, the level of output, Q, is also relatively constant, but may grow on average about 3–4% in a given year for a rich country economy. Thus, as V and Q are stable, M, the money supply, is the primary influence on P, the price level.

Should the money supply be expanded too much, price levels will increase. If the money supply is held too tightly, the size of the overall economy might contract. Thus, Friedman and the monetarists began to advocate a monetary rule, which limits the expansion of the money supply to a range of 3–4% per year. This, they argue, allows for stable real economic growth, and avoids the temptation of central banks to over-manage the economy with the money supply.

Some economists have, in recent years, expanded on the theme of caution when it comes to monetary policy. In times of recession, governments may find that expansionary fiscal and monetary policy, in the traditional sense of managing interest rates, is not sufficient to stimulate a recovery. They can and often do resort to printing money (a power reserved for central banks) to encourage spending.

This policy is sometimes called quantitative easing; its effect is an increase in the money supply. More specifically, the inflationary effect lowers the buying power of everyone holding money. It is, therefore, an inflation tax, because all holders of money now have less purchasing power. The effect of the policy to print money may be relatively slight during recessionary times, but to attempt to lower debts by printing money in healthier times may risk serious price increases or even hyperinflation.

However, other classical economists question whether price changes matter in the long run. David Hume, writing about it in the 1800s, anticipated the quantity theory of money by making the distinction between real variables and nominal variables. This might be read as the distinction between P and Q in the quantity theory.

Milton Friedman was famous for his belief that 'inflation is always and everywhere a monetary phenomenon'. He opposed counter-cyclical use of monetary policy because he believed fluctuations in money supply only contributed to the business cycles' booms and busts.

The quantity theory of money is a monetarist concept that the money supply has a direct and positive relationship on the price level.

To access Worksheet 18.2 on 'easy money', please visit www. pearsonbacconline.com and follow the onscreen instructions.

Money neutrality is the concept that while the money supply affects price levels it will not affect the level of output.

To learn more about monetary policy, visit www.pearsonhotlinks.com, enter the title or ISBN of this book and select weblink 18.5.

However, Hume and economists who have followed him have come to a different conclusion. They assert that if the money supply were, perhaps, doubled compared to the amount of real output, real output would be likely to stay the same. Prices may double, but the standard of living based on the economy's productive capacity would be unlikely to change much. This concept of money neutrality states that manipulation of the money supply may affect price levels, but not production, in the long run (N Gregory Mankiw, *Principles of Economics*, 2008).

Even if this is the case, most economists believe that the money supply can have significant impact on short-run decisions. Inflationary spikes can lead to disruptions, crises of confidence and psychological gloom in the short run. And besides, most economists argue, price stability is achievable in any case through prudent implementation of sound monetary policy.

EXERCISES

3 Draw one investment demand curve that shows elastic demand, and a second one that shows inelastic demand.

4 Show exactly the same interest rate increase on each. What does the change in quantity demanded suggest about the condition of the economy?

5 Show an interest rate decrease on each. What does the change in quantity demanded suggest about the condition of the economy?

6 List and explain the advantages and disadvantages of using monetary policy to stop inflation.

7 Explain why the effect on net exports can contradict the original purpose of monetary policy changes.

To access Quiz 18, an interactive, multiple-choice quiz on this chapter, please visit www.pearsonbacconline.com and follow the onscreen instructions.

PRACTICE QUESTIONS

1 **a** List and explain the three methods or tools used by central banks to control the money supply. (10 marks) [AO4]

    b Assess the effectiveness of monetary policy in fighting a recession. (15 marks) [AO3]

2 **a** Using appropriate diagrams, show how the central bank may fight inflation. (10 marks) [AO2], [AO4]

    b Evaluate the effectiveness of monetary policy in managing inflation. (15 marks) [AO3]

3 **a** Analyse the methods by which the central bank might decrease the money supply. (10 marks) [AO2]

    b Discuss the likely impact on an economy of a substantial decrease in the level of interest rates. (15 marks) [AO3]

19 SUPPLY-SIDE POLICIES

Role of supply-side policies

Learning outcomes

- Explain that supply-side policies aim at positively affecting the production side of an economy by improving the institutional framework and the capacity to produce (that is, by changing the quantity and/or quality of factors of production).
- State that supply-side policies may be market-based or interventionist, and that in either case they aim to shift the LRAS curve to the right, achieving growth in potential output.

 Nanpu Bridge, Shanghai; a massive infrastructure project.

If it sometimes seems that aggregate demand (AD) gets all the attention, this is with good reason. From the 1940s onwards, Keynesian demand-management policies dominated the macroeconomic management schemes of finance ministers. These policies put heavy emphasis on the use of government spending to stimulate the economy, spending that often required increases in either taxes or government debt to finance the resulting deficits. Until well into the 1960s, healthy growth rates among many rich and developing countries appeared to validate the Keynesian demand-management approach.

However, by the late 1960s and early 1970s, as rich economies sputtered and inflation grew more serious, the protests of neo-classical scholars were gaining a wider audience. What followed, in the macroeconomic debates of the 1980s and beyond, emphasized a variety of new perspectives, including an emphasis on money and inflation control (evident in the work of the monetarist school), as well as a renewed focus on creating a healthier environment for business to flourish. This emphasis on the supply side of the

> Supply-side policies are a combination of government-led and free market policies designed to increase the productive capacity of the country.

macroeconomic equation would eventually shake, if not reorient, the centrality of the Keynesian paradigm.

Types of supply-side policy

Supply-side policies aim at positively affecting the production side of an economy by improving the quantity or the quality of the factors of production. These policies attempt to develop a healthier institutional framework for production to occur. On an aggregate diagram, successful supply-side policies shift the long-run aggregate supply (LRAS) curve to the right, increasing the overall productive capacity of the economy (Figure 19.1). This pushes future full-employment income, Y_{FE}, out to the right to Y_{FE1}. A higher standard of living and greater employment results.

Figure 19.1
Supply-side policies and LRAS.

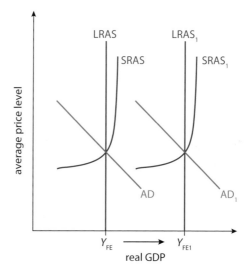

Supply-side policies are of two types: government based and market based. Governments can act directly to improve the economy's capacity to produce. Government intervention seeks to provide capital goods or services where, it is believed, the market itself has failed to provide them. In contrast, market-based policies seek to unleash the full power of open markets to improve competition, open labour markets, and create better incentives.

The appeal of supply-side policies

In theory, supply-side policies are especially desirable because they improve the overall macroeconomic environment in which individual actors operate. Good policies would encourage productivity as well as create more and better factors of production. In this environment of productive surplus, growth is the logical outcome. Furthermore, increasing LRAS manages to expand the economy without generating inflation, a typical problem with expansionary demand-side policies.

In particular, supply-side policies appear to answer one of the most serious challenges of macroeconomic policies – stagflation (Figure 19.2). A loathsome combination of economic recession with rising inflation, stagflation easily resisted demand-side approaches. By increasing aggregate supply (AS), however, both problems can be eased and the economy returned to full employment.

In the 1970s, the economy was widely seen as locked into a period of stagflation where the equilibrium price levels (PL_E) were high and increasing, while output was below full

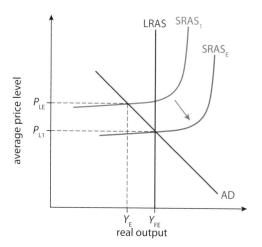

Figure 19.2
Stagflation and supply-side
policies.

employment (Y_E). Movement of AD would have either (in the case of expansionary policy) increased inflation further or (in the case of deflationary policy) driven the country into deeper recession. Successful supply-side policies would instead push SRAS to the right to SRAS$_1$, easing prices to PL_1 and encouraging recovery to full employment at Y_{FE}.

To learn more about supply-side economics, visit www.pearsonhotlinks.com, enter the title or ISBN of this book and select weblink 19.1.

19.2 Market-based supply-side policies

Learning outcomes
- Explain how factors including deregulation, privatization, trade liberalization and antimonopoly regulation are used to encourage competition.
- Explain how factors including reducing the power of labour unions, reducing unemployment benefits and abolishing minimum wages are used to make the labour market more flexible (more responsive to supply and demand).
- Explain how factors including personal income tax cuts are used to increase the incentive to work, and how cuts in business tax and capital gains tax are used to increase the incentive to invest.

US President Ronald Reagan and UK Prime Minister Margaret Thatcher were champions of the supply-side school of economic theory.

Origins of market-based supply-side policies

The impetus behind the criticism of Keynesian policies came from an influential group of neo-classical economists. Among the most prominent was Milton Friedman, who also became renowned for contributions to thinking about the money supply. Friedman and the other neo-classical economists followed in the tradition of Friedrich von Hayek, an Austrian economist who had openly clashed with Keynesian approaches since the 1940s. The term 'neo-classical' implied a harking back to old, accepted classical economics precepts. Energized by the economic crises of the 70s, neo-classical economists fiercely criticized the heavy regulation of markets,

To learn more about neo-classical economics, visit www.pearsonhotlinks.com, enter the title or ISBN of this book and select weblink 19.2.

Market-based supply-side policies are intended reduce government intervention thereby allowing the free market to increase efficiency and improve incentives.

government ownership of major industries, and protectionist policies that had become the calling card of Keynesianism.

Their protests took root as politicians in the UK and US began to advocate freer markets and less government control. Margaret Thatcher in the UK and Ronald Reagan in the US both took decisive and unpopular stances on the basis of supply-side influence. Most notably, Thatcher privatized and shrank the coal industry in the UK, causing large-scale strikes and subsequent unemployment in the industry. Reagan, meanwhile, crushed a prominent strike by air traffic controllers in 1981, sending a signal that the days of trade union ascendancy were over.

Whether these policies reflected pure supply-side approaches or a hybrid of supply-side economics and conservative politics in their respective countries is still debated. However, the guiding principles of supply-side economics were clearly at work. These policies aimed to open up competition, free up markets from government involvement, and return influence to the private sector.

Types of market-based supply-side policy

Market-based supply-side policies include:

- policies to encourage competition
- labour market reforms
- incentive-related policies.

CASE STUDY

Say's law: supply creates its own demand

Champions of free markets often point to some of the basic principles of what is now called supply-side economics to emphasize the importance of businesses in creating wealth. Among the more popular are ideas credited to Jean-Baptiste Say. When considering commodity markets, Say noted that business initiative could be an important first step. A carpenter who creates the first chairs (as opposed to benches), may well hire woodcutters to chop down more trees, employ extra workers to do some of the basic cutting, and so on until a new group of people have income as a result of the supply of these new chairs.

In turn, these newly employed people now have income that can be spent on (among other things) the chairs they helped produce. Thus, an extreme simplification of Say's law has been that *supply creates its own demand*. Throughout modern economic history, Say's law is often cited by business groups to justify deregulation of industry, reductions in taxes, and a general loosening of the restrictions placed on market activity.

▲ Jean-Baptiste Say, 18th-century French economist and businessman.

EXERCISES

1   Explain Say's law using a more modern example.

2   To what extent do you see Say's law as being a good guide for law or policy?

Policies to encourage competition

This group of policies aims to open the market to greater competition. They flow from the free market philosophy that greater competition encourages harder work, more innovation, lower prices and better quality in an attempt to earn money and win customers.

Deregulation

It is argued by supply-siders that governments can discourage business by applying stringent or unnecessary regulation to markets. Deregulation can be applied to a variety of situations in order to reduce bureaucracy as well as the required costs of complying with government rules. The rules under attack are typically intended as protection against some negative externality of production to do with product quality and safety, worker safety, or pollution control.

Anti-monopoly regulation

Where monopoly power exists, it gives producers the ability to restrict output and increase prices. Anti-monopoly laws (also called anti-trust laws) seek to prevent or dismantle monopolies in the market. It was with this approach that the governments of the US and others were successful at opening up the market for air travel. Until the 1970s, most countries operated heavily regulated, often state-owned airlines, with fixed prices and regulated routes. After deregulation, the market grew considerably, with more choice and a decrease in prices, at least for the first several years.

Privatization

One legacy of World War II industrial policies in many countries has been government control of the 'commanding heights' of the economy. For example, steel and iron, energy, and the transportation industries were under government ownership and control. Supply-siders believed that most of these had become bloated with unnecessary employees and operated inefficiently because they lacked the right incentives. Privatization, it was argued, would encourage owners to lower costs and thus prices. Prominent examples of implementation include the coal industry in the UK, as well as telecommunications and airlines in many countries.

Trade liberalization (free trade)

Supply-side economists applied the free market principle to international trade as well. They opposed tariffs, quotas, and subsidies that encouraged dependence on the government. They encouraged free trade, reduction of trade barriers and open competition.

Labour market reforms

Supply-side economists see government efforts to regulate and manage labour relations as an intrusion into the operation of free markets, and believe that inefficiencies result. Reforms in this area are intended to make labour markets more responsive to supply and demand.

Reducing trade union power

This could be viewed as the counterpart to anti-monopoly rules, with trade unions attempting to

These labour rights advocates of 1910 would certainly reject supply-side attempts to reduce union power today. Some 20 000 women garment workers went on strike in the winter of 1909–10 demanding better wages and conditions and union recognition.

assume a collusive or monopolistic control over the market for their work. Trade unions, where successful, keep wages above the market level, and reduce overall employment as a result. Restricting trade union power to organize or bargain collectively with employers would decrease their wage-setting power. In theory, more workers would then move more freely among employers and more employment will result.

Reducing unemployment benefits

Unemployment benefits, according to supply-side economists, reduce the incentive to find employment. This creates a disincentive for workers to accept jobs at lower wages during periods of unemployment, and thus prolongs the economy's return to full employment. Supply-siders argue for benefits that are smaller and shorter in duration.

Ending the minimum wage

The minimum wage sets a price floor for labour, which creates a surplus of workers who will not be hired at the government-enforced wage rate. The unemployed workers require more unemployment benefits, which require more tax revenue. Higher wages reduce the profits of business and thus lower supply, and may reduce employment even further.

Incentive-related policies

Supply-siders have argued that taxes discourage work and production, and that reducing income and business taxes encourage productivity and the expansion of business.

Reducing income tax

Lowering taxes increases the after-tax income of those affected. It should, therefore, increase the incentive to work since every hour of work results in greater pay. Generally, it is believed that a reduction in the tax rate will reduce the amount of tax revenue earned by the government. However, in the 1970s, American economist Arthur Laffer began advocating lower taxes on the basis that lower taxes (at the high end of the tax rate) would actually raise tax revenue (Figure 19.3).

Figure 19.3
The Laffer curve.

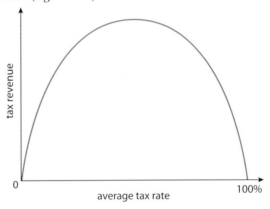

Taxes had grown too high, according to Laffer, and a reduction would stimulate work to the extent that the greater income of workers would bring in increased tax revenue. The key, it was said, was to find the optimal tax rate, the point at the top of the curve. Too far to the right, the higher the average income tax rate, and lower revenue results. Too far to the left, the lower the tax rate, and lower revenue results.

Reducing business taxes and capital gains taxes

A tax on business profits obviously diminishes profits. Cutting corporate taxes, it is said, encourages firms to produce more, shifting supply to the right, and possibly encouraging

To access Worksheet 19.1 on Obama vs Bush, please visit www. pearsonbacconline.com and follow the onscreen instructions.

more employment. Taxes on capital gains can apply to individual investors or businesses. It taxes the gain made on a capital investment, such as the profit made when selling property or shares in a company. These taxes discourage investment. So reducing the tax will make these entrepreneurial risks more rewarding and encourage investment.

19.3 Evaluation of market-based supply-side policies

Learning outcomes
- Evaluate the effectiveness of market-based supply-side policies through consideration of factors including the ability to create employment, the ability to reduce inflationary pressure, the impact on economic growth, the impact on the government budget, the effect on equity, and the effect on the environment.

Policies to encourage competition

The record of market-based supply-side policies varies according to specific policies and places. In the aftermath of World War II, it now seems clear that large parts of the US and UK economies were uncompetitive and stagnant under government control. The breaking up of anti-competitive markets like those of airlines and telecommunications appears to have yielded more consumer choice and better value for consumers. The effectiveness of privatization, however, depends largely on the manner in which it is enacted. Effective privatization should introduce the profit motive and create incentives to improve service and lower costs.

In several prominent cases, however, extremely valuable national assets were auctioned off cheaply to connected officials and bureaucrats. Many of these companies enjoy significant monopoly power and have little need to make the desired changes. This is understood to have happened rather often in the transitional economies of Eastern Europe and Russia. In other cases, the new private firms negotiate loose and lucrative ownership deals with the country (often with the bribed complicity of local officials). These deals allow them to raise prices well above current levels and reduce service to costly areas. This kind of scandal sparked rioting in Bolivia over water rights in 2000 and 2005 (Chapter 29).

Labour market reforms

The deregulation of industry can indeed yield economic benefits in countries where markets are regulated for the sake of preserving bureaucratic power. However, the social costs of deregulation may be borne out in unsafe products, dangerous work places and polluted environments. Striking the balance between these two goals is among the more difficult aspects of good governance.

In labour markets, the withdrawal of government intervention in the forms of minimum wages, trade union rights and unemployment benefits may indeed make the labour market more flexible and responsive to market forces. It also, however, exposes a country's most vulnerable people to the quixotic consequences of the market. Workers paid below minimum wage would be ever-more dependent on their employers, and therefore at more risk of exploitation. While trade unions explicitly and openly exist to drive up wages, they

In the spring of 2011, the Republican Party of the US government published *A Roadmap for America's Future*, a budget proposal that slashes government spending on social programmes such as healthcare and unemployment benefits. The roadmap is largely viewed as a supply-side policy because it reduces the role of government in the market for goods that many Americans depend on. At the same time, it reduces government budget deficits and, in theory, frees up for use by the private sector resources that would otherwise be employed by the government. While the plan is unlikely to be approved by the Democrats in the government, it has led to a revival of the supply-side argument for smaller government and a larger role for the private sector in the market for goods such as education and health.

also help to protect workers from illegal and coercive treatment by employers. Dropping unemployment benefits may inspire the jobless to take whatever work is available. However, those out of work for structural reasons need time to retrain or even relocate to new jobs.

Incentive-related policies

With regard to incentive-based supply policies, the specifics of a country's situation are very relevant to the question of whether such policies are effective. Countries with extremely high tax rates on corporations, individuals and investment (e.g. Sweden) may yield more tax revenue by lowering their rates and stimulating growth. In countries where marginal rates are lower, the results do not appear to support tax cuts. When the Reagan administration lowered tax rates in the US, the revenue earned from taxation actually dropped at the same time incomes rose.

This points to one of the more severe criticisms of supply-side policies. When tax rates for the upper-income groups are reduced, more of the tax burden must, by definition, fall on the lower-income groups. More of the total tax revenue, in other words, is now paid by the poor. This has a redistributive effect, one that is accentuated if the welfare safety net is reduced at the same time. If union power is reduced, unemployment benefits are reduced, and other government services to the poor are also cut, then the effect is a reduction in the standard of living for lower-income groups, in favour of reduced taxes for the relatively rich.

This is why supply-side economists are burdened with the need to demonstrate the reality of the Laffer curve, and show that a given country will indeed recoup lost tax revenues with increased growth. Otherwise, these policies will be regarded as simply a move to redistribute income from poor to rich. Critics have labelled this approach a trickle-down view of the economy, suggesting that tax gains by the rich generate very little (a trickle) economic growth. Over time, there is very little evidence to support the idea that lower tax rates actually increase tax revenues. Even Milton Friedman, whose support of free markets appears to be unbounded, agreed during the debate over major US tax breaks in 2003, that cutting taxes reduces government revenue. The best one could argue, he said, was that reducing tax revenues would compel governments to reduce spending, 'cutting their allowance.'

 19.4 # Interventionist supply-side policies

Learning outcomes

- Explain how investment in education and training will raise the levels of human capital and have a short-term impact on aggregate demand, but more importantly will increase LRAS.
- Explain how policies that encourage research and development will have a short-term impact on aggregate demand, but more importantly will result in new technologies and will increase LRAS.
- Explain how increased and improved infrastructure will have a short-term impact on aggregate demand, but more importantly will increase LRAS.
- Explain that targeting specific industries through policies including tax cuts, tax allowances and subsidized lending promotes growth in key areas of the economy and will have a short-term impact on aggregate demand but, more importantly, will increase LRAS.

Types of interventionist supply-side policy

Interventionist supply-side policies require some kind of government action to improve the factors of production. Note that most of these require immediate spending, which will initially stimulate AD. However, well-crafted policies should create an enduring expansion of LRAS. Such policies include:

- investment in human capital
- investment in new technology
- investment in infrastructure
- industrial policies.

Interventionist supply-side policies are government-led attempts to increase the productive capacity of the country.

Investment in human capital

Education is investment in human capital.

Labour and entrepreneurship are two of the four factors of production, and can collectively (if somewhat coldly) be called human capital. Enhancing the productivity of that capital is likely to require significant government investment.

Education

Public education is a common policy in most countries. This has not always been true, but has gradually become accepted as a necessary ingredient of a modern economy. Learning basic literacy and numeracy, in particular, is rewarded with large jumps in the incomes of those so educated. Education improves the skills and productivity of the workforce as well. High levels of educational achievement are highly correlated with national income.

Training

Specific training for some jobs may not be offered in schools, and may be offered by special job training centres established by the government. This helps businesses find productive employees and thus should enhance economic growth.

Health services

In countries where public health is poor, it is difficult for children to regularly attend school, and worker absenteeism is chronic. Government efforts to improve healthcare

To access Worksheet 19.2 on unemployment in Spain, please visit www.pearsonbacconline.com and follow the onscreen instructions.

can improve labour productivity in these situations. For example, at a basic level, prenatal care and inoculations can help ensure healthy births and childhoods. Most governments recognize this benefit, although some poorer countries find the costs difficult to manage.

Investing in education, training and health services will, by the building and staffing of these institutions, stimulate AD. However, the lingering effects of a well-trained, educated and healthy workforce should endure into the future, pushing LRAS outwards by improving labour and entrepreneurship.

Investment in new technology

Policies that encourage research and development have an immediate impact on AD. However, the more enduring effect should come through the resulting new technologies that will increase LRAS. When the government hires or sponsors the hiring of scientists and engineers to work in a particular area, this government spending stimulates AD in the immediate term. When their work results in new life-enhancing drugs, increased food production, and safer or cleaner technologies, the entire productive capacity is enriched, pushing LRAS outwards. This can be accomplished by public/private sector partnerships, as well as tax incentives for research and development.

Investment in infrastructure

Infrastructure is the building of large-scale public projects such as ports, highway systems, bridges, communications networks, as well as power and water systems. This kind of spending most certainly increases AD in the short run, but should also expand the capital base of the country in the long term, increasing LRAS in the process. The creation of a port, for example, makes it easier for the country to import goods, which may enhance the capital base of that country. At the same time, exports of goods will also be improved. The expanded market for domestic goods spurs investment to produce for overseas markets.

Industrial policies

Governments may support specific industries; perhaps an industry where the country has comparative advantage, or one with good long-term prospects.

Financial incentives

The government can support the industry with reduced taxes, subsidized loans, and even direct subsidies. These all reduce the costs to the firms, and encourage more production.

Protection for 'infant industries'

Industries believed to be potentially competitive in the world market may get this special treatment. Compared to their global competitors, they may currently be too small to enjoy the benefits of economies of scale. Governments can put down protective tariffs or quotas to keep foreign competition out until the firm is sufficiently large and developed.

 In 2008, in the midst of a global economic downturn, the Communist government of China announced a $586 billion fiscal stimulus, the largest relative to a country's GDP initiated in modern times. The stimulus went towards investments in housing, rural infrastructure, transport, health and education, environment, industry disaster remediation, income-building, tax cuts, and finance. The purpose was to avoid a slow-down of China's growth rate by stimulating both aggregate demand and aggregate supply. Which components of the stimulus would you consider to be demand-side? Which would you consider to be supply-side?.

Evaluation of interventionist supply-side policies

Learning outcomes

- Evaluate the effectiveness of interventionist supply-side policies through consideration of factors including time lags, the ability to create employment, the ability to reduce inflationary pressure, the impact on economic growth, the impact on the government budget, the effect on equity, and the effect on the environment.

The use of interventionist supply-side policies should always take into account the specific needs of a country. The needs of developed nations may be different from the needs of less-developed nations. Resource bases and tax revenue situations are likely to differ as well. That said, after decades of trial in some form or another, it is possible to make some generalizations about specific interventionist policies.

Investment in human capital

Investment in human capital by way of education is rather universally supported, as it empowers people to better their own lives in their own way. Job training is regarded as a necessary method of easing the adjustment for the structurally unemployed. However, the costs can be considerable, and questions arise about the degree to which governments are well equipped to know which skills are needed and to ably train for those skills. While most countries support some kind of government-assisted healthcare, either by subsidies or the guarantee of health services, the costs and quality vary widely. However, in the poorest countries, it is clear that specific types of health services would significantly improve life spans, standard of living, and worker productivity.

Investment in new technology

The sponsorship of research and development is largely (though not exclusively) considered the domain of developed countries. The best case for such funding is that productive scientific research will not be undertaken by the market alone. This can be a result of imperfect information, as perhaps the true benefits of research are unknown until the research is completed. Or it can be that such research is so expensive that firms cannot expect to earn a sufficient return on the effort.

An example of both problems is the lack of research into the treatment and cure for common poor-country diseases like malaria. While costly, this kind of investment in knowledge can yield unexpected positive externalities in the forms of new technologies. The internet itself, developed over time through partly government-sponsored projects in various countries, is the latest and most common example.

Investment in infrastructure

Questions of cost also arise with the provision of infrastructure, though the benefits and costs are much more clear for these projects. Economists can estimate the prospective revenue and growth from construction of a new highway to relieve traffic, or from a rail system to improve the movement of goods. A strong case is made for infrastructure projects as public or merit goods that will not be undertaken if left to the market. Such

To access Worksheet 19.3 on Singapore, please visit www.pearsonbacconline.com and follow the onscreen instructions.

projects can be the source of enormous expenditure, especially in the case of major works like river damns and railways, and thus can be subject to significant corruption and waste as well.

CASE STUDY

Big dam projects = big d* corruption**

The allure of large-scale infrastructure investments is understandable. Politicians and voters are drawn by exhortations to national progress, the elevation of national status, and the potential for economic growth. Others have less admirable aims. Many of the biggest infrastructure projects are reported to have extravagantly looted public funds. Itaipu Dam, the world's largest hydroelectric power facility jointly built by Brazil and Paraguay, has been described in a report to the UK government as 'possibly the largest fraud in the history of capitalism. Itaipu was originally projected to cost some $3.4 billion, but skim-offs by the military rulers of Paraguay and Brazil and their colleagues contributed to the cost skyrocketing to around $20 billion.' (*Recent cases of corruption involving UK companies and UK-backed international financial institutions*, The Stationary Office, 2001).

More recently, in China the construction of the even larger Three Gorges Dam has been subject to quieter, but similar claims. In 1999, *The Guardian* reported that over 100 cases of official corruption in the dam's construction were being investigated. At the time, *China Daily* noted that while the project was a mammoth task for the construction industry, it had also become 'a challenge of similar scale for the (public) prosecutors'.

EXERCISES

3   To what extent does corruption in infrastructure projects diminish the case for such supply-side investments?

4   Speculate as to what kind of policies and institutions might reduce the scale of corruption on such projects.

Industrial policies

Industrial policies also have a mixed record of success. Countries such as Japan and South Korea can claim to have acted wisely in promoting specific industries that now mean a great deal to their national income. Japan, in the wake of World War II, offered many favourable tax, subsidy, and lending policies to its electronics industry, with famous results. South Korea, partly in imitation of Japanese success, did the same with electronics as well as developing the world's premier shipbuilding industry. However, industrial policies can also create entrenched corporate interests who regard national support as a corporate right. When such industries grow complacent or uncompetitive, they may still remain potent politically. Thus they can draw resources away from more competitive parts of the economy, or compel governments to protect them from competition well beyond their maturity into economic adulthood.

- How can we know whether government should support pure research, which might contribute to the sum total of human knowledge but which might never have an impact on technology?
- What other knowledge issues are relevant to investment in pure research?
- Investment in education and training is a common supply-side policy. What other reasons could there be for supporting the education of the population?
- What knowledge issues arise in answering the question as to whether government should shoulder this responsibility or whether it should be left to the market?

PRACTICE QUESTIONS

1 Using an appropriate diagram(s), explain how supply-side policies are expected to affect national income. (10 marks) [AO2], [AO4]

2 Distinguish between market-based supply policies and interventionist policies. (10 marks) [AO2]

3 a Explain two possible supply-side factors that may cause an increase in the level of unemployment. (10 marks) [AO2]

b Evaluate the view that demand-side policies are more effective than supply-side policies in reducing the level of unemployment. (15 marks) [AO3]

4 a Explain the difference between demand-side and supply-side economic policies. (10 marks) [AO2]

b 'Higher economic growth can only be achieved through the implementation of supply-side policies.' Discuss. (15 marks) [AO3]

© International Baccalaureate Organization 2006

To access Quiz 19, an interactive, multiple-choice quiz on this chapter, please visit www.pearsonbacconline.com and follow the onscreen instructions.

INTERNATIONAL TRADE

The benefits of trade

Learning outcomes
- Explain that gains from trade include lower prices for consumers, greater choice for consumers, the ability of producers to benefit from economies of scale, the ability to acquire needed resources, a more efficient allocation of resources, increased competition, and a source of foreign exchange.

A morning tale of two teenagers

Kaja's home.

Elise's home.

The sky is going from black to purple, and Kaja knows that it's time to get up. She wakes up her brother. The reeds under his head, she notices, are still wet from the blowing rains of last night. Her brother moans and crawls towards the opening of the hut. Together, they make the long, sleepy hike to the water. An hour later, the sky lighter with the rising sun, Kaja and her brother wade through the shallow water with harpoons in hand. Time passes without any luck, then Kaja spears something. A big fish, she wishes, because that would make her parents happy and they would reward her with a handful of nuts gathered the previous day. But it's a small one, though enough for breakfast, and it's getting late. The pair head back home, stopping at a stand of trees to pick up some coconuts. Their early morning chores complete, they continue home. They greet their parents an hour later, as their mum tends to their younger sisters in the hut. Soon, breakfast will be ready, and the day can begin.

At 07:00, a mechanical bird chirps; Elise reaches across her bed and pinches her phone. Ten minutes later, the bird chirps again; Elise takes the phone and starts checking her messages. She starts with text messages from her friends at school, emails from soccer pals, and then a look at the weather information for today. She checks her closet, pulls out two items and a t-shirt from under her bed. As she steps into the hallway, she's surprised by the cold. Her brother, who is always 'hot,' has turned the air conditioning up again. In 20 minutes, she has cleaned up and is taking some extra time with her makeup. From the kitchen, she can smell her mum's coffee, the frying eggs, and a whiff of toasting bread. After a call from her mother, she rushes to breakfast. Elise skips the eggs, but eats two pieces of toast with butter and jam. Minutes later, she's on the train to her school, nearly 3 kilometres away. As she walks in, greeting friends and chatting, she checks the time: nearly 8 o'clock. Time to get to class.

Two lives could hardly be more different, but what accounts for this difference? You probably see Elise's morning as that of a typical modern teenager, while Kaja's seems to belong to an ancient time. Elise is any middle-class European teenager, while Kaja's story is based on what we know of the Sentinelese people, an isolated tribe living on one of the Andaman Islands. Elise sleeps in comfort in a secure apartment, Kaja in a hut made of thatch. Elise enjoys bread from France, butter from Germany, and jam from England. Kaja's entire food menu comes from what is available nearby. Elise sleeps late and takes the train to school. Kaja wakes early and walks nearly two hours before breakfast. Elise communicates with dozens of people every day; most are from outside her family, some are from other parts of her country, other parts of Europe, even other continents. Kaja may see a few non-family members of the tribe in the evening, but she will probably never speak to anyone outside the few hundred other Sentinelese.

The Sentinelese are among the most isolated people on earth, resisting any contact with outsiders. Only a few photos exist of them, and even the Indian government has given up on contacting them. It goes without saying that the Sentinelese have a closed economy. Their entire standard of living comes from the resources available to them and their own labour. And if we acknowledge that the simplicity of such an existence may be attractive, we must also see the limitations, inconveniences, hardships, and difficulties that go with it.

Elise, meanwhile, floats along contentedly, without direct knowledge of where her food, phone, clothes, and all the other elements in her life come from. She's aware, of course, of her father's and mother's jobs, and has a sense she will need to find one herself some day, something she's good at. She expects of course, that she will be very good at her job, maybe among the best, and will get everything she needs, materially speaking, from the money she earns doing it. In short, Elise will eventually specialize in something, and will trade her wages for everything else.

As it is with these two representative stories, so it goes with countries and trade. Economists have long argued that what is true on the individual level is true for whole nations as well: countries grow rich through trade. All countries have valuable assets or resources. Using their different resources to the fullest, through specializing and trading, should yield extra wealth for all.

Voluntary trade is mutually beneficial

The buying and selling of goods and services across country borders is called international trade. Trade has a long history, before countries as we know them existed, and even before recorded history. From the trading of flint for obsidian, to the age of empires and colonialism, and into today's modern era of globalization, the impulse to improve one's life through trade has endured. Trade increasingly accounts for greater and greater amounts of a country's well-being. Exports, the selling of goods and services to buyers outside the country, have increased tremendously worldwide, particularly in the last 20 years. Imports, the buying of goods from sellers outside the country, have also increased. Economists generally believe that this growth occurs because it benefits both parties to the transaction, and that the benefits to trade are many. These benefits are discussed below.

 Free trade is a market environment where buyers and sellers can make transactions without government intervention.

Lower prices

Countries, just like individuals, can specialize in particular areas of expertise. This means they produce more efficiently than if each country tried to produce enough of everything for all its needs. Thus, a global division of labour takes place, where these multiplied efficiencies add to the overall wealth of consumers everywhere. In short, we get more output for less resources. Trade, it can be said, drives down real prices of the goods and services we all want.

Taking advantage of different factor endowments

No two countries share exactly the same resource base. Some are by the sea, some blessed with fertile farmland, some with ample deposits of minerals, and others placed well for trading between the others. Trade takes advantage of these differences between countries. The owner of a pin factory sells pins to his town, whereas the farmer from the country sells his milk and grain, which the factory owner would have enormous difficulty making on his own. Saudi Arabia, flush with oil deposits, buys technology from Japan, which has few natural resources but a very skilled technical and technology sector. Both are better off.

Economies of scale

As production levels grow ever larger to meet international demand, the specialization of managers and the introduction of expensive technology can help improve the productivity of a given business sector. The benefits of extreme specialization bring lower and lower average costs. These low costs drive down the prices of these goods. But these gains come from large-scale production and would not be likely to occur if production were limited to the domestic market.

Increased variety/choice

A brief check around your room or class will reveal an array of goods from many countries. A computer assembled in China; a glass from Russia; clothes from Thailand, Egypt and the Dominican Republic. As the number of countries in the global market has grown, so has the amount of choice. Even a simple desk lamp is now available in nearly any size, colour, design and wattage. While some find these choices overwhelming, others enjoy the power it gives to consumers to make decisions about their own purchases.

Acquisition of needed resources

Some economists have claimed that since China entered the global economy in the 1980s, it has been the greatest counter-inflationary force in the world. China's low-cost labour and abundant natural resources have led to it emerging as the largest manufacturer of cheap secondary goods in the world. How has China's emergence in the global economy benefited consumers in the West?

Some countries lack critical goods to improve their standard of living. In some cases, production of a needed good is simply impossible. Trade is the only way to get it. This need can range from a vital natural resource like natural gas for heating, to the need to import capital goods that might improve industry or agriculture. Adding these imported goods can improve production or improve everyday life for buyers.

Competition can improve efficiency

When a company controls a market, it lacks the competitive incentive to provide good service and lower costs. To maximize profits, it seeks to set prices as high as possible and reduce service costs. With no opposition to challenge its practices, such a company thrives at the expense of consumers who have no choice. However, when domestic markets are opened to foreign competition, companies are pressed into lowering prices and improving service, or they suffer from the competition with the foreign firms.

Political benefits

'Merchants have no country. The mere spot they stand on does not constitute so strong an attachment as that from which they draw their gains.' So wrote Thomas Jefferson in 1814. Indeed, trade requires relationships and attachments. Merchants want predictable supply of their imported resources and hope to maintain steady and reliable output to customers abroad. They abhor disruptions to everyday business and future planning. This, economists believe, helps keep the peace. This idea has been popularized by Thomas Friedman in *The Lexus and the Olive Tree* as 'the golden arches theory of conflict resolution', which holds that no two countries with a McDonald's have ever fought a war.

The updated version of this analogy suggests the same sort of pacifying effect to countries who are part of Apple's iPhone supply chain. However, more profound examples exist. After hundreds of years of conflict, reaching an apex of destruction and misery in two world wars in the 20th century, most of western Europe has since enjoyed a period of relative quiet and peaceful relations. They have also, not coincidentally, embarked on an extraordinary experiment in economic integration. Decade by decade, the six founding countries of the original European Common Market (1957), have been joined by 21 others while lowering barriers and opening borders to goods, services, and now workers. While this period of calm may seem small compared to the ages of bloody rivalry that preceded it, economists and political thinkers generally agree that trade and integration have consistently encouraged compromise and resolution over conflict and antagonism.

Efficiency and exports = growth and development

Development economists have concluded that exports can be a path to significant economic growth. When countries develop their comparative advantages, they become competitive and export to world markets. This results in a source of foreign exchange and a more efficient allocation of resources. The foreign exchange revenue boosts GDP, and allows more consumption of needed goods from foreign markets.

Furthermore, the growth can lead to an increase in incomes and, potentially, an overall increase in the average standard of living if devoted to education, infrastructure and healthcare. Figure 20.1 shows how exports regularly 'stay ahead' of GDP, suggesting that without consistent gains in exports, GDP might stagnate or even drop.

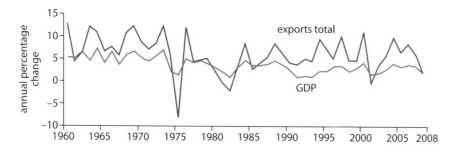

Figure 20.1
Export growth *vs* GDP growth.

A brief history of international trade theory

The Scottish economist and moral philosopher Adam Smith further developed our view of the division of labour at the village level with his analogy of the pin maker:

… a workman not educated to this business, nor acquainted with the use of the machinery employed in it, could scarce, perhaps, with his utmost industry, make one pin in a day, and certainly could not make

twenty. ... But if they had all wrought separately and independently, and without any of them having been educated to this peculiar business, they certainly could not each of them have made twenty, perhaps not one pin in a day; that is, certainly, not the two hundred and fortieth, perhaps not the four thousand eight hundredth part of what they are at present capable of performing, in consequence of a proper division and combination of their different operations ...

Adam Smith, *The Wealth of Nations* (Book 1), 1776

To Smith, the benefits of specialization were obvious. Everyone develops special efficiency, and auctions off that efficiency in the free market. Thus, through self-interest and trade, prosperity is made possible.

Smith's efforts were seconded by the work of David Ricardo just a few decades later. Ricardo, a banker and Member of Parliament, disliked the British Corn Laws, which he believed protected wealthy landowners and drove food prices up for everyone else. In particular, he viewed the laws as a redirection of income and resources away from relatively new and dynamic industries. In the process of fighting the Corn Laws, Ricardo developed the theory of comparative advantage. The theory holds that even countries that are more productive in all aspects should still trade with their otherwise inferior partners. This theory is explored later in this chapter (pages 420–423).

The French economist and philosopher Frédéric Bastiat took up the theme nearly 100 years later, on the national level. In the *Petition of the Candlemakers*, Bastiat satirizes the impulse to protect this or that market. The candlemakers in this work see the Sun as a rival and propose that the illumination of buildings with natural light be made illegal, as this would benefit the candle trade. Furthermore, by protecting candlemakers, all suppliers of candle-related goods would benefit: tallow producers, whale hunters who sell the blubber, the shipping industry, by extension all of France would benefit from the new rule. However, Bastiat's ridicule did not end the impulse to restrict markets.

More recently, James Ingram presented another way to demonstrate the benefits of trade, with the story of Mr X. This secretive and mysterious businessman tells the world he can turn simple primary goods like grain, coal and cotton into TVs, radios and cars, very cheaply. Mr X opens his factory, and the results stun the world. True to his word, the basic goods go in and the relatively advanced ones roll out. Consumers love the cheaper prices, competitors loathe the competition. Mr X jealously guards his trade secrets but a little boy wanders onto the property one day and discovers the truth: there are no miraculous manufacturing techniques, no special processes. The company, it turns out, is one big import–export business. The gains Mr X produced were made by trade alone.

The Corn Laws were protectionist tariffs placed on imported grain to protect British land owners from foreign competition. Their repeal in 1846 marked a significant shift towards freer trade by the British empire, which had previously pursued mercantilism. This economic theory believed a country's wealth and power was derived primarily from the sale of exports and the hoarding of monetary wealth at home (primarily gold bullion).

To access Worksheet 20.1 on gains from trade, please visit www.pearsonbacconline.com and follow the onscreen instructions.

To learn more about trade, visit www.pearsonhotlinks.com, enter the title or ISBN of this book and select weblink 20.1.

20.2 Absolute and comparative advantage (HL only)

Learning outcomes
- Explain the theory of absolute advantage.
- Explain, using a diagram, the gains from trade arising from a country's absolute advantage in the production of a good.
- Explain the theory of comparative advantage.
- Describe the sources of comparative advantage, including the differences between countries in factor endowments and the levels of technology.

- Draw a diagram to show comparative advantage.
- Calculate opportunity costs from a set of data in order to identify comparative advantage.
- Draw a diagram to illustrate comparative advantage from a set of data.
- Discuss the real-world relevance and limitations of the theory of comparative advantage, considering factors including the assumptions on which it rests, and the costs and benefits of specialization (a full discussion must take into account arguments in favour and against free trade and protection).

Absolute advantage

It is important to acknowledge what may be obvious: some countries are simply more efficient at some forms of production than other countries. This efficiency is called absolute advantage.

Countries that possess an absolute advantage in a good are wise to specialize and produce that good. Table 20.1 shows two countries with clear absolute advantage in their respective specialities. This table shows the limits of production for these countries: Country S can produce 30 units of oil *or* 5 units of wheat; Country U can produce 3 units of oil *or* 15 units of wheat. Country S is far superior to Country U in oil production, whereas the Country U is much more efficient at growing wheat.

Absolute advantage is the situation that occurs in comparative advantage theory, when one country can produce more of a given product with the same or less resources than another country.

TABLE 20.1 ABSOLUTE ADVANTAGE		
Country	Oil/units produced per unit of time	Wheat/units produced per unit of time
Country S	30	5
Country U	3	15

A glance at this two-country trading scenario immediately tells you that each country should specialize and trade. With a total of 30 units of oil and 15 of wheat on the market, global output is at the highest possible point. Country S could never produce that much wheat on its own, nor could Country U produce that much oil. Absolute advantage theory states that Country S should specialize in oil and trade it for wheat from Country U, which should specialize in wheat production.

However, the world rarely has such extreme cases of clear absolute advantage. A more common real-world occurrence is when one country has absolute advantage in several types of production. Some countries, it would seem, are better at making nearly everything. Should those countries bother to trade with their inferiors?

To better grasp the problem, imagine the following scenario. Lawyer J worked her way through school as a data entry clerk. She was extraordinary, typing 110 words per minute. When she became a lawyer, she was the best in her area, but she never seemed to find a typist worth hiring. None, compared to her, were any good. It was frustrating for her to see the mistakes being made, and she found it tedious to wait for the typist to catch up with her as she dictated legal briefs. 'What a waste of money!' she would sometimes say to herself. So occasionally, after work hours, she would sit down and do some of the typing work herself. From an economic perspective, should Lawyer J do her own typing?

This demands some thought. In economic terms, Lawyer J possesses an absolute advantage in both typing and lawyering. In other words, she can produce more output, is more efficient, at each task. This suggests that perhaps she should do both things, as she is more efficient at both.

However, she is rewarded very differently for each activity. When she does her own typing, she saves the $40 per hour she would normally pay her secretary. When she is working as a lawyer, she is paid an average of $300 per hour. If the answer seems a little clearer now, let's clarify the reasons why.

If we assume that Lawyer J does one hour of typing instead of lawyering, what does she lose? What is her opportunity cost of typing? She saves $40, but loses $300 in lawyering fees. Therefore her opportunity cost is $260. When she hires a typist, she loses the $40 paid to her secretary, but keeps the $300 for attorney fees. Therefore her opportunity cost for lawyer work is only $40.

Because she earns so much more as a lawyer (and would lose it if she chose to type for that hour), it is logical to conclude that she should work always as a lawyer. This is the activity with the lower opportunity cost. Therefore, even though she has an absolute advantage in both jobs, her *comparative advantage* lies in lawyering.

Comparative advantage and opportunity cost

Comparative advantage is when a country produces a good at a lower domestic opportunity cost than another country.

The same principle applies to countries. Comparative advantage theory says that countries should specialize in the production of whatever has the lowest opportunity cost (saying something has the lowest opportunity cost naturally implies that it is the good whose production has the most value). Countries that specialize produce more efficiently and should trade their output with other countries to enjoy a higher standard of living.

David Ricardo was the first to show the benefits of comparative advantage mathematically, in the early 1800s. With countries, it is possible to demonstrate comparative advantage with a simplified example involving two countries producing only two goods. For a country to produce more of good A, it must sacrifice some portion of good B. This is the opportunity cost of more of good A, and the reverse holds true for shifting resources to more of good B.

Comparative advantage matrix: output model

Table 20.2 shows the output possible for each product and each country, if each produced *only* that good. For example, if Country C produced only TVs, it could produce 10 TVs and no smartphones. If Country J produced 15 smartphones, it could not make any TVs. If either country wanted to produce more of one, it would need to sacrifice some of its production of the other. In this regard, Table 20.2 represents the countries' production possibilities.

TABLE 20.2 COMPARATIVE ADVANTAGE MATRIX: OUTPUT METHOD		
Country	**Output of TVs**	**Output of smartphones**
Country C	10	5
Country J	20	15

Based on their output, it is rather easy to determine who has the absolute advantage. Which country produces more efficiently? Country J produces more TVs, as well as more smartphones. Therefore, Country J has the absolute advantage in both industries. Like Lawyer J, Country J is better at both tasks. However, Country J may still benefit from trade with the clearly inferior producer, Country C.

Domestic opportunity cost

To find out who has the comparative advantage, we need to calculate the domestic opportunity costs in each country of both TVs and smartphones. In other words, what is the trade-off for production inside Country J and Country C?

In calculating domestic opportunity cost for an output problem, we use the equation:

$$\text{opportunity cost X} = \frac{\text{output Y}}{\text{output X}}$$

Worked example

For Country C:

$$\text{opportunity cost of producing 1 TV} = \frac{5 \text{ smartphone}}{10 \text{ TV}} = 0.5 \text{ smartphone}$$

$$\text{opportunity cost of producing 1 smartphone} = \frac{10 \text{ TV}}{5 \text{ smartphone}} = 2 \text{ TV}$$

For Country J:

$$\text{opportunity cost of producing 1 TV} = \frac{15 \text{ smartphone}}{20 \text{ TV}} = 0.75 \text{ smartphone}$$

$$\text{opportunity cost of producing 1 smartphone} = \frac{20 \text{ TV}}{15 \text{ smartphone}} = 1.33 \text{ TV}$$

We can now place opportunity cost values inside the matrix to clarify the choices. Table 20.3 shows the trade-offs for making one good, in terms of another. For Country C, to produce 1 TV would require the sacrifice of 0.5 of a smartphone. For Country C to make 1 smartphone, it would lose 2 TVs. For Country J, making 1 TV would require the sacrifice of 0.75 of a smartphone. Making 1 smartphone would require the sacrifice of 1.33 TVs.

TABLE 20.3 COMPARATIVE ADVANTAGE MATRIX: OUTPUT METHOD WITH OPPORTUNITY COSTS				
Country	Output of TVs	Opportunity cost of producing 1 TV	Output of smartphones	Opportunity cost of producing 1 smartphone
Country C	10	0.5 smartphone	5	2 TV
Country J	20	0.75 smartphone	15	1.33 TV

Cross-market comparison

Next, to determine which country has the lowest opportunity cost of production, we make a comparison across the market for each product.

In the market for TVs, Country C has the lower opportunity cost, giving up only 0.5 of a smartphone for every TV made, whereas Country J gives up 0.75 of a smartphone for every TV made. Thus, Country C has the comparative advantage in TVs, because it has the lower opportunity cost.

In the market for smartphones, Country J has the lower opportunity cost, giving up only 1.33 of a TV for every smartphone made, whereas Country C gives up 2 TVs for every smartphone made. Thus, Country J has the comparative advantage in smartphones, because it has the lower opportunity cost.

Specialize and trade

With comparative advantage determined, it is rational for each country to specialize in the production of the good for which it has the lowest opportunity cost. This maximizes production between the two countries, which then trade their goods with each other. What is the price of these goods? Each country sells the good at some price between their own opportunity cost and the opportunity cost of the other country.

Therefore, Country C sells its TVs at a price somewhere between 0.5 and 0.75 smartphone per TV. The exact trade price is negotiable, but it is clear that Country C must get a price better than 0.5 smartphone for each TV. Otherwise it would produce smartphones itself.

Country J trades its smartphones at a price somewhere between 1.33 and 2 TVs per smartphone. The exact trade price is negotiable, but it is clear that Country J must get a price better than 1.33 TVs for each smartphone. Otherwise it would produce TVs itself.

Comparative advantage matrix: input model

● **Examiner's hint**

When analysing production possibilities tables, you need to be clear whether the data in them are about quantity of output produced or the number of inputs needed to produce one unit of output. If the table contains output data, then the goal is to *maximize the total output* of the goods being produced. Thus, to determine absolute advantage, we look for the country with the higher number. If the table contains input data, then the goal is to *minimize the use of inputs*. Thus, to determine absolute advantage, we look for the country with the lower number.

Calculations and determinations of comparative advantage can also be made using factor inputs, rather than market production or output. This measure of efficiency is demonstrated by how relatively few inputs go into the production of one unit of the good. In this type of matrix, high numbers reflect inefficiency, as more resources are being used; low numbers show efficiency, with fewer inputs per unit of output.

Table 20.4 shows the amount of labour needed to produce one unit of iron and one unit of butter. It is clear that Country A has the absolute advantage in both iron and butter production. It produces each product with fewer hours of labour.

Country	Input time for output of 1 unit iron/hours	Input time for output of 1 unit butter/hours
Country A	25	15
Country Z	10	5

TABLE 20.4 COMPARATIVE ADVANTAGE: INPUT METHOD

Domestic opportunity cost

To find out who has the comparative advantage, we need to calculate the domestic opportunity costs for each country. When calculating the opportunity cost for factor input values, we use the following equation:

$$\text{opportunity cost X} = \frac{\text{input X}}{\text{input Y}}$$

Worked example

For Country A:

$$\text{opportunity cost of producing 1 unit iron} = \frac{25 \text{ hours iron}}{15 \text{ hours butter}} = 1.67 \text{ butter}$$

$$\text{opportunity cost of producing 1 unit butter} = \frac{15 \text{ hours butter}}{25 \text{ hours iron}} = 0.6 \text{ iron}$$

Country Z:

$$\text{opportunity cost of producing 1 unit iron} = \frac{10 \text{ hours iron}}{5 \text{ hours butter}} = 2 \text{ butter}$$

$$\text{opportunity cost of producing 1 unit butter} = \frac{5 \text{ hours butter}}{10 \text{ hours iron}} = 0.5 \text{ iron}$$

We can now place opportunity cost values inside the matrix to clarify the choices (Table 20.5).

TABLE 20.5 COMPARATIVE ADVANTAGE MATRIX: INPUT METHOD WITH OPPORTUNITY COSTS

Country	Input time for output of 1 unit iron/hours	Opportunity cost of producing 1 unit iron	Input time for output of 1 unit butter/hours	Opportunity cost of producing 1 unit butter
Country A	25	1.67 butter	15	0.6 iron
Country Z	10	2 butter	5	0.5 iron

Cross-market comparison

Next, to determine which country has the lowest opportunity cost of production, we make the comparison across the market for each product.

In the market for iron, Country A has the lower opportunity cost, giving up only 1.67 of a butter unit for every unit of iron made, whereas Country Z gives up 2 butter units for every unit of iron produced. Thus, Country A has the comparative advantage in iron, because it has the lower opportunity cost.

In the market for butter, Country Z has the lower opportunity cost, giving up only 0.5 units of iron for every butter unit made, whereas Country A gives up 0.6 units of iron for every butter unit produced. Thus, Country Z has the comparative advantage in butter, because it has the lower opportunity cost.

Specialize and trade

With comparative advantage determined, it is rational for each country to specialize in the production of the good that has the lowest opportunity cost. This maximizes production between the two countries, which then trade goods with each other. Although this is a simplification of real-world realities (only two products per country), it reflects the potential benefit a country gets if it can incur lower opportunity costs to get the same or greater levels of output. After specializing, each country sells the good at some barter price between its own opportunity cost and the opportunity cost of the other country.

Therefore, Country Z trades butter at a price somewhere between 0.5 and 0.6 units of iron per unit of butter. Accordingly, Country A trades iron at a price somewhere between 1.67 and 2 units of butter per unit of iron. Country Z must get a price better than its domestic opportunity cost for butter (0.5 iron units) and Country A must get a price better than its domestic opportunity cost for iron (1.67 butter units). Assuming they both negotiate and trade, each is better off.

To access Worksheet 20.2 on payoff matrices, please visit www.pearsonbacconline.com and follow the onscreen instructions.

Absolute and comparative advantage with production possibilities curves

The concepts of absolute and comparative advantage can also be demonstrated using production possibilities curves (PPCs). Because simple PPCs assume the production of two goods, and show the trade-offs between those goods, we can deduce the relative opportunity costs.

Using the data in Table 20.1 (page 419), Figure 20.2 demonstrates the concept of absolute advantage for Country U and Country S. For the sake of simplicity, the trade-offs in each case are assumed to be constant. Thus, opportunity costs are constant, and the slope of the PPC line is a straight line.

With a fixed set of resources, Country U produces 15 units of wheat while Country S produces only 5 units. Country U has the absolute advantage in wheat. In the market for oil, however, Country S produces 30 units, compared to the Country U's 3 units. Thus, Country S has the absolute advantage in oil. From this, we deduce that Country U should produce wheat and sell it to Country

Figure 20.2
Absolute advantage on a PPC.

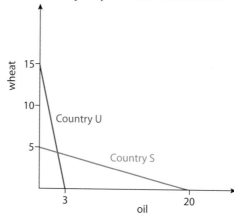

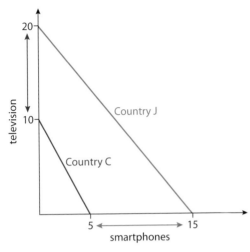

Figure 20.3
Production possibility curves to show comparative advantage.

Figure 20.4
Expanded consumption possibilities with specialization and trade.

S in exchange for its oil. The calculation of relative opportunity costs would support this, but it is hardly necessary since the choice of specialized goods for each country is obvious.

It is less obvious when one country is more productive in each area. Figure 20.3 shows the same information as Table 20.2. The PPC demonstrates Country J's possession of absolute advantage in both industries by having a PPC beyond Country C's in every direction. If we did not have the values to give us specific information, the slope of lines would give us a clue to the relative trade-offs for each country. Country C's line is steeper, suggesting that it probably gives up TVs more rapidly as it tries to increase its production of smartphones. We could then infer that Country J had the lower opportunity cost of smartphones. Logically, Country C would then have the better opportunity cost of TVs.

Let's assume that Country C and Country J find a trade price that's mutually agreeable. It should be something between the opportunity cost ratios they were previously experiencing. A rate of 1.5 TVs per smartphone is between 1.33 (the Country J's opportunity cost) and 2 (Country C's opportunity cost). The smartphone for TV rate would be the reciprocal of 1.5 (0.67) smartphones for every TV. In Figure 20.4, we assume that Country C specializes in TVs and makes 10, and Country J specializes in smartphones and makes 15. Each country now can trade at the new price, which means a new opportunity cost for each. This expansion of the PPC, in the area where the other country specializes, demonstrates the new, greater consumption possibilities for each country.

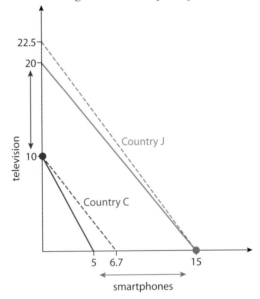

However, it is important to note that gains from comparative advantage only apply when the domestic opportunity cost ratios are different. When they are the same, when the trade-offs of one good for another are equal, there are no apparent benefits to trade. The domestic opportunity cost is the same for both countries, so there's no advantage to trading with the other country. Therefore, there is no comparative advantage.

● **Examiner's hint**

The production possibilities tables and curves here are unrepresentative of the real world. They would look more realistic if, instead of two specific goods, they represented two categories of goods. For instance, if we examined the output of agricultural goods and consumer electronics in South Korea and Australia, we would find that South Korea had a clear comparative advantage in consumer electronics, whereas Australia had the advantage in agricultural goods.

Sources of comparative advantage

What, then should a country produce? Where, in reality, do its comparative advantages lie? Resource endowments play a large role. A country that possesses most of the farmable land in the region is likely to have a comparative advantage in agriculture. One that has vast quantities of untapped fossil fuel or other natural resources may have a potential comparative advantage there. Other countries may have little natural resources or land, but have highly skilled workforces that provide financial, merchant, and other services to the world. Whether a country's possession of particular resources gives it a comparative advantage rests on two factors. First, the relative abundance of the resource. Second, the value of the good produced from the resource to the world market. An abundant resource that is highly valued is an obvious source of comparative advantage. Production will be efficient and opportunity costs low. A scarce resource with little value on the world markets has no advantage. Production will be costly and opportunity costs high. In selecting which industries to develop, many countries struggle to determine and exploit their true comparative advantages.

Limitations of comparative advantage

While recognized as essentially valid in theoretical form, the theory of comparative advantage is heavily criticized for not being an accurate representation of real trade.

Perils of extreme specialization

In theory, a country might devote its entire resources to the production of a single good. This makes the relative prosperity of the country dependent on the value of that good. If the good is a commodity, the country's entire income is bound to the price of the commodity. This would bring extraordinary risk to the population's well-being and potentially place the country on a roller-coaster of volatility. This overspecialization is just one of the risks of comparative advantage. A long-term concern is whether a country will be trapped in a certain type of production, thus limiting its potential for full development.

Many countries may find themselves with a comparative advantage in agricultural goods, in part because the developed world has already developed efficiencies in the making of many services and manufactured goods. With the rich world already in possession of this head start, poor agricultural economies are left producing commodities of relatively low market value while obeying the law of comparative advantage. Were they to strictly follow the law, the kind of structural change that is believed to be necessary for development might never happen. The country, in other words, might never develop industry or service sectors, and be relegated to a low standard of living and relative dependency.

> W To learn more about specialization, visit www. pearsonhotlinks.com, enter the title or ISBN of this book and select weblink 20.2.

Unrealistic assumptions

Comparative advantage theory is also heavily criticized for being an inaccurate representation of the actual world of trade. Many of the assumptions underlying the theory, it is said, are simply invalid, as briefly discussed below.

- Transport costs, assumed to be irrelevant in theory, cannot be ignored in practice. They can raise costs enough to eliminate a comparative advantage.
- Goods are assumed to be identical. Wheat is wheat, whether from the USA or Ukraine. However, goods often have some differentiation, especially in the world of manufactured goods. It is difficult to assess true comparative advantage when the goods are not the same.

- Perfect information about the availability and prices of all available goods is impossible, given the vast nature of global markets. Thus, determining one's own comparative advantage is challenging at best.
- The theory assumes relatively constant costs. This is reflected in the PPCs with constant slopes. However, one would expect improvements in production that may lead to significant economies of scale. Constant cost assumptions might mask potential comparative advantages for industries that appear uncompetitive, or may overestimate an advantage that is actually less extreme than it appears.
- The two-country model is unrealistic, making the determination of comparative advantage rather difficult. However, multi-country analysis is possible with appropriate mathematical modelling.
- Full employment, a necessary condition of the theory, rarely occurs in practice. Developing countries, in particular, have massive unemployment and inefficiency.
- Finally, the assumption that countries practise free trade is highly debatable. While tariffs and other forms of protectionism have been significantly reduced in recent decades, many countries still protect markets with tariffs, subsidies, quotas and bureaucratic barriers. These practices distort the market, making the gains from comparative advantage difficult to discern, and even harder to realize.

To access Worksheet 20.3 on the Dominican Republic, please visit www.pearsonbacconline.com and follow the onscreen instructions.

HL EXERCISES

1   a   Given a fixed amount of resources, Country U and Country M can produce the number of soy beans and avocados indicated in the table below. Using the data in this table, draw two production possibilities curves, one for each country.

Country	soy beans/tons	avocados/tons
Country M	60	15
Country U	90	30

   b   Calculate the opportunity cost of producing soy beans and avocados in each country.

   c   Identify which country has a comparative advantage in soy beans and avocados.

   d   If the two countries were to trade, suggest a rate of exchange between soy beans and avocados, which would be favourable to both countries.

   e   Based on the rate of exchange you identified in **d**, draw a new production possibilities curve on the graph you drew in **a** showing the level of consumption in both countries with trade.

20.3 The World Trade Organization

Learning outcomes
- Describe the objectives and functions of the World Trade Organization.

A brief history

The World Trade Organization (WTO) advertises itself as the 'only international organization dealing with the global rules of trade between nations. Its main function is to ensure that trade flows as smoothly, predictably and freely as possible.' The WTO originated from negotiations on trade that followed World War II. It was generally thought that a wave of protectionism in the 1930s drew countries closer to the war that followed. Thus, in 1948, 23 countries signed the General Agreement on Tariffs and Trade (GATT).

During the same negotiations, held in Bretton Woods, New Hampshire USA, the International Monetary Fund (IMF), the World Bank, and the Bretton Woods exchange rate system were also established with the aim of creating stability and order to world trade and income flows. In time, the GATT developed from an agreement to a forum for future negotiations, and eventually an organization in its own right.

Every few years, GATT negotiations were staged with the goal of creating standardized trade rules. After holding seven rounds of negotiations, the final round culminated in the creation of the WTO in 1993. The WTO extended and expanded the GATT mission, with greater scope over services and capital flows, as well as increased authority. It is based in Geneva, Switzerland, and has a staff of over 600. It is currently working on the Doha Round, and the stated purpose of this round is to expand the benefits of trade to less developed countries (LDCs).

Logos at the headquarters of the World Trade Organization.

The Doha round started in 2001 and is still unfinished without an end in sight. Already the longest trade round yet, the main barriers continue to be the reluctance of rich countries to reduce their heavy subsidies and protection of agricultural markets. In turn, rich countries are seeking reductions in allowable tariffs on developing country protectionist measures. At stake are hundreds of billions of dollars in new markets for developing countries.

Aims of the WTO

The WTO seeks to expand international trade by lowering trade barriers and improving the flow of trade. It has specific objectives (in bold, below) that enhance this overall goal.

- **Trade without discrimination**. WTO members are all asked to subscribe to Most Favoured Nation status. This means that goods from all WTO member countries are treated equally. A tariff applied to one is applied to all, and there are thus no real favourites. At the same time, foreign goods should be treated the same as domestic goods.
- **Freer trade through negotiation**. The success of each trade round is attributed to the combined efforts of continuous negotiation. This ensures that changes to trade policy are done by direct dealing, and also that they are done gradually. This allows affected countries to prepare for the adjustments that will probably be enacted when the new agreement comes into force.
- **Predictability through binding and transparency**. Binding refers to the commitment among members to keep tariffs at or below certain rates. This allows importers to assess markets more accurately and make better decisions about trade. Openness about trade rules also encourages more trade.
- **Promoting fair competition**. While devoted to free trade, the WTO also claims to seek trade that is more fair. Rules against dumping and intellectual property theft, for example, are aimed at increasing fair competition. More generally, the creation of a system of trade rules promotes fair play by establishing some fundamental guidelines for most trade.
- **Encouraging development**. Nearly two-thirds of WTO members are developing countries. These countries are granted special trade concessions because it is assumed that their industries need time and space to grow to a level of direct global competition.

With these objectives in mind, the WTO performs the following functions:

- provide a forum for trade negotiation
- execute WTO agreements
- evaluate and rule on trade complaints by member countries
- provide technical assistance to developing countries on trade issues
- track changes in member trade policies.

To learn more about WTO members, visit www.pearsonhotlinks. com, enter the title or ISBN of this book and select weblink 20.3.

EXERCISES

2 Use weblink 20.3 (see hotlinks box) to access the WTO site, select a WTO country and research its trade partners and overall trade ranking. Choose a country from the 153 current WTO members. Under 'trade statistics' for each country, identify the following aspects of your country's trade profile:

i the top five countries of export

ii the top five importing countries

iii overall rank in merchandise trade

iv overall rank in exports and imports

v by percentage, the top type of goods exported

vi by percentage, the top type of goods imported.

Competing views of the WTO

Because the WTO is the only organization devoted to the expansion of trade, it is difficult to evaluate the achievements of the organization. There is no basis for direct comparison. However, it may be possible to arrive at some measure of understanding by evaluating the arguments and evidence of those on both sides of the issue.

Europe's Common Agricultural Policy (CAP) is one of the largest obstacles to free trade in the world. This massive system of subsidies and tariffs supports the largest farms in Europe to the tune of millions of euros every year, providing European farmers with massive support from taxpayers. Such subsidies are a major obstacle to economic growth in the developing world because it is incredibly difficult for poor farmers to compete in global food markets.

Supporters' view

The WTO makes specific claims about its value, claims that are often synonymous with the benefits of free trade generally.

- The WTO system promotes peace. By increasing trade relationships between countries, the WTO helps reduce conflict as 'sales people rarely fight their customers'. 1930s Europe competed to raise barriers, which contributed to World War II, while post-war Europe has grown increasingly integrated by trade and is at peace.
- The WTO provides a place to handle disputes constructively. By providing a dispute process, with a schedule of negotiation as part of the early stages, the WTO encourages compromise.
- The WTO system is based on rules rather than power. The WTO often judges rich countries to be violators of trade policy. This rules-based system helps protect smaller, poorer trade partners when disputes arise.
- Free trade cuts the cost of living. When countries produce based on efficiencies and comparative advantage, the costs of food, clothes and other necessities are cheaper. The WTO notes that rich countries, primarily the EU and US, subsidize their farmers with nearly $1 billion per day, enough to fly all their cows around the world first class one and a half times.
- Trade provides greater consumer choice and variety. Trade gives consumers worldwide access to goods, meaning any consumer can shop according to their preferences. More luxury goods are available, as well as a greater variety of cheaper consumer goods.

- Trade boosts incomes. Agreements in the 1994 Uruguay round resulted in an income increase of between $109 billion and $510 billion. This income can be used by governments, in part, to improve services and infrastructure. However, domestic producers protest when inefficient industries face competition.
- Trade increases economic growth, which can increase employment. While trade can increase GDP, the effect on jobs, according to the WTO, is more complicated. Countries that lose jobs can smooth the adjustment with good transitional policies, or perhaps this is because countries with good policies tend to be the ones that are more likely to respond to job losses anyway. The results are, according to the WTO, mixed.
- The WTO system encourages efficiency and simplicity. Certainty about trade rules, transparency about the rules, and predictability about the trading environment all encourage trade and efficiency.
- WTO agreements shield countries from narrow interests. When asked to enact forms of protectionism, national governments resist the temptation because they want to be seen playing by international rules. Thus, governments are in a better position to ignore powerful special interest groups that would distort trade in their favour.
- The same rules create good incentives for better government. Short-term, special-interest lobbying and corruption are more difficult to enact when everyone knows the rules (transparency) and the government is pledged to support them.

Critics' view

While relatively few critics argue with the view that international trade makes everyone better off in theory, many critics take issue with the way that trade is organized by the WTO in practice.

- Despite claims to equalize the trade environment, WTO negotiations favour rich countries. These countries bring large groups of trade negotiators, far more than smaller countries. Furthermore, it has been charged that many agreements are made without consultation or involvement of poor countries. This has escalated in recent years during the Doha round – Brazil and India formed the 'G20' group to represent developing countries' needs.
- It is argued that most of the gains in trade have come from trade between rich countries, negating the claim that trade benefits everyone.
- Poor countries sometimes cannot afford trade representatives, and so have no representation in trade negotiations.
- Rich countries and individuals are getting richer faster than everyone else. Studies have shown that the rich–poor gap has been growing since 1990. Oxfam International notes that 'with only 14% of the world's population, high-income countries [still] account for 75% of global GDP, which is approximately the same share as in 1990' (*Rigged Rules and Double Standards*, 2002).
- The Uruguay round has not addressed tariff escalation. This refers to the practice of developed countries keeping tariffs on raw materials and primary goods (imported by these countries) low, while maintaining much higher tariffs on the semi-processed and higher-value goods made from the raw materials. This keeps away low-cost competition from LDCs in these semi-processed and higher-value industries. It also prevents LDCs from diversifying their production, increasing the risk of overspecialization.
- Agricultural subsidies in rich countries have not been reduced, despite pledges by countries signing up to the Uruguay round. These subsidies depress world prices, and reduce production in developing markets that would otherwise export to the developed world.

During the 1999 meeting of the WTO in Seattle, USA, protesters from around the world and all levels of society, demonstrated their opposition to the WTO's mission. When the protests turned violent, the Seattle police responded with force. Protesters would later argue that they were successful in stalling the WTO's progress towards enacting measures to reduce trade union power, endanger the environment and lead to the exploitation of poor workers in developing countries.

- The protection of intellectual property rights, an issue of far greater interest to the capital-intensive rich world, keeps innovation from spreading quickly to developing countries. In the area of pharmaceutical drugs, this issue is felt rather acutely, as it directly affects healthcare levels for countries that cannot afford to pay the prices of new drugs.
- As tariffs are dropped by successive rounds of trade agreements, rich countries appear to be resorting to other bureaucratic barriers such as product standards to keep goods out.
- Because the WTO has primarily commercial interests in mind, its agreements ignore cases of worker exploitation, as well as rights and safety issues. The WTO does little to encourage environmental protection. The promotion of trade empowers multinational corporations to campaign for relaxed environmental and worker standards. Creating and enforcing these standards is considered a local problem. Meanwhile, local authorities often compete to soften the standards to encourage companies to relocate.

A hot topic

To learn more about free trade, visit www.pearsonhotlinks.com, enter the title or ISBN of this book and select weblink 19.3.

Free trade, in theory and in practice, is among the more hotly debated international topics of our time. Research continues to inform this debate, with more and more data employed to establish some reliability to its conclusions. For one economist at least, several notions that surround trade need to be challenged. Others, it seems, tend to be true after all.

- ***Economies that are open to trade grow faster****. Poor countries grow richer when more open to trade, as recent successes in India and China have helped to demonstrate.*
- ***Rich countries are more protectionist than poor ones****. Not true, since poor countries tend to have higher average tariffs than rich ones. This does not address the problem of tariff escalation.*
- ***Agricultural protectionism in the rich world worsens global poverty****. If subsidies were removed, food prices will rise. These increases could hurt nutrition levels in some poor countries that rely on food imports.*

Are there moral as well as economic arguments in favour of free trade?

Arvind Panagariya, Think again: international trade, *Foreign Policy*, 1 November 2003

To access Quiz 20, an interactive, multiple-choice quiz on this chapter, please visit www.pearsonbacconline.com and follow the onscreen instructions.

PRACTICE QUESTIONS

1 **a** Explain three benefits (gains) which might arise from international trade.
(10 marks) [AO2]

  b Assess the proposition that the WTO failed in its mission of liberalizing world trade.
(15 marks) [AO3]

© International Baccalaureate Organization 2003 (part a only)

2 (HL only) Using a production possibilities table, explain the concepts of absolute and comparative advantage.
(10 marks) [AO2], [AO4]

3 **a** (HL only) Using appropriate diagrams, explain the concepts of absolute and comparative advantage.
(10 marks) [AO2], [AO4]

  b Evaluate the degree to which comparative advantage theory usefully reflects the reality of modern global trade.
(15 marks) [AO3]

21 PROTECTIONISM

The case for protectionism

Learning outcomes
- Discuss the arguments in favour of trade protection, including the protection of domestic jobs, national security, protection of infant industries, the maintenance of health, safety and environmental standards, anti-dumping and unfair competition, a means of overcoming a balance of payments deficit and a source of government revenue.

 Protectionist barriers prevent free trade. Once built, they are difficult to tear down.

Despite the obvious gains made possible by trade, all countries try to protect some industries from unpredictability and the threat of foreign competition. This is protectionism. It can take many forms and is waged to varying degrees. Some of the most ardent free-trade countries still shelter or support large portions of their economies with a variety of protectionist methods. Other countries openly promote protectionism as their fundamental economic growth policy. Why is protectionism so popular? This chapter explores the arguments around protectionism and evaluates the effects of protectionist policies.

Protectionist measures run counter to the principle of comparative advantage explained in Chapter 20, where countries specialize in the goods with the lowest opportunity cost, and then trade those goods with others. The term 'free trade' describes the process of lowering protectionist barriers and thereby realizing those gains from trade. Countries work out these agreements through tedious negotiation at the global level through the World Trade Organization (WTO) and on the regional level through trade blocs such as the European Union, the North American Free Trade Agreement (NAFTA) or Mercado Común del Sur (MERCOSUR), also known as the Common Market of the South.

Protectionism is the placement of legal restrictions on international trade, and includes tariffs, quotas, subsidies and other bureaucratic barriers.

Arguments for protectionism

The proponents of protectionism argue that their vulnerable domestic markets face unfair and damaging foreign competition. As global trade has expanded dramatically in recent decades, many of the following arguments continue to be raised, especially in times of economic turmoil.

To protect domestic employment

Among the most loudly promoted rationales for protectionist measures is that they will keep local jobs safe from foreign competition. It is most likely to be heard from industries that are in a 'sunset' stage of relative decline compared to their international competition. They typically argue for more time to adjust to the market, to modernize and improve efficiency. Rather ironically, this kind of modernizing would usually eliminate many of the jobs these industries profess to want to save. However, in most situations, these firms are in long-term decline and are merely holding off an inevitable loss of market share. Nevertheless, industries threatened in this manner will often see management and labour unions join forces to press parliament or congress for protectionist advantages.

To protect sunrise or infant industries

Infant industries are those that are newly developed and have not had an opportunity to develop the economies of scale and low costs that are achieved by selling to a large market.

Many countries, perhaps especially less developed countries (LDCs), believe they have industries that are future champions. Countries can argue that their industries are as yet underdeveloped, and have not grown large enough to achieve lowered costs through economies of scale. These industries should therefore be sheltered until they can face on more equal terms the powerful multinational corporations and highly developed industries of rich countries. The strategy is to block imports with tariffs and other trade barriers. It may also include subsidies to the infant industry. In theory, these firms will eventually grow strong enough to compete without such assistance.

Advocates of the sunrise industry perspective point to the success of countries that have developed dramatically in a relatively short period, citing the Asian tigers of South Korea, Singapore, Taiwan and Hong Kong. Major industrial powers like the US, Germany and others have histories of protecting their heavy industries as they grew. These countries identified potential growth industries and supported them with state subsidies, as well as discouraged domestic consumption by levying high import tariffs. Critics take issue with these results, citing evidence of higher education levels and lower wages as the drivers of productivity in the tiger economies in particular. At the same time, critics of the sunrise industry view also note that most sunrise industries never grow up fully, and often require state support long after their infancy or even adolescence has passed. These dependent firms, they argue, will continue to draw government subsidies and will cry out for protectionism long into the future.

To counteract relative domestic tax differences

Some economists have recently argued that domestic tax policies can reduce or enhance the competitiveness of a country's exports. Countries that rely heavily on value added taxes have a competitive advantage over those that do not sell their goods in this system. It is said that where a country does not have VAT, the tax burden falls on domestic producers in other ways (payroll taxes, for example), ways that are not directly reflected in the price. When a VAT country exports its goods to a non-VAT country, it sends goods that have less of a built-in tax burden than the domestic goods of the non-VAT country.

Furthermore, when a non-VAT country tries to export to a VAT country, its goods carry with them a much higher built-in tax burden.

For example, an electric fan from a VAT country might cost $20 domestically, including the VAT. The non-VAT country might also produce an electric fan that would sell domestically at $20. When the fan with VAT is exported to the world market for fans, the VAT comes off so the export price is $17. Meanwhile, the non-VAT country would still be selling its electric fans at $20, because the payroll and other taxes are embedded into the price.

Advocates of tariff duties argue that the extra levies merely equalize tax differences and make competition fairer rather than distorted. However, it should be noted that it can be very difficult to determine the relative tax differences between countries and within specific industries.

To access Worksheet 21.1 on the possible beginning of a trade war, please visit www.pearsonbacconline.com and follow the onscreen instructions.

To prevent the dumping of foreign goods onto the domestic market

Dumping occurs when one country exports goods at a price below their average costs (Figures 21.1 and 21.2). This implies that exporters are losing money on these goods and are therefore preying on domestic producers hoping to steal away domestic consumers with unsustainably low prices. Dumping does occur, although with perhaps less frequency than complaining countries would admit. Some firms dump goods in an attempt to drive competition off of the market. The dumping firms then raise prices when domestic competition has been destroyed. Dumping firms might also be selling off surplus goods, having extracted higher prices for them in their domestic markets. For example, in recent years, the sell-off of excess clothing and textiles to African countries has prompted cries of dumping from domestic clothing makers there. If this were only an occasional instance, there would be little harm done. But when the practice is sustained over time, long-term damage to domestic sellers can occur. In contrast, the benefit to domestic consumers, in the form of cheaper clothes in the long run, is debatable.

Countries which believe they are victims of dumping can take their case to the WTO. Allegations of dumping, however, have proven difficult to confirm. Across countries, wide

Dumping is the selling of goods to another country at a price below the original domestic production costs.

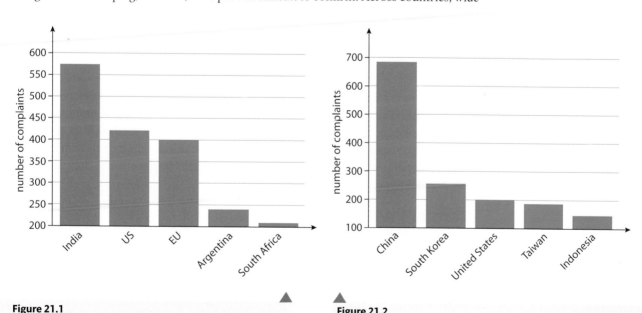

Figure 21.1
Dumping complaints: countries filing most complaints, 1995–2003.

Figure 21.2
Dumping complaints: countries most accused of dumping, 1995–2003.

To learn more about dumping, visit www.pearsonhotlinks.com, enter the title or ISBN of this book and select weblink 21.1.

differences in cost structures, as well as a lack of transparency and uniform accounting procedures, can make the calculation of relative costs exceptionally complicated. If one country wins a dumping complaint against another in the WTO, it can establish peremptory protectionist measures against the offender. However, this approach, as with any escalation of protectionist barriers, can lead to bitter and counter-productive trade wars.

To diversify the production base of a developing country

Many poor countries export a limited range of goods, and typically these goods are basic commodities. When the market price drops dramatically, this can cause significant loss of income for the country that relies on it. As a result, it is argued that some poor countries would benefit from selectively protecting some domestic markets in an attempt to diversify the economic base. With such protection, perhaps for sunrise industries, the country would be less vulnerable to wide swings in global market prices for their goods.

This argument, like most others, ignores the benefits gained by comparative advantage by demonstrating the risks of over-specialization. It also values a form of economic security rather than income gains. At the same time, it is understandable that any country would not want its entire economic future to be dependent on one industry. Brazil in the 1960s feared that coffee would be its only viable export, a situation that currently concerns Ethiopia. Furthermore, where these countries rely on extraction industries like mining, the worry can become rather acute as the resource is depleted.

To enforce product standards

Product standards exist to protect consumers from hazardous products as well as to ensure a reputation of quality production across an industry. These standards are likely to raise the cost of production. In recent years, countries have used product standard rules to challenge the import of goods, arguing that those products threaten the national safety or health. These claims can be derived from scandals in the news, such as the poisonous dog food and toothpaste produced in China in 2008. Or they can be based on disputed scientific claims about new methods of production, such as the long-running conflict over US hormone-injected beef. Several European countries, as well as Japan, have restricted such imports from the US, citing public health concerns.

To raise government revenue

A nation can raise revenue through a variety of tax methods. In poor countries, where income tax compliance is low, customs duties can provide a vital source of money. Nevertheless, the additional taxes still distort the market by taxing goods that are wanted or needed by the domestic population. By raising import prices, they may also limit the importation of important resources needed for growth and development to flourish by taxing needed capital goods or health products.

To protect against unfairly low labour costs

A popular argument among wealthy countries is that many imported goods are produced at wage rates far below those paid in their own domestic industries. This argument can be further extended to include hiring and working conditions that would be considered unacceptable at home. The combination of lower wages and reduced labour standards makes it impossible for industries at home to pay a living wage to their workers and provide them with safe and reasonable work environments.

However, for many countries a surplus of labour is their primary comparative advantage, allowing them to produce competitively in industries where they may lack technological knowledge or the latest capital equipment. The Chinese coastal town of Datang has become known as Sock City for its massive share of the global sock market. Many of Datang's workers sewed socks by hand in the 1970s, and the industry grew in large part because of its labour-cost advantage. All the while, China and other low-cost labour markets have won this share from Europe and the US – countries with a high labour cost.

To protect strategic industries

Plausible arguments can be made that military or defence needs should be produced domestically for security reasons. Buying sophisticated telecommunications equipment from foreign suppliers, for example, could make a country vulnerable if relations grow strained between the buying and selling countries. This argument can be used, less convincingly, to protect commodity industries such as food and metals. In these instances, it is more likely to be a case of protection of domestic employment or outright fears of foreign competition than legitimate strategic worry.

To overcome a balance of payments deficit

The balance of payments measures the flow of money into and out of a country. The export and import of goods and services, called the trade balance, is normally a major part of that accounting. Therefore, countries that find they are spending excessively on imported goods, thereby worsening their trade deficit, may enact protectionist policies to address this imbalance.

This approach, called expenditure-switching, is regarded by most economists as only a temporary solution. While it may lower imports for a short time, the structural problems that are causing the imbalance are not addressed by this policy. In the meantime, higher tariffs or stricter trade barriers continue to distort trade and deny the potential gains from comparative advantage.

To improve the terms of trade

Terms of trade is defined in detail in Chapter 25. Briefly, it is the ratio of export prices to import prices. The idea is that a large country might block access to its market with a tariff that could harm import demand enough to reduce demand for the imported good and reduce the price of those imports. For this to be true, the reduction of demand must outweigh the increased price effect of the tariff. The relatively small gains in terms of trade are only true for larger countries, however. It is also debatable whether countries would want to antagonize smaller neighbours over such limited gains. The weakened relations between the two countries could lead to retaliation and an escalating trade dispute.

To learn more about protectionism, visit www. pearsonhotlinks.com, enter the title or ISBN of this book and select weblink 21.2.

As trade globalizes, the share of trade (as measured by exports) is likely to shift from region to region, country to country. Figure 21.3 (overleaf) shows the regional changes from 2000 to 2007. Remember that the shares of the various regions are derived from an ever-growing export market. In other words, a region may lose a portion of its export market share but still be exporting more in absolute terms because overall global trade is growing.

To access Worksheet 21.2 on a call for protectionism, please visit www. pearsonbacconline.com and follow the onscreen instructions.

Sometimes, protectionism serves no purpose whatsoever. The US has had a shoe tariff since the 1930s. And what has happened over the years is that the world's shoe production has moved to China. The tariff, still in place today, protects no one – it simply harms American shoe consumers.

Figure 21.3
Shares of world exports by region.

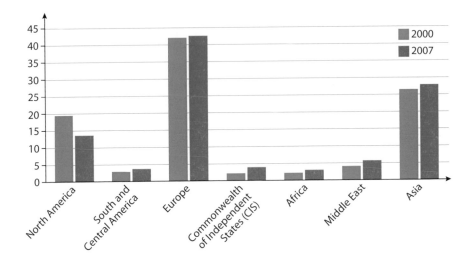

 21.2   # The case against protectionism

Learning outcomes
• Discuss the arguments against trade protection, including a misallocation of resources, the danger of retaliation and 'trade wars', the potential for corruption, increased costs of production due to lack of competition, higher prices for domestic consumers, increased costs of imported factors of production and reduced export competitiveness.

Arguments against protectionism

While Chapter 20 outlined the virtues of free trade, this section deals with the specific disadvantages of protectionist policies.

Misallocation of resources

Countries that protect declining industries compel their consumers to pay higher prices. This is an unnecessary misallocation of income to inefficient producers. Furthermore, because such industries are larger than they would otherwise be, they draw more workers and capital than would occur under free trade conditions. It follows that industries with the potential to realize their comparative advantage do not get these workers, nor the benefit of access to capital. It all goes to the inefficient but politically connected dinosaur firm.

Escalation to a trade war

What might start out as a dispute over subsidies or unfair bureaucratic barriers can degenerate quickly into a damaging trade conflict. When this occurs, trade can grind to a halt and economic growth is imperilled. This kind of escalation took hold during the Great Depression, as desperate governments resorted to protectionism as a way to prevent unemployment from deepening. Many economists have blamed this rapid shutdown of world trade as a major factor in the entrenchment of the crisis.

In the more recent troubles of 2008, trade complaints grew rapidly, while many governments and the WTO urged everyone to stay calm and avoid sparking a round of retaliatory policies. Despite a few isolated incidents of a tariff or quota, trade remained largely as free as it was before the crisis. Though it may seem paradoxical that WTO rulings actually allow retaliatory policies, it is believed that the WTO's role in adjudicating trade disputes tends to lower the chance of bad policy being made in the heat of the moment.

Protectionism as a corruption magnet

Industries that appeal for protection have a distinct economic interest in securing as much of it as they can. Higher tariffs mean more revenue for those producers, which creates a potentially very large incentive to bribe lawmakers to enact such laws. An industry that gets $300 million in extra profits from a quota against their competitor can surely spare some of that money to help their political allies. This opens the door to special political favours for any constituency, and erodes the integrity of the government.

Domestic complacency causes higher prices and costs

Protected firms quickly understand that their real profits come from staying protected, and thus put more energy into persuading the public and politicians of their case. They have less of an incentive to actually modernize or innovate for greater efficiency. After all, that would weaken their case for assistance the next time the laws are up for renewal. With such poor incentives, firms tend to be complacent and resist change. Thus, consumers and firms that buy from the protected firm pay higher prices. These higher costs, if borne by domestic producers, harm the ability of other domestic firms to supply products, reducing potential output. For consumers, this can result in a lower standard of living, especially when the protected goods are necessities.

Higher import costs

Protectionist measures directly affect the firms and consumers who buy imported goods. These higher prices might drive some imports out of the market entirely, relegating domestic producers and consumers to higher prices and possibly inferior quality goods. Again, these costs cause lower output levels for firms and lower standard of living for consumers.

Reduced export competitiveness

Firms that use imported resources pay higher costs. Firms that hope to export suffer the indirect harm of having workers and resources (capital) drawn away by inefficient producers. These related effects suggest that protectionism can corrode seemingly unrelated export-based businesses. A recent example occurred when China expanded its quota on cotton imports, allowing in more cotton than ever before. This occurred under pressure from textile makers who were paying ever-higher prices on a market protected by strict quotas.

Gains from trade: from closed economy to free trade

Before examining the types and effects of protectionism, let's look briefly at the gains from trade. Figure 21.4 shows a closed economy domestic market price and quantity at P_E and Q_E. Were this market open to trade, foreign suppliers would supply at the world price of P_{WORLD}. This price is established by a multitude of sellers and buyers worldwide. This means that the domestic market for this country, being a relatively small piece of a large market, can import as much as it wants of the product at the world price. Thus, the P_{WORLD} price reflects a perfectly elastic supply curve for these imported goods.

Figure 21.4

From closed economy to open economy.

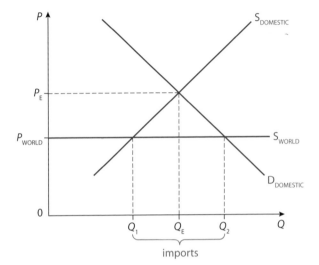

At the lower world price, far fewer domestic suppliers can afford to produce, so domestic production stops at Q_1. But more is demanded at that lower price as well. The country imports the amount the domestic firms cannot supply, as well as the extra quantity demanded. In Figure 21.4, this is shown as quantity Q_1 to Q_2 – imports supplied by foreign producers. As a result, the outcome of free trade is to improve the welfare of consumers, who enjoy more of the product at a lower price. Another outcome is to reduce the revenue of the relatively inefficient domestic producers, who produce less at the new lower world price. It is this loss in revenue, or rather the fear of it, that prompts domestic producers to request protectionist help from their governments.

21.3 Types of protectionism

Learning outcomes
- Explain, using a tariff diagram, the effects of imposing a tariff on imported goods on different stakeholders, including domestic producers, foreign producers, consumers and the government.
- Explain, using a diagram, the effects of setting a quota on foreign producers on different stakeholders, including domestic producers, foreign producers, consumers and the government.

- Explain, using a diagram, the effects of giving a subsidy to domestic producers or different stakeholders, including domestic producers, foreign producers, consumers and the government.
- Describe administrative barriers that may be used as a means of protection.
- Evaluate the effect of different types of trade protection.
- (HL only) Calculate from diagrams the effects of imposing a tariff on imported goods on different stakeholders including domestic producers, foreign producers, consumers and the government.
- (HL only) Calculate from diagrams the effects of setting a quota on foreign producers on different stakeholders including domestic producers, foreign producers, consumers and the government.
- (HL only) Calculate from diagrams the effects of giving a subsidy to domestic producers on different stakeholders including domestic producers, foreign producers, consumers and the government.

Tariffs

A tariff is a tax charged on imported goods. Taxes are viewed as an added cost of production by firms, so a tariff shifts the supply curve to the left or backwards. In Figure 21.5, a tax on imported goods shifts the supply curve S_{WORLD} upwards, reflecting higher costs imposed by the tax.

A tariff is an import tax placed on a good produced abroad.

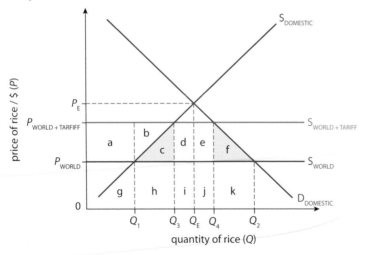

◀ **Figure 21.5**
Tariff designed to reduce the quantity of imported rice.

Domestic producers

Before the tariff, the domestic supply was 0–Q_1, from which the revenue earned is shown by the box g. Now at the new tariff price, domestic producers can afford to produce more, and so increase production to 0–Q_3, and earn greater revenue at $a + b + c + g + h$.

Foreign producers

Before the tariff, foreign production (imports) was Q_1–Q_2 and earned revenue $h + i + j + k$. At the higher tariff price, domestic producers take the share of the market shown by Q_1–Q_3, and the consumer quantity demanded decreases from 0–Q_2 to 0–Q_4. So now foreign production (imports) drops to Q_3–Q_4 and import revenue declines to $i + j$. Foreign producers do not, however, enjoy the benefit of the higher prices, as the government collects the difference between the world import price and the new tariff price, shown by d + e.

Government

Government collects the import tax, which can be a substantial benefit to the country's revenue base. This tariff revenue is shown in the boxes d + e.

Consumers

Consumers pay higher prices, from P_{WORLD} to $P_{WORLD + TARIFF}$ and now buy less of the product, from $0-Q_2$ to $0-Q_4$.

Welfare loss

The new market share enjoyed by domestic producers only occurs because of the artificially high tariff price. The area of the blue triangle c represents an inefficiency form of welfare loss, because that amount would already be produced at the world price, but now consumers must pay more for domestic producers to supply it. At the same time, consumers restrict their overall demand from $0-Q_2$ to $0-Q_4$ as a result of the tariff price, and so consume less. The reduced consumption overall represents another welfare loss, the loss of consumer surplus enjoyed before the tariff raised prices. This lost surplus is represented by the blue area f.

In sum, the tariff causes the price of the good to rise. If this product were a factor cost in other products (e.g. tyres for cars) then the price of the final goods (cars) would rise as well. Smaller quantities of the good are consumed, harming domestic consumers and reducing their welfare. Domestic producers enjoy the benefits of this protection, earning more revenue and producing more output, but they do so inefficiently and at the expense of consumers paying the higher tariff prices. Meanwhile, the government can gain some tax revenue that was not possible before imposing the tariff.

It is logical to conclude that domestic producers have a strong incentive to keep the tariff in place, while the government also enjoys the benefit of the tariff. Consumers, however, may not be aware of the impact of the tariff. If consumers are conscious of the tariff, it still represents a relatively minor impact on their welfare when measured against the gains made by the producer. The result is that consumers feel a relatively smaller incentive to fight the tariff politically. Foreign producers, while not having a political voice on the issue, can urge their governments to retaliate against the country imposing the tariffs. This can result in arbitration with the WTO or an outright trade war should the matter escalate beyond this dispute.

To access Worksheet 21.3 on tariffs, please visit www.pearsonbacconline.com and follow the onscreen instructions.

To learn more about tariffs, visit www.pearsonhotlinks.com, enter the title or ISBN of this book and select weblink 21.3.

EXERCISES

4   For decades, the EU has levied high tariffs on bananas imported from Latin America. Create an appropriate diagram to show this situation. To the left of your diagram list the beneficiaries of this policy under the heading 'Helped,' and to the right of the diagram make a list of the injured parties under the heading 'Hurt.' Be prepared to explain the reasons for each item on your list.

Quotas

Governments can decide to simply restrict the amount or number of a good allowed into the country. This restriction of the quantity imported is called a quota. For example, in the recent past, the US has placed strict quotas on imported textiles, a limit that most profoundly affected Taiwan and, more recently, China. Like a tariff, a quota tends to raise both domestic and import prices, but in ways that are unusual compared to the other protectionist diagrams.

In a closed market (Figure 21.6), producers will produce Q_E at a price of P_E. If that market is open to trade, world producers can sell at a much lower price, P_{WORLD}. Among domestic producers, relatively few can produce at P_{WORLD}, and they produce only the amount $0-Q_1$. World producers can sell the rest, Q_1-Q_2. Note that the world supply is perfectly elastic at that price, reflecting the fact that for most commodities, the size of the market is quite large compared to the demand of any single country. Therefore, the world market can supply as much as this country is willing and able to buy, represented by domestic demand, at the market price P_{WORLD}. For domestic producers, this marks a dramatic fall in revenue. Now they only receive a, where the foreign sellers receive b + c + d + e.

A quota is a limit on the physical quantity of a good that can be imported into the country.

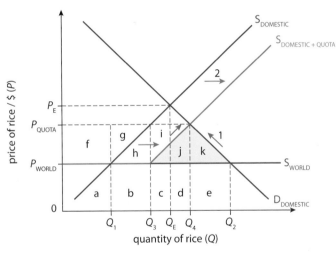

Figure 21.6
Quota to reduce the quantity of imported rice.

At this point, domestic rice producers are likely to call for protection from the overwhelming competition of foreign suppliers. If they convince the government to implement a quota, world producers will be limited to a specific amount, Q_1-Q_3. So, at P_{WORLD}, the domestic market still supplies only $0-Q_1$, and Q_1-Q_3 is imported.

From this point onwards, there is a gap between the amount demanded, $0-Q_2$, and the amount supplied, which has stopped at $0-Q_3$. This shortage will cause producers, including foreign ones, to start raising prices. Producers begin to supply more to the market at higher prices, and consumers reduce their quantity demanded along the demand curve. This process, denoted by the two green arrows, continues until the market is cleared at P_{QUOTA} and Q_4. As producers supply more, this creates a new extension of the domestic supply curve, $S_{DOMESTIC + QUOTA}$, shown by the red arrows. Therefore, the market settles at a price below the domestic equilibrium P_E, but above the free trade price P_{WORLD}.

This situation creates clear winners and losers, as well as market inefficiencies and deadweight losses.

Domestic producers

Before the quota, domestic producers earned revenue represented by box a. After the quota, they earn a + f, and i + j + c + d where domestic suppliers resumed production.

Foreign producers

Before the quota, foreign producers earned revenue represented by boxes b + c + d + e. After, foreign producers sell fewer units, but get a higher price (P_{QUOTA}) for each of them. Their new revenue is shown by areas b + g + h. This could be viewed as an improvement over the alternative of a similar tariff, where the increased revenue from higher prices (g + h) would all go to the government. Here, the foreign producer receives that revenue.

Consumers

Before, consumers paid the lower price P_{WORLD} and could buy more on the market, $0–Q_2$ rather than $0–Q_4$. The quota causes higher prices and less consumption.

Government

Government gains no obvious advantage from a quota, although it is possible that any sales tax receipts would be lower with fewer goods on the market.

Market inefficiency

Where domestic supply resumes and begins to rise again, at Q_3, domestic producers only supply more with the incentive of higher prices. Before the quota, that same quantity was produced at the lower world price. This unnecessary increase in prices marks a global market inefficiency, where consumers pay more than the market would otherwise require, and is denoted by the blue triangle j.

Welfare loss

When the post-quota quantity demanded decreases to Q_4, it represents a loss of consumer surplus previously enjoyed by buyers of the good. This loss is marked by the blue triangle k.

Over the long term, like all forms of protectionism, quotas can lead to the dependence of domestic industries on government assistance rather than their own efforts.

Voluntary export restraints (VERs)

When a trade dispute is looming, the exporting country can offer to voluntarily limit the amount of their exports. This has the exact same effect as a quota of a similar size, and is also shown by Figure 21.6. This may pre-empt a worse outcome for the foreign producer, and may satisfy the protectionist demands of the domestic industries. A VER has advantages for the exporting country. Like a quota, any increase in market prices goes to the foreign producers. Politically, it prevents a tariff or quota from becoming law, and as a result is more likely to be flexibly applied in the future.

A voluntary export restraint is self-imposed quota, put in place by the importing country or industry.

Legally formed barriers can become entrenched and are much more difficult to change or remove. In recent decades, Japanese producers of cars and microchips have agreed to such restraints in US markets. Meanwhile, US beef producers have sought out a voluntary restraint on exports to South Korea, in an effort to prevent an outright ban.

EXERCISES

5 In the 1900s and early 2000s, the US imposed quotas on imports of textile goods from Taiwan and China. Create a diagram that shows an active quota on US imports of Chinese textiles. To the left, list beneficiaries of this policy; to the right, list injured parties. Be prepared to explain the reasons for your lists.

Subsidies

A country can also choose to protect domestic producers by subsidizing them. Subsidies are sums paid to firms by government to produce a particular good. A review of simple, closed economy subsidies is found in Chapter 2. These subsidies can be of two types: lump sum or per unit. A lump-sum subsidy has the effect of lowering overall costs and encouraging production. Per-unit subsidies are payments made for every extra unit produced. We will consider protectionist subsidies from the per-unit perspective. If the country in question were to subsidize its rice market, it would pay a specific amount for each level of output (number of bushels, kilograms, or tons).

A subsidy in the international context is a government payment to a firm that can be used to promote exports and/or reduce the quantity of imports.

Figure 21.7 demonstrates the effects of a subsidy intended to reduce the amount of imported rice. Facing open competition before the subsidy, domestic production only measures $0–Q_1$. The rest of the market is satisfied by foreign producers selling $Q_1–Q_2$ at a market price of P_{WORLD}. Domestic producers earn far less, represented by box a, whereas foreign producers earn b + c + d. This kind of potent competition could devastate local production, so domestic rice farmers request government help.

American cotton farmers are the largest beneficiaries of agricultural subsidies, at a great cost to the American taxpayer.

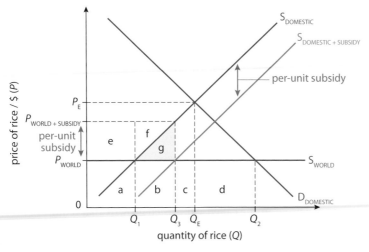

◀ **Figure 21.7**
Subsidy to reduce the quantity of imported rice.

If that help takes the form of a subsidy, the government would pay a subsidy that can be seen as the distance between the two supply curves, or as the distance between P_{WORLD} and $P_{WORLD + SUBSIDY}$. That amount would be paid for each unit of production. This has the effect of lowering the production costs for rice farmers, increasing supply to a new level of production, $0–Q_3$. Foreign supply drops to $Q_3–Q_2$. Note: the price of rice has not changed. Domestic producers are merely now able to produce more at the world price than before.

This significantly changes the amount of revenue earned by each group. Domestic producers now earn a + b + e + f + g, while foreign revenue drops to just c + d. The total amount of government expenditure on the subsidy is shown by the amount of the per-unit subsidy multiplied by the amount produced domestically, which is ultimately $0–Q_3$. So the government spends $e + f + g$ on rice subsidies.

Just as with tariffs and quotas, this form of protectionism ignores comparative advantage and distorts the market. In the market for rice, the amount $Q_1–Q_3$ switches from foreign, low-cost production, to domestic higher-cost production. Foreign producers would have produced that amount without a subsidy, but domestic producers could only enter the market because they were paid the subsidy. The triangle g shows the area of inefficiency, where resources are being misallocated.

Export promotion subsidy

In a more extreme fashion, if the subsidy is high enough, a country can promote the export of their domestic production. Figure 21.8 shows how the domestic price could be lowered to a point beneath the world price and the country can export the excess.

Figure 21.8 ▶
Subsidy to promote exports (export subsidy).

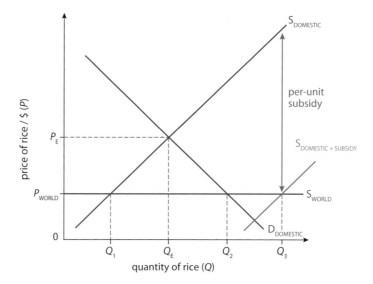

In this case, domestic producers receive such a large subsidy that they can produce more at P_{WORLD} than is demanded by their home market. Before the subsidy, they imported $Q_1–Q_2$. After the subsidy, they export $Q_2–Q_3$. The same outcomes still apply, although with much more extreme effect. Domestic producer revenue soars, foreign revenue is completely eliminated. The amount of the subsidy rises significantly. The extent of market inefficiency grows, as resources are more pervasively misallocated.

This policy is part of a programme called 'export-led growth' that requires governments to select likely export 'winners' from their domestic industries. Ideally, such winners would be somewhat competitive on world markets and need only a relatively small subsidy to become export competitive. If this were true, the difference between P_E and P_{WORLD} would be smaller than in Figure 21.8, and a smaller subsidy would accomplish the same goal.

To access Worksheet 21.4 on tariffs, quotas and subsidies, please visit www.pearsonbacconline. com and follow the onscreen instructions.

It is worth noting that such subsidies will come at significant cost to taxpayers, and mark a major redistribution of resource from those taxpayers to the favoured industries. In recent years, it has often been claimed that successful export economies such as Korea and China have resorted to this kind of extraordinary subsidy. If true, these countries are expending considerable resource in the process. This form of export promotion also ignores comparative advantage, and is likely to lead to industry dependence on the subsidies.

Administrative barriers

Bureaucratic barriers

Countries may impede the penetration of their markets with waves of paperwork and legal requirements that raise the cost of importing. While any imported good must clear appropriate customs checks for health, safety and valuation, it is possible to extend and amplify these requirements so as to frustrate potential importers. The time and energy required may prevent potential importers from making the attempt, so imports are effectively reduced.

Product standards

Health, safety and environmental considerations can also be used to exclude goods from the local market. Imports may be expected to meet specific technical standards, and importers may be required to test and prove the safety and quality of their goods. This may raise costs to the point where many importers decide the extra cost is not worth it, and thus quit their attempt to enter the market. Where domestic producers and government regulatory agencies create these import standards with the goal of limiting imports, they are engaging in protectionism.

Among the more famous examples of this type of dispute is the resistance, on the grounds of health safety, of the UK, the EU and Japan to imports of hormone-fed US beef. In another instance, on entering the EU, small farmers in Romania had exports of their milk products to other EU countries blocked on the grounds of hygiene, and had their EU subsidies withheld until they agreed to milk their cows by machine.

Environmental standards

Environmental standards provoke passionate debates in trade matters. The depletion of common-access resources, with endangered species being particularly controversial, sparks fierce argument. Japanese whalers, for example, have long argued that theirs is a legitimate activity, based on the use of available resources, and that restrictions against it are disguised protectionism. In these cases, the WTO is asked to rule on the legitimacy of the claims.

Qualifications

To learn more about barriers to trade, visit www.pearsonhotlinks.com, enter the title or ISBN of this book and select weblink 21.4.

The providers of domestic services such as teachers, physicians, lawyers, electricians and many others typically require specific qualifications to work legally in any given country. While justified on the grounds of raising professional standards of practice and expertise, such qualifications may also prevent capable workers from relocating to other countries. This keeps domestic prices (wages) high and protects domestic employment in these fields.

Exchange rates

Exchange rates are covered more extensively in Chapter 22. An exchange rate is basically the amount one currency commonly and currently accepted in exchange for a unit of another. As the price of your own currency decreases, in terms of what other countries must pay to receive it, so do the price of your exports to the rest of the world. Low exchange rates make all your exports less expensive and, therefore, more attractive. They also make imports less desirable, effectively protecting domestic markets at the same time. In theory, these rates would adjust automatically. As quantity demanded for these low-priced exports grows, there would be upward pressure on the exchange rate as well.

To access Worksheet 21.5 on protectionism data response questions please visit www. pearsonbacconline.com and follow the onscreen instructions.

Countries can choose to intentionally manipulate their exchange rates to encourage exports, as China has allegedly done in recent years. But, in doing so, a country runs the risk of over-pricing significant imported resources and therefore limiting aggregate supply, possibly negating the boost that lower exchange rates might provide.

Nationalistic campaigns

An industry desperate to regain market share may also promote their products in patriotic terms. In theory, this should boost the domestic demand for locally produced goods. These campaigns often claim product superiority, or appeal to fellow countrymen to protect domestic employment. Such campaigns can gain substantial energy from the perception that one or more foreign countries are competing unfairly. As such, the campaigns may have initial temporary success in making marginal market gains for domestic producers. However, the cost in terms of advertising and promotion can be significant when measured against the results. Moreover, consumers can tire of these campaigns if they see little difference between competing goods over time.

Calculating the effects of protectionist policies (HL only)

When given specific values for price and quantity, we can calculate the effects of protectionist policies on all the relevant stakeholders: domestic and foreign producers, consumers, and the government.

Tariffs

Worked example

Figure 21.9 shows a tariff of $15 per unit placed on steel.

Figure 21.9
Tariff of $15 per unit placed on steel.

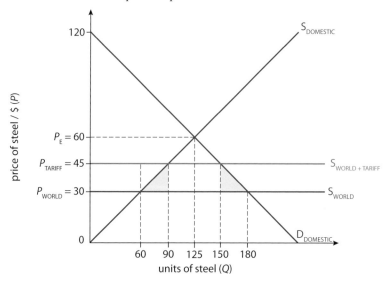

Domestic producers previously sold 60 units at the world price of $30. After the tariff, they are paid $45 and sell 90.

Domestic producer revenue before tariff:

$$P_{\text{WORLD}} \times Q_{\text{DOMESTIC}} = \$30 \times 60 = \$1800$$

Domestic producer revenue after tariff:

$P_{TARIFF} \times Q_{NEW\ DOMESTIC}$ = $45 × 90 = $4050

Foreign producers receive the world price of $30, but their imports are reduced from 120 units to 60.

Foreign producer revenue before tariff:

$P_{WORLD} \times Q_{IMPORTS}$ = $30 × (180 − 60) = $3600

Foreign producer revenue after tariff:

$P_{WORLD} \times Q_{NEW\ IMPORTS}$ = $30 × (150 − 90) = $1800

Consumer surplus is calculated as the area of the consumer surplus triangle, $\frac{1}{2}(b \times h)$.

Consumer surplus before tariff:

½(highest price − P_{WORLD}) × Q_{WORLD} = 0.5(120 − 30) × 180 = $8100

Consumer surplus after tariff:

½(highest price − P_{TARIFF}) × Q_{WORLD} = 0.5(120 − 45) × 150 = $5625

Government revenue is calculated as the amount of the tariff multiplied by the number of imports.

Government revenue before tariff:

0 = no tax collected

Government revenue after tariff:

(P_{TARIFF} − P_{WORLD}) × $Q_{NEW\ IMPORTS}$ = ($45 − $30) × (150 − 90) = $900

The two blue triangles represent the net loss of social welfare resulting from the tariff.

Welfare loss of tariff = 2(0.5(30 × 15)) = 2 × 225 = $450

Quotas

Worked example

Figure 21.10 shows a quota of 30 imported units of steel.

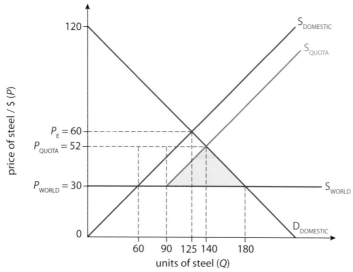

Figure 21.10 Quota of 30 imported units of steel.

Domestic producers previously sold 60 units at the world price of $30. After the quota, they are paid $52 and sell 110.

Domestic producer revenue before quota:

$P_{\text{WORLD}} \times Q_{\text{DOMESTIC}} = \$30 \times 60 = \$1800$

Domestic producer revenue after quota:

$P_{\text{QUOTA}} \times Q_{\text{NEW DOMESTIC}} = \$52 \times ((60 - 0) + (140 - 90)) = \$5720$

Foreign producers receive the same quota price of $52, but their imports are reduced from 120 units to 30.

Foreign producer revenue before quota:

$P_{\text{WORLD}} \times Q_{\text{IMPORTS}} = \$30 \times (180 - 60) = \$3600$

Foreign producer revenue after quota:

$P_{\text{QUOTA}} \times Q_{\text{NEW IMPORTS}} = \$52 \times (90 - 60) = \$1560$

Consumer surplus is calculated as the area of the consumer surplus triangle, $\frac{1}{2}(b \times h)$:

Consumer surplus before quota:

$\frac{1}{2}(\text{highest price} - P_{\text{WORLD}}) \times Q_{\text{WORLD}} = 0.5(120 - 30) \times 180 = \$8100$

Consumer surplus after quota:

$\frac{1}{2}(\text{highest price} - P_{\text{QUOTA}}) \times Q_{\text{QUOTA}} = 0.5(120 - 52) \times 140 = \$4760$

Government revenue is calculated as the amount of the tariff multiplied by the number of imports.

Government revenue before quota:

$0 =$ no tax collected

Government revenue after quota:

$0 =$ no tax collected

The blue triangle represents the net loss of social welfare resulting form the quota.

Welfare loss of quota $= 0.5(50 \times 22) + 0.5(40 \times 22) = \$990$

Subsidy

Worked example

Figure 21.11 shows a per-unit subsidy of $15, the same value as the per-unit tariff above. This subsidy is designed to reduce the number of imports.

Figure 21.11
Subsidy.

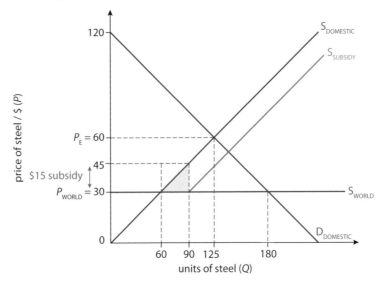

Domestic producer revenue before subsidy:

$P_{WORLD} \times Q_{DOMESTIC} = \$30 \times 60 = \$1800$

Domestic producer revenue after subsidy:

$P_{SUBSIDY} \times Q_{NEW\ DOMESTIC} = \$45 \times 90 = \$4050$

Foreign producers receive the world price of $30, but imports are reduced from 120 to 90.

Foreign producer revenue before subsidy:

$P_{WORLD} \times Q_{IMPORTS} = \$30 \times (180 - 60) = \$3600$

Foreign producer revenue after subsidy:

$P_{WORLD} \times Q_{NEW\ IMPORTS} = \$30 \times (180 - 90) = \$2700$

Consumer surplus is calculated as the area of the consumer surplus triangle, $\frac{1}{2}(b \times h)$:

Consumer surplus before subsidy:

$\frac{1}{2}(\text{highest price} - P_{WORLD}) \times Q_{WORLD} = 0.5(120 - 30) \times 180 = \$8100$

Consumer surplus after subsidy:

$\frac{1}{2}(\text{highest price} - P_{WORLD}) \times Q_{WORLD} = 0.5(120 - 30) \times 180 = \$8100$

(Note that because equilibrium P and Q remain constant, the consumer surplus is unchanged.)

Government expenditure is calculated as the amount of the subsidy multiplied by the number of imports.

Government expenditure before subsidy:

0 = no subsidy paid

Government expenditure after subsidy:

per-unit subsidy $\times Q_{DOMESTIC} = \$15 \times 90 = \$1350$

The blue triangle represents the net loss of social welfare resulting form the subsidy.

Welfare loss of subsidy $= 0.5(15 \times 30) = \$225$

To access Worksheet 21.6 on Vietnam's shrimpers please visit www.pearsonbacconline.com and follow the onscreen instructions.

Extension topic: quotas *vs* tariffs (HL only)

Figure 21.12 is a quota diagram employing the same supply and demand as the original tariff diagram, Figure 21.9 (page 446). The tariff of $15 limited imports to 60 units; here, a quota of 60 imported units is set.

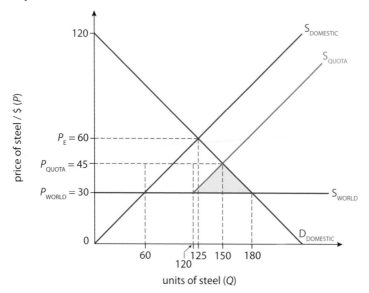

Figure 21.12
A quota of 60 units.

We can now compare quotas and tariffs. Most of the equilibrium effects are the same. Even the price rises by exactly the same amount, $15. Here's where the results diverge. To whom goes the increase in price? Domestic producers, of course, receive their share. But instead of the government receiving their tax revenue of $900, that revenue goes to the foreign producers.

This reinforces an important point about trade negotiations. For the importing countries, a quota is far better than a tariff because the importers receive the price differential. Better yet, when an importing country sees that quotas are to be established, it might volunteer to impose its own quota (a VER) to avoid any trade restrictions becoming law. Once legislated, trade rules like tariffs and quotas become difficult to repeal, unless done under orders from the WTO. A voluntary restraint, on the other hand, can be eased or lifted through diplomatic negotiation, and tends to be more flexible in the long run.

HL EXERCISES

6 Create a free trade diagram that has the following values:

    a a supply curve with quantities of 45 units at $15, 30 units at $10, 15 units at $5

    b a demand curve with quantities of 15 units at $15, 30 units at $10, 45 units at $5

    c world price: $5; domestic price $10

    d @ the world price, domestic quantity of 15 units

    e @ the world price, foreign imports of 30 units.

7 Impose a tariff of $3.

    a Draw in the expected results for domestic/import quantities on your diagram (you may estimate these, based on how your diagram is drawn).

    b Based on your diagram, calculate the following:

        i domestic producer revenue before the tariff

        ii domestic producer revenue after the tariff

        iii foreign revenue before the tariff

        iv foreign revenue after the tariff

        v the total tariff amount

        vi the areas of inefficiency and welfare loss.

8 Using the same starting values as in question 6, create a new diagram. Impose a quota of 15 units.

    a Draw in the expected results for domestic/import quantities on your diagram (you may estimate these, based on how your diagram is drawn).

    b Based on your diagram, calculate the following:

        i domestic producer revenue before the quota

        ii domestic producer revenue after the quota

        iii foreign revenue before the quota

        iv foreign revenue after the quota

        v the amount of dollars representing area of inefficiency.

9 Using the same starting values as in question 6, create a new diagram. Place a subsidy of $2 on domestic production.

    a Draw in the expected results for domestic/import quantities on your diagram (you may estimate these, based on how your diagram is drawn).

    b Based on your diagram, calculate the following:

        i domestic producer revenue before the subsidy

        ii domestic producer revenue after the subsidy

        iii foreign revenue after the subsidy

        iv the area of inefficiency

        v the total amount of the subsidy.

1

Court backs EU anti-dumping duties on Chinese shoes

r A European court has ruled that a decision to impose anti-**dumping** measures on shoes from China and Vietnam was sound, a court statement in Brussels said on Thursday.

s Beijing has filed a complaint with the World Trade Organization accusing the European Union of imposing illegal duties after the EU extended for 15 months, at the end of 2009, penalty taxes that were first imposed in October 2006 on shoes with leather uppers from the two countries.

t The General Court, a branch of the European Court of Justice, ruled against Chinese footwear producers in a series of six cases where 'applicants requested annulment of the 2006 regulation,' the statement said.

u 'The anti-dumping measure ... thus remains in force,' it added.

v The challenges cited what were faulty and erroneous analyses of the costs of Chinese and Vietnamese imports to European Union producers, who include some of the biggest brand names in the footwear world.

w The court 'rejected all of the applicants' claims and dismissed the actions for annulment,' ordering them 'to pay their own costs and the costs incurred by' the EU in defending the cases.

x Beijing announced at the start of February that it was filing a complaint with the **WTO**. If the two sides do not reach an agreement within 60 days, the WTO complaints body will rule on the case.

y European Trade Commissioner Karel De Gucht was in Hanoi on Tuesday to open negotiations with Vietnam on a free trade agreement with the EU.

z He said there that the European Commission had a 'very solid case' in its imposition of anti-dumping measures against shoes from China and Vietnam.

Agence France-Presse, 4 March 2010

a Define the following terms (indicated in bold in the text) from the text:

   i dumping (paragraph r)   (2 marks) [AO1]

   ii WTO (paragraph x).   (2 marks) [AO1]

b Using a diagram, show the effect of dumping on the market for shoes in the EU.

                                                       (4 marks) [AO2], [AO4]

c Using a diagram, show the effect of the EU rulings that allow tariff duties on imported shoes in the eurozone.   (4 marks) [AO2], [AO4]

d Evaluate the effectiveness of the EU's anti-dumping measures.   (8 marks) [AO3]

2

Let's keep the steel tariffs

This is a letter to the editor written by Leo Gerard, International President, United Steel Workers of America.

u Eighteen months ago, the US steel industry was in ruins. Years of unfair foreign trade and **dumping** had devastated our domestic market, and the results were grim: more than 30 companies bankrupted, 17 companies sold out, more than 50 000 jobs destroyed and the healthcare benefits of more than 200 000 retiring workers were lost.

v President Bush recognized this grave danger and put in place a three-year program of tariffs on certain steel products. His goal was to protect American manufacturing jobs, to

To access Quiz 21, an interactive, multiple-choice quiz on this chapter, please visit www.pearsonbacconline.com and follow the onscreen instructions.

help the steel industry to recover by regaining its **comparative advantage**, and to stand up for the principle that free trade must be fair trade.

w Across our industry, companies are benefiting. Labour and management have made agreements that increase worker productivity and reduce unnecessary levels of management. Productivity is up, and billions of dollars have been invested in new technologies and improved facilities. None of this would have been possible without the extra time provided by the three-year steel tariff program.

x Just as important, the gloomy predictions of opponents of the tariff program have not become reality. Steel prices in America are among the lowest in the world. Steel supplies are readily available. Above all, the industries that are the biggest consumers of steel are in better competitive shape today than they were before the program was introduced.

y We have made great progress, but significant work remains. Rebuilding an industry isn't an event; it's a process. And we are very much in the middle of that process.

z The president's steel program planned for three years of gradually declining tariffs. Despite the critics, the challenge now is to continue with the program so that the sweeping changes made possible by the tariffs can be fully realized and turned into a foundation for long-term strength. We are confident that the president will continue to be true to his word so that this vital industry can continue its recovery, and manufacturing jobs will remain secure in America.

Source: adapted from *The Washington Post*, October 2003

a Define the following terms indicated in bold in the text:

  i dumping (paragraph u) (2 marks) [AO1]

  ii comparative advantage (paragraph v). (2 marks) [AO1]

(Total 4 marks)

b Using an appropriate diagram, explain how the domestic and foreign producers of steel will be affected by the US tariff. (4 marks) [AO2], [AO4]

c Using an appropriate diagram, show how an import quota might be used to protect the domestic producers. (4 marks) [AO2], [AO4]

d Using information from the text and your knowledge of economics, evaluate the validity and effectiveness of protectionist arguments and policies. (8 marks) [AO3]

© International Baccalaureate Organization 2005 (part **a** only)

22 EXCHANGE RATES

22.1 Determination of exchange rates

Learning outcomes
- Explain that the value of an exchange rate in a floating system is determined by the demand for, and supply of, a currency.
- Distinguish between a depreciation of the currency and an appreciation of the currency.
- Draw a diagram to show determination of exchange rates in a floating exchange rate system.
- (HL only) Calculate the value of one currency in terms of another currency.

Imagine you have just landed in New Delhi. You have big plans to see the sights, visit museums, try new foods and generally make the most of your time in India. As your plane begins to land, you wonder how much money you will need. As you enter the terminal, you observe that the banks are charging different rates from those back home. Are the banks making big profits at your expense, or did something happen to change the value of the currency while you were travelling?

An exchange rate shows the price of one currency in terms of the amount of another. For example, if the pound sterling (the British pound, GBP) is valued at $1.50, then the exchange rate between the pound and the US dollar is 1.5 USD = 1 GBP.

This valuation can also be expressed in reverse, as the amount of pounds needed to buy one US dollar. To determine this number, take the reciprocal of the original ratio. In this example, 1 USD/1.5 GBP, or 0.666 pounds would be needed to buy one US dollar. Table 22.1 shows a range of currency values, with the reciprocal values noted.

How much money should I exchange to cover holiday expenses? Should I change cash, or withdraw money using my credit card?

An exchange rate is the value of one country's currency expressed in terms of the amount of another country's currency needed to buy it (e.g. the amount of euro per dollar).

	USD	EUR	GBP	INR	AUD	CAD	ZAR	NZD	JPY	SGD	RMB
TABLE 22.1 SELECTED EXCHANGE RATES											
1 USD	1.00000	0.74993	0.64936	44.5798	1.08044	1.00076	7.48278	1.40721	93.0339	1.37308	6.82730
inverse	1.00000	1.33345	1.53997	0.02243	0.9255	0.99924	0.13364	0.71063	0.01075	0.72829	0.14647
1 EUR	1.33345	1.00000	0.86590	59.4450	1.44071	1.33446	9.97794	1.87644	124.056	1.83094	9.10388
inverse	0.74993	1.00000	1.15487	0.01682	0.69410	0.74937	0.10022	0.53292	0.00806	0.54617	0.10984
1 GBP	1.53997	1.15487	1.00000	68.6515	1.66384	1.54113	11.5233	2.16706	143.269	2.11450	10.5138
inverse	0.64936	0.86590	1.00000	0.01457	0.60102	0.64887	0.08678	0.46146	0.00698	0.47292	0.09511

The foreign exchange market

Currency as a free market commodity is relatively new. At the close of World War II, in an attempt to organize the post-war global financial system, the Allied nations created a fixed-rate system of foreign exchange. In this system, the value of currency was pegged in relation to other currencies, and that rate was backed up by the country's gold reserves. Since the 1970s, countries have increasingly freed their currencies to float with supply and demand.

The foreign exchange market, also known as the forex or currency market, is said to be as close to a perfectly competitive market as there is. Prices are widely known because of easy telecommunication. Products are homogeneous. As a market, it is certainly unusual in many respects. There are millions of buyers and sellers on any given day. It spans the globe and operates 24 hours a day except for weekends. Prices are updated constantly through the use of rapid telecommunications and the internet. Profit margins tend to be low, and profits tend to be made through volume of sales. The market is enormous. The average daily turnover in global foreign exchange markets is estimated at $3.98 trillion, as of April 2007.

The market has a variety of actors, from the smallest retail currency traders up to the most powerful central banks (Figure 22.1).

Figure 22.1
Actors in the foreign exchange market.

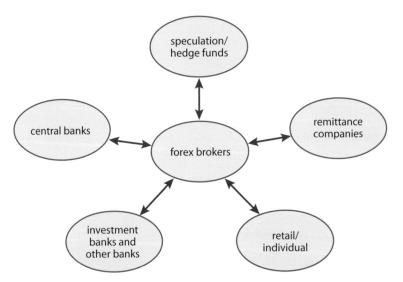

An individual buying currency on the streets of Delhi is probably buying at the retail level, from a small trader who buys from a forex broker. These brokers, at the highest levels, buy and sell currency to nearly all the other actors on the market. The brokers normally make profits from charging an explicit service fee of some fixed or percentage amount. They can also create spread (a gap) between the buying and selling prices, from which they take their profit.

Central banks buy and sell currency to influence the exchange rate, but sometimes have less power over the rate than the brokers themselves. Remittance companies exchange money for foreign workers who are sending money back home, and therefore need it to be converted to their home currency. Investment banks and hedge funds account for a very large share of forex trading, and often do so with pure speculation in mind. In other words, they buy currency with the specific intent of trading it later at a higher value. At its most dynamic, the forex market is highly speculative and subject to wide swings in values, as well as to panic-selling and runs on a currency when the value of one currency suddenly drops.

Floating exchange rates

A floating exchange rate is one where the value of a currency is determined by the demand for and supply of that currency on the foreign exchange market. Currency floats freely when the government does not intervene on the market, and allows the exchange rate to fluctuate.

Figure 22.2 shows the market for the most heavily traded currency, the US dollar, in terms of the second most heavily traded one, the euro. The dollars bought and sold are priced in terms of the euro. Just as with the demand for any commodity, the demand is downward sloping and the supply is upward sloping. Those demanding dollars are presumably holding euros and seeking to purchase dollars, whereas the suppliers of dollars are holding dollars and are willing to exchange them for euros. Where the supply and demand intersect is the equilibrium exchange rate. Using the rate noted in Table 22.1, this would make the rate 0.749 euro (75 euro cents) for every dollar. (Note that Figure 22.2 has been slightly truncated in order to magnify the area of equilibrium.)

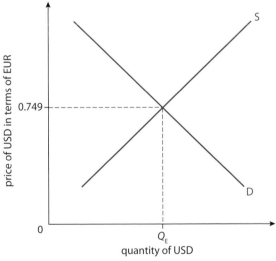

This exchange can also be viewed from the perspective of the market for euros. As noted in Table 22.1, the reciprocal of the euro value of dollars is the dollar value of euros. In this case, dollars are purchased for euros at the prevalent rate of 0.749 euros per dollar. Conversely, euros purchased with dollars will be bought at a rate of 1.33 dollars per euro.

Appreciation and depreciation

When floating exchange rates change, the increase in the value of one currency against another is called appreciation. It follows that the relative decrease in value of the other currency is called depreciation. Using our dollars and euros example, let's assume that one

To learn more about currency, visit www. pearsonhotlinks.com, enter the title or ISBN of this book and select weblink 22.1.

A floating exchange rate is one where the price of a currency is determined by the free market interaction of supply and demand for the currency.

Figure 22.2
Floating currency equilibrium.

The most heavily traded currencies in 2009 were:

- US dollar (USD)
- European euro (euro)
- Japanese yen (JPY)
- British pound (GBP)
- Swiss franc (CHF)
- Canadian dollar (CAD)
- Australian dollar (AUD)
- South African rand (ZAR)

Depreciation is a decrease in the free market exchange rate of a currency.

Figure 22.3 ▶

Depreciation: demand decrease.

of the factors influencing the demand for dollars diminishes, reducing overall demand for dollars. As with all other demand curves, the demand for dollars shifts to the left to D_1 (Figure 22.3).

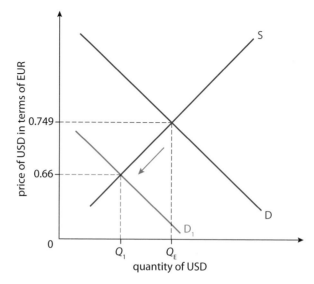

At the new euros-for-dollars exchange rate, it takes 0.66 euros to buy a dollar, rather cheaper than before. The price of dollars, in euro terms, has decreased, and we can say that the dollar has depreciated against the euro. In turn, this sets the dollars-for-euros exchange rate at approximately 1.50 dollars, rather higher than before. Correspondingly, we can say that the euro has appreciated against the dollar.

In Figure 22.4, the dollar depreciates for a different reason – an increase in supply. The holders of dollars are putting more on the foreign exchange market to be sold. Thus, supply shifts to the right to S_1, and the equilibrium price falls from 0.749 euros per dollar to 0.66 euros per dollar.

Figure 22.4 ▶

Depreciation: supply increase.

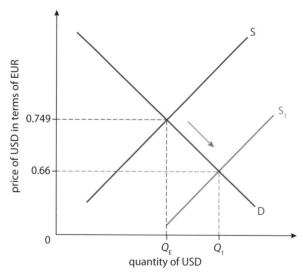

Appreciation is an increase in the free market value of a currency.

For an exchange rate to appreciate (rise in value), either demand must increase or supply must decrease. In the first instance, an increase in demand for the currency shifts demand to the right, raising the amount of the opposite currency that is needed to buy each unit of this currency. Figure 22.5 shows an increase of demand for dollars, shifting demand out to the right. At the new equilibrium, more quantity (Q_1) of dollars is traded, and the price has risen from 0.749 euros per dollar to 0.80 euros per dollar.

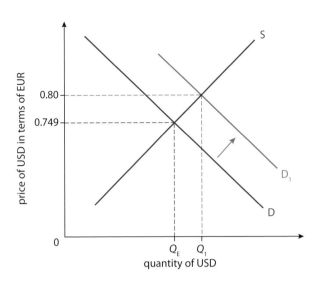

Figure 22.5
Appreciation: demand increase.

The other cause of appreciation is a decrease in supply, causing the price of the currency to rise. In Figure 22.6, the supply of dollars contracts, reducing the amount of dollars traded (Q_1) and increasing the price in euros paid for each dollar. The exchange rate for dollars appreciates from 0.749 to 0.80 euros per dollar.

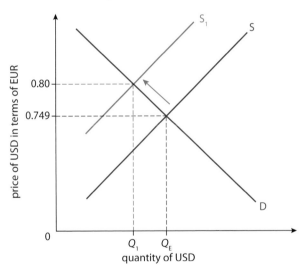

Figure 22.6
Appreciation: supply decrease.

 ## 22.2   Causes of change in the exchange rate

Learning outcomes
- Describe the factors that lead to changes in currency demand and supply, including foreign demand for a country's exports, domestic demand for imports, relative interest rates, relative inflation rates, investment from overseas in a country's firms (foreign direct investment and portfolio investment) and speculation.
- Draw diagrams to show changes in the demand for, and supply of, a currency.

Determinants of exchange rate

Like the supply and demand for any good, the non-price factors that shift supply and demand are called the determinants. Some of the principal determinants of exchange rates are discussed below.

Demand for goods and services

The relative demand for imports and exports can directly influence the purchase of currencies, and so alter the exchange rate. When demand for a country's exports increases, it increases demand for the currency itself. To buy the exports, the importers first need to buy the exporting country's currency to pay for them. To import Canadian maple syrup, for example, the importer first needs to buy Canadian dollars.

Thus, demand for a country's currency is partially derived from the relative demand for its exports compared to that of the trading country. For example, an increase in European demand for Thai goods should increase the demand for the Thai baht, and cause an appreciation of the baht in euro terms. Correspondingly, it would result in a depreciation of the euro versus the Thai baht.

Furthermore, the interaction of imports and exports with the exchange rate can be self-correcting. As the Thai baht climbs, the price of Thai goods in euro terms rises and makes them less attractive. European consumers, if sensitive to the price change caused by the new exchange rate, may reduce overall Thai imports and lower demand for baht again. Thus, extreme levels of appreciation and depreciation can be balanced out by the export price and demand changes that are the result. This can have implications for the balance of payments and specifically the current account (Chapter 23).

Demand for foreign direct investment

Foreign investors may find it necessary to buy a foreign currency to make particular kinds of investment in that country. To make any kind of significant foreign direct investment (FDI) by opening a branch location, starting a new firm, or creating a joint venture in another country, requires that country's currency to buy capital equipment, rent space, pay salaries and purchase materials. This suggests that increases in FDI appreciate a currency, and the loss of FDI depreciates it.

Demand for financial investments and capital flows

Financial investments such as the buying of foreign company shares, or interest-earning deposits in a foreign bank, are also likely to require purchase of the home currency. In other words, demand for a country's financial investments appreciates the currency.

In particular, a change in a country's interest rate can attract or repel foreign financial investors. Should the interest rates offered to depositors increase, individuals and banks would be attracted to the higher relative interest rate and buy the local currency to deposit in the bank. This event would be called a capital inflow, and would appreciate the currency, as long as the difference in interest rates exceeds whatever exchange fees are paid in the transaction.

The reverse could also be true: a decrease in relative interest rates at home could cause some depositors to flee domestic banks and buy other currencies in search of a better rate of return. This would, in turn, depreciate the value of the currency. In other words, if the Bank of Turkey were to raise interest rates relative to other countries, some investors would buy Turkish lire and deposit the amount to earn higher returns. This capital inflow would raise the value of the Turkish lira and relatively depreciate other currencies.

Relative inflation rates

As the prices of one country rise faster than those of another, its exports become more expensive and, therefore, less desirable. At the same time, imports will be relatively cheaper than before and more attractive. If Paraguay's prices were to soar relative to its neighbour Argentina, the demand for Paraguayan exports and the corresponding demand for the Paraguayan guarani would decrease. And Paraguay would seek out more imports from Argentina, increasing demand for the Argentine peso. This higher relative inflation would also hurt the trade balance (Chapter 23). Simply put, higher inflation tends to depreciate a currency, and lower relative inflation tends to appreciate it.

Speculation

The holders of foreign currencies can also speculate on future values. As with the buying and selling of shares, speculators may buy a currency hoping it will appreciate, sell it when they believe it has reached peak value, and take the resulting profits. The exact portion of forex trading devoted to speculation is unknown, but it is believed to make up the majority of a market that was worth 4 trillion USD in 2007, and expected to rise.

The actions of speculators can cause large swings in the value of the currency, particularly downward during a run. For this reason, forex speculation has been criticized for worsening currency crises like the Asian financial crisis of 1997. Defenders of currency speculation have pointed out that speculators provide a service because they have an interest in rationally assessing a currency's true value. Speculators, they argue, merely accelerate a process that would otherwise take much longer.

With this in mind, it is important to remember that speculators not only make their bets on a variety of purely economic factors such as the balance of payments situation and relative budget deficits, but also on political events and other less tangible factors.

Central bank intervention on the forex market

The central banks may buy or sell large amounts of foreign exchange with several goals in mind. They may seek to prop up the value of their currency by using foreign currency reserves to buy up their own. They may also sell their own currency if they seek to reduce its value, perhaps to increase the desirability of their exports and reduce the domestic consumption of imports. Indeed, they may also seek an overall balance between the current and capital accounts in the balance of payments.

Most countries' central banks do this to some extent, and economists call this intervention a managed float system (page 465). In this system, a country may target an acceptable range of exchange rate values and use reserves to keep the currency within that range. In the most extreme cases, the range is narrow and the country is essentially pursuing a fixed exchange rate (page 461).

To access Worksheet 22.1 on exchange rate determinants, please visit www.pearsonbacconline.com and follow the onscreen instructions.

22.3 Effects of change in the exchange rate

Learning outcomes
- Evaluate the possible economic consequences of a change in the value of a currency, including the effects on a country's inflation rate, employment, economic growth and current account balance.

Assuming a generally free-floating exchange rate, a change in the value of a currency can have significant consequences for the country's economy.

Appreciation
Advantages to appreciation
Less expensive imports

The increased value of the currency means that buying imported goods is now relatively less expensive than before. With increased buying power in these terms, a country can enjoy cheaper foreign consumer goods and capital goods. This can help those firms that import raw materials and capital goods, lowering their costs of production. At the same time, increased consumer goods can improve the standard of living and round out the economy in helpful ways. For developing countries, the ability to buy cheaper capital goods and energy resources could be a significant advantage. Where a country relies heavily on imports of any kind, an appreciation of the exchange rate can put downward pressure on inflation.

Competitive pressure on domestic exporters

An indirect effect of the higher exchange rate is that domestic firms exporting to other countries are at a price disadvantage relative to their foreign competitors. As the exchange-rate-adjusted price of their exports rises, they are compelled to seek out new ways of cutting costs and innovating. As a result, the company may find that it is a more robust and energetic competitor should the exchange rate ever return to previous levels.

Disadvantages to appreciation
Export levels reduced

The distinction between competitive pressure and competitive disadvantage is blurred, and companies attempting to export at consistently high exchange rates may come to believe that while their import costs are low, it may not compensate for the challenge of selling at the higher exchange rate. As a result, many export industries may find that their overall sales revenues drop considerably. Significant unemployment in these industries can be a consequence.

Greater imports hurt domestic production

Relatively cheap imports may hurt even non-exporting domestic industries. If those industries cannot match the exchange rate discount now available on imported goods, their share of the market and their sales may drop as well. This could also result in unemployment in those industries.

Effect on major economic goals

To summarize, appreciation reduces inflationary pressure where the demand for imports is relatively inelastic (e.g. energy resources). This may eventually help with economic growth. However, the more immediate impact on growth is to reduce exports and decrease real gross domestic product (GDP). This is likely to reduce employment, especially in exporting industries. Furthermore, the trade balance of exports to imports is likely to move towards a deficit, as exports slow down and cheaper imports increase.

Depreciation

Advantages to depreciation

Expansion of domestic industries

Foreign consumers view exports as relatively cheap, and are likely to import more. This raises revenues in those exporting companies and could increase employment. However, even non-exporting domestic industries benefit because the increase in the relative price of imported goods makes their domestic products seem cheaper. Therefore, non-exporting domestic industries are also more likely to expand and hire more workers, perhaps lowering domestic unemployment rates.

Disadvantages to depreciation

Imported inflation

Where countries need to import significant levels of raw materials or resources, a decrease in the exchange rate can bring on a certain amount of imported inflation. In particular, when the country has a relatively inelastic demand for those goods and therefore cannot adjust its expenditures, imports can be a persistent source of inflation, as long as the exchange rate stays high. Therefore, any decision by interventionist governments to devalue the currency should consider this possible result as a realistic consequence.

Effect on major economic goals

To summarize, appreciation increases inflationary pressure when demand for imports is relatively inelastic (e.g. energy resources). This may slow down economic growth. However, to the degree that a country already offers exports, the reduced price is likely to increase exports and increase real GDP. This should add to employment, especially in export industries. Furthermore, depreciation should improve the trade balance of exports and imports, with increased exports and a decreased demand for relatively more expensive imported goods.

 To learn more about exchange rates, visit www. pearsonhotlinks.com, enter the title or ISBN of this book and select weblink 22.2.

 ## 22.4 Government intervention

Learning outcomes
- Describe a fixed exchange rate system involving commitment to a single fixed rate.
- Distinguish between a devaluation of a currency and a revaluation of a currency.
- Explain, using a diagram, how a fixed exchange rate is maintained.
- Explain how a managed exchange rate operates, with reference to the fact that there is a periodic government intervention to influence the value of an exchange rate.
- Examine the possible consequences of overvalued and undervalued currencies.

 A fixed exchange rate is one that, through government action, is held to a narrow band of possible prices. Managed rates are those that are manipulated to fall within a wide band of prices.

Fixed exchange rates

In a fixed exchange rate system, the value of a currency is locked into (pegged) to the value of another currency. The central bank determines this value and enacts massive and constant intervention to maintain the established rate. This can be done by buying and selling currency reserves, as well as making other adjustments to currency and monetary policy.

Let's imagine that the Argentine central bank decided that the currency (Argentine peso) should be at par with the American dollar, so that 1 Argentine peso = 1 USD. If the equilibrium level happened by chance to be at that rate, no intervention would be required. However, if there were a surge in US beef productivity that lessened demand for Argentine beef exported to the US, then demand for pesos would decrease (Figure 22.7).

Figure 22.7
Fixed exchange rates.

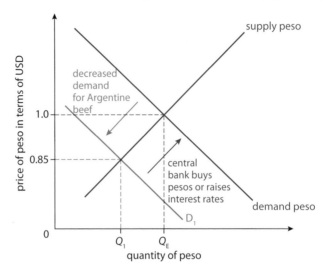

If the value of the peso were floating freely, this would decrease the value of pesos priced in dollars to 0.85 USD per Argentine peso. In that event, to maintain the 1 to 1 value of the peso and avoid depreciation, the Argentine central bank could immediately buy up the surplus pesos on the market using their reserve of US dollars. This would shift demand for the peso back to the desired price of 1 peso to 1 USD.

There are two possible directions in which a country could go in the process of maintaining its exchange rate. These are exemplified by Argentina (which, in the early 2000s, sought to maintain an exchange rate that was seen by many as artificially high) and China (which, for many years, has been seen as manipulating its currency to be artificially low). These two cases are examined below.

Government methods to sustain a high fixed exchange rate: Argentina

Official reserves

If Argentina wanted to keep its currency at par with the dollar, despite a tendency for the peso to drop below that value, it could buy up pesos with its reserve of dollars. This tactic alone is probably unsustainable as it can put tremendous pressure on the foreign exchange reserves.

Interest rates

Argentina could also use a tool of monetary policy by increasing interest rates offered by domestic banks. This would offer a higher relative rate of return and attract foreign depositors. Such depositors must buy pesos to get the higher interest rates. The resulting capital inflow would increase the demand for and price of the peso. A disadvantage to using interest rates primarily for this purpose is that it puts significant limitations on the degree to which monetary policy can be used to manage the domestic money supply and, correspondingly, the levels of domestic employment and inflation.

Exchange controls

Exchange controls are limits imposed by a country on the amount of foreign currency that can be bought by domestic residents. This serves to slow the amount of pesos leaving the country by decreasing the amount available for the purchase of imports, travel purposes, or the purchase of financial assets abroad. Exchange controls thus restrict the supply of pesos on the market and reduce the downward pressure on the exchange rate. While these controls can be effective, they can frustrate domestic consumers and producers who seek opportunities in foreign markets. They can also discourage investors and speculators from buying the currency in the first place.

Import limits

Argentina could also augment the value of the peso by cutting back demand for imports and slowing the demand for foreign currency. This can be done by expenditure reduction, or reduction in aggregate demand (AD) by contractionary fiscal policies. The higher interest rates noted above can also achieve this by lowering consumption and investment. Of course, this policy brings significant trade-offs in the loss of domestic national income and employment. A second method of import limitation would be to impose trade barriers against imported goods. These barriers, discussed at length in Chapter 21, may be effective at reducing demand for foreign currency but can severely limit the market for important imported resources, inspire retaliation among affected countries, and run foul of WTO rules.

<aside>
In 2001, Argentina's one-to-one peso-to-dollar peg collapsed after fraud, money laundering and capital flight made it impossible for the central bank to maintain the artificially high rate. By 2002, the peso had devalued by 75%, traded on the street at 4 pesos per dollar.
</aside>

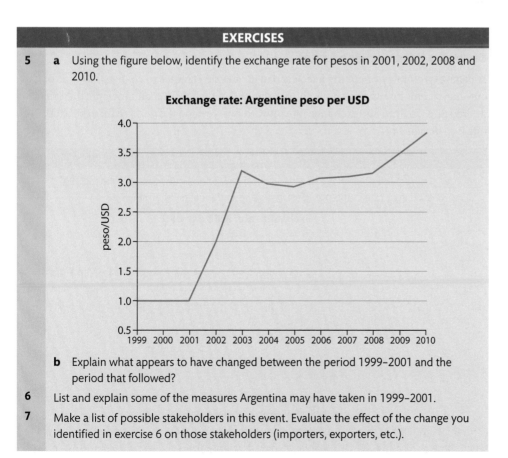

EXERCISES

5 **a** Using the figure below, identify the exchange rate for pesos in 2001, 2002, 2008 and 2010.

Exchange rate: Argentine peso per USD

b Explain what appears to have changed between the period 1999–2001 and the period that followed?

6 List and explain some of the measures Argentina may have taken in 1999–2001.

7 Make a list of possible stakeholders in this event. Evaluate the effect of the change you identified in exercise 6 on those stakeholders (importers, exporters, etc.).

Government methods to sustain a low fixed exchange rate: China

Official reserves

China can keep its exchange rate low by consistently supplying extra yuan to the market and thus buying up foreign currency in exchange. This must be done carefully as it can lead to an overall increase in the money supply and have an inflationary effect. At the same time, the country must keep foreign reserves on hand, or may use them to selectively buy other foreign capital assets.

Import/export policy

Lower exchange rates can be a significant export advantage and tend to lower the demand for imported goods. If the promotion of exports is especially successful, it can breed resentment among the importing countries. In this case, China has seen a dramatic rise in protectionist measures taken against it over the years. As a result, there is pressure on China to voluntarily limit its exports, to revalue its currency or to face charges in the WTO.

Interest rates

To keep the exchange rate low, interest rates must not be allowed to rise too much. Keeping interest rates consistently low could have a stimulative effect on AD and cause inflation.

Exchange controls

A country wishing to keep its exchange rates low may restrict the amount of domestic currency that can be held by foreign enterprises doing business there. For example, China could restrict the amount of yuan held by foreign banks operating in China. This would limit demand for the domestic currency as well, and keep exchange rates low. It also poses a significant bureaucratic and economic barrier to foreign firms operating in the country, and can limit foreign direct investment.

To access Worksheet 22.2 on China's silver bullet, please visit www. pearsonbacconline.com and follow the onscreen instructions.

Changing fixed exchange rates

Whenever a country operating fixed exchange rates determines to change the value of its currency, it employs the methods above to move supply and demand towards their new desired rate. To drive the exchange rate upward is to revalue it, and to reduce the exchange rate is to devalue it.

EXERCISES

8 a Using the figure below, how would you characterize the change in the RMB's exchange rate in the pre-1994 years and in the years that followed?

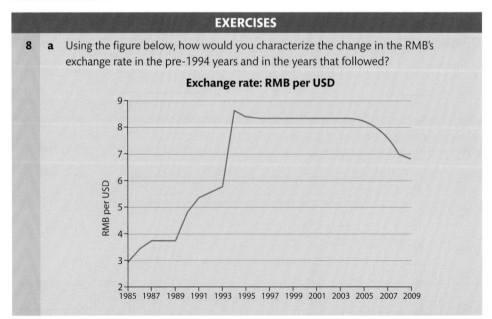

Exchange rate: RMB per USD

---

b Is the rate for 1994 onward a higher or lower exchange rate than before?

What advantages did China possibly gain from making this change? Disadvantages?

9 List three possible policy measures that China might have used to put this change into

10 effect.

Managed exchange rates

Managed float system

While fewer and fewer countries fix their currencies in the way described above, most are still willing to intervene should the exchange rate climb too high or fall too far for their liking. These countries may still peg their own currency to the value of another or to a basket of several currencies. However, they have a much wider acceptable range of values than a strictly fixed system. When the exchange rate approaches either the upper or lower limit, the central bank acts to keep the value within that range.

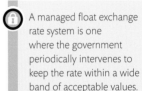

A managed float exchange rate system is one where the government periodically intervenes to keep the rate within a wide band of acceptable values.

The degree to which a country can manage its currency depends on the same factors that determine whether or not it can fix its rate: in particular, the amount of foreign and domestic reserves and relative interest rates. The more narrow the band, the more potential difficulty in maintaining the rate.

Why enact this halfway measure between fixed and freely floating exchange rate policies? The managed system puts a priority on stability, particularly between two pegged currencies. This stability could be an advantage, depending on the degree of trade and other economic integration with the other country. For example, it is rather common for countries seeking to adopt the euro to peg their currencies. This allows for stable import and export prices between countries and is viewed as a necessary step to joining the eurozone club.

Currency valuation

When the supply and demand of a currency meet, as they do at equilibrium, there is no overvaluation or undervaluation. However, any time a country holds a currency above or below that equilibrium, the resulting overvaluation or undervaluation can have significant effects on its overall economy.

Overvalued currencies

In Figure 22.7, Argentina initially lost value from the target rate of 1 USD to 1 peso. If it tried to maintain this as the official rate, without intervention to prop up its value, we would say that the peso is overvalued. It is likely that black markets would arise, where the actual street price for pesos would be between the equilibrium of 0.85 USD and 0.99 USD.

Overvaluing a currency presents some advantages. Developing countries may wish to import capital goods or materials at a cheaper price, something the higher rates would enable. However, overvaluation almost certainly hurts exports which, combined with greater import purchasing power, is likely to lead to a trade balance deficit. Overvaluation can also hurt domestic industries, which now face competition from cheap imports. Should a country decide that these costs are too great, it must either intervene to revalue the currency or be prepared to devalue the currency.

Undervalued currencies

Keeping a currency undervalued can have advantages. By keeping exports relatively cheap, undervaluation can improve exports and reduce the attractiveness of importing goods.

To access Worksheet 22.3 on managed exchange rates, please visit www. pearsonbacconline.com and follow the onscreen instructions.

This may improve the trade balance, but can also create an opportunity for imported inflation. Countries have employed this as a means to gain access to greater amounts of foreign exchange and to accelerate economic growth. However, as a sustained practice, undervaluation can be viewed by competitors as a form of unfair trade promotion and protectionism, since it both encourages exports and discourages imports by distorting prices. This can lead to charges of unfair trade and retaliatory protectionism.

22.5 Evaluation of different exchange rate systems (HL only)

Learning outcomes
- Compare and contrast a fixed exchange rate system with a floating exchange rate system, with reference to factors including the degree of certainty for stakeholders, ease of adjustment, the role of international reserves in the form of foreign currencies and flexibility offered to policymakers.

Fixed exchange rate

Advantages of a fixed rate

Stability

With fixed exchange rates, foreign investors do not have to take into account possible changes in exchange rates when calculating costs and sales. This simplifies business plans and reduces the cost of potential FDI companies. It can also help domestic companies with significant foreign sales or imported cost components.

Inflation control

When locked into a fixed rate, exports are vulnerable to the effects of domestic inflation, which would raise export prices and could reduce the demand for those exports. Governments are, therefore, compelled to manage inflation to keep their export prices competitive.

Protection against speculation

Free-floating rates are at the mercy of the market, where large speculators can heavily influence the buying and selling of a currency. When a government pledges to support the value of a currency, as under a fixed system, speculators have less incentive to make speculative actions against the currency's value. However, this does occasionally happen in fixed-rate systems.

Disadvantages of a fixed rate

Limitations on domestic policy
- Where the fixed-rate system is managed largely by manipulation of interest rates, the option of using those same interest rates for domestic policy purposes is significantly restricted. For example, if a fixed-rate country faces a recession, it would normally enact expansionary monetary policy, lowering interest rates to stimulate consumption and investment. However, to attract foreign deposits and keep demand for the currency

high, it would be compelled to leave interest rates high. This could deepen a recession and possibly limit economic growth overall.

- If the rate is kept low, it is possible that continued buying of high-priced imports would cause imported inflation. This inflation could not be addressed in the traditional manner, with higher interest rates, because the interest rates are being kept low to suppress the exchange rate.

- When the currency is fixed too high, it can cause a trade deficit because exports are priced uncompetitively. This imbalance cannot be corrected by devaluation (that would defeat the purpose of maintaining the high fixed rate), so countries must either enact protectionism (increasingly difficult) or enact expenditure-reducing policies. These policies aim to reduce national income, and thus reduce the demand for imported goods. While solving the trade deficit, this could also have severe effects on economic growth and employment.

Limited options with external shocks

In times of economic crisis, the single-minded pursuit of a fixed exchange rate can limit the range of options available to respond to the crisis. For example, a spike in the price of an imported energy resource could trigger a current account deficit. This happened in 2008 when Russia shut of supplies of natural gas to a range of nearby countries, most especially Ukraine. With more import money going out, there is a drain on foreign exchange reserves. If reserves are running low, more dramatic and potentially damaging measures such as protectionism and export controls are required to maintain the fixed rate.

Need to hold foreign reserves

Fixed-rate regimes require large amounts of foreign reserves to protect against speculators. In the absence of such reserves, foreign governments and investors will not be confident that the government can properly defend the currency. So, reserves lie dormant for the sake of market confidence in the fixed rate when they could be better used to buy and sell needed resources.

Risk of speculation

If a country has fixed a high exchange rate and is running low on reserves, speculators aggravate the problem by betting against the currency. They believe that the government must inevitably devalue, so they sell the currency, which depreciates it further. This forces the government to defend the currency by spending more reserves, weakening its position further, and inviting more speculation that it will default. These are the makings of a run on a currency.

Setting the rate

Determining what the ultimate fixed rate should be is an enormously complex decision, and includes a number of unknown factors. A high rate can hurt exporters and domestic industry, while a low rate may help exports but cause imported inflation.

Vulnerability to charges of unfair competition

If a country can sustain a low relative exchange rate that dramatically increases its exports, it may encounter resentment from competitor nations. This can result in poor trade relations, trade sanctions or protectionist policies being levied against the fixed-rate country.

Floating rate

Advantages of a floating rate

Domestic policy freedom

Overall growth and inflation management is enormously difficult even under normal conditions, without the need to factor in the management of exchange rates as well. Allowing the exchange rate to float freely means that one is free to manipulate monetary policy, specifically interest rates, to manage the balance between domestic growth rates and inflation. This also means that it will not be necessary to use fiscal policy to manage exports and thus the exchange rate.

Self-adjustment and balance of payments

A surge in demand for exports can lead to a surplus trade balance. The increased demand for the currency leads to appreciation, however. And the higher valued currency may discourage continued export sales. This could, therefore, reduce some of the accumulating trade surplus. This demonstrates the self-adjusting nature of the balance of payments when the exchange rate is allowed to float according to market wishes.

No surplus currency reserves

Because floating rate schemes do not require the stockpiling of currency reserves to prop up or devalue a currency, financial resources are allocated more efficiently. Foreign exchange can then be used to more productive ends, such as purchasing capital goods or imported resources.

Flexible response to external shocks

Sudden disruptions to the economy can be managed without the need to devote resources to fixing a rate. In the event of a massive debt relief package, such as that agreed by the EU for some of its members in 2010, countries would normally see their currency depreciate as faith and expectations for growth fall. This depreciation would allow for greater exports, and for growth to return. This growth would help the debtor country pay off its debts. (Because many EU countries have the euro as currency, they cannot do this independently. Unless the euro itself depreciates significantly, these countries will find it difficult to get enough export-led growth to pay off debts quickly.)

Disadvantages of a floating rate

Uncertainty for investors

When entering new or unfamiliar markets, foreign investors put a priority on holding as many factors as possible stable and predictable. Exchange rates are very important here because the foreign company may need to import materials and capital equipment. Simultaneously, it will be paying wages and property costs in local currency. This would also be true of domestic companies with foreign sales or investment aspirations. Navigating wide fluctuations in the exchange rate adds administrative cost and makes both predicting costs and setting product prices very difficult.

Influence of random events prevent automatic adjustment

While floating rates permit a flexible response to economic crises, not all shocks can be solved by exchange rate self-adjustment. Severe international political tension, domestic social turmoil, and other random events can depress markets and limit growth, despite any self-adjustment in exchange rates.

Risk of imported inflation

Countries that have constant need of foreign resources may find themselves with a persistently low exchange rate. In that situation, where the country has little opportunity to change the nature of its imports, it will import inflationary pressure on the economy as a whole. This is true of countries importing natural resources like oil, and those importing capital resources to build industry. The resulting cost-push inflation can slow economic growth on the supply side.

Volatility

Wide swings in currency values make doing business much more difficult, especially for those who import or export on a regular basis. With this in mind, developing countries often seek to peg their currency to a large trading partner. In extraordinary circumstances of great volatility, a rescue of the currency is required. Typically administered by the IMF, these rescue plans can come with significant conditions that may dictate the management of domestic fiscal policy (Chapter 28.)

HL EXERCISES

11 **a** From the information provided in the chart below, estimate the USD-per-euro exchange rate at the start of 2000, 2002, 2004, 2007 and 2008.

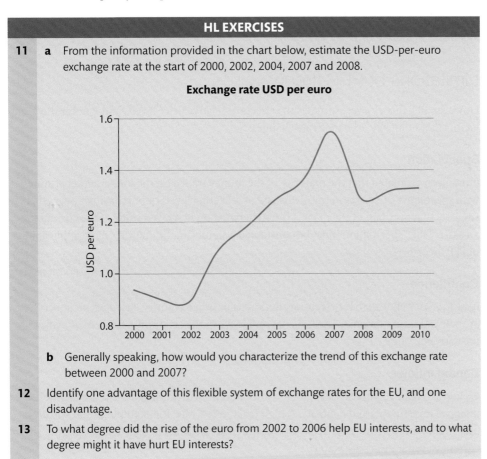

Exchange rate USD per euro

b Generally speaking, how would you characterize the trend of this exchange rate between 2000 and 2007?

12 Identify one advantage of this flexible system of exchange rates for the EU, and one disadvantage.

13 To what degree did the rise of the euro from 2002 to 2006 help EU interests, and to what degree might it have hurt EU interests?

Purchasing power parity theory of exchange rates

Purchasing power parity (PPP) theory takes the view that exchange rates should reflect comparable buying power in two respective countries. In other words, one should be able to purchase a basket of goods in one country with the same amount of money, either in local currency or in the exchange rate equivalent in foreign exchange.

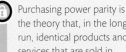
Purchasing power parity is the theory that, in the long run, identical products and services that are sold in different countries should cost the same.

For example, if the exchange rate between the Japanese yen (JPY) and the US dollar were 100 JPY per USD, then a 1000 USD computer should cost 100 000 JPY. Likewise, any Japanese item priced at 100 000 JPY would cost 1000 USD.

Because inflation affects purchasing power domestically, it can affect this relationship. If US inflation grew by 10%, then US dollars would buy less at home and it would require 1100 USD to buy the computer. PPP theory argues that the exchange rate should reflect this loss of purchasing power, so that the exchange rate would now be 1.1 USD per 100 JPY, and that approximately 91 JPY would be equal to 1 USD.

Deviations from the PPP exchange rate may indicate that a country's currency is overvalued or undervalued. Using the above example, if the value of the yen does not rise to reflect purchasing power, if it trades at 97 JPY per USD despite US inflation, then PPP theory would imply that the yen is undervalued at that rate, and should, over time, appreciate to match the purchasing power parity rate of 91 JPY per dollar.

PPP theory thus suggests that steady inflation tends to depreciate a country's currency. It also suggests exchange rates would not be necessary, if the value of currency reflected exact purchasing power. Currency would be easily exchanged to buy a good without concern for any losses or gains from overvaluation or undervaluation.

Limitations of PPP theory

However, PPP theory overestimates the effects of relative price levels, and ignores the other factors that influence exchange rate changes.

Speculation

It has been estimated that the majority of the money traded on the forex market is done with speculative purposes in mind. Instead of reflecting levels of purchasing power, this suggests that over half of the market is traded based on perceived value of the currency as an asset. Thus, speculation must be considered a significant limitation on the applicability of PPP theory.

Confidence

Investors may choose to buy factories or do business in a country based on prospects for growth and future income. The level of confidence in the economy plays a major role in the currency value.

Capital inflows

Changes in relative interest rates can enhance or diminish the attractiveness of domestic financial investments and deposits. A high real interest rate, for example, could still drive up demand for the currency, while low real interest rates may hinder demand for the currency even if prices are stable.

Much trade is not international

PPP theory is based on the idea of arbitrage. This means if a good were priced cheaply, in exchange rate terms, the good would be purchased at the low exchange rate price and be resold where it can bring a higher price. This will eventually equalize prices and drive the actual exchange rate to be equal to the PPP rate. However, the percentage of goods traded internationally (while growing) is still unlikely to make up a majority of GDP for most countries. With that in mind, the validity of the price equalization aspect of PPP is in question.

Barriers to trade

Further limiting the drive towards price equalization across borders is the continuing practice of protectionism. Limits to the free trade of goods impede the trend towards free movement of goods and, therefore, towards true purchasing power parity.

Goods not always comparable

PPP theory works best when the goods traded or compared are excellent substitutes. Indeed, the most famous test cases of PPP theory involve highly standardized products – the McDonald's Big Mac, and Starbucks coffees. Comparing prices between these goods can be instructive, since the products are the same. However, differences in product types and quality make further comparison significantly more problematic.

 To learn more about purchasing power parity, visit www.pearsonhotlinks. com, enter the title or ISBN of this book and select weblink 22.3.

22.6 Exchange rate calculations and linear functions (HL only)

Assessment statements
- Calculate the exchange rate from linear demand and supply functions.
- Plot demand and supply curves for a currency from linear functions and identify the exchange rate.
- Using exchange rates, calculate the price of a good in different currencies.
- Calculate the changes in the value of a currency from a set of data.

Supply and demand for currency with linear functions

As you learned in Chapter 2, the supply and demand for a product can be calculated using linear demand functions. We can do the same with exchange rates because foreign exchange is traded in much the same manner as any other product.

Calculating exchange rates from linear functions

Just as with product and labour markets, the market for foreign exchange can be understood and expressed using linear equations for supply and demand. Again, the linear demand equation format is:

$$Q_D = a - bP$$

However, in this function, P stands for the exchange rate of the currency, in terms of another currency. So, using this demand function we can derive a specific demand function for the currency, in this case the euro:

$$Q_{D\ EURO} = a - bP$$

Again, P represents the exchange rate of the currency. For our example, a plausible demand function might be:

$$Q_{D\ EURO} = 100 - 10P$$

TABLE 22.2 EXCHANGE RATE DEMAND SCHEDULE	
Exchange rate / USD per euro	**Quantity of euros demanded / billions**
2	80
1.75	82.5
1.5	85
1.25	87.5
1	90

EXCHANGE RATE SUPPLY SCHEDULE	
Exchange rate / USD per euro	**Quantity of euros supplied / billions**
2	95
1.75	90
1.5	85
1.25	80
1	75

Using this demand function, we can calculate the quantity demanded of euros at several USD-per-euro exchange rates, and then show them on a demand curve. Table 22.2 shows the amount of euros demanded at each exchange rate.

Before plotting the demand schedule, let's compute the supply schedule as well. Recall that linear supply functions look like this:

$$Q_S = c + dP$$

So, for the euro:

$$Q_{S\,EURO} = c + dP$$

Which, for our example, might be:

$$Q_{S\,EURO} = 55 + 20P$$

Therefore, a linear supply schedule for the supply of euros is shown in Table 22.3.

We can determine the equilibrium by solving for the equilibrium exchange rate (P) and quantity (Q) by setting supply equal to demand.

Worked example

$$55 + 20P = 100 - 10P$$
$$30P = 45$$
$$P = 1.5$$

So, the exchange rate is $1.50 per euro.

Putting the exchange rate (P) into both functions, and we get the equilibrium quantity of 85.

Diagramming exchange rates using linear demand functions

Now that we have the quantities supplied and demanded, we can plot the market diagram for euros. Figure 22.8 shows the intersection of supply and demand to be at $1.5 per euro, with 85 billion euro traded.

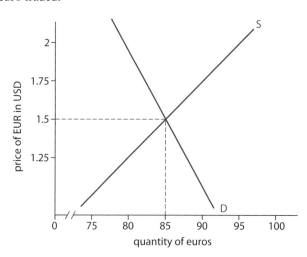

Changes in foreign exchange equilibrium using linear functions

Freely floating exchange rates are subject to change, of course. And these changes can also be expressed using linear functions. In the linear demand function, *a* represents the level of autonomous demand. When this amount changes, demand has changed, and a new curve representing a new set of prices and quantities must be created. The same is true for *c* in linear supply functions. A change in *c* is a change in supply, requiring a new supply schedule and new supply curve.

For example, let's consider the demand function above when the *a* variable has increased by 7.5 from 100 to 107.5; the new demand function is:

$$Q_{D\,EURO} = 107.5 - 10P$$

This increases demand at all prices and results in a new demand schedule (Table 22.4).

TABLE 22.4 EXCHANGE RATE DEMAND SCHEDULE

Exchange rate / USD per euro	Quantity of euros supplied / billions
2	87.5
1.75	90
1.5	92.5
1.25	95
1	97.5

Notice, that all the quantities demanded have increased by 7.5 units. Again, we can solve for equilibrium exchange rate (*P*) and quantity (*Q*) by setting supply equal to demand.

Worked example

$$55 + 20P = 107.5 - 10P$$

$$30P = 52.5$$

$$P = 1.75$$

The exchange rate is $1.75 per euro

When paired with the old supply numbers, the new market equilibrium becomes apparent (Table 22.5). At $1.75 per euro, 90 billion euros are bought and sold.

TABLE 22.5 EXCHANGE RATE MARKET SCHEDULE

Exchange rate / USD per euro	Quantity of euros demanded / billions	Quantity of euros supplied / billions
2	87.5	95
1.75	90	90
1.5	92.5	85
1.25	95	80
1	97.5	75

Figure 22.9 (overleaf) shows the new equilibrium, created by a shift of the demand for euros to the right or upwards by 7.5 billion euros at every price.

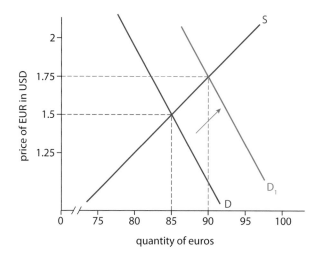

Supply shifts can be represented in the same way. For example, let's go back to the original supply and demand functions and change the supply variable c by 15 units. This represents a major increase in supply, as something like a panic sets in about the strength of the euro. Many euro holders are offering up their currency on the market, shifting supply to the right. The new linear supply function is:

$$Q_{S\,EURO} = 70 + 20P$$

The resulting supply schedule is shown in Table 22.6

We can determine the equilibrium by solving for the equilibrium exchange rate (P) and quantity (Q) by setting supply equal to the original demand function.

TABLE 22.6 EXCHANGE RATE SUPPLY SCHEDULE

Exchange rate / USD per euro	Quantity of euros supplied / billions
2	110
1.75	105
1.5	100
1.25	95
1	90

Worked example

$$70 + 20P = 100 - 10P$$

$$30P = 30$$

$$P = 1$$

So, the exchange rate is $1.00 per euro.

All supply quantities have increased by 15 units. This represents an increased supply at all prices and a parallel shift in the supply curve for euros. When paired with the old demand numbers, the new equilibrium is apparent at $1 per euro, and 90 billion exchanged (Table 22.7).

TABLE 22.7 EXCHANGE RATE MARKET SCHEDULE

Exchange rate (USD per euro)	Quantity demanded euros (billions)	Quantity supplied euros (billions)
2	80	110
1.75	82.5	105
1.5	85	100
1.25	87.5	95
1	90	90

Figure 22.10 shows the new equilibrium for euros.

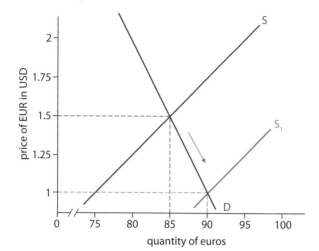

Figure 22.10
Exchange rate shifts, linear functions.

It is possible to express the supply and demand for any currency in terms of a linear function. At the same time, these functions can help calculate full supply and demand schedules, diagrams and market equilibrium from these functions.

Calculating exchange rates from a set of data

Currency information is reported in many forms and can be deduced from various sources of information. Therefore, you need to be able to calculate exchange rates from different types of data.

Changes in the price of traded goods and services

Sometimes, the prices of imported and exported goods change because the exchange rate has changed. For example, if the Mexican peso appreciates by 20%, you would expect the price of Mexican exports to increase by the same amount. To look at it from the other side, if the price of Mexican imports increased by 20%, you might, all other things being equal, conclude that the peso has appreciated by that amount.

You are expected to be able to calculate the inferred change in the exchange rate, given the change in the price of exports. Consider a box of matches imported from Thailand into the eurozone. The price of the matches is 75 Thai baht (THB), which is equivalent to 1.5 EUR, assuming that there are no exchange fees or import duties. This price is in accordance with a baht-to-euro exchange rate of 50 THB per EUR.

Suddenly, the price of matches increases in the eurozone. It now requires 2 EUR to buy one box, which is still priced at 75 THB. What must have happened to the exchange rate? Clearly the euro has depreciated against the baht, but how far? We can calculate the new exchange rate based on this change in prices.

Worked example

At the old exchange rate: 1 EUR = 50 THB

This could be inferred from the fact that Thai matches cost: 1.5 EUR or 75 THB

$$\frac{\text{forex price of the good}}{\text{domestic price of the good}} = \text{exchange rate for foreign currency}$$

$$\frac{75\ \text{THB}}{1.5\ \text{EUR}} = 50\ \text{THB per EUR}$$

Using the same formula, we can derive the new exchange rate:

$$\frac{75 \text{ THB}}{2 \text{ EUR}} = 37.5 \text{ THB per EUR}$$

So the euro has depreciated against the baht, and the baht has appreciated against the euro. It now takes more euros to buy Thai baht, and to buy imported Thai goods like a box of matches. The exchange rate has changed from 50 THB per EUR to 37.5 THB per EUR.

HL EXERCISES

14 Given the following linear demand and supply functions for the USD in terms of Chinese RMB: $Q_S = 10 + 3P$; $Q_D = 50 - 2P$

  a Calculate the exchange rate for USD in terms of RMB.

  b Plot the linear supply and demand curves on a diagram, indicating the equilibrium price and quantity.

15 Assume that the exchange rate for British pounds and USD is 1.60 USD per GBP.

  a Calculate the value in GBP for 1 USD.

  b For the information given above, calculate how many pounds would be received in exchange for 1200 USD.

  c Calculate in USD the price of a Manchester United football jersey that costs 45 GBP.

  d Assume that large pack of US writing pens costs 10 GBP. A change in the exchange rate raises their price to 11 GBP. Calculate the value of the new USD per GBP exchange rate.

16 Last year, Japan could import athletic jerseys from China costing 60 RMB, which cost 720 JPY at current exchange rates. Now the same 60 RMB jersey costs 780 JPY. What is the current exchange rate?

To access Quiz 22, an interactive, multiple-choice quiz on this chapter, please visit www.pearsonbacconline.com and follow the onscreen instructions.

PRACTICE QUESTIONS

1   **India faces rising currency**

  1 The Indian economy has performed remarkably well in the past 10 years, achieving levels of growth only beaten by China. However, India is not without problems including rural poverty and the lack of infrastructure, which threaten to limit the gains from **economic growth**. Now the strength of the Indian economy and its attractiveness to foreign investors is causing a new and unexpected problem – a rising currency. This week the Indian rupee reached its highest value against the US$ since 1998.

  2 During 2007, foreign investment into India increased by more than 80% to a record US$44 billion. India is an attractive place for investment because it is a developing economy with the potential for future economic growth. The relatively cheap labour available in India makes it an attractive place for manufacturing and call centres. For these reasons, the Indian rupee has appreciated 15% against the US$ in the past year.

  3 While large capital inflows are beneficial for the economy, the rising currency may cause increasing hardship for exporters, especially India's labour-intensive manufacturing industries. Exports account for 10% of the US$854 billion economy and the government is counting on strong exports to support economic growth in India. India's economy expanded by 9.2% in the past year, the highest growth rate in two decades.

  4 The nation's largest computer-services provider said the Indian rupee's 'drastic' gains will reduce earnings by over US$7 billion. The Federation of Indian Exporters says 'the currency is overvalued and we are asking the government to intervene'.

5   India's central bank, which sold a record US$11.9 billion [worth of] Indian rupees in February in a bid to slow the currency's gains, is, however, also concerned about India's rising inflation rate.

6   The Reserve Bank of India is torn between the need to contain inflation, which accelerated at 7 % in February, the fastest pace for more than two years, and the need to limit the appreciation of the currency. To reduce inflation, one policy response is to increase **interest rates** but this is likely to further strengthen the Indian rupee.

adapted from *The Economist*, 13 December 2007;

Bloomberg, 17 April 2008;

Economics Help, 12 November 2008

a   Define the following terms indicated in bold in the text:

   i   economic growth (paragraph 1)   [2 marks] [AO1]

   ii interest rates (paragraph 6).   [2 marks] [AO1]

b   Using an appropriate diagram, explain why the Indian rupee has 'increased 15% against the US$ in the past year' (paragraph 2).   [4 marks] [AO2], [AO4]

c   Using an aggregate supply and demand diagram, explain how the rupee's appreciation will affect exports and overall economic performance (paragraph 3).

[4 marks] [AO2], [AO4]

d   Using information from the text/data and your knowledge of economics, evaluate the extent to which the Indian government should intervene to manage the value of the Indian rupee.   [8 marks] [AO3]

© International Baccalaureate Organization 2010 (part **a** only)

2   **The benefits of a lower dollar**

1 The current decline in the US dollar ($) will provide a much-needed stimulus to the US economy. The depreciation of the dollar will bring especially welcome relief to the US manufacturing sector, which has suffered the disastrous consequences of lost jobs, reduced profits, and decreased investment as a result of the dollar's overvaluation for the past several years. However, although the dollar has come down significantly from its peak in February 2002, it has not yet fallen nearly enough to reverse the damage caused by its high value since the late 1990s.

2 The high value of the dollar since the late 1990s has acted like a massive tax on US exports and a huge **subsidy** to US imports. As a result, although US manufacturing firms have made substantial investments in new technologies and US manufacturing workers have vastly increased their productivity, these achievements have not been successful because foreign products have been selling at artificially low prices due to the overvalued dollar. Specifically, the overvalued dollar has resulted in:

- About 740 000 lost jobs in the manufacturing sector by 2002 – more than one quarter of the 2.6 million jobs lost in manufacturing since 1998.

- A decrease of nearly US$100 billion in the annual profits of US manufacturing companies by 2002.

- A fall in investment in the domestic manufacturing sector by over US$40 billion annually as of 2002, representing a loss of 25 % of US manufacturing investment.

3 There is a situation where the United States of America is running up foreign debt at a rate unseen in history. In the fourth quarter of 2002, the **current account deficit** of the world's largest economy hit an annualized rate of 5.2% of GDP, well above the 3.4% deficit reached in 1987, the last time the USA faced an international financial crisis.

adapted from Blecker, RA. *The benefits of a lower dollar*, 30 May 2003, EPI Briefing Paper;
Bulletin with *Newsweek*, 13 May 2003, 121(6372):20

a Define the following terms indicated in bold in the text:

i current account deficit (paragraph 3)   (2 marks) [AO1]

ii subsidy (paragraph 2).   (2 marks) [AO1]

b Using an appropriate diagram, explain why the value of the US dollar has declined (paragraph 1).   [4 marks] [AO2], [AO4]

c Using an appropriate diagram explain why the increased value of the dollar appears to be harming the overall economy (paragraphs 1 and 2).   [4 marks] [AO2], [AO4]

d Using information from the text and your knowledge of economics, discuss the degree to which the US government should intervene to lower the US dollar exchange rate.   [8 marks] [AO3]

23 THE BALANCE OF PAYMENTS

23.1 Meaning of the balance of payments

Learning outcomes
- Outline the role of the balance of payments.
- Distinguish between debit items and credit items in the balance of payments.

If you've ever walked through a retail superstore like a Wal-Mart, a Carrefour or a Tesco, you may have wondered, 'Where did all this STUFF come from?' The cheap tennis rackets, kitchen utensils, picture frames, home entertainment systems and countless other items you pass in the aisles were very likely manufactured in an Asian country; perhaps China, maybe Indonesia or Vietnam or Japan. In 2004, over 70% of the products sold in the more than 3000 Wal-Mart stores in the US were manufactured in China.

Wal-Mart has 'Low prices, every day': What impact does all that spending by Americans on cheap imports from China have on the US economy?

Chinese goods are not only sold in these giant stores known for their low prices. Walk across the street to a tyre shop and see where most of the tyres were made. Then check out the fine print on the frozen seafood at the grocery store. Check the labels on the designer handbags on sale at the mall. What did you discover? Chances are, most of the manufactured goods you've purchased anywhere lately were made in a country other than the one you live in (unless, of course, you live in an Asian country).

The flow of goods across national borders has become ever more imbalanced as the world's economies have integrated in the last several decades. Free trade agreements between nations and the efforts of international organizations like the WTO have reduced or eliminated the barriers to trade that, only a generation ago, ensured that many of the consumable goods produced in Asia today were then made domestically. The liberalization of trade, combined with the extremely low costs of labour, land and capital in less developed countries, have led to a global trading system in which many countries' expenditures on imports have, for years, far outpaced their incomes from the sale of exports.

The balance of payments

The balance of trade in goods between nations is just one of the factors measured in a nation's balance of payments. According to the International Monetary Fund, the 'balance of payments (BoP) is a statistical statement that summarizes, for a specific time period, the economic transactions of an economy with the rest of the world.' Trade in manufactured goods is just one of the components of a nation's BoP. Also included are exchanges

To learn more about the balance of payments, visit www.pearsonhotlinks. com, enter the title or ISBN of this book and select weblink 23.1.

between a nation and all other nations of services, income, gifts, capital, and financial assets (e.g. currencies, government bonds and company stocks). Each of these transactions is recorded for a given year in one of three accounts:

- the current account
- the capital account
- the financial account.

23.2 Components of the balance of payments

Learning outcomes
- Explain the four components of the current account, specifically the balance of trade in goods, the balance of trade in services, income and current transfers.
- Distinguish between a current account deficit and a current account surplus.
- Explain the two components of the capital account, specifically capital transfers and transactions in non-produced, non-financial assets.
- Explain the three main components of the financial account, specifically, direct investment, portfolio investment and reserve assets.
- (HL only) Calculate elements of the balance of payments from a set of data.

Accounts in the BoP

A nation's balance of payments measures the exchanges that take place in three separate accounts.

- The current account measures the balance of trade in goods and services and the flow of income between a nation and all other nations. It also records monetary gifts or grants that flow into or out of a country.
- The capital account measures the transfer of ownership of capital goods between a nation and all other nations.
- The financial account measures the flow of funds for investment in real assets (such as factories or office building) or financial assets (such as stocks and bonds) between a nation and the rest of the world.

The official foreign exchange reserves balance the three accounts in the balance of payments. This measures the net effect of all the money flows from the three accounts above. In years when the sum of all three accounts above is greater than zero, a nation's central bank experiences a build-up of foreign exchange. In years when the above accounts' sum total is less than zero, the central bank must draw on its reserves of foreign exchange to make up the imbalance.

In this chapter we examine New Zealand's balance of payments in some detail to determine how the balance on each of the above accounts is determined. Most of the information that follows is adapted from Colin Danby's *Balance of Payments: Categories and Definitions*.

Balance of payments information is extremely important when it comes to the formulation of national and international policy by any country. Knowledge of foreign investment and payments imbalances informs most policy decision-making in a world where national economies are becoming increasingly interdependent.

Understanding how BoP is measured: debits and credits

Any transaction between a country's residents and the rest of the world results in either a debit or a credit towards one of the accounts in its balance of payments. Whenever a transaction brings money into the country, it is recorded as a credit. This means that someone in the country is getting paid for something. Whenever the transaction involves a flow of money out of the country, it is recorded as a debit. This means that someone in the country is paying someone abroad for something.

Figure 23.1 shows how each of the possible transactions between New Zealand's residents and the rest of the world is recorded in New Zealand's balance of payments. Exchanges that result in money flowing into New Zealand are indicated by green arrows; transactions that send money out of New Zealand are indicated by red arrows.

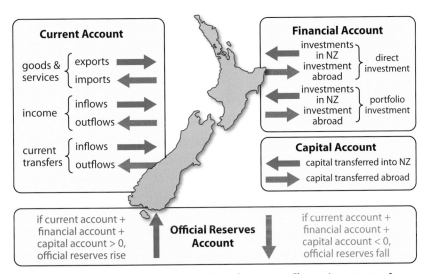

Figure 23.1 New Zealand's balance of payments accounts.

Current account + Financial account + Capital account + Change in reserves = 0

The balance of payments must always be in balance. This means that the net outcome of all the money flows in Figure 23.1 is a balance of zero. For instance, in a given year, New Zealand's total balance in its current account might be negative (the country has spent more on imports than it earned from exports). The balance in New Zealand's financial and capital accounts must then be positive.

The reason for this is simple. Every dollar New Zealanders spend on foreign goods and services ultimately ends up being spent again on something from New Zealand. The country's currency, the New Zealand dollar (NZD), cannot be spent by foreigners on anything other than New Zealand's goods, services or assets. Therefore, the money spent by New Zealanders on the rest of the world's stuff is ultimately spent on New Zealand's stuff. If NZD held by foreigners are not spent on New Zealand's goods and services (measured in the current account), then they are spent on financial or real assets (recorded in the financial account). In this way, a current account deficit is offset by a financial account surplus, hence the *balance* of payments.

This explanation is, of course, an over-simplification. To better understand the confusing matrix of a nation's economic interactions with the rest of the world, let's first examine each of the accounts and identify its components in detail.

The current account

A nation's current account has four components measuring transactions between the residents of one nation and the residents of all other nations. The account measures:

- the flow of goods
- the flow of services
- the flow of income
- the flow of transfers.

Sometimes a nation's current account balance is referred to as the balance of trade because it records the transactions involving goods and services actually produced by workers in one country and sold to or bought from consumers in another country.

If the sum of the four components of the current account is greater than zero, then a nation has a current account surplus, which means the total income from foreigners spending on its output is greater than its own spending on foreign output. On the other hand, a current account deficit results when residents of a nation spend more on imported goods and services than they earn from their sale of exports to the rest of the world.

Balance of trade in goods

The balance of trade in goods measures the spending by consumers and firms in one nation on another nation's goods (both consumer and capital goods) as well as spending by consumers in the rest of the world on the recording nation's goods.

> The current account measures the flow of funds between a nation and the rest of the world for the purchase of goods and services and income transfers. The current account includes the visible (goods) and the invisible (services) balance, and is sometimes simply referred to as the balance of trade.

- **Goods credits (+)**. Goods exports count as a credit in the current account because they require that foreigners make payments to the exporting nation. Exports, as a component of aggregate demand (AD), also contribute to employment and output of a nation. However, the level of exports depends primarily on economic conditions abroad, such as foreign incomes and growth in foreign consumer and capital markets. Note that the export of both consumer and capital goods counts as a credit in the current account.
- **Goods debits (–)**. Spending by domestic consumers on goods produced in foreign nations counts as a debit in the current account, since it requires a payment to foreign producers. Spending on imports subtracts from domestic AD, since it is a leakage of national income from the importing nation. The main determinant of imports is the level of income of domestic households; as incomes rise, domestic consumers and firms spend more on both imported consumer and capital goods, as well as on domestic output.

Balance of trade in services

Services refer to non-tangible purchases such as tourism, banking, consulting, legal services, and transportation. Services can be imported and exported, although there is no physical movement of a product involved. Many services can be bought and sold remotely thanks to the high-speed communication made possible by broadband internet.

- **Services credits (+)**. Services bought by foreigners, either within the nation or from abroad, count as a credit in the current account, since they require that a foreign consumer makes a payment to a domestic producer. Earnings from the tourist industry in Thailand are a credit in Thailand's current account because foreigners are spending on transport, accommodation, entertainment and leisure services within Thailand. On the other hand, an X-ray examination of a patient in the US analysed overnight by a medical student in Mumbai, India, is a service export for India that did not require the presence of a foreign consumer within India's borders.

- **Services debits** (–). Services purchased from foreigners and consumed by domestic households are a debit in the current account because they require a payment to a foreign producer. The spending by a German tourist travelling in Thailand and spending income earned in Germany on Thai services, counts as a debit in Germany's current account. The Chicago hospital that outsources its X-ray analysis to India has imported the service from India, so the US experiences a debit in its current account.

The term 'balance of trade' usually refers to a nation's goods and services balance in the current account. However, these are not the only flows that are measured in this account.

To learn more about the balance of trade, visit www.pearsonhotlinks.com, enter the title or ISBN of this book and select weblink 23.2.

Income balance

When citizens of one country earn income from activities in another country, the transfer of income back to the income earners' country of origin is also measured in the current account. This includes the wage income earned by a country's citizens from employment by foreign companies abroad. For instance, an American teacher working at an international school in Germany may send home a portion of his or her wages to the US; this would be measured in both the US and Germany's current accounts. Income also refers to investment income, such as interest and dividends earned on investments in foreign bonds or stocks. If a British citizen living in the UK has a savings account in a Swiss bank, the interest earned on his savings counts as a credit for the UK current account and a debit for Switzerland's.

- **Income credits** (+). This includes wages earned by a country's workers employed abroad which are sent home, interest on a country's residents' savings and investments in foreign banks and financial markets, and dividends earned abroad from domestic investors purchasing stocks in foreign firms. Each of these transactions requires that foreigners make payments to residents in the country in question, so they are counted as a credit in that country's current account.
- **Income debits** (–). Wages that are paid by firms in one country to foreign workers in that country and which are then sent abroad count as a debit in the current account. In addition, interest paid to foreign savers in domestic banks and dividends paid to foreign shareholders in a domestic company are all considered 'leakages' and therefore are counted as a negative (debit) in the current account.

Current transfer balance

A transfer refers to a payment made from one nation to another that is not in exchange for any good or service, such as a gift or a grant. New Zealand's central bank explains why such monetary, non-production transfers are measured in the balance of payments: 'Current transfers directly affect the level of disposable income and influence the consumption of goods and services for the donor and the recipient economies.'

Transfers are divided into two categories: official transfers are payments from one government to another, sometimes known as 'aid'. Private transfers are payments made by citizens of one country to residents of any other country.

Current transfers can be recorded as either a credit or a debit in the current account.

- **Transfer credits** (+). Official and private transfers from foreign governments or households to the government or individuals in a country count as a credit in the current account. All such transfers require a payment from foreigners to domestic stakeholders, increasing the level of disposable income at home and reducing it in the foreign country.
- **Transfer debits** (–). Official and private transfers by the government or individuals within a nation to foreign governments or households count as a debit in the current account. Both transfers require a payment from domestic stakeholders to interests abroad, and increase disposable income abroad while reducing it at home.

Substantial transfer payments from one country to another give the recipient nation the ability to import more from abroad. In Chapter 28, we evaluate the intentions of certain types of tied aid in which the donor nation transfers income to a less developed country with conditions, usually requiring that the aid money be spent on imported goods and services produced by the donor nation's firms. In this regard, official transfers may do more harm than good for the recipient nation, whose producers may be harmed by the increased spending on imports by aid recipients.

Worked example

To calculate the components of the current account for NZ in 2004, you need to consider the given debits and credits and add them up to find the current account balance (as shown in Table 23.1, column 4).

TABLE 23.1 NEW ZEALAND'S CURRENT ACCOUNT: 2004			
Component of current account	Credits / millions of NZD	Debits / millions of NZD	Balance / millions of NZD
goods	29 109	-29 706	-597
services	11 966	-9 777	2 189
income	2 844	-8 851	-6 007
current transfers	1 318	-1 128	190
current account balance			-4 225

Figure 23.2 is an alternative way of showing the same information.

Figure 23.2
New Zealand's current account balance.

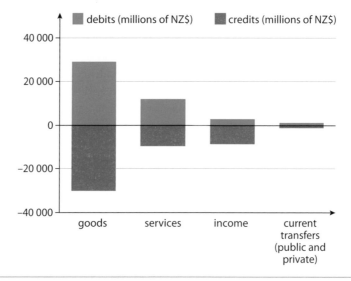

The capital account measures the transactions involving ownership of capital, forgiveness of debt, or the acquisition and disposal of non-produced, non-financial assets between a nation and all other nations.

To learn more about the current account, visit www.pearsonhotlinks. com, enter the title or ISBN of this book and select weblink 23.3.

Economics as a science generally focuses on positive analysis. That is to say, it examines the world through an objective lens aimed at examining what is, rather than what should be. An example of a positive statement is: New Zealand spent more on imports in 2004 than it sold in exports to the rest of the world.

Normative statements are more subjective in nature, expressing an opinion or arguing for what should be, rather than what is. For instance, it would be a normative statement to say: New Zealand would be better off with greater balance in its current account.

To what extent is it appropriate for economists to make normative statements such as this? Should economics stick to analysis of what is and leave what should be up to politicians and the media? Or is it appropriate for economists to determine what should be based on their analysis of data such as that of a nation's balance of payments?

The capital account

The capital account measures the transactions involving ownership of capital, forgiveness of debt, or the acquisition and disposal of non-produced, non-financial assets between a nation and all other nations.

Capital transfers

When a nation's government or private sector gives money to another nation for the purchase of fixed assets or directly donates capital goods to residents of another country, this is recorded as a debit by the donor country and a credit for the recipient country. The capital account does not measure the purchase or sale of capital between nations, rather the actual transfer of fixed assets from one nation to another.

- **Capital transfer credits (+).** If the Canadian government were to make a $2 million donation to the Ministry of Education in Tanzania to build schools in rural areas, the transaction would involve the transfer of money from Canada to Tanzania for the purpose of helping Tanzania acquire fixed assets in the form of new school buildings. Tanzania would record this as a capital account credit.
- **Capital transfer debits (–).** If the US development agency, USAID, were to finance the construction of a new port facility in Liberia's capital city, Freetown, the money provided would be recorded as a debit for the US, because it would require transfer of income from the US to a foreign country.

Debt forgiveness

Besides the transfer of cash to acquire new capital or of capital itself, the capital account also measures the forgiveness of debt from lenders in one country to debtors in another. Debt owed by one nation to a lender in another nation, if forgiven by the lender, counts as a credit for the debtor's nation and a debit for the lender's nation in their capital accounts.

- **Debt forgiveness credit (+).** If the government of Rwanda were to be relieved of its debts on a loan made to the previous government by the African Development Bank, this would be recorded as a credit in Rwanda's capital account.
- **Debt forgiveness debit (–).** If a bank in Switzerland which made a loan to the government of Sierra Leone 10 years ago were to decide to forgive the debt still owed by the Sierra Leonean government, the balance owed to the Swiss bank would be measured as a debit for Switzerland.

Exchanges of non-produced, non-financial assets

Finally the capital account measures the flow of non-produced, non-financial assets. This includes, as defined by the New Zealand central bank, 'the purchase or sale of intangible, non-financial assets, such as patents, copyrights, trademarks, franchises and licences; and the acquisition of land by a government or international organization or the disposal of such land.'

 To learn more about the capital account, visit www.pearsonhotlinks.com, enter the title or ISBN of this book and select weblink 23.4.

 The capital account of the balance of payments records the transactions involving ownership of capital, forgiveness of debt, or the acquisition and disposal of non-produced, non-financial assets between a nation and all other nations.

Worked example

To calculate the capital account balance for NZ in 2004, you need to consider the given debits and credits and add them up (as shown in Table 23.2, column 4).

TABLE 23.2 NEW ZEALAND'S CAPITAL ACCOUNT: 2004			
Account	**Credits / millions of NZD)**	**Debits / millions of NZD)**	**Capital account balance / millions of NZD)**
capital account	1576	–814	762

The financial account

A nation's financial account measures the exchanges between a nation and the rest of the world that involve ownership of financial and real assets. Foreigners may buy and sell a country's real assets, including real estate, factories, office buildings and other factors of production. Such transactions are recorded in the financial account because they involve the ownership of assets, not the purchase of the nation's output of goods or services. If an office building in Auckland were sold to a Chinese textile manufacturer, none of New Zealand's output would actually be consumed by China; this explains why such an investment is not measured in the current account. Ownership would be transferred, and there would be a flow of money into New Zealand, moving the country's financial account towards surplus.

In addition to real assets, much of the activity measured in the financial account is the buying and selling of financial assets such as company stocks and government bonds. If an investment bank in New Zealand were to invest in Spanish government bonds, the transaction would require a payment from New Zealand to the government of Spain, but no goods or services would be exchanged, so the transaction is purely financial. Such a bond purchase would be recorded as a credit for Spain and a debit for New Zealand.

The financial account measures two broad types of investment (direct investment and portfolio investment).

Direct investment

This means acquiring a significant ownership stake in a foreign business. Foreign direct investment (FDI) refers to the buying and selling of a minimum of 10% of a company's shares by a foreign investor in the domestic economy or by a domestic investor in another nation's economy.

Whether direct investment counts as a positive or a negative in the financial account depends on who is buying what.

Direct investment abroad: investors from one country may buy or sell ownership stakes in foreign firms.

- **Credits (+)**. When domestic investors sell shares in foreign firms there is an inflow of financial capital, moving the financial account towards the positive.
- **Debits (−)**. When domestic investors acquire an ownership stake in foreign companies there is an outflow of financial capital, which moves the financial account towards the negative.

Direct investment at home: foreign investors may buy or sell ownership stakes in domestic firms.

- **Credits (+)**. When foreign investment in shares of domestic firms increases, there is a net inflow of financial capital, moving the financial account towards the positive.
- **Debits (−)**. When foreigners sell their ownership stake in domestic firms to domestic investors, there is an outflow of financial capital, moving the financial account towards the negative.

The dividends and interest income earned from direct investments abroad or paid to foreign investors at home are counted in the balance of payments in the income section of the current account. But the flow of financial capital into or out of a country for the acquisition of ownership of firms as described above is part of the financial account.

Portfolio investment abroad

Portfolio investment consists of small investors, both domestic and foreign, buying and selling equity shares of companies abroad as part of their portfolio of assets. It

FDI refers to the buying and selling of a minimum of 10% of a company's shares by a foreign investor in the domestic economy or by a domestic investor in another nation's economy.

also includes ownership of foreign debt, issued either by governments or private firms. The difference between portfolio investment and FDI is that to be considered FDI, the investment must result in a minimum of 10% equity ownership in the foreign firm, whereas equity ownership of less than 10% is considered portfolio investment. In addition to stocks and shares, portfolio investment includes ownership of foreign debt certificates, both public and private, such as government and corporate bonds and treasury bills.

Portfolio investment measures the investments of foreigners in businesses in the domestic economy and domestic investors investing in businesses and government debt abroad.

Portfolio investment abroad: the money spent by domestic investors in foreign equity and debt counts as an asset to the investor's home country. Since domestic investors own equity or debt in a foreign firm or government, such investment is considered an asset to the home country and a liability to the foreign firm or government.

- **Credits (+)**. When investors sell those assets, foreigners make a payment to the domestic investor, so there is an addition to the financial account.
- **Debits (–)**. When domestic investors buy foreign assets, there is a subtraction in the financial account, since it requires a payment to a foreign stakeholder.

Portfolio investment at home: the money spent by foreigners on domestic stocks, shares and bonds counts as a liability for the home country. Since a share of a domestic firm or government's debt is transferred to a foreign stakeholder, such investment is considered a liability to the home country, an asset to foreigners.

- **Credits (+)**. A foreign investor buying domestic securities makes a payment to the home country, creating a positive entry in the financial account.
- **Debits (–)**. When the foreign investor sells his domestic securities, there is a subtraction from the financial account because domestic firms or the government must make a payment to the foreign investor.

Just as the profit income earned from direct investment is measured in the current account, so are the interest and dividend incomes earned from portfolio investments. However, the financial flows involved in the acquisition of private and public securities and debt are not considered income, so they are measured by the financial account.

Other investment

Other investment usually refers to loans made by banks to foreign borrowers or money saved in banks across national borders.

Loans from domestic banks to foreign borrowers and savings by domestic households in foreign banks count as assets for the home country, since foreign interests owe money to domestic interests.

- **Credits (+)**. When a foreign borrower pays back a loan to a domestic bank, it counts as a positive in the financial account since it requires a payment from foreigners to domestic interest.
- **Debits (–)**. When a domestic bank makes a loan abroad, it counts as a negative in the financial account since it requires a payment to a foreigner.

Domestic borrowing from foreign banks and foreign savings in domestic banks are considered liabilities for the home nation and an asset for the foreign nation.

- **Credits (+)**. Money borrowed from a foreign bank counts as a positive for the domestic financial account, since it requires a payment from abroad to a domestic interest.
- **Debits (–)**. When a loan is repaid to a foreign bank, there is an outflow of financial capital, resulting in a shift towards the negative in the financial account.

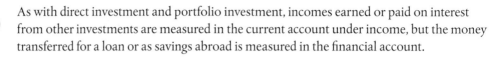

> The financial account of the balance of payments measures the exchanges between a nation and the rest of the world involving ownership of financial and real assets.

As with direct investment and portfolio investment, incomes earned or paid on interest from other investments are measured in the current account under income, but the money transferred for a loan or as savings abroad is measured in the financial account.

Worked example

To calculate the components of the financial account for NZ in 2004, you need to consider the debits and credits and add them up to find the financial account balance (Table 23.3).

TABLE 23.3 NEW ZEALAND'S FINANCIAL ACCOUNT: 2004			
Component of financial account	**Credits / millions of NZD**	**Debits / millions of NZD**	**Balance / millions of NZD**
direct investment	3895	−1293	2602
portfolio investment	3920	−6947	−3027
other investments	1850	−289	1561
financial account balance			1136

Foreign exchange reserves

Foreign exchange reserves refer to the assets of other nations held by a country's central bank. Reserves consist primarily of foreign financial assets such as government bonds and foreign currency.

In a given year, if the flow of money into a country due to its exchanges in the current and financial accounts exceeds the flow of money out of the country, the difference is added to the central bank's official reserves of foreign exchange. If the there is a net outflow of money in a year, the difference is made up by a withdrawal from the central bank's reserves of foreign exchange.

In the case of New Zealand, in 2004 the outflow of money in the current account exceeded the inflow money from the foreign ownership of New Zealand's financial and capital assets by 2327 million NZD. The central bank of New Zealand had to draw on its reserves of foreign assets to make up for this imbalance. To fill the hole left from its current account deficit, the central bank sold 2.3 billion NZD of the foreign currency and government bonds it held, resulting in an inflow of 2.3 billion NZD back to New Zealand from abroad.

The country's ownership of assets denominated in foreign exchange actually decreased because of its large trade deficit, but the resulting inflow of NZ dollars from the sale of these assets corrected the imbalance in the current and financial accounts, achieving a balance of zero in these two accounts.

It should be pointed out that, contrary to common sense, a net deficit in the current, capital and financial accounts actually results in an inflow (thus, a positive sign) in the official reserves account, since the deficit country must sell its reserves of foreign currency to make up for the net deficit. On the other hand, if a country has a net balance of payment surplus, as in China, then the change in the foreign exchange reserves is recorded as a negative since China's ownership of assets denominated in foreign currencies actually increases each year China's current account surplus exceeds its capital and financial account deficits. From an accounting standpoint, China's growing ownership of foreign exchange and foreign-denominated assets counts as a negative in China's official reserves account.

The presence of foreign exchange reserves in a nation's central bank allows the government to draw on these reserves to intervene in the market for their nation's currency to influence the exchange rate, or to balance out the financial account in years when the current and financial accounts do not balance. Additionally, foreign assets can be sold and converted to the domestic currency to finance government spending in times of fiscal need. For instance, in 2009 China launched a $535 billion fiscal stimulus package financed partly by its massive reserves of US dollars accumulated over 20 years of current account surpluses with the US.

Foreign exchange reserves refer to the assets of other nations held by a country's central bank. Reserves consist primarily of foreign financial assets such as government bonds and foreign currency.

Worked example

To calculate the official reserves balance for NZ in 2004, you need to consider the given debits and credits and add them up (Table 23.4).

TABLE 23.4 NEW ZEALAND'S OFFICIAL RESERVES ACCOUNT: 2004

Account	Credits / millions of NZD	Debits / millions of NZD	Change in reserve assets
reserve assets abroad	2327	–	2327

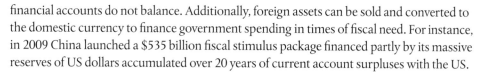

23.3 Relationship between the accounts

Learning outcomes
- Explain that the current account balance is equal to the sum of the capital account and financial account balances.
- Examine how the current account and the financial account are interdependent.
- (HL only) Calculate elements of the balance of payments from a set of data.

Looking at Tables 23.1–23.4, we can see that the large current account deficit is countered by financial and capital account surpluses. This supports the assertion that the sum of the current, capital and financial accounts plus the change in official reserves should equal zero:

current account + capital account + financial account + change in official reserves = 0

Another way to look at this equation is to notice that a nation's current account balance equals the inverse of the capital, financial and reserve account balances.

current account = –(capital account + financial account + change in reserve assets)

Figure 23.3 shows the relationship between the capital and financial accounts and the reserve assets using the figures from Tables 23.2–23.4.

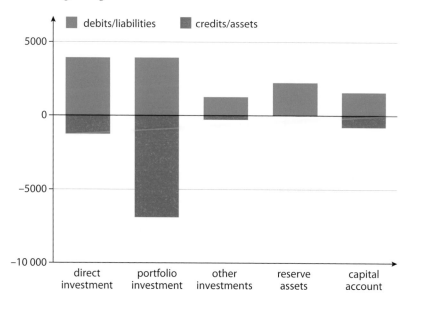

◄ **Figure 23.3**
New Zealand's financial and capital accounts and reserve assets: balance = $4225 billion.

Worked example

To calculate the official balance of payments for NZ in 2004, you need to consider the components of the balance of payments and add them up (Table 23.5).

TABLE 23.5 NEW ZEALAND'S BOP = 0.	
Account	**Balance / millions of NZD**
current account	−4225
capital account	762
financial account	1136
change in official reserves	2327
total balance of payments	0

Notice that New Zealand's current account balance of −4225 is the inverse the sum of the capital, financial and reserve accounts: 762 + 1136 + 2327 = 4225.

HL EXERCISES

1   Prepare the balance of payments for the country whose international exchanges are shown in the table below.

Category	Balance / billions of $
imports of goods	550
import of services	400
export of goods	380
export of services	550
income	−130
current transfers	70
direct investment	40
portfolio investment	−80
capital transfers	90
transaction in non-produced, non-financial assets	−25
reserve assets	?
balance of payments	?

a   Calculate the following balances:

   i   current account

   ii   financial account

   iii capital account

   iv   reserve assets

   v   balance of payments.

b   Does the country have a trade deficit or surplus? Interpret the meaning of the current account balance for the nation's households and firms.

c   Describe how you determined the change in reserve assets and explain why this number is either negative or positive.

Current account deficits

If the total spending by a nation's residents on goods and services imported from the rest of the world exceeds the revenues earned by the nation's producers from the sale of exports to the rest of the world, the nation is likely to be experiencing a current account deficit. The situation is not at all uncommon among many of the world's trading nations. Figure 23.4 shows nations by their cumulative current account balances over the years 1980–2008. The brown countries all accumulated current account deficits over the three decades, with the largest by far being the US, which has a cumulative deficit of $7.3 trillion. The green countries are ones which have had a cumulative surplus in their current accounts, the largest surplus belonging to Japan at $2.7 trillion, followed by China at $1.5 trillion.

Figure 23.4
Current account deficit and surplus nations.

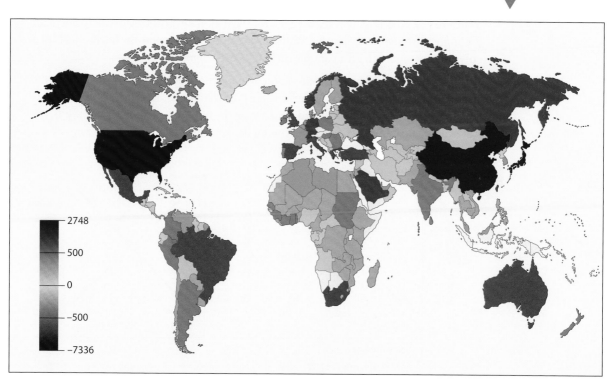

The top 10 current account deficit nations are shown in Figure 23.5. It is obvious that the US alone accounts for a larger current account deficit then the next nine countries combined. At $7.3 trillion dollars in deficits over 28 years, the US deficit surpasses Spain's (at number 2) by 1000%.

Figure 23.5
The top 10 current account deficit nations.

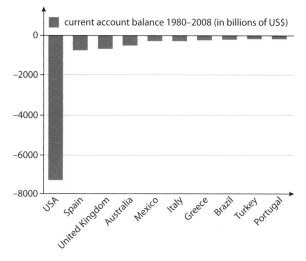

The consequences of a nation having a current account deficit are not immediately clear. And it is debatable whether a trade deficit is necessarily a bad thing. Let's examine some of the facts and implications about current account deficits, and evaluate the pros and cons for countries that run deficits in the short run and in the long run.

> A nation experiences a current account deficit when it spends more on imported goods and services from the rest of the world than it earns from the sale of its exports to the rest of the world.

Effect of a current account deficit on the exchange rate

You have already learned about the determinants of the exchange rate of a nation's currency relative to another currency (Chapter 22). One of the primary determinants of a currency's exchange rate is the demand for the nation's exports relative to the demand for imports from other countries. With this in mind, let's examine the likely effects of a current account deficit on a nation's currency's exchange rate.

When households and firms in one nation demand more of other countries' output than the rest of the world demands of theirs, there is upward pressure on the value of trading partners' currencies and downward pressure on the importing nation's currency. In this way, a movement towards a current account deficit should cause the deficit country's currency to weaken (Figure 23.6).

Figure 23.6
A persistent current account deficit puts downward pressure on the deficit country's currency. **a** Market for NZD in Japan; **b** market for JPY in New Zealand.

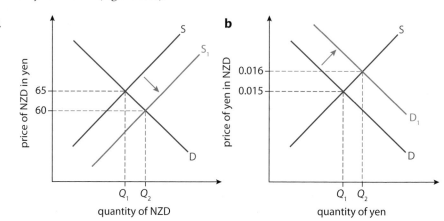

Suppose New Zealand's imports from Japan begin to rise due to rising incomes in New Zealand and a corresponding increase in demand for imports. Assuming Japan's demand for New Zealand's output does not change, New Zealand will move towards a deficit in its current account and Japan towards a surplus. In the foreign exchange market, demand for Japanese yen (JPY) will rise while the supply of NZD now made available to buy JPY increases, depreciating the NZD.

The downward pressure on exchange rates resulting from an increase in a nation's current account deficit should have a self-correcting effect on the trade imbalance. As the NZD weakens relative to its trading partners' currencies, consumers in New Zealand start to find imports more and more expensive, while consumers abroad, over time, find products from New Zealand cheaper. In this way, a floating exchange rate system should, in the long run, eliminate surpluses and deficits between nations in the current account. The persistence of global trade imbalances illustrated in Figure 23.5 is evidence that in reality, the ability of flexible exchange rates to maintain balance in nations' current accounts is quite limited.

Implications of a persistent current account deficit (HL only)

When a country experiences deficits in the current account for year after year, there are some predictable consequences that may have adverse effects on the nation's macroeconomy. These include foreign ownership of domestic assets, higher interest rates, currency depreciation and foreign indebtedness.

Effect on foreign ownership of domestic assets

By definition, the balance of payments must always equal zero. For this reason, a deficit in the current account must be offset by a surplus in the capital and financial accounts. If the money spent by a deficit country on goods from abroad does not end up returning to the deficit country for the purchase of goods and services, it will be re-invested into that country through foreign acquisition of domestic real and financial assets, or held in reserve by surplus nations' central banks.

Essentially, a country with a large current account deficit cannot export enough goods and services to make up for its spending on imports. Instead, it ends up exporting ownership of its financial and real assets. This could take the form of FDI in domestic firms, increased portfolio investment by foreigners in the domestic economy, and foreign ownership of domestic government debt, or the build-up of foreign reserves of the deficit nation's currency.

Effect on interest rates

A persistent deficit in the current account can have adverse effects on the interest rates and investment in the deficit country. A current account deficit can put downward pressure on a nation's exchange rate, which causes inflation in the deficit country because imported goods, services and raw materials become more expensive. In order to prevent massive currency depreciation, the country's central bank may be forced to tighten the money supply and raise domestic interest rates to attract foreign investors and keep demand for the currency and the exchange rate stable. Additionally, since a current account deficit must be offset by a financial account surplus, the deficit country's government may need to offer higher interest rates on government bonds to attract foreign investors. Higher

Many people in New Zealand, the US, and other countries with large financial account surpluses argue that foreign ownership of domestic assets poses a threat to their countries' economic and political sovereignty. To what extent is the freedom of a nation's people determined by the level to which foreign interests have control over the country's domestic financial and real assets? Does political, social and economic freedom become jeopardized as foreign interests gain greater ownership of the domestic economy?

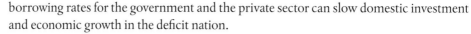

The interest rate effect of a large current account deficit should be negative (i.e. cause interest rates to rise in the deficit country). However, in recent years, the country with the largest trade deficit, the US, has actually experienced record low interest rates even while maintaining persistent current account deficits. This can be understood by examining the macroeconomic conditions of the US and global economies, in which deflation posed a greater threat than inflation over the years 2008–10. Among international investors, the fear of deflation combined with low confidence in the private sector has kept demand for US government bonds high even as the US trade deficit has grown, allowing the US government and central bank to keep interest rates low and continue to attract foreign investors.

borrowing rates for the government and the private sector can slow domestic investment and economic growth in the deficit nation.

Under normal macroeconomic conditions, a build-up of US dollars among America's trading partners would require the US to raise interest rates to create an incentive for foreign investors to re-invest that money into the US economy. However, in the environment of uncertainty and low confidence in the private sector that has prevailed over the last several years, America's trading partners have been willing to finance its current account deficit without requiring high interest rates. In fact, the US has borrowed at record low interest rates during this period.

Effect on indebtedness

A large current account deficit is synonymous with a large financial account surplus. One source of credits in the financial account is foreign ownership of domestic government bonds (i.e. debt). When a central bank from another nation buys government bonds from a nation with which it has a large current account surplus, the deficit nation is essentially going into debt to the surplus nation.

For instance, as of August 2010, the Chinese central bank held $868 billion of US Treasury Securities (government bonds) on its balance sheet. In total, the amount of US debt owned by foreign nations in 2010 was $4.2 trillion, or around 40% of the country's total national debt and 25% of its GDP.

On the one hand, foreign lending to a deficit nation benefits the deficit nation because it keeps demand for government bonds high and interest rates low, which allows the deficit country's government to finance its budget without raising taxes on domestic households and firms.

On the other hand, every dollar borrowed from a foreigner has to be repaid with interest. Interest payments on the national debt cost US taxpayers over $400 billion in 2010, making up around 10% of the federal budget. Nearly half of this went to foreign holders of US debt (Figure 23.7), meaning almost $200 billion of US taxpayer money was handed over to foreign interests, without adding a single dollar to aggregate demand in the US.

Figure 23.7
Foreign-owned US debt (2010): $4.2 trillion.

Some argue that personal debt is higher in countries with higher levels of national debt because the government sets an example for the nation's households. If a government accumulates large amounts of foreign debt, are individuals in society more likely to accumulate debt themselves? To what extent is the behaviour of individuals in society modelled after the behaviour of the government?

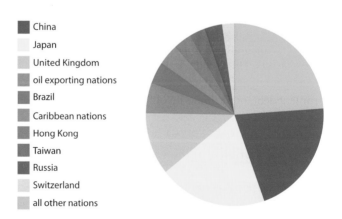

- China
- Japan
- United Kingdom
- oil exporting nations
- Brazil
- Caribbean nations
- Hong Kong
- Taiwan
- Russia
- Switzerland
- all other nations

The opportunity cost of foreign-owned national debt is the public goods and services that could have been provided with the money that instead is owed in interest to foreign creditors. If the US current account were more balanced, foreign countries like China would not have the massive reserves of US dollars to invest in government debt in the first place, and the taxpayer money going to pay interest on this debt could instead be invested in the domestic economy to promote economic growth and development.

Effect on international credit ratings and demand management

A large current account deficit requires a nation to run a financial account surplus. As explained above, a surplus in the financial account may consist of foreign ownership of the deficit nation's government debt. Over time, budget deficits financed through foreign borrowing reduce the attractiveness of the deficit country's government bonds to foreign investors, harming its international credit rating, forcing the government to offer ever increasing interest rates to foreign lenders.

In 2010, Spain's credit rating was downgraded by the international credit ratings agency Moody's. As a result, Spain's borrowing costs rose.

The outlook for Spain's already troubled economy has darkened after Moodys' downgraded its credit rating by one notch, stripping the country of its triple-A debt status.

The move to cut Spain's local and foreign currency government bond ratings to Aa1 from Aaa followed similar action taken by major rating agencies Fitch and Standard & Poor's, reflecting concerns about weak growth prospects and the country's "deteriorating" public finances.

Moody's accepted that while Spain's high external debt and persistent current account deficit are slowly being corrected, they still remain larger than for most of its EU competitors.

Spain's economy is expected to grow more slowly than Germany, France and the UK where borrowing costs are lower. Spain's cost of borrowing has doubled in a year and it now pays twice as much to investors for its benchmark 10-year bonds than Germany.

Adapted from news sources, September 2010

Higher rates must be offered to investors in Spain, reducing the Spanish government's ability to manage the level of AD in the nation through fiscal policy to promote its macroeconomic objectives. A more balanced current account in which Spain's export revenues were higher would reduce the pressures on the budget deficit, improve Spain's credit rating and give the government greater flexibility in its use of demand-management policies.

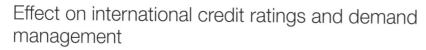

In April 2011, when US sovereign debt reached over $14 trillion, one credit rating agency lowered the credit outlook for the US to negative. While the US kept its AAA rating, the negative outlook says that there is a 33% chance the rating will need to be lowered in the next two years. Are the days of cheap borrowing by the US coming to an end? It would seem so.

Methods to correct a persistent current account deficit (HL only)

The existence of a persistent current account deficit can have many detrimental effects on a nation's economy. For this reason, a government or central bank may find it necessary to intervene to promote greater balance in the nation's current account. At the very least, reducing a current account deficit promotes domestic employment as it leads to an increase in the nation's net exports, meaning more demand for the nation's output and a reduction in unemployment.

Expenditure-switching policies

Any policy by a government aimed at reducing domestic spending on imports and increasing spending on domestically produced goods and services is known as an expenditure-switching policy. Such policies could also be called protectionist since essentially they are aimed at reducing demand for imports and increasing domestic employment, albeit in the name of promoting a balanced current account.

Exchange rate manipulation

As you know, it is possible for governments and central banks to intervene in foreign exchange markets to manipulate the value of their own currency relative to their trading partners (Chapter 22). A central bank may supply a greater quantity of its own currency on forex markets by demanding more of other currencies so as to devalue its currency and make imports less attractive to domestic consumers. Alternatively, it may lower domestic interest rates to make foreign investment less appealing, reducing demand for its currency and lowering the exchange rate.

Either of these policies will make imports more expensive to domestic households, who will switch their expenditures to domestically produced goods and services. Likewise, foreign consumers will find the nation's output more affordable, and over time exports should rise, moving the current account towards balance.

Increased protectionism

Another method for switching expenditures from imports to domestically produced output is to increase the barriers to trade with other nations. Import tariffs or quotas, or subsidies to domestic producers will all make domestically produced goods more attractive to consumers at home and reduce demand for imports.

In the short run, net exports may rise and the current account move towards surplus, but in the long run, such policies promote inefficiency among domestic producers who enjoy artificially high prices due to government protection. Over time, the comparative advantage of foreign producers is likely to increase as domestic firms can get away with being productively inefficient. Instead of focusing on efficiency, domestic producers have strong incentives to devote resources to preserving or expanding protectionist laws. In the meantime, foreign producers grow stronger and more efficient by competing in the world market. Protectionism leads only to a misallocation of resources and ultimately the costs it imposes on society are greater than the benefits it brings.

Expenditure-reducing policies

A second set of policies available to governments hoping to reduce a current account deficit involves the reduction of overall expenditures by firms and households in the nation. This reduces spending on imports and thus restores balance in the current account. Clearly, expenditure-reducing policies have adverse effects on domestic output and employment, and are thus not desirable except as a last resort.

Contractionary fiscal policies

Raising taxes on domestic households and firms reduces disposable income and reduces overall AD, including demand for imports. Reductions in government spending would also reduce disposable incomes and overall AD in the nation. In addition, the fall in import demand, the lower rate of inflation (or, if the decline in AD is great enough, the deflation) that occur as a result of contractionary policies actually make the country's exports more attractive to foreign consumers, further improving the current account deficit.

Contractionary monetary policies

Another means of reducing overall demand for imports in a nation is to raise interest rates to discourage consumption of imported durable goods (financed by borrowing) and firms' investment in imported capital goods. Higher interest rates also have a disinflationary (or deflationary) effect, making the nation's exports more attractive to foreign consumers.

On the other hand, higher interest rates may attract foreign investors, shifting the nation's financial account further towards surplus and appreciating the currency as foreign demand for domestic assets rises. This could have the opposite effect of that intended by the central bank, as a stronger currency might make imports even more attractive, offsetting any improvement in the current account achieved by reducing consumption of durable goods and investment in foreign capital goods.

Expansionary supply-side policies

Contractionary fiscal and monetary policies will surely reduce overall demand in an economy and thereby help reduce a current account deficit. But the costs of such policies are likely to outweigh the benefits, as domestic employment, output and economic growth suffer due to reduced spending on the nation's goods and services. A better option for governments worried about their trade deficit is to pursue supply-side policies that increase the competitiveness of domestic producers in the global economy.

In the long run, the best way for a nation to reduce a current account deficit is to allocate its scarce resources towards the economic activities in which it can most effectively compete in the global economy. In an environment of increasingly free trade between nations, countries like the US and those of Western Europe will continue to confront structural shifts in their economies that at first seem devastating. However, over time, such shifts are likely to be seen as both inevitable and beneficial to the overall level of efficiency and welfare in the global economy.

The auto industry in the US has changed forever due to competition from Japan. The textile industry in Europe long since passed its apex of production, and the UK consumer will never again buy a television or computer monitor made in the UK. The reality is, much of the world's manufactured goods can and should be made more cheaply and efficiently in Asia and Latin America than they ever could be in the US or Europe.

The question Europe and the US should be asking, therefore, is not 'how can we get back what we have lost and restore balance in our current account', but 'what can we provide for the world that no one else can?' By focusing their resources towards providing the goods and services that no Asian or Latin American competitor is capable of providing, the deficit countries of the world should be able to reduce their current account deficits and at the same time stimulate AD at home, while increasing the productivity of the nation's resources and promoting long-run economic growth.

That may sound easy to say, and it is fair to ask 'how can they achieve this?' This is where supply-side policies come in. Smart supply-side policies mean more than tax cuts for corporations and subsidies to domestic producers. Smart supply-side policies that would promote more balanced global trade and long-run economic growth include the following.

Investments in education and healthcare

Nothing makes a nation more competitive in the global economy than a highly educated and healthy workforce. Exports from Europe and the US will increasingly come from the highly skilled service sector and less and less from the manufacturing sector. Highly educated and skilled workers are needed for future economic growth and global competitiveness, particularly in scientific fields such as engineering, medicine, finance, economics and business.

Public funding for scientific research and development

Exports from the US and Europe have increasingly depended on scientific innovation and new technologies. Copyright and patent protection ensure that scientific breakthroughs achieved in one country are allowed a period of time during which only that country can enjoy the sales of exports in the new field. Green energy, nano-technology, and biomedical research are emerging technologies that require sustained commitments from the government sector for dependable funding.

Investments in modern transportation and communication infrastructure

To remain competitive in the global economy, the countries of Europe and North America must assure that domestic firms have at their disposal the most modern and efficient transport and communication infrastructure available. High-speed rail, well-maintained inter-state or international highways, modern port facilities, high-speed internet and telecommunications; these investments allow for lower costs of production and more productive capital and labour, making these countries' goods more competitive in the global marketplace.

Benefits of reducing a current account deficit

Reducing a current account deficit will have many benefits for a nation like the US, Spain, the UK or Australia. A stronger currency ensures price stability, low interest rates allow for economic growth, and perhaps most importantly, less taxpayer money has to be paid in interest to foreign creditors. Governments and central banks may go about reducing a current account deficit in many ways: exchange rate controls, protectionism, contractionary monetary and fiscal policies, or supply-side policies may all be implemented to restore balance in the current account. Only one of these options promotes long-run economic growth and increases the efficiency with which a nation employs its scarce factors of production.

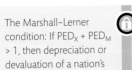

To access Worksheet 23.1 on currency manipulation, please visit www.pearsonbacconline. com and follow the onscreen instructions.

Supply-side policies are clearly the most efficient and economically justifiable method for correcting a current account deficit. Unfortunately, they are also the least politically popular, since the benefits of such policies are not realized in the short run, but take years, maybe decades, to accrue. For this reason, time and time again governments turn to protectionism in response to rising trade deficits.

The Marshall–Lerner condition and the J-curve effect (HL only)

When a nation runs a persistent deficit in its current account it should put downward pressure on the country's exchange rate (page 492). In a system of floating exchange rates, such fluctuations between the currencies of deficit and surplus countries should correct the imbalances by altering relative prices of imports and exports in a way that moves both deficit and surplus countries towards a more balanced current account. However, such shifts do not always occur.

The Marshall–Lerner condition: If $PED_X + PED_M > 1$, then depreciation or devaluation of a nation's currency shifts the balance on its current account towards surplus.

Whether or not depreciation of a nation's currency reduces a trade deficit depends on the combined elasticity of demand for imports and exports. If $PED_X + PED_M > 1$, then depreciation in the currency will move a country's current account towards surplus. This is known as the Marshall–Lerner condition (MLC). If the MLC is not met, then depreciation of a nation's currency will worsen a country's current account deficit.

Common sense might indicate that if a country's currency depreciates relative to other currencies, this should lead to an improvement in the country's balance of trade. For Country Z whose currency is the dollar, the reasoning is as follows.

- A weaker dollar means foreigners have to give up less of their money in order to get one dollar's worth of Country Z's output.

- At the same time, since Country Z's dollar is worth less in foreign currency, imports become more expensive, as Country Z's residents have to spend more dollars for a certain amount of another country's output; hence, imports should decrease.
- The decrease in imports and increase in exports should reduce Country Z's current account deficit.

Fewer imports and more exports should mean an improvement in the country's balance of trade, but this is not necessarily the case. What matters is not whether a country is importing less and exporting more, but whether the increase in revenues from exports exceeds the decrease in expenditures on imports. Here is where the Marshall–Lerner condition can be applied.

The following is an example of a situation in which the MLC is met and depreciation of Country Z's dollar results in an improvement in the current account.

- Import spending exceeds export revenues in Country Z, causing depreciation of Country Z's dollar.
- If foreigners' demand for Country Z's exports is relatively elastic, then a slightly weaker dollar should cause a proportionally larger increase in foreign demand for Country Z's output, causing export revenues in Country Z to rise.
- Likewise, if Country Z's residents' demand for imports is relatively elastic, then a slightly weaker dollar should cause their demand for imports to decrease proportionally more than the increase in price of those imports, reducing overall expenditures on imports.
- If the combined elasticity of demand for exports and imports is elastic (i.e. the coefficient is greater than 1), then depreciation of Country Z's currency will shift its current account towards surplus. In this case, the MLC is met.

So what if the MLC is not met? Demand for exports and imports may not always be so responsive to changes in prices brought on by changes in exchange rates. Imagine a scenario in which a weaker dollar does little to change foreign demand for Country Z's output. In this case, income from exports may actually decline (since it now takes fewer units of foreign currency to buy Country Z's exports) as Country Z's dollar depreciates.

Likewise, if Country Z's residents' demand for imports is highly inelastic, then more expensive imports have a proportionally small effect on import demand. In which case, expenditures on imports may actually rise as they become more expensive. If the combined price elasticity of demand for exports and imports is inelastic, depreciation of the currency actually worsens a trade deficit. Country Z's import expenditures rise while export revenues fall, worsening the current account deficit.

The MLC is basically an application of the total revenue test of elasticity (Chapter 4). If demand for a country's exports is inelastic, a fall in price leads to a decrease in total revenues from the sale of exports. The same depreciation that caused the price of exports to fall causes the price of imports to rise, and if demand for imports is inelastic, then their higher prices causes total expenditures on imports to rise. Thus, the MLC is not met (Figure 23.8, overleaf).

If MLC is met, depreciation of a nation's currency causes revenues from export sales to rise and expenditures on imports to fall, moving the country towards a trade surplus (Figure 23.9, overleaf).

Figures 23.8 and 23.9 show how price elasticity is a critical element in any decision to devalue currency. In reality, the MLC can be met even when the elasticities of demand for exports and imports are separately somewhat inelastic. For example a PED_X of 0.5 and a PED_M of 0.6, both relatively inelastic by themselves, combine to have a value of 1.1, enough to satisfy the MLC.

To access Worksheet 23.2 on the MLC, please visit www.pearsonbacconline.com and follow the onscreen instructions.

Figure 23.8
The effect of depreciation on imports and exports depends on their PED: if demand is inelastic, depreciation may worsen a current account deficit. **a** Market for Country Z's exports; **b** market for imports in Country Z.

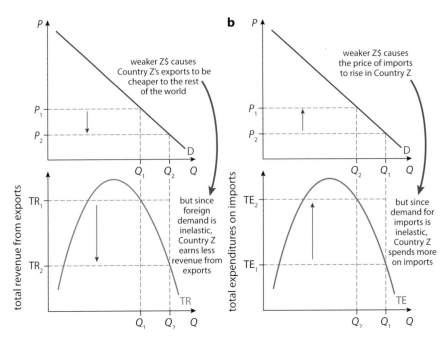

Figure 23.9 The effect of depreciation on imports and exports depends on their PED: if demand is elastic, depreciation may move a country towards a current account surplus. **a** Market for Country Z's exports; **b** market for imports in Country Z.

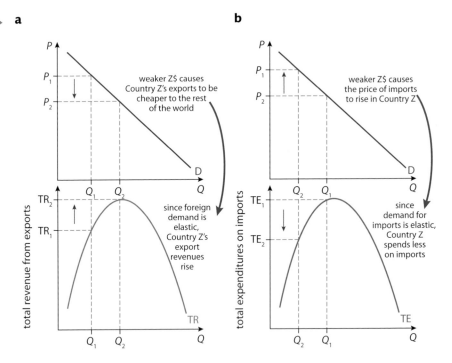

The J curve

The MLC analysis above suggests that a country with an inelastic import and export demand combination would never want to devalue its currency, because that would lead to a worsening of its current account. However, PED changes over time. As consumers have time to adjust to changes in the price of particular goods, they are able to change their behaviour to consume either more or less of the good in question depending on how the price changed.

For example, when the price of a particular brand of toothpaste goes up, consumers who are used to buying that toothpaste may continue to do so for a while until they have found a suitable substitute. Over time, the responsiveness of consumers to a change in price increases as consumers can alter their decisions about what and where to buy.

When the exchange rate between two nations changes, consumers in both nations will be more responsive to the changing price of imports as time goes by. For example, if the value of the Swiss franc were to fall relative to the British pound, British consumers would not immediately notice that Swiss goods were getting cheaper in the UK. Chocolate consumers in the UK would continue to buy, say, French and Belgian chocolate in the short run. However, over time, they would begin to take notice of the relatively cheaper Swiss chocolates, and therefore become more responsive to the lower price of Swiss imports in the long run. Likewise, Swiss consumers would find British goods more expensive, but Swiss consumers who are used to buying British beers would be more responsive to the higher prices over time, once they've been able to find suitable substitutes, such as Belgian and German beers.

The PED for both imports and exports increases over time. Therefore, following depreciation of a nation's currency, it is likely that in the short run, demand for imports and exports will be inelastic, the MLC will not be met, and therefore the weaker currency actually moves a country towards a current account deficit. As time passes, however, and the currency remains weak, consumers at home and abroad begin to alter their demand based on the changing price of imports and therefore PED becomes more elastic, the MLC is met, and the nation whose currency weakened moves towards a current account surplus.

The implication is that in the short run, depreciation of a nation's currency is likely to move its current account towards a deficit, whereas in the long run, the current account balance should begin to improve. This is illustrated in a simple diagram known as the J curve (Figure 23.10).

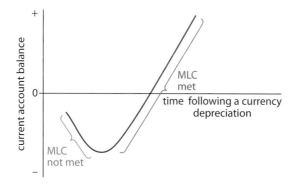

Figure 23.10
The J curve shows how depreciation of the nation's currency is likely to affect the current account balance over time.

The J curve is simply a line showing the change that is likely to occur in a nation's current account following a currency depreciation over time. Due to the inelasticity of demand for imports and exports in the short run, a weaker currency moves the current account deeper into deficit for a while. But over time, consumers at home and abroad adjust to the changing prices of imports and exports and the current account deficit begins to decline as the balance of trade moves towards surplus.

23.5 Current account surpluses

Learning outcomes

- Explain why a surplus in the current account of the balance of payments may result in upward pressure on the exchange rate of the currency.

- (HL only) Discuss the possible consequences of a rising current account surplus, including lower domestic consumption and investment, as well as the appreciation of the domestic currency and reduced export competitiveness.

Selling more goods and services to the rest of the world than a nation consumes in imports results in a surplus in the nation's current account. It is said that one country's deficit is another country's surplus. This could not be more clearly illustrated than in Figure 23.11 showing the combined current account surpluses and deficits of the world over the last several years.

Figure 23.11
Global trade imbalances have grown over the last 15 years.

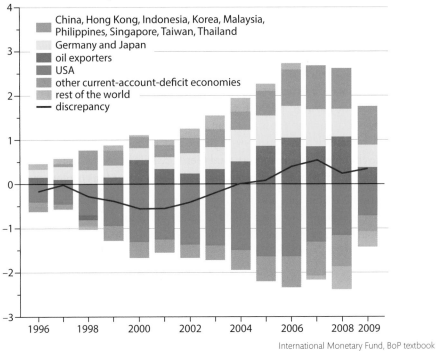

International Monetary Fund, BoP textbook

The coloured bars above the zero line represent the total trade surplus (in trillions of dollars) of the handful of countries that have the largest current account surpluses. These include China, Germany, Japan and the oil-exporting nations of the Middle East. The bars below the zero line represent the trade deficit nations, most notably the US.

The ten countries with the largest current account surpluses over the last three decades are shown in Figure 23.12.

Figure 23.12
The top 10 current account surplus nations over the last 30 years.

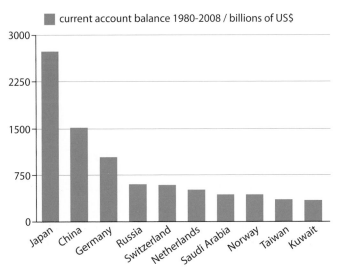

The major source of the trade surpluses in Japan, China, Taiwan, Germany and Switzerland is the export of manufactured goods and services, while the surpluses of Russia, Saudi Arabia, Norway and Kuwait are accounted for by large exports of oil, gas, and other primary commodities.

The consequences of a persistent surplus in a nation's current account are basically the reverse of those occasioned by a persistent deficit. They include currency appreciation, increased ownership of foreign financial and real assets, as well as lower overall levels of domestic consumption and the increased likelihood of protectionist policies being imposed by trading partners attempting to reduce their trade deficits.

A nation's current account of the balance of payments is in surplus when the nation's total export revenues exceed its expenditures on imports.

Effect of a current account surplus on the exchange rate

If a nation consistently sells more of its output to foreigners than it demands of foreign output, demand for the exporting nation's currency will eventually rise and appreciate. In addition, since the surplus nation demands relatively little of foreign goods, the supply of its currency in foreign exchange markets will fall, contributing to the currency's appreciation.

Over time, an appreciating currency will reduce the export industry's competitiveness with the rest of the world and force domestic producers to become more efficient or shut down as foreign demand for their goods eventually falls.

This adjustment assumes, of course, that exchange rates are floating and the currency is allowed to appreciate. China, the country with the largest current account surplus (in 2009, $297 billion, down from $426 billion in 2008) prevents its currency from appreciating as it would under a floating exchange rate system by intervening in the forex market to peg the exchange rate to the US dollar. By closely managing the RMB's value through its use of its foreign exchange reserves to buy and sell dollars and RMB in the forex market, the Chinese government ensures that the country's large trade surplus does not cause an appreciation of its currency, which would reduce demand for Chinese exports and slow the country's economic growth.

Under a system of floating exchange rates, current account surpluses should be kept in check by the appreciation of the surplus nation's currency and the corresponding decrease in demand for its exports and the increasing appeal of imports among domestic consumers. However, in a global economy in which governments actively intervene in foreign exchange markets to devalue their own currencies, massive imbalances can persist for years and even decades.

Effect of a current account surplus on domestic consumption and savings (HL only)

Persistent current account surpluses imply that households in the surplus nation are consuming at a lower level over time than households in countries with current account deficits. The reason for this may not be immediately clear. Essentially, the high levels of investment in foreign assets, plus the large reserves of foreign exchange held in the central bank of a surplus nation add up to a form of forced savings among the surplus country's households.

Think of it this way: money earned from the sale of exported goods but *not* spent on imported goods is money saved by the nation with the trade surplus. The financial account deficit needed to maintain a current account surplus reduces households' consumption by re-investing money earned from export sales in foreign assets rather than spending it on goods and services.

China's national savings rate is around 45%. This does not mean that the average Chinese household saves 45% of its income earned in the workplace. It means that of the Chinese GDP of $5 trillion, nearly half was invested in real and financial assets at home or abroad (in 2009). Only around 40% of China's GDP was accounted for by household consumption. Compare this to the US, where 12% of GDP was accounted for by savings and investment, and 70% was made up of household consumption.

The high levels of savings and investment at home and abroad necessary to maintain China's massive current account surplus result in less of the country's hard-earned income going towards domestic consumption or spending on imports. Another way to think about this situation is as follows. Nearly half of the stuff produced in China is exported to and consumed by the rest of the world, but China imports far less than it exports, meaning nearly half of China's output is *not* consumed by Chinese households, but by foreigners. A trade deficit nation, on the other hand, may actually be able to consume *more* than it produces, since many of the goods and services its households enjoy are produced abroad and are imported using money borrowed from foreigners in the financial account.

To access Worksheet 23.3 on China's billions, please visit www. pearsonbacconline.com and follow the onscreen instructions.

Evaluating the global trade imbalance

Many people around the world are worried about the large imbalances that exist in nations' current and financial accounts. Figure 23.11 shows the roughly three trillion dollar surplus that has emerged over the last decade among a handful of exporting nations, compared with the equally large deficits of another handful of importing nations. Many consider this to be a worrying trend. If the trend continues and these imbalances grow ever larger, the implications for the global economy could be severe.

Continued decline in secondary and tertiary sectors in the West

Some worry that the continued dependence on imports will completely wipe out any remaining manufacturing-sector jobs in Western Europe, the US and other countries with large trade deficits. The loss of manufacturing jobs due to free trade, argue some, has wiped out the middle class and lowered median incomes for hundreds of millions of Americans and Europeans who only 20 years ago could have counted on a strong domestic manufacturing sector for life-long employment offering generous wages and benefits.

This era of globalization is characterized by a growing trend in outsourcing and off-shoring jobs in both the secondary and tertiary sectors from the deficit nations to the surplus nations. Many foresee only growing imbalances as more and more of the world's output is produced in Asia, Latin America, and perhaps, in the future, Africa.

Persisting poverty in the developing world

From the exporting nations' perspectives, persistent trade surpluses promise continued economic growth, but such export-oriented growth may come at the expense of improvements in the typical household's standard of living if this growth is continually fuelled by more and more investment abroad.

Financial account deficits in these nations mean that households are forced to consume less than they would be able to if their currencies were allowed to appreciate and the current account were in better balance. Increased imports to countries like China and its Asian neighbours may mean slower growth as their export sectors adjust to more competition from abroad, but it would also mean higher standards of living for the households in these nations as they begin to enjoy the increased purchasing power of their stronger currencies and the variety of imported goods available from the rest of the world.

The threat to economic sovereignty

Perhaps most worrying to some, particularly in the US, is the continued increase in foreign ownership of domestic assets and the corresponding threat to economic sovereignty that results from persistent financial account surpluses. We must keep in mind that a surplus is not always good, just as a deficit is not always bad. America's growing financial account surplus means that increasingly, ownership of American corporations, factories, office buildings, real estate, and the national debt itself is in the hands of foreign interests.

Additionally, the build up of US dollar assets in Asian central banks is frightening to Americans who realize that should these governments decide to reduce their holding of US dollars, the corresponding increase in supply of the currency on foreign exchange markets would cause such a massive depreciation of the US dollar that Americans would find the imports they so desperately depend on becoming increasingly expensive. Take into account the $200 billion of taxpayers' money being paid in interest to foreign holders of US government bonds each year, and the desire to achieve greater balance in the nation's current and financial accounts becomes quite understandable.

Blame it on the RMB

So how can better balance be achieved? It may sound harsh to make this claim, but until China relinquishes control over the value of its currency, the trade imbalances of today are likely to continue.

Twenty years ago, the growth of Chinese exports posed little threat to the more developed economies of the world. China was just like other developing economies of the time (Russia, Brazil, Indonesia, India): a huge country with a tiny economy. But as China's exports have moved up the value chain, from toys and T-shirts to airplanes and auto parts, its continued growth has posed ever-increasing threats to the more developed economies of the world.

Today, China competes for business not only with other low-income countries flush with cheap labour (e.g. India and Brazil), but with the manufacturing giants of the 20th century as well (e.g. Germany and the US). As China has risen to the ranks of the largest and most advanced economies in the world, its policy of directly managing the exchange rate of the RMB relative to the US dollar has caused increasing disruption in the efficient allocation of the world's resources across national borders.

A weak RMB hurts American producers *and* those in other less developed countries, who find it ever harder to compete with China's low-cost producers, whose costs are kept even lower thanks to the artificially weak RMB. To compete with China, other low-cost, developing countries have had to resort to currency devaluations of their own, further accelerating the flow of productive resources from Europe and the US to Asia and Latin America.

Only when the RMB is allowed to appreciate against the dollar and the currencies of China's other trading partners will the massive imbalances of the last decade begin to diminish. Following such an adjustment, the price of Chinese goods in Europe and America would certainly rise in the short run but, over time, other less developed economies whose growth has been stifled by the weak RMB will begin to meet the global demand for low-cost, labour-intensive goods. Perhaps with a stronger RMB, China's textile industry would decline as Cambodia, Lao People's Democratic Republic, and Bangladesh offer cheaper exports to the West. In the meantime, high-tech industries that have recently declined in the West and relocated to China will be more likely to remain in Europe or America, allowing those countries to once again provide more of the advanced goods and services in which they truly hold a comparative advantage to the global marketplace.

China might stand to benefit as well. Revaluing the currency should improve buying power, making imported consumer goods more affordable. It could also reduce the inflationary pressure that is expected to grow as China seeks out greater quantities of imported resource materials to feed its manufacturing colossus.

Until the Chinese government decides it can safely loosen the noose on the RMB, however, the imbalances that have seen the decline in manufacturing in the West and the corresponding rise of foreign indebtedness and dependence on imports will continue. For now, unfortunately, it does not appear such a correction will begin any time soon.

CASE STUDY

BoP surplus hit in Sept quarter on rising spend abroad

MUMBAI: Despite doubling of net portfolio inflows, India's overall balance of payments surplus slumped in the July–September quarter because consumption surged and long-term stable FDI slowed down.

Preliminary data released by the Reserve Bank of India (RBI) on Friday showed current account deficit – net of cross-border transactions of goods and services – during July–September 10, which rose to $15.8 billion compared to $9.2 billion in July–September 09.

This was because imports rose faster than exports and net services income was lower during the period.

There was a sharp rise in portfolio inflows, but net capital flows remained almost at same levels as last year as other flows, particularly FDI were muted and outward investment increased. Net FDI inflow in the period was $2.5 billion against $7.5 billion a year ago.

The net capital inflow in the period was $20.4 billion against $19.3 billion in corresponding period last year.

After taking into account the larger current account deficit, the increase in foreign exchange reserves on balance of payments basis was $3.3 billion in July–September 10 against $9.4 billion in the year-ago period.

The current account records transactions related to purchase of goods and services or income from a service, while capital account inflows include investments or debt creating flows.

The balance of payments is the sum of the current and capital account transactions in a given period.

The RBI, in its latest Financial Stability report released on Thursday, had warned about a potential threat to the external sector. 'Accelerated capital flows to the economy have helped finance the widening current account deficit. However, a potentially worrying feature of capital flows to India has been the dominance of portfolio flows and debt flows as compared to the more stable investment flows on gross basis,' it said. 'Such flows require watchful management as they are prone to sudden stops and reversals.'

'The deficit is being increasingly financed by short-term capital, rather than FDI, which is enlarging short-term debt and raising external vulnerability,' said Tushar Podar, chief India economist, Goldman Sachs, in a recent note to clients. 'We flag the deterioration in external balances as the biggest risk to India's growth story, and one that investors should follow closely.'

The trade deficit (excess of imports over exports) was higher at $35.4 billion in July–September against $29.6 billion a year ago.

The surplus on the invisibles account (items like software, travel and tourism income and remittances by the Indian diaspora) was lower at $19.6 billion compared to $20.4 billion in the same period last year.

Remittances also dropped to $13 billion from $13.8 billion but net software earnings for the quarter rose to $12.3 billion from $10.8 billion.

Economic Times, India, 1 January 2011

EXERCISES

2 According to the article above, India has a current account deficit. What must be true about India's capital and financial account balances? Why must this be true?

3 The article says 'a potentially worrying feature of capital flows to India has been the dominance of portfolio flows and debt flows as compared to the more stable investment flows on gross basis'. Why would inflows of FDI be more likely to contribute to long-term economic growth in India than the short-term investments and the accumulation of debt for India?

4 India has a deficit in the balance of trade in goods, but a surplus in the balance of trade in services. Why, then, does India still have a current account deficit overall?

PRACTICE QUESTIONS

1 **Item 1** **Fighting the slowdown in Chile**

- A reduction in inflationary pressures because of slow growth of international demand, and a deceleration of the world economy, has allowed the Central Bank of Chile to cut interest rates to their lowest level for 14 years. The low interest rates have in turn contributed towards the peso (the Chilean currency) hitting a record low; and the **depreciation** of the peso is raising import prices.

- The Chilean government would like to see foreign trade add to growth, and is planning to eliminate its remaining controls on **capital flows** to stop the decline in FDI, and to provide funds for businesses.

- A bilateral free trade agreement with the USA will help in the long run, but Chile's economy could use a boost now, which may leave expansionary monetary policy as the main instrument available.

Adapted from *Business Week*

Item 2 **Chile's real GDP and current account balance**

Real GDP (annual % change)			Current account balance (% of GDP)		
2000	2001	2002	2000	2001	2002
5.4	4.0	3.3	−1.4	−2.2	−2.6

a With reference to Item 1, explain the following terms which are in bold in the passage:

i depreciation (2 marks) [AO1]

ii capital flows. (2 marks) [AO1]

b With reference to Item 2, briefly describe what has happened to the current account balance since 2000. Using any of the data provided, give one possible reason for this change. (4 marks) [AO2]

To access Quiz 23, an interactive, multiple-choice quiz on this chapter, please visit www.pearsonbacconline.com and follow the onscreen instructions.

c Explain the relationship between low interest rates and the depreciation of the peso.

(4 marks) [AO2]

d Use the data and your knowledge of economics to evaluate the decision of the Chilean government to enter trade agreements and reduce controls on capital flows.

(8 marks) [AO3]

2   **OECD survey, Czech Republic**

According to the OECD's latest survey of the Czech Republic, structural reforms with their emphasis on supply-side measures aided a strong recovery in 2000 and early 2001 after the **recession** from 1997–99. Efforts to fight inflation through monetary policy have also been quite successful. However, the large **current account deficit** is putting downward pressure on the exchange rate and this may be inflationary. This, along with a loose fiscal policy is posing a challenge to monetary policy in stabilizing demand in the medium term. In order to maintain its inflation targets, it is recommended that the Czech Republic continue using supply-side measures along with fiscal tightening.

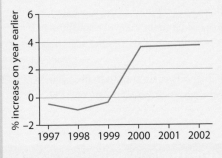
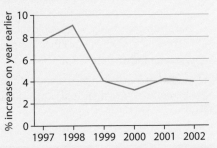

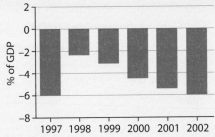

adapted from *The Economist*, 4 August 2001

a Define following terms that appear in bold in the text:

   i recession (line 3)   (2 marks) [AO1]

   ii current account deficit (line 4).   (2 marks) [AO1]

b Analyse the relationship between GDP and the current account balance between 1999 and 2001.   (4 marks) [AO2]

c Using an exchange rate diagram, explain why 'the large current account deficit is putting downward pressure on the exchange rate'.   (4 marks) [AO2], [AO4]

d Using the data and your knowledge of economics, discuss possible consequences of a persistent deficit balance in the Czech Republic's current account.   (8 marks) [AO3]

© International Baccalaureate Organization 2003 (part of **a** only)

ECONOMIC INTEGRATION

Forms of economic integration

Chapters 20–23 discuss the theories and the realities of free trade in the world today. Economists tend to believe that trade is generally beneficial for those nations that participate in it. Of course, there are always losers whenever nations engage in exchanges of goods and services but, in most cases, the gains of trade for society outweigh the costs.

Free trade based on the principle of comparative advantage is an ideal that would promote maximum allocative efficiency of the world's scarce resources. Unfortunately, it is an ideal that is far from being achieved. Since the industrial revolution and the end of colonialism, the *status quo* for most of the world's nations is generally protectionist and anti-trade.

During much of the 20th century, many of the world's economies were ideologically aligned in opposing camps, divided by the Iron Curtain into capitalist and communist systems. But, on the break-up of the Soviet Union, the ideological battle seemed to end as the vast majority of nations pursued free market reforms in an effort to promote long-run economic growth and development in their economies.

However, while free market reforms have prevailed within nations and trade has flourished among the citizens of the emerging market economies, free trade between nations has grown more slowly than many would have hoped. Nations often act out of the fear of losing current industry, rather than seeing the opportunities and benefits of open trade. And so they resist further economic integration.

The hesitancy among nations to open their borders to international trade has led to the need for clearly articulated agreements between nations as a precursor to economic integration. Trading blocs represent arrangements between two or more nations through which tariffs, quotas, and other barriers to trade of most goods and services are either reduced or eliminated altogether. Trading blocs may take several forms and can be categorized by the stages of economic integration achieved. The lowest stage represents the first steps between two or more nations at integrating their economies, while the highest stage is complete economic integration.

The European Free Trade Area is one of many such trading blocs meant to promote the free flow of goods and services between nations.

 A trading bloc is an agreement between governments of two or more nations where regional barriers to trade (tariffs, quotas and non-tariff barriers) are reduced or eliminated in the participating states.

Levels of economic integration

Completely free trade between nations is the ideal but, in reality, countries tend to take small steps towards eliminating barriers to trade between one another. The types of trading bloc nations may enter into with other nations are, in order of level of economic integration:

- preferential trade agreement
- free trade area
- customs union
- common market
- economic and monetary union
- complete economic integration.

These trading blocs can be either bilateral (between two nations) or multilateral (between more than two nations). Typically, preferential trade agreements are agreed between two nations or between a group of nations that are part of a free trade area and another nation. At the other end of the scale, there is only one major economic and monetary union in the world today – the eurozone: European nations using a common currency, the euro. However, several economic and monetary unions are in various stages of proposal and development.

24.2 Preferential trade agreements

Learning outcomes
- Distinguish between bilateral and multilateral (WTO) trade agreements.
- Explain that preferential trade agreements give preferential access to certain products from certain countries by reducing or eliminating tariffs, or by other agreements relating to trade.

Preferential trade agreement

A preferential trade agreement (PTA) is when two or more countries reduce or remove tariffs on particular goods or services produced in participating countries, or make other agreements reducing the barriers to free trade between the nations. This is the first stage of economic integration, and differs from higher stages in that not all goods are necessarily exempt from tariffs, nor must tariffs be eliminated completely on the goods included.

The term 'preferential' points to the fact that when nations sign up to such an agreement, the result is that one nation ends up preferring to buy goods and services from the other rather than from countries not included in the agreement. Preferred trade differs from free trade in that the trade is clearly not free since tariffs are not completely eliminated on all goods and services, and tariff reductions only apply to select nations, not all of a country's trading partners. Therefore, PTAs result in increased trade between participating nations at the expense of trade with the rest of the world. PTAs fall short of achieving an efficient allocation of resources, even between their members.

PTAs can be either bilateral or multilateral. Table 24.1 shows some contemporary PTAs.

TABLE 24.1 PREFERENTIAL TRADE AGREEMENTS			
Name of PTA	**Countries involved**	**Coverage**	**Year created**
Asia Pacific Trade Agreement	Bangladesh, China, India, Lao People's Democratic Republic, Republic of Korea, Sri Lanka	Goods only	1976
Latin American Integration Association (LAIA)	Argentina, Bolivarian Republic of Venezuela, Bolivia, Brazil, Chile, Colombia, Cuba, Ecuador, Mexico, Paraguay, Peru, Uruguay	Goods only	1981
Lao PDR–Thailand	Lao People's Democratic Republic; Thailand	Goods only	1991
Economic Cooperation Organization (ECO)	Afghanistan, Azerbaijan, Islamic Republic of Iran, Kazakhstan, Kyrgyz Republic, Pakistan, Tajikistan, Turkey, Turkmenistan, Uzbekistan	Goods only	1992
Melanesian Spearhead Group (MSG)	Fiji, Papua New Guinea, Solomon Islands, Vanuatu	Goods only	1994
South Asian Preferential Trade Arrangement (SAPTA)	Bangladesh, Bhutan, India, Maldives, Nepal, Pakistan, Sri Lanka	Goods only	1995
Chile–India	Chile; India	Goods only	2007

Two of the agreements in Table 24.1 are bilateral, many are multilateral. Some PTAs are regional (such as ECO), others include nations in very different geographical locations (Chile–India). All the agreements involve reductions in or removal of tariffs on selected goods. Services are not included in any of these PTAs.

A PTA represents a step towards free trade but it must be noted that it is a rather small step. Such a pact between two or more nations promotes increased integration of the small number of countries involved, but only on selected goods and at the expense of increased integration with the rest of the world's economies.

When two countries like Chile and India enter into a PTA, the reduction in tariffs on Indian goods in Chile will certainly increase the demand for Indian imports in Chile, but this may mean a decline in demand for other countries' goods. For instance, Indian rice is cheaper for Chilean consumers because of the PTA between the nations. This may mean that Chile imports more Indian rice, but also means that Chile imports less Thai rice. This is why these agreements are called preferential and not free trade agreements. Under totally free trade, Chile would import rice from the country that has the lowest opportunity cost in rice production, and this could be any country in the world. Under a PTA, Chile imports more rice from India, even if India does not have the lowest opportunity cost, simply because the tariff on Indian rice is lower than that on rice from other countries.

 A preferential trade agreement is when two or more countries reduce or remove tariffs on particular goods or services produced in participating countries, or make other agreements reducing the barriers to free trade between the nations.

To what extent does a preferential trade agreement achieve the ideals of free trade? Does it seem ethical for one country to prefer a particular country in its trade relations over all the other countries with which it could potentially trade more freely?

24.3 Trading blocs

Learning outcomes
- Distinguish between a free trade area, a customs union and a common market.
- Explain that economic integration will increase competition among producers within the trading bloc.
- Compare and contrast the different types of trading blocs.

Free trade area

A free trade area (FTA) is formed when two or more nations make an agreement to completely eliminate tariffs on most (if not all) goods and services traded between them. FTAs are at the second level of economic integration, closer to truly free trade than a PTA where tariffs are reduced or eliminated only on certain goods.

Countries in an FTA agree to eliminate tariffs on goods and/or services produced in other member countries, but maintain the right to set their own tariffs on non-member countries.

According to the World Trade Organization (WTO), there were 168 FTAs existing in 2010, some bilateral, some multilateral. Some are shown in Table 24.2 (overleaf).

Each of these FTAs requires the removal of tariffs in the member countries on goods and/or services produced in and imported from all other member countries. The intended effect of such an agreement, of course, is to allow for a more efficient allocation of resources based on the principle of comparative advantage among the member states.

 A free trade area is formed when two or more nations make an agreement to completely eliminate tariffs on most (if not all) goods and services traded between the member nations.

Name of FTA	Countries involved	Coverage	Year enacted
Australia–New Zealand (ANZCERTA)	Australia; New Zealand	Goods and services	1989
Ukraine–Russian Federation	Ukraine; Russian Federation	Goods only	1994
North American Free Trade Agreement (NAFTA)	Canada, Mexico, US	Goods and services	1994
EC–Egypt	Austria, Belgium, Bulgaria, Cyprus, Czech Republic, Denmark, Estonia, Finland, France, Germany, Greece, Hungary, Ireland, Italy, Latvia, Lithuania, Luxembourg, Malta, Netherlands, Poland, Portugal, Romania, Slovak Republic, Slovenia, Spain, Sweden, UK; Egypt	Goods only	2004
South Asian Free Trade Agreement (SAFTA)	Bangladesh, Bhutan, India, Maldives, Nepal, Pakistan, Sri Lanka	Goods only	2006
US–Morocco	US; Morocco	Goods and services	2006
ASEAN–Japan	Brunei Darussalam, Myanmar, Cambodia, Indonesia, Lao People's Democratic Republic, Malaysia, Philippines, Singapore, Vietnam, Thailand; Japan	Goods only	2008
China–New Zealand	China; New Zealand	Goods and services	2008
Canada–Peru	Canada; Peru	Goods and services	2009
Japan–Switzerland	Japan; Switzerland	Goods and services	2009

TABLE 24.2 FREE TRADE AREAS

Evaluating the effects of a free trade agreement

The North American Free Trade Agreement (NAFTA), signed in 1994, drastically altered the structures of the three economies involved. The manufacturing sectors in the US and Canada shrank due to the reduction of tariffs on goods imported from Mexico, the country with the lowest labour costs of the three member states. The reduction in tariffs on Mexican goods imported to the US was significant, increasing the percentage of Mexican goods entering the US duty free by nearly 500% between 1990 and 2001 (Figure 24.1).

Figure 24.1
The effect of NAFTA on US–Mexico trade. **a** Share of US goods imported from Mexico entering duty free; **b** average US tariff on dutiable goods imported from Mexico; **c** average US tariff rate on total goods imported from Mexico; **d** average Mexican tariff rate.

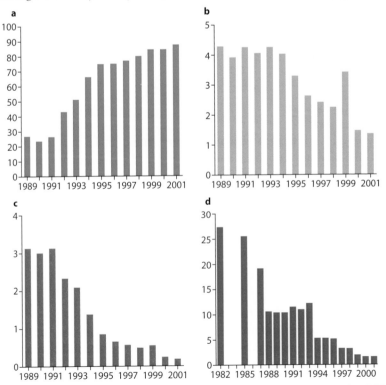

US Congressional Budget Office, *The effect of NAFTA on US–Mexico trade and GDP*, May 2003

Between 1991 and 2001, the percentage of Mexican goods entering the US duty free increased from 25% to almost 90%, while the tariff rate on the few goods still taxed fell from 4% to around 1%. Mexico also reduced or removed its tariffs on US imports, the average rate declining from 12% in 1991 to around 2% in 2001.

Needless to say, not everyone in the US was thrilled with the reduction or elimination of tariffs on goods from Mexico. Many of the goods imported duty free after the signing of NAFTA were labour-intensive manufactured goods that had previously been produced in the US, including auto parts, consumer electronics and clothing. The US Congressional Budget Office defends NAFTA by arguing as follows.

The most direct economic benefits from international trade arise from the fact that countries are not all equally adept at producing the same products. The reasons they are not lie in differences in natural resources, in education levels of their workforces, in relative amounts and qualities of physical capital, in confidential technical knowledge, and so on. Without trade, each country must make everything it needs, including things it is not very efficient at producing. When trade is allowed, each country can concentrate its efforts on what it does best relative to other countries and export some of the output in exchange for imports of products it is less good at producing. As countries do that, total world output increases.

US Congressional Budget Office, *The effect of NAFTA on US–Mexico trade and GDP*, May 2003

Despite the sound economic rationale expressed in this report, opposition to NAFTA in the US continues today. Besides the shrinking effect on employment in labour-intensive industries in the US, opponents point to the effect that NAFTA has had on the US current account balance with Mexico. Figure 24.2, from the same Congressional Budget Office report, shows the US current account balance with Mexico before and after NAFTA, as well as the size of the trade deficit relative to the US GDP.

Figure 24.2
US current account balance with Mexico before and after NAFTA.

US Congressional Budget Office, *The effect of NAFTA on US–Mexico trade and GDP*, May 2003

The effect of increased free trade between the US (a rich country) and Mexico (a middle-income country) could not be more clear. Spending by Americans on goods produced in Mexico grew far more rapidly after the signing of NAFTA in 1994 than US sales to Mexico did. The US current account deficit with Mexico ballooned to $35 billion (or 0.3% of US GDP) by 2001. You will remember from Chapter 23, that a trade deficit has several negative effects including depreciation of the currency (USD), declining employment in the manufacturing sector, and increased foreign (Mexican) ownership of home (US) assets (i.e. a financial account surplus).

On the other hand, the growth in imports from Mexico increased the variety of goods and services available to American consumers, and since Mexico can produce most goods at a much lower cost, the shift in the balance of trade was also accompanied by lower prices and increased real incomes among American households, who enjoyed cheaper manufactured goods due to NAFTA.

Besides NAFTA, the US is currently involved in another 13 free trade agreements. These agreements do not all harm employment in the US; in fact many US producers benefit greatly from increased free trade with the rest of the world. Figure 24.3 shows the relatively small total size of the 14 economies with which the US has free trade agreements.

Figure 24.3
Countries with which the US has free trade agreements produce 7.5% of world output.

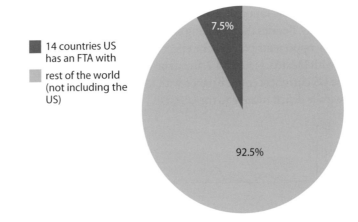

Despite the fact that the 14 economies with which the US has free trade agreements make up only 7.5% of the world's total GDP, they make up a much larger percentage of the total demand for US exports (Figure 24.4).

Figure 24.4
Countries with which the US has free trade agreements consume 42.6% of US exports.

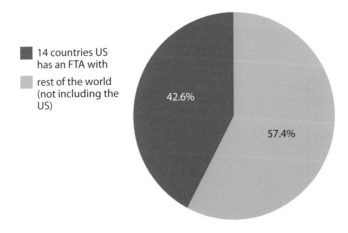

Countries with which the US has free trade agreements: Australia, Bahrain, Canada, Chile, Dominican Republic, El Salvador, Guatemala, Honduras, Israel, Jordan, Mexico, Morocco, Nicaragua and Singapore.

Free trade agreements like NAFTA and the 13 others the US has signed are controversial because of the effect they can have on member countries' domestic producers, but the resulting reallocation of resources between nations can have major benefits for both consumers and producers in all member nations. The US producers who were harmed by the decline in demand due to cheap imports from Mexico under NAFTA may very well have benefited due to increased demand from the 13 other countries with which the US has free trade agreements.

Free trade agreements and the FTAs they form move countries one step closer towards achieving the ideal of free trade espoused by the principle of comparative advantage.

Customs union

Next on the spectrum of economic integration is the customs union. A customs union joins member economies in an agreement whereby tariffs on all goods and services produced by one another are traded duty free, while the member nations must also agree on common duty rates on imports from all non-member countries.

Thus, a customs union differs from a free trade agreement in that:

- in a free trade agreement, each member nation maintains the freedom to determine the barriers to trade it will impose on imports from nations that are not part of the FTA
- in a customs union, member nations adopt common tariffs on non-member nations' goods and services.

In 2010, there were 20 customs unions in effect worldwide – a selection is shown in Table 24.3.

To access Worksheet 24.1 on a customs union, please visit www.pearsonbacconline.com and follow the onscreen instructions.

TABLE 24.3 CUSTOM UNIONS			
Name of customs union	**Countries involved**	**Coverage**	**Year enacted**
East African Community (EAC)	Burundi, Kenya, Rwanda, Tanzania, Uganda	Goods only	2000
Economic and Monetary Community of Central Africa (CEMAC)	Cameroon, Central African Republic, Chad, Congo, Equatorial Guinea, Gabon	Goods only	1999
Gulf Cooperation Council (GCC)	Bahrain, Kuwait, Oman, Qatar, Saudi Arabia, United Arab Emirates	Goods only	2003
Eurasian Economic Community (EAEC)	Belarus, Kazakhstan, Kyrgyz Republic, Russian Federation, Tajikistan	Goods only	1997
Southern Common Market (MERCOSUR)	Argentina, Brazil, Paraguay, Uruguay	Goods and services	1991 (goods) 2005 (services)

Like a free trade agreement, a customs union improves the efficiency with which resources are allocated between member states, increases the variety of goods available in each nation, broadens the market for a nation's producers, and is likely to result in lower prices and greater employment in the economies involved. On the other hand, the common tariffs on non-member nations might divert trade away from more efficient producers in nations not included in the customs union. Such unions could, therefore, decrease overall efficiency resulting from international trade.

A customs union is an agreement between nations through which tariffs on all goods and services produced by member nations are traded tariff free, while the member nations agree on common tariff rates on imports from all non-member countries.

Common market

The fourth type of trading bloc is the common market. This is like a customs union in that goods and services are traded without tariffs but, in addition, the four factors of production flow freely between member nations. In other words, the barriers to the flow of labour, land, capital resources and entrepreneurial talent are also reduced or eliminated. The aim is to improve the allocation of resources *within* member nations and *between* them.

To access Worksheet 24.2 on trading blocs, please visit www.pearsonbacconline.com and follow the onscreen instructions.

To learn more about trading blocs, visit www.pearsonhotlinks.com, enter the title or ISBN of this book and select weblink 24.1.

The most successful example of a common market is the European Economic Area (EEA), which includes the 27 countries in the European Union plus Switzerland, Norway and Liechtenstein. Proposed common markets include the Association of South East Asian Nations and the East African Community. In order to facilitate the flow of productive resources between nations in a common market, shared regulations and policies regarding labour and capital employment must be adopted by member nations.

24.4 Monetary unions

Learning outcomes
- Explain that a monetary union is a common market with a common currency and a common central bank.
- Discuss the possible advantages and disadvantages of a monetary union for its members.

Monetary union

The penultimate stage of economic integration is the monetary union, which comprises a common market in which member states also adopt a common currency managed by a single central bank. A monetary union, for all intents and purposes, joins the economies of member states into one combined economy. Two examples of a monetary union are the USA (which essentially combines the economies of America's 50 states under one central bank sharing one currency, the US dollar) and the eurozone, which includes the 14 European nations that have foregone their own currencies to adopt the euro.

Monetary unions share all the characteristics of lower stages of economic integration:
- tariffs between member states are eliminated
- common tariffs on non-member nations are adopted by member states
- land, labour and capital resources may flow free of intervention between member states
- regulations regarding labour and capital are shared between member states.

A monetary union is a trading bloc in which member states eliminate all barriers to trade between them, allow for the free flow of the factors of production, adopt common tariffs on non-member states, and use a common currency managed by a shared central bank.

In addition, members abandon their monetary sovereignty and the ability to control the money supply in their own economy, since monetary policy is determined by the shared central bank. The states in the US long ago abandoned separate currencies, and, since 1913, the US money supply has been managed by the Federal Reserve. In 1999, the year in which the euro was adopted, eurozone nations lost the ability to independently determine monetary policy; it is determined by the European Central Bank, which controls the supply of the euro and thus influences interest rates among euro states.

While a monetary union represents nearly complete economic integration, the states in such a pact may maintain their fiscal sovereignty, or their ability to control their own fiscal policies, albeit with strict guidelines established by the central bank which are required to assure stability in the exchange rate of the shared currency against other currencies.

Complete economic integration

This is the final stage of economic integration, in which member states completely forego independence of both monetary and fiscal policies. The difference between the US and the eurozone is that the 50 states in the US are subject to the monetary *and* fiscal policies of the US federal government, while the eurozone nations are subject only to the monetary policies of the European Central Bank.

The US therefore represents an example of complete economic integration; but since each nation in the eurozone is free to determine its own government budget and allocate government tax revenues as it sees fit, the eurozone is not a completely integrated economy. The 14 euro nations are integrated economically and monetarily, but not fiscally. Each nation's government can decide its own fiscal policies, unlike each US state government. A group of states joined in complete economic integration essentially become one state, foregoing economic sovereignty over the majority of the economic policies and activities in the nation.

The loss of fiscal sovereignty may explain why the euro countries have thus far avoided complete economic integration; it is not yet politically viable to the culturally and socially diverse citizens of Europe to accept the sacrifice of fiscal freedom and hand over control of their governments' budgets to a federal European government.

 To what extent is a nation's cultural identity dependent on its economic independence? Does joining an economic union like the eurozone require a nation to abandon some of its cultural identity?

Benefits of complete economic integration

It is worth noting that, in early 2011, the value of the euro reached its lowest level relative to other major currencies in several years. The fact that the eurozone is *not* a completely integrated economic area is the major cause for global uncertainty over the future of the currency itself. The fiscal irresponsibility of several euro nations, most notably the PIIGS (Portugal, Ireland, Italy, Greece and Spain), has threatened the stability of the euro as a globally traded currency. These five countries have, for years, run large and persistent government budget deficits, financed through the sale of government bonds to international lenders, and all have national debts that exceed 100% of their GDP.

As their debts have ballooned, the willingness of the international community to continue to finance these governments' profligate social welfare and pension programmes has waned, forcing these governments to offer higher and higher interest rates on their debt. The rise in interest rates needed to attract lenders threatens to crowd out private sector spending that is already depressed due to the global financial crisis, and to throw these economies (and their more fiscally responsible eurozone neighbours) into periods of government austerity. Such austerity will be accompanied by slow growth and a reduction in the standard of living of citizens whose governments will be forced to balance their budgets by cutting spending on social benefits and public goods of all sorts.

Under a system of complete economic integration, nations like Greece and Portugal would not be allowed to continue year after year running massive deficits and building up the level of debt they have accumulated. Had the eurozone been both a monetary *and* a fiscal union from the beginning, it is likely that the continent's current economic woes would be much less severe.

Advantages and disadvantages of economic integration

Countries that trade with other countries tend to experience increases in output, income and the standard of living of their people. From the lowest level of integration in which nations reduce tariffs on only certain products produced abroad to complete economic integration in which all barriers to trade are eliminated and monetary and fiscal policies are shared across member states, the benefits of increased economic integration are the same as those of free trade in general.

Advantages of economic integration

- **Greater efficiency**. Resource allocation is more efficient when artificial barriers to trade are eliminated and goods and services are produced in the nation with the lowest domestic opportunity cost.
- **Higher real incomes**. Cheaper imports lead to higher disposable incomes for consumers in nations that trade, improving the quality of life and the variety of goods and services available.
- **Larger export markets**. A broader consumer base allows domestic industries that are able to compete internationally to increase their output, hire more workers, and expand to meet the demands of the international marketplace.

On the other hand, increased economic integration can have some detrimental effects, which are also the disadvantages of free trade in general.

Disadvantages of economic integration

- **Fall in employment in certain industries**. Increased competition from producers abroad may force some domestic firms to shut down or move their operations overseas, reducing domestic employment.
- **Exploitation of workers**. At lower levels of economic integration in which labour regulations are not common between nations, disparities in the working conditions and wage rates between nations may create an environment in which low-skilled labour is exploited in the nations with large populations of low-income, low-skilled workers.
- **Environmental effects**. Environmental regulations may also differ between nations in a free trade area, which may cause producers to open factories in countries with the lowest standards, increasing pollution and greenhouse gas emissions overall.
- **Rising trade imbalances**. If economic integration causes a nation's imports to rise faster than its exports, then large current account imbalances between countries could result, as was the case with the US and Mexico following the signing of NAFTA.

Loss of economic sovereignty

At the higher levels of integration, such as a monetary union, member nations must give up the ability to control their own monetary policies. This reduces a country's ability to manage demand in its domestic economy by raising or lowering interest rates or manipulating the exchange rate of its currency relative to its trading partners' currencies. Since no single nation in a monetary union can determine the level of interest rates or the exchange rate on its own, control of the nation's macroeconomy is to some extent essentially handed over to a multinational central bank, a sacrifice many nations are not eager to make.

This explains why some of the nations in the EU are not currently seeking to become a part of the eurozone. Giving up its own currency prevents a country from increasing its attractiveness to foreign consumers and investors by keeping domestic interest rates low and the value of its currency weak.

24.5 Trade creation *vs* trade diversion (HL only)

Learning outcome
- (HL only) Explain the concepts of trade creation and trade diversion in a customs union.
- (HL only) Explain that different forms of economic integration allow member countries to gain from economies of scale.

To further evaluate the effects of economic integration, we must look more closely at the impact trading blocs have on overall efficiency in the allocation of resources. In fact, it is not always the case that economic integration through bilateral or multilateral trading blocs increases *overall* efficiency in the use of the world's resources. Trading blocs do create trade between member nations, but this may come at the expense of overall efficiency if increased trade between nations causes diversion of trade from other, more efficient, lower-cost nations.

Nations that join a trading bloc experience increased trade with other nations in the trading bloc, which improves the efficiency with which resources are allocated between member nations. However, the full effect of economic integration must be examined to determine whether what results is *trade creation* or *trade diversion*. The latter occurs when a trade agreement between two or more nations diverts trade from non-member nations to member nations.

Trade creation

Trade is created if the formation of a trading bloc, bilateral or multilateral, shifts production of certain goods or services from a high-cost country to a low-cost country, thus improving efficiency, increasing the overall level of output and increasing international trade.

Take, for instance, the effect on the US television industry when NAFTA was signed. TVs had been produced in the US for decades when Mexico and the US agreed to eliminate tariffs under their free trade agreement in 1994. Since NAFTA was signed, the TV industry in the US has all but disappeared. Americans are consuming more televisions than ever, but many of those TVs are now produced in Mexico rather than in domestic factories. NAFTA created more global trade and increased the level of output of televisions as production moved from a high-cost nation (the US) to a low-cost nation (Mexico).

 Trade creation is when a free trade agreement shifts production of certain goods or services from a high-cost country to a low-cost country.

Trade diversion

Trade diversion occurs if the formation of a trading bloc between two or more nations results in the production of a good or service transferring from a nation with a lower opportunity cost to one with a higher opportunity cost. Such a scenario may seem unlikely, but it occurs rather commonly at the higher levels of economic integration, such as in a customs union.

When two or more nations agree to eliminate barriers to trade between themselves, but to maintain common external tariffs on all other nations, it is possible that the result will be the diversion of trade from low-cost producers to high-cost producers.

Take, for instance, the European Economic Area (EEA), which includes the 27 countries of the EU plus Norway, Switzerland and Liechtenstein. All 30 countries in the EEA are middle- or high-income nations that have agreed to eliminate tariffs between all member nations. However, the EEA has common tariffs on non-member nations, many of which are low-income countries that may have a comparative advantage in the production of certain goods over high-income EEA nations. Due to the nature of agreement between member nations, the existence of external tariffs could increase trade between one European nation and another at the expense of trade with low-cost nations.

For example, Poland, a middle-income country with a comparative advantage in the production of intermediate manufactured goods such as auto parts, joined the EEA in 2004. As a member of the EEA, Poland enjoys duty-free exports to Germany, its largest trading partner, also a nation with a large auto industry. Germany most likely began importing more auto parts from Poland after its entry into the EEA in 2004 than it had before, since these goods could now be obtained duty free. But if this increase in trade with a middle-income European neighbour came at the expense of trade between Germany and a lower-cost non-European nation, such as China, then trade was not created, it was diverted.

Assume China had been producing auto parts at even lower cost than Poland, then Poland joined the EEA and all German tariffs on Polish goods were eliminated. Since Chinese goods are still subjected to tariffs in Germany, demand for Chinese output in Germany would fall following the elimination of tariffs on Polish goods. In this way, European economic integration under the EEA may have diverted, rather than created, international trade from a low-cost producer (China) to a higher-cost producer (Poland). When trade is diverted due to the formation of a trade bloc, overall allocative efficiency is reduced.

CASE STUDY

NAFTA keeps Mexico's economy afloat

In the global economic slump, exporting nations have suffered as incomes in Europe and North America stagnate. But Mexico is confounding the trend. In 2009, Mexico's exports shrank, but they recovered quickly in 2010, its share of the American import market growing to its highest level ever – 12.2%.

Mexico has many advantages over other exporting nations. Geographical proximity to its largest trade partner means low shipping costs despite rising oil prices. NAFTA allows Mexican imports to enter the US tariff-free, a major advantage that Chinese exporters do not enjoy. Despite Chinese producers' other cost advantages, the tariffs on Chinese goods give Mexican producers an edge in the US market. Chinese paving stones, for example, cost $5.20 per square metre compared to $5.29 for Mexican ones. But the 8.5% US tariff levied on Chinese paving stones makes them more expensive than Mexican ones. The same is true for other Mexican goods including cloth, glassware, chemicals and cars.

For over two decades, China's major advantage has been low labour costs; but this is changing – factory-workers' wages are now rising at double-digit rates. Mexico offers highly skilled labour in many industries and the wage gap with the US remains large – Mexico is increasingly appealing to American importers.

At present, 80% of Mexican exports go to the US, despite trade agreements with many other nations. One downside for the Mexican export sector is in the fine print of trade agreements with some European nations: Mexican goods entering Europe tariff-free must have originated in Mexico (or the EU). But many exporters rely on parts from the US, so they do not qualify for tariff-free access to European markets. However, as Mexican parts manufacturers expand, this may change and new markets open to Mexican exporters.

Sixteen years after NAFTA was signed, Mexico has benefited greatly from its free trade relationship with the US. But for its exporters (and the millions of workers they employ) to benefit from further trade with Europe and reduce their dependence on the American market, Mexican industry must produce more of the parts that go into the finished products.

HL EXERCISES

1   According to the case study above, how does Mexico's ability to export paving tiles tariff-free to the US benefit Mexico? How does it harm China?

2   Would you describe the effect of NAFTA on trade between the US, Mexico and China as an example of trade creation or trade diversion? Use evidence from the case study to support your answer.

3   Why is Mexico not able to take full advantage of its free trade agreements with countries other than the US (e.g. the EU)? What does the article suggest as a strategy for Mexico to begin enjoying the full gains of its existing free trade agreements?

4   How will continued economic integration help Mexico? Discuss the impact of FTAs on Mexican firms and Mexican households.

To access Quiz 24, an interactive, multiple-choice quiz on this chapter, please visit www.pearsonbacconline.com and follow the onscreen instructions.

1 **Item 1**   **South American trading bloc under pressure**

Only a few months ago, MERCOSUR, South America's main **trading bloc**, looked to be near collapse. Argentina called for sanctions against the many firms that were closing their factories and rushing to Brazil, attracted by big subsidies and a devalued currency. Brazil for its part was threatening to take Argentina to the World Trade Organisation over the import quotas that Argentina had imposed against 'dumped' textile exports.

MERCOSUR went through a difficult time when the region slipped into recession in 1998, and intra-bloc trade slumped. It nearly collapsed after the January 1999 devaluation of the Brazilian currency made Argentina's goods up to 40% dearer in their largest market. Brazil has since recovered from recession, helping Argentina: in the first three months of this year, Argentina clocked up a trade surplus with Brazil of $300 million. Even so, Argentina has been struggling to pull out of the recession, in part because the new government raised taxes in December in an effort to help cut the fiscal deficit.

But hysteria has given way to common sense. Argentina and Brazil have agreed to bring their economies into closer harmony. They have set a timetable for a set of **economic-convergence** targets similar to those in the Maastricht treaty that led to the euro. The first targets will cover public debt, government borrowing and inflation. Others, such as the balance of payments, may come later. In the long term, the aim is supposed to be a common currency.

Where does that leave MERCOSUR's smaller members? Shut out of a market dominated by the giants, Uruguay has so far refused to back the Argentine–Brazil car deal, which imposes a 35% tariff on non-MERCOSUR cars from 2006.

Further progress is likely to depend on economic performance. Meeting the convergence targets will involve keeping to unpopular austerity programmes, and approving difficult domestic reforms. Neither Argentina nor Brazil may find that very appealing.

adapted from *The Economist*, 27 May 2000

Item 2

Consumer prices, % change from previous year

Budget balance, % GDP

graphs from The Economist Intelligence Unit

a Define the following terms that appear in bold in the text:

   i trading bloc   (2 marks) [A01]

   ii economic convergence.   (2 marks) [A01]

b At one point, MERCOSUR came close to falling apart. Briefly explain why this was happening.   (4 marks) [A02]

c Using an appropriate diagram, explain the effects on various stakeholders of the common tariff on non-MERCOSUR cars that was being proposed by Argentina and Brazil.
                                                                              (4 marks) [AO2], [AO4]

d Using the data and your knowledge of economics, evaluate the degree to which trading blocs increase efficiency and move the global economy toward free trade.
(8 marks) [AO3]

2   **Protecting shrimp farmers**

The USA has started talks with Thailand on a **free trade area**.

The US International Trade Commission (ITC) has said it has evidence to suggest that Thailand and five other Asian countries were selling shrimps at below market prices, and gave a warning that it might impose tariffs. This threatens to complicate the free trade talks expected to start soon.

The tariffs are being demanded by the Southern Shrimp Alliance that represents thousands of shrimp catchers from the USA. The alliance is seeking tariffs up to 349% on imported shrimps. Critics of this action argue that it will do little to benefit struggling American shrimp catchers, while making it very difficult for small scale shrimp farmers in these Asian countries.

Thailand and the other leading shrimp exporters to the USA insist they are not **dumping**. They say their labour costs are lower and they are more productively efficient because they farm shrimp in ponds rather than fishing in the ocean as the Americans do.

If an anti-dumping ruling is successful, it is estimated that Thailand's 35 000 shrimp farmers will need to reduce output by 20–30%, and hundreds of small scale producers and feed producers will go out of business.

TABLE 1 INCREASE IN ASIA'S MAJOR SHRIMP EXPORT VALUES TO THE USA			
	2002 / thousands of $	2003 / thousands of $	% Change
Thailand	399.9	445.3	11.3
Vietnam	282.9	394.4	39.4
India	293.4	327.7	11.7
China	131.6	245.3	86.4
Indonesia	118.0	141.1	19.5
Total US imports	2075.5	2460.9	18.6

TABLE 2 HOURLY LABOUR COSTS		
	Shrimps / US$	Shirts / US$
Thailand	0.50	2.00
USA	17.00	26.00

adapted from 'Free Trade runs into Protectionism', Murray Heibert and Shawn W Crispin, *The Far Eastern Economic Review*, 4 March 2004

a Define the following terms indicated in bold in the text:
  i free trade area (paragraph 1)   (2 marks) [AO1]
  ii dumping (paragraph 4).   (2 marks) [AO1]
b Using an appropriate diagram, explain effect of the proposed US tariff on imported shrimp.   (4 marks) [AO2], [AO4]
c Using the data in Table 2, calculate the opportunity cost of shrimps and shirts in the US and Thailand. Based on your calculation, indicate which country has a comparative advantage in the two goods.   (4 marks) [AO2], [AO4]
d Using information from the text and your knowledge of economics, examine the degree to which Thailand and the US would mutually benefit from a free trade arrangement.   (8 marks) [AO3]

25 TERMS OF TRADE (HL ONLY)

25.1 Meaning and measurement of terms of trade

Learning outcomes
- Explain the meaning of terms of trade.
- Explain how terms of trade are measured.
- Calculate the terms of trade using the equation: index of average export prices / index of average import prices × 100.
- Distinguish between an improvement and a deterioration in the terms of trade.

If the average price of exports increases relative to the average price of imports, it is called an improvement in the terms of trade. If the reverse occurs and the average price of imports rises relative to the average price of exports, it is called a deterioration of the terms of trade.

One way of understanding the concept is to view it in terms of how much of an average unit of imports you could buy with an average unit of exports. It suggests that if export prices are increasing relative to import prices, the country will find importing goods relatively easy and cheap. More imports can be bought with the previous level of exports. If the reverse were true and import price increased relative to export prices, the average export would buy less in terms of imported goods.

In simplified terms, if Country G's average export prices increase by 10% compared to the average price of imports from Country K, then Country G would be able to buy 10% more of Country K's goods with its export revenue. This suggests Country G now has more buying power, or a more favourable terms of trade relative to Country K. Country K has relatively less buying power, and must sell more of its exports to get the previous level of imports from Country G.

This implies that terms of trade can be directly related to a country's standard of living and potential for economic growth. Specifically, countries that depend on imports for essential consumer goods or critical capital resources have a keen interest in their own terms of trade.

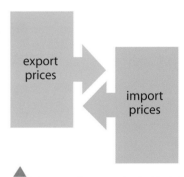

Terms of trade is the ratio of export prices to import prices.

Terms of trade refers to the ratio of a country's average price of exports to the country's average price of imports.

Meaning of terms of trade

The terms of trade ratio compares the prices received for export goods to the prices being paid for imported goods. It is expressed as:

$$\text{terms of trade} = \frac{\text{index of average export prices}}{\text{index of average import prices}} \times 100$$

The export and import averages are calculated in much the same way a consumer or producer price index is calculated, by compiling the weighted averages for export goods and import goods over a period of time.

Calculating terms of trade

Table 25.1 shows how terms of trade can be calculated from year 1 (the base or index year) over a period of six years. The calculation column uses the equation we looked at above.

	TABLE 25.1 CALCULATING TERMS OF TRADE				
Year	Index of average export prices	Index of average import prices	Calculation of terms of trade	Terms of trade	Improvement or deterioration?
Year 1	100	100	$\frac{100}{100} \times 100$	100	index year
Year 2	100	105	$\frac{100}{105} \times 100$	95.2	deterioration
Year 3	109	105	$\frac{109}{105} \times 100$	103.8	
Year 4	116	112	$\frac{116}{112} \times 100$	103.5	
Year 5	120	110			
Year 6	120	125			

HL EXERCISES

1 Explain what it means to have a 95.2 terms of trade value for year 2.

2 What does it mean to have a 103.8 terms of trade value for year 3?

3 Complete the rest of the table. What does the ultimate value of the terms of trade for year 6 tell you?

25.2 Changes in the terms of trade

Learning outcomes
- Explain that the terms of trade may change in the short term due to changes in demand conditions for exports and imports, changes in global supply of key inputs (such as oil), changes in relative inflation rates and changes in relative exchange rates.
- Explain that the terms of trade may change in the long term due to changes in world income levels, changes in productivity within the country and technological developments.

Reasons for change in terms of trade

Short-run causes

Demand changes

All of the factors that can affect the demand for both exports and imports can affect their prices as a result. Consumer taste for exports may change. Other countries may see their incomes rise, increasing demand for your exports. If the demand for Country Z's butter increases, Country Z's terms of trade improves. In short, any determinant that shifts the demand for exports or imports outwards increases those prices.

Supply changes

If many countries join a market and create a surplus, then a country's export prices are likely to drop. This was true throughout the late 1980s in the market for coffee, as new producers joined an attractive market and consequently pushed down world coffee prices and depressed their relative terms of trade.

Relative inflation rates

If a country's domestic price levels rise relative to other countries, its terms of trade improves as well. However, this improvement will make those exports less attractive and competitive globally.

Changes in exchange rates

Short-term and long-term changes in the exchange rate can influence the terms of trade. Changes in the exchange rate effectively change the prices paid by foreigners, so the prices of exports and imports fluctuate, affecting the terms of trade.

For example, let's suppose Peru and Chile were trade partners, exchanging Peruvian sweet potatoes for Chilean wine. At the original exchange rate, 1 Peruvian sol might be equal to 200 Chilean pesos. At this rate, let's say it takes 10 Peruvian soles (= 2000 Chilean pesos) to buy a bottle of wine; and for 2000 pesos, Chile can import one kilogram of the best and rarest camotes (sweet potatoes). However, suppose the Peruvian sol rises against the peso to the point where 1 sol buys 250 pesos. For the terms of trade, it means that Peru can sell fewer camotes to get the same amount of wine, and Chile must sell more wine to get the same amount of camotes. Peru's terms of trade has improved. Chile's has declined.

Long-run causes

When global demand is altered by income changes

You will remember that income growth for a country leads to an increase in demand for exports. In particular, income growth tends to increase demand for secondary and tertiary products. This trend favours the terms of trade of developed countries which produce these products, and harms less developed countries (LDCs) which are dependent on primary products. Therefore, as global income is expected to grow over time, the terms of trade of most LDCs will continue to deteriorate.

Productivity changes

Sustained increases in relative productivity can lower a country's export prices and drive down its terms of trade. If a country is somehow able to produce more with the same or fewer inputs, the result is increased productivity. This can be derived from improvements in labour productivity, technological progress, more education or better management techniques. This is a good reason to have a deterioration of the terms of trade. However, if the demand for the country's exports is elastic, the price fall may increase exports sufficiently for total export revenue to increase. Conversely, it is also possible that productivity may decline as a result of high wages or other increased input costs. This may increase the terms of trade, but does so at the expense of productivity and competitiveness. Though the terms of trade increases, it is not good news for the economy.

Monopoly power

In industries where price-setting power is concentrated among a relatively small group of firms (most likely an oligopolistic industry), the increased prices can drive down the terms of trade for LDCs. For example, when producers of manufactured goods with significant oligopoly price-setting power manage to effectively raise prices, this can improve the terms of trade in countries where the producers reside. If certain producers of food and household goods held such oligopoly power, their ability to hold prices up while penetrating developing country markets would have the effect of increasing the terms of trade of their US and European home countries, while diminishing the terms of trade in less developed countries where they sell their goods. Oil producers, most obviously, when acting as a cartel can exert their monopoly power to drive up prices and enhance their terms of trade in the process.

Trade protectionism

Protectionist policies may have an effect on the terms of trade, but only to the extent to which the country makes up a share of the export or import market. Large market-share countries like the US have greater power to affect terms of trade through trade policy than small-share countries such as Bolivia. The precise effect of such manoeuvres depends on the specific policy. Tariffs and quotas that protect a large domestic market can effectively raise import prices relative to export prices for that country, as well as reducing import competitiveness. This will shift the terms of trade in favour of the large protectionist power.

However, export subsidies work slightly differently, but can still undercut the terms of trade of smaller producer countries. Such subsidies (e.g. EU and US farm subsidies) allow rich countries to promote their exports and lower the effective prices of their agricultural goods. This puts downward pressure on the price of those commodities, lowering prices of primary goods of many poorer countries – goods that make up the major portion of such countries' exports. Thus, even export subsidies tend to drive down the terms of trade for poorer, primary-good-producing countries.

25.3   Consequences of changes in the terms of trade

Learning outcomes
- Examine the effects of changes in the terms of trade on a country's current account, using the concepts of price elasticity of demand for exports and imports.
- Explain the impacts of short-term fluctuations and long-term deterioration in the terms of trade of economically less developed countries that specialize in primary commodities, using the concepts of price elasticity of demand and supply for primary products and income elasticity of demand.
- Explain how changes in the terms of trade in the long term may result in a global redistribution of income.

Whether or not a change in the terms of trade is a positive development depends on a variety of factors, most importantly on the cause of the change and its effect on the balance of payments. These results are affected by the relative elasticities of demands for the goods involved.

Terms of trade and the trade balance

Changes in the terms of trade are not necessarily good or bad. To understand more fully the precise effects of any terms of trade change, it is important to ascertain the likely effect on a country's trade balance. In Chapter 23, you learned that the trade balance consists primarily of export revenues (an inflow of money) and import expenditures (an outflow of money), as well as other lesser factors. Because the two income flows are forms of total revenue, we can view them in simplified total revenue terms.

total export revenue = average $P_X \times Q_X$

total import expenditure = average $P_M \times Q_M$

Therefore, if the price of either imports or exports increases, it could influence the overall total value of either side of the trade balance. We might assume, for example, that an increase in the price of exports would enhance total export revenue and improve the trade balance. However, this would run counter to what we know of the law of demand – as price increases, quantity demanded falls. Therefore, it is possible that an increase in export prices (and thus implicitly an improvement of the terms of trade) might actually result in a decrease in export revenue, and a decrease in the trade balance. That all depends, of course, on the value of the price elasticity of demand for exports in that case. So before we can make any determination about the effect of an improvement of the terms of trade, we would also need to know the elasticity of demand for both exports and imports.

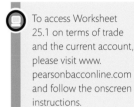

To access Worksheet 25.1 on terms of trade and the current account, please visit www.pearsonbacconline.com and follow the onscreen instructions.

Elasticity of demand for exports and imports

It should be clear that the elasticity of demand for exports is critical to both the balance of payments and the terms of trade. In Chapter 23, you learned that the price elasticity of exports and imports can influence the effectiveness of devaluation through the Marshall–Lerner condition and the J curve.

Price elasticity of demand for exports

With that in mind, let us remember that the price elasticity of demand for exports is the responsiveness in the quantity demanded of exports to changes in the price of exports.

$$PED_X = \frac{\text{percentage change in demand for exports}}{\text{percentage change in average price of exports}} = \frac{\%\Delta Q_X}{\%\Delta avgP_X}$$

If PED_X is inelastic, then changes in the average price of exports do not significantly affect demand for them. Where export prices are falling, this would lead to a decrease in export revenues. This typically applies to the exports of energy commodities like coal, natural gas and oil. With a PED that is less than one, price drops hurt overall revenue. However, in industries where the demand is actually elastic, price decreases can result in improved revenue.

More explicitly, if the value of $PED_X > 1$, meaning relatively elastic demand, then a decrease in export prices (which corresponds to a decrease in terms of trade) results in an overall increase in export revenue. However, where $PED_X < 1$, relatively inelastic export demand, export price increases (and terms of trade improvement) reduce the total export revenue.

Price elasticity of demand for imports

The price elasticity of demand for imports is the responsiveness of import demand to the changes in the average price of imports. It is shown by the equation:

$$PED_M = \frac{\text{percentage change in demand for imports}}{\text{percentage change in average price of imports}} = \frac{\%\Delta Q_M}{\%\Delta avgP_M}$$

Where demand for imports is price inelastic, those countries would continue to buy the goods in similar proportions, and thus spend significantly more on imports, if import prices were to increase. However, decreasing import prices will cause an overall decrease in total import spending when demand for imports is inelastic. While commodities tend to have inelastic demand, most other products tend to be price elastic in the long run.

More explicitly, if the value of $PED_M > 1$, meaning relatively elastic demand, then an increase in import prices (which corresponds to a decrease in terms of trade) results in an overall decrease in import revenue, an outflow from the economy. Conversely, where $PED_M < 1$, relatively inelastic import demand, import price increases (and terms of trade deterioration) increase the total import expenditure.

HL EXERCISES

4 Draw the two diagrams, one representing relatively inelastic demand for exports, one with relatively elastic demand.

5 On each, show the same increase in price, and draw total revenue boxes that reflect the change in total revenue before and after the price change.

6 Draw two more diagrams in the same fashion, now representing inelastic and elastic demand for imports.

7 On each show the same increase in price, and draw total revenue boxes that reflect the change in total revenue before and after the price change.

Causes of improvement in the terms of trade
Increase in demand for exports

Demand for exports can increase for all the usual reasons: a change of taste in favour of certain exports, increased prices for a competitor's goods, perhaps rising incomes abroad. If the increased export prices are a result of increased demand, it is likely to improve the balance of payments.

In Figure 25.1, the increased demand for exports has caused price to increase from P_E to P_1, and quantity to increase from Q_E to Q_1. Overall total export revenue increases from the area delineated by P_E–a–Q_E–0 to the larger area P_1–b–Q_1–0. The increased total revenue for exports, *ceteris paribus*, increases the flow of export revenue to the trade balance as well.

Figure 25.1
Increase in demand for exports.

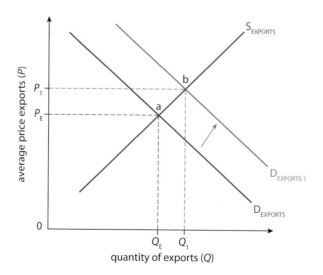

Decrease in supply of exports

Should domestic production of exported goods decrease, the result would be an increase in export prices that would improve the terms of trade. However, as you might guess, the effect of this change on the total export revenue and the trade balance depends on the price elasticity of demand for exports.

In Figure 25.2, a decrease in the supply of exports increases the price to P_1. The relatively elastic demand for exports means that a decrease in supply increases prices but actually results in less total export revenue, from area x + z to area x + y.

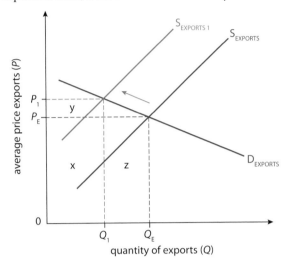

Figure 25.2
Decrease in supply of exports: elastic demand.

But what if export demand is inelastic? When demand is inelastic (as in the case of an important resource export like petroleum) and the price rises, total export revenue increases (Figure 25.3). in this case, when price increases from P_E to P_1, the total revenue (x + y) is much larger than the previous export revenue (x + z). Thus, as the price of exports increases, increasing the terms of trade, the trade balance also improves.

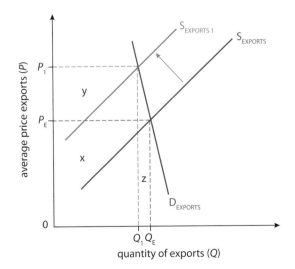

Figure 25.3
Decrease in supply of exports: inelastic demand.

This indicates that a rise in export prices, *ceteris paribus*, improves the terms of trade but that the effective export revenue is conditional on the elasticity of demand for exports. One implication is that countries with inelastic demand for exports (perhaps those exporting energy resources) can enjoy a terms of trade increase with less worry than countries whose export demand is price elastic, in particular those exporting goods such as agricultural commodities.

Domestic inflation raises export prices

High domestic inflation, relative to a country's trading partners, encourages an improvement in the terms of trade. Whether this leads to an improvement in the trade balance depends on the elasticity of demand for the country's exports.

It is also true that the PED of a good varies as the price of the good falls (Chapter 4). PED is high at the higher range of prices, drops as the price drops and eventually reaches a unit elasticity point (PED = 1), then becomes relatively inelastic at the lower prices (Figure 25.4).

Figure 25.4
Domestic inflation raises export prices.

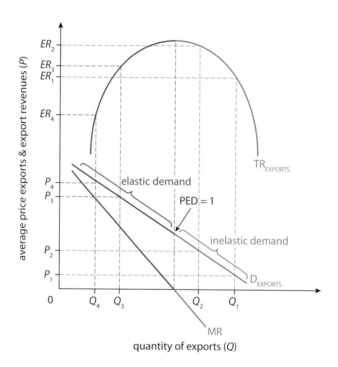

As average export prices increase from P_1 to P_2, where demand is relatively inelastic, the total export revenue grows from ER_1 to ER_2, which will improve the export side of the trade balance. This continues until the point on the demand curve where MR = 0. From that point, any price increase (and, therefore, any improvement in the terms of trade) is in the elastic price range of demand. Therefore, an increase in export prices from P_3 to P_4 results in a decrease in export revenue from ER_3 to ER_4, and a decrease on the export side of the trade balance.

With this in mind, we can draw the following conclusions.

- Terms of trade improvements caused by inflation improve the trade balance when demand is inelastic. Price rises do litle to discourage export consumption and, therefore, export revenue grows.
- Improvements to the terms of trade caused by inflation reduce the trade balance when demand for exports is elastic. In this case, price rises significantly discourage export purchases and cause a lowering of export revenue.

In theory, these instances could be good news for LDCs selling commodities because domestic inflation should improve both the terms of trade and trade balance. In practice, however, LDCs selling commodities can rarely afford to charge higher prices for commodity goods sold worldwide. With ample substitutes on the global market, there is little room for price increases. Thus, there are good reasons for LDCs to keep control of domestic inflation.

Changes in the exchange rate

Depreciation of the exchange rate makes exports more inexpensive, and imports more expensive. Therefore, depreciation effectively decreases a country's terms of trade. Appreciation does the opposite: exports become more expensive to the world while imports become cheaper. Therefore, appreciation effectively increases a country's terms of trade. How does this affect the trade balance? That depends on the price elasticity of demand for exports and imports.

In Figure 25.5, depreciation leads to an effective decline in the terms of trade. From that point, the change in the trade balance depends on the combined price elasticity values for both exports and imports. If elastic, depreciation and worsening terms of trade improve the trade balance by moving it towards a surplus. If inelastic, depreciation and worsening terms of trade hurt the trade balance by moving it towards a deficit.

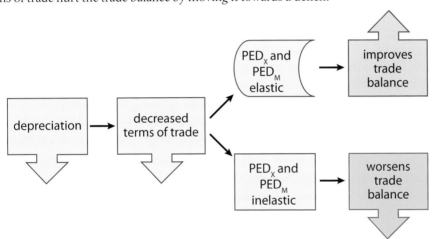

Figure 25.5
Effects of depreciation on the terms of trade.

In Figure 25.6, appreciation leads to an effective improvement in the terms of trade. From that point, the change in the trade balance again depends on the combined price elasticity values for both exports and imports. If elastic, appreciation and improved terms of trade worsen the trade balance by moving it towards a deficit. If inelastic, appreciation and improving terms of trade help the trade balance by moving it towards a surplus.

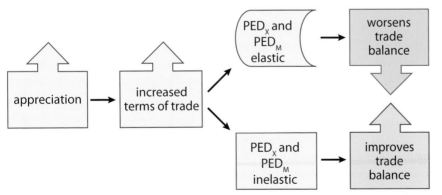

Figure 25.6
Effects of appreciation on the terms of trade.

This result is directly related to the Marshall–Lerner condition, which states that the combined elasticities of demand for exports and imports must be greater than 1 for a currency depreciation (and, therefore, terms of trade deterioration) to improve the trade balance. When the combined elasticities are relatively elastic, then depreciation (implying a terms of trade deterioration) causes more export revenue and reduced import expenditure, improving the trade balance. If the combined elasticities are less than 1, depreciation and the resulting terms of trade reduction worsen the trade balance.

In practice, LDCs are often encouraged by economists and lenders to attempt to depreciate their currency and increase export revenue. They therefore find themselves in the above situation. Not only does this worsen the terms of trade and make the consumption of imports more difficult, it can also hurt the trade balance when the PED of exports and imports is inelastic.

In the reverse scenario, appreciation improves the terms of trade. But it will only improve the trade balance if the combined elasticities of demand for exports and imports is relatively inelastic. Thus, the appreciation results in higher export revenue and reduced import revenue.

Short-term fluctuations in the terms of trade

LDCs are tied to primary goods and commodity goods, and these markets can be volatile. Short bursts of commodity activity can cause sudden increases in some countries' terms of trade. These sudden bursts are called commodity booms; they can occur for a variety of reasons, depending on the particular market. In the years from 2000 to 2008, the prices of many metals, chemicals, fuels and food items rose significantly. A major reason for this boom was increased demand from the growing economies of China and India: as these economies began to more fully exploit their domestic resources, they increasingly sought to import more commodity goods.

Commodity speculation heightened the price increases as speculators bet on ever-higher prices. Also adding to the problem was the interrelated nature of food and fuel. Higher demand for food increased the demand for fertilizers that are made from oil products. This increased the demand for oil, increasing its price. Then, as countries sought substitutes in the form of biofuels (Chapter 6), the demand for biofuel inputs such as corn and sugar grew as well. To grow these required more petroleum-based fertilizers, and so the cycle became self-reinforcing.

Commodity booms affected countries in different ways, depending on whether the country was the beneficiary of price increases or suffered the burden of these increases. Commodity importers of food, in particular, suffered when food prices rose dramatically in 2007. Political unrest from high food prices led to food riots in many countries, including Burkina Faso, Cameroon, Egypt and Morocco. Some buyers resorted to hoarding goods, which pushed prices up further. As a result, countries in this predicament attempted export tariffs and other means to prevent the flow of food out of the country.

For countries getting higher prices for their commodity exports, the increased terms of trade could be an advantage. For food-exporting countries, this may mean a rare rise in their incomes. They can afford to import more and better capital goods, pay down international debts faster, and make brief advances towards a better standard of living. However, these advantages may dwindle fast, if the boom fades, so countries must be quick to take advantage of the short-term gains. The danger is that countries may not see the opportunity and may squander the gains on imported consumer goods.

Whether a country exports or imports commodities during a boom, governments tend to struggle to make effective policies to handle the disruptions. Commodity exporters face decisions about how to manage their sudden increase in income, and worry about the appreciation of their currency. Commodity importers tend to panic at the sudden increase in necessary consumption or production costs, and worry about paying for a spike in the trade deficit.

Long-term deterioration of terms of trade and LDCs

 To access Worksheet 25.2 on terms of trade and the BoP, please visit www. pearsonbacconline.com and follow the onscreen instructions.

Many LDCs have experienced a long-term trend towards deteriorating terms of trade. We have established that an improving or deteriorating terms of trade is neither unequivocally good nor bad. We have also observed that the degree to which any change in terms of trade helps or hurts a country depends a great deal on the nature of its export and import patterns, specifically the relative price elasticities.

Relatively developed countries experiencing a terms of trade downturn can take solace in the fact that the vast majority of what they produce for export has a relatively elastic demand, and therefore the lower export prices will eventually result in enough overall increased total export revenue to compensate for the initial decreased terms of trade purchasing power. Moreover, these export goods tend to be income elastic, which means that the growth of global income will ensure a growing demand for these goods.

Even middle-income countries are likely to either benefit from an improved terms of trade, or at least suffer less under a deterioration. Because middle-income countries are somewhat diversified, the price of their exports does not change uniformly in one direction, but is likely to vary more randomly. As such, these countries may not suffer such wide fluctuations in the terms of trade.

Developing countries, however, have no such comfort. LDCs often gain most of their export revenue from commodities and, in many cases, these are few for any given country. The market for commodities has relatively low-income inelasticity, meaning that as global income grows, the demand for these goods grows rather slowly, while more advanced and specialized products see their market demand grow much faster. Because the increased demand for higher value goods is likely to outpace the demand for commodities, the terms of trade of poor undiversified countries is likely to deteriorate over the long term. Thus, in simple terms, if the demand for goods produced in developed countries increases 10% over time, and the demand for poor country products increases only 5%, then the terms of trade is likely to continue to move away from LDCs.

 To learn more about terms of trade, visit www. pearsonhotlinks.com, enter the title or ISBN of this book and select weblink 25.1.

As a result, LDCs experience an ever-decreasing share of world output and resources. The consumption of needed imports of capital goods, healthcare items, and necessary resources is more difficult and requires more and more export sales (at lower prices). Without access to the imported goods, economic development is likely to be stifled indefinitely.

HL EXERCISES				

8 Consider the table below.

LOWEST NET BARTER TERMS OF TRADE, 2005–08				
Country	**2005**	**2006**	**2007**	**2008**
Pakistan	75	70	66	58
Bangladesh	80	75	68	58
Japan	83	75	72	62
Korea	79	74	72	62
Haiti	93	90	86	62
Philippines	86	77	76	67

based on data from the World Bank

a Explain how the terms of trade have changed for all of the above countries since 2005.

b Speculate on what may have caused this change.

c For each country, do you think the decreasing TOT is an advantage or disadvantage? Why?

d What other information would help you answer part c?

9 Consider the table below.

HIGHEST NET BARTER TERMS OF TRADE, 2005–08				
Country	2005	2006	2007	2008
Angola	172	198	203	255
Brunei	164	198	193	253
Venezuela	156	184	202	249
Qatar	156	187	188	249
Algeria	164	191	183	239
Niger	158	206	322	233

based on data from the World Bank

a Explain how the terms of trade have changed for all of the above countries since 2005.

b Speculate on what may have caused this change.

c For Venezuela and Brunei, do you think the improving terms of trade is an advantage or disadvantage?

d For those same countries, what do you expect to be the effect on the trade balance? Why?

To access Quiz 25, an interactive, multiple-choice quiz on this chapter, please visit www.pearsonbacconline.com and follow the onscreen instructions.

PRACTICE QUESTIONS

1

Terms of trade impress – even without dairy spike

The relative purchasing power of New Zealand's exports is the highest it has been since 1974.

The **terms of trade** improved 0.6% in the June quarter, Statistics New Zealand said yesterday, to be 2.4% higher than a year ago and 12.4% higher than five years ago.

And economists expect further gains in coming quarters as higher world prices for dairy products flow through to the data.

'We are still in the midst of a structural shift to higher terms of trade, courtesy of higher soft commodity prices,' said ANZ National Bank chief economist Cameron Bagrie.

'This is a positive development for New Zealand's longer-term economic development and living standards.' The exchange rate climbed 4.7% during the quarter, so both export and import prices fell in New Zealand dollar terms.

But import prices fell 1.7% (despite a 3.1% rise in oil prices), outstripping a 1.2% fall in export prices (despite a 3.4% rise in dairy prices).

The terms of trade have yet to reflect much of the recent surge in world dairy prices. They show dairy prices 4% lower than in the June quarter last year, whereas ANZ's commodity price index recorded a 48% increase, in New Zealand dollar terms, over the same period. Overall sales in terms of volume have increased, as well as prices in the last several months.

Despite the most favourable terms of trade in 33 years New Zealand ran a **trade deficit** of $5.6 billion in the year ended June. Export volumes rose just 0.4%, as pastoral products and fish all declined even in seasonally adjusted terms.

Import volumes by contrast rose 3.3%, driven by increases in capital goods and motor vehicles.

'Firms have been taking advantage of cheaper capital goods to boost investment spending,' ASB economist Daniel Wills said.

Bagrie said that if there was any comfort for the Reserve Bank it was in the 4.2% fall in imports of consumer goods – an indication that domestic demand was waning. 'In addition a strong 15.9% increase in capital goods import volumes points to more investment by businesses, which will help alleviate some of the capacity constraints in the economy.'

New Zealand Herald, 12 September 2007

a Define:

   i terms of trade (paragraph 2) (2 marks) [AO1]

   ii trade deficit (paragraph 8). (2 marks) [AO1]

b Using an appropriate diagram, explain the increase in terms of trade as it relates to the increase in dairy sales. (4 marks) [AO2], [AO4]

c Explain how New Zealand can have a favourable terms of trade and still run a trade deficit. (4 marks) [AO2], [AO4]

d To what extent will the surge in terms of trade be an advantage (or disadvantage) to New Zealand's economy in the short and long run? (8 marks) [AO3]

2   Israel Business Arena: Index shows exporters face tougher times

Israeli exports competitiveness worsened during the first quarter of 2010, due to the ongoing **deterioration in the terms of trade**. The Terms of Trade Index, the ratio between the dollar price of industrial exports and the dollar price of imported raw materials, was 2% lower in the first quarter than in the preceding quarter, the Manufacturers Association of Israel Research Department reports. The decline represents the drop in purchasing power of Israeli exports in terms of imports.

The drop in Terms of Trade Index in the first quarter is a direct continuation in the deterioration in Israel's terms of trade, which resumed in the third quarter of 2009. The terms of trade improved in the fourth quarter of 2008 and first quarter of 2009, thanks to a sharp drop in fuel prices. Israel's terms of trade have been deteriorating steadily since the fourth quarter of 2001 and reached a low point in the third quarter of 2008, after a fall of 40% over seven years. The Terms of Trade Index fell 27% between the end of 2001 and the first quarter of 2010.

In addition to the drop in the Terms of Trade Index since the third quarter of 2009, exporters' competitiveness has also been hurt by the shekel's **appreciation**. Between May 2009 and March 2010, the shekel rose 10% against the dollar, resulting in fewer shekels earned for every dollar in foreign sales.

Globes' correspondent, *Israel Business News*, 13 April 2010

a Define:

   i deterioration in the terms of trade index (paragraph 1) (2 marks) [AO1]

   ii appreciation (paragraph 3). (2 marks) [AO1]

b Using a diagram, explain the effect of the shekel's appreciation on the terms of trade (paragraph 3).   (4 marks) [AO2], [AO4]

c Explain why Israel's terms of trade might have improved with the decrease in fuel prices (paragraph 2).   (4 marks) [AO2], [AO4]

d Using your knowledge of economics and information from the article, assess the effects of Israel's changing terms of trade on its balance of payments and other key economic indicators.   (8 marks) [AO3]

26 INTRODUCTION TO ECONOMIC DEVELOPMENT

26.1 Economic growth and economic development

Learning outcomes

- Distinguish between economic growth and economic development.
- Explain the multidimensional nature of economic development in terms of reducing widespread poverty, raising living standards, reducing income inequalities and increasing employment opportunities.
- Explain that the most important sources of economic growth in economically less developed countries include increases in quantities of physical capital and human capital, the development and use of new technologies that are appropriate to the conditions of the economically less developed countries, and institutional changes.
- Explain the relationship between economic growth and economic development, noting that some limited economic development is possible in the absence of economic growth, but that over the long term, economic growth is usually necessary for economic development (however, it should be understood that under certain circumstances economic growth may not lead to economic development).

Four-fifths of the world's population live in poverty. Is this good news or bad news?

▼

Consider the following assertion: our modern era of globalization has made it possible for more people to live lives of greater wealth, health and comfort than at any time in history. Globally speaking, people have longer life spans and enjoy comforts and conveniences only imagined by people living as recently as 100 years ago. However, this obvious fact runs alongside another, very unpleasant one. Approximately four-fifths of the world's people live in developing countries, many of them in abject poverty. That's nearly 4.8 billion people. Furthermore, developing countries account for less than one-fifth of total world income. Development economics, as a field of inquiry, attempts to understand and address that disparity. It is enormously encouraging to see the progress made by so many so quickly. Surely something can be learned of this success, and surely these lessons can be applied in service to the unlucky billions who are just getting by?

Figure 26.1 (overleaf) shows relative development levels geographically. Its findings are based on scores for countries on the Human Development Index, a composite indicator of development (page 561).

 Economic development is the sustainable increase in living standards for a country, typically characterized by increases in life span, education levels, and income.

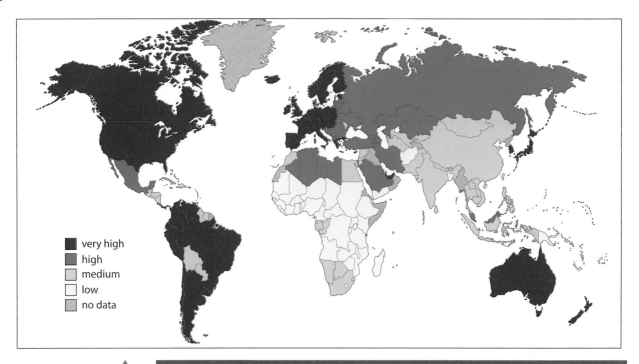

Figure 26.1
Development by country.

1   Using Figure 2.61, rank the geographical regions in order of level of development.

2   Based purely on the geographic depiction of developed countries in Figure 26.1, list three generalizations you might make with regard to development.

3   To what extent do you believe these generalizations to be true?

4   What information or data would help you assess whether those generalizations were true?

Development over the years

For the decades that followed the Great Depression of the 1930s, most macroeconomists focused on economic growth. Growing economies, it was logically reasoned, would improve the lives of most citizens. The emphasis was on investment in infrastructure, creating productive capacity, stimulating spending, and generally improving income level. In Chapter 11, the many measures economists have devised to assess those levels are discussed, from GDP to *per capita* GDP, to adjusting for purchasing power and the creation of purchasing-power-parity-adjusted *per capita* GDP. The limits of GDP or GNI to assess the activity it claims to record have been acknowledged. Economists, it could be said, grew better and better at keeping score, but only in a particular way.

Beginning in the late 1940s and early 1950s (the end of the colonial era in many poor countries) there emerged a concern that growth alone did not always provide a better quality of life. Sheer economic growth had a mixed record in terms of improving health, education and other basic living standards. Economists began seeking out new ways to look at economic well-being, especially for poor countries, which had either missed out on growth or found its promises unfulfilled.

Development can be defined as a broad measure of economic well-being, one that takes into account factors beyond monetary income to include health, education and other social indicators. Development economics is a branch of economic theory that has grown up around the idea that it is possible to understand what makes poor countries poor (and rich countries rich) and to make policy changes that can turn poor countries into richer ones.

A sign of the growing interest in a wider focus came in 1966, when the United Nations created the UN Development Programme, and by 1971 had consolidated most of its development-related agencies together. Funded by voluntary contributions of UN members, the UNDP has contributed technical assistance, consultants' services, equipment, and fellowships for advanced study abroad. It has funded projects in resource planning, training institutes, the application of modern technology to development, and the building of the economic and social infrastructure.

In 1990, influenced by the work of Amartya Sen, the UNDP began to compile and publish the Human Development Index, a broader evaluation of economic well-being that has become the standard international benchmark measure for quality of life. This drive towards a development focus, rather than pure growth, has gathered momentum through the work of the UN as well as from a wide variety of academics in the last few decades. It culminated in the UNDP's Millennium Development Goals Project, an ambitious effort to draw attention and resources to the struggles of poor countries (page 558). This chapter elaborates on the relationship between growth and development, defines characteristics that less developed countries (LDCs) share and considers the ways in which they are different. It also describes and explains the common methods of measuring economic development.

To learn more about development, visit www.pearsonhotlinks.com, enter the title or ISBN of this book and select weblink 26.1.

Growth and development

Economic growth is rather strictly defined as an increase in real GDP over the previous year. Economists strive to refine and clarify the idea by measuring it against population size and relative spending power. But it remains the defining characteristic of a country's economic success. Growth, because it usually means more money and activity and employment, generally suggests that something is going right with the economy. A recession, a lack of growth or a decrease in the economy's size, triggers attention and policy changes.

Development, in contrast, emphasizes specific changes in aspects of people's lives in many different dimensions. A primary focus of development economics is the reduction of poverty, the raising of incomes among the world's poorest. Furthermore, development economics seeks the improvement of general living standards. Typically, living standards are measured by long life, general health, education achievement and opportunities, as well as measures of income. Development economics, like mainstream views of growth, also focuses on employment, in particular on the types of employment offered in poor countries, and how countries can adapt and respond to the challenges of their workforces.

Economic growth

While economic growth occurs with any increase in GDP over the previous year, it is relevant to make a distinction between the growth of actual production and growth of potential production. Potential output is an increase or shift to the right of long-run aggregate supply (LRAS) or a country's production possibilities frontier (PPF) (Figure 26.2, overleaf).

Figure 26.2
Economic growth: **a** PPF;
b LRAS.

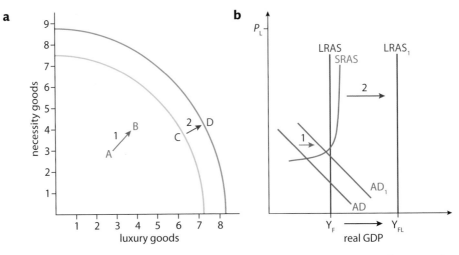

Growth in production is shown on a PPF (Figure 26.2a) as a movement (1) from A, where resources are not being used efficiently, to B where there is more activity (and GDP) and more efficiency. On Figure 26.2b, the AD/AS diagram, it can be shown as a deflationary gap that is partially reduced by an increase in aggregate demand (1) from AD to AD_1. In contrast, growth in the long-term potential of the economy is shown as a shift of the PPF outwards from point C to D (2), or a shift to the right of the LRAS curve (2). In either long-run case, an increase in the quantity or quality of the factors of production, perhaps encouraged by growth in productivity, has improved the overall productive capacity of the economy. It is long-run growth that we are concerned with here.

Sources of economic growth

The natural resource base

When it comes to natural resources, each country must do its best with what it has. Some countries are blessed with an abundance of water, arable land, timber, and other natural resources. The US attributes some part of its enormous wealth to a breadth and depth of natural bounty. Other countries, like Singapore and the Netherlands, resort to increasing resources like land by means of impressive technological achievement. Still other countries toil away in hopes of discovering a precious new resource, as happened in Afghanistan in 2009 when vast mineral deposits, some including lithium (which is used to power all kinds of modern batteries) were discovered. The estimated worth of Afghan deposits is nearly 3 trillion dollars. Such a windfall is extremely rare; the only practical alternative is to seek out ways to improve resources already known about.

Physical capital

Growth can be achieved by increasing or improving the amount of physical capital. This includes buildings, machinery, vehicles, offices, and equipment. The resources to purchase these goods come from savings (and the income earned from savings); the intellectual power to improve them comes from a more highly educated workforce. Some technology can be imported from overseas capital products and by hiring foreign expertise. Capital widening refers to the extension of capital goods to a larger segment of workers (e.g. more farmers using simple tools). Capital deepening refers to increases in the ratio of capital per worker, so that workers have more capital to work with (all farmers using better farm tools). Some combination of capital widening and capital deepening is necessary for growth to occur.

Appropriate technologies

It is often assumed that poor countries benefit from the technological improvements being made by rich ones. This is certainly true, and advancements in information technology hold promise for poor countries to improve market access and price information. However, other examples point to technology that can be detrimental to growth. Multinational agricultural companies, for example, have created highly productive seeds. These seeds should improve farm yields in the short term, but the plants they produce do not set seed themselves. Seeds for the next planting must be purchased from the corporation. In other cases, foreign aid agencies may be forced by their countries to provide certain types of technology, regardless of the recipient country's needs. As a result, expensive new tractors lie rusting, unused after breaking down and requiring expensive repairs, when more appropriate intermediate technology would have moved the country forwards. Rather than assert that more is always better, the emphasis is now on appropriate technology.

Human capital

The quantity of human capital can be increased by encouraging childbirth with better prenatal and maternal healthcare. It can also be accomplished by encouraging immigration to the country, adding to the labour force. However, many countries have too large a population and are seeking ways of reducing it. China's one-child policy and Singapore's incentive system for families are two prominent examples.

The quality of human capital can be improved through a variety of approaches to make the average person more productive. Improved healthcare keeps children healthy, and parents able to care for them. It also lowers the amount of time workers are absent or ill during working hours. Furthermore, education and worker training are all investments in human capital, and thus should contribute the productive capacity (LRAS) of the country.

Institutional factors

Enduring economic growth can only occur when minimum levels of legal and institutional factors are in place. Political stability is a prerequisite. A stable banking system ensures the flow of capital. A minimum level of infrastructure is necessary, so that goods can be transported, and a minimum level of public health is required. An orderly legal system that affirms property rights encourages investment. A reasonably good education system, one that successfully trains students in numeracy and literacy, is also important.

To access Worksheet 26.1 on economic development myths, please visit www.pearsonbacconline.com and follow the onscreen instructions.

CASE STUDY

People in economics: Amartya Sen

What does it mean to be free? For Amartya Sen, the question has been personal, political and professional. Sen was born in West Bengal, then a colony of Great Britain. As a child, he witnessed the devastating Bengal famine of 1943, an event that lingered with him and shaped his research as an economist. Sen achieved top marks at prestigious prep schools in Bengal and India, and eventually studied at Cambridge. His early years of graduate work were marked by intense debates between the advocates of Keynesian and neo-classical economics. Eventually, though, Sen made his mark by pursuing a different perspective on national economic well-being. His study of famines and deprivation led him to conclude that most famine was unnecessary, a consequence of factors that had little to do with a lack of resources. More important, he argued, were the capabilities of the people to fend for themselves. Freedom, he argued, was more than the lack of government interference in one's life, but rather the ability to positively do something to help oneself. To Sen, it is on this basis that all governments should be evaluated. Famine, he later noted, was far less likely in functioning democracies because the government is compelled to respond to its people in times of critical shortage. Sen also promoted a focus on gender inequality, writing famously that 'more than

◀ Amartya Sen (b. 1933): the 'conscience of his profession'.

100 million women are missing,' in China and India because of preferential healthcare for men and sex-selective abortion of girls. Among the most influential economists, if not intellectuals, of the 20th century, Sen questioned the view of *homo economicus*, of humans as purely self-motivated actors. He was awarded the 1998 Nobel Prize for his work on social choice theory and his interest in poverty and development. His work in the causes of famine and on social welfare, drove much of the thinking behind changes in United Nations development policy in recent decades, including the formulation of the Human Development Index.

A country seeking progress can follow many paths. A brief review of macroeconomic trends in different countries yields many combinations of growth, inequality, health, and other standard-of-living results. Indeed, all the sources of economic growth are useful components of economic development. However, the outcomes of economic growth can be very different.

Growth without development

Economic growth means more production and income for a country. This, in principle, should yield an increase in the standard of living. However, sometimes growth is achieved along with very disagreeable outcomes related to the basic economic questions of what to produce, how to produce it, and to whom the results of production are actually distributed.

Many poor countries have limited choice about the types of good to produce. They are generally limited to resource extraction and production of agricultural commodities, often with problematic results. How production occurs (i.e. choice of production methods) can cause serious environmental harm that deepens poverty. Meanwhile, the benefits of production frequently go to a tiny elite, rather than being more generally spread across income levels.

What to produce: limited benefits to LDC production

Too much of some resources might even be considered a bad thing. Some economists say there is a resource curse when countries have an abundance of a non-renewable mineral or fuel resource. Why a curse? Because exchange rates are driven up by demand for the resource, crowding out other exports, and also because governments that rely on the easy money from these found resources tend to be inefficient and corrupt.

The theory of comparative advantage directs countries to produce the goods and services for which they have the lowest opportunity costs. In other words, countries should do what is most valuable to them, based on the market value of that activity. This, the theory states, is the surest path to economic growth. However, this type of production may not yield enduring or extensive economic benefits, nor is it certain that this type of growth can keep countries competitive in terms of income relative to rich countries. Most LDCs gain the majority of income and export revenue from resource extraction and the production of agricultural commodities. Each has limitations.

- **Resource extraction**. Precious timber is sold from Burma to China, copper extracted from mines in Zambia, diamonds from South Africa, oil from Indonesia. Ideally, resource wealth should translate into income and a higher standard of living. However, because most poor countries lack the capital resources and infrastructure to extract resources, they auction extraction rights to multinational corporations (MNCs). Because mineral extraction is more capital intensive than labour intensive, the increased employment benefit is not very great. At the same time, capital flight occurs when the profits earned are repatriated to the home country headquarters of the MNC. Furthermore, while it is hoped that these activities will require and result in infrastructure improvements, many of the gains in infrastructure are industry specific, or limited to the area where the resource extraction occurs.
- **Agricultural commodities**. It is estimated that 40% of the world's population work in agriculture. Most live in poor countries. This ties most of the world's poor citizens directly to the fortunes of agricultural production and these markets are notoriously

volatile. Weather changes, blights, and surges in productivity are all responsible for wild swings in commodity prices, and thus affect the incomes of many poor countries. As discussed in Chapter 25, this can be a losing game for two main reasons: increased productivity has generally suppressed prices in the last several decades and, as global income continues to grow, demand for these commodities is relatively income inelastic. Therefore, the demand for these goods grows much more slowly than demand for manufactured goods and services. As a result, the relative incomes of poor, agriculture-based countries continue to fall behind. Also dampening prices are the massive protectionist subsidies lavished on farmers in the EU and the US. Yet poor countries are driven to commodity production because this is where their comparative advantage exists. Even if they wanted to, however, they have few options to diversify. The structural change from primary to secondary production requires capital goods. Buying capital goods requires foreign exchange, and these countries need the revenue earned from extraction and agriculture to buy the capital goods. With the export prices falling and demand growing slowly, their terms of trade is in decline. Thus, many LDCs find themselves trying to earn more and more from agricultural production that has less and less market demand from the rest of the world.

How to produce: production and environmental destruction

The diminished terms of trade contributes to environmental degradation in many LDCs. Because the resources or crops LDCs are producing have a declining terms of trade value, such countries must produce more of their decreasing-price exports to buy the relatively more expensive import goods from around the world. This problem can easily degenerate into a vicious cycle: the pressure to produce more crops contributes to deforestation, soil depletion, and even water contamination. In broader terms, the pressure on resources in LDCs leads producers to seek ever-lower costs with regards to many types of production. The result is the daunting array of environmental damage discussed below.

- **Deforestation**. The dramatic rise in forest cutting coincided with the industrial revolution, beginning in the second half of the 19th century. It has continued, at varying rates, ever since. While the rates of forest destruction are sometimes disputed, it is generally agreed that deforestation is a serious environmental problem. The World Bank, whose estimates are viewed as conservative, says that forest area has decreased by 1% since 1989. Rainforests in Brazil, Central America, Madagascar, West Africa and South Asia have been particularly ravaged in recent decades. Because more developed countries (MDCs) have already cut their forests, the world has turned to LDCs as a source of timber products. At the same time, population growth and the pressure to clear land for agricultural use have apparently accelerated deforestation in LDCs. The effects are serious, including the disruption of the water cycle, increased soil erosion, and decreased biodiversity. In addition, it is likely that LDCs are trading short-term gains from deforestation for the long-term preservation and maintenance of natural resources.
- **Land degradation**. LDC land resources are declining in natural value as a result of land clearance, livestock production and overgrazing, commercial development and urbanization, clear cutting and deforestation, as well as agricultural overuse. This results in a depletion of minerals and nutrients from the soil, making farming more difficult and expensive. Soil erosion, as a result of deforestation and urbanization, contributes to a loss of organic matter, compounding the depletion of soil quality. The destruction of soil resources obviously hinders poor countries, which rely heavily on agricultural production for income.
- **Water pollution**. Population growth, combined with the pollution of fresh-water sources, has caused some to view water as the speculative good of the future, akin to oil and gold. Lack of fresh water is a major cause of disease and premature death, very

seriously affecting those in LDCs. In China, several hundred million people lack an uncontaminated water source. In India 1100 children die every day from diarrhoea from contaminated water. Globally, it is estimated that 14 000 people die every day from lack of access to clean water. Economic growth contributes to the problem with agricultural production causing increased fertilizer runoff, increased use of insecticides, and increased animal waste. Industrial waste in the form of heavy metals, detergents, chemical wastes, and petroleum fluids also contribute to water contamination.

- **Over-fishing**. As global income rises, the demand for fish has grown. To meet that demand, industrial fishing has significantly increased its capacity to catch fish. Repeated crashes of fish populations in recent decades have caused many to worry that global fish stocks are on the verge of collapse. Because open-sea fishing is considered a common good, fish can be taken from the oceans without concern for the replenishment of stocks. LDCs that earn significant foreign exchange from fish exports are susceptible to over-fishing. They are thus more vulnerable to fish depletion and a long-term threat to this food and income source.

- **Air pollution**. Most air pollution is associated with human economic growth. Among the major causes of air pollution are methane (produced by livestock), car exhaust, and manufacturing and power plant exhaust. Air pollution affects the health of many people, causing the death of up to 2 million each year. Air pollution also exacerbates many illnesses, including lung disease, pneumonia, asthma, emphysema and bronchitis. At minimum, this puts a strain on healthcare services in LDCs, and most certainly lowers productivity rates among workers in those countries.

- **Climate change**. Perhaps the most daunting environmental challenge is posed by the rising temperature of the planet's surface and air. The scientific consensus is that the average temperature of the planet increased significantly in the 20th century. Some estimates of 21st-century warming suggest the increase will be greater, from 1.1–6.4 °C (2.0–11.5 °F). The effects are expected to be catastrophic; here are a few examples:
  - increased frequency and severity of extreme weather events such as drought and heavy precipitation
  - rising sea levels destroy coastal cities and increase the spread of airborne disease
  - disrupted weather patterns devastate crop yields and threaten global food security.

Such changes will cause rapid changes to whole ecosystems, with unpredictable but dire results for all species, especially humans.

Economic growth, as currently practised, is widely accepted to be a major contributor to climate change. Carbon dioxide and other greenhouse gases are produced by many different types of economic activity, including burning fossil fuels for energy, deforestation, and animal farming.

CASE STUDY

The top 10 of the world's most polluted places

- Sumgayit, Azerbaijan: organic chemicals and mercury, from petrochemical and industrial complexes
- Linfen, China: particulates and gases from industry and traffic
- Tianying, China: heavy metals and particulates, industry
- Sukinda, India: chromium, chromite mines
- Vapi, India: industrial effluents
- La Oroya, Peru: lead and heavy metals; metal mining and processing
- Dzerzhinsk, Russia: chemicals, toxic by-products; lead; chemical weapons manufacturing
- Norilsk, Russia: heavy metals, particulates; mining and smelting

- Chernobyl, Ukraine: radioactive materials
- Kabwe, Zambia: lead; mining and smelting

Blacksmith Institute, 2007

The Blacksmith Institute is an environmental non-governmental organization that tracks pollution problems. This alphabetical (by country), unranked list of 30 sites (the 'dirty thirty') was published in 2007. Countries with the most entries were China, India and Russia. The Middle East and Oceana had no sites on the list.

EXERCISES

5   To what extent does the Blacksmith Institute's list prove the contention that growth can cause environmental damage?

6   Assess the validity of the following statement.

Poor countries are merely going through the states that rich countries went through. Once they are rich, they will fix these problems just as the rich countries have.

For whom: who benefits from production?

- **Income inequality**. Growth in overall GDP and even growth in *per capita* measures of income may obscure who really receives the higher income. Economists use measures such as the Gini coefficient and Lorenz curve to assess and illustrate the distribution of income (Chapter 16). Recent trends show that inequality in many countries is growing. In other words, those earning the most money are seeing their incomes rise the fastest, while those earning lesser incomes are seeing their share of national income decrease.

The effect of income inequality on growth and development has been the subject of philosophical debate as well as academic study. Some view efforts to redistribute income through tax policies that take higher proportions from the top earners as anti-capitalistic and contrary to free market principles. Some research augments this view, arguing that the relatively rich tend to save more of their income and thus provide more capital from which more growth can occur. This perspective has not held up well and more recent research suggests that extreme levels of inequality tend to retard growth because of the disruption of social cohesion and the encouragement of social unrest. Other research suggests that both very high and very low inequality tends to slow growth, and therefore recommends a moderate approach to income redistribution. Growth tends to be more self-sustaining when the Gini coefficient is between 25 and 40 (the former typical of Northern Europe, the latter of France, Germany, the UK, and the US).

These results suggest that countries with very high (and also very low) inequality have a harder time sustaining the growth that will fund greater development. Also, because lack of redistributive tax policies is most often the cause of income inequality, the base of tax revenue is smaller than it could be. Development, for a country at a given income level, may be harder to achieve because it is less well funded than in a country that actively redistributes income through tax policies.

Growth with development

There is an overwhelmingly high correlation between high income and high levels of development. This is to be expected, as income is typically a core measure of development. But the variety of results, and especially high-income development failures, leads to the conclusion that may have seemed obvious from the start: growth is a necessary, but

 The top five countries with the most equal distributions (averaged between 1997 and 2008) are: Norway, Australia, Iceland, Canada and Ireland. These are all countries high on the Human Development Index (HDI). The bottom five countries, those with most unequal distributions of income, are all low-ranking HDI countries: Mali, the Central African Republic, Sierra Leone, Afghanistan and Niger.

not sufficient, condition for true development. Growth should be expected to enhance many aspects of the standard of living in a country, provided the money is well spent. For example, high growth provides increased tax revenues, which can be used to improve schools and basic healthcare services.

Figure 26.3 illustrates the relationship of growth and development. Growth, if managed effectively, can yield the expected positive outcomes of longer lives, more education, and an overall better standard of living. However, if managed poorly, environmental damage, high inequality of income, inattention to the basic necessities and corruption can ensure that growth runs afoul of its supposed logical ends.

Figure 26.3
Growth, with and without development.

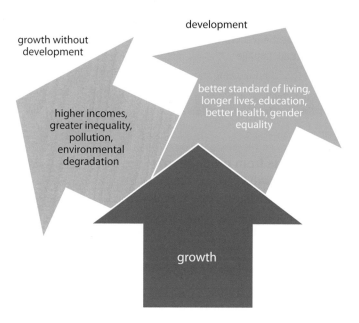

Development without growth

As growth can lead in so many bad directions, is it possible to achieve development without it? The evidence suggests that it is. Some countries with low GDP *per capita* can score very well on composite development indicators, rather better than their high-growth and richer counterparts. So perhaps growth is not a prerequisite for development (Table 26.5, page 562).

One way to interpret such a result is to allow that some countries may overachieve, relative to their *per capita* GDP, because of attention to institutional factors such as their court system or banking system. Perhaps, despite a lack of MDC levels of income, their educational attainment is quite high. Perhaps these countries make wise investments in prenatal care of mothers and children, lowering infant mortality levels and extending life spans. Perhaps development is possible without growth.

Another look at the list of overachievers and underachievers in Table 26.5 suggests that the underachievers derive significant levels of income from resource extraction, typically oil revenues. The Emirates, Kuwait and Venezuela, most conspicuously, have underachieved in development terms despite large inflows of foreign exchange. So perhaps the more relevant lesson is to understand why so many countries like these misspend their incomes and achieve only 'uneconomic growth.' This term is attributed to American economist Herman Daly; it describes economic growth that actually reduces the standard of living rather than enriching it. The list of development overachievers is rather small, compared to that of the underachieving, high-income, growth-development failures.

To access Worksheet 26.2 on economic growth, please visit www. pearsonbacconline.com and follow the onscreen instructions.

26.2 Common characteristics of economically less developed countries

Learning outcomes

- Explain, using examples, that economically less developed countries share certain common characteristics (noting that it is dangerous to generalize as there are many exceptions in each case), including low levels of GDP *per capita*, high levels of poverty, relatively large agricultural sectors, large urban informal sectors and high birth rates.
- Explain that in some countries there may be communities caught in a poverty trap (poverty cycle) where poor communities are unable to invest in physical, human and natural capital due to low or no savings; poverty is therefore transmitted from generation to generation, and there is a need for intervention to break out of the cycle.

Levels of development

Setting foot in a less developed country might provide some instant clues about the level of development: poor housing, bad sanitation, children running in the streets during school hours. But poor areas exist in every country, so it is important to use aggregate statistics to comprehend the magnitude of the problem in any given country. The degree to which LDCs share common characteristics allows economists to devise and test common policies to address their concerns. With this in mind, economists have identified several traits that are likely to be evident in a typical LDC. At the same time, it is important to note that there is quite a variety between these countries. In other words, all LDCs do not look alike: differences are discussed in section 26.3. Here, we are going to look at some similarities.

Some traits associated with poverty

High birth rates/large dependency ratios

Measured as the crude birth rate (CBR), global birth rates have dropped steadily over the last 100 years, but the rates for developing countries have dropped much more slowly. The global average CBR for 2010 is approximately 20 births per 1000 women of child-bearing age per year. In LDCs, this figure is far exceeded, with CBRs as high as 40–55 births per 1000 women of child-bearing age per year. In other words, birth rates in many LDCs can be 2–3 times higher than the global average.

The dependency ratio is the combined number of people not in the labour force compared to those who are in the productive population (labour force). High birth rates tend to lead to high dependency ratios, another common characteristic of LDCs. Countries with high birth rates and large populations of younger people fall easily into this category. At the same time, richer countries with ageing populations are also seeing their dependency ratios climb. Countries with high dependency ratios are likely to struggle to meet the needs of their relatively large dependent population. The highest ratios, typically at or above 80%, imply that for every productive, working person there is another person to support.

 Dependency ratio is the percentage of old-age adults and below-working-age children relative to the number of working-age adults.

Low *per capita* GDP

There is a high positive correlation between levels of development and attainment of GDP *per capita*. Thus, the countries which rank at the bottom of the Human Development Index tend to have low average levels of income. Perhaps not surprisingly, these same countries tend to have high rates of extreme and moderate poverty.

Table 26.1 shows the percentage of the population living in extreme and moderate poverty in selected middle- and low-income countries (defined by their GDP *per capita*). Note the correlation of low average income and extreme poverty.

TABLE 26.1 EXTREME AND MODERATE POVERTY LEVELS, 2007		
Country	**% population living in extreme poverty**	**% population living in moderate poverty (includes those in extreme poverty)**
Middle-income countries		
Romania	0.5*	4.1
Costa Rica	0.7*	4.3
Brazil	4.3*	12.7
Low- and very low-income countries		
Cambodia	25.8	57.8
Indonesia	27.4	56.6
Timor Leste	37.2	72.8
Liberia	83.7	94.8

* Figure for 2008 as no data available for 2007.

High agricultural dependence

Developing countries rely heavily on agricultural production which can be the main source of labour income as well as export earnings. More specifically, a larger percentage of labour is employed in agriculture in LDCs. Generally speaking, developed countries tend to employ less than 10% of the population in agriculture, while the proportion in LDCs may be 50–80%. These countries, along with a large portion of their employed population, remain vulnerable to weather changes and the typically volatile market for agricultural commodities.

Large urban informal sector

The informal sector is defined as being unorganized, unregistered, and unsupported by the state and its institutions. It may include subsistence production, cottage industry, unreported merchant activity, and black market trade. Most LDCs have relatively high proportions of their economy operating informally.

Poverty cycle

Because poor countries lack income, they can become trapped in a cycle of poverty from which it is difficult to escape (Figure 26.4).

Without surplus income, it is difficult to accumulate any savings. Without a base of savings on which to draw, there are no resources to invest in the physical, human, and natural capital needed for increased productivity. When productivity is stagnant, wages and income stay low. Thus the cycle repeats itself from one generation to the next. It is for this reason that many LDCs seek foreign investment and foreign aid to inject flows of money and capital into the cycle.

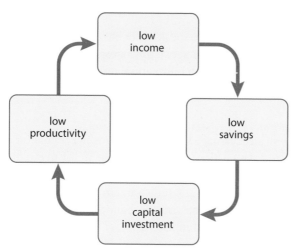

Figure 26.4
The poverty cycle.

EXERCISES

7   Select one country each from the categories of middle income and low/very low income. Make a short table that lists the relevant statistics for each of the following: crude birth rate, dependency ratio, percentage of employment by industry (sometimes broken down into statistics for men and women.)

26.3 Diversity among economically less developed countries

Learning outcomes

• Explain, using examples, that economically less developed countries differ enormously from each other in terms of a variety of factors, including resource endowments, climate, history (colonial or otherwise), political systems and degree of political stability.

LDCs are not all the same

While many LDCs share the imposing challenges discussed above, they can differ quite profoundly in other ways. These differences are important to bear in mind as the policies recommended to LDCs cannot be applied without consideration for the differences.

Differences between LDCs

Resource endowments

While it is understandable to think that a country is poor because it has little in the way of natural resources, this is not necessarily true. Angola, a country disrupted by decades of civil war, was once considered the breadbasket of its region and holds major oil reserves. Burma is known to possess large quantities of oil, natural gas, teak wood, and gems, yet it still languishes in poverty. Brazil, considered to be as resource-rich as nearly any country in the world, has considerably underperformed in development terms given its resource endowment. At the same time, some countries have done rather well despite limited natural resources. Japan, with little arable land and no in-ground resources to speak of, has consistently been ranked among the top few developed countries in the world. Famously,

Singapore has almost no resources to speak of but has expanded its land base by increasing its shoreline. Lichtenstein and Andorra, two tiny European principalities, enjoy very high development levels with perhaps their only natural resource being their geographical location in Europe.

Climate

Countries blessed with an advantageous balance of sunshine, rainfall and moderate temperature appear to have a natural advantage in their ability to exploit agricultural resources. Many of the very least developed countries are in the region of the Sahara desert, where temperature extremes and little water make life hard. Generally, LDCs can have warm summers or moderate ones, be arid, humid or monsoonal, have cold winters or moderate ones. There is not a shared climate.

History

Many developing countries were once colonies of developed countries. However, the effects of colonization are varied, as well as being disputed. It has been argued that countries with lingering occupation, like India and Hong Kong, benefited by the establishment of legal order and effective institutions. In contrast, countries that were used primarily for resource extraction, such as Burma and Vietnam, have fared less well. Other studies suggest that the duration of colonization played a significant role, and that the terms of independence also made a difference.

Political systems

LDCs have a wide range of political systems. There are large democracies such as Brazil, India and Indonesia. Some have monarchical absolutist leaderships, as in Brunei, Bhutan and North Korea. Others have single party rule, as in China and Cuba. Many have disputed governments, where conflict has rendered government almost completely ineffective, as in Somalia, Haiti, Afghanistan, Sudan and Chad. Iran is a military theocracy. With such variety it is necessary to create policies with consideration of the distinctive political structure in any given developing country.

Degree of political stability

Civil war or inter-state conflict certainly interferes with plans for prosperity and development. Many of the countries at the bottom of the Human Development Index have suffered from one or the other of these dangers. Zimbabwe, Congo, Burundi, Mozambique, Chad, Somalia, Ethiopia, Afghanistan and Sudan, all in the final 30 countries in development terms, have all been at war internally or externally in the last decade or so. However, many other countries have had relatively stable governments, with little conflict over changes in power. This, of course, does not confirm the relative efficacy of these governments – some of the most stable can be among the most corrupt.

- Does the term 'economic development' mean different things in different cultures?
- Are there two ways of thinking about economics: from the point of view of an economically more developed country and from that of an economically less developed country? If so, what is the difference?
- Are there two different sets of values in which such a distinction is grounded?
- How can we decide if the distinction between economically more developed countries and economically less developed countries is a meaningful one given that economic development itself might not be so clearly defined?

26.4 Single indicators of economic development

Learning outcomes
- Distinguish between GDP *per capita* figures and GNI *per capita* figures.
- Compare and contrast the GDP *per capita* figures and the GNI *per capita* figures for economically more developed countries and economically less developed countries.
- Distinguish between GDP *per capita* figures and GDP *per capita* figures at purchasing power parity (PPP) exchange rates.
- Compare and contrast GDP *per capita* figures and GDP *per capita* figures at purchasing power parity (PPP) exchange rates for economically more developed countries and economically less developed countries.
- Compare and contrast two health indicators for economically more developed countries and economically less developed countries.
- Compare and contrast two education indicators for economically more developed countries and economically less developed countries.

How do economists objectively classify countries at various stages of development? Countries are usually first ranked by their *per capita* income levels (Chapter 11). However, one measure alone fails to render an accurate portrait of any country's overall development. Because development involves so many facets of economic life, most summary evaluations of a country must involve many indicators taken together. Economic indicators are specific points of data gathered systematically and continuously to better inform economists and policymakers. For a single area (e.g. health) there may be dozens of different ways of assessing the level of development.

Much like the gathering of national income data, the compilation and study of measurement data is useful because:

- baseline indicator data can help set an agenda for progress, with specific goals
- indicator data measured from one year to the next can indicate the level of progress on that goal
- continued data gathering enables policymakers to reformulate and adjust policies to improve performance
- indicators across countries allow for cross-country comparisons of relative development.

Single indicators cover a specific area. For example, 'doctors per 100 000 people' is an indicator of the level of healthcare. Composite indicators gather a group of indicators and put them together in an attempt to get a broad picture of a country's level of development. Typically, composite indicators draw on income, health and education data to rank countries on levels of development. An example of a composite indicator is the United Nations Human Development Index (page 561).

It is important to bear in mind that conclusions based on statistics gathered from LDCs must be read with caution. Many countries cannot afford the resources needed for consistent and rigorous gathering of information. For this reason, many countries provide only limited data. Still more challenging is the extraordinary variety of development indicators. The language and purposes of these can vary significantly. As a result, some scepticism with regard to the reliability of the data is warranted. However, where a long-term trend is evident, it is likely that the data have a certain level of reliability and validity.

Income indicators

National income data are usually the starting point for understanding development levels. You will recall from Chapter 11 that real gross domestic product (real GDP) is the inflation-adjusted value of all the goods and services produced in the country in the past year. As such, it provides an indicator of the level of activity within a country's borders. Real gross national income (real GNI) takes the ownership of resources into account. Rather than tracking production geographically, it considers the flow of incomes across borders. Real GNI is the inflation-adjusted value of all production from factors of production owned by a country. In short, GNI = GDP – net income flows. Furthermore, to get a better understanding of the average level of production or income, *per capita* measures are used. These divide national totals by the population to get average income levels.

Per capita GDP *vs per capita* GNI

Compared to national income totals, *per capita* income data provides a better sense of the average standard of living. Large economies can overstate the relative affluence of a country when their income is 'divided' by a much larger population. Much smaller countries, in contrast, may do quite well considering their smaller overall economy is 'spread' over a very small population base.

When viewed comparatively, a number of high-income countries have rather different *per capita* GDP and GNI results. Figure 26.5 shows such a selection, where Luxembourg, the highest *per capita* income in terms of GDP, has over $20 000 less income *per capita* in GNI terms. What does this mean? It suggests that there is far more economic activity happening within Luxembourg than is actually being paid to Luxembourger-owned factors of production. This also appears to be true, to a lesser extent, for Ireland and Japan. Meanwhile, for Norway and Sweden the opposite appears to be true. Norwegian and Swedish-owned factors of production (including repatriated corporate profits and salaries), earn significantly more than the income generated solely within the boundaries of each country.

Figure 26.5
Per capita GDP and *per capita* GNI, selected developed countries, 2009.

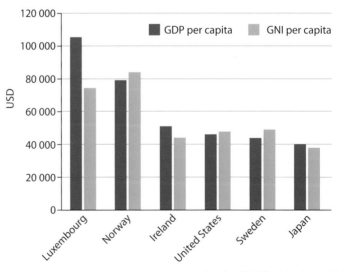

based on World Bank development indicators database

In the case of richer countries, GNI may be higher than GDP because firms in those countries have spread overseas and now generate significant profits that are sent back to their corporate homes. In Luxembourg, famous as a banking centre, it appears that the economic activity in the country exceeds the income accrued to its firms and citizens.

Developing countries may also have a discrepancy between GDP and GNI numbers. The income generated by production within China slightly outpaces the income generated by Chinese-owned factors. The same is true for Nicaragua and Burundi as well. At the same time, for India, Nepal and Ghana, net factor income pushes GNI above the output income generated by GDP (Figure 26.6).

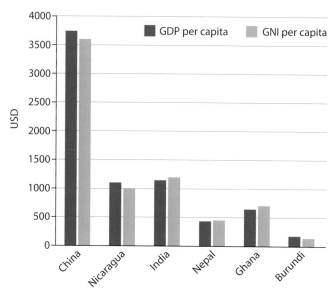

based on World Bank development indicators database

Figure 26.6
Per capita GDP and *per capita* GNI, selected developing countries.

For relatively less developed countries, the differences between GDP and GNI may be for different reasons. China, with increasing amounts of foreign direct investment (FDI), may see a significant amount of corporate profits sent out of country. In the case of poor countries with higher GNI numbers, it is possible that many have citizens living abroad as guest workers who repatriate salaries home. These migrant salaries can be a significant source of income for developing countries.

Purchasing power parity (PPP) comparisons

Of course, when doing any national income accounting, statisticians first calculate output and incomes in the local currency. But comparisons between Norwegian kroner and Thai baht, for example, would seem meaningless without being translated into a single currency, usually the US dollar.

While this translation makes comparisons more useful, the spending power of money in Norway may be very different from that in Thailand. Resources, goods and services may be more expensive in Norway than in Thailand, which means that more income is needed in Norway to enjoy the same standard of living as in Thailand.

To more accurately reflect the buying power of any amount of income, and so to better assess the standard of living in a country, economists use a comparison called purchasing power parity (PPP). Purchasing power parity is based on the law of one price, which states that an identical good in one country should cost the same in another country, and that the exchange rate should reflect that price. This has implications for the way we look at exchange rates (Chapter 22). For our purposes here, PPP is a tool to assess more accurately the standard of living available for a given amount of income in a country.

For example, the Norwegian equivalent of $100 (Nk588) may buy a certain amount of food, perhaps three pizzas. The Thai baht equivalent of $100 (THB2994) may buy six pizzas, because staple goods are cheaper in Thailand. This means that every $100 of income earned in Norway will buy less in goods and services than the same amount in Thailand. Therefore, Norway's high GDP *per capita* may overrate the standard of living there.

When the purchasing power is factored into national income measures, it produces a refined view of the GDP data. Table 26.2 shows *per capita* GDP adjusted for purchasing power in five European countries. In each case, PPP adjustments reduce the *per capita* GDP. All are countries where the cost of living tends to be high.

TABLE 26.2 MDCS *PER CAPITA* GDP ADJUSTED DOWNWARDS WITH PPP ACCOUNTING			
Country ranked by *per capita* GDP	**Per capita GDP / thousands USD**	**PPP-adjusted *per capita* GDP/ thousands USD**	**PPP-adjusted *per capita* GDP/ rank**
1 Luxembourg	105 350	84 003	1
2 Norway	79 089	55 672	3
3 Denmark	55 992	36 762	13
4 Ireland	51 049	41 278	6
5 Netherlands	47 917	40 715	7

Table 26.3 shows *per capita* GDP adjusted for purchasing power in five countries whose *per capita* GDP is revised upwards when purchasing power is taken into account.

TABLE 26.3 LDCS *PER CAPITA* GDP ADJUSTED UPWARDS WITH PPP ACCOUNTING		
Country	**Per capita GDP / thousands USD**	**Per capita GDP PPP adjusted/ thousands USD**
China	3 744	6 838
Romania	7 500	14 198
India	1 134	3 275
Ethiopia	345	936
Russia	8 800	18 945

When PPP-adjusted *per capita* GDP is greater than nominal GDP, it suggests that the potential standard of living is underestimated. What these countries also share is some underdevelopment. In countries such as Ethiopia and perhaps India, the vast majority of the population live in conditions of absolute poverty. In others, like Romania and Russia, portions of the country are underdeveloped, although the country itself is considered a low-middle-income country.

It is with this in mind that economists pay attention to PPP-adjusted GDP levels to better understand the attainable quality of life, and to compare one country with another in this regard.

Health indicators

A critical skill for development workers is to understand the benefits and limitations of any single piece of data. Data can be useful for what it does not reveal as well as for what it does tell us. The reporting of a single indicator may provide answers but it also raises more questions.

Using health indicators

Let's consider a single indicator of health. The World Bank tracks the adolescent fertility rate (number of births per 1000 women aged 15–19 per year). There is an extremely high negative correlation between the number of births in this age group and the level of development. Figure 26.7 shows three countries at the top of this measure and three countries at the bottom.

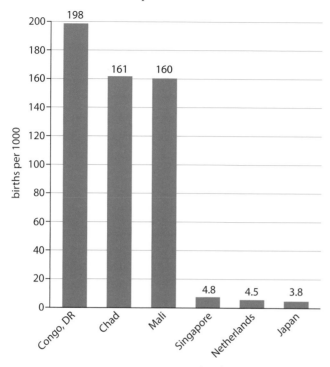

Figure 26.7
Adolescent fertility rate, 2009.

The high correlation between births and level of development could suggest that lowering adolescent fertility would improve standards of living, and that policymakers should take steps to make that happen. But it also raises questions. First, are high fertility rates a symptom or a cause of lack of development? Do extra children strain family resources and prevent progress? This would indicate that people in those countries would like to have fewer children. Or are children considered assets in farming communities, workers who can help plant and harvest? Should development work focus on supporting these children with healthcare and education, or at redirecting the economy away from these types of production methods and cultural beliefs? Clearly, a deeper understanding of the country itself is required to make use of such a piece of data as this. Other data that support or inform the policy action would be welcome.

Let's compare the figures for adolescent fertility rate to another health indicator as a validity check. How do the same countries perform on female life expectancy? If the data on adolescent fertility actually indicated a lack of development, we would expect to see women living shorter lives in countries with higher fertility rates, and longer lives where fertility is lower. Figure 26.8 shows female life expectancy in the same countries.

Figure 26.8
Female life expectancy, 2009.

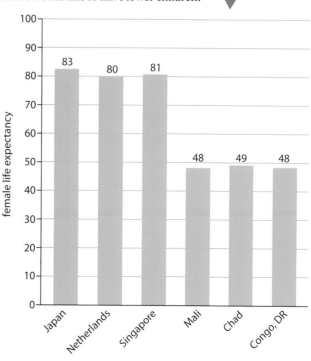

The results are striking. It appears that in countries where adolescent fertility is very low, women live, on average, nearly 64% longer than women in countries where high adolescent fertility is the norm. Taken together, this might lead one to conclude that adolescent fertility is a cause of a short life span for women. However, it is also possible that this is a coincidence, that there are other, more direct causes of the disparity. High infant mortality, for example, would bring down the average age considerably. Perhaps a high incidence of malaria or other serious disease also reduces life spans. Adolescent fertility might be less of a risk than the initial comparison might suggest.

As you can see, there are risks to making inferences, judgements and policy based on single indicators. Generally speaking, wise policy is made only when many points of data are cross-referenced with other data to derive a thorough understanding of the causes of development problems.

Education indicators

Income and health data are two of the three most important areas to be focused on when looking at development indicators. The third is education data. Educational attainment levels tend to correlate highly with development. It is widely believed that education builds up the level of human capital. Productivity rises because the labour force is more skilled and capable. Furthermore, education is widely accepted to be a merit good with positive externalities. A more informed public is thought to vote and participate politically, yielding better policy outcomes.

Using education indicators

It is again instructive to compare education data from developed and developing countries. Figure 26.9 shows one such indicator, primary pupil to teacher ratio. This, at the very least, is an indicator of the resources a society devotes to education. The countries with the highest ratios have many more students per teacher, so that less attention and instruction can be given to each child.

Figure 26.9
Primary pupil to teacher ratio, selected countries.

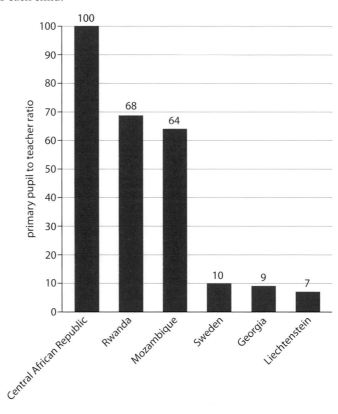

Figure 26.10
Adult literacy rates, 2008.

Chart: adult literacy rate / % for six countries:
- Liechtenstein: 100
- Georgia: 100
- Sweden: 99
- Mozambique: 54
- Rwanda: 70
- Central African Republic: 55

Do other education indicators produce similar results for the same countries? Figure 26.10 (above) shows the adult literacy rate for the same countries.

How might these two measures be related? Primary education years are when basic literacy and numeracy are learned. Therefore, we would expect countries that devote more resources (teachers) to primary education to have better literacy results. And, as expected, countries with six and seven times more students per teacher do fare comparatively poorly. However, it might be surprising to see that the Central African Republic did as well as Mozambique, despite having so many more students per teacher. Furthermore, a look at the full adult literacy data shows that 10 other countries performed worse than the Central African Republic, with Chad having only a 33% literacy rate. Indicators do not prove a cause and effect relationship. It may be that other factors influence educational achievement, besides pupil/teacher ratios. The quality of instruction, the duration of a typical student's education every year, or over their lifetime, may also strongly influence the result.

To learn more about the World Bank's development indicators, visit www.pearsonhotlinks.com, enter the title or ISBN of this book and select weblink 26.2.

EXERCISES

8 Using the World Bank site (see hotlinks box above), select one education indicator.

  a List three countries and their indicator data from the top and bottom of the group.

  b Compare and contrast the results.

  c Speculate what other information would be useful to inform any policy action on this indicator.

9 Select another education indicator. Using the same six countries, compare and contrast their performances on both indicators.

26.5 Multiple indicators of economic development

Learning outcomes
- Outline the current status of international development goals, including the Millennium Development Goals.

World Bank: a source of development indicators

There are many agencies and non-governmental organizations that try to assess levels of development in different ways, but few measure development in as many ways as the World Bank. The Bank was founded at the Bretton Woods conference in 1944 as part of the Allies' attempt to create a new financial order. Its stated goal is the reduction of poverty, and it regularly makes loans to LDCs in an attempt to fill gaps in capital financing and to promote development. The World Bank's database of development indicators has continuously expanded and now includes:

Improving help in LDCs is one of the goals of the World Bank.

- % of rural citizens with access to water source
- % of mobile and fixed line telephones
- ratio of girls to boys in education
- contraceptive prevalence
- expenditure per student on education
- pump price for diesel fuel
- carbon dioxide emissions
- plant and animal species threatened
- immunization rates
- % of births attended by skilled health staff
- internet users and use
- poverty rates
- dependency ratios
- patent applications.

To access Worksheet 26.3 on visualizing economic growth, please visit www. pearsonbacconline.com and follow the onscreen instructions.

Taken together, the breadth of data creates a bigger, more detailed picture than any single indicator alone. It serves the bank and other development agencies when setting goals and assessing the success of their goals.

United Nations: Millennium Development Goals

To that same end, in 2000, the United Nations embarked on the most ambitious development programme in history, the UN Millennium Development Goals (MDG) Project. The eight goals below were agreed by all 192 member states as well as 23 international organizations. They are to be accomplished by 2015:

- eradicate extreme poverty and hunger
- achieve universal primary education
- promote gender equality and empower women
- reduce child mortality rate
- improve maternal health
- combat HIV/AIDS, malaria, and other diseases
- ensure environmental sustainability
- develop a global partnership for development.

In the process, the MDG project also sets out to measure its success with a similarly large collection of single indicators. To accomplish these goals, a series of targets is established, each with appropriate indicators, against which the success of the programme can be measured. Here are two examples.

- **Goal** Eradicate extreme poverty and hunger
    Target Halve the proportion of people living on less than $1 a day
        Indicators:
        – Proportion of population below $1 per day (PPP values)
        – Poverty gap ratio [incidence × depth of poverty]
        – Share of poorest quintile in national consumption
- **Goal** Promote gender equality and empower women
    Target Eliminate gender disparity in primary and secondary education preferably by 2005, and at all levels by 2015
        Indicators:
        – Ratios of girls to boys in primary, secondary and tertiary education
        – Share of women in wage employment in the non-agricultural sector
        – Proportion of seats held by women in national parliament

The target generally defines the way in which success will be measured. Thus, eradicating poverty will be measured against the number of people living on less than $1 per day, reduction of the poverty ratio and improving the consumption levels of the poor. Promotion of gender equality and the empowerment of women will be measured by equalizing the number of girls to boys attending school, the share of women working, and the proportion of women holding office.

- What knowledge issues are involved in compiling a list of development goals?

EXERCISES

10 For the MDG 'improve maternal health,' speculate on the kind of indicators that could be used to measure success. List three indicators you created.

11 Pick any other MDG and imagine the kind of data you would want to gather if you were trying to achieve this goal. List three indicators that you created.

12 Using the United Nations website (below) check your answers for exercises 10 and 11 against the UN's list of development goals indicators.

13 Compare and contrast your indicators to the actual MDG indicators. What do you like about yours? What do you like about the MDG indicators?

Amid the many very ambitious goals, a lesser but valuable end is the pursuit of better and more valid forms of measuring development. Better data should, in turn, lead to better evaluation of policies, and more real success in meeting development goals. With this in mind, the UN publishes a report card to assess its progress. Reproduced overleaf is a small section, reporting progress on goals 1–4. Green areas indicate targets already met (light green indicates the target will be met by the 2015 deadline). Yellow areas show insufficient

To learn more about the United Nations Millennium Development Goal indicators, visit www. pearsonhotlinks.com, enter the title or ISBN of this book and select weblink 26.3.

progress and the target may not be met by 2015. Red areas show no progress has been made towards the target (or there has been a regression).

Progress to date in pursuit of MDGs 1–4; 2010.

Goals and Targets	Africa		Asia			
	Northern	Sub-Saharan	Eastern	South-Eastern	Southern	Western
GOAL 1 | Eradicate extreme poverty and hunger						
Reduce extreme poverty by half	low poverty	very high poverty	high poverty	high poverty	very high poverty	low poverty
Productive and decent employment	very large deficit in decent work	very large deficit in decent work	large deficit	very large deficit in decent work	very large deficit in decent work	very large deficit in decent work
Reduce hunger by half	low hunger	very high hunger	moderate hunger	moderate hunger	high hunger	moderate hunger
GOAL 2 | Achieve universal primary education						
Universal primary schooling	high enrolment	moderate enrolment	high enrolment	high enrolment	moderate enrolment	moderate enrolment
GOAL 3 | Promote gender equality and empower women						
Equal girls' enrolment in primary school	close to parity	close to parity	parity	parity	parity	close to parity
Women's share of paid employment	low share	medium share	high share	medium share	low share	low share
Women's equal representation in national parliaments	very low representation	low representation	moderate representation	moderate representation	low representation	very low representation
GOAL 4 | Reduce child mortality						
Reduce mortality of under-five-year-olds by two thirds	low mortality	very high mortality	low mortality	moderate mortality	high mortality	low mortality

part of UN MDG Report 2010

EXERCISES

14   Explain why you think the United Nations publishes this report card.

15   What questions would you ask, after viewing this information?

16   What is the next step for policymakers, after reading and interpreting the report?

26.6   Composite indicators of economic development

Learning outcomes

- Explain that composite indicators include more than one measure and so are considered to be better indicators of economic development.
- Explain the measures that make up the Human Development Index (HDI).
- Compare and contrast the HDI figures for economically more developed countries and economically less developed countries.
- Explain why a country's GDP/GNI *per capita* global ranking may be lower, or higher, than its HDI global ranking.

Composite indicators attempt to aggregate groups of different indicators into a single ranking. They are usually expressed as an 'index.' The index value indicates the relative distance between countries on the list. Because they measure several values at once, these indicators are generally regarded as a superior wide-view picture of a country's development level.

The Human Development Index

The most influential and important composite indicator is the Human Development Index (HDI). It was created by the UN Development Programme (UNDP) in the late 1980s and put into use in 1990. It was created as a response to dissatisfaction with the emphasis on economic growth as the sole means to measure development. According to the UNDP:

The Human Development Index is a composite indicator of development, created by the United Nations, which ranks country development on the basis of average income, education levels, and life span.

- *[there was] growing evidence that did not support the then prevailing belief in the 'trickle down' power of market forces to spread economic benefits and end poverty*

- *the human costs of Structural Adjustment Programmes became more apparent*

- *social ills (crime, weakening of social fabric, HIV/AIDS, pollution, etc.) were still spreading even in cases of strong and consistent economic growth*

- *a wave of democratization in the early 90s raised hopes for people-centred models.*

UNDP, Human Development Reports website, Home page, accessed May 2011

The UNDP was thus attempting to shift the paradigm for development away from a purely growth-based model to a broader view, one that encompasses health and education levels. Amartya Sen, whose work is recognized as providing the intellectual framework of the HDI, put it this way:

To learn more about the standard of living, visit www.pearsonhotlinks.com, enter the title or ISBN of this book and select weblink 26.4.

Human development, as an approach, is concerned with what I take to be the basic development idea: namely, advancing the richness of human life, rather than the richness of the economy in which human beings live, which is only a part of it.

Amartya Sen, UNDP, Human Development Reports website, Home page, accessed May 2011

With this ideal in mind, the HDI evaluates the performance of a country in three areas:

- long life – measured by life expectancy
- education – measure by adult literacy and combined primary, secondary and tertiary enrolment ratio
- standard of living – measured by GDP *per capita* (PPP-adjusted).

Each country's performance in an area earns a score between 0 and 1; 0 is lowest, 1 the highest. These areas are then compiled for the composite HDI ranking. Table 26.4 shows the top five and bottom five countries, according to their score on the HDI.

A casual look at Table 26.4 confirms the connection between economic prosperity and development. The top five countries are all economically wealthy, while the bottom five are all desperately poor. This may merely state the obvious – that improvements in the quality of life require societies to make something of their productive resources. For income, long life and a chance at an education, the land, labour and capital of a country need to be employed in building homes, hospitals and schools. Still, while acknowledging the obvious we can also observe that some

TABLE 26.4 TOP AND BOTTOM FIVE HDI, 2010	
Country	**HDI score, 2010**
Norway	0.938
Australia	0.977
New Zealand	0.907
United States	0.902
Ireland	0.895
Guinea-Bissau	0.284
Burundi	0.282
Niger	0.269
Congo	0.239
Zimbabwe	0.140

countries seem to do quite well with relatively little income, and others rather poorly considering their relative income levels.

To underscore the distinction between purely economic activity and human development activity, Table 26.5 shows selected pairs of countries in order of descending HDI level. If growth alone were the determinant of economic development, we would expect to see the countries at the top of the HDI to also be at the top of the GDP *per capita* list and income level to descend with lower development levels.

The country pairs show how well some countries have done with less income resources. Notice that Australia is only slightly behind Norway for the top spot on the HDI, but has 45% less income *per capita*. Slovakia, at number 31 on the HDI, outscores the United Arab Emirates, while earning nearly 43% less. Perhaps most startling is Argentina at number 46 on the HDI outscoring Kuwait while generating 70% less GDP *per capita*.

TABLE 26.5 HDI INDEX RANKING COMPARISON WITH *PER CAPITA* GDP				
Country	HDI rank	HDI value	*Per capita* GDP	GDP rank
Norway	1	0.938	58227	3
Australia	2	0.937	40286	13
New Zealand	3	0.907	27520	34
United States	4	0.902	46852	9
Korea	12	0.877	29325	28
Switzerland	13	0.874	43109	12
Slovakia	31	0.818	22340	44
United Arab Emirates	32	0.815	56485	4
Argentina	46	0.775	14930	55
Kuwait	47	0.771	50283	5
Bulgaria	58	0.743	11547	73
Trinidad and Tobago	59	0.736	25161	37
Georgia	74	0.698	4946	110
Venezuela	75	0.696	11819	71
Paraguay	96	0.640	4629	115
Botswana	98	0.633	13462	65
Kyrgyzstan	109	0.598	2332	139
South Africa	110	0.597	10139	78
Madagascar	135	0.435	958	170
Papa New Guinea	137	0.431	2395	140

Table 26.5 yields several possible conclusions.

- GDP *per capita* alone is an unreliable predictor of the level of human development one should expect from a country.
- Some countries clearly under-perform in development terms compared to their relatively high income levels. These countries have the resources to improve on health and education standards, and should revisit their policies in this regard.
- Some countries clearly over-perform in development terms compared to their relatively low income levels. Policymakers may benefit from a closer study of what explains their achievements.

While the HDI is the most widely accepted measure of overall development, it also has limitations. Its emphasis on income, life span, and education enrolment is still overly simple. Broader measures of development may yield data that give more insight into a particular country's challenges. Although not factored into the HDI, the UNDP often gathers additional data about gender equity, income equality, sustainability and governance.

To learn more about the Human Development Index, visit www. pearsonhotlinks.com, enter the title or ISBN of this book and select weblink 26.5.

Gender Inequality Index

In 2010, the UNDP created the first Gender Inequality Index, a composite indicator of the disparity in well-being between women and men in three areas: reproductive health, empowerment and the labour market. The health dimension is measured by two indicators: maternal mortality ratio and the adolescent fertility rate. The empowerment dimension is also measured by two indicators: the share of parliamentary seats held by each gender and their secondary and higher education attainment levels. The labour dimension is measured by women's participation in the workforce. According to the UNDP, the Gender Inequality Index 'is designed to reveal the extent to which national human development achievements are eroded by gender inequality, and to provide empirical foundations for policy analysis and advocacy efforts.'

Comparison of overall HDI rank to Gender Equity rank reveals that in some countries, gender equity performance is holding back total development; other results indicate that gender equity is bringing overall development forwards (Table 26.6).

TABLE 26.6 COUNTRIES WITH LARGE DISPARITIES BETWEEN HDI RANK AND GENDER EQUITY RANK			
Country	**HDI rank**	**Gender equity rank**	**HDI-GER disparity**
Large negative disparity			
Saudi Arabia	55	143	–88
Slovenia	29	104	–75
Korea	12	76	–64
Japan	11	74	–63
Iran	70	133	–63
Ireland	5	59	–54
US	4	57	–53
Large positive disparity			
Rwanda	152	10	+142
South Africa	110	16	+94
Tajikistan	141	47	+94
Namibia	105	20	+85
Kyrgyzstan	109	24	+85

The top seven countries in Table 26.6 have a gender equity rank well below their HDI rank. This suggests that the HDI scores for these countries would be even higher if there were to be some improvement in women's healthcare, women's comparative education levels, female employment or political representation.

The bottom five countries in Table 26.6 have scored extremely highly on gender equity compared to their overall HDI rank. As the HDI rankings attest, none of these are especially wealthy or highly developed. But gender equity scores are 'better than expected' when compared to their HDI rankings.

 What criteria could we use to determine whether a particular method for measuring development is effective?

 What knowledge issues might be encountered in constructing a composite indicator to measure development?

To access Quiz 26, an interactive, multiple-choice quiz on this chapter, please visit www.pearsonbacconline.com and follow the onscreen instructions.

EXERCISES

17 **a** Is there any one common theme that might explain the negative disparities for countries shown in Table 26.6?

   b List some specific reasons that might explain some of these specific results.

   c What kind of data might support or undermine your hypothesis?

18 **a** Is there any one common theme that might explain the positive disparities for countries shown in Table 26.6?

   b List some specific reasons that might explain some of the specific results.

   c What kind of data might support or undermine your hypothesis?

PRACTICE QUESTIONS

1 Distinguish between economic growth and economic development. (10 marks) [AO2]

2 Describe how less developed countries can have similar and different characteristics. (10 marks) [AO2]

3 Explain the distinction between GDP *per capita*, GDP *per capita* with purchasing power parity. (10 marks) [AO2]

4 List and explain three single indicators of development. (10 marks) [AO2]

5 Explain how the Human Development Index is derived, and how it functions as a measurement of development. (10 marks) [AO2]

27 DOMESTIC AND INTERNATIONAL FACTORS AND ECONOMIC DEVELOPMENT

27.1 Domestic factors and economic development

Learning outcomes

- With reference to a specific developing economy, and using appropriate diagrams where relevant, examine how the following factors contribute to economic development:
    a   education and health
    b   the use of appropriate technology for industry and agriculture
    c   banking, credit and micro-credit
    d   the empowerment of women
    e   income distribution.

The line between economic growth and economic development is not always clear. Many of the factors that may promote economic growth in a nation also contribute to economic development. Growth itself, defined as an increase in the average income of a nation, contributes to development in that when people's incomes rise, their ability to consume education, afford healthcare and thereby improve the quality and length of their lives improves.

School children in Nepal.

In the same way that higher incomes can improve people's well-being, improvements in education, health and social harmony can contribute to economic growth. In summary, without growth, there can be no development; but without development, economic growth is far less likely. The two objectives are not mutually exclusive, so the pursuit of both should be the utmost priority of economic policy.

In their pursuit of macroeconomic objectives aimed at increasing national income and output (economic growth), governments may also achieve improvements in households' well-being by promoting policies that improve health and education. Both these measures increase productivity of the nation's workforce in the long run and help achieve the objectives of full employment, price stability and growth.

Economic development

Economic development requires a solid foundation of institutions provided by or closely regulated by the government, even in an economy in which economic growth is already happening. The most important source of economic development is almost certainly the quality and the quantity of resources available domestically in a nation. Resources, in this sense, comprise the human, technological and natural capital possessed by a nation. By improving these domestic factors, a country can promote economic development, improve the well-being of its people and simultaneously promote economic growth.

The domestic factors that contribute to economic development include the promotion of education and health among a nation's people, the acquisition and improvement of technology used in industry and agriculture, access to a stable banking system able to provide credit to businesses and entrepreneurs, a societal acceptance of the importance of women in achieving economic objectives, and a functioning tax system which allows the government to provide public goods that would not otherwise be provided by the free market.

Each of these domestic factors is explored below, with evidence from developing countries to provide you with a framework for the analysis of the importance of each factor.

Domestic obstacles to economic development

Before examining domestic and international sources of economic development, we must consider some of the obstacles poor countries face in achieving meaningful improvements in the standard of living of their people. Obstacles to development, like sources of development, can be both internal (domestic) and external (international).

Poverty traps

A poverty trap is a self-perpetuating mechanism that contributes to the persistence of poverty in a nation.

A poverty trap is any self-reinforcing mechanism that contributes to the persistence of poverty in nation. If a country finds itself in a poverty trap over a long period of time, it is unlikely to escape unless meaningful steps are taken either domestically or initiated by an outside force to allow the country to escape the trap.

Poverty traps usually have at their core a fundamental obstacle that perpetuates itself and thereby keeps the country poor. Some examples of poverty traps include the natural resource trap, the geography trap, the poor education/poor governance trap, and the conflict trap.

To learn more about poverty, visit www. pearsonhotlinks.com, enter the title or ISBN of this book and select weblink 27.1.

Natural resource trap

A poor country with few natural resources may find itself in a poverty trap for two reasons. First, without mineral, energy, forest, or marine resources it cannot sustain its domestic need for such resources. Secondly, it cannot export resources to earn much-needed foreign exchange.

Without a developed secondary, manufacturing sector, many poor countries (such as Congo and other mineral-rich countries in Africa) depend greatly on the export of raw materials to Europe and East Asia. A country without a secondary sector and a poor supply of natural resources, however, could find itself in a particularly difficult situation in which the foreign capital required to invest in its secondary sector is inaccessible due to the lack of exchangeable commodities from within the country.

The natural resource trap is visualized in Figure 27.1.

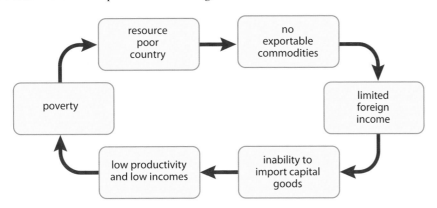

◀ **Figure 27.1**
The natural resource trap.

Poverty persists because of the lack of access to capital goods from abroad. Since the country has few valuable natural resources to exchange with the rest of the world, it has only limited access to the foreign exchange it would need to acquire the capital goods needed to develop a secondary sector. Without capital, worker productivity and incomes remain low, and the people remain impoverished.

Paul Collier, an economics professor at Oxford, proposes another kind of natural resource trap, in which a poor country is kept poor because of its abundance of natural resources. His seemingly contradictory theory is explained by the fact that if all a poor country has to offer the global market is one valuable natural commodity (such as diamonds from Sierra Leone or Liberia), this breeds domestic conflict over the control of the one natural resource. Political and social upheaval may result from the struggle for control of the exportable commodity, creating conditions completely antithetical to those necessary for economic development.

Geography trap

Collier also suggests that a major source of persistent poverty for some nations is their geographical location. If a nation is land-locked and surrounded by poor countries, that country is extremely likely to be poor itself. Being landlocked alone does not mean a country is poor. There are several landlocked countries in Europe that are among the richest in the world, such as Luxembourg, Switzerland, Austria and Liechtenstein. But all these countries are fortunate to have rich neighbours with whom they have good economic relations.

A look at the map of Africa, Asia or South America identifies many landlocked countries that are among the poorest in the world, including Bolivia, Paraguay, Niger, Zambia, Nepal and Afghanistan. Each of these countries is landlocked and surrounded by other poor countries, a situation that makes it incredibly difficult for the landlocked country to begin a journey on the path of economic development. Figure 27.2 (overleaf) illustrates the geography trap.

Figure 27.2
The geography trap.

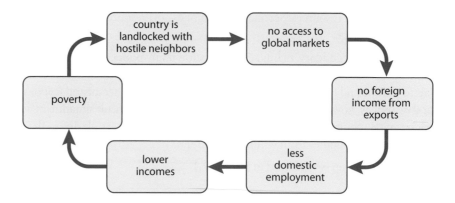

The key to the geography trap is the lack of access to sea ports even in neighbouring countries. Without access to sea ports, it does not matter how politically stable and economically attractive a country is to foreign producers and consumers. If there are no means to safely and reliably export their output to the rest of the world, such a country would not even be on the radar of international investors looking for places to produce goods for the global market. Without reliable demand from other countries, it would be nearly impossible for a poor country to increase its national income and the standards of living of its people.

Education / poor governance trap

One of the most important functions of government is to collect taxes and provide public goods to the nation's people, including education, healthcare and infrastructure. In a poor country with a corrupt government, an ineffective tax system and a poor education system, economic development is nearly impossible to achieve. And under-provision of education perpetuates the bad governance and poverty, as can be seen in Figure 27.3.

Figure 27.3
The education/poor governance trap.

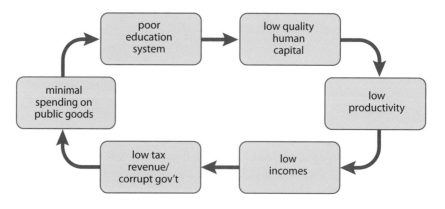

Poor countries are poor because their leaders keep them poor. To what extent is this statement true? Is a good leader all that is needed to achieve economic development in a poor country?

A poorly educated workforce makes a country less attractive for foreign direct investment, limiting the amount of capital available to workers. Low skill levels and limited capital make the nation's workforce unproductive, meaning lower incomes, less tax revenue, and less ability for the probably corrupt government to provide the very public goods needed to get the country on the road to economic development.

The education and poor governance trap persists until a responsible government comes to power, is able to reduce corruption and waste, and ensure that any tax revenues generated by the economy are allocated responsibly towards improving education and thus the human capital of the nation's workforce.

Conflict trap

The worst poverty trap for a country to find itself in is a conflict trap. Unfortunately, any of the three poverty traps described above can easily evolve into conflict, and if a country finds itself in all three situations (landlocked with poor natural resources and a corrupt government) the likelihood of conflict arising is extremely high. Civil unrest perpetuates poverty for many reasons, but Figure 27.4 shows the basic problem with conflict in a developing nation.

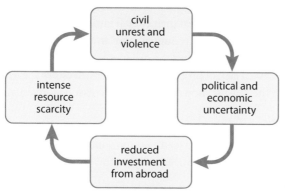

Figure 27.4
The conflict trap.

Much of the conflict in the poor world is over the resources that are needed to generate income that could then be put to work improving people's lives. But the existence of conflict ultimately intensifies the scarcity of resources and creates an environment of political and economic uncertainty that makes the country unattractive to foreign investors who might otherwise invest in the nation's economy. In this way, conflict born from scarcity actually intensifies scarcity and thereby fuels more conflict. A country in which many resources are going towards waging an internal war is most certainly going to remain poor until stability is achieved and an atmosphere deemed safe for international investors is restored.

> **W** To learn more about news in Africa, visit www. pearsonhotlinks.com, enter the title or ISBN of this book and select weblink 27.2. Follow links to the following news categories: conflict, corruption, education, business.

EXERCISES

1   The poverty traps described above are only some of the possible traps a poor country may find itself in. Identify three other possible traps that may cause poverty to persist in a poor country.

2   **a**   Use the link in the hotlinks box above to discover some African news stories. Identify three headlines that you think might be about stories relating to economic development. Read the three articles you have discovered and determine whether or not they relate to one of the obstacles to development discussed above.

   b   Discuss with your class the headlines you found and determine whether they could be used to formulate an alternative poverty trap to those described above.

Institutional and political obstacles to economic development

Other domestic obstacles to economic development are rooted in the failure of institutions to lay the groundwork for meaningful improvements in people's lives.

Ineffective taxation structure

With an unclear or ineffective tax structure, a nation is unattractive to foreign investors who might otherwise invest in the country. Uncertainty about how taxes are collected deters investment and reduces the amount of foreign capital in the country. In addition, rich domestic households may choose to save their incomes and wealth abroad in a country whose tax structure is more stable and predictable. An ineffective tax structure may allow domestic firms and households to hide their income from the government, depriving the country of much-needed funds for investment in public goods.

Lack of property rights

If foreign investors cannot be sure that their property rights will be respected by the domestic government, they are unlikely to invest their capital into a poor country. The guaranteed protection of property rights makes a country more attractive to foreign investors and increases the amount of capital and thus the productivity and income of the nation's workforce. Domestically, a lack of property rights deters investors at even the lowest levels. Poor farmers neglect their fields; shop owners have no reason to invest in their businesses.

Political instability

An unstable political structure could lead a country into conflict and push a developing country into a cycle of conflict and uncertainty, perpetuating poverty.

Inequality in the distribution of income

An unequal distribution of income, demonstrated by a nation's Gini coefficient, is common in poor countries. While the vast majority of the population remains poor, what little income is generated by the economy is often enjoyed by a tiny elite. Unequal income distribution may be a result of an ineffective tax system, without which an equitable distribution of income is impossible. And without a system of transfer payments, the ability of the poor to escape poverty by improving their human capital is limited, keeping the majority of the country's population in poverty.

Lack of infrastructure

Infrastructure includes roads, highways, airports, rail track, sea ports and communications infrastructure such as cellular towers, phone lines and internet. Without these much-needed capital goods, a country is less attractive to foreign investors and subsequently the supply of productivity-enhancing foreign capital is limited. Infrastructure improves the efficiency with which a nation's economy functions; improved efficiency leads to lower costs and higher incomes. Lack of infrastructure is a major obstacle to economic development.

Lack of access to credit

Many developing countries lack an effective banking system able to offer secure deposits to savers and access to credit to borrowers. Without a functioning domestic financial system, households with money to save will likely save it abroad, a phenomenon known as capital flight. Without a supply of loanable funds domestically, it becomes nearly impossible for small businesses to access credit to finance productivity-enhancing investments. Consumers also find it impossible to borrow money to invest in real estate or consumer durable goods, both of which make up significant proportions of more developed countries' economies' total demand.

Social and cultural obstacles to economic development

The challenges to be overcome by a poor country in achieving development are many. From its geography to the composition of its exports, to corruption and conflict, the formula that must be satisfied for development to occur is exceedingly complex. But even if all the above obstacles are overcome, there remain several social and cultural issues that must be addressed for a nation to achieve meaningful economic development.

Religion

Religious differences within a nation can create an obstacle to economic development. This is particularly the case if members of the different religions are in conflict with one another. Israel's West Bank is a good example of a region in which two religious groups (Muslims and Jews) have yet to overcome their religious differences and begin working towards meaningful development. Other examples include Sri Lanka, where only recently has a 25-year conflict between Hindus and Buddhists ended; Southern Thailand, where tensions between Muslims and Buddhists have slowed progress towards economic development; and the Philippines, where Muslim rebel groups have staged attacks on the predominantly Christian population for over two decades. In each of these countries, many of the ingredients needed to promote development are in place, but the ongoing conflicts between religious groups create an environment in which economic uncertainty prevails and therefore actual development is limited.

Tradition

In some cultures, the objectives of economic growth and development are questioned by the more traditional members of society; progress towards development in a modern sense of the word is undermined by those who wish to promote a more traditional society. The Taliban in Afghanistan wishes to turn the country into a religious theocracy ruled by Islamic Sharia law. In other countries, the perceived Westernization that economic development entails could form the basis for movements that promote a traditional societal structure in opposition to the ethics of economic growth and development.

Aid workers complain that religious objections to medical practices and treatments can get in the way of progress. For example, the Catholic Church forbids its followers to use condoms, even in parts of Africa where AIDS is most destructive. Secondly, recent efforts to eradicate polio have been set back in several Islamic countries (e.g. Pakistan and Nigeria) where religious leaders denounced the vaccines as 'impure' and 'an American plot', and urged followers to avoid them.

Domestic factors that contribute to economic development

Understanding the obstacles developing countries face in achieving improvements in their people's welfare allows economists to focus on the strategies needed to overcome these obstacles. Some of the domestic factors that may promote development are discussed below.

Education

An educated population is able to contribute more to the economic output of a developing country more than if the population has less access to education. There is a strong correlation between education and income; as access to education increases, productivity of workers rises allowing them to contribute to the nation's output and increase their own income in the process.

Figure 27.5 shows how the rising literacy rate in Nepal, a developing country, has coincided with growing *per capita* income since 1981, when only around 20% of the adult population could read and write and the *per capita* GDP was just $148. By 2008, literacy rates had tripled to 58% and tiny *per capita* income had grown to $440. Clearly, Nepal is still a very poor country, in which 80% of the population lives below the poverty line, but

Figure 27.5
There is a direct correlation between improved education and income in Nepal.

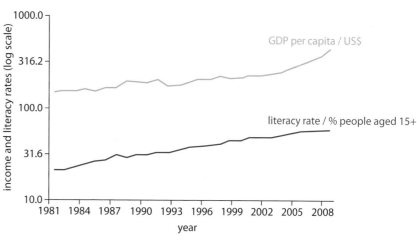

To learn more about education, visit www. pearsonhotlinks.com, enter the title or ISBN of this book and select weblink 27.3.

continued improvements in literacy will improve the population's ability to contribute to the nation economically and politically.

Health

Improved health and a longer life are not only the result of economic development; they also contribute to development in areas such as income and education. When factors such as life expectancy and infant mortality improve, the people of a nation can shift their focus towards becoming more productive members of the economy and improving their incomes and quality of life.

Figure 27.6 looks at Nepal between 1960 and 2008. As infant mortality plummeted from nearly 250 deaths per 1000 live births in 1960 to around 40 in 2008, and life expectancy increased from 40 years to 64 years, the *per capita* income in the nation increased around ten-fold. Fewer deaths in childbirth and a longer life point to improved health of the Nepalese people, while larger GDP *per capita* represents an improvement in the variety and quantity of goods and services to the average Nepali household. It should be pointed out that Nepal is still a very poor country. It is ranked 138th out of 169 by the United Nations Development Project's Human Development Index. However, Nepal's people today are far better off than they were 50 years ago.

Figure 27.6
The correlation between improved health and income.

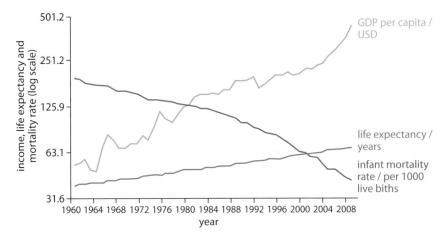

To learn more about health, visit www. pearsonhotlinks.com, enter the title or ISBN of this book and select weblink 27.4.

Banking, credit and micro-credit

Micro-credit is a much talked about and widely used development strategy that provides financial credit or technology loans to entrepreneurs in poor communities to create small businesses – ideally businesses with a socially beneficial purpose. Loans (credit) may be issued by community banks or by international micro-finance institutions. Community banks act like local banks in the developed world, collecting deposits from local savers and using them to make loans to local borrowers.

International micro-credit organizations match lenders in the developed world with borrowers in the developing world. There are even online organizations that allow individual lenders to peruse loan requests from individual entrepreneurs in developing nations, most of whom are women, and make loans directly to the borrower of their choice. Such a programme differs from regular commercial credit, which is either unavailable or very expensive. The benefit for poor country entrepreneurs is that without the existence of micro-credit institutions, they would have little access to credit, severely limiting the extent to which the human capital of poor countries can be put to work promoting economic growth and development.

Entrepreneurs with access to financial capital, either through a community bank or an international micro-credit institution are able to put their business skills to work employing others in providing goods and services that are in demand in their local communities. Often, the loans entrepreneurs receive are very small, as little as $100 or $200, which may be all that is needed to acquire some simple capital equipment such as a sewing machine or a vendor stand from which the entrepreneur can begin producing output demanded by her community. The more successful borrowers eventually gain access to larger amounts of credit, allowing them to expand their businesses, employ more workers and add more value to the developing nation's output.

Micro-lending is not always in the form of financial capital. Some development projects aim to put physical capital directly into the hands of poor entrepreneurs. In Kenya, for instance, an NGO known as WISER aims to match young entrepreneurs with the tools they need to start their own businesses using donated technology such as copy machines, laptop computers with cellular internet connections, foot pumps for water, and digital LCD projectors. The technology is sold on credit to entrepreneurs who are required to pay back the value of the capital through their business revenues.

The capital, once in the hands of local entrepreneurs, is immediately put to use providing services to the community. Here are some examples.

- The copy machine was installed and powered by a generator. It was the first such machine ever installed in the community. Local businesses, students, job seekers and others could, for a few cents, photocopy their documents locally, avoiding the two-hour drive previously required for such a service.

- The laptops were installed in an internet café and made available to local students and businesses. Farmers and fishermen could check product prices in the cities hours away, increasing efficiency and bargaining positions when middle men came to town to buy their produce. Job openings in the city newspapers' classifieds could be printed and posted for the local community to see, improving information symmetry between the poor countryside and the cities where job opportunities existed. The cost of access to these services was cheap, yet the entrepreneurs who were granted the laptop loan were able to pay back the cost of the technology in no time at all, and the community as a whole benefited from their existence.

- The LCD projector was the first of its kind ever seen in the community. The entrepreneur who received the projector hooked it up to a satellite dish in order to capture and project English Premier League football matches onto the wall of a large room in a local building. The business was to sell tickets to local football fans who were more than happy to pay to watch English football matches in full colour on a wall-sized screen. Before the projector arrived in the community, football fans had huddled around tiny black-and-white televisions with poor reception to watch football matches. The football-theatre business was the most successful of all, and paid back its loan fastest.

 What do you think of the choice of an LCD projector for investment lending money? Do you think entertainment spending is any better or worse than other investment? On what basis did you answer initially, reason or emotion?

Community banking, micro-credit and micro-lending all promote the entrepreneurial talents of the people in less developed countries (LDCs), and for that reason promise great potential for long-run economic development. Whereas many of the obstacles to development and strategies for overcoming them outlined in this chapter require a top-down approach, micro-finance and micro-credit are purely grassroots in nature, empowering individuals within the poorest communities in the developing world to create their own opportunities while meeting the demands of their community and creating income and employment for others in the process.

The empowerment of women

The role of women in society could play a crucial role in determining whether a developing country is able to achieve meaningful improvements in the standards of living of its people. Female education in particular should be a goal of poor countries wishing to promote development. Better-educated women mean improved chances at development for many reasons, including the two discussed below.

Reduced fertility rates

The more educated women become, the fewer children they are likely to have. This is important for several reasons; notably it reduces the burden on working members of society when there are fewer mouths to feed in the home. Lower fertility rates also mean the children women do have are likely to be better nourished and provided with more education themselves, which in the long run will improve the productivity of a nation's workforce. Slower population growth promises to increase the *per capita* income of a nation over time, improving the standards of living of the people.

Women in the work force

Does the protection of human rights automatically lead to increased development? Are freedom, liberty and property rights enough to improve the lives of people in a poor country?

When a developing country views women as an economic asset in themselves, the productive capacity of the nation is instantly increased. Women tend to be equally as productive as men in poor countries, contributing to economic activity and creating jobs and income through small enterprises and as members of the larger workforce. Better-educated women are, of course, more productive and able to earn incomes that can be used to provide health, education and a better life for their children, promoting future economic growth and development in the process.

27.2 International obstacles to economic development

Learning outcomes
- With reference to specific examples, explain how the following factors are barriers to development for economically less developed countries:
  a over-specialization on a narrow range of products
  b price volatility of primary product prices
  c inability to access international markets.
- (HL only) With reference to specific examples, explain how the following factor is a barrier to development for economically less developed countries:
  a long-term changes in the terms of trade.

Besides the internal obstacles to development detailed above, there are several external obstacles to a country achieving improvements in the income, health and education of its citizens.

Narrow range of exports

LDCs in which education and health are lacking and the value of human capital (i.e. the economic potential of the people of the nation) is therefore limited, often depend on a narrow range of exports for a major component of their total economic activity. A poor country with a currency that is non-convertible on foreign exchange markets must export to the rest of the world to gain hard currency that can then be used to acquire much-needed imported necessities for its people.

In addition, most LDCs are capital poor, meaning they have a workforce deprived of the technology and tools needed to increase productivity and incomes. In order to acquire capital goods, many of which are produced in more developed countries, poor countries must earn foreign currency through the sale of their exports to the rest of the world.

Being able to produce and offer a diversity of goods and services to foreign consumers is a valuable attribute for a developing country. Unfortunately, many poor countries have a very narrow range of exports, often primary or low-tech manufactured goods such as textiles. A narrow range of exports poses an obstacle to economic development for many reasons – two are discussed below.

Over-dependence on primary products

When a country specializes in the production of a single primary commodity, whether a food crop (e.g. coffee or cocoa) or an energy resource (e.g. oil or gas) or a mineral resource (e.g. copper or diamonds), the ability of that country to achieve meaningful improvements in its people's standards of living is limited by the extent to which it can earn steady income from its exports of its one commodity. The problem with primary commodities is that their prices tend to fluctuate greatly on the global commodity markets. Most poor countries specializing in a particular commodity have very little price-making power in the global market.

Being price-takers, a decrease in global demand and a fall in price of the commodity can have devastating effects on the country's net exports and overall level of aggregate demand and economic output. The highly inelastic supply of most agricultural and mineral resources means that even a slight fall in global demand can cause the price of the good to fall dramatically, reducing a poor country's income levels and its ability to purchase the imported consumer goods its people depend on.

Figure 27.7 shows how a decrease in demand for coffee grown in Country B from one year to the next can lead to a massive decrease in Country B's export revenues. Because the coffee farmers of Country B are highly unresponsive to a fall in demand for coffee in the short run, they must accept a lower price for their output in order to sell it. The alternative of taking their supply off the market by storing it is expensive and unrealistic for most farmers.

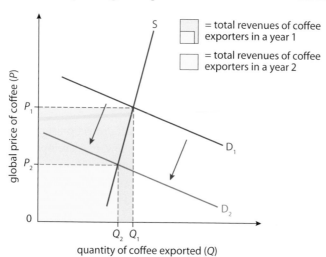

◀ **Figure 27.7**
Over-dependence on a primary commodity poses an obstacle to growth and development.

If Country B depends heavily on the export of this one commodity, even a slight decrease in the world demand for coffee can devastate the country's economy and drastically reduce the standard of living of its people.

Consequences of adverse terms of trade (HL only)

A nation's terms of trade measures the value of its exports relative to the value of its imports. If a nation is heavily dependent on a particular primary or secondary commodity for a major component of its total exports and income, and the value of that export declines relative to the value of imports, the people of that nation will find their standard of living declining over time. Chapter 25 has a detailed explanation of how this occurs.

Once again the importance to a developing country of diversifying the composition of its output is emphasized. Along with becoming over-dependent on a primary commodity, a nation in which income and employment depend heavily on any particular type of good or service is likely to be harmed when global demand for its exports shrink, reducing revenues from exports and worsening the nation's terms of trade.

27.3 International factors that contribute to economic development

Learning outcomes
- With reference to specific examples, evaluate each of the following as a means of achieving economic growth and economic development:
  - **a** import substitution
  - **b** export promotion
  - **c** trade liberalization
  - **d** role of WTO
  - **e** bilateral and regional preferential trade agreements
  - **f** diversification.

To overcome the external obstacles to economic development, the government of a poor country may pursue several strategies to achieve economic growth and development. The effectiveness of the various external strategies for development is evaluated below.

Protectionism in international trade
Import substitution policies

> Import substitution policies are protectionist policies meant to reduce domestic consumers' dependence on imported goods, for which they substitute domestic goods and services, thus promoting the development of domestic industries.

If a developing country's government chooses to enact protectionist policies, it could harm the economy's potential to achieve meaningful steps towards development. Protectionism is seen in a strategy for economic growth known as import substitution. Here, a country attempts to reduce domestic consumers' dependence on imported goods by setting strict tariffs and quotas on the import of certain goods and then promoting the development of domestic industries.

At first glance, it looks as though an import substitution policy could promote development. However, it can lead to retaliatory tariffs from countries whose imports are restricted in the developing nation. Thus the impact of protectionism at home may be reduced demand abroad for the developing nation's goods, a situation that reduces the level of domestic income and output and limits households' access to the goods, services and foreign capital that would improve their standards of living.

Export promotion policies

Export promotion policies are an alternative set of policies for promoting economic growth and development. They aim to increase the overseas market for domestic producers by employing subsidies, tariffs, and exchange rate controls that allow domestic producers of international commodities to gain the upper hand in foreign markets. Such a policy can be highly effective if done right, but once again the threat is that the resources allocated to producing goods for the foreign market might have been more efficiently allocated by the free market towards producing goods and services to meet the needs and wants of domestic consumers.

 Export promotion policies are protectionist measures aimed at increasing the competitiveness of domestic producers in foreign markets. Subsidies for domestic producers of exportable goods and intentional devaluation of the nation's currency give domestic producers an advantage in international markets and promote export-oriented growth.

Export promotion has been employed by LDCs, particularly those of East and Southeast Asia, for decades with varying degrees of success. Malaysia, Thailand and the Philippines have all aimed to grow their export sectors through currency devaluation and targeted subsidies for domestic industries. All three countries have achieved strong economic growth over two decades, albeit economic development has at times been slow to follow and all three countries still face many social, institutional, cultural and political challenges before they join the ranks of the high-income countries of Europe, North America and East Asia.

Trade liberalization

An alternative to using protectionism to promote growth and development is for an LDC to embrace trade liberalization. The risks associated with a developing country opening its market to free trade are of course substantial. There is no guarantee that one country's opening itself to trade will be reciprocated by its trading partners.

For example, African Country K may choose to remove tariffs on imported grain from Europe in the hope that European nations will remove protectionist duties on Country K's exports, thereby liberalizing trade of goods to and from Country K. However, without some tariffs on European grain, heavily subsidized, capital-intensive food products from Europe will flood Country K's market at prices too low for its farmers to compete with.

While the intention of trade liberalization was to make imports cheaper for Country K's residents and to make Country K's products more attractive to foreign consumers, the result may be a reduction in the welfare of the primarily rural population of Country K who find it increasingly difficult to compete with subsidized food from Europe.

Role of World Trade Organization

The WTO (Chapter 20) has tried to alleviate poverty in LDCs by addressing the constraints to global trade that put poor countries at a disadvantage in the global economic system. Some of the challenges the WTO has attempted to address and will continue to address in future rounds of trade negotiations include the following.

- Encouraging LDCs to refocus their development agendas away from high tariff barriers and towards strategies relying on trade liberalization and integration into the global trading system.
- Getting developed countries to take into account the needs of developing countries when considering their own trade policies.

- Promoting access to new markets for manufactured goods and primary commodities from developing countries.
- Working towards meaningful cuts in protectionist agricultural subsidies in developed countries.
- Making sure that future bilateral or multilateral trade agreements do not undermine the industrialization prospects of developing countries.
- Providing duty-free and quota-free access to imports from LDCs in the developed world.
- Promoting increased movement of labour, both high skilled and low skilled, among LDCs and between LDCs and the developed economies.

The WTO's role in poverty alleviation is to bring countries together to develop a fair trade framework that promotes meaningful development in poor countries.

Bilateral and regional trading blocs

In the absence of progress at the multilateral or WTO level, a better option for a developing nation than removing all barriers to trade with other nations may be to start locally in trade liberalization by joining regional trading blocs or entering into preferential trade agreements with neighbouring countries.

The East African Community (EAC) is a common market agreement that includes Kenya, Burundi, Uganda, Tanzania and Rwanda. The aim of the EAC is to enable free movement of labour, services and capital to significantly boost trade and investments and make the region more productive and prosperous.

By embracing free trade first with its neighbours, and from there entering into additional preferential and free trade agreements with geographically more distant trading partners, developing countries may begin to enjoy the benefits of trade liberalization without being subjected to the unfair disadvantages that would result from the failure of more developed countries to reciprocate the removal of protectionist policies such as agricultural subsidies and import tariffs.

Diversification of national output

Perhaps the best strategy for a developing country to overcome the external obstacles to economic growth and development is to diversify the composition of its output. A poor country that is overly dependent on one or a few primary commodities, or even low-skilled manufactured goods, faces great obstacles in growing its economy in a manner that ensures higher incomes, better health and improved education among its people.

Investing in human capital may be the best way a government can achieve the diversification of its national output. Better-educated workers attract foreign investment from multinational corporations eager to tap the relatively low-wage, but well-educated workforce available. The inflow of foreign investment allows the LDC to acquire much-needed foreign capital and productivity-enhancing technology that can be employed in the production of manufactured goods, thus providing the nation's households with higher incomes. Higher incomes increase the level of savings in the nation, providing loanable funds to entrepreneurs and businesses at home, and further contributing to the nation's growth and development.

To access Worksheet 27.1 on Haiti, please visit www.pearsonbacconline. com and follow the onscreen instructions.

The key for a developing nation's government is to identify the poverty trap in which it is ensnared, and then pursue policies that enable it to escape that trap and begin the journey towards growth and development. This may be harder than it sounds, but some of the strategies described here will help a nation improve the standard of living of its people.

Overcoming the obstacles to economic development: the big picture approach

None of the challenges described above can be completely overcome in the short term. Many LDCs in the world today will still be poor a century from now; poverty will always exist in some form regardless of the gains from increased trade, growth and development.

There is great hope, however, that life will continue to improve for the great majority of the world's poorest people over the next 50 years, as it has in the last 50 years. Since 1960, the gap between the developed and developing world has become much less evident than it has been throughout most of history. Using available data from the World Bank, the Swedish statistician Hans Rosling has demonstrated the sweeping changes that have taken place. A quick review of Rosling's development data shows that despite what many in the developed world think, the poorest people today are actually much better off than they were just a couple of generations ago.

Human health

In 1960, for example, there was a clear gap between the countries with long life expectancy and low fertility rates and those with short life expectancy and high fertility rates. In 1956, just about all of sub-Saharan Africa, South Asia, Southeast Asia and Latin America experienced short lives and large families. Figure 27.8 shows the relationship worldwide between total fertility (expressed as average number of births per woman) and life expectancy (years) in 1960.

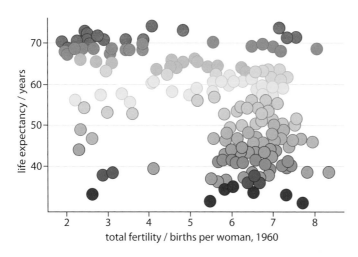

The World Bank

Figure 27.8
Total fertility and life expectancy in 1960: dots represent countries. Notice the gap between the countries with large families and short life and those with small families and long life.

Each coloured dot represents a country. The red countries (upper left) include the more developed countries (MDCs) of Western Europe and North America, where long life and small families were the norm 50 years ago. The blue countries (lower right) include those in the developing world 50 years ago, with larger families (more than five births per woman) and shorter lives (typically, less than 50 years). Fifty years ago, the gap between MDCs and LDCs was quite clear. The bunch in the upper left were the rich nations, the group in the lower right were the poor nations.

If not much had changed in the last 50 years, then we would expect there to be a similar relationship still visible today, with the poorest countries living short lives with large families. However, when we look at the data for the same two indicators of human welfare in 2009, we see that the world has changed dramatically (Figure 27.9, overleaf).

Figure 27.9
Total fertility and life expectancy in 2009: dots represent countries. Notice that many countries that had large families and short lives have now moved to the upper left.

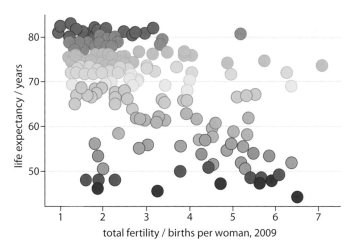

The World Bank

Today, there are far more red countries than there were 50 years ago. The majority of the nations that were then characterized by large families and short lives have managed to bring down fertility rates and simultaneously increase life expectancy. There is no longer a clear gap between the rich world and the poor world. Many of the countries in the upper left of the chart for 2009 are ones that in 1960 would have been in extreme poverty characterized by high fertility rates, high infant mortality rates, rampant disease and short life expectancy.

We can conclude from the analysis of simple, available data that over the last half century, some economic development has indeed come to the world's poorest countries. But there is more to be done. The people of countries represented by blue dots in Figure 27.9 still live in absolute poverty, many surviving on less than $2 per day. The bottom billion of people live lives still characterized by disease, poverty and suffering; they have enjoyed none of the benefits from economic globalization, growth and development. To continue to improve the lives of the world's poorest, governments and international development organizations must continue to employ the same strategies that have brought billions out of despair over the last 50 years.

Income

Figure 27.10
World *per capita* GDP has increased over 20-fold in 50 years.

The gap between the *per capita* incomes in the world's richest nations today and that in the developing world is still large, but much smaller than it was 50 years ago. Along with longer lives and smaller families, many of the world's poorest countries have experienced

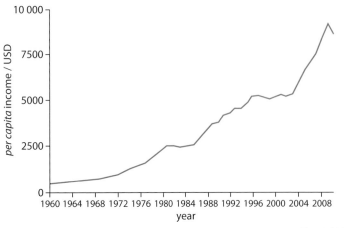

The World Bank

significant increases in *per capita* income during an era of globalization and market liberalization. The global *per capita* income has grown from just $446 50 years ago to nearly $9000 today (Figure 27.10). While this figure tells us nothing about the distribution of world income, it is a clear indication that, on average, people in 2010 are nearly 20 times richer than their grandparents were just 50 years ago.

Global income growth has come about because of many factors, and often in spite of bad governance, geographical or natural resource traps. The sheer demand from the international marketplace for raw materials, minerals, and goods manufactured using low-skilled labour has meant that foreign investment from the more developed economies to the less developed economies has increased incomes, output and the productive capacity of poor countries more than any domestic government policy could have.

Gains from trade

Of course, the degree to which an LDC benefits from globalization depends on the effectiveness of its government in managing trade flows, capital and financial investments from abroad and protecting the well-being of their workforce in a competitive global marketplace that is more than willing to exploit low-wage workers to benefit multi-national corporate interests. In addition, the revenues that flow to governments from the investments of foreign firms must continue to be invested in the human and physical capital of the developing nation if integration into the global economy is to bring development to the nation's people.

Many developing countries have looked to the success stories of East Asia for inspiration in their own journeys towards economic development. In China alone, more than 300 million people have been lifted out of poverty as three decades of rapid economic growth have increased the *per capita* income of the Chinese household seven-fold. But such economic miracles driven by ever-growing demand for cheap manufactured goods in the West is not likely to be realized by smaller developing nations without the access to international markets and the abundant workforce enjoyed by China.

A path to prosperity

A path towards development for the poorest countries today, namely those in sub-Saharan Africa, South and Central Asia and parts of Latin America, will require great attention by governments to the basic needs of their nation's people. Without sound investments in health, education, and financial and physical infrastructure, along with a reliable legal and political framework that reassures foreign investors of the nation's stability, economic development will continue to elude the poorest nations today.

The poverty traps outlined earlier are all able to be overcome if one of the components of the cycle can be broken. But without strong, stable and right-minded political leadership, poverty will endure in the LDCs of today.

 For each of the domestic and international factors discussed in this chapter, what would you consider to be sufficient evidence that it plays a role in enhancing or inhibiting economic development?

 27.4 **Development section research project**

In preparation for the IB examinations, it is important that you achieve a strong understanding of the domestic and international obstacles to and factors contributing to the economic development of a specific country. This project will help you become an expert on a particular country, which in turn will help you be better prepared for examination papers 2 and 3, which include questions on economic development.

World Bank Development Project Proposal
Introduction

The following research assignment will help you learn more about the obstacles facing countries and the strategies they can employ to achieving economic development. You will have approximately four class periods dedicated to in-class research and preparation. In addition, to produce a high-quality proposal, you will need to spend some time outside the class on this assignment.

Overview

You will assume the role of the Chief Development Officer (CDO) in charge of implementing an economic development project in a less developed country (LDC) of your choice. As the CDO, it is your duty to submit development project proposals to international lending agencies such as the World Bank and the African Development Bank. However, not all proposals from all countries can be granted, so before submitting a proposal, you must prepare a detailed report for the lending agency.

Objective

To win a concessionary loan from the World Bank to put towards a specific development project in the LDC you represent. Funds are extremely limited, so whether or not you receive aid and, if you do, how much aid you receive will be determined by a panel of judges consisting of your classmates.

You must prepare a detailed report, which should include the following sections.

- Part 1 Development data: an overview of your country's current level of economic development.
- Part 2 Obstacles to development: information on some of the obstacles to economic development faced by your country.
- Part 3 Resources and potential: an identification of existing resources within your country.
- Part 4 The proposal: a proposal for a specific development project that will improve human welfare in your country.

You will then make an appeal to lenders at the World Bank, requesting financing for your project. A panel of judges (your classmates) will decide whether to approve requests and bring them to the chief economist of the bank (your teacher). The best proposals (accurate, appropriate, achievable) will receive the limited financing available – the best marks. Less realistic proposals will receive fewer funds than they request or none at all.

The report may take any form you wish. It could be a written report to be delivered orally, it could be a slide presentation, or it could be a video. You could even choose to create a website or blog containing the details of your report. Any appropriate media can be used to prepare and present the report.

Resources online

The following hotlink boxes will take you to useful websites.

To learn more about World Bank Countries and Regions, visit www.pearsonhotlinks.com, enter the title or ISBN of this book and select weblink 27.5.

 To learn more about the CIA's World Factbook, visit www.pearsonhotlinks.com, enter the title or ISBN of this book and select weblink 27.6.

 To learn more about African Development Outlook, visit www.pearsonhotlinks.com, enter the title or ISBN of this book and select weblink 27.7.

To learn more about the African Development Bank, visit www.pearsonhotlinks.com, enter the title or ISBN of this book and select weblink 27.8.

  To learn more about UNDP Human Development Reports, visit www.pearsonhotlinks.com, enter the title or ISBN of this book and select weblink 27.9.

Part 1 – Development data

From the website UNDP choose one of the countries listed under 'Low Human Development' to focus on in your research. This is the country for which you will act as the CDO.

1.1 Social and economic data

Using the websites above, research and include in your presentation the following data for your country. Along with each item, you must provide a brief explanation of its importance to your nation's economic development.

Social indicators of development:

- Human Development Index (HDI) ranking and value
- population growth rate
- school life expectancy
- life expectancy at birth
- total fertility rate
- education expenditures.

Economic indicators of development:

- GDP *per capita*
- GDP – composition by sector
- unemployment rate
- public debt
- stock of direct foreign investment – at home
- labour force – by occupation.

1.2 Dependency ratio

A nation's dependency ratio is the percentage of its population under the age of 15 and over the age of 64 (i.e. those not of working age) divided by the percentage of the population between 15 and 64 (i.e. those of working age).

A nation's dependency ratio tells you something about the ability of members of the nation's workforce to provide necessities for themselves and their dependants. Typically, LDCs have a higher dependency ratio than more developed countries (MDCs). The lower a nation's dependency ratio, the greater the ability of its workers to accumulate savings. Savings lead to investment, accumulation of capital, greater productivity, higher income and more economic development.

To calculate your nation's dependency ratio, you must find demographic information on its population. You may need to do additional research beyond the websites listed above to find this data.

Once you have calculated your country's dependency ratio, briefly describe the importance of this measure to your country's ability to achieve meaningful economic development.

1.3 Income distribution

The Lorenz curve (Chapter 16) is a graphical representation of a country's income distribution. It plots the percentage of a nation's total income (GDP) against its total population. The line of absolute equality is the 45-degree line, which indicates a nation where each quintile (each 20% of the population) earns exactly the same income as each other quintile. No country is absolutely equal, so the line of equality is only used for comparison. As an example, Figure 27.11 (overleaf) shows the Lorenz curve for Cambodia.

Figure 27.11
Lorenz curve for Cambodia.

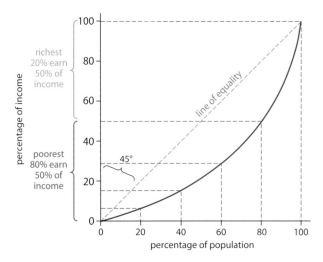

The Gini coefficient is the ratio of the area below the line of equality and above the Lorenz curve to the total area of the triangle below the line of equality. A country with perfect income equality would have a Gini coefficient of zero. A country in which the top 1% of the population controlled all of the nation's income would have a Gini coefficient of nearly 1.

Example: Country A's income is distributed across its population as follows:

- 1st 20% – 5.9%
- 2nd 20% – 12%
- 3rd 20% – 17.2%
- 4th 20% – 23.6%
- 5th 20% – 41.3%
- Gini coefficient = 0.352.

Illustrating your country's Lorenz curve may require research beyond the websites suggested above. Try to find data on the share of national income earned by the richest and poorest households in your country. You may not find the percentages earned by each quintile, but you may find that richest 10% of the population earn, say, 70% of income while the lowest 10% earn only 3% of the income. This data can be applied to a Lorenz curve. Using the best data you can find, draw your country's Lorenz curve and include it in your report along with an explanation of the importance of income distribution as an indicator of economic development.

1.4 Development data analysis

To emphasize the importance of data in determining your country's development status and needs, answer each of the following questions at the end of Part 1 of your report.

To what extent does your country exhibit:

- low standard of living?
- low incomes?
- inequality?
- poor health?
- inadequate education?
- low levels of productivity?
- high rates of population growth and dependency burdens?
- high levels of unemployment?
- dependence on agricultural production and primary product exports?
- imperfect markets?
- dependency on foreign developed countries for trade, access to technology, foreign investment and aid?

Part 2 Obstacles to economic development

This section of your report focuses on the obstacles to further economic development faced by your nation. Answer the following question using your findings in Part 1 as support.

- What are the major domestic and international obstacles preventing your country from achieving economic development?

You can choose to create and present visual representations of poverty traps to show the major obstacles to development in your country. Poverty traps include:

- conflict trap
- natural resource trap
- geography trap
- education/poor governance trap.

Other domestic obstacles to development you may discover your country faces include institutional and political obstacles, ineffective taxation structure, lack of property rights, political instability, corruption, unequal distribution of income and lack of infrastructure.

International trade obstacles to development you may focus on include overdependence on primary products, adverse terms of trade, narrow range of exports, or protectionism in international trade.

You may also discuss the various social and cultural obstacles to development faced by your country, including religion, culture, tradition, or gender issues.

Part 3 Resources and potential

This section of your report describes the internal and external advantages your country possesses that will enhance its chances for development. What geographical, social, institutional/political, economic, technological, or other advantages does your country already possess that make it a viable candidate for external aid?

Your goal is to convince the panel from the World Bank that your country is a worthy aid recipient and will put resources to use responsibly towards socially and economically beneficial ends. Why should *your* country receive scarce foreign aid?

Part 4 Formal proposal

The final section of your report proposes a specific project to promote economic development and improve the standards of living of your nation's people. Your proposal must include each of the following components.

- **Project type**. What exactly are you requesting financing for? Possible project types include infrastructure investments, fair-trade organizations, micro-credit schemes, health or education initiatives, environmental and social projects.
- **Project goals**. Include specific details about who will be involved from your country and from the international community, what resources are needed to make your project possible, when and where exactly your project will take place, and how the project will promote human development in your country.
- **Examples of similar projects**. To convince your lenders that your project is realistic, you must include at least one example of a similar project that has been successfully implemented somewhere in the world. This will require some additional research into examples of development projects.
- **Financial analysis of the project**. Your proposal must include a financial breakdown of your project. Detailed cost estimates, expected rates of return, a repayment schedule detailing how and when the development loan will be repaid must all be estimated and

included in your proposal. Remember, the World Bank does not make donations to developing countries, it makes loans. And all loans are expected to be repaid. Therefore, only those projects that have a realistic chance of success will be granted financing.

Timeline for completion

The research and preparation of this report will take several class periods plus quite a bit of time outside of class. The timeline below is only a suggestion. Your teacher will decide on his or her own timeline as is appropriate with your school calendar.

- **Week 1**. Choose the medium you will use for your report and the country you will represent. Complete research for Part 1.
- **Week 2**. Continue research on Parts 2 and 3.
- **Week 3**. Research is now complete. Create your formal proposal with required detail. One day should be dedicated for peer-editing of reports. You should peer-edit two other students' reports and have yours reviewed by two classmates.
- **Week 4**. Completed reports presented in first class of the week. You present your report to the World Bank panel (classmates).

Distribution of funds

After each presentation, the panel members (students) complete a brief evaluation, which is submitted to the World Bank's chief economist (teacher) for review. Final distribution of funds (and grades) is determined by the chief economist. The countries whose reports best fulfil the above criteria will receive the most funds and the highest grades. Reports failing to adequately fulfil the above criteria will receive less funding (and a lower grade).

To access Quiz 27, an interactive, multiple-choice quiz on this chapter, please visit www.pearsonbacconline.com and follow the onscreen instructions.

PRACTICE QUESTIONS

1   **Karnataka tourism set to gain from admissions fever**

i   Being admitted to professional courses in medical, dental and engineering institutions in India is the biggest ambition of most of the academically brilliant students and their parents. Given the limited number of places available in Indian Institutes of Technology (IIT), there is a huge demand for admission to professional colleges – as in the State of Karnataka where thousands apply every year, not only from within the state, but also from other parts of India and even from abroad.

ii   Despite a fee of R30 000, there is **excess demand** for places. This year, a record number of 127 343 students have applied to Karnataka's colleges. Of these, as many as 59 299, or roughly 46.7%, are from outside the state. These candidates are competing with each other for the 26 000 places in the state's professional colleges – medical, dental and engineering.

iii With such large numbers of non-Karnataka students, possibly accompanied by at least one parent or adult to guide them, it is natural that there will be enormous business opportunities for the hotels, lodgings and travel operators. The state-owned Karnataka Tourism Development Corporation (KTDC) has taken the initiative to offer an elaborate and attractive package.

iv   A spokesperson for the KTDC said, 'We believe there are many **social benefits** arising from the demand for places at IIT and it is our intention to take advantage of them'.

adapted from *The Economic Times*, India, 6 May 2001

a   Define the following terms indicated in bold in the text:

i   excess demand (paragraph ii)   (2 marks) AO1

ii   social benefits (paragraph iv).   (2 marks) AO1

b With the aid of a diagram, explain how the social benefits resulting from the provision of education promote economic development in India. (4 marks) [AO2], [AO4]

c Identify and explain two possible government responses to the shortage of spots at the Indian Institute of Technology (4 marks) [AO2]

d To what extent is education an essential requirement for reducing poverty in LDCs such as India? (8 marks) [AO3]

© International Baccalaureate Organization 2003 (part **a** only)

2 **Bitter coffee**

Item 1 The price slump has created some winners. Trans-national companies and global coffee cafes (such as Starbucks) are making record profits as the price of their main raw material slumps. Over the past three years the export price of coffee as a proportion of the retail price has fallen.

adapted from Celine Charveriat, *Bitter Coffee – How the poor are paying for the slump in coffee prices*, Oxfam, 2001

Item 2 What has happened to the price of coffee is a disaster. Years back, when coffee prices were good, we could afford to send our children to school. Now we are taking our children out of school because we cannot afford the fees. How can we send our children when we cannot afford to feed them well?

a coffee grower in Tanzania, in *Bitter Coffee*, Oxfam, 2001

Item 3 Developed countries often have no tariffs on coffee beans, but impose tariffs on processed coffee products to keep out these higher value products that return more income to job-starved poor countries.

adapted from *The Guardian*, 5 August 2002

Item 4

International coffee prices (US cents per unit weight of coffee, 1998–2001)

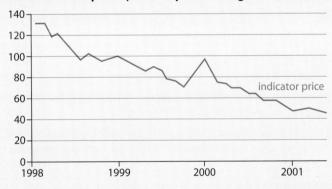

adapted from *Bitter Coffee*, Oxfam, 2001

Item 5

Dependence on coffee exports, selected countries (% of total exports, 1998)

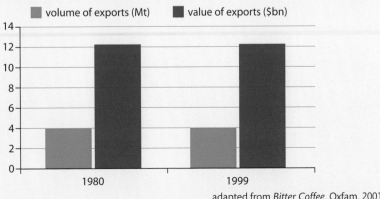

adapted from *Bitter Coffee*, Oxfam, 2001

Item 6

Coffee exports from developing countries (volume and value, 1980 and 1999)

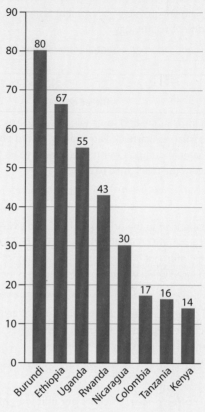

adapted from *Bitter Coffee*, Oxfam, 2001

a   Explain the effects of the fall in coffee prices on:

    i   a coffee grower   (2 marks) [AO1]

    ii   global coffee cafes.   (2 marks) [AO1]

b   Using a supply and demand diagram, explain the change in the volume and value of coffee exports between 1980 and 1999 (Item 6).   (4 marks) [AO1], [AO2]

c   Using an appropriate diagram, explain how the coffee-processing market is blocked to coffee-producing countries because of the high tariffs the processing countries put on these goods.   (4 marks) [AO2], [AO4]

d   Use evidence from the text and your knowledge of economics to discuss the importance for a developing country of diversifying the composition of its output in promoting stable economic growth and development.   (8 marks) [AO3]

© International Baccalaureate Organization 2004 (part **a** only)

FOREIGN INVESTMENT, AID, TRADE AND DEBT

The meaning of FDI and MNCs

Learning outcomes
- Describe the nature of foreign direct investment (FDI) and multinational corporations (MNCs).

 Foreign food aid being delivered.

Foreign direct investment

As you now know, countries can become trapped in the poverty cycle. In its simplest form, the poverty trap shows how limited income makes it difficult to accumulate savings. Without savings, there is little available capital to grow the economy. To break free, many countries seek out foreign injections of money and capital goods. These injections take the form of foreign direct investment (FDI) and foreign aid (Figure 28.1, overleaf). Countries often incur significant foreign debt in the process. This chapter describes each strategy and explores its effectiveness.

Figure 28.1
Aid and FDI can break the poverty trap.

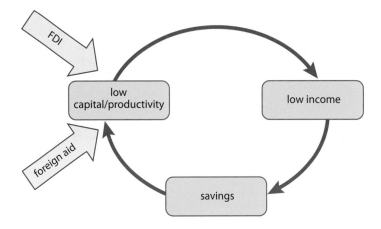

FDI refers to the long-term investment by a company into the market of another country. Inward flows of FDI to a country are when foreign companies invest in the domestic market of that country. Outward flows of FDI are when domestic companies do the same in foreign markets.

 Foreign direct investment is the long-term investment by foreign firms into the domestic markets of other countries.

Typically, FDI occurs when foreign companies purchase productive assets, such as factories, mines and land. These private companies are, by the act of FDI, multinational corporations (MNCs) that are seeking profits by moving or expanding operations to new countries. FDI can be classified as either greenfield investment (when companies construct new facilities from scratch) or brownfield investment (when investors purchase or lease existing facilities).

28.2 Conditions that favour MNC investment

Learning outcomes
- Explain the reasons why MNCs expand into economically less developed countries.
- Describe the characteristics of economically less developed countries that attract FDI, including low-cost factor inputs, a regulatory framework that favours profit repatriation and favourable tax rules.

MNCs and developing countries

There are tens of thousands of multinational corporations, with hundreds of thousands of branch affiliates all over the world. A multinational corporation is typically a large company with trading, manufacturing or service operations across several countries. They are also called trans-national corporations (TNCs). Their initial growth happened in the 1950s as the US moved company offices and factories to Europe at the end of World War II and the start of the Cold War. After steady growth for several decades, FDI exploded in the 1990s.

 A multinational corporation is a large company with trading, manufacturing, or service operations across several countries.

While trade has increased four times more rapidly than GDP, FDI has increased even more quickly. This is partly due to the liberalization policies of many developing countries during the 1980s and early 1990s, as well as to the newly emerged transitional economies moving from central control to market-based systems. Table 28.1 shows the 10 largest multinational corporations, ranked on the basis of their foreign holdings.

TABLE 28.1 TOP 10 MULTINATIONAL CORPORATIONS (NON-FINANCIAL), BY FOREIGN ASSETS.				
Corporation	**Home**	**Industry**	**Foreign assets / millions $**	**Foreign employment**
General Electric	US	Electrical and electronic equipment	401 289	171 000
Royal Dutch / Shell	Netherlands	Petroleum expl. / ref. / distr.	222 323	85 000
Vodafone Group	UK	Telecommunications	201 570	68 747
BP	UK	Petroleum expl. /ref. / distr.	188 969	76 100
Toyota	Japan	Motor vehicle manufacture	169 568	121 765
ExxonMobil	US	Petroleum expl. / ref. / distr.	161 244	50 337
Total	France	Petroleum expl. / ref. / distr.	141 442	50 858
E.On	Germany	Utilities (electricity, gas and water)	141 168	57 134
Electricité de France	France	Utilities (electricity, gas and water)	133 697	51 385
Arcelor Mittal	Luxembourg	Metal and metal products	127 127	239 455

UNCTAD, *World Investment Report*, Annex Table 26

Clearly, the largest MNCs come from developed countries. Inflows are expected to total more than 1.1 trillion USD in 2010, and potentially up to 2 trillion USD as soon as 2012. Currently, much FDI flows back and forth between developed countries. However, in 2010, nearly half of FDI inflows went to developed countries, with the other half going to developing countries. Flows of FDI dropped in 2001 and again, because of the recession, in 2008–09 but, in each case, the rebound of FDI has been due to increased flows to developing countries. This suggests that future growth of FDI will be in developing countries.

Figure 28.2 shows the flows of FDI by developed nations and developing regions. A few items stand out. First, China receives more FDI than nearly all of Latin America, more than all of its East Asian neighbours combined, and more than all of South and Southeast Asia, which includes India. Also, note that FDI inflows for Asian countries are nearly double that of the rest of the developed world, including Latin America, the Caribbean, and North and South Africa.

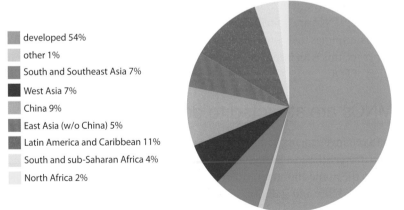

- developed 54%
- other 1%
- South and Southeast Asia 7%
- West Asia 7%
- China 9%
- East Asia (w/o China) 5%
- Latin America and Caribbean 11%
- South and sub-Saharan Africa 4%
- North Africa 2%

Figure 28.2
FDI inflows by economy type and region.

based on UNCTAD, *World Investment Report*, Annex Table 1

Assuming that developed countries continue to invest in developing ones in the future, which regions will benefit most? Already some regions are rather reliant on FDI as a percentage of their overall investment. Figure 28.3 (overleaf) shows selected regions and the percentage of total private investment that is made up of FDI.

Figure 28.3
FDI as a percentage of private investment.

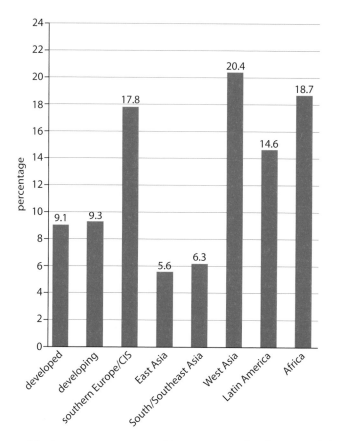

FDI makes up roughly the same percentage of investment in developing and developed countries. But there is wide variation in the importance of FDI to different regions. For East, Southeast, and South Asia, private investment is not especially dependent on FDI. West Asia, Africa, Southern Europe/CIS, and Latin America all depend more heavily on FDI for investment.

It is also relevant to compare the size and power of the largest MNCs to the economies into which they are investing. In 2009, the sales of the top 10 MNCs (Table 28.1) nearly equalled the GNI of all of South America, and were nearly double that of all of African countries combined. These MNCs are quite large when compared to the countries in which they are investing. This amplifies their importance and influence and, as FDI is expected to grow in the coming years, this is an important factor in developing sound policies for the attraction and retention of FDI.

Why MNCs are attracted to developing countries

The gap between investments in different regions suggests that MNCs are seeking particular characteristics in a host country. Whether the aim is to produce locally and export back to the home country, or to produce and sell in the host country, all MNCs are seeking profitability and stability. The chief attractions of an LDC as an FDI host are discussed below.

Low-cost labour

Many MNCs choose to relocate production to countries where the per-unit labour costs are much lower. This lowers overall costs of production for these goods, even when transport costs are included. In labour-intensive industries, such labour costs are critical and, as wages rise in one country, MNCs seek out lower-wage production elsewhere.

Natural resources

Access to natural resources – be they mineral, metal, timber, or fossil fuel – can draw the interest of many foreign investors. Some countries in Africa and Southeast Asia have recently been recipients of attention from China, in the form of aid and foreign investment. Typically, these countries are resource rich, reflecting China's need to create new supply lines for its growing economy.

Political stability

MNCs generally cannot afford to make substantial investments in areas where the political order is not clear. They prefer countries where the political environment (democratic, autocratic, single-party state, or otherwise) is stable.

Large domestic market

Part of the attraction of emerging markets is that the MNCs' products can be sold to the local population as well. Thus, for some MNCs, the attraction of foreign investment is to export to the rest of the world (and perhaps back to the home country) and to expand the market for the MNC's goods by direct presence in the country. This explains the natural advantage that China and India possess, having huge domestic markets and major growth potential as incomes rise.

Relaxed regulatory environment

Developing countries may relax their regulation of markets in the hopes of garnering more FDI. This deregulation can take several forms.

* **Profit repatriation**. Relaxing of rules on the repatriation of profits, so MNCs can more freely redirect profits to the home country.
* **Tax rules**. Tax rules for corporate profits may be reduced to entice investment. Ireland, which has one of the lowest corporate tax rates in Europe, has resisted increasing this rate, despite a major budget deficit, because it attracts FDI.
* **Property rights**. A respect for property rights, so that firms are not dissuaded from investing by the fear of government takeover or the confiscation of assets through corrupt practices.
* **Health and safety regulations / pollution control**. MNCs may be drawn to a country because the reduced health, safety and pollution regulations mean lower production costs for the firm.

Liberalized free market conditions

Firms also want to see markets open in the general sense. This means they want to see the following conditions.

* **Free trade**. Foreign firms that need to secure imported factor inputs will want open trade, free of tariffs and other protectionist measures.
* **Privatization**. Some MNCs see opportunity in countries that are in the process of privatizing their state industries. Privatization theoretically means new opportunities for outside firms whether their presence is as a purchaser of the industries, or as a supplier of services.
* **Tradable foreign exchange**. Firms prefer to convert domestic currency profits into their home country currency. Exchange controls that limit the amount of foreign capital flow discourage investment.

Evaluation of FDI

Learning outcomes
- Evaluate the impact of foreign direct investment (FDI) for economically less developed countries.

Because the expansion of FDI is expected to continue, it is critical for developing countries to assess the value of FDI for their own development plans. Keeping in mind the variety of developing countries, as well as the differences between types of FDI, it is still possible to make some generalizations about the desirability of foreign investment.

Advantages of FDI

Capital improvements

- Capital injections can help to break the poverty cycle by injecting much-needed capital goods and finance.
- The foreign purchase of domestic assets brings money into the capital account of the balance of payments, enabling more imports of foreign consumer and capital goods.
- Foreign investment can induce LDC governments to invest in infrastructure to support the new firms. This may have spin-off benefits to the country at large if the works projects have other useful applications.
- Some forms of FDI provide opportunities for enhanced research and development, which may expand technical capital in the greater economy.
- FDI can stimulate domestic industry when the MNC buys locally produced capital goods and services.
- Technology transfer improves the country's capital stock. As foreign firms bring in new and more advanced technology, domestic rivals and suppliers are inspired to adapt technologically as well.

Income, employment and training

- Employment is increased:
  - where foreign firms hire significantly from the domestic workforce; this increased employment increases incomes and tax revenues
  - where firms improve the skills of workers; here FDI can increase human capital through training.
- The increased income accruing to workers and to the MNC is subject to taxation. These increased tax revenues might be used for development purposes such as improved healthcare and education.

Market efficiency and choice

- MNCs may compete with complacent domestic industries. The added competition should lower prices and increase market efficiency domestically.
- If MNCs help a country realize its comparative advantages, world trade is enhanced and lower prices result.
- For domestic consumers, the arrival of foreign firms may initiate meaningful choice in the market for goods and services.

Disadvantages of FDI

Muted effects on employment

- Foreign firms may choose to bring large amounts of management personnel to launch and administer the company. In this case, the employment growth only comes to the low-skilled and low-wage labour force.
- Where foreign management stays in place, the expected training and skills transfer effect is limited.
- Some industries do not hire workers extensively as they are capital intensive. Thus, some FDI companies that earn large revenues have relatively few domestic workers.

Limited income benefits

- **Repatriation of a foreign firm's profits limits the income growth benefits of FDI.** For example, the Swedish house-goods firm IKEA sends its profits home to Sweden. Thus, the impact of IKEA's presence in any country is limited to employment, input sourcing, and perhaps infrastructure benefits.
- **Foreign firms use accounting methods to avoid taxes.** To pay less in tax in a high-tax country, firms try to show that they are making smaller taxable profits. The method used is called transfer pricing: firms show that they pay for resources from affiliates with prices higher than actually paid. For example, Company X in India might claim that it bought an input resource like steel from the Company X factory in Korea at $500 a beam. In reality, the Korean branch of Company X produces the beam at a much lower cost. This makes Company X in India appear less profitable, and thus pay lower corporate taxes in India. It is in this way that LDCs gain less tax revenue than they might otherwise hope.

Limited capital injections

- Countries like China sometimes require that the foreign affiliate be paired with a domestic company in a joint venture, in the hope that some transfer of managerial and technical skills will take hold. In other instances, domestic companies are bought through transfers of share ownership in the new foreign parent company. In either case, the benefit of supposed capital injections is lost. Rather than receive cash for their shares, domestic owners are merely tied to the fate of the new parent firm.
- There is no guarantee that the investment spending from FDI companies comes from outside the domestic economy. In reality, many firms borrow from local financial markets. This pushes up borrowing costs and crowds out domestic firms who are seeking credit. It also limits the expected benefits of external credit injections.

MNC power

Some MNCs earn more in revenue than the GDP of many small LDCs. They come armed with highly skilled lawyers, accountants and political lobbyists, seeking the best return on their investment. Many development economists, politicians and non-governmental organizations have concerns that this presents opportunities for predatory behaviour by MNCs.

- **Influence over regulatory environment.** Through the reduction of tax revenues, environmental degradation and exploitation of workers, it is believed that governments may achieve 'uneconomic growth' in the race to attract FDI. This process is known as the 'race to the bottom': companies seeking the lowest possible costs pressure the governments of LDCs to relax their regulatory policies over taxes, and over environmental and worker protection.

- **Taxes**. Attempting to lure investors, countries often compete to reduce tax burdens for foreign firms. They may also create special investment zones with discounted land purchase and other financial enticements such as easy repatriation of foreign exchange profits.

To learn more about the Electronic Wasteland, visit www.pearsonhotlinks.com, enter the title or ISBN of this book and select weblink 28.1.

- **Environment**. It is suspected that MNCs seek out countries where environmental rules are relaxed. This allows companies to pollute in a variety of ways, without making recovery efforts. A clear example of this is the business of selling the rights to dump rich-world garbage in poor countries. Whatever is salvageable in this waste, particularly hi-tech products like computer parts, is often highly toxic to extract and expensive to do properly. It is shipped to cities like Guiyu, China, where it is broken down cheaply but dangerously. However, it should also be said that some evidence has emerged that the movement of MNCs to China, for example, has coincided with a reduction in pollution levels because of enhanced production technology.
- **Worker rights**. It is often argued that MNCs move production to low-wage countries where it is difficult to organize unions, and where workers' rights are not valued. While the employment offered by MNCs increases incomes above what was previously available, the common practice of subcontracting (outsourcing) means that large MNCs can practise 'deniability' when their subcontractors exploit workers by withholding wages or creating poor work conditions.
- **Overwhelming competition with local industry**. Large multinationals already enjoy many of the benefits of economies of scale. With their production, marketing, inventory control, and distribution systems already established, they often have an enormous competitive advantage over domestic firms. This may kill local industry and eliminate the possibility of domestically owned firms.

CASE STUDY

Big sporting events: real investment or all flash?

Just how much international sporting events such as the World Cup contribute to human development is debatable.

Poor and middle-income countries hoping for a taste of international prestige must have been inspired by South Africa's hosting of the World Cup in 2010. Millions of visitors streamed into the country, injecting large amounts of foreign cash and cachet. The games went off without serious incident or technical problems or violence and were, to most observers, a shining success. But to others, the allure of major competitions like the World Cup and the Olympics are more mirage than substance. Hosting such tournaments offers up all the glitter of foreign direct investment, with few of its benefits and all of its drawbacks.

Such events promise large amounts of foreign exchange, but this is usually a one-time injection. Rather than receiving foreign capital, countries typically go deeply into debt, diverting local capital away from local needs to build the necessary infrastructure to host these events. In poor countries, this may result in some new roads and mass transit links, but it also requires expensive stadium projects that are luxurious by regional standards. These hulking 'white elephants' are often barely used again, and live on as ugly memories of an expensive party the country hosted years before: Greece's white elephants from 2004 are famous, and as early as 2009 the glorious 'Bird's Nest' in Beijing was falling into disrepair from lack of use. Suspicions about the predatory nature of some FDIs were further bolstered when it was revealed by the Dutch government that FIFA, the World Cup governing body, pressed it and other bidding countries to implement special laws for the World Cup – including blanket tax exemptions for FIFA and FIFA sponsors, as well as limits on workers' rights.

If this can happen under the public spotlight of a major sporting event, critics wonder, then what kind of deals and exemptions might apply during the routine approval of more mundane investment projects in more remote places? Better to win on the pitch, it is said, than to play a losing game off of it. South Africans, who spent $5.1 billion on the games, are prepared for a spending hangover, but appear to be pleased with the results. And it is expected that the quest to host such events will continue. The cost, it is argued, is well worth it in the name of enhancing a country's 'brand.' At the same time, it could be said that such tournaments are rarely justified economically, unless one counts the losses as 'psychic income,' and believes that LDCs should have the same opportunities to misspend their money that rich ones have.

EXERCISES

1   To what degree is the comparison between FDI and the hosting of a major sporting event a valid one?

2   If we assume that staging these events is a net loss for the countries involved, to what degree is this economically justifiable? In what ways is it not?

3   How might developing countries protect themselves from the abuses and waste these events typically see?

Foreign aid

Learning outcomes

- Explain that aid is extended to economically less developed countries either by governments of donor countries, in which case it is called official development assistance (ODA), or by non-governmental organizations (NGOs).
- Explain that humanitarian aid consists of food aid, medical aid and emergency relief aid.
- Explain that development aid consists of grants, concessional long-term loans, project aid that includes support for schools and hospitals, and programme aid that includes support for sectors such as the education sector and the financial sector.
- Explain that, for the most part, the priority of NGOs is to provide aid on a small scale to achieve development objectives.
- Explain that aid might also come in the form of tied aid.
- Explain the motivations of economically more developed countries giving aid.
- Compare and contrast the extent, nature and sources of ODA to two economically less developed countries.

Official aid

Foreign investment is one way to inject capital into the poverty cycle experienced by many countries. Foreign aid is another. It can be defined as financial, technical and in-kind assistance to other countries. Aid can be given by foreign governments – when it is called official development assistance (ODA). Or it can be given by non-governmental organizations (NGOs). Aid flows are tracked by the Organization for Economic Cooperation and Development (OECD).

 Development aid is the name for long- or short-term loans, grants, and technical assistance for the purpose of increasing the living standard of another country.

Development aid tends to have a longer-term focus and consists of outright grants or concessional long-term loans. It includes project aid that could involve support for schools and hospitals. It can involve programme aid that supports continuing efforts to build whole sectors such as education, healthcare and finance.

Government aid

Donor country governments can give directly to another country – this is called bilateral aid. Alternatively, donors can contribute to multilateral organizations like the United Nations, World Bank, IMF, or regional development banks like the Inter-American Development Bank. Subgroups with specific goals (e.g. UN Children's Fund) can also be the focus of specific giving. These organizations administer the flow of aid according to their aims and goals. In 2007, about two-thirds of ODA was bilateral aid. Figure 28.4 shows the flow of aid according to these distinctions.

Figure 28.4
Sources and types of aid, 2000–07, shown cumulatively.

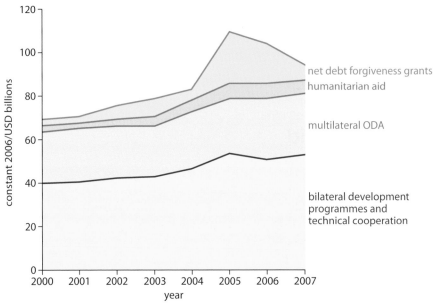

OECD, *Aid targets slipping out of reach?*, 2008

ODA flows are concessional in nature: they are required to consist of at least 25% grant money, and the rest in long-term loans with relatively easy terms. These loans can be in some combination of local currency and the currency of the donor. In reality, up to three-quarters of ODA funding is grant money, the rest is loans.

Types of aid

Foreign aid takes many forms, but can generally be classified as follows.

- Debt relief grants to heavily indebted LDCs.
- Technical assistance to LDCs such as engineers, doctors, agricultural experts.
- Development assistance in the form of aid to whole sectors such as education or healthcare or specific institutions such as hospitals, schools, and economic cooperatives.
- Humanitarian aid given for emergency relief in disaster areas after tsunamis, earthquakes and famine. This can consist of emergency help, medical aid and food aid.
- Commodity assistance such as the purchase of seeds, fertilizer, equipment, building materials or other essential commodities to encourage the smooth operation of some markets as well as to prevent economic or health sector shocks.

Aid from NGOs

Aid provided by NGOs typically has a more specific purpose or operates on a smaller scale than ODA. Oxfam, which is dedicated to poverty relief and the advocacy of fair trade, is one of the more famous NGOs. Also well known is *Médecins Sans Frontières*, which sends medical relief to areas of emergency and long-term need.

 A non-governmental organization is typically a non-profit group that is created for a set of specific, public-action purposes, including development work.

NGOs focus on areas that official aid may not reach. Poverty relief, accomplished by working closely with desperate communities, is a major emphasis. Many NGOs focus specifically on women's issues, in particular prenatal care, abuse prevention, childcare, and women's healthcare.

Donor motivation for giving aid
Political and strategic

In some instances, previous colonial powers might provide aid to their former colonies, in part because of business and political relationships stemming from the colonial years. In general, Cold War calculations motivated most of the post-World War II assistance thinking. The US justified expensive reconstruction efforts in South Korea, Japan and Western Europe based on Cold War strategy. An extension of this tendency in modern aid is the fact that bilateral aid, where one country gives directly to another, is perhaps more likely to be politically or strategically motivated. Table 28.2 shows the top 10 recipients of foreign aid by country.

TABLE 28.2 TOP RECIPIENTS OF FOREIGN AID, BY COUNTRY, 2008	
Country	**Aid / billions of dollars**
Iraq	9.8
Afghanistan	4.8
Ethiopia	3.3
Palestine	2.5
Vietnam	2.5
Sudan	2.3
Tanzania	2.3
India	2.1
Bangladesh	2.0
Turkey	2.0

Money spent on Iraq and Afghanistan is given with the stated objectives of securing peace, preventing conflict and building stability, democracy and economic growth through military and development means. The large amounts given to Palestine, Sudan, India, Bangladesh and Turkey could arguably be considered in the same light.

Economic

Countries may provide aid as a means of conducting good business in countries where business relationships are valued and perhaps natural resources are coveted by the donor country. Australia, for example, gives substantial aid to Indonesia and other nearby Asian trading partners when other countries have greater need.

In other instances, aid given to countries without special economic ties to the donor country may be linked to the commercial interests of the donor. Called tied aid, this can take the form of sending equipment and materials from the donor country. This may have the benefit of stimulating demand in the donor country, but probably limits the effectiveness of the aid, particularly when the donations are of goods inappropriate to the recipient country's level of technology (e.g. sophisticated tractors in lieu of simple farm equipment). On a per-dollar basis, the receiving country receives less value and derives less benefit from such transactions.

Humanitarian

Emergency assistance to disaster-stricken areas after tsunamis, earthquakes and hurricanes all qualify as short-term humanitarian aid. Other, more enduring aid efforts are aimed at the relief of long-term poverty in much of the developing world. For instance, the United Nations Development Programme has championed the refocusing of growth policies towards development goals. This effort culminated with the UN Millennium Goals for 2015. Nevertheless Figure 28.5 (as well as Figure 28.4) suggests that political and economic interests form most of the motivation for donor aid. If the needs of the poorest countries were a priority, one would expect ODA funding to go predominantly to LDCs. But this is not the case. Less than one-third of ODA funding goes to LDCs.

Figure 28.5
Proportion of ODA given to LDCs and non-LDCs.

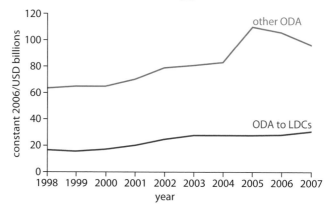

CASE STUDY

Afghanistan and Uganda

OECD statistics make it possible to see more clearly the differences in the scope and nature of aid in different countries. The OECD 'at a glance' files give information about the donor sources of aid, amounts, and areas where aid is directed within a recipient country. Figures 28.6 and 28.7 show the situation in two countries at similar levels of development. On the 2010 HDI, Afghanistan is 155th, while Uganda is ranked 141st. However, they are in different parts of the world, with rather different aid profiles.

Afghanistan

Receipts	2006	2007	2008
net ODA (USD million)	2956	3965	4865
bilateral share (gross ODA)	84%	79%	86%
net ODA / GNI	36.1%	39.0%	..
net private flows (USD million)	19	13	37

Receipts	2006	2007	2008
population (million)	no data available		
GNI *per capita* (Atlas USA)	no data available		

Top ten donors of gross ODA (2007-08 average)	(USDm)
1 United States	1816
2 EC	328
3 United Kingdom	296
4 Canada	277
5 Germany	256
6 IDA	251
7 Japan	155
8 Norway	112
9 Turkey	107
10 Netherlands	100

bilateral OAD by sector (2007-08)

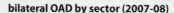
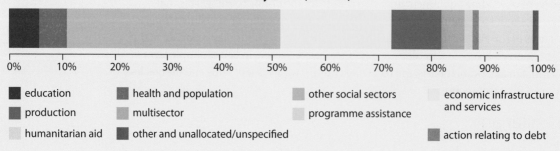

- education
- production
- humanitarian aid
- health and population
- multisector
- other and unallocated/unspecified
- other social sectors
- programme assistance
- economic infrastructure and services
- action relating to debt

OECD

Figure 28.6 Afghanistan ODA 'at a glance'.

Uganda

Receipts	2006	2007	2008
net ODA (USD million)	1539	1737	1657
bilateral share (gross ODA)	61%	58%	61%
net ODA / GNI	15.8%	14.9%	11.7%
net private flows (USD million)	20	38	112

Top ten donors of gross ODA (2007-08 average)	(USD m)
1 United States	327
2 IDA	277
3 EC	210
4 United Kingdom	116
5 AfDF	116
6 Denmark	97
7 Netherlands	77
8 Ireland	73
9 Norway	72
10 Sweden	60

Receipts	2006	2007	2008
population (million)	29.7	30.6	31.7
GNI *per capita* (Atlas USA)	340	370	420

bilateral OAD by sector (2007-08)

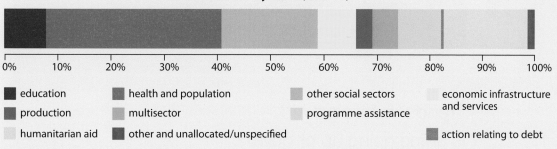

education · health and population · other social sectors · economic infrastructure and services · production · multisector · programme assistance · humanitarian aid · other and unallocated/unspecified · action relating to debt

Figure 28.7 Uganda ODA 'at a glance'.

OECD

The two countries have similar population numbers – roughly 30 million people. Both have extremely low GNI *per capita*. Afghanistan's GNI is not listed in Figure 28.6 because reliable statistics are hard to come by; it is estimated to be about $1100 per year. Uganda's GNI *per capita* is much less, between $340 and $420 per year. It would seem that Uganda is significantly poorer in income terms, although roughly equal in development terms. However, the developed world sent Afghanistan between 3–5 billion dollars per year between 2007 and 2009, while Uganda received from a half to a third of that amount.

We can infer reasons behind this discrepancy. Afghanistan, a centre point of conflict against the terrorist group Al-Qaeda, is likely to be receiving much more aid because of its perceived strategic importance. The recent discovery of more than $1 trillion of mineral deposits has added economic incentives to the motivation for aid giving. Although Uganda has also been made aware of significant oil deposits, it does not possess the strategic 'advantage' of Afghanistan.

Who is donating to each country? If we look at the bilateral share of ODA, we can determine how much aid is bilateral compared to how much is from multilateral organizations. Most of the aid in each case each is bilateral; Afghanistan's bilateral ODA is over 80% while Uganda's bilateral share is 60%. On the individual country donor list, it is clear that the US gives nearly $1.5 billion more to Afghanistan than Uganda. This makes up a large portion of the discrepancy between the two countries, and can be understood in terms of the US role in counter-insurgency efforts in Afghanistan since 2002.

Other differences emerge when the areas receiving aid money are compared. While the percentage of aid spent on education is similar, less than 10%, Uganda spends much more on health and population issues than Afghanistan. Afghanistan spends far more on the category called 'other social sectors,' which includes water and sanitation, other population and health spending, government and civil society, and conflict, peace and security. One might guess that the last several categories are particularly important in Afghanistan, as the members of the North Atlantic Treaty Organization (NATO) – including the top five donors to Afghanistan – have attempted to rebuild the country's institutions and government in the wake of the attacks on the Twin Towers (11 September 2001), several years of destructive Taliban rule, and nearly 20 years of guerrilla war against the USSR.

In other areas, spending on infrastructure is higher in Afghanistan, while programme assistance is a priority in Uganda. At the same time, aid in Uganda goes somewhat more directly to humanitarian efforts. Finally, it appears that ODA forms a larger share of total national income for Afghanistan (shown by the net ODA/GNI figure). Afghanistan relies on foreign aid for nearly a third of national income (or more), while for Uganda the figure ranges from about 12% to 15%.

As these two case studies suggest, every country's development story is different. With regard to foreign aid, some countries may receive significant international attention and resources for reasons that are quite separate from need. Uganda appears, with its lower income and greater use of resources on humanitarian efforts, to be more desperate in terms of poverty than Afghanistan. However, it may also be that the requirements of some countries, particularly conflict zones which have difficulty maintaining stability, cost quite a bit more for some periods. For our purposes, the above examples do illustrate the tendency of the developed world to focus on areas of strategic or economic importance. But they also serve as a caution to regard each development tale as one that requires more insight and information for a proper assessment.

To learn more about ODA and the countries it is given to, visit www.pearsonhotlinks.com, enter the title or ISBN of this book and select weblink 28.2.

EXERCISES

4   **a**   Use the link in the hotlinks box (left) to find ODA information 'by country.' Pick two countries that share some characteristics but have some differences to their profiles as well.

b   List the similarities between the two aid profiles.

c   List the differences between the two aid profiles.

d   Make inferences and attempt to draw conclusions about the similarities and differences you have identified.

Trends in foreign aid
Is giving going up or down?

In global terms, rich-country giving to poor countries has grown, from just under $40 billion in 1960 (constant dollars) to nearly $120 billion in 2008. However, this growth in absolute terms masks the relative decline in giving observed when aid is measured as a percentage of rich-country income.

Figure 28.8

Net ODA by total and % GNI, 1960–2008.

▼

Figure 28.8 shows that aid totals have increased steadily, but not at a rate that keeps pace with income growth. Rich-country giving was about 5% of GNI in 1960. That percentage grew slightly, but then declined rather steadily until just after the start of the new millennium. Current aid levels are at nearly 0.3% of GNI, still significantly less than the early commitments of aid in the 1960s.

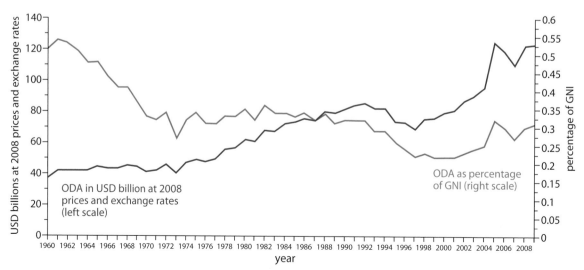

OECD

5   Why do you think that aid has decreased in relative terms since 1960?

6   Suggest several reasons why it may have increased recently.

7   Is it possible that factors other than aid have contributed to development? If so, what factors?

Who gives foreign aid?

The OECD also keeps track of the countries donating foreign aid. This can be viewed in absolute or relative terms (Figure 28.9). In terms of total contributions, the US clearly gives more than any other country; France, the UK, Japan and Germany all contribute less than half the amount from the US. However, when considered as a percentage of GNI, the largest contributors are Sweden, Norway, Luxembourg and Denmark, along with the Netherlands. Only these five countries (shown in green) have reached the OECD guideline of 0.7% of GNI to be donated as aid. Several OECD countries, chief among them the US, fall well below the 0.7% level.

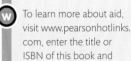

To learn more about aid, visit www.pearsonhotlinks. com, enter the title or ISBN of this book and select weblink 28.3.

Figure 28.9
a Net ODA in 2009; **b** ODA as % GNI in 2009.

a

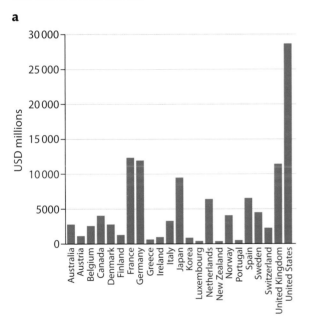

b

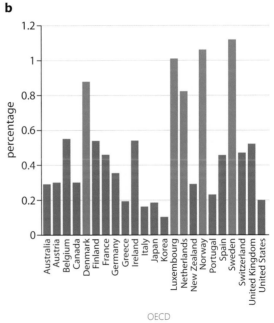

OECD

Evaluation of foreign aid

Learning outcomes

- Evaluate the effectiveness of foreign aid in contributing to economic development.
- Compare and contrast the roles of aid and trade in economic development.

Is foreign aid effective?

There are several factors that limit the effectiveness of aid. Aside from the dwindling quantity of aid, several objections are levied against the continuance or expansion of foreign aid among rich countries.

Criticisms of aid

Aid is inefficient

Too often, aid money is set aside for large-scale showcase projects that embellish the reputations of the project administrators and donors, despite the fact that smaller or medium-scale projects would do the job at a lower cost. Large infrastructure projects like dams and airports have the attraction of tangible outcomes, but may well be redundant or extravagant.

Corruption squanders aid

In many instances, enormous amounts of money and resources are diverted by corrupt leaders. The money can be stolen, rerouted through friendly political organizations, or kicked back to decision-making officials. Humanitarian goods can be withheld and sold off for profit, or passed around to government officials and the military.

Aid rarely gets to those who need it

Figure 28.5 (page 600) shows that most aid money goes to relatively well-off countries. Among poor countries receiving aid, some evidence suggests that assistance money is concentrated in more affluent urban areas rather than poorer rural ones.

Aid displaces local investment and markets

LDCs are notoriously poor at tax compliance (i.e. the degree to which society pays taxes on its income). Foreign aid discourages governments to enforce the tax code and generate revenue for itself. Furthermore, some kinds of commodity aid may depress local markets and reduce incentives for domestic production.

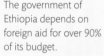

The government of Ethiopia depends on foreign aid for over 90% of its budget.

Aid fosters dependency

For some of the poorest countries, aid accounts for a majority of government revenue, a situation that is chronic rather than temporary. Rather than raise revenue by collecting taxes, countries come to expect aid to fill the gap in government budgets.

Arguments for foreign aid

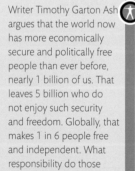

Writer Timothy Garton Ash argues that the world now has more economically secure and politically free people than ever before, nearly 1 billion of us. That leaves 5 billion who do not enjoy such security and freedom. Globally, that makes 1 in 6 people free and independent. What responsibility do those 1s have to the other 5s? To what degree do the 1s have the power to help the other 5s?

Nevertheless, part of the Millennium Development Goals Project is a push to encourage governments to step up and meet the stated goal of 0.7% of GNI. Economists and the UN are therefore encouraging more aid, rather than less.

Delivery of aid is the problem

Champions of development point out that aid programmes are relatively new areas of social policy, and attempt to solve very complex problems. Some argue that with the advent of new NGOs, which are applying many new ideas, the quality of aid work will improve.

Aid addresses areas where growth alone will not

Many pro-growth policies can create significant negative externalities (Chapter 26, pages 542–545). Income inequality is one area where aid can redress and support vulnerable populations. Technical assistance can improve health services or help guide environmental policy.

Successes not celebrated because the need is still great

Improved malaria treatment has lengthened lives and enhanced quality of life in many countries; the Millennium Development Goals Project has made progress on a number of fronts. Most of this work has been supported by aid-funded policies, through the UN, the

World Bank and many NGOs. However, by advertising success, aid agencies and the UN risk reducing the sense of urgency that might motivate countries to give more. Promoters of aid must balance the desire to know that aid is working against the desperate need for aid that still persists in much of the world.

Trade *vs* aid

Led by the EU and the US, the rich world spends nearly $1 billion per day on agricultural subsidies and at the same time has protective tariffs on agricultural goods. These policies have been protected under WTO rules for decades. The subsidies and trade rules have two, mutually reinforcing and harmful effects on poor countries. For most LDCs, agricultural commodities are their most likely source of comparative advantage, yet rich-world subsidies artificially build up the competition when rich-world agriculture already has competitive advantages in capital and technology. Furthermore, the subsidies often result in overproduction and the dumping of rich-world produce on world markets. This drives world commodity prices downwards, reducing the income of LDCs that are dependent on agricultural goods, which is to say most of them.

To access Worksheet 28.1 on the bottom billion, please visit www. pearsonbacconline.com and follow the onscreen instructions.

The case for trade

Reducing or eliminating rich-country subsidies and trade barriers would expand the market for poor-country agricultural goods. With larger export markets, the farming industry in these countries could grow and build up capital, and perhaps begin to take advantage of some economies of scale. More efficient and mature agricultural sectors would earn more foreign exchange for the country itself. This might also allow countries to diversify into other areas of production, reducing their dependency on a few staple goods. The increased income might, in fact, reverse the trend in the poverty cycle (Chapter 26) and stimulate more savings and investment. At the same time, the increased income might reduce dependence on foreign aid.

Limitations of trade

Some economists have noted that while poor countries produce food, many also import it. Net food-importing LDCs could be hurt, they argue, if rich-country agricultural subsidies are rapidly eliminated. A major cut in subsidies could cause a rise in food prices, which could cause instability. As food prices soared in late 2007 and early 2008, food riots broke out in parts of Asia and Africa, lending credibility to this claim.

To learn more about fair trade, visit www. pearsonhotlinks.com, enter the title or ISBN of this book and select weblink 28.4.

Even fair-trade advocates like Oxfam are wary of the bargain that might be struck in order to obtain open agricultural markets. They worry that, in the name of trade liberalization, rich countries would demand that LDCs further reduce the exceptions to free trade rules allowed by the WTO. This could result in the swamping of LDC infant industries under a deluge of established foreign competitors, mostly the developed world's MNCs.

Still others argue that the trade *vs* aid argument presents a false trade-off. The prominent development economist Jeffrey Sachs, for instance, consistently rejects the idea that trade and aid are mutually exclusive. Trade and aid are both necessary for the poorest countries to break the poverty cycle and make large strides in development. Trade is necessary for income growth and self-sufficiency. But aid, he argues, will go where trade does not reach.

To learn more about micro-finance, visit www. pearsonhotlinks.com, enter the title or ISBN of this book and select weblink 28.5.

Beyond aid?

Economists are increasingly looking for new ways to measure the degree to which countries are supporting development efforts around the world. One policy research group, the Center for Global Development (CGD), has created the Commitment to Development Index (CDI). This composite measure is based on the premise that aid itself is insufficient, and that policies of rich countries in many different areas will influence development as well. The ranking adds trade policy, immigration, investment, technology, security, environment, and technology contributions as well (Figure 28.10).

Figure 28.10
Commitment to development index, 2010.

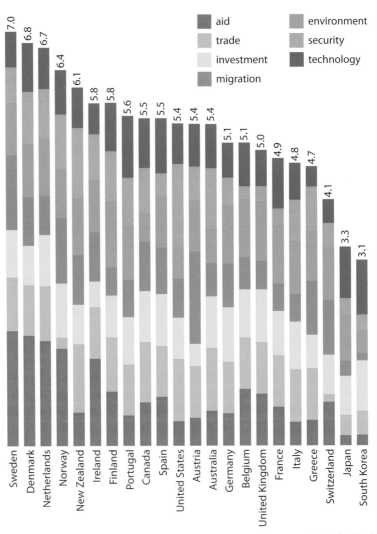

Center for Global Development

While the results are rather similar overall to the ODA/GNI figures (Figure 28.9, page 603) the CDI provides more specific insight into the nature of rich-country contributions to overall development. Its creators hope that the CDI will refocus rich-country perspectives on development in the same way that the Human Development Index altered the way we assess what constitutes a better standard of life. Interesting further research by the CGD indicates that there is a high correlation between indicators of donor country democracy and the level of commitment to development.

28.6 Major institutions in development

Learning outcomes

- Examine the current roles of the IMF and the World Bank in promoting economic development.

The World Bank

The World Bank is an international development assistance organization that was created with the purpose of enhancing economic development and structural change. The Bank was created at Bretton Woods, at the same conference as the system of international exchange rates, the International Monetary Fund (IMF) and the General Agreement on Tariffs and Trade (GATT), which later evolved into the World Trade Organization (WTO). These institutions were developed as a system of economic order that would prevent further economic collapses like the Great Depression of the 1930s, which created the conditions for World War II.

The World Bank was initially made up of a handful of countries, with the former Allied countries forming its core. It has since grown to 187 members. Membership influence is directly related to the amount of donor money given to the bank. In 2010, the bank revised voting rules to allow a greater voice from developing countries. Currently the largest voting shares go to the US (15.8%), Japan (6.84%), China (4.42%), Germany (4.00%), the UK (3.75%) and France (3.75%).

A brief history of the World Bank

1947 to the 1960s

In the early years, a sort of fiscal conservatism dominated the Bank's thinking and lending. Making safe loans with an emphasis on projects that would repay the loans easily, the Bank focused on infrastructure projects that would directly increase economic growth. This approach established the financial credibility of the Bank but limited its impact on broader development issues.

1970s

Under new leadership from 1968, the Bank changed priorities to emphasize the meeting of basic needs in poor countries. Spending on social programmes increased significantly, including healthcare, education and poverty alleviation. Lending increased significantly, as did the debt levels of many LDCs, during this period.

1980s

The Bank revisited its fiscally conservative roots under the leadership of AW Clausen. During this period, the increasing debt loads of LDCs inspired the bank to create significantly restrictive conditions on the granting of new loans. The comprehensive economic reforms required, called Structural Adjustment Programmes (SAPs), required major changes in macroeconomic and international economic policy for the countries that took loans at this time. A typical SAP required the liberalization of exchange rates and capital flows, reduced protectionism and open markets. SAPs normally required significant spending cuts by governments (in order to repay the loan), cuts that reduced levels of education, healthcare and support for the poor or unemployed. These policies were later criticized for being harsh and anti-development in practice.

1990s to the present

The Bank responded to criticism of its SAPs by expanding the focus of its lending and assistance activities. The Bank now emphasizes sustainable development methods as opposed to pure economic growth. It supports poverty alleviation and debt relief for poor countries as well. With these aims in mind, the Bank has supported the work of the UNDP to reach the Millennium Goals of 2015.

Evaluation of the World Bank

The influence and role of the World Bank has received regular criticism, especially after the introduction of the SAPs in the 1980s. What follows is a discussion of some of the more common complaints about the Bank.

Conditionality

Conditionality refers to the macroeconomic requirements made by the World Bank (and the IMF) before the granting of loans.

World Bank loans come with conditions attached. Recipient countries must follow the often strict guidelines to receive the funding. The cutting of budget deficits, in particular, in order to pay back the loans, force large cuts in social welfare spending on unemployment relief, medical services and education subsidies. These cuts hit the poorest and most vulnerable rather hard, critics say. These policies may be mixed with compulsory liberalization of domestic industry and trade. Privatization may be causing increased unemployment, with fewer resources available (because of budget cuts) to help the jobless. Increased foreign competition may also cause domestic industries to fold, creating more unemployment and suffering. While this criticism of the World Bank has softened in recent years, as the Bank has adapted its conditions to more specific circumstances, it remains probably the chief complaint of borrowers and critics.

Loss of sovereignty

A related issue to World Bank conditionality, separate from the effectiveness of the conditional requirements, is that these loan terms may dramatically reduce a country's economic sovereignty. The scope of the change can be all-encompassing. When monetary, fiscal and international trade policies are all apparently dictated by non-elected international officials, the borrowing country's people will question the legitimacy of the policies.

Dominance of rich countries

The voting procedures of the Bank give heavy weight to donor countries, most of them highly developed countries, and chief among them the US. Such countries, it is argued, know little of the choices faced by poor countries, and thus World Bank policies are disconnected from poor-country needs. More worrisome is that policy prescriptions too often resemble the harsh medicine that is easier for a doctor to give than to take. During

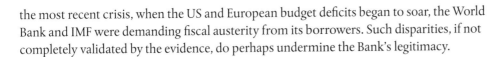

the most recent crisis, when the US and European budget deficits began to soar, the World Bank and IMF were demanding fiscal austerity from its borrowers. Such disparities, if not completely validated by the evidence, do perhaps undermine the Bank's legitimacy.

Mixed results

The free market emphasis of the World Bank's approach has, according to some economists, led to rising inequality in a number of recipient countries. Even further, the resulting cuts in social spending have potentially lowered some countries' performance on the HDI, in effect worsening the quality of life in those countries. More pointed criticism has come from a former chief economist of the Bank, Joseph Stiglitz. While serving for three years in the late 1990s, Stiglitz reported dismay at the results of the 10-year studies of World Bank policy towards former communist countries. He left the Bank, and has since advocated a much greater government role in creating economic growth and development.

To Stiglitz, the timidity of poor-country businesses and individuals to spend or invest results in a lack of growth that can be compensated for only by governments. However, such a role is practically impossible when World Bank/IMF conditionality forces austere fiscal and monetary policy, as well as compulsory liberalization. In part as a reaction to these lingering critiques from Stiglitz and many others, the Bank has refocused its efforts on a broad array of specific development issues that are designed to more directly target development goals. These include sustainable development through carbon-trading funds, conservation efforts and water–sanitation initiatives. The Bank has sought to fortify institutions by working against corruption, and for the promotion of legal reform and property rights. It spends on human development by funding childcare projects, malaria treatment, and HIV/AIDs projects worldwide. Thus the World Bank appears to be changing tactics and strategy as the development consensus changes, even if these changes are occurring rather slowly.

The International Monetary Fund (IMF)

The International Monetary Fund is an organization of 187 countries, whose dues go towards funding IMF activities. Among the stated aims of the IMF are to be working towards fostering global monetary cooperation, securing financial stability, facilitating international trade, promoting high employment and sustainable economic growth, and reducing poverty around the world.

Role of the IMF

Created alongside the World Bank and GATT (page 607), the IMF's initial purpose was to act as the overseer of the Bretton Woods fixed-exchange rate system. The IMF was to monitor the balance of payment situations of member countries and when necessary, act on behalf of those countries to solve current account problems. Typically, this involved the risk of some kind of rapid currency depreciation. The IMF would then loan the country money (an inflow on the financial account) to finance the current account deficit that is a symptom of the depreciation. Without this financing, countries with current account deficits might need to devalue their currencies and upset the fixed-rate system.

The IMF, to some extent, still plays this role, as the international lender of last resort. In the 1980s, the IMF expanded its role beyond management of exchange rates to a form of debt relief. Many LDCs experienced crippling debt crises, and the IMF worked with these countries and the countries and banks that had lent to them. By acting as a final guarantor of privately loaned funds, the IMF provided a backstop for many debt crises. Furthermore, most countries avoided defaulting on IMF loans because this would eliminate their financial safety should any future crisis arise. However, complying with the IMF's loan rules proved challenging for many countries. The stabilization policies associated with these rules could be far-reaching. This resulted in most of the criticism directed at the agency.

Stabilization policies

The recent economic crisis has demonstrated that IMF repayment policies will continue to be debated. The agency may well be the world's 'financial fire department' but it does not work for free, nor is it considered a kind of public good. The policies, according to the IMF, are justified because they are aimed at:

- paying back the IMF so that funds will continue to be available for countries in need
- enabling the IMF to impose unpopular policies that would have prevented the crisis in the first place.

The policies include a range of market-oriented reforms that, depending on the country in question, could have enormous impact.

Government budget austerity

In order to pay back loans, governments need to cut their spending. This nearly always results in significant cuts to social programmes, often in times of crisis, when the need is greater than usual.

Supply-side policies

The IMF may insist on the reduction of minimum wage laws, the privatization of industries, and the cutting of state subsidies to firms.

Inflation control

To establish stability and to reduce the drag downwards of exchange rates, governments may be urged to control inflation with significantly higher interest rates. These high rates could reduce investment and consumption and usher in a period of recession, with all the unemployment and social dislocation that goes with it.

Currency floating

Since the ending of the Bretton Woods system, currencies are encouraged to float to avoid over- or under-valuations. For many, floating rates could lead to a painful depreciation of the currency.

Trade liberalization

This includes reductions in protectionist tariffs, quotas and subsidies, as well as ending restrictions on foreign direct investment.

Evaluation of the IMF

Because countries in need of IMF help have such poor credit reputations, the IMF's willingness to lend offers a hard-won seal of approval, a kind of stamp of credit-worthiness. This makes countries ever more desperate to land IMF help when international consensus determines it is necessary for foreign credit and investment to return to the country. Nevertheless, many of the same criticisms levelled at the World Bank have been applied to the IMF, including the following.

Rich-country dominance

Voting is done according to IMF rules, with the percentages of votes being, in line with those

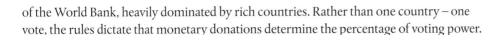

of the World Bank, heavily dominated by rich countries. Rather than one country – one vote, the rules dictate that monetary donations determine the percentage of voting power.

Moral hazard

IMF lending, it is argued, frees countries from fiscal responsibility, and allows them to mismanage their monetary and fiscal policies. With the IMF around to help, the consequences of poor management are one step removed from short-run concerns.

Harsh policies

IMF stabilization polices have a reputation for hitting hardest when the population is most vulnerable. The decreased spending on merit goods, the cutting of already low wages, cuts on food and medical subsidies, and reduction in unemployment benefits at times of greater unemployment, all these have been cited as extraordinary and inhumane policies, especially when applied to developing countries where the reserves of savings and private help are low to begin with.

IMF today

IMF lending surged in 2008, as the world financial crisis hit many countries hard. As of 2010, the IMF was committed to lending nearly $200 billion. The largest outstanding loans from the IMF are to Romania, Ukraine, and Hungary. This highlights the role of the IMF as primarily a financial institution, lending where crises arise rather than with a specific development focus. It also underscores the concerns with IMF stabilization policies, as the politicians and people of each country have railed against the forced spending cuts that are a condition of IMF loans. As each country laid off public-sector employees such as doctors and teachers, and cut by 30% the salaries of the remaining government workforce, there has been the usual talk of defaulting and protesting and even defaulting on the IMF loans. In early 2011, Ireland, a country with one of the highest *per capita* incomes, agreed to accept an IMF/EU bailout worth $85 billion. Its government collapsed the following day.

 To learn more about the International Monetary Fund, visit www.pearsonhotlinks.com, enter the title or ISBN of this book and select weblink 28.6.

28.7 Foreign debt and its consequences

Learning outcomes

- Outline the meaning of foreign debt and explain why countries borrow from foreign creditors.
- Explain that in some cases countries have become heavily indebted, requiring rescheduling of the debt payments and/or conditional assistance from international organizations, including the IMF and the World Bank.
- Explain why the servicing of international debt causes balance of payments problems and has an opportunity cost in terms of foregone spending on development objectives.
- Explain that the burden of debt has led to pressure to cancel the debt of heavily indebted countries.

How indebtedness happens

A country's level of international or external debt determines the level of its indebtedness. This refers to the total amount of external debt, both public and private. Poor-country

International debt comprises short- and long-term loan obligations owed to foreign governments, NGOs and private sources.

debt tends to be more public than private. When a country borrows internationally, it is recorded as an inflow of funds in the financial account (Chapter 23). This foreign borrowing, with the influx of foreign income it provides, can help to balance out deficits of the current account. So, when a country incurs a trade deficit by spending greater sums on foreign imports, foreign borrowing helps to balance the books.

This money can be an important source of investment income, as it represents an injection into the poverty cycle. Normally, a poor country's low income results in low savings, which reduce the pool of money to be borrowed. With access to international loans, a poor country can bridge the savings gap and borrow for investment and capital growth.

The foreign debt, however, only helps in the short term. These debts must be repaid, both the principal loan amount and the interest. Paying interest (called servicing the debt) can be among the most debilitating long-run costs of debt, and is the problem that the most severely indebted countries now face.

Origins of the debt problem

LDCs have not always had a reputation for being heavily in debt. In 1973–74, the petroleum-exporting countries of OPEC put in place an oil embargo that drove oil prices to new highs. The inelastic demand of oil resulted in large export revenues for the oil producers, and massive import expenditure increases for many oil importers.

Large amounts of the 'petrodollars' from OPEC countries were deposited in rich-country banks, which sought to reinvest them. These banks were seeking to make loans, and many oil-importing LDCs were in need of the foreign exchange to shore up their capital accounts and finance their newly inflated trade deficits.

What followed was a rush of lending and borrowing from rich-world banks to poor-country governments. However, the flood of petrodollars blinded banks to the risky nature of many of these loans. In hindsight, it seems clear that many of the countries involved were not financially capable of paying back the loans. Additionally, the loans transacted during this period were not made on the traditionally concessional terms. Instead, countries were borrowing at higher, private market interest rates that would be more difficult to repay. Even in good times and with the funds being spent wisely, these debts would have been a significant burden. In the event, many of the funds were poorly used, and did little to help grow the economies of their recipients.

Consequences of indebtedness

Countries trapped in the poverty cycle may find that large foreign debt acts as an anchor to their development hopes, keeping them in one place. Resources that could be devoted to economic growth and development are instead diverted to the paying down of old debts. Heavily indebted countries suffer from many of these related problems.

Figure 28.11 shows the flow of consequences for many LDCs burdened by massive debt. First, the large loans with market interest rates incur larger than usual debt repayments. The LDC is likely to struggle with repayment, which could jeopardize its credit rating. This makes future borrowing more difficult, as new lenders want even higher interest rates, and are less likely to make loans.

This slows the flow of investment funding in both the private and public sector. Private entrepreneurs find it difficult to borrow for expansion or capital formation. This slows down economic growth and makes debt repayment harder. For governments, debt service and

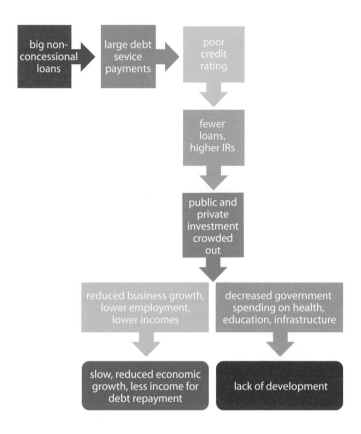

Figure 28.11
The debt trap.

the lack of new funding requires a reduction in spending on merit goods such as education, healthcare and infrastructure. This, in turn, reduces opportunities for development.

Attempted reform: HIPC initiative

Debt burdens reached crisis levels in the 1990s. A combination of NGOs, economists and missionary organizations mounted a campaign for debt relief to poor countries. In 1996, with debt burdens in poor countries threatening the stability of poor nations throughout the developing world, the World Bank and the IMF created the Heavily Indebted Poor Country (HIPC) Initiative. This marked a change in the approach by what had been considered traditional and conservative lending institutions. Countries that qualify are eligible for special assistance in the form of concessionary loans and direct debt relief.

By early 2010, 36 countries had qualified and received at least partial debt relief and low-interest loans. To qualify, countries have to prove that their debts are unsustainable, as measured by their exports-to-debt ratio and other income-to-debt measurements. It also must be shown that the debt cannot be handled by the normal methods. Finally, countries must meet certain macroeconomic stability targets to be eligible for relief.

Early implementation of the programme earned criticism because of the time it takes to fully qualify for relief, on the basis of the sometimes challenging macroeconomic limitations placed on countries that are already in trouble in development terms. After adjustments to the programme to address these problems, the IMF/World Bank have reported the following results:

- nearly $102 billion debt relief spread across 40 HIPC countries
- reduction of the debt stocks of HIPC countries down to $21 billion
- reduction in the debt-to-export ratio of 457% in 1999 to 127% in 2010
- reduction in the debt-to-GDP ratio from 114% in 1999 to 29% in 2010.

Additionally, the HIPC programme has created initiatives that attempt to ensure that the savings from reduced debt service and repayments get channelled back into poverty-relief areas. Nonetheless, in recent years some very public campaigns have been waged by NGOs and celebrities who have argued that the HIPC initiatives have not gone far enough to relieve the morbid debt under which many poor countries labour.

Arguments against debt relief have focused on the inefficacy of the above initiatives, as well as the moral hazard issue. Critics say that debt-relief savings will be recycled into the banking system or will go towards expensive prestige public spending projects, with the benefits going to the upper-income classes. Moreover, they argue that debt relief encourages the taking on of more debt. Poor-country governments can borrow freely, they say, immune to the risks of heavy debt because the HIPC will soften the pain of repayment later on.

One view of the indebtedness problem suggests that it was a unique set of circumstances that led to the debt explosion of the 70s and 80s, and that a repeat is unlikely. But the financial crisis of 2008 suggests that financial bubbles like the petrodollar years are still possible. Thus, indebtedness cannot be written off as a one-time event. Furthermore, it appears that the IMF and World Bank have, if belatedly, developed some skill at handling this relatively new and complex problem. If measured by the results published by the IMF and World Bank, it would appear the HIPC has made significant strides in the reduction of debt levels for member countries. The conditions of stability have, at times, rather harshly reduced the level of social services in already strained countries. But more countries that need debt relief have struggled to meet the terms, and so still face significant growth and development stagnation.

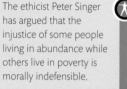

The ethicist Peter Singer has argued that the injustice of some people living in abundance while others live in poverty is morally indefensible.

Evaluate the validity of this viewpoint using your own knowledge of economics and your understanding of morality.

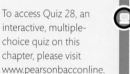

To access Quiz 28, an interactive, multiple-choice quiz on this chapter, please visit www.pearsonbacconline.com and follow the onscreen instructions.

PRACTICE QUESTIONS

1

Crisis in Africa

Item 1

i   The World Bank and the International Monetary Fund have played a major role in Africa's development through their Structural Adjustment Programmes. The stated aim was to bring export-led recovery and a reduction in poverty.

ii   However, Africa has suffered a worsening debt crisis, with looming bankruptcy. Increasingly, the IMF has assumed responsibility for national budget policies, and has insisted on **strict deflationary targets**. At the same time, the World Bank has overseen moves towards **trade liberalization** and deregulation of agricultural markets.

iii The IMF and the World Bank now have a chance to resolve the debt crisis which is destroying lives across sub-Saharan Africa and other developing regions. However, a new policy course will need to be charted in which reform of the heavily indebted poor countries is undertaken, along with an abandonment of the almost religious faith in the power of market forces to generate development and reduce poverty.

adapted from various newspaper articles

Item 2

	Guinea–Bissau	Sierra Leone	Singapore
Debt service ratio (debt service as a % of exports of goods and services)	67	60	Not applicable
Adult literacy / %	54.9	31.4	91.1
Real GDP per capita / $	811	625	22604
% labour force in agriculture	85	67	0
Terms of trade (1987 = 100)	89	92	89
Current account balance before official transfers / $ millions	−41	89	15 093

Human Development Report, UN, 1998

a With reference to Item 1, briefly explain the following terms indicated in bold in the text:

i strict deflationary targets (paragraph ii)   (2 marks) [AO1]

ii trade liberalization (paragraph ii).   (2 marks) [AO1]

b With reference to Item 2, briefly explain why the adult literacy rate of Sierra Leone will make it difficult for the country to grow and develop.   (4 marks) [AO2]

c Use your knowledge of economics to explain two of the significant problems faced by Sierra Leone and Guinea–Bissau (other than the literacy rate problem).(4 marks) [AO2]

d Using information from the text and your knowledge of economics, evaluate the effectiveness of the IMF/World Bank's market-based Structural Adjustment Programmes toward Sierra Leone and Guinea–Bissau.   (8 marks) [AO3]

© International Baccalaureate Organization 2001 (part **a** only)

2   **Fighting poverty in Africa**

Item 1 There are those, not least in Africa, who fear this massive debt relief will produce the same circumstances that have followed smaller debt write-offs. Incompetent governments will run-up large new debt, spend the money on unrealistic projects and place spare cash into Swiss bank accounts.

Arab News, Editorial, Saudi Arabia, 12 June 2005

Item 2 Doubling official aid, even if it is **tied aid** and cancelling Africa's debt are theoretically very attractive proposals. They fail because they are based on a misguided faith that you can rely on human unselfishness to end human misery. Tony Blair and his partners would do the continent a lot of good if they promoted trade, removed agricultural subsidies and encouraged investment relationships, rather than offering kindness and generosity through more aid and debt relief.

Andrew M Mwenda, *Sunday Monitor*, Uganda, 12 June 2005

Item 3 If we are serious about addressing Africa's poverty, far more money and effort will be needed as well as freeing these countries from debt repayment, which then allows them to invest in economic development and improve the health and education of their citizens. Africa has 11% of the world's population, but accounts for only about 1% of the world's economic output. Export-led growth is needed. Without more help from the developed countries, the future looks bad.

Seattle Times, Editorial, US, 12 June 2005

Item 4 Africa is not poor. As the Africa commission report has noted, while it lacks **infrastructure**, Africa is rich in human and natural resources. The problem is that Africans have been forced to live in countries that have not wanted to enrich the lives of people within them, but rather to transfer resources abroad. The struggle of Africa is to be part of the world economic order based on mutual respect, not exploitation.

Ken Wiwa, *The Observer*, 12 June 2005

© International Baccalaureate Organization 2001

a Define the following terms indicated in bold in the text:

i tied aid (Item 2)   [2 marks] [AO1]

ii infrastructure (Item 4).   [2 marks] [AO1]

b Using an appropriate diagram, explain how domestic farmers would be affected by the removal of their subsidies.   (4 marks) [AO2], [AO4]

c Using an AD/AS diagram, explain the effect of a successful export-led growth policy.   [4 marks] [AO2], [AO4]

d Using information from the text and your knowledge of economics, evaluate the effectiveness of increased aid and debt forgiveness policies.   [8 marks] [AO3]

© International Baccalaureate Organization 2008 (part **a** only)

29 THE BALANCE BETWEEN MARKETS AND INTERVENTION

29.1 Markets and intervention: the debate continues

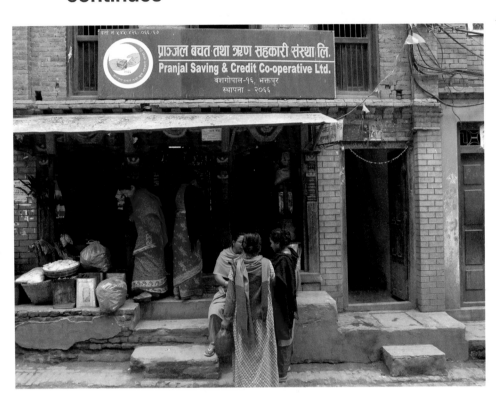

Not all development requires government intervention. In Nepal, local women access credit through local banks.

Role of government in the microeconomy

From the early chapters in this book, we have examined the impact of government intervention in the free market. From the loss of welfare that results from price controls to the dead weight loss of excise taxes and subsidies, government intervention in the free market tends to reduce overall efficiency in a market, leading to either an over- or an under-allocation of resources and a net loss of consumer and producer welfare. In its attempt to help consumers or producers, a government ultimately harms society as a whole when it picks winners and losers in the nation's economy.

The exception to the general rule that government intervention in free markets reduces overall welfare is when government intervenes in a market in which resources are inefficiently allocated when left alone. Government may be able to increase overall welfare in society by regulating the production or consumption of:

- demerit goods (those which create negative externalities through their production or consumption and so are over-provided by the free market)
- merit goods and public goods (those which create positive externalities through their consumption or production and so are under-provided or not provided at all by the free market).

In the case of public goods, government may simply provide them in lieu of the free market.

The role of government in the provision of particular goods that improve the well-being of the nation's people, particularly merit goods such as education, health and infrastructure, must be examined to determine the extent to which government intervention improves on or interferes with the nation's economic development.

Role of government in the macroeconomy

In macroeconomics, there is no consensus among economists with regard to the extent of government intervention necessary to make a national economy function efficiently at its full employment level. The issue of the government's role is the subject of debate between two competing schools of economic thought:

- the demand-side, Keynesian school
- the neo-classical, supply-side school.

Keynesians believe that the overall level of economic activity in a nation is determined by the level of aggregate demand (AD) and that government should play an active role in regulating the level of demand to meet the macroeconomic objectives of full employment, price stability and economic growth.

Neo-classical economists, on the other hand, believe that any attempt by government to manage demand results in a misallocation of resources and reduces the efficiency and ability of the free market economy to correct itself in times of high inflation or high unemployment. Therefore, argue the neo-classicals, the government that governs best is that which governs least. Leave the economy be, argues this school of thought, and the demands of consumers in society will be most efficiently met through the market mechanism and the pursuit of profits by firms.

 Can anyone truly know what is 'good' and what is 'bad'? To what extent can government policies improve on the behaviour of free-willed individuals in sociey?

Role of government in the international economy

Much like government intervention in individual markets within a country, government intervention in the free trade of goods and services between nations generally reduces overall welfare and efficiency in the long run. Interventionist policies include:

- protectionist tariffs and quotas
- subsidies aimed at improving the competitiveness of domestic producers in international markets
- exchange rate manipulation aimed at making one country's goods more attractive to foreign consumers or at making imported capital goods more affordable to domestic consumers.

Of course, this does not keep governments from regularly intervening in the functioning of the free market. And in some cases, government intervention has improved the welfare of the people; for example:

- by increasing employment and income through exchange rate controls (China's export-fuelled economic growth of the last two decades)
- through state sponsorship of domestic industries that with government support have achieved economies of scale and cornered the market in several key global industries (heavy industries in South Korea and Japan).

Government intervention in the free market has certainly benefited the economic superpowers of the 21st century, from Germany's export-driven economy, to China's state-run enterprises, and the American defence industry, which will receive $80 billion of government spending on research and development in 2011.

29.2 Market-oriented and interventionist policies

Learning outcomes

- Discuss the positive outcomes of market-oriented policies (such as liberalized trade and capital flows, privatization and deregulation), including a more efficient allocation of resources and economic growth.
- Discuss the negative outcomes of market-oriented strategies, including market failure, the development of a dual economy and income inequalities.
- Discuss the strengths of interventionist policies, including the provision of infrastructure, investment in human capital, the provision of a stable macroeconomic economy and the provision of a social safety net.
- Discuss the limitations of interventionist policies, including excessive bureaucracy, poor planning and corruption.

The need for government and the free market

The fact is, without any government at all, many of the goods and services that society truly needs would be under-provided by the free market. In addition, without the watchful eye of government regulators, firms with only their private costs and benefits in mind would surely over-produce many of the goods that in fact are very harmful for human health and the environment.

Despite what the most ardent free market advocates believe, there is an important role for government in any economic system. While the majority of the goods and services households demand can be provided efficiently by the free market, many of the goods necessary to promote long-run, sustainable economic development and growth must be provided by, or at the very least supported by, the government.

In this chapter, we examine in detail the delicate balance in today's world between the free market and the government, focusing on economic development.

- On the one hand, to what extent is it within the power of the free market to increase the standard of living by improving health, education, and the availability of consumer goods and services (all measures which form the basis for economic development)?
- On the other hand, to what extent can government promote development through its own policies and interventions in a nation's economy?

To learn more about free markets, visit www.pearsonhotlinks.com, enter the title or ISBN of this book and select weblink 29.1.

There is no easy answer to these questions, and the best we can hope to achieve is some guidance on how to evaluate the roles of government and the free market in promoting sustainable, achievable economic development.

Market-oriented *vs* interventionist policies

A market-oriented growth and development policy is generally any policy that requires little or no role for government in promoting economic development through the unregulated activities of the free market. Individual consumers and producers interact with one another free of government intervention, regulation or control. Market-oriented development policies often require the deregulation or privatization of state-owned enterprises, handing the production of certain goods and services to private businesses. These seek to maximize their profits through the provision of their products to the rest of society, and thereby provide society with goods and services that improve human welfare.

In the context of economic development, we must examine the effectiveness of private enterprises at providing the goods needed to promote improvements in human welfare: healthcare, education and infrastructure.

Strengths of market-oriented policies
Privatization and deregulation

The major argument for privatization and deregulation of industries previously managed or regulated by the government is that the incentives of a private firm will always be to reduce costs, achieve efficiency, and provide a quality product to consumers.

In contrast, it is believed that when important services are provided by the government, the incentives do not always align with the goals of efficiency and meeting the demands of consumers. When government attempts to provide goods such as education, health and basic utilities (water, sanitation, electricity), there is always the possibility that corruption, bureaucratic red tape and misaligned incentives will result in wastefulness. This in turn will reduce the likelihood that these essential goods will be provided in an efficient manner that meets the nation's development goals.

The trade-off between efficiency and equity (fairness) is at the core of the debate over whether the government or the free market best promotes development through the provision of these goods. While a state-run enterprise providing an essential good (e.g. water) to a nation's citizens may aim to provide services in a fair and equitable manner, it is likely that it will fail to provide its services in a low-cost, efficient manner. The objectives of efficiency and equity are not easy to achieve together.

Improved efficiency in the provision of public goods

One way to analyse the effects on efficiency of a market-oriented approach to providing goods that improve human welfare is to apply the microeconomic models which examine marginal benefit and marginal cost of a particular good (Chapter 6).

Let's consider Ukraine. This country is undergoing a transition from government-provided healthcare (a guaranteed benefit under the Soviet Union, of which the Ukraine was a state until 1991) to a free market for healthcare. Today, Ukraine has a dual healthcare system: a publicly funded service available to all citizens, and a private health system available to those willing and able to afford private insurance premiums. The state-run health programme is subject to price controls determined by government policies aimed at

To access Worksheet 29.1 on fair trade, please visit www.pearsonbacconline.com and follow the onscreen instructions.

Since the decline of the Soviet Union in 1991, the formerly communist nations of Eastern Europe have undergone the greatest period of privatization of state-owned enterprises in history. Whereas for most of the 20th century, most consumer goods and services were provided by the state, beginning in the 1990s and continuing through the 2000s, private industry has taken over the provision of countless essential (and non-essential) products for these nations' consumers.

Beds line a hallway inside a public hospital in the Ukraine.

making healthcare affordable to all Ukrainian citizens. On the other hand, in the market for private healthcare, hospitals and clinics are allowed to charge consumers higher prices, and thus the providers are willing and able to supply a greater quantity of healthcare than the public system.

Figure 29.1 shows Ukraine's transition from a regulated, national healthcare monopoly to a more competitive, private healthcare system.

Figure 29.1
Ukrainian healthcare.
a Under government
provision; **b** under
competitive free market
provision.

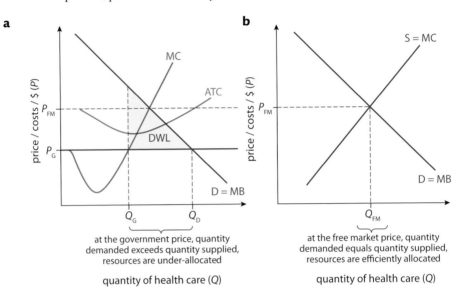

a   b

at the government price, quantity
demanded exceeds quantity supplied,
resources are under-allocated

quantity of health care (Q)

at the free market price, quantity
demanded equals quantity supplied,
resources are efficiently allocated

quantity of health care (Q)

Under the government-provided healthcare programme, the state-run hospitals essentially held a monopoly on healthcare in Ukraine. The state-run monopoly was not able to charge the price it would have set under a free market system (P_{FM}), since the goal of equity required a lower price (P_G). However, because the government system was under-funded, the quantity demanded (Q_D) far exceeded the quantity supplied (Q_G). The result was a shortage of healthcare for the Ukrainian people and a large loss of welfare (blue triangle, DWL, dead weight loss).

The government's goal of equity, supposedly achieved by keeping healthcare prices low, conflicted with the economic objective of efficiency, since without large enough subsidies from the government, the public healthcare system operated at a level at which it actually earned economic losses (at Q_G and P_G, the average cost of healthcare is greater than the price). Ultimately, the inefficient public healthcare system also failed to achieve equity in the provision of a good vital to human welfare. Misaligned incentives and the inability of the price mechanism to allocate resources efficiently created an environment ripe for corruption.

The question was, then, what would happen if the provision of healthcare in Ukraine were completely turned over to the free market? In fact, just such a transition has been underway over the last two decades.

Through a system of healthcare privatization, hundreds of private health clinics have opened up in Ukraine serving customers who are able to afford private health insurance or are able to pay directly for medical services themselves. The incentives of a private health clinic do not lie in making healthcare affordable to all Ukrainians, but rather in maximizing their own profits. At first, this may appear less desirable for the Ukrainian healthcare consumer, but on close inspection it is apparent that despite the higher price of healthcare under the privatized free-market system, there is a significantly greater quantity of healthcare provided (Q_{FM} compared to Q_G) than under the government system.

In addition, assuming the private market for healthcare is competitive, the dead weight loss (efficiency loss) under the government system is reduced or eliminated when the market is privatized. The quantity of healthcare demanded has fallen under the free-market system because the prices charged by private clinics are higher than the prices set by the government. However, the quality and the quantity of care provided has increased because private hospitals and clinics are able to charge a price that reflects the true market demand and supply of healthcare.

To learn more about public goods, visit www. pearsonhotlinks.com, enter the title or ISBN of this book and select weblink 29.2.

Each individual in society is responsible for taking care of his or her own health. Therefore, healthcare should be considered a purely private good. In the world around you, what evidence is in support of arguments for and against this idea?

The price mechanism works, price controls don't

As the situation in Ukrainian healthcare shows, price controls in a market for a good essential to human welfare lead to shortages. Price controls are a standard method of government intervention that is supposed to help either the consumers or the producers of essential goods. Governments may attempt to increase equality and help those who need help most by using price ceilings in the markets for essential goods such as food or fuel.

The problem with such intervention is that a price set by a government means nothing in a market economy. Prices set lower than those that would be determined by the market lead to shortages; price floors set above equilibrium lead to surpluses.

Of course, consumers who are able to get the essential good (often food or fuel) at the official prices are certainly better off than if they had paid the free market price, but the unfortunate truth of price controls is that very few people are able to buy the desired good at the government's price. As a result of prices set below equilibrium, black markets emerge in which consumers buy the good at a price much higher than that set by the government.

In 2014, the new government of Venezuela, led by President Maduro, announced price control laws in an attempt to halt rising prices and food shortages. The new measures followed a decade of price controls under former President Hugo Chavez to introduce 'fair prices', with devastating consequences.

Queues snake around the state-run supermarket as people wait for hours to buy staples like rice and milk, and basic hygiene products like toilet paper. But the shelves are empty – stripped by the 'fair prices' that have made the cost of importing food too expensive and the lure of the black market too tempting.

New laws promise clampdowns on the hoarders, on those who overcharge and on the food traffickers who smuggle subsidised essentials over the border to Colombia.

But it is the black marketers who thrive – ordinary Venezuelans forced to turn to the buhoneros (street peddlers), paying prices vastly inflated above the government's price ceilings. The result is scarcity and hunger – the two devils 'fair prices' were meant to slay.

Adapted from various news sources, 2014

Empty shelves and frustrated customers.

This story is one of inefficiency of government intervention in the free market. Venezuela was facing extreme shortages of basic foodstuffs and other goods that were intensified by the government's attempt to maintain fair and reasonable prices. But as a result of its interventions, the welfare of the Venezuelan people was made far worse than it would have been had prices been allowed to rise. The rising prices would have incentivized producers of food, medical supplies and essential primary commodities to increase their production to reap the rewards higher prices would have promised. But in the absence of a

● **Examiner's hint**

Price controls make an excellent topic for an IA commentary. Governments try to control more prices than you might immediately realize. In addition to key products like food and fuel, governments regularly intervene in markets for items ranging from tuition for universities to rents for inner-city apartments and electricity, gas and water utility rates. In almost every case, attempts at improving equity by controlling prices leads to shortages or surpluses of the goods in question. The subject offers an excellent topic for analysis and evaluation in a commentary.

functioning price mechanism, the market economy simply could not work, and despite the government's good intentions, Venezuelans suffered.

A similar attempt at government price controls took place in China in 2007 when the world price of oil reached its all-time high of $150 per barrel. In an attempt to keep fuel affordable for Chinese households and businesses, the government in Beijing imposed strict price controls on diesel and petrol. The outcome was predictable for anyone familiar with the way markets are supposed to work.

China has been forced to reverse its policy of controlling the price of oil after its fuel cap brought long queues and rationing to filling stations across the country.

In the wake of a record surge in global oil prices, the government announced in September that it would intervene to keep fuel prices at current levels amid fears of their impact on already record levels of inflation. But just two months later Beijing has ordered a U-turn and raised prices in an attempt to alleviate the supply crisis that has gripped much of the country.

The fuel cap prevents Chinese oil refiners from passing on rising crude oil costs to consumers, but the lower fuel prices has led to increased demand from consumers while incentivising the refiners to scale back production to limit their losses. The government's relaxation of its fuel price controls is intended to encourage refiners to increase supply in the hope of shortening the long queues of trucks waiting to fill up that have become commonplace across many parts of China.

Despite the increase in fuel prices, state-run refiners such as Sinopec witnessed dramatic knock-on effects as profits slumped 77% in the first six months of 2008.

Adapted from various new sources, 2007 and 2008

It is ironic that one of the consumers supposed to benefit from government price controls seems to favour the efficiency of the free market over the equity of government control. The price mechanism is one of the greatest attributes a market-oriented approach to economic development and growth offers. Without the signals and incentives made clear by a functioning system of prices, government has no hope of providing human welfare-improving goods and services more efficiently than the free market.

Improved efficiency in the international flows of goods, services and capital

Beyond the gains in efficiency resulting from the privatization of vital industries that relate to economic development, a market-oriented approach to international trade policies also has a beneficial effect on efficiency and resource allocation that may improve the level of development for a nation's people.

Economist Milton Friedman once declared 'We economists don't know much, but we do know how to create a shortage. If you want to create a shortage of tomatoes, for example, just pass a law that retailers can't sell tomatoes for more than two cents per pound. Instantly you'll have a tomato shortage. It's the same with oil or gas.'

In Chapter 27, you learned about two strategies for economic development that require the use of protectionist policies to promote the development of domestic industries either among domestic consumers (import substitution) or among foreign consumers (export promotion). Under import substitution, the government must erect barriers to trade that make foreign produced goods less attractive to domestic households in a developing country. Consumers then substitute domestically produced goods for the imports they might otherwise have consumed. Under export promotion, domestic industries of interest to the government receive large subsidies that would give them a competitive advantage over foreign competitors in international markets, growing the developing country's export sector, presumably creating jobs and income that otherwise would not exist for the nation's households.

While both policies at first appear to have merit, we must analyse again the effect on efficiency of such interventionist methods for promoting economic development.

Tariffs on imports (aimed at increasing demand for domestic goods) and subsidies (aimed at making domestic firm's products more attractive to foreign consumers) are inefficient in that they lead to an over-allocation of resources towards the goods the government decides the nation should produce more of.

Let's consider a decision by the government of Country V, a rice-producing nation, to impose a tariff on all imported rice. The aim is to improve the welfare of the country's rice growers and reduce dependence on foreign rice. Assume that the world price of rice, P_W, is lower than the domestic price of rice in Country V, indicating that other countries are able to produce and export rise at a lower cost. Figure 29.2 shows the effect of such a tariff, a development strategy commonly employed by the governments of poor countries.

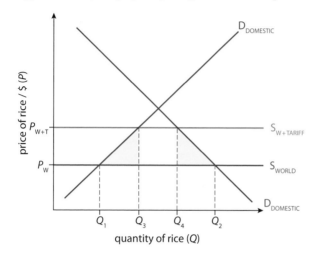

◀ **Figure 29.2**
Protective tariffs lead to higher prices for essential commodities, reducing welfare of poor households.

The tariff on imported rice has the intended effect of increasing domestic rice output from Q_1 to Q_3, but has it improved the level of economic development in Country V? It is more likely that the average Country V citizen is worse off because of the tariff on rice. The two blue triangles in Figure 29.2 represent the loss of total welfare, in this case of consumer surplus, in Country V. Since good nutrition and affordable food are indicators of economic development, the higher price of rice, meant to help Country V's rice farmers, in the end makes the citizenry as a whole worse off. Economic development is actually hindered due to a protectionist import substitution policy aimed at promoting economic development.

Export promotion policies for economic development also demonstrate the inefficiency of government intervention and the limitations of government at promoting economic development. Export promotion policies are those which aim to make certain domestic industries more competitive in global markets, typically through the use of targeted government subsidies.

In the 1990s, Malaysia was experiencing rapid economic growth with the stated goal of achieving developed nation status in a very short period of time. *Vision 2020* was an ambitious government plan to make Malaysia the economic powerhouse of Southeast Asia by the year 2020. In order to achieve this goal, the Malaysian government believed it needed a large export sector, able to compete with its more developed Asian rivals, Singapore, South Korea, Taiwan and Japan.

The Malaysian government believed the nation needed a large exporting automobile sector in order to be a developed country. The government aimed to develop the country's automobile sector through an aggressive set of protectionist policies focusing on both import substitution and export promotion. Substantial tariffs were levied on imported

While import substitution and export promotion policies are generally thought of as inefficient, they have been used successfully by developing nations in the past. Japan, South Korea, Taiwan and Malaysia are all middle- or high-income Asian countries which, during their own periods of development, employed strategic protectionism to achieve national economic objectives that increased overall income and improved the welfare of the nation's people.

Protons on the assembly line in a Malaysian factory.

automobiles, sometimes as high as 100%, while the state-owned automobile company, Proton, received billions of Malaysian ringgit over two decades.

Malaysia car manufacturer Proton has announced an ambitious new five-year plan to massively boost exports in a drive to halt falling profits due to declining domestic sales.

The government-backed company hopes new models such as the Suprema S will prove popular with foreign consumers as it earmarks half of total volume for overseas markets. Proton currently sells to over 20 countries but its sales lag at below 5%.

Proton's share of the Malaysian car market dipped below 25% in 2013 as sales stalled, while exports have also slumped in recent years, with only 6,000 units sold in 2013 compared to over 16,000 in 2011.

The Malaysian government, however, remains committed to bucking this downward trend.

"Although running at a loss, Proton will continue to export its models to create future markets," trade minister Mustapa said.

Adapted from various new sources, November 2013 to April 2014

Figure 29.3 is a subsidy diagram (Chapter 5) which we can use to analyse the effects on efficiency and total welfare in the Malaysian car market, and to evaluate the use of export-promotion as a strategy for economic development.

Figure 29.3

Malaysia's automobile market with and without subsidies: subsidies for domestic producers impose a greater cost on society than the benefit created.

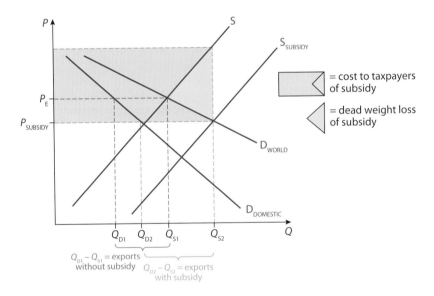

It is clear from Figure 29.3 that the government's effort to promote the export of cars is causing over-allocation of resources to the automobile market.

World demand for Malaysian cars is greater and more elastic than domestic demand, since the world market includes consumers in China and India who have a wide selection of cars produced all over the world to choose from. Without subsidies, Malaysia would export $Q_{S1}-Q_{D1}$ cars to the rest of the world at price P_E.

However, under the government's policy of export promotion, Proton receives billions in subsidies, increasing the supply of Malaysian cars to $S_{SUBSIDY}$ and reducing the price to $P_{SUBSIDY}$. The greater supply and lower price of Malaysian cars leads to an increase in the quantity of Protons demanded by Malaysian consumers to Q_{D2} and the quantity demanded by the rest of the world to $Q_{S2}-Q_{D2}$. Malaysian car exports increase, Proton's revenues rise and employment in the Malaysian car industry grows.

But has the government's policy of export promotion led to an overall improvement in the welfare of the Malaysian people and therefore promoted economic development? To answer this question, we must look at the overall cost to society of increased car exports and compare it to the benefit the policy added.

The cost to the Malaysian taxpayer to achieve the government's objective of greater car exports and thus a stronger industrial sector is clearly greater than the added benefit to the Malaysian economy. The cost of the subsidy (the distance between the S curve and the $S_{SUBSIDY}$ curve multiplied by the quantity of cars produced Q_{S2}) represents Malaysian households' tax money that was given to Proton to increase the supply of cars in Malaysia.

The benefit to Proton of increased sales and lower costs plus the benefit to Malaysian households of lower prices for Protons is represented by the green area in Figure 29.3. But the total cost is shown by the green and pink areas. The deadweight loss represents the difference between the amount of Malaysians' taxes spent on the subsidy and the added benefit the subsidy provided to the Malaysian people. Therefore, we can conclude that the total cost exceeded the total benefit in monetary terms.

But what was the opportunity cost of the government's decision to promote the export of automobiles? This requires us to consider what could have been provided to Malaysian households with the tax money that went to the car industry. Economic development requires improvements in human health, education and access to life-improving goods and services; the cheaper cars resulting from the subsidy clearly fall short of these goals.

Malaysian households would have benefited more in economic development terms if their tax money had gone towards improving the Malaysian education system, building more hospitals, training more doctors or providing access to sanitation to the poorer parts of Malaysia. These are just a few examples of what government could have done to bring more economic development to Malaysia than its decision to promote the export of Protons to China and India.

Market-oriented policies: many strengths

Whenever a government influences the allocation of resources through the use of price controls, tariffs or subsidies in a market for consumer goods the outcome is always suboptimal for society as a whole. In the case of protective tariffs, consumers of the protected good are harmed at the expense of increased domestic production. In the case of a subsidy aimed at promoting exports and growing a nation's manufacturing sector, the nation's people are also negatively affected because taxpayer money going to support the government's favoured industry could instead have been used to provide public goods such as education and healthcare, both of which are under-supplied by the free market.

In all the examples we have looked at here, government intervention resulted in less allocatively efficient levels of output than would have been achieved by the free market. Free trade, on both the micro-level and the international level, eliminates inefficiency as competition forces producers to allocate resources efficiently towards the products most in demand domestically and internationally.

Should we, therefore, conclude that the government should always keep its hands out of the market and let private firms pursue their profits and thereby allow the needs of society to be met entirely by the free market? Unfortunately, as we now know, free markets often fail to achieve allocative efficiency on their own. We must, therefore, examine the situations in which government intervention may actually improve on the allocation of resources achieved under the market system.

Weaknesses of market-oriented policies

To understand when it is beneficial for the government to intervene in the markets for certain goods and services, we must look more closely at a market for a merit good such as healthcare. In Ukraine, we saw that under a system of government price controls, there was an under-allocation of resources towards healthcare. Privatizing and deregulating the healthcare market, it was assumed, would eliminate the inefficiency of government provision because the higher prices attracted more healthcare providers and reduced the quantity demanded until it equalled the quantity supplied.

But such a simple analysis overlooks that fact that healthcare is a merit good – one that creates positive benefits for society when consumed by private individuals. A healthier population makes for a more productive workforce and thus generates greater income and employment opportunities for the nation as a whole. Healthier parents are better able to raise children and provide them with a good education, which further improves the level of well-being of the population over time.

When left to the free market, however, a merit good such as healthcare in the Ukraine will be under-provided, much as it was under government provision, since the market fails to account for the external benefits of such a good when determining the price of healthcare and the quantity provided by private clinics. But the government also failed to account for these external benefits, and its meagre attempt to make healthcare available to the people through the use of price controls failed as well.

Figure 29.4 looks at the healthcare market in Ukraine under the assumption that the consumption of healthcare creates external social benefits that are not realized by the individual healthcare consumer.

Figure 29.4
The market for healthcare in the Ukraine: Because of the positive spillover benefits of healthcare, resources are under-allocated towards the good by the free market.

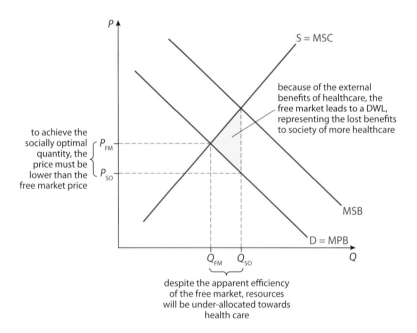

to achieve the socially optimal quantity, the price must be lower than the free market price

because of the external benefits of healthcare, the free market leads to a DWL, representing the lost benefits to society of more healthcare

despite the apparent efficiency of the free market, resources will be under-allocated towards health care

The analysis in Figure 29.4 seems to contradict our original conclusion that the free market results in greater efficiency than the government's attempt to provide healthcare. This would only be true if the marginal private and marginal social benefits of healthcare were the same – in other words, if there were not external benefits. But as with many goods whose consumption improves human welfare and thus promotes economic development (such as education and infrastructure), the external benefits of healthcare are only realized when the government intervenes in the free market to make it more affordable to consumers.

A price ceiling, however, is not enough, since it only intensifies the shortage that already exists by distorting the price signal to healthcare providers. What is needed in markets like that for healthcare in Ukraine is a complementary approach to promoting economic development: an approach involving both the efficiency of the price mechanism achieved through the free market and the watchful eye of a government aware that certain goods may be under- or over-produced without an active role for government.

29.3 Complementary approach: a market with government intervention

Learning outcomes
- Explain the importance of good governance in the development process.
- Discuss the view that economic development may best be achieved through a complementary approach, involving a balance of market-oriented policies and government intervention.

To promote economic development in a manner that respects the efficiency of free markets while simultaneously recognizing that in certain cases they fail to achieve the socially optimal level of output of human welfare-improving goods, governments should adopt a complementary approach to economic development.

The market mechanism involving demand, supply, and equilibrium price should be allowed to function, even in markets for goods such as healthcare. Government provision in Ukraine proved even more inefficient than when the market underwent privatization. But even the free market failed to achieve the socially optimal level of healthcare provision. Therefore, the role for government should be to assist the free market in achieving a socially optimal price and quantity for the good, through a combination of subsidies and price controls that respects supply and demand, rather than undermining it.

For example, a government policy that reduces the costs of private providers to the level at which they can provide healthcare at price P_{SO}, or a policy that increases the marginal private benefit to the level at which it intersects supply at Q_{SO} would correct the market failure using market mechanisms. Subsidies for healthcare providers or consumers would help reduce the dead weight loss in the Ukrainian healthcare market (Figure 29.5, overleaf).

This analysis points to the fact that government intervention in the market is not always inefficient. If done responsibly, recognizing the efficiency of the price mechanism and the interaction of supply and demand that underlies the functioning of a free market, government intervention can improve efficiency and welfare and thus lead a nation towards economic development.

But when undertaken irresponsibly, without paying attention to the importance of prices in determining the quantity of a merit good demanded and supplied, government provision of the goods and services important to development in a poor country can lead to an even greater misallocation of resources than under the free market.

 The role of government in the market for healthcare is one of the most controversial issues facing some nations today. The US has higher healthcare costs than anywhere in the world, and nearly 1 in 6 Americans live without any health insurance coverage whatsoever. Even there, however, many oppose any government involvement in the market for healthcare, claiming that any intervention distorts incentives and reduces the quality and variety of services available.

Figure 29.5
Market for healthcare in Ukraine. A government subsidy increases the supply of healthcare and reduces the externality resulting from its under-provision.

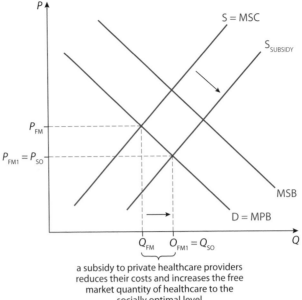

a subsidy to private healthcare providers reduces their costs and increases the free market quantity of healthcare to the socially optimal level

Where government intervention is needed

When we recognize that certain goods simply cannot be provided at the level that is socially optimal by the free market, the need for a complementary approach to provision in which the government improves on the efficiency of the free market becomes clear. Market failures tend to exist in markets for goods without the provision of which a nation's economy is unlikely to achieve the objective of economic development. Besides healthcare, other merit or public goods without which a country would not achieve the objective of economic development include education, social safety nets and infrastructure.

Education

Without government support, education would be under-provided in many developing countries.

Education is a good with countless external benefits of consumption. When a nation educates its children, the nation's human capital is improved and they are more likely to grow up to become productive members of the workforce, contributing to the production of goods and services that benefit fellow citizens, and paying taxes that can in turn be used to provide more education to future generations.

Without government intervention in the market for education, resources would be vastly under-allocated towards schooling for the nation's youth. Most developed nations provide education as a benefit for all citizens to at least the secondary level.

Less developed countries (LDCs) can learn from the model that has successfully contributed to the economic growth and high living standards of Western European, East Asian and North American countries. A private education system has many benefits for a nation, but without the support of government, only the most privileged and richest members of society are able to improve their human capital to a level that leads to a higher standard of living. A publicly supported education system reduces inequalities in society and improves the well-being of all members of a nation.

Social safety nets

Social insurance is another area of the economy that would be inefficient without the presence of government. Social insurance includes those systems that transfer the risks of an individual becoming unemployed, disabled, or retiring without an income to society as whole. While markets for private insurance exist in most countries, the countries with the highest level of human development tend to have strong and stable systems of social safety nets.

A report prepared by the International Labour Organization in 2000 found that 75% of the 150 million people unemployed around the world lack any unemployment insurance protection. The report showed that the countries providing the most generous support to unemployed workers were Austria, Belgium, Denmark, Finland, France, Germany, Iceland, Luxembourg, Netherlands, Norway, Portugal, Spain, Sweden and Switzerland. These 14 countries provide unemployed workers with benefits averaging 60% of their last salary for more than one year following the loss of their job. This benefit allows workers and their families to maintain a suitable standard of living during their period of economic hardship while they have time to look for a new job.

Countries with medium-level systems included Australia, Canada, Ireland, Japan, New Zealand, the UK and the US. In these countries, fewer of the unemployed workers received benefits and the compensation provided was lower, averaging around 40% of salaries earned before being laid off.

In the countless countries not mentioned above, there are literally tens of millions of unemployed workers receiving no benefits whatsoever from the private or public sectors during their times of hardship. The total lack of any social insurance is an obstacle to economic development in a low-income country. The families of unemployed workers in a country without a social safety net suffer:

- children are more likely to go undernourished
- children are more likely to supplement the family income by working rather than going to school
- healthcare is out of reach for a family with no income.

This all tends to perpetuate poverty in LDCs and reduce the likelihood that human welfare will improve over time.

The International Labour Organization argues that social insurance could and should be used in LDCs to further promote development through government-guaranteed employment of those who lose their private-sector jobs. Such individuals could be put to work building projects that improve the nation's infrastructure, education and health systems. The costs of such programmes are far outweighed by the benefits:

Workers who are fortunate enough to be covered by unemployment benefits are mainly concentrated in industrialized countries. But for those who work in the rural or urban informal sectors in developing countries – including 750 to 900 million underemployed workers – hardly any unemployment protection exists at all.

... these groups of workers should be assisted through employment in labour-intensive infrastructure programmes – feeder roads, land reclamation, minor dams, wells and irrigation systems, drainage and sewerage, schools and health centres. Employment provided under such programmes can be organized so that workers can obtain an employment guarantee for a number of days per year ...

... social protection, even in the supposedly expensive forms to be found in most advanced countries, is affordable in the long term. It is affordable because it is essential for people, but

It may be the case that a very strong social safety net can reduce growth and development in a nation. In 2010, Denmark was forced to examine closely its system of benefits, which provides unemployed workers with up to 90% of their salary for up to four years following the termination of their employment. Such a generous benefit can create a disincentive to seek employment, which may slow the growth of a nation and reduce its competitiveness in the global economy.

To access Worksheet 29.2 on poverty alleviation, please visit www.pearsonbacconline.com and follow the onscreen instructions.

also because it is productive in the longer term. Societies which do not pay enough attention to security, especially the security of their weaker members, eventually suffer a destructive backlash.

International Labour Organization, 2000

Infrastructure

A nation's infrastructure includes more than its roads and railways, although such capital goods are also necessary for a nation to achieve economic development. Infrastructure includes telecommunications, transportation, and utilities such as sewage, running water, electricity and gas. When private firms are given control of a nation's infrastructure, the results can be detrimental to the nation's economic development and growth. Without government provision or subsidies to providers, such capital goods as electricity and water systems will be under-provided.

Certain types of infrastructure such as roads and railways, it could be argued, are in fact public goods. Very few private firms would find it economically feasible to construct highways across a poor, developing country, for instance. It would simply be too difficult to recover the costs of production through charging for the use of such a system of roads. Therefore, without government provision, such major capital investments would simply not take place.

Lack of infrastructure, such as roads, poses an obstacle to economic development.

On the other hand, certain types of infrastructure can be provided by the free market in a cost-effective, profitable manner. The market for cellular phone service, for instance, has been a hotly contested one in many developing countries. For instance, in the Democratic Republic of the Congo (DRC), a nation with one of the lowest Human Development Index rankings in the world, there were 5.9 million cellular service subscribers in 2007, representing 9.3% of the population. Of the four providers of cellular service in the DRC, only one (in fact the one with the fewest subscribers, Congo Chine Telecoms) was partially controlled by the DRC government. The three leading providers of this service, so vital to the nation's human development and economic vitality, were private multinational corporations.

CASE STUDY

Cellphones and electricity in Africa

Cellphones have led to huge improvements in the well-being of the rural poor all over the developing world. Cellphones provide poor Africans with:

the means to communicate, apply for a job, get product prices and availability, and access health information.

In some African countries the ability to transfer money has transformed lives. This is especially widespread in Kenya where over 60% of mobile owners use their device for money transfers. At a click, millions of Kenyans are bypassing the lengthy bank queues and making small transfers that would otherwise take hours to complete.

Adapted from www.pewglobal.org and the *Economist*, 10 June 2010

The ability of remote, poor communities to engage in economic activities across vast distances quickly and efficiently with a cellphone increases the incomes of the poor and empowers them as contributors to the economic well-being of the country.

While mobile phones and the network infrastructure needed to operate them have been sufficiently provided by the private sector, a much more basic, related good needed to operate the phones has been grossly under-provided. Many of the remote, rural communities that benefit most from cell phones are so far off the grid that they do not have even have access to the electricity needed to charge mobile phones. Ironically, the phones, provided efficiently by the free market, depend on electricity, which has historically been provided by government, but is currently under-provided in much of Africa. This poses problems for the rural poor in Africa:

Africa's 48 sub-Saharan countries have the same electricity generation capacity as Spain. But dilapidated infrastructure means as much as a quarter of even this capacity is unavailable, meaning power shortages and regular interruptions to supply. These outages are particularly acute away from the main urban centres.

Adapted from the African Development Bank Group, 2008

The inefficiency of having to spend hours or even days just to charge a cell phone poses an obstacle to the extent to which this technology can improve the well-being of those with access to it. The cost to the government of a rural African country of providing the most remote communities with electricity on the national grid is prohibitive. But it turns out the free market has recently come up with a possible solution to a problem traditionally solved by government infrastructure spending. Entrepreneurs have begun to provide the rural poor in Africa and other parts of the world with low-priced solar electricity units.

Manufactured cheaply in China, a solar electricity unit can be purchased in Africa for as little as $80. One unit provides enough electricity for a household to power several electric lights, a few common appliances and to charge electronics such as cellphones. The benefits enjoyed by households that have acquired such systems quickly outweigh the costs. The renewable electricity provided by solar panels has reduced poor families' dependence on increasingly scarce heating and cooking fuel, improved health and provided children with the ability to study under electric lights after dark, thereby improving the quality of education received.

Solar electricity and other such sustainable, low-cost methods of providing the rural poor with access to those goods traditionally provided by big, government infrastructure projects are still emerging. Markets have popped up around the developing world, but there is no reliable supply of resources to meet the ever-increasing demand of the hundreds of millions of poor households still living without electricity in the world.

CASE STUDY

Water in Bolivia

While the private sector is able to provide certain goods that improve human welfare efficiently and in a far more effective manner than the government, other merit goods are better left to the government to provide. If the very survival of the population depends on access to a particular good, such as safe drinking water, then handing the provision of such a good over to the free market could have dramatically harmful effects on human welfare. Privatizing goods traditionally provided by the public sector does not always lead to the most efficient or equitable outcome.

Protesters in Cochabamba, Bolivia demand lower rates for their water.

In order to receive an infrastructure development loan from the World Bank, the government of Bolivia agreed to privatize its water systems in late 1999. The rights to the water supply in Bolivia's third largest city Cochabamba were sold to the American corporation Bechtel. In January 2000 Bechtel suddenly restricted the supply of water to the city and increased the usage rates charged to residents. The impact this privatization had on the well-being of Bolivians is illustrated in the following extract from a report on what became known as the Cochabamba Water Revolt:

The World Bank had coerced Bolivia to privatize its water, as a condition of further aid. The new company, controlled by Bechtel, the California engineering giant, announced its arrival with a huge overnight increase in local water bills. Water rates leapt by an average of more than 50%, and in some cases much higher. Bechtel and its Spanish co-investor, Abengoa, priced water beyond what many families could afford.

The people demanded that the rate hikes be permanently reversed. The Bolivian government refused. Then the people demanded that the company's contract be cancelled. The government sent out police and soldiers to take control of the city and declared a state martial law.

In the face of beatings, of leaders being taken from their houses in the middle of the night, of a seventeen-year-old boy being shot and killed by the army – in the face of it all, the people did not back down. In April of 2000, Bechtel's company was forced to leave and the people won back control of their water.

WW4 Report, 2006

A profit-seeking firm like Bechtel would probably have done a very good job providing water to Bolivians in the most efficient manner possible. It would be in the company's interest, after all, to eliminate any inefficiencies in the provision of water to reduce its costs and thereby maximize its profits.

Since large utilities such as water markets are typically natural monopolies, the market for water in Bolivia can be illustrated by Figure 29.6. Demand intersects the average total cost of water provision while it is still downward sloping, indicating a scenario in which it makes sense for only one firm to provide the good to the market.

Figure 29.6
The water market in Cochabamba, Bolivia: A natural monopoly under-provides important goods, thus government regulation is required.

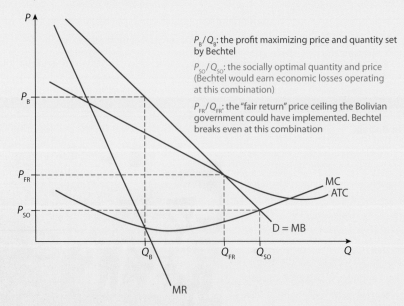

P_B/Q_B: the profit maximizing price and quantity set by Bechtel

P_{SO}/Q_{SO}: the socially optimal quantity and price (Bechtel would earn economic losses operating at this combination)

P_{FR}/Q_{FR}: the "fair return" price ceiling the Bolivian government could have implemented. Bechtel breaks even at this combination

The high price that Bechtel tried to charge Bolivians for water probably reflected their actual private cost and the private benefits of water provision. The problem was, once privatized, Bechtel became a purely monopolistic seller of a merit good. To an economics student, this can be understood as a double market failure. Monopolists always prefer to restrict output and charge a price higher than that which would be charged in a competitive market. Granted, the Bolivian government was itself a monopolist before selling the rights to Bechtel but, unlike Bechtel, the government at least placed the interests of Bolivians above those of private shareholders and charged a lower price closer to the socially optimal level.

If Bechtel or any private company is left to provide a merit good like water (needed for sanitation, health and human welfare), strict government regulation is needed. The Bolivian government could have implemented a 'fair return price' for water in Cochabamba. This would have established a price ceiling equal to Bechtel's average total cost and allowed the firm to break even while providing water at a quantity and a price closer to the socially optimal level than the purely monopolistic quantity and price.

Such a regulated private monopoly would still have the incentive to reduce its costs and provide water as efficiently as possible, since the profit motive still underlies the business of providing water to the people of Cochabamba. This is in contrast to a state-run monopoly providing water, in which the possibilities for corruption and waste are likely to undermine the economic objective of efficiency achieved in a competitive market.

The outrage at the government's privatization of Cochabamba's water supply reflects the double market failure under Bechtel's control, since in addition to the output being restricted in Bechtel's pursuit of profits, water is a merit good for which the marginal social benefit of consumption exceeds the marginal private benefit. To the citizens of Cochabamba, the unregulated privatization of the water supply presented an unacceptable step backwards away from economic development, demonstrating yet another situation in which the unfettered free market was unable to meet the development needs of a poor country's people.

In the end, the Bolivian government recognized the benefits of cheap water and took over its provision once more, making sure that it remained affordable and available in quantities more socially optimal than the price and quantity provided under Bechtel.

Efficiency is of greater importance than equality. Therefore, even in markets for goods such as water, infrastructure and healthcare, private firms can do a better job of providing goods to a nation's people than the government could possibly hope to achieve. What evidence would be required to prove this statement correct?

Striking a balance between government and market

Economics is sometimes called the dismal science. Originally this term referred to the fact that it dealt with the inevitable problem of scarcity faced by all human societies and the myriad conflicts that arise over the use and allocation of scarce resources. Throughout your course, you have explored situations both micro and macro, local, national and international, ranging from the efficiency of the elusive perfectly competitive market to the inefficiency of protectionism.

You have learned about the theories, models, graphs and other tools economists employ to try and deal with scarcity efficiently and equitably, with the well-being of society as the ultimate goal. The competing objectives of efficiency and equity may not always coincide but the outcome achieved by Adam Smith's invisible hand of the market can be improved on. This can be brought about through the implementation of re-allocative policies such as taxes, subsidies and price controls by an economically informed and well-intentioned government.

In this regard, economics is hardly dismal at all. It offers a toolkit for making the world a better place. By quantifying the seemingly unquantifiable, such as the 'marginal social benefit of healthcare', economists are able to present realistic, achievable solutions to challenges affecting human welfare. The central problem of scarcity is dismal indeed but economics is ultimately a hopeful science offering market-based solutions to humankind's biggest problems.

Yet the dismal truth is that good economics is not always valued by those in power who have the greatest ability to affect the allocation of the scarce resources we depend on. In reality, good politics does not always equal good economics – a claim for which the poor decisions of politicians and leaders in countless countries, day after day, present ample evidence.

Whether it's a decision to cut taxes and increase government spending in a country on the brink of a debt crisis, or the decision to control the price of fuel in a city where long queues are already forming at petrol stations, or to privatize a water system in a region where poor people already find it difficult to maintain health, government decisions often reflect poor economic judgement.

And the free market itself rarely has all the answers to the problem of scarcity. The idea that markets promote efficiency and therefore achieve a socially desirable outcome places great faith in the assumption that competition exists to ensure that efficiency emerges. In reality, a market system driven by individuals pursuing self-interest does not always lead to the most desirable outcomes for society as a whole, despite Adam Smith's belief in the allocative power of the invisible hand.

Markets tend to experience cyclical fluctuations over time, evolving from periods of innovation and competition to periods of increasing concentration of market power among a few large firms, stagnation and inefficiency. The creative destruction of the free market and innovation in welfare-improving technologies sometimes requires the guiding hand and watchful oversight of a socially conscious government.

The markets for goods which are vitally important to a nation's economic development (healthcare, education, infrastructure, social insurance) and certain welfare-improving technologies must all be examined carefully with the tools and models of economics so as to decide the extent to which the free market is capable of promoting human welfare and development. The motives of the free-market pursuit of profits lay the foundation for efficiency, while the interests of society must be attended to by watchful government regulators.

Development will not be achieved in any country left entirely to the free market; nor will total government control promote improvements in human welfare. The complementary approach of a market-oriented development strategy combined with careful government oversight is the most likely to promote economic development while creating an atmosphere for sustainable economic growth.

Dismal science or a sliver of hope?

Despite all your reading, the conversations in class, the diagrams you've drawn in your notes, and the pages and pages of analysis and evaluation you have laboured over, the theories and tools of economics only get us so far in our understanding of how to make the world a better place. The welfare of human societies ultimately rests in the establishment and maintenance of economic systems that take into account the costs and benefits of human behaviour on society, on the environment including other species with which we share the planet, and on generations of humans both present and in the future.

Sustainability is defined as 'the ability to endure'. The ability of any economic system to endure depends on the extent to which it accounts for the future in its decisions as to how resources should be allocated in the present. Unfortunately, neither the free market nor government intervention has done a sufficiently good job of accounting for future generations in the economic interactions and policies of the 20th and 21st centuries.

In the film *The Corporation*, the economic and environmental challenges the world has faced since the industrial revolution are compared to the challenges faced by the earliest pioneers of human flight. Those intrepid adventurers would push their crafts off high cliffs, flap their mechanical wings, and think they were flying because the ground was still so very far away. But eventually they would crash to the ground, as they were doomed to from the moment they pushed off the cliff's edge. Without knowledge of flight mechanics and good design, their craft could never fly. Like the early flight pioneers, society has yet to develop an economic system that allows all human civilization to soar.

Again, like those pursuing the dream of flight, Western civilization pushed itself off a massive cliff into the unknown when it embarked on the path towards industrialization that began in England over 300 years ago. Today, LDCs around the world are travelling the same path. The ground in this analogy is the point at which the world's resources are depleted to a degree beyond which they are unable to be replenished. It once seemed so far away that very few people ever considered the likelihood of civilization crashing into it. But today it is growing ever closer.

The economic systems we have developed, some argue, are as unsuited to making our civilization sustainable as mechanical wings were to flight. Eventually, if we do not realize that the ground is growing nearer, human civilization will crash. The question is, at what point will our civilization realize it is on a path towards total resource depletion and self-destruction? At what point will we begin implementing much-needed reforms to the economic systems that govern our allocation of resources?

Sustainability in economics

When will good economics – an economics that accounts for all stakeholders, those living now and those of future generations – prevail in our exchanges with one another on a local, national and international level? Only when an economic system prevails that accounts for the true costs and benefits of our behaviour to society, to the environment, and to future generations will human civilization enter an era in which it can truly fly and thereby avoid the fate of the flight pioneers and their flapping mechanical wings.

Economics is only dismal insofar as it is ignored by policymakers and politicians. Economics offers a design for a civilization that could truly fly, allowing humans to survive indefinitely in a world in which resources are allocated efficiently between the competing wants and needs of society in a sustainable manner.

The ability of humankind to endure, to sustain itself into the future, is increasingly questionable. A greater understanding of economic theories, and an implementation of the models and tools economics teaches us can help ensure that future generations will live in a world in which human societies everywhere can live happy, healthy lives, free of fear and conflict. In this regard, economics is the most hopeful science of all.

To learn more about sustainability, visit www.pearsonhotlinks.com, enter the title or ISBN of this book and select weblink 29.3.

What criteria can economists use to decide on the balance between markets and intervention? Is development economics dependent on external normative notions such as what constitutes a good or fulfilled life?

To access Quiz 29, an interactive, multiple-choice quiz on this chapter, please visit www.pearsonbacconline.com and follow the onscreen instructions.

PRACTICE QUESTIONS

1

EU's secret plans target markets in developing countries

i The European Union (EU) has drawn up secret plans aimed at opening the service sector markets in the world's poorest countries in return for reducing its farm subsidies.

ii The demands made by the European Union would allow European firms to charge for providing water to some of the 1.2 billion people living on less than a dollar a day. Water has always been regarded as a free good, but this idea is changing. It would give large gains to European banks, telecommunication businesses and business service firms.

iii The European Union is under intense pressure to remove **export subsidies** that depress global food prices and impoverish farmers in the developing world. Reform of Europe's agricultural policy is a top demand from developing countries.

iv Supporters for less developed countries argue that the EU proposals are not pro-development, nor do they encourage sustainable development. Many poor countries would be tied to unfair and irreversible commitments if they agree to European requests. If these economic decisions go wrong developing countries would be affected for generations to come. A more effective approach would be to encourage **export-led growth**.

v While the privatization of water would result in a higher price for the consumer, the advantage is that the water will be clean and filtered, enabling the population to be healthier and live longer, acting as a positive externality. Against this is the cost of implementing the privatization, possible social and economic upheaval, and institutional and political factors that would act as significant barriers to economic growth and development.

vi Among its demands, the EU wants Bolivia to let in more overseas water companies despite a recent case where a multinational company increased water prices by 200% in one city. The EU is also looking at Panama with similar plans where water privatization plans were scrapped in 1998 after strikes and demonstrations.

adapted from Gary Duncan, *The Times*, 26 June 2003

a Define the following terms indicated in bold in the text:

   i export subsidies (paragraph iii)   (2 marks) [AO1]

   ii export-led growth (paragraph iv).   (2 marks) [AO1]

b Using an appropriate diagram, explain the effect of EU export subsidies on the market for agricultural commodities.   (4 marks) [AO2], [AO4]

c Using an appropriate diagram, explain why consumers will buy nearly constant quantities of water despite higher prices.   (4 marks) [AO4]

d Using information from the text and your knowledge of economics, evaluate the degree to which market failure and externality theory applies to the market for water and whether it should be produced privately or publicly.   (8 marks) [AO3]

2 **Drug companies bring hope for HIV/AIDS sufferers**

i 'Industry puts the average cost of developing a new drug at around US$800 million. Were it not for a patent system that rewards companies for risking millions on research, anti-HIV/AIDS drugs would not exist', said **World Trade Organization's** (WTO) director general, Mike Moore.

ii 95% of individuals worldwide who are infected with the HIV/AIDS virus live in poor countries, with almost no access to life-prolonging treatment because of barriers such as the high cost of drugs.

iii One possible solution to the high cost of drugs seems to be through differential pricing schemes [a form of **price discrimination**] that charge poor countries less than the rich. This form of legal price discrimination is already used for vaccines and contraceptives, with prices as low as 1% of those in the USA. Major pharmaceutical companies have recently promised to cut prices to cost levels in Africa. The aim is to cut the price for HIV/AIDS therapy by as much as 95%.

iv The big multinational corporations (MNCs) do not, in theory, object to differential pricing for their pharmaceutical products. But they still want patent protection and guarantees to prevent the re-entry of low-priced drugs back to developed countries.

v Delay can spell disaster when dealing with HIV/AIDS. A recent forecast sees South Africa heading for an economic collapse within three generations, as the number of wage-earners is dramatically reduced and parents die before they can teach their children the basics of life. Thankfully, the chance of this problem happening was reduced last week, when the South African government announced a serious, well-funded and long-term plan for treating its sick citizens with HIV/AIDS drugs. If the plan is competently implemented, HIV-positive parents should survive long enough to put their children through school, and South Africa should pull back from the brink of catastrophe.

adapted from *Science*, 17 March 2000, Vol 287, Issue 5460;
Lancet, 7 April 2001, Vol 357, Issue 9262;
The Economist, 29 November 2003, p11;
Time, 2 February 2004, Vol 163, Issue 5, p44

a Define the following terms indicated in bold in the text:

   i   World Trade Organization (paragraph i)   (2 marks) [AO1]

   ii price discrimination (paragraph iii).   (2 marks) [AO1]

b Using a production possibility curve or aggregate demand and supply diagram, explain the impact on economic growth of a lack of progress in dealing with the HIV/AIDS problems described above for a country like South Africa. (4 marks) [AO2], [AO4]

c Using an appropriate diagram, explain why HIV/AIDS drugs might be under provided by the free market.   (4 marks) [AO2], [AO4]

d Using information from the text and your knowledge of economics, examine the benefits and costs to various stakeholders of government intervention in the market for HIV/AIDS drugs in less developed countries.   (8 marks) [AO3]

Chapter 30

Theory of knowledge and economics

Why study economics?

The obvious answer: The vast majority of economics students are fulfilling a prerequisite for their business school degrees! Economics has long been an essential field for understanding the economy, which has been synonymous with the interests of business.

Indeed, quite a lot of IB economics has these aspects of economics as its focus: how individuals and firms operate on the micro-level (section 1 of your syllabus), how entire economic systems function (section 2), and how a dynamic global economy works (section 3).

However, as the number of economists grows, and their interests diverge from the traditional subject matter, economics has branched out into a variety of fields. Nobel Prize winners for economics have increasingly done work that applies in areas like psychology, criminology and social behaviour. At the same time, many economists now focus on very specific questions of human behaviour and use sophisticated mathematical analysis to test out their hypotheses. So right now, with pretty much the entire world as the subject of some economics question or other, seems to be a good time to be an economist.

Still, economics as a science has often been the subject of ridicule. One reason is the tendency among economists to give highly qualified advice rather than direct counsel. Harry Truman, US President at the end of World War II, once said that he'd like to meet a one-handed economist because he kept hearing 'on the one hand' this and 'on the other hand' that. George Bernard Shaw famously claimed that if 'all the economists in the world were laid end-to-end, they would never reach a conclusion.'

Economics, news and business – is this what make the world go round?

Economy is the art of making the most of life.

George Bernard Shaw

Economists do seem to find convoluted ways to state obvious truths. Another joke asks what it takes to be a good economist. The answer – an unshakable grasp of the obvious. Think of the law of demand or the puffily named 'law of diminishing marginal utility' and this criticism tends to resonate.

More serious, however, are the obvious failures of economists to adequately foretell the greater economic crises of the modern era: most notably the Great Depression of the 1930s and the crisis of 2008. Ronald Reagan famously uttered the sceptical view, when he said that an economist 'sees something working in practice and asks if it will work in theory.' Economists flock to the scenes of economic disasters like the ones mentioned above, dissect and analyse the various parts, and seemingly the whole thing can happen again without anyone seeing it coming.

Economics and ways of knowing

The TOK diagram alongside shows a knower developing knowledge through four methods of input: emotion, reason, sense perception, and language. To what extent does economics derive its knowledge claims from these inputs?

Emotion

At first glance, it would appear that economists view humans as super-rational creatures (*Homo economicus*, page 644), who are constantly weighing costs and benefits to find optimal outcomes. However, economists do assume that emotion plays a part in the human decision-making process, so emotion is brought into the analysis. Perhaps the more appropriate question is: Do economists develop their theories from emotional beginnings, and justify them through through reason and language?

Questions of wealth and income redistribution, to take the most potent example, often draw forth some of the most heated and unscientific language. One could argue that major schools of macroeconomic thought such as Keynesianism and the neo-classical approach, spring from emotional or philosophical debates about who gets what.

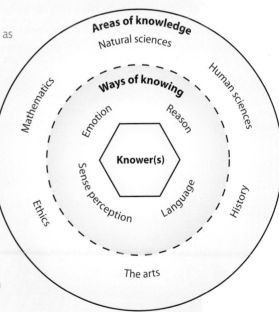

Areas of knowledge.

Reason

Economics presents many reasonable propositions, and extends them into bodies of theory. Principles such as the law of demand, for example, appear to be articles of sheer common sense that are dressed up in fine language. From its origins in political philosophy, economics has always had a basis in logic and reason.

Language

As a body of knowledge, economics has been populated with its own lexicon, one that aims to describe aspects of behaviour more accurately. Like any area of knowledge, one's understanding of the subject is coloured by the language employed. Terms like 'full employment' and 'tax burden' tell us perhaps more than is intended about how economics views each situation: one is desirable (full), while the other is not (burden.)

The language of economics sometimes requires economics students to re-define terms that are used outside the field in a different way. 'Efficiency' means something entirely different in economics from what its meaning might be in a different context. Similarly, long after a recession has ended – according to the economic definition – citizens of a nation still feel they are in the midst of a catastrophic economic meltdown. When the US and European economies returned to growth in late 2009, unemployment remained in double digits; when the recession was technically over, those most adversely affected continued to feel the pinch – and do so to the present day.

Economists must be aware of the limitations of their own terminology when they want to encapsulate and convey the importance of economics (i.e. understanding the world in a productive and useful way) to the non-economics community.

Sense perception

Economics, like other social sciences, seeks to understand what motivates human behaviour and interactions, focusing on the commercial realm.

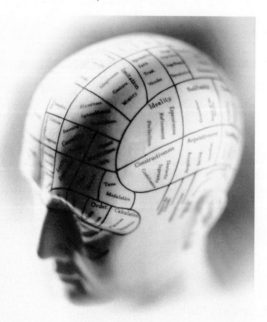

Economists observe and experience life like anyone else. These perceptions can sometimes be at odds with the reality described by economic data. For example, the recent recession of 2008–10 has been described as among the worst in decades for many countries. During this period, social scientists were careful to track the happiness levels in countries experiencing high unemployment. They found that while people were growing poorer, they were not significantly less happy; in fact, they were happier than they had been at periods of stronger economic performance. This research gained credibility because it confirmed what people were perceiving generally, through life experience.

The degree to which economics can 'know' something is true depends on many assumptions that may not be agreed on by the non-economics community. The economic doctrine that higher incomes lead to more happiness has been challenged by other social sciences and from within the economics field. Perceptions of happiness itself may vary and are not always rooted in material consumption. Such challenges to the ways of defining human welfare from beyond the economics field certainly strengthen the pursuit of knowledge in economics, while posing a challenge to economists who must continuously strengthen their methods of analysis of human behaviour to adapt to humans' ever-evolving understanding of what it means to be happy.

Economics as a science

The problems economists face in conveying their views and theories to the general public are understandable. Economics is a social science and has as its subject one of the most complex of problems: understanding and predicting human behaviour.

The physical sciences benefit from the ability to control one group and experiment on another. By isolating causal factors and testing them, physical sciences have built up, bit by bit, a huge reservoir of specific knowledge about the world. Such precise experimentation is impossible in economics. Humans, unlike bacteria or chemicals, rarely interact with their surroundings in a consistent or predictable manner.

Testing hypotheses in economics

Testing the effectiveness of a reduced interest rate, for example, can provide some predictive information about future decisions. The law of investment demand predicts that lower interest rates will lead to more investment, greater output and employment and economic growth. But this economic law is influenced by many other factors, most obviously the circumstances surrounding a change in interest rates.

Rarely will the economic conditions at the time of an interest rate cut be identical to those at the time of a previous cut in rates; for this reason, the precise outcome of a cut in rates is impossible to predict. Consumer confidence, consumption levels, debt levels, unemployment rates, and other variables might be controlled for (and economists can attempt to statistically control for these factors) but when it comes down to it, there is no way to know precisely how an economy will respond to a cut in interest rates.

A national economy is dynamic and, as Heraclitus said, no one steps into the same river twice. The passage of time guarantees that random variables will alter the validity of predictions based on current experience. That said, the evolution of statistical econometric analysis (econometrics), which uses forms of regression analysis, has made some of this kind of predictability much more possible than before.

The other side of the argument goes that the management of macroeconomics, a particularly challenging environment for prediction, has advanced significantly. Witness the massive increases in global income and wealth over the last 50 years. As our discussion of economic development made clear, more people live free from hunger and absolute poverty today than ever before, even if this progress is incomplete. Consider the scope of economic expansion over the past 60 years.

It has been argued that the extraordinary expansion of financial markets has actually created a new set of problems, problems that financial economists and regulators are still grappling with. The assumption among economists that markets are efficient led to economic policies that deregulated financial markets in the belief that private investors and borrowers, interacting in a purely free market, would allocate financial capital efficiently. Instead, deregulation led financial markets into dangerous new territory, culminating in an economic crisis.

Perhaps the closest that economics comes to the more specific and verifiable findings of hard science is in the realm of behavioural economics. In particular, economists in recent years have taken 'found evidence' where large amounts of data are collected, and used statistical regression analysis to assess the relative weight given to causal factors. This type of economics may test whether a certain policy is effective (e.g. awarding tax credits rather than spending vouchers).

Economists studying crime have shown that longer prison terms tend to reduce crime, along with a few lesser causal factors. As a form of positive economics, these types of finding have real benefits. They should lead to better public policy and a better society. But at the same time, some have lamented the lack of ideological fire in this research. Determining the effectiveness of birth control policies in rural areas might be interesting, some say, but it is the big themes of normative economics, the battle over government's role in our lives, for example, that should still require our greatest attention.

Cost–benefit analysis in economics

How much is a human life worth? Our instinct is to answer that all human life is priceless, and this is indeed a noble instinct. However, it quickly melts away in the heat of everyday choices. The cost of a life is, in our modern age, a figure that is coldly calculated for the purposes of risk determination by all kinds of business. The life-value of a person is calculated by their life expectancy and earning power, and includes other variables.

Automobile companies, for example, build cars that are reasonably safe, but not perfectly safe in all situations. The cost of a perfectly safe car would be enormous, so companies must have some way of knowing how much they stand to lose if their cars fail and they are sued for the losses incurred by their customers. This is where a car manufacturer can do a cost–benefit analysis on the safety of their cars.

For automobile companies, the question of how safe is too safe is a matter of financial reality. To extend the example even further, in the US there are approximately 35 000 fatal car crashes each year. This number could surely be reduced if speeds were reduced or if driving at night were abolished or any of many other restrictions on behaviour were introduced.

Society weighs the costs and benefits of lifestyle choices like this all the time, whether it is acknowledged or not. Economics can, at the very least, inform these debates over conduct and policy.

Discussion questions

- Is it wrong to put a financial value on human life?
- From which way of knowing did you answer the first question: reason, emotion, logic, or language/symbols?
- Are there any areas where the estimation of a cost of a life is inappropriate, or does not apply?
- Does the value of a human life change, depending on the situation or the society?

Utilitarianism in economics

Among the more direct attempts to apply economic principles to moral thinking was that of John Stuart Mill, who in the 19th century formalized a philosophy of human interaction rooted in the very economic concept of the pursuit of utility. Working as a philosopher and social theorist, Mill developed a moral viewpoint called utilitarianism.

Mill wrote that a fundamental method of evaluating moral questions was based on the greatest happiness principle. In other words, the course of action that is most morally justified is that which creates the greatest happiness for the most people.

John Stuart Mill (1806–73); British philosopher and civil servant ▶

While the utilitarian philosophy has been eclipsed by many others since Mill's time, the pursuit of utility (happiness) has become embedded in modern economic theories which hold that individuals in a market economy (whether consumers or producers) will engage in activities that help them achieve the greatest level of utility (profit).

Mill was influenced by thinkers like Jeremy Bentham (1748–1832, an English philosopher and political radical) and his own father, the Scottish philosopher and economist James Mill). His moral philosophy was applied controversially. On questions of women's rights and slavery, for instance, Mill's thinking was viewed by many as radically progressive and even dangerous.

Discussion questions

- Utilitarianism holds that the individual pursuit of utility is itself morally good. How is this similar to and different from the economic view of utility and profit maximization?
- Does modern economic theory attach moral values to the behaviours of individual consumers and producers in a market economy?
- To what extent does the pursuit of individual happiness contribute to or interfere with the achievement of social harmony?

A market for everything

Since the 1950s, and especially in the era of advanced statistical analysis, economists have moved from the traditional into more complicated areas of human interaction. Among the more popular areas of study has been the market for marriage. This area can be provocative, as it touches on sensitive cultural issues.

In countries such as India and China, where there are growing shortages of women available for marriage, economists are examining how cultural practices such as the paying of a dowry (from the family of a bride to that of a groom) or a bride price (from the family of the groom to that of the bride) affect the supply of and demand for suitable mates between the sexes.

Other economists have studied the economics of polygamy (men keeping several wives) as well as the influence of greater education and job opportunities for women on their own marriage possibilities. Furthermore, some game theory economists have attempted to calculate why women live in greater numbers in big cities, and have concluded that opportunities for marriage play a role.

▲ Crown Princess Victoria of Sweden marries Daniel Westling, June 2010.

Discussion questions

- Are you participating, perhaps without consciously knowing it, in a 'marriage market'? Explain.
- To what degree is it appropriate to view such culturally specific issues such as marriage through the lens of market theory?
- Is this market perspective itself a cultural bias, or a scientific approach?

The bonds of matrimony are like any other bond – they mature slowly.

Peter de Vries

Homo economicus

In the course of studying economics, you may have noted that economists make several assumptions in order to more easily observe and draw conclusions from the interactions of individuals in a market economy. *Ceteris paribus*, for instance, which economists regularly employ when examining the relationship between two variables, holds all else equal apart from the two variables being studied. Of course, in the real world, all else is rarely equal, a fact economists may ignore so as to get a clearer understanding of a particular economic relationship. The tendency of economics to make broad, unrealistic assumptions about the world may challenge the efficacy of economics as an area of study.

Among the most egregious of the assumptions made by economists is that all human beings are perfectly rational individuals who always act in their own self-interest. The assumption of rational behaviour underlies nearly every significant economic theory, from the idea that there is a socially optimal level of output (where MSB = MSC, Chapter 6) to the concept of profit maximization, which assumes all rational firms produce at the quantity at which their marginal revenue equals the marginal cost.

For markets to be efficient, the individuals interacting in them must be perfectly rational and in pursuit of their own self-interested aims: a system in which no one is in control but through which the chaotic behaviours of rational individuals aggregate to result in an optimal provision of the goods and services required for society to survive and prosper.

Rationality and the pursuit of self-interest form the foundation of Adam Smith's market theories: that in pursuit of their own selfish objectives, individuals will inadvertently provide society with the goods which make everyone around them better off.

Irrational behaviour is like a virus in an otherwise healthy economy; as soon as individuals (firms, consumers, governments) pursue objectives that are not in the best interest of themselves or which are clearly irrational, inefficiencies begin to emerge and resources are misallocated. The very foundation of the market system is thus undermined.

Philosophical foundations of *Homo economicus*

Homo economicus, economic man, is the concept underlying many economic theories. It holds that all humans are purely self-interested, rational actors who have the ability to make judgements that fulfil their subjectively defined ends. In modern economic theory, the end humans seek is generally accepted to be increasing monetary well-being and material wealth.

The philosophical foundation of *Homo economicus* comes from a long tradition of Western philosophy, long before Adam Smith formalized the theories of market economics. Hints of the economic man can be found in the words of Aristotle in the 4th century BC:

... how immeasurably greater is the pleasure, when a man feels a thing to be his own; for surely the love of self is a feeling implanted by nature and not given in vain, although selfishness is rightly censured; this, however, is not the mere love of self, but the love of self in excess, like the miser's love of money; for all, or almost all, men love money and other such objects in a measure.

Aristotle *Politics*, Book I, c. 340 BC

The observation of humans' tendency to rationally pursue their own self-interest was continued by Adam Smith:

By the 19th century, the assumption of rationality in humans fully encapsulated the pursuit of self-interest, as articulated by John Stuart Mill:

What is now commonly understood by the term 'economics' is not the science of speculative politics, but a branch of that science. It does not treat of the whole of man's nature as modified by the social state, nor of the whole conduct of man in society. It is concerned with him solely as a being who desires to possess wealth, and who is capable of judging of the comparative efficacy of means for obtaining that end.

John Stuart Mill, Of the definition of political economy; and on the method of investigation proper to it, in *Essays on Some Unsettled Questions of Political Economy*, 1844

Whoever offers to another a bargain of any kind, proposes to do this. Give me that which I want, and you shall have this which you want, is the meaning of every such offer: and it is in this manner that we obtain from one another the far greater part of those good offices which we stand in need of. It is not from the benevolence of the butcher, the brewer or the baker that we expect our dinner, but from their regard to their own interest.

Adam Smith, *The Wealth of Nations*, 1776

The formulation of the concept of the economic man was solidified in the 20th century by several Austrian economists, notably Friedrich von Hayek, who in 1933, in the midst of the Great Depression, argued that markets guided by rational, self-interested individuals could achieve a more efficient allocation of resources than could be achieved under any attempt at state intervention.

The assumption of *Homo economicus* has formed the basis for many economic theories which have influenced economic policies that governments and central banks have put in action and which, in turn, have had significant impacts on the global economy over the last 100 years. But is economic man a reasonable assumption? Are humans always the coldly calculating, rational and well-informed pursuers of self-interest that economists assume they are? Recent observations of the failures of several markets in the global economy indicate that perhaps economists' most fundamental assumption, that of *Homo economicus*, is drastically flawed.

We will benefit our fellow man most if we are guided solely by the striving for gain. For this purpose we have to return to an automatic system which brings this about, a self-directing automatic system which alone can restore liberty and prosperity.

Friedrich von Hayek, interview with Bernard Levin, 31 May 1980

Homo economicus and the financial crisis of 2008

Homo economicus is always rational and, therefore, only pursues activities in markets that enable maximization of well-being and self-interest. It would be irrational, therefore, for an industry to create a product to sell to its customers at a price that did not reflect the true value. When buyers eventually realize that the product is worth far less than they paid for it, demand will fall and the product's manufacturers experience economic losses, and eventually shut down. It would be unthinkable for a rational businessman to attempt to build a successful firm on a total lie.

It may, therefore, come as a surprise that in recent years, it has been realized that one of the most important industries in the global economy was built on just such a lie: the financial services industry.

Between 2000 and 2007 investment banks, most notably on Wall Street, created bonds made up of home mortgages that were given to low-income American home buyers. Many of these loans were made to individuals who had very little hope of ever paying them back, information which the banks issuing the mortgages knew very well. But because the investment banks could package thousands of these mortgages into 'asset-backed securities' and sell them on to large investment funds, such as the national pension fund of European countries and the public employees' pension funds of many US states, the investment banks did not worry too much about the true underlying value of the mortgages making up the bonds they assembled and sold.

In early 2007, the borrowers on whose monthly payments the value of the bonds was based began defaulting on their mortgages; the banks began foreclosing on their homes. Predictably, the value of the bonds began to plummet. Pension funds around the world lost trillions of dollars and the Wall Street banks that created the bonds were stuck holding hundreds of billions of dollars' worth of worthless products that nobody wanted to buy. Ultimately, in the US, the investment banks had to be bailed out by the government to the tune of nearly $1 trillion of US taxpayer money.

The problem for the financial industry during the years leading up to the global financial crisis in 2008 was that it assumed that all stakeholders involved were acting rationally and in their own self-interest. The households looking to buy new homes, the banks making the loans, the investment banks packaging the loans into securities, the investors buying the securities and even the government regulators who neglected to look closely at the bonds' underlying assets – all were assumed to be acting rationally. In other words, it was assumed that the market was efficient because of the freedom of the individuals engaged in the buying and selling going on. As it turned out, however, the whole financial system was acting irrationally, buying and selling assets without considering what was in either their own or society's best interests.

Several economic theories based on the assumption of *Homo economicus* can be pointed to for fuelling the bubble in the US housing market that provided fuel for the fire of the financial crisis. Here are two of them.

- **Rational expectations theory (RET)**. Rooted in the concept of *Homo economicus*, this economic theory assumes that humans acting generally in their own self-interest make rational decisions based on the best available information. Therefore, it assumes that people (and, hence, markets) do not make systematic errors when predicting the future.

- **Efficient markets hypothesis (EMH)**. Rooted in rational expectations theory, EMH says that prices in markets, particularly financial markets, represent the best possible estimates of the risks attached to the ownership of various assets (e.g. stocks, shares, bonds). Asset bubbles are, therefore, impossible, since the term 'bubble' implies an irrational and unsustainable increase in the value of an asset which will ultimately burst. Markets are therefore self-correcting, and the most effective tool for assuring economic stability is free markets, rather than government regulation or oversight.

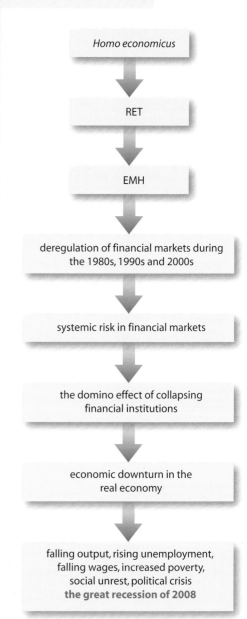

Connecting the dots: from *Homo economicus* to the financial crisis of 2008.

The general acceptance of theories rooted in the concept of *Homo economicus* led to the de-regulation of financial markets, which allowed money and resources to go whichever way the market (rational or not) determined. The series of events can be roughly summarized as follows.

- During the last decade, the market decided that more and more money and resources should go towards particular assets, specifically the US mortgage market (the market for new homes in the US).
- As money flooded the US home mortgage market, it became cheaper and easier for Americans to get loans to build a home. *Great! Right?!* Well, only until it came time to pay back those loans.
- Trillions of dollars worldwide became tangled up in the US mortgage market, representing households' savings from around the globe.
- When Americans suddenly found their loans coming due, they found it hard to repay them due to adjustable interest rates and falling home prices (supply had grown more rapidly than demand).
- Many Americans and Europeans began defaulting on their mortgages, meaning all that money that had been lent to home buyers literally disappeared.
- Banks and financial markets faced a liquidity crisis, meaning they had no money.
- Lending stopped to households, firms, and other banks, meaning spending on goods and services decreased, meaning jobs were lost and economies entered recession.

▲ There are many species of early hominid such as (from left) *Homo erectus, Homo rudolfensis, Homo ergaster* and *Homo habilis*.

How could any of this have happened if the concept of *Homo economicus* and the economic theories based on it are correct? Are humans always rational, calculating, perfectly informed, self-interested beings acting purely in their own self-interest?

The concept of *Homo economicus* has formed the basis for economic theories for centuries and for major macroeconomic policies over the last 30 years. Policies of market liberalization (freeing the market from the guiding, regulatory hands of government) led to great prosperity, but to greater risk and volatility as irrational exuberance over asset prices led to inefficient market outcomes, bubbles, and financial shocks plunging the real economies of the world into recession.

A more complete understanding of humans is needed as the human science of economics enters a new era. The human being as a cold, rational, calculating creature interested in only its own gain is an over-simplification, and forming theories and policies on such an assumption is dangerous. The future of economics must incorporate a more complete and complex understanding of human behaviour if the economic crises of the last few years are to be avoided down the road.

Discussion questions

- Do people (or organizations) consistently and accurately weigh the costs and benefits of their actions?
- How has the formulation of economic theories rooted in the assumption of humans as rational, self-interested actors led to inefficient outcomes in financial markets?
- To what degree is the view of *Homo economicus* a logically consistent one?
- To what extent to you agree with the concept of humans as rational actors?

Theory of knowledge is all about discussion, debate and collaboration. Consider working with your classmates to brainstorm and formulate ideas for the TOK essay.

TOK essay and economics

As much as any other course of study you undertake as part of the IB Diploma, economics offers you a perspective on the world that is rich with models built on assumptions about human beings and their interactions in the commercial realm. As seekers of knowledge capable of reflecting on how you know, you must become a critical, objective analyst of the ways of knowing offered by the field of economics.

You will be asked to grapple with assigned TOK questions in a theory of knowledge essa These questions can be addressed using your economics knowledge and perspectives.

Here are three TOK essay questions each with a brief analysis of how you might tackle the question. They are just a sample of the type of reflection you may undertake on the economic way of knowing in a Theory of knowledge essay.

To what extent are the various areas of knowledge defined by their methodologies rather th their content?

from *Theory of Knowledge Prescribed Titles, November 2010, May 20*
© International Baccalaureate Organization 20

You could argue that the methodologies are more critical than the knowledge itself. The natural sciences attempt to establish verifiable truth, or scientific laws. They do so using methods that allow for peer review and must be open to the possibility that the theory wrong. Do such methodologies apply, for example, to the arts? The arts would appear t be more defined by a search for self-knowledge and introspection.

For economics, the scientific approach drives the way in which many economists try to establish knowledge. Cost–benefit analysis takes quantification to its rationalist extreme. The risk that practitioners of any science (physical or social) run is that their methodologies may get in the way of their content.

A model is a simplified representation of some aspect of the world. In what ways may mode help or hinder the search for knowledge?

from *Theory of Knowledge Prescribed Titles, November 2010, May 20*
© International Baccalaureate Organization 20

Economists cannot run controlled experiments on humans, at least not very easily. For this reason, models are especially important for isolating variables and controlling for them. In this way economists can answer questions about the degree of effect of one variable (e.g. income growth) on another (e.g. consumer debt levels).

In practice, many of the graphical models depicted in this course (such as the money market) are simplifications of principles demonstrated with advanced mathematical models and statistical research. At the same time, a model is only as good as the variables it studies. Not all aspects of an issue are included in the model and, as a result, the predictive power of the model is diminished.

In the years leading up to the great recession of 2008–10 economists failed, by and large, to incorporate inflated property markets and their link to the derivatives being sold to investors by Wall Street banks. So when the housing bubble burst, economists had no idea of the extent to which the real economy would be affected. Economic models were flawed and, as a result, very few economists, policymakers, or government regulators attempted to slow the rise in home prices and the growth in derivative markets that fuelled the financial bubble of the early 2000s.

Compare and contrast our approach to knowledge about the past with our approach to knowledge about the future.

from *Theory of Knowledge Prescribed Titles, November 2008, May 2009*
© International Baccalaureate Organization 2009

Does understanding what has happened in the past prepare us for what will happen in the future? This question has great relevance to the study of economics. It is a well-established fact, for instance, that for the seven decades following the Great Depression in the US in the 1930s, home prices never fell significantly nationwide. Many economic models were built on the assumption that home prices could not fall nationwide, and that homes were therefore a safe, stable foundation on which to build a market for financial derivatives.

When economic policies are based on information economists have observed about the past, we run the risk of thinking we are able to predict the future. The economic turmoil of the last several years shows the extent to which economists are unable to predict the future. Understanding the limitations of our own knowledge would make us more humble and aware of the shortcomings of our economic theories and models.

Discussion question

An economist is someone who sees something that works in practice and wonders if it would work in theory. (Ronald Reagan, US President)

- Interpret the joke. What does the speaker seem to be saying?
- Try to reformulate the sentence to be more accurate.
- Assess the degree to which you think this is true.

31 ADVICE AND SKILLS FOR THE INTERNAL ASSESSMENT PORTFOLIO

The Internal Assessment (IA) is a very important part of the IB Economics course. It is required of all students, and many find the task enjoyable and challenging. You are free to pursue personal interests within the boundaries of the course syllabus, and because each commentary is researched outside class time, more deliberation and planning are possible. This means that the IA process provides an opportunity to enrich your knowledge.

Your portfolio

Building your IA portfolio requires you to engage with real news items and to apply the economic concepts you have learned. You will write economics commentaries on three news items.

To find appropriate articles, you will need to read a variety of news items from various sources, and judge their relevance to economics topics. For each of the three articles that you choose, you will identify in your commentary the concepts and aspects of economic theory that are at work in the article. The commentary will analyse the event, apply the concepts in detail, and explain how the theory works. This requires good evaluation skills and good command of diagrammatic skills.

Besides this review of the internal assessment writing process, you are advised to read and review the IA section of the IB *Economics Guide*, which should be available from your teacher.

Details and requirements

The IA portfolio is worth 20% of your final mark whether you are an SL or HL student.

The IA writing process should be integrated into your class and use 20 hours of class time; it is not an independent project. The IA process is summarized as follows.

- You will produce *three commentaries* from a variety of news sources.
- Each commentary will focus on a *different part of the IB syllabus*.
- Articles must come from print news media that include *newspapers, magazines, and internet news sites*. Television or radio broadcasts are not suitable. Blogs or other opinion or editorial articles are strongly discouraged.
- Articles should be *brief*. Long articles are very much discouraged. If you do select a longer article, the commentary should focus on a short section indicated by highlighting in the portfolio.
- Articles should be in the *same language as the commentary*. If different from the commentary language, a translation and the original article should be attached to the commentary.
- Articles must be *current*, published within one year of the writing of the commentary.
- Articles must be from a *variety of news sources*, a different one for each commentary. You may not choose two articles from, say, *The Financial Times*.
- You are encouraged to choose articles from a *mixture of local, national and international news sources*.

- Commentaries should be no longer than 750 words (the IB *Guide* has a list of items that are *not* included in the word count).
- Commentaries should be *your own work*, not done in collaboration. Try not to use the same articles as anyone else. Your teacher may not assign articles for you to use.

Rubric requirements

Your commentaries will be marked by your teacher against a set of rubric requirements defined by the International Baccalaureate Organization (IBO). Table 31.1 shows you the five criteria that apply to each of your three commentaries, the skill area each criterion tests, the marks available for each criterion, and the highest descriptor for each criterion.

TABLE 31.1 INTERNAL ASSESSMENT RUBRIC REQUIREMENTS			
Criterion	**Skill area**	**Marks**	**Top level descriptor**
A	Diagrams	3	Relevant, accurate and correctly labelled diagrams are included, with a full explanation.
B	Terminology	2	Terminology relevant to the article is used appropriately throughout the commentary.
C	Application	2	Relevant economic concepts and/or theories are applied to the article appropriately throughout the commentary.
D	Analysis	3	There is effective economic analysis relating to the article.
E	Evaluation	4	Judgements are made that are supported by effective and balanced reasoning.
	Total:	14	

In addition to the criteria in Table 31.1, criterion F (worth 3 marks) is applied to the entire portfolio. Criterion F assesses your complete portfolio on the following five points:

- each commentary is not more than 750 words
- each article relates to a different section of the syllabus
- each article comes from a different and appropriate source
- each article is no more than a year old
- the portfolio has a summary coversheet, each commentary has a coversheet, and each article is included in the portfolio.

So, each commentary is marked on criteria A–E and is given a score out of 14 marks. The entire portfolio is then given a score out of 3 marks for criterion F. Thus, the full portfolio is scored out of 45 marks (3 commentaries × 14 marks + 3 marks).

Teacher assistance

You can expect guidance from your teacher at critical stages of the IA process. Your teacher can advise you about article selection, but the final selection is up to you. You should ask questions about the appropriate application of theory to the issues in your articles. And your teacher will comment on the initial draft of each commentary – these comments won't be extensive and won't rewrite any portion of the draft. But the advice should guide you to the goal of achieving a clear and insightful piece of work.

It is also up to your teacher to ensure that your work is authentically produced and that the process adheres to IB norms of academic honesty.

How to write a high-quality commentary

Step 1 Find an appropriate article

Finding a suitable article may seem like the easiest part of the process, but you'll be surprised at just how difficult it can be.

Information balance

For IA purposes, a useful news article should say neither too little nor too much. The article should describe an issue sufficiently to allow room for analysis and discussion of an event's implication. But the article should not provide that analysis itself – that's your job. This is why general news articles from daily newspapers (or news agency services) can work out very well, while articles from more economics-focused publications (e.g. *The Economist*) or scholarly journals are often less suitable.

Conduct an effective search

The internet has made it possible to search far and wide with incredible speed, but the volume of information can be overwhelming and stall your progress at a very early stage. With this in mind, search for a good article with care.

Where to look

Search engines are well suited for finding articles on specific topics. So rather than going to the home page of your favourite search engine, begin your search in the news section. For example, don't start at www.google.com, begin at http://news.google.com, which ensures that your search results will already be filtered from news websites.

But beware – not all news sites are appropriate for an IB commentary. Additional filtering is needed to select an appropriate article. Some search engines specialize in economics news. Surfwax Economics News (http://news.surfwax.com/economics/) is popular and helpfully categorizes current articles by economics topics from a typical course syllabus.

Use keywords

Often, a web search for a topic from the syllabus that is commonly referred to in the media (e.g. demand, taxes, trade) will turn up thousands of hits. Searching for an article by browsing the results of such a broad search will prove tedious and you are not likely to find more than a very few appropriate articles. However, terms such as 'income elasticity of demand' or 'aggregate supply' are not typically used by the news media, even though the concepts themselves are regularly the subject of reports in the business and economic news. To find articles relating to such concepts, you must be critical and flexible in your browsing of search results; move on quickly if your first search attempts fail to yield any promising results. When this happens, try out associated terms that are linked with the overall concept. And ask your teacher if there is another way of phrasing your searches to get better results for the topic you are interested in.

Collaborate with classmates

The chances are good that in the search process your classmates will come across and pass on several articles that could be appropriate for a commentary. Collaborate on the search process, share with each other articles you have found, even begin class discussions over the articles found. Online social bookmarking tools such as Diigo and Stumbleupon can be excellent for collaborative discussions on potential articles.

Use databases

Most schools' libraries or media centres now subscribe to news-only web databases that purify an article search by allowing only results from established news organizations, such as EBSCO Host or JStore. Try speaking with your school librarian or media centre specialist to learn more about how to conduct effective searches using these subscription-based services. More and more online news sources are putting their best articles behind a pay shield (or pay wall) that requires users to pay a subscription to read entire articles. Don't let this frustrate you; the chances are, your school already pays to get you access to such articles. Take advantage of the resources available in your library or media centre to ensure your search is as efficient and successful as possible.

Manage resources

Online social bookmarking services (e.g. Diigo, Delicious or Stumbleupon) can significantly improve your learning experience. Social bookmarking enables you to organize, store, manage and search for online resources in a shared environment. You may create a group with some classmates, or you may encourage your teacher to set up a social bookmarking group that allows the class to add articles with highlights and comments to a shared webpage where you can browse one another's found articles and choose the ones you think are best for your commentaries.

Once articles are bookmarked on the class page, then you, your fellow students and your teacher can engage in forum-style discussions beneath the link to each article, building understanding and generating ideas for application, analysis and evaluation to be done in the commentary. It may be that your teacher already requires your class to find and bookmark articles relating to topics on which the class is engaged. But whether or not this is the case, you will all benefit from seeking out several articles before deciding on the ones for your commentaries. Organizing and cataloguing the vast quantities of news and information encountered in the article search process is important to success in the IA, and social bookmarking sites provide a simple and engaging way to manage information.

Using social bookmarking to have a conversation around the news.

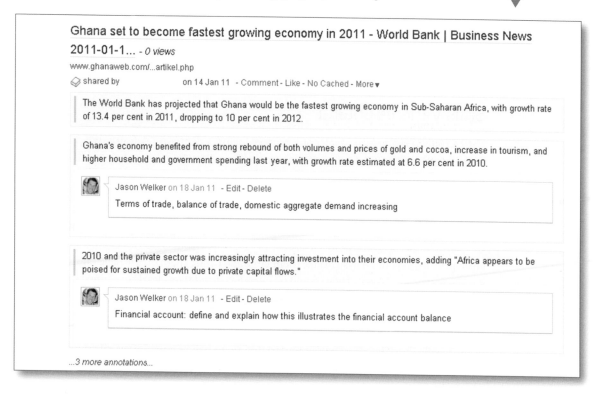

...3 more annotations...

Vet your article

So how can you tell if your article is a worthy candidate for a commentary? The more articles you have read and collected, the more skilled a reader you will have become. Of the many articles you have saved, you are likely to have decided early on that a few have the right balance of not-too-little / not-too-much information and analysis. Once you have narrowed down your options to two or three for each choice, vet the articles for final selection. You might take the following steps.

- **Brainstorm**. Pull out a copy of the current IB *Guide* and turn to the list of topics. Or you might want to use the vocabulary list for the relevant unit. As you read the article, check off the relevant terms.
- **Identify concepts**. As you read each article, make notes in the margin (or on the website if you're using a social bookmarking tool) of the concepts from the syllabus to which the article relates. This will help you decide if the article is appropriate for the section of the syllabus you wish to address.
- **Identify diagrams**. Typically, a high-quality commentary includes at least two (but perhaps more) diagrams. Diagrammed items should be part of the core topics of the commentary, not merely introductory material or of tangential interest. As you read the article, take note of potential diagrams you can include in your analysis. If you are not able to identify at least two relevant economics graphs to include in your commentary, the article may not be of use to you.
- **Outline**. Create a simple outline of each section of your commentary. List what each paragraph will do, including the types of explanation and areas of evaluation. Remember that diagrams must be clearly explained in the body of the text, and not merely attached to the commentary.

After completing these steps for each potential article, it should be clear which of your options is best suited to be the subject of an economics commentary that meets the requirements of the IA.

Step 2 Write the draft

Now that you've outlined the key ideas for each paragraph, you can begin to link together the main ideas in complete prose for your draft commentary.

Satisfy the IA criteria

The IA criteria require that each commentary includes diagrams, definitions, application, analysis and evaluation of relevant economic theory. The discussions below will help you more clearly understand these requirements.

Diagrams

Diagrams must be highly relevant and fully explained in the text. Explanations must make specific reference to graph points (e.g. quantity increases from Q_1 to Q_2.) Graphs should be given priority in your analysis. Make them large and centre them on the page rather than writing text around them. They should be introduced and then clearly explained in the text.

Define and explain

Definitions of *relevant* terms should be included in each commentary. Not all economics terms need to be defined – it would be easy to use up half of your 750 word count defining terms. Only define terms that are integral to the analysis and evaluation you plan to conduct in each commentary. Once a term has been defined, *do not define it again* in a later commentary in the same portfolio. Explanations require students to describe clearly, make intelligible and give reasons for an economic concept or idea. It is your job to bring clarification to the economic concepts relating to your article.

Analysis

Analysis requires you to closely examine the events laid out in your article through the tools and theories learned in your economics course. A clear analysis will identify the interrelationships that exist between different variables presented in the article. Economic diagrams should form the heart of your analysis; anything that *can* be explained graphically *should* be explained graphically. With only 750 words, you must be concise and selective in how you analyse the news on which your commentary is based.

Evaluation

This is your opportunity to discuss the implications of an economic issue, and to assess the effects the issue (or policies to redress it) have on stakeholders. Evaluation is the skill many students find most difficult. It requires you to *make a judgement based on evidence*. In your commentaries, you can evaluate throughout the text, or you may choose to conduct the evaluation at the end of each commentary. To make an evaluation, you can:

* weigh the advantages and disadvantages of certain economic policies
* discuss the effects on different stakeholders in society of a particular policy or event
* compare the short-run and long-run effects of an economic policy or a decision by a particular stakeholder in a market
* critically assess the validity of the economic theories you have applied to your commentary.

Critically assessing the validity of economic theories is the thing many students find the most difficult to do successfully. Evaluation requires that you *call into question the economic theories themselves*. For instance, economic theory would argue that a progressive tax system is inefficient due to its negative effect on the incentive to work and earn higher incomes. However, you may argue that in reality there is little evidence that progressive taxes reduce efficiency, and that the resulting reduction in income inequality more than justifies the use of such a system in a modern, developed economy. You have now called into question the economic view that taxes are inefficient.

Evaluation is the most heavily weighted criterion of the five applied to each commentary (it is given 4 out of the 14 available marks), so it is of the utmost importance that you pay particular attention to the quality and depth of evaluation in your portfolio. There are more ideas on how to evaluate effectively in Chapter 32.

Avoid unnecessary summary

The article supplies the fundamental information for your commentary. The grader will read the article you have supplied, so it is not necessary for you to recap that information. To do so would waste precious words that count against your limit. You *should* reference the article by including direct quotes and references to data.

Reference the article

In each commentary, it is critical that you cite the article in several instances. Each commentary should include references to the specific circumstances as laid out in the article. Include at least one direct quote, and whenever there are numbers such as prices, quantities or percentage changes mentioned in the article, attempt to incorporate them into the analysis in your commentary.

For example, if there is mention of airline ticket prices changing for a particular route, then in your graph of the airline market, include the original price and the new price on the y-axis, rather than a generic P_1 and P_2. This demonstrates that you are a skilled economist able to apply economic theory to real examples. If you use direct quotes, they should be a brief phrase, or a word or two. Avoid long quotes that will count against your word limit.

Step 3 Revision

When you have finished your draft, you submit it to your teacher. He or she will provide you with brief but useful advice about how to improve each commentary. Take this help seriously – it can significantly improve your marks. You should continue to seek advice, but remember your teacher can give only limited help from now on. Be sure to observe all the appropriate language conventions and you can ask a classmate to help copy-edit your work. Finally, use the following checklist of requirements before handing in your final draft.

- Do I have a cover sheet with all the appropriate information? What is my word count?
- Are all the relevant economic terms defined? Have I used economic terminology throughout my commentary, not just occasionally?
- Have I included at least two diagrams? Have I explained them carefully in the body of the text?
- Have I referenced the article to a degree that makes it clear my commentary is on the particular circumstances described in the article, not just a repetition of what I read in my textbook or took notes on in class?
- Is my analysis complete? Have I considered the major areas of theory that are related to this topic?
- Have I evaluated effectively? Have I considered the short run and the long run, the implications for various stakeholders, and the validity of the economic theory itself?

The IA portfolio is intended to be an enriching learning experience. Feel free to seek out articles in areas of your own interest. You are far more likely to bring insight to issues in which you are already interested. However, another equally important motivation is to encourage you to broaden your knowledge of economics and the world by reading widely.

Exemplar economics commentary

Below is a sample commentary to guide you in your portfolio creation. It is divided into the three parts that must be included for each of the three commentaries in your portfolio: the cover page, the extract and the commentary.

Part 1 The cover page

Each of the three cover pages in your final portfolio should be formatted identically. Use the same font and font size consistently throughout your portfolio. Include the essential information below on every cover page. The word count covers all words except those used in diagrams (for example, labels or brief descriptions you include on or immediately next to a graph). Your extract must be cited using appropriate MLA or APA citation techniques. These are easily found on the web. Be sure to include the date the commentary was submitted on each commentary's cover page.

Course: IB Economics HL

Commentary number: I

School name: _____

Candidate name: _____

Candidate number: _____

Date commentary was written: 23 October 2010

Section of the syllabus to which the commentary relates:
Section 2 – Microeconomics

Word Count: 750

Source of extract: Matthew Allen, 11 November 2008, Where is Switzerland's cheapest place to live?
Swissinfo.com at: www.swissinfo.ch/eng/search/Result.html?siteSe
ct=882&ty=st&sid=9958380h

Part 2 The extract

Each extract for which you've written a commentary must be included in its entirety. When copying articles from the internet into your commentary, be sure to select only the text of the article. If possible select 'print article' on the website, then copy the text on the print screen. This helps you avoid copying advertisements, pictures, text boxes or other features from the web page that are not related to your article.

It is very important that you highlight the relevant text in your article. This is particularly important for longer articles, as the reader does not want to have to read lots of irrelevant text in preparation for each commentary. Use a standard font and font size for each of your three extracts. Uniformity is a simple way to make your portfolio more attractive and easier to read.

Where is Switzerland's cheapest place to live?

While Switzerland may not be known for its low cost of living, a study has revealed the most affordable place to set up home.

Inhabitants of canton Appenzell Inner Rhodes, in the east of Switzerland, enjoy the highest levels of disposable income after tax and fixed costs such as housing. Geneva residents have less in their pockets than people in any other region.

The survey by Credit Suisse bank measured a range of expenses – from tax rates, social security payments, health insurance premiums to utility bills, house prices and rent – in a number of communities.

It found the cost of living varied enormously depending on where people chose to reside. For example, individual cantons and local municipalities have the power to set their own tax rates.

The rural canton of Appenzell Inner Rhodes again topped the list as the most inexpensive place to live, as it did in 2006 when the survey was last conducted.

The report said the canton was 'the most appealing place to live for the broad middle classes' thanks to relatively low real estate prices, moderate tax rates and the country's lowest health insurance premiums.

Geneva remained rooted to the bottom of the league table of the 26 cantons owing to high property prices and hefty taxes. Obwalden climbed five places to second after slashing taxes in 2007 while Zug fell 13 places to 18 as the cost of real estate rocketed in the past two years.

Foreign influence

The influx of wealthy foreigners has made a big impact on the demographic landscape in Switzerland. The Credit Suisse report said that more people have left Zug since 2006 than any other canton, but the population has been rising thanks to its international attraction.

'Zug has the lowest tax rate in Switzerland so it is more attractive for foreigners with high incomes despite the high cost of property,' Credit Suisse senior economist Thomas Rühl told swissinfo.

'In tourist regions, such as Valais and Graubünden, there are a lot of second homes owned by both foreigners and Swiss, and that has substantially increased real estate prices and rents.'

The disparity in the amount of disposable income enjoyed by inhabitants has increased the trend of people moving cantons for financial reasons.

The survey gave a hypothetical example of a family with two children and a gross income of SFr156 600 ($133 000) living in a bought home.

Commuter trend
The report calculates that such a family would have SFr36 800 left over from taxes and fixed costs in the community of Bettingen, canton Basel City, but SFr61 400 if it lived in Rheinfelden, canton Aargau.

Thomas Rühl told swissinfo that economic necessities had led to an increase in the number of people moving address and opting to commute into work.

'There has been a dramatic increase in the number of commuters in the last 40 years,' he said.

'This is a direct result of the financial optimisation of households. If someone can increase their disposable income they will move to another canton and this has happened on a very large scale.'

Part 3 The commentary

Each commentary should begin on a new page within the portfolio. Try to begin your commentary with a *brief* (i.e. one or two sentences) identification of the theories that your commentary discusses. Next, include a very brief summary of the extract. In this exemplar, the extract is summarized in a single sentence (Recently, Credit Suisse conducted ...).

Graphs are of the utmost importance in an IB economics commentary. Give each diagram a clear introduction, followed by a detailed explanation of what it shows. Check that each graph includes all necessary labels. Try to include colour in your diagrams and whenever there is a shift of a curve, include an arrow indicating the direction of the shift.

Define terms where necessary, but be sure not to use up your whole word count with definitions. Not every single economic term needs to be defined, only those integral to your analysis.

Application, analysis and evaluation are embedded throughout the commentary below, but it should be clear that the bulk of the analysis and evaluation occurs in the final four paragraphs.

Finally, the commentary concludes with a re-statement of the main ideas introduced in the first paragraph. The IB economics commentary is not unlike other essays you have written in the past. Using sound essay-writing techniques will ensure that your commentary flows from beginning to end. Pay attention to how easy it is to read and understand. One way to determine if your commentary is ready for submission is to have a non-economics student friend or family member read it over. If it makes sense to them and they can summarize your main points after reading it, then you have probably written a strong commentary. However, if they put it down more confused about economics than when they started reading it, you have some work to do!

● **Examiner's hint**

Using colour on diagrams can certainly enhance your presentation, particularly of the IA portfolio. However, the IBO's current system of scanning and distributing papers does not support colour. So be sure that your diagrams also include clear labelling that supports your analysis.

Commentary

Demand, supply and elasticity are basic economic concepts that, when applied to different markets, can help governments and individuals make informed decisions about things as basic as where to live and how to collect taxes.

Recently, Credit Suisse conducted a survey and determined that Switzerland's most expensive canton is Geneva, while the cheapest place to live is Appenzell Inner Rhodes (AIR).

Demand is a curve showing the various amounts of a product consumers want and can purchase at different prices during a specific period of time. Supply is a curve showing the different amounts of a product suppliers are willing to provide at different prices. Equilibrium price and quantity are determined by the intersection of demand and supply. Price elasticity of demand (PED) indicates the responsiveness of consumers to a change in price, and is reflected in the relative slope of demand.

In the graph below, the markets for housing in Geneva and AIR are shown.

Housing markets in Geneva (G) and AIR (A).

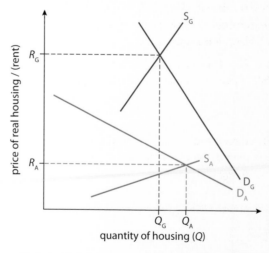

Demand for housing in Geneva (D_G), is high because of the many employment opportunities there. In addition, Geneva's scarce land means supply of housing is low, resulting in a high equilibrium rent (R_G). Demand for housing in Geneva is inelastic, since renters in Geneva are less responsive to changes in rent compared to AIR, perhaps due to the perceived necessity of living close to their work.

Demand for housing in AIR (D_A) is low, but supply is high due to the abundance of land. AIR is a rural canton with few jobs, therefore fewer people are willing and able to live there than in Geneva. Since living in the countryside is not a necessity, demand is relatively elastic, or responsive to changes in rent. The lower demand and greater supply make the AIR's equilibrium rent relatively low.

The effect of a tax on property is a shift of the supply curve to the left and an increase in rents as landowners, forced to pay the canton a share of their rental incomes, raise the rent they charge residents.

In Geneva, property taxes are high, but this has little effect on the quantity demanded.

Geneva's property tax shifts the supply of housing leftwards, as fewer landlords will be willing and able to supply properties to renters when the canton taxes rental incomes. However, the decrease in quantity demanded is proportionally smaller than the increase in the price caused by the tax, since demand for housing in Geneva is highly inelastic, or unresponsive to the higher price caused by the tax.

Housing market in Geneva.

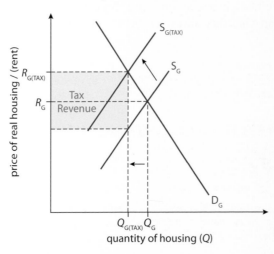

Renters in AIR are far more responsive to higher rents caused by property taxes, perhaps because living in AIR is not considered a necessity and there are more substitutes for rural cantons to live in. Renters in Geneva do not have the freedom to live in one of Switzerland's many rural cantons, and are therefore less responsive to higher rents resulting from cantonal taxes.

Housing market in AIR.

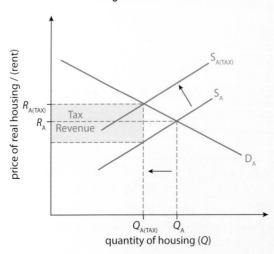

A tax decrease in AIR could lead to a significant increase in the number of people willing to live there, since renters are highly responsive to lower taxes. To some extent, housing in AIR and Geneva are substitutes for one another. Lower taxes in AIR would make living there more attractive, and subsequently the demand for housing in Geneva would fall putting downward pressure on rents there. People would move to AIR, attracted by lower rents, and commute to work in the cities. According to the article, this is already happening:

'The disparity in the amount of disposable income ... has increased the trend of people moving cantons for financial reasons ... Economic necessities had led to an increase ... of people moving address and opting to commute into work'.

There are many determinants of demand for housing in Switzerland, the primary one being location. High rents in Geneva are explained by the high demand for and the limited supply of housing. On the other hand, residents in AIR enjoy much lower rents, due to the weak demand and abundant land. Cantons should take into consideration the PED for housing when determining their property tax levels. Raising the tax in Geneva will have little effect on rentals but could create substantial tax revenue. On the other hand, reducing taxes in AIR may attract many households away from the city to the countryside, drawn by the lower rents and property taxes.

Applying the basic principles of demand, supply and elasticity to Switzerland's housing market allows households and government alike to make better decisions about where to live and how much to tax citizens.

Marked student commentary

Below is an IA commentary from a portfolio written by an IB economics student. Following the commentary is a completed IA criteria rubric with the marks earned for each of the five criteria, a total score, and teacher comments for each area of assessment.

Course: IB Economics HL

Commentary number: 3

School name: _____

Candidate name: _____

Candidate number: _____

Date commentary was written: 1 December 2009

Section of the syllabus to which the commentary relates:
Section 4 – International economics

Word Count: 726

Source of extract: Cornelius Rahn, 9 November 2009, German exports rose in September as global economy strengthened Bloomberg News at: http://www.bloomberg.com/apps/news?pid =20601100&sid=aRBd_2ZdeMs

German Exports Rose in September as Global Economy Strengthened

By Cornelius Rahn

Nov. 9 (Bloomberg) – German exports rose more than economists forecast in September as a global recovery stoked demand for goods made in Europe's largest economy.

Sales abroad, adjusted for working days and seasonal changes, increased 3.8 percent from August, when they fell 2.8 percent, the Federal Statistics Office in Wiesbaden said today.

Economists expected a gain of 2.5 percent, the median of 13 forecasts in a Bloomberg News survey showed. Exports still declined 18.8 percent from a year earlier.

Germany emerged from recession in the second quarter and growth probably accelerated in the third as exports picked up and government stimulus measures bolstered domestic spending. The euro's 19 percent appreciation against the dollar since mid-February may undermine the recovery by making exports more expensive.

'The exchange rate shouldn't play a role in the coming months,' said Andreas Rees, an economist at Unicredit SpA in Munich. 'Exports are the growth driver and we believe that will continue into the fourth quarter. But if the euro strengthens further, and when the impact of the inventory cycle wears off, exports will feel the pinch.'

Imports rose 5.8 percent in September from August, the statistics office said. The trade surplus widened to 10.6 billion euros ($15.8 billion) from 8.1 billion euros in August. The surplus in the current account, a measure of all trade including services, was 9.4 billion euros, up from a revised 4.4 billion euros in the previous month.

Car Sales Surge

Germany's Daimler AG, the world's second-largest maker of luxury vehicles, said on Nov. 6 that sales in China rose 55 percent in the 10 months through October from the same period a year earlier.

Still, HeidelbergCement AG, Germany's biggest cement maker, on Nov. 4 predicted lower operating profit and sales for the fourth quarter as demand from Asia fails to balance weaker business in other areas.

German wine growers on the banks of the river Moselle exported 10 percent less of their famous Riesling in the year through July as demand from the U.S. and the U.K. declined.

The Economy Ministry raised its outlook for the economy on Oct. 16, forecasting growth of about 1.2 percent in 2010 after a 5 percent contraction this year.

Commentary

Germany's glimmer of hope grows as their highly demanded exports could aid their recovery from the recession. Europe's largest economy is now widening its trade surplus with increasing sales in countries like China where there's been a 55% rise in sales. However, Germany might not be so lucky if the dollar continues to depreciate against the euro.

The statistics office presented a 5.8% increase in imports from August to September with the trade surplus reaching €10.6 billion in the same amount of time. At this rate, the recession will become an event of the past; however, the floating exchange rates between the United States and Germany might interfere in Germany's recovery.

The German and American governments do not interfere in the currency market and leave it up to the demand and supply of the currency on the foreign exchange market. An exchange rate is the value of one currency in terms of another and at the moment they are being influenced by interest rates in the US and Europe, a determinant. The low US interest rates are causing investors, foreign households and firms to invest elsewhere where the return is higher.

Another determinant of exchange rates, speculation of the public, will find Americans investing in German assets, stocks, bonds and currency because they predict the euro to keep rising and therefore be of more value than the dollar. This is shown on the diagram below by an outward shift of demand (from Q_E to Q_1) in the euro market in America. The example given in the diagram shows the euro appreciating, gaining value against the dollar, from 1.2 to 1.5. Meaning that before one euro was worth $1.20 and now it's worth $1.50.

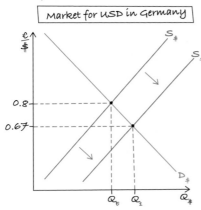
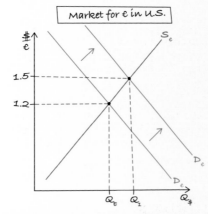

As a result, the supply of dollars in Germany will increase as Americans have to supply more dollars for Germans to be able to exchange into euros. This increase in the supply of dollars is what causes the dollar to depreciate (when a currency decreases in value).

However, the article sees flaws in this currency exchange, '*The euro's 19 percent appreciation against the dollar since mid-February may undermine the recovery by making exports more expensive*'. This appreciation of the euro is going to act as a tariff on exports to America, which might eventually slow down the economic growth in Germany, as net exports make up part of the GDP.

However, a closer look reveals this appreciation to be beneficial for the country. Andreas Rees indirectly states foreign countries' inelastic demand for Germany's exports, '*The exchange rate shouldn't play a role in the coming months. Exports are the growth driver and we believe that will continue into the fourth quarter.*' He goes on to say exports will feel a pinch in the future, were the euro to stay high revealing all the classic signs of the Marshal–Lerner condition. This rule calculates how successful a country is in improving their current account deficit with the re-evaluation of their currency if:

$$PED_{EXPORTS} + PED_{IMPORTS} > 1$$

If the price elasticity of demand for exports and imports is smaller than one, then the Marshal–Lerner condition is not met and the proportionate decrease in the price of exports demanded is less than the proportionate increase in the price of exports leading to an increase in revenue (shown by the rectangle of the price × the quantity).

This diagram shows the increase in export prices due to the euro's appreciation and by how little the quantity demanded changes because of the inelastic demand. The green rectangle is the revenue of both scenarios, but the increase in export prices gains the revenue indicated by the yellow rectangle.

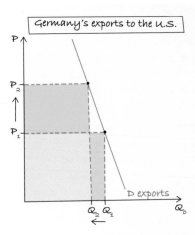

As a result Germany's current account surplus of €10.6 billion would continue to move towards surplus. This low elasticity could be due to German and foreign trading firms having contracts to finish off before they can purchase cheaper exports from another country. Or, simply that foreign consumers are accustomed to German products and will take some time to adjust to newer cheaper ones.

However, in the long run, PED of exports and imports increase so that eventually they equal more than one. Therefore, the Marshal–Lerner condition is achieved and consumers become more responsive to the increase in German export prices. This is a disadvantage because consumers will start to replace European products with either domestic products or substitutes from other countries if the euro were to stay strong.

Table 31.2 shows you how this commentary was marked.

Criteria	Skill Area	Marks	Top level descriptor	Teacher comments
A	Diagrams	2/3	Relevant, accurate and correctly labelled diagrams are included, with a full explanation.	Diagrams are correctly labelled, but could be integrated more smoothly into the commentary.
B	Terminology	1/2	Terminology relevant to the article is used appropriately throughout the commentary.	Some terms requiring definitions are not defined (such as current account surplus).
C	Application	2/2	Relevant economic concepts and/or theories are applied to the article appropriately throughout the commentary.	The determinants of exchange rates and the Marshall–Lerner condition are applied well to the article.
D	Analysis	3/3	There is effective economic analysis relating to the article.	Good analysis is demonstrated when examining the likely impact on Germany's trade balance of the stronger euro.
E	Evaluation	2/4	Judgements are made that are supported by effective and balanced reasoning.	The evaluation is brief and incomplete. An attempt at evaluating the long-run effects of a strong euro is made, but not enough attention is paid to other impacts of the currency's appreciation.
	Total:	10/14		Overall this commentary demonstrates sound analysis using the economic concepts learned in section 4 of the IB course. Definitions are missing, and evaluation is brief and one-sided.

ADVICE AND SKILLS FOR THE EXAMS AND EXTENDED ESSAY

The majority of your IB Economics marks are derived from your performance in the examinations at the end the course. This chapter shows you how the exams are assessed and the skills you need to get the best marks.

If you are pursuing the full IB Diploma, you can elect to write your Extended Essay on an economics subject. This chapter also provides you with information and advice on how best to tackle an Extended Essay in economics. You should also consult the IB *Economics Guide* for detailed information on the requirements of the examinations and Extended Essay.

Examinations

Exams count for 80% of your overall mark whether you are an HL or an SL student although the number and relative value of each paper breaks down differently between HL and SL. To do well, you should pursue the appropriate testing skills with the same energy with which you pursue knowledge of economics concepts.

Assessment objectives

The diploma programme has four assessment objectives (AO1, AO2, AO3, AO4), each defining the need for a particular skill (Table 32.1). Each exam paper requires the demonstration of the four skills, although specific questions may require only one or two at a time.

TABLE 32.1 IB ECONOMICS ASSESSMENT OBJECTIVES		
Assessment objective	**Skill**	**Students will be able to ...**
AO1	knowledge and understanding	demonstrate knowledge and understanding of the common SL/HL syllabus demonstrate knowledge and understanding of current economic issues and data HL only: demonstrate knowledge and understanding of the higher level extension topics
AO2	application and analysis	apply economic concepts and theories to real-world situations identify and interpret economic data demonstrate the extent to which economic information is used effectively in particular contexts HL only: demonstrate application and analysis of the extension topics
AO3	synthesis and evaluation	examine economic concepts and theories use economic concepts and examples to construct and present an argument discuss and evaluate economic information and theories HL only: demonstrate economic synthesis and evaluation of the extension topics
AO4	selection, use and application of a variety of appropriate skills and techniques	produce well-structured written material, using appropriate economic terminology, within specified time limits use correctly labelled diagrams to help explain economic concepts and theories select, interpret and analyse appropriate extracts from the news media interpret appropriate data sets HL only: use quantitative techniques to identify, explain and analyse economic relationships

from *Economics Guide* © International Baccalaureate Organization 2010

These skills are assessed in two exams for SL students, and three exams for HL students.

Exams summary

SL and HL examination assessment have much in common. Paper 1 parts A and B focus on microeconomics and macroeconomics, respectively. Paper 2 parts A and B examine international and development economics, respectively. Both papers require all four assessment objectives to be addressed. Also, within each section A and B, students have a choice between two questions. At both HL and SL, the internal assessment requirement is for a portfolio of three commentaries on recent news items (Chapter 31).

Table 32.2 outlines the assessment types and weights for the standard level programme.

TABLE 32.2 STANDARD LEVEL (SL) ASSESSMENT	
SL assessment component	**Weight**
Paper 1 (90 minutes) Extended response (essay) paper; total = 50 marks AO1, AO2, AO3, AO4 *Section A* • syllabus content: section 1 microeconomics • students answer one question from a choice of two (25 marks) *Section B* • syllabus content: section 2 macroeconomics • students answer one question from a choice of two (25 marks)	40%
Paper 2 (90 minutes) Data response paper; total = 40 marks AO1, AO2, AO3, AO4 *Section A* • syllabus content: section 3 international economics • students answer one question from a choice of two (20 marks) *Section B* • syllabus content: section 4 development economics • students answer one question from a choice of two (20 marks)	40%
Internal assessment (20 teaching hours) Maximum 750 words × 3; total = 45 marks Internally assessed by the teacher; externally moderated by IB at end of course • students produce a portfolio of three commentaries on published extracts from the news media, each relating to different sections of the syllabus	20%

from *Economics Guide* © International Baccalaureate Organization 2010

The HL assessment model diverges from the SL with the addition of Paper 3, and consequently a recalibrating of the weights accorded to each paper (at SL each of papers 1 and 2 carry 40% of the total IB mark, at HL papers 1 and 2 are accorded 30% each, and Paper 3 makes up the remaining 20%).

Table 32.3 outlines the assessment types and weights for the HL programme.

TABLE 32.3 HIGHER LEVEL (HL) ASSESSMENT	
HL assessment component	**Weight**
Paper 1 (90 minutes) Extended response (essay) paper; total = 50 marks AO1, AO2, AO3, AO4 *Section A* • syllabus content: section 1 microeconomics • students answer one question from a choice of two (25 marks) *Section B* • syllabus content: section 2 macroeconomics • students answer one question from a choice of two (25 marks)	30%

Paper 2 (90 minutes) Data response paper; total = 40 marks AO1, AO2, AO3, AO4 *Section A* • syllabus content: section 3 international economics • students answer one question from a choice of two (20 marks) *Section B* • syllabus content: section 4 development economics • students answer one question from a choice of two (20 marks)	30%
Paper 3 (1 hour) HL extension paper; total = 50 marks AO1, AO2, AO4 • syllabus content: HL extension material from all sections of the syllabus • students answer two questions from a choice of three (25 marks per question)	20%
Internal assessment (20 teaching hours) Maximum 750 words × 3; total = 45 marks Internally assessed by the teacher; externally moderated by IB at end of course • students produce a portfolio of three commentaries on published extracts from the news media, each relating to different sections of the syllabus	20%

from *Economics Guide* © International Baccalaureate Organization 2010

You should bear in mind that even though each section of papers 1 and 2 focuses primarily on a particular section of the syllabus, it is likely that you will be required to draw on your knowledge of other areas to round out your answers. Don't be tempted to compartmentalize your knowledge too exclusively.

Paper 1 requirements

A paper 1 question is typically divided up into two sub-questions on a related topic.

Part (a) usually requires you to demonstrate the skills in AO1, AO2 and AO4 (knowledge and understanding, application and analysis, and the use of appropriate skills and techniques). Part (a) is always worth 10 marks.

Part (b) often requires some combination of all four AOs, with a heavy emphasis on AO3 (synthesis and evaluation). Part (b) is always worth 15 marks.

A typical paper 1 question might look like this.

1 a Explain the concepts of price floors and price ceilings. (10 marks)

   b Evaluate the effectiveness of price control policies designed to improve producer and consumer welfare. (15 marks)

Part (a) asks you to *explain*. This suggests a heavy emphasis on defining terms, diagramming as needed, and explaining how the concepts work.

Part (b) is different; it asks you *evaluate* – to make a critical judgement on the policies in question, based on evidence from the real world, and demonstrating your understanding of, in this case, the economic concept of price controls.

Evaluation of price controls requires you to measure the effectiveness of price-control policies against their stated goals of helping either producers or consumers. You also need to apply relevant knowledge of price control programmes, and explain the advantages and disadvantages of such schemes. To properly demonstrate the skills of synthesis and evaluation required by AO4 can involve many different approaches (page 672).

Paper 2 requirements

Paper 2 is a data response paper. You are asked to read a selection of information from a news story and/or study a selection of international or development economic data; you then answer questions based on the readings. Your answers should also demonstrate your own knowledge of course topics. Data response questions are more specific and directed than the extended response questions of paper 1.

There are four parts to a paper 2 question.

Part (a) always requires you to define two terms from the document or data supplied. No more than a definition is required to receive the full two marks for each definition. Part (a) totals 4 marks.

Part (b) typically requires you to use an appropriate diagram or to use data in the tables given to explain something relating to the document or data. Part (b) totals 4 marks.

Part (c) is similar to part (b). You are usually asked to use a diagram or to explain an economic concept using appropriate skills and techniques (A04). Part (c) totals 4 marks.

Part (d) typically begins with the words 'Using information from the text/data and your knowledge of economics, evaluate …'. Clearly, the assessment objective assessed here is AO3, synthesis and evaluation. To earn top marks, you must refer to evidence from the given text, *and* make an informed judgment regarding the issue addressed. Part (d) totals 8 marks.

A typical paper 2 question series might look like this (note that the informative text/data is not included here).

2 a Define the following terms indicated in bold in the text:

    i   public good   (2 marks)

    ii foreign direct investment.   (2 marks)

  b Using an appropriate diagram, explain why public goods tend to be under-provided by the free market and sometimes 'require government support' (paragraph 4).   (4 marks)

  c With reference to Figure 1, explain why there is a difference between the Human Development Index for Bangladesh and Afghanistan.   (4 marks)

  d Using information from the text/data and your knowledge of economics, evaluate trade liberalization as a means of promoting human development in Bangladesh.   (4 marks)

There are several important points you should note about the form of paper 2 questions

1   Part (a) is almost always about two definitions. You should answer this section quickly and in a straightforward manner; no explanation, analysis or evaluation is required.

2   Parts (b) and (c) are similar; important here are clear and methodical explanations of how a concept works. You should focus on incorporating clear and correctly labelled graphs where they are required. Neither part requires the skills of AO3 (synthesis and evaluation).

3   Part (d) *does* assess AO3 (synthesis and evaluation). Examiners are looking for judgement and assessment of the issue, not more of the same explanations given in answer to parts (b) and (c). This section often prompts you to use 'information from the text and your own knowledge of economics'. There are some easy and distinct ways to indicate you are doing so, and that you know the difference between the two.

- You can cite relevant portions of the text as you write by using very brief quotes. For example, you might say:

- the effectiveness of aid in Haiti is further hampered due to the country's 'poor infrastructure and ... weak and corrupt national government'. Careful oversight is therefore needed to make sure that aid reaches those it is intended to help.

  Small quotes like this, signal to the examiner that you are drawing from the text.

- You can draw on real examples from the world with which you are familiar to show that you are 'using your own knowledge of economics'. Examples may be from class discussions that you have engaged in, articles you have read, or even from the commentaries you wrote as part of the IA portfolio.

- The best evaluation requires more than just a 'textbook explanation' of the relevant economic theories. You may be asked to argue for or against a controversial economic theory or policy. You responses should examine *both* sides of an argument or debate, but ultimately come to a conclusion drawn by you based on your informed opinion on an economic issue.

Paper 3 requirements

The HL-only paper 3 assesses the quantitative methods section of the syllabus. The topics span the entirety of course content, from the computation and plotting of linear demand and supply functions, to the calculation of elasticities and calculating the effects of a tariff. For practice in these skills, you should be sure to attempt the HL exercises in this book, and ask your teacher about the extra resources online.

Paper 3 questions require the 'selection, use and application of appropriate skills and techniques.' What the appropriate skills and techniques are, is indicated by the AO4 command terms. Table 32.4 lists the command terms typical of the AO4 questions that may appear on paper 3.

TABLE 32.4 AO4 COMMAND TERMS FOR PAPER 3	
Term	**What it asks you to do**
Calculate	Obtain a numerical answer showing the relevant stages in the working.
Construct	Display information in a diagrammatic or logical form.
Derive	Manipulate a mathematical relationship to give a new equation or relationship.
Determine	Obtain the only possible answer.
Draw	Represent by means of a labelled, accurate diagram or graph, using a pencil. A ruler (straight edge) should be used for straight lines. Diagrams should be drawn to scale. Graphs should have points correctly plotted (if appropriate) and joined in a straight line or smooth curve.
Identify	Provide an answer from a number of possibilities.
Label	Add labels to a diagram.
Measure	Obtain a value for a quantity.
Plot	Mark the position of points on a diagram.
Show	Give the steps in a calculation or derivation.
Show that	Obtain the required result (possibly using information given) without the formality of proof. 'Show that' questions do not generally require the use of a calculator.
Sketch	Represent by means of a diagram or graph (labelled as appropriate). The sketch should give a general idea of the required shape or relationship, and should include relevant features.
Solve	Obtain the answer(s) using algebraic and/or numerical and/or graphical methods.

from *Economics Guide* © International Baccalaureate Organization 2010

The AO4 command terms you are most likely to meet on paper 3 are: calculate, label, construct and draw. In addition, some AO2 command terms may appear on paper 3; the most likely are listed in Table 32.5.

TABLE 32.5 AO2 COMMAND TERMS FOR PAPER 3	
Term	**What it asks you to do**
Distinguish	Make clear the differences between two or more concepts or items.
Explain	Give a detailed account including reasons or causes.
Suggest	Propose a solution, hypothesis or other possible answer.

from *Economics Guide* © International Baccalaureate Organization 2010

Other Paper 3 considerations

- Carry-over points may be awarded, where appropriate, if you make a calculation error in the first part of a question.
- Because many of the questions require computation, you are allowed a calculator.

Assessment advice
Using diagrams effectively

There are a number of ways you can maximize your effectiveness in the economics exam-writing process. Among them is understanding how to use diagrams.

Diagrams are the most powerful tools of explanation available to economists, and learning their appropriate use is important. It is often said that a picture is worth a thousand words, and it is certainly true that the abstractions contained in a supply and demand diagram would take several dozen words to explain. Keep the following tips in mind to help you employ these diagrams to their fullest power.

Make sure your diagram is fully labelled

The absence of labels and points of reference casts doubt on your knowledge of the topic. Fully labelled diagrams have the opposite effect, and reassure the examiner of your economic prowess. Figure 32.1 shows you the areas of labelling required to make a diagram useful. A diagram also needs a title.

Figure 32.1
Supply and demand diagram for orange juice.

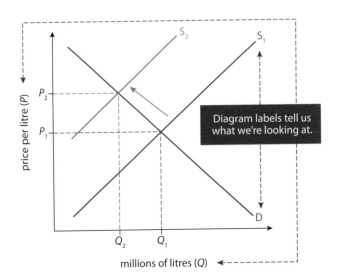

Diagram labels tell us what we're looking at.

Draw dynamic diagrams

Diagrams should show something happening. Nearly all questions that call for diagrams are asking you to show a change – one that implicitly tells a story. Static diagrams have little to say. Figure 32.2 shows a price increase; you might try to explain a price increase without demonstrating the change, but it is much clearer to show the change explicitly on the diagram. In Figure 32.2a, not much information is communicated. In contrast, Figure 32.2b communicates quite a lot of information.

Both diagrams indicate two prices and two quantities. But only in Figure 32.2b is it apparent what has caused the change in price and quantity, and in which direction they have changed.

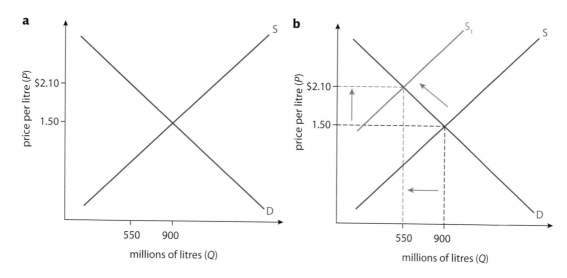

Figure 32.2
Rising productions costs reduce the supply of orange juice and increase the price.

Include arrows and ordinal notation

In diagrams showing changes, arrows and dashed lines tell the examiner that you are in command of the action. Arrows showing the movements of curves and use of ordinal notation (D, D_1, D_2) demonstrate your understanding of the process underway. Figure 32.3 leaves little doubt as to how this market changed.

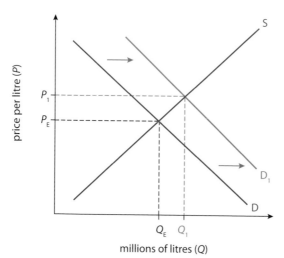

Figure 32.3
An increase in the demand for orange juice causes the price and quantity to increase to P_1 and Q_1.

Integrate your diagrams into the text of your answer

Even the best diagrams cannot tell the whole story by themselves. You must make explicit references to the diagram to get full credit for an answer (e. g. 'as can be seen in the diagram below, a decrease in the price from P_1 to P_2 leads to an increase in the quantity of hybrid cars demanded'). Graphs that are floating on the page without mention in your text will earn only partial credit.

Remember to draw your diagrams where you need to use them – that is, immediately after you first mention the change. Introduce your diagram. Then explain with appropriate detail the changes that are happening in the diagram.

Effective evaluation and synthesis (AO3)

Several components of the SL and HL assessments (both external and internal) require you to employ effective evaluation. In the examinations, it is required to reach the highest mark bands for part (b) of paper 1 questions and part (d) of paper 2 questions. In the internal assessment, 4 of the 14 marks available for each commentary are awarded for effective evaluation. *Consequently, this discussion of evaluation is relevant to the IA component of your course as well as to the examinations.*

Evaluation is perhaps the most challenging skill to master. Along with the related skill, synthesis, it requires that you go beyond the explanation, application and analysis of economic theory that is required for AO1 and AO2.

Effective evaluation requires you to make a judgement based on evidence. This sounds simple enough, but making a well-informed, intelligent judgement based on evidence from the real world is one of the most challenging tasks you face.

Here are some examples of examination questions that require the skill of evaluation.

* Discuss the economic and social consequences of globalization.
* Which is the most effective way to encourage development – aid or trade? Justify your answer. © International Baccalaurate Organization 1999
* Critically examine the view that the control of inflation should always be the most important objective of governments. © International Baccalaurate Organization 1999
* Suggest and evaluate measures to deal with high unemployment.
* Evaluate the alternative ways in which a trade deficit might be reduced or eliminated. © International Baccalaurate Organization 2009
* Discuss the view that the benefits of economic growth will always 'trickle down' into people's lives.
* Examine the strategies that may be used to reduce unemployment, referring to more developed countries and less developed countries in your answer. © International Baccalaurate Organization 2002

These questions are all either from or are in the style of part (b) of paper 1 questions or part (d) of paper 2 questions. The first thing to notice is that only a few of them actually use the word 'evaluate'. Some other prompts that require you to 'use economic concepts and examples to construct and present an argument' include:

* discuss
* critically examine
* justify
* suggest.

There are several approaches you can take when answering a question that requires you to evaluate. The four most trusty and true methods are considered below. In each case, one of the above questions is given an example answer.

Consider short run *vs* long run

The concepts of short run and long run in economics have different applications depending on whether the question relates to micro- or macroeconomics. Depending on the period of time following a particular policy or economic decision by an individual, a firm or a government, there may be very different outcomes.

Worked example

- Evaluate the alternative ways in which a trade deficit might be reduced or eliminated.

  In the short run, a government may choose to employ protectionist policies to reduce a current account deficit. Higher taxes on imported goods and services will make them less attractive to domestic consumers, reducing expenditures on imports and moving the current account towards surplus.

  However, due to the misallocation of resources resulting from protective tariffs, and the likelihood that trading partners will impose retaliatory tariffs on the deficit country, a longer-term solution to a current account deficit requires investments in human capital, infrastructure and technology.

  Such investments will increase the productivity and international competitiveness of the deficit country, reducing the country's dependence on cheap imports and making its own exports more attractive to foreign consumers. Such a strategy will, in the long run, reduce the nation's current account deficit, increase net exports, and in the process grow the economy, creating more jobs and a more productive workforce.

Examine the impact on different stakeholders

Throughout the economics course, various stakeholders are mentioned. Discussing the impacts of a particular economic decision, policy or action on the various stakeholders involved is an effective method for evaluation.

Worked example

- Discuss the economic and social consequences of globalization.

  It is helpful to first identify all the stakeholders who are affected by globalization. These may include:

  - domestic households
  - domestic firms
  - government
  - foreign households and firms
  - workers in the primary, secondary and tertiary sector
  - foreign workers
  - the environment.

  Globalization is generally beneficial for those who experience it; however, not everyone is necessarily better off as the world's markets become increasingly interconnected.

  In a globalizing world, in which different countries have comparative advantages in different goods and services, the opening of domestic markets to international trade can lead to major social and economic disruptions for domestic households, firms, workers and the government. In Europe and North America, globalization has led to the loss of millions of manufacturing jobs which, over the last two decades, have increasingly shifted to low-cost developing countries in which labour-intensive production is relatively cheap.

On the other hand, skilled workers in the developed world, particularly those with high levels of education, have benefited greatly from globalization as the demand for services such as banking, law, finance and business has expanded dramatically in the global marketplace.

This evaluation could continue by examining the effects of globalization on workers and firms in the developing world. It could even discuss the environmental effects that international trade has wrought, including increased greenhouse gas emissions and the unsustainable extraction of primary commodities in less developed countries.

Discuss advantages and disadvantages

This may be the easiest and most obvious way to evaluate. Throughout the IB course you have read about and discussed with your class the advantages and disadvantages of various economic policies. This approach is best suited to macroeconomics questions. In approaching a question such as the one below, you may choose two or three policy options, and weigh the advantages and disadvantages of each.

Worked example

- Suggest and evaluate measures to deal with high unemployment.

  Both fiscal and monetary policies can be used to reduce unemployment in an economy. Both policies have their advantages and disadvantages. Expansionary fiscal policy, for instance, has the advantage of directly stimulating aggregate demand through government spending and higher disposable incomes among households who enjoy lower taxes. With greater consumption and government spending, job creation is highly likely and unemployment should fall.

  On the other hand, expansionary fiscal policy financed through increased government borrowing may have the effect of driving up interest rates in the private sector, as the government must offer lenders higher rates on its debt. The corresponding increase in demand for loanable funds may drive up interest rates and thereby crowd out private investment. In this way, the fall in unemployment that may have resulted from increased government spending might not occur if private sector investment decreases at the same time.

Such an approach as this to evaluation is highly effective, especially if the response were to evaluate the advantages and disadvantages of monetary policy and, based on the evaluation, draw a conclusion which argued for one type of policy response over the other.

Prioritize the arguments

This approach to effective evaluation involves prioritizing the arguments for a particular position which you have taken in your response. For example, in answer to the question below, you may decide to identify and then rank according to importance the threats posed by a high rate of inflation.

Worked example

- Critically examine the view that the control of inflation should always be the most important objective of governments.

  The most important reason a government should keep inflation under control is that a rapidly rising price level drastically reduces the standard of living of a nation's people.

A high rate of inflation erodes the purchasing power of households' nominal incomes; therefore, if incomes are rising at a rate slower than that of the price level, then the real incomes of the nation's households decline and the average citizen is actually getting worse off over time.

Secondly, inflation makes a country's exports less competitive in the global market, and, therefore, over time a high rate of inflation will lead to an increasing deficit in the nation's current account. The higher price of the nation's goods makes imports more attractive to domestic consumers, and exports less attractive to foreigners. The growing current account deficit will require the nation to sell increasing amounts of its assets to foreign investors, whose funds will flow back into the nation in the financial account.

The above evaluation could continue by identifying a third and perhaps even a fourth argument for why low inflation should be the most important objective of governments. On the other hand, you could have taken a very different approach to the question and argued that inflation should not be the most important objective, and then prioritized the arguments for why unemployment, economic growth, or income distribution should be of greater importance to governments.

Extended Essay in economics

The Extended Essay is an exciting and rewarding component of the IB diploma programme. In it, you get to research and write a detailed paper on a topic in a subject that interests you. As part of this requirement, it is your responsibility to choose a topic that fits into one of the subjects on the approved Extended Essay list, which can be obtained from your school's IB coordinator.

Once you have chosen your subject area, you must meet the following requirements.

- **Observe the relevant regulations**. You must have an Extended Essay supervisor, who ideally is a teacher of the subject you have chosen to write on and who works at your school. This teacher, or your school's IB coordinator, is responsible for providing you with the *Extended Essay Guide*, an official IB publication in which the regulations relating to the Extended Essay are laid out.
- **Meet deadlines**. You and your supervisor should agree deadlines for intermediate and final drafts of your Extended Essay. It is likely that your school will have internal deadlines agreed by all IB teachers. Make sure you are aware of these deadlines, and plan accordingly to meet the requirements of each deadline so as to ensure your final essay is of the best quality possible.
- **Acknowledge sources in an approved academic manner**. The easiest way to fail the IB diploma programme is to be caught plagiarizing. In your research and writing of the Extended Essay, it is crucial that you acknowledge all sources of information and ideas in an approved manner, most likely through footnotes or a bibliography following either the APA or the MLA structure.

In addition to these requirements, you are strongly recommended to:

- start work early
- think very carefully about the research question for your essay
- plan how, when and where you will find material for your essay
- plan a schedule for both researching and writing the essay, including extra time for delays and unforeseen problems
- record sources as your research progresses (rather than trying to reconstruct a list at the end)

- have a clear structure for the essay before beginning to write
- outline your essay before starting to write it
- check and proofread the final version carefully
- make sure that all basic requirements are met (e.g. word count, abstract).

Preparing for your Extended Essay

Before starting work

- Read the assessment criteria in the *Extended Essay Guide* (see also pages 679–681).
- Read previous essays to identify strengths and possible pitfalls. Your supervisor should be able to provide you with past, marked essays to give you ideas of how to begin your own.
- Spend time working out the research question. A strong research question is essential – without one, your essay will be weak at best.
- Work out a structure for your essay. Before you begin writing in earnest, create a comprehensive outline of the essay.

During the research and writing

- Start work early and stick to deadlines.
- Maintain a good working relationship with your supervisor. Check in with your supervisor often, at least once every two weeks. Remember, it is your responsibility (not your supervisor's) to make sure you have regular meetings. Without initiative on your part, you won't benefit from your supervisor's guidance.
- Construct an argument that relates to the research question. The research question is only the starting point for your essay. In attempting to answer it, you must construct a reasoned argument supported by evidence gathered in your research.
- Use the library and online resources, and consult librarians for advice. Librarians today deal with more than just books. Most school libraries have access to online databases of scholarly journals, which could be great sources for research. Using search engines successfully requires sound search technique; be sure to consult a specialist in your school to get tips on how to go about conducting your online and library research.
- Don't be afraid to change your topic and research question if there is a problem with your original one. If you start early enough, there should be plenty of time to change topics a few weeks or a month or two into the process if you decide you cannot successfully write an essay on your original topic.
- Use the appropriate language for the subject. Keep the course syllabus, a textbook, and your class notes in front of you at all times while writing. The biggest threat to your success is writing 4000 words that repeatedly drift away from the topics covered in your chosen subject. Keep your essay grounded in the subject by continuously checking your progress against the course syllabus.
- Let your interest and enthusiasm show. Hopefully you have chosen a topic that genuinely interests you. It is perfectly acceptable to express interest and emotion in your writing. Some of the best essays are those in which the writer's voice and personality are clearly visible.

After completing the essay

- Write the abstract. The abstract is intended to encourage you to examine closely the arguments you have developed within the Extended Essay and the significance of any conclusions you have reached. It is also designed to allow readers to understand quickly the contents of your essay. The *Extended Essay Guide* will tell you what the abstract must include.

- Carefully proofread your essay. Try to have at least one or two of your classmates also proofread your essay for you (perhaps you can agree to proofread theirs for them). In addition, you should ask your supervisor to give your final draft one last look before you submit the true final copy.

Following all this advice will ensure you have a successful experience researching and writing your Extended Essay and that you produce an essay you can truly be proud of. In addition to being an important component of your ultimate IB score, the essay's greatest value is the preparation it gives you for the most common form of assessment you are likely to encounter in the university system. The research process you experience in writing your Extended Essay is very much like that most undergraduate and even graduate students undertake in writing university essays.

The topic you choose to research is likely to be in a subject area that interests you personally, and the experience you gain in researching and writing a 4000-word essay may help prepare you to enter a programme of study in a similar subject area at university level. Many IB students subsequently find the opportunity to incorporate their Extended Essay research into college essays and interviews. A successful essay experience will increase the likelihood of you getting onto a programme in an area of study that you are truly passionate about pursuing at a higher level.

Extended Essay in economics
Is economics right for you?

Economics is a very popular subject for the Extended Essay at many schools. Some students are under the impression that economics is an easier subject in which to write an essay in than, say, the physical sciences such as physics or chemistry.

Let it be known, right now, that this is a myth. There is no sound evidence to support the assumption that economics is any easier to write a strong Extended Essay for than the physical sciences. In fact, the best economics Extended Essays tend to be those which take a highly scientific approach to the research and writing process.

Why is this? The higher levels of economics are extremely empirical in their analysis. Economics is a social science, yes, but in their study of humans' interactions with one another in markets, economists seek to quantify human behaviours to as great an extent as possible. By collecting, organizing, displaying and then analysing data representing the interactions of individuals, firms or governments in a mathematical way, economists are able to observe the interactions between two or more variables and develop hypotheses about human behaviour.

In this regard, a top-notch economics essay may appear very scientific indeed; students hoping to avoid doing experiments and gathering data should perhaps avoid writing an economics essay.

What does an economics essay look like?

- An Extended Essay in economics should employ the core principles of economics as a basis for researching a particular topic. Both primary and secondary research should be conducted to gather data and background information for the essay. Theories outlined in the course syllabus, as well as the tools, models, graphs and skills learned during the IB Economics course should be applied to the topic.

- You should avoid writing an historical, narrative essay, even on an economic topic. For instance, an essay exploring the use of contractionary monetary policy to bring down inflation by the US Federal Reserve in the early 1980s is less desirable than an essay examining the effect of the European Central Bank's expansionary monetary policy in 2009 on the level of investment in Germany's automobile sector. The latter is more current and more relevant to the economy today.

- Essays should be analytical rather than descriptive. The purpose is not so much to tell a story as to analyse events in the world around you through the lens of economics. To this end you can employ the tools and models of economics to develop a deeper understanding of human interactions and behaviour.

- It is important that you can answer your research question using economic concepts and theories. Often, students choose a topic they think is appropriate for economics, but which would be more suited to business and management. For instance, you may wish to analyse the costs and revenues of a particular firm in which you have a relative who is employed. Caution is needed in such a situation: the microeconomic models covered in the economics course are highly conceptual, and would be very difficult to apply to an individual firm in a particular market. A better idea would be to examine the market as a whole, developing and analysing a hypothesis relating to market demand, price, and quantity, rather than the costs and revenues of an individual firm.

- Data are very important. The primary research component should be of primary focus. An essay in which you undertake an analysis of a particular product market, for example, may include historic price and output data for the market, surveys of consumers in the market, interviews with sellers in the market, and so on. Data should be presented in a visually appealing manner. Where possible, create charts and graphs rather than presenting large tables full of small numbers.

- Do not waste too many words summarizing your data. If presented well, it doesn't need it. Focus on analysing your data. Attempt to find and explain patterns within the data, and once identified, apply the tools of micro- or macroeconomics to explain those patterns.

- Secondary research should include analyses of data that already exist from studies done by others on topics similar to yours. Successful secondary research can bolster your argument, offering evidence found through similar studies that either supports or refutes your own hypothesis.

Choosing your research question

In developing your research question, it is important to be focused. Do not choose a question that is too broad to be answered in a 4000-word essay. For instance, of the following two questions, which do you think is more appropriate for an economics extended essay?

- Is the market for international schools in London an example of an oligopoly, and if so, do the schools collude with each other?
- What effect does Spain's large budget deficit have on the economy and what should Spain do to increase aggregate demand?

Bit of a trick question! In fact, neither is appropriate for an economics Extended Essay. Here is why. The first is actually two questions, and in order for you to be able to answer the second one, the answer to the first must be 'yes'. Avoid yes/no questions altogether if possible. This question would be improved if it read:

- To what extent does the market for international schools in London demonstrate the characteristics of an oligopolistic market?

This question is more focused, and it is not a yes/no question. The characteristics and models of oligopolies can be analysed in the context of the market for international schools in London, and a reasonably accurate conclusion can be drawn based on analysis of the evidence gathered through primary research.

The second of our original questions is inappropriate because it is too broad to answer in 4000 words. In addition, it is a two-part question, the second part being only somewhat related to the first part. Avoid two-part questions. This question would be improved by narrowing its focus and making it a one-part question:

- How did Spain's record budget deficit affect the wages and benefits of public sector employees in Barcelona in the second half of 2010?

This question focuses on the impact of a macroeconomic variable (the budget deficit) on a microeconomic indicator (public sector employment in Barcelona). Data on both the deficit and public sector employment can be found, workers can be interviewed, hypotheses can be formed, and possible solutions to the challenges faced by Spain can be evaluated.

For further guidance on choosing a topic and developing a research question, along with more information on treatment of the topic in an economics Extended Essay, check the IB *Extended Essay Guide*.

Interpreting the assessment criteria

Extended Essays are externally assessed on assessment criteria by examiners appointed by the IBO. Essays are marked out of 36 points allocated between 11 criteria as shown below. The total score for your essay is used in conjunction with your Theory of knowledge score to determine the number of points awarded jointly to these two components of your diploma.

Criterion A Research question: 2 points

You are strongly recommended to state your research topic as a question. You must be able to answer the question using contemporary economic theory. The question must be clearly focused and sufficiently narrow that it can be answered within the word limit. The question should not be trivial, nor should the answer be patently obvious. It should be neither a double-barrelled question (with two parts) nor a yes/no question.

Criterion B Introduction: 2 points

Your introduction should succinctly explain the significance of the subject, why it is worthy of investigation, and how the research question is appropriate for economic analysis. The introduction should not be seen as an excuse for padding out an essay with a lengthy superficial account of the reasons for choosing the subject. Your personal experience or particular opinion is rarely relevant here.

Criterion C Investigation: 4 points

The range of resources available is influenced by various factors, but above all by the topic. At the very least, you should provide evidence that appropriate economic sources have been consulted. Wherever possible, you should use primary sources , with secondary sources as evidential support. Statistical data collected from books or the internet (e.g. from national statistical agencies, the IMF, the ILO, the World Bank, the WTO) may be very valuable and can be effectively used to answer the question. If you carry out a survey, the questions must reflect appropriate and sensible economic analysis. For example, any conclusions about the elasticity of demand for a good would be highly suspect if your survey asked about a hypothetical change in a quantity demanded based on a hypothetical change in price.

You can demonstrate good planning by using appropriate information to support a well-structured argument. Your essay should not include theory or information that is not used to answer your research question directly. For example, it would not be appropriate to include large sections of textbook economic theory without showing how and why the theory can be applied to your particular research question.

Criterion D Knowledge and understanding of the topic studied: 4 points

Having chosen a topic of interest and carried out an appropriate amount of research, you should be able to demonstrate in-depth knowledge of the topic. This is another reason why your research question has to be suitably focused. Your essay should be comprehensive and thorough.

You should fully label the axes and curves on diagrams and accurately draw the relationships between curves. For example, the relationship between marginal and average values should always show the correct mathematical link. If appropriate, you should show an appreciation of the ideological underpinning of a diagram. For example, if your essay looks at demand management as a way of reducing unemployment, you should use an appropriate AS curve.

Criterion E Reasoned argument: 4 points

You should make it evident throughout your essay that you are answering your research question. Relevant economic theory, concepts and data or information must be integrated in a logical and coherent manner. You need to develop a valid and persuasive argument in a clear and structured way, with awareness that there may be alternative viewpoints.

Criterion F Application of analytical and evaluative skills appropriate to the subject: 4 points

Essays that are highly descriptive will score poorly here. You should use data or information in the context of the appropriate economic concepts and theories. Effective analysis occurs if the information you have gathered is examined using economic theories.

You should show critical awareness of the validity of your information and the possible limitations of your argument. Very importantly, the essay should clearly note any assumptions you have made in setting out your argument and reaching your conclusions.

Don't include diagrams if there is no evidence to support their relevance to your research question. For example, if your essay looks at a non-collusive oligopoly, you shouldn't indiscriminately include a kinked demand curve if there is no evidence of the behaviour associated with such a curve. If you do include theories or diagrams that are not supported by evidence, you should note that the situation might be explained by the theory, but that there is no evidence to prove firmly that the theory is valid. For example, if it appears that a firm is operating in a monopolistically competitive market and is not making abnormal profits but you do not have proof of this, then your explanation should make clear that this is an assumption and has not been empirically proven.

You must properly integrate your diagrams into your essay. Real data should be used on diagrams wherever possible. For example, if your essay is about using taxes to reduce the negative externalities caused by smoking in Canada, then the y-axis label should read 'the price of cigarettes / C$ per package' and any real numbers (for example, 25% tax) should show on the diagram.

Criterion G Use of language appropriate to the subject: 4 points

It is extremely important that you use economic terminology and provide definitions of key terms. This will clearly enhance the academic tone of your essay. Definitions should be precise. For example, a discussion of elasticity should refer to percentage or proportionate changes as opposed to big or small changes.

Criterion H Conclusion: 2 points

Consistent is the key word here: the conclusion should develop out of the argument and not introduce any new material. Any obvious limitations to your analysis or argument should be restated here, as evidence of your critical awareness. For example, if you carried out a survey but the sample size was rather small, then you could state that the sample size might limit the validity of your conclusion drawn. If you carried out interviews, you could note that the ideological bias of the interviewees might limit the validity of the conclusions drawn.

Criterion I Formal presentation: 4 points

This criterion relates to the extent to which your essay conforms to academic standards about the way in which research papers should be presented. If you present an essay that omits a bibliography or does not give references for quotations, it will be deemed unacceptable (level 0). If your essay omits one of the required elements – title page, table of contents, page numbers – it will be deemed no better than satisfactory (maximum level 2). If your essay omits two required elements it will be deemed poor at best (maximum level 1). Additionally, if your diagrams are poorly presented or if the information shown on the diagram is unclear, one mark will be deducted.

Criterion J Abstract: 2 points

The abstract is judged on the clarity with which it states the research question, explains how the investigation was carried out and summarizes the conclusion. However, the *quality* of the research question or the conclusion is *not* judged here. For example, if your essay has a very broad research question (e.g. What were the effects of the Asian financial crisis?) it is likely to score poorly on several criteria simply because it is far too broad and unfocused. However, if you clearly state the (poor) question and include the other two required elements in your abstract, then the abstract can still receive full marks.

Criterion K Holistic judgment: 4 points

Qualities that are rewarded under this criterion include the following.

- **Intellectual initiative**. Ways you can demonstrate this in your economics essay include undertaking appropriate primary research, for example, the construction of a meaningful and relevant survey with an appropriate sample, or interview(s) with relevant people, drawing meaningful conclusions based on an analysis of a large amount of statistical data and the choice of an original topic (although it should be noted that less original topics should not be penalized here).
- **Insight and depth of understanding**. You are most likely to demonstrate these qualities by drawing mature and balanced conclusions from the research you undertook, showing awareness of the limitations of your research, and evaluating the applicability of economic theory.

ANSWERS TO QUANTITATIVE EXERCISES

Chapter 2

11

Price in $ (P)	Quantity demanded (Q_D)
0	300
3	210
5	150
7	90
9	30

12

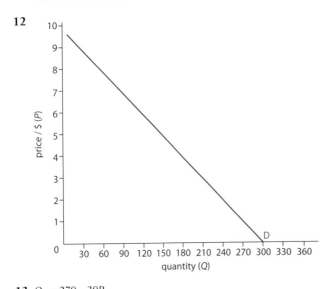

13 $Q_D = 270 - 30P$

Price in $ (P)	Quantity demanded (Q_D)
0	270
3	180
5	120
7	60
9	0

14

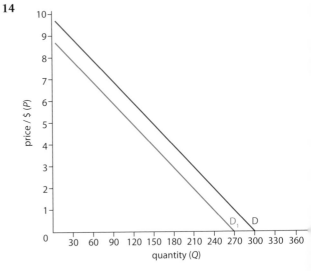

15 $Q_D = 300 - 10P$

Price in $ (P)	Quantity demanded (Q_D)
0	300
3	270
5	250
7	230
9	210

16

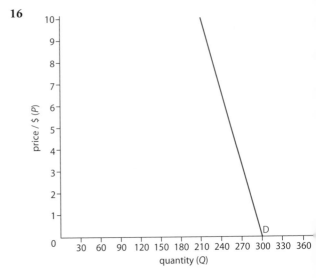

22

Price in $ (P)	Quantity supplied (Q_S)
10	0
20	100
30	200
40	300
50	400

23

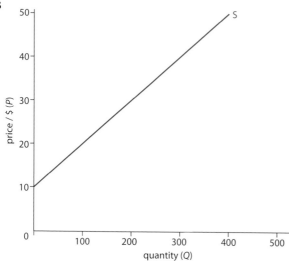

24 $Q_S = -50 + 10P$

Price in $ (P)	Quantity supplied (Q_S)
10	50
20	150
30	250
40	350
50	450

25

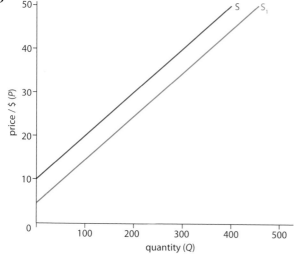

26 $Q_S = -100 + 30P$

Price in $ (P)	Quantity supplied (Q_S)
10	200
20	500
30	800
40	1100
50	1400

27

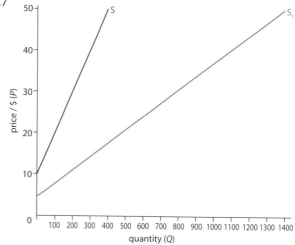

 # Chapter 3

2 a $-400 + 50P = 800 - 30P$

$50P = 1200 - 30P$

$80P = 1200$

$P = 15$

$Q_D = 800 - 30(15) = 350$

b $-240 + 40P = 660 - 20P$

$40P = 900 - 20P$

$60P = 900$

$P = 15$

$Q_D = 660 - 20(15) = 360$

c $-50 + 25P = 90 - 10P$

$25P = 140 - 10P$

$35P = 140$

$P = 4$

$Q_D = 90 - 10(4) = 50$

3 **a**

Price in $ (P)	Quantity demanded (Q_D) $Q_D = 300 - 30P$	Quantity supplied (Q_S) $Q_S = 100 + 10P$
0	300	100
3	210	130
5	150	150
7	90	170
9	30	190

4 **a** $Q_S = 100 + 10P$; $Q_D = 380 - 30P$

Price in $ (P)	Quantity demanded (Q_D) $Q_D = 380 - 30P$	Quantity supplied (Q_S) $Q_S = 100 + 10P$
0	380	100
3	290	130
5	230	150
7	170	170
9	110	190

b

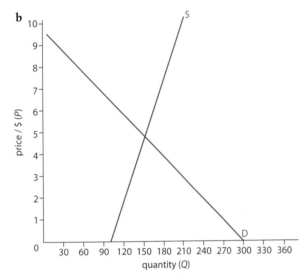

b

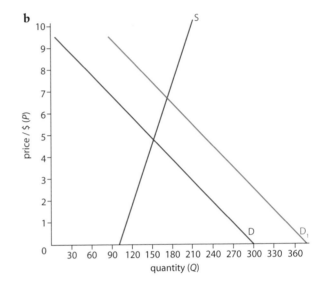

c The equilibrium quantity bought and sold is given by the intersection point on the graph above.

d $Q_S = 100 + 10P$; $Q_D = 300 - 30P$

$100 + 10P = 300 - 30P$

$100(-100) + 10P = 300(-100) - 30P$

$10P = 200 - 30P$

$10P(+30P) = 200 - 30P(+30P)$

$40P = 200$

$40P/40 = 200/40$

$P = 5$

$Q = 150$

c

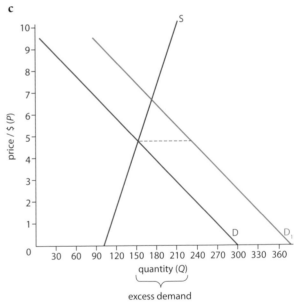

excess demand

d $Q_S = 100 + 10(5)$; $Q_D = 380 - 30(5)$

$Q_S = 150$; $Q_D = 230$

$230 - 150 = 80$ units excess demand

Chapter 4

1. The PED = absolute value of % change in quantity over % change in price. Quantity falls by 40% following an increase in price of 50%: PED = 40/50 = 0.8

2. First, calculate % change in price: $(10 − 8)/8 = 0.25 × 100 = 25\%$. Now plug this into the PED formula with the PED = 1.5: 1.5 = %ΔQ/25. Simplify by multiplying 1.5 × 25 = 37.5. The % change in quantity resulting from a 25% increase in price is 37.5%. Therefore, the new quantity is 200 − (0.375 × 200) = 125. The increase in price from $8 to $10 leads to a decrease in the quantity demanded from 200 to 125 units.

3. PED is always negative because the law of demand says that there is an inverse relationship between quantity demanded and price. When price increases, quantity falls, and *vice versa*. To simplify, PED is usually expressed as an absolute value, and the PED coefficient is therefore positive.

4. a $Q_{D1} = 500 − 20(5) = 400$

   $Q_{D2} = 500 − 20(6) = 380$

   % change in Q = (380 − 400)/400 = 0.05 × 100 = 5%

   % change in P = (6−5)/5 = 0.2 × 100 = 20%

   PED = 5/20 = 0.25

   b $Q_{D1} = 500 − 20(10) = 300$

   $Q_{D2} = 500 − 20(11) = 280$

   % change in Q = (280 − 300)/300 = 0.067 × 100 = 6.7%

   % change in P = (11 − 10)/10 = 0.1 × 100 = 10%

   PED = 6.7/10 = 0.67

5. The PED increases as the price of the good increases.

6. When the good gets more expensive, it makes up a larger proportion of consumers' income and it becomes more exclusive in the eyes of consumers (more of a luxury). Both the proportion of income the price of a good represents and its status as a luxury are determinants of PED.

7. A PED of 1 indicates unit elasticity. If the price falls and demand is unit elastic, then the percentage increase in quantity equals 5% and there will be no change in the revenues of sellers.

8. XED = % change in the quantity of one good over % change in the price of a related good. Therefore, XED = −5/15 = −0.33. Since the XED is negative, the goods must be complements. An example of complementary goods is charcoal and charcoal barbecues. If charcoal prices rise, we would expect barbecue sales to fall.

9. $\dfrac{(1000 − 600)/600}{(20 − 25)/25} = 0.67/−0.2 = −3.35.$

   The two goods must be complementary goods, because the XED coefficient is negative. An example is footballs and football shoes. The two goods in this example are cross-price elastic, since the absolute value of the XED coefficient is greater than one.

10. $−0.8 = \dfrac{\%ΔQ}{(5 − 4)/4} = \%ΔQ/0.25$

    To find the % change in tennis rackets, simplify the equation: −0.8 × 0.25 = −0.2.

    So a 25% increase in the price of tennis balls led to a decrease in demand for tennis rackets of 20%.

12. $XED = \dfrac{(350\,000 − 250\,000)/250\,000}{(130 − 110)/110} = 0.4/0.18 = 2.22$

14. YED = % change in quantity demanded for a good resulting from a particular % change in consumers' income.

    YED = 12/8 = 1.5.

    Since YED is positive, this good must be a normal good, such as restaurant meals.

15. a % change in Q = (40 − 45)/45 = −0.11 × 100 = −11%

    % change in Y = (55 000 − 40 000)/40 000 = 0.375 × 100 = 37.5%

    YED = −11/37.5 = −0.293

    Since YED is negative, this must be an inferior good.

    b An example of such a good is discount toothpaste.

16. a YED for gourmet ice cream is income inelastic because the coefficient is less than 1. Since YED is positive, ice cream is a normal good.

    b YED for fast food hamburgers is income elastic because the absolute value of the coefficient is greater than 1. Since YED is negative, fast food hamburgers are an inferior good.

    c YED for air travel is income elastic because the coefficient is greater than 1. It is also a normal good, since YED is positive.

17. PES = % change in quantity divided by % change in the price of a good. PES = 3/9 = 0.33.

18. PES = 0.5

    % change in P = (3 − 4)/4 = −0.25

    To find the change in the quantity supplied, we plug the % change in price into the PES formula:

    0.5 = %ΔQ/−0.25 = 0.5 (−0.25) = −0.125 × 100 = −12.5%

    The % change in quantity supplied resulting from a fall in price of 25% is −12.5%.

19. a $Q_1 = 30 + 2.5(10) = 55$

    $Q_2 = 30 + 2.5(11) = 57.5$

    % change in Q = (57.5 − 55)/55 = 0.045 × 100 = 4.5%

    % change in P = (11 − 10)/10 = 0.1 × 100 = 10%

    PES = 4.5/10 = 0.45

b $Q_1 = 30 + 2.5(5) = 42.5$

$Q_2 = 30 + 2.5(4) = 40$

% change in Q = $(40 - 42.5)/42.5 = -0.058 \times 100 = -5.8\%$

% change in P = $(4 - 5)/5 = -0.2 \times 100 = -20\%$

PES = $-5.8/-20 = 0.29$

20 Over time, producers are better able to respond to a change in the price of the goods being produced. If demand falls and price falls, producers can shut down plants or close factories over time, reducing their output by more than they can in the short run. If demand and price rise, producers can open new plants or factories and increase output by more over time.

Chapter 5

8 $-8 + 6P = 37 - 3P$

$-8(+8) + 6P = 37(+8) - 3P$

$6P = 45 - 3P$

$6P(+3P) = 45 - 3P(+3P)$

$9P = 45$

$9P/9 = 45/9$

$P = 5$

$Q = 22$

9 $Q_S = -8 + 6P; Q_D = 37 - 3P$

Price in $ (P)	Quantity demanded (Q_D) $Q_D = 37 - 3P$	Quantity supplied (Q_S) $Q_S = -8 + 6P$
0	37	-8
1	34	-2
3	28	10
5	22	22
7	16	34
9	10	46

10

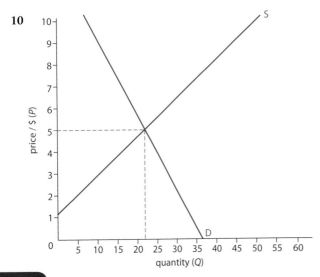

11 The market equilibrium price and quantity are given by the intersection point on the graph in answer 10.

12

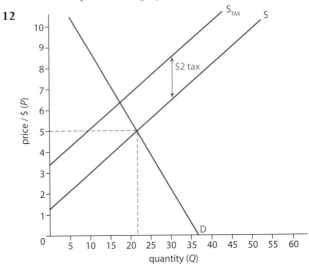

13 $P = 6.30$, $Q = 16$, as shown in the graph below.

14

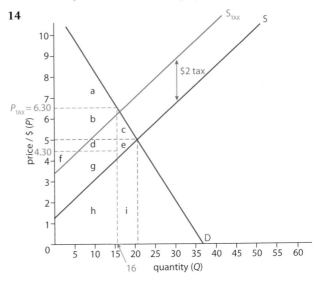

consumer surplus before tax: a + b + c

consumer surplus after tax: a

producer surplus before tax: d + e + f + g

producer surplus after tax: f

area of the tax: b + d

deadweight loss: c + e

15 consumer tax: $6.30 - 5 = 1.30$ per unit ($\times$ 16 units) = $20.80

producer tax: $5.00 - 4.30 = 0.70$ per unit ($\times$ 16 units) = $11.20

total tax: 2.00×16 units = $32

16 a before tax: $5 \times 20 = \$100$

b after tax: $6.30 \times 16 = \$100.80$

17 a before tax: $5 \times 20 = \$100$

b after tax $4.30 \times 16 = \$68.80$

18 a more elastic demand = lesser consumer tax burden

less elastic demand = greater consumer tax burden

b The value of b in a linear function should increase to make demand more elastic (the rate of change in Q_D increases).

The value of b in a linear function should decrease to make demand less elastic (the rate of change in Q_D decreases).

24 $-3 + 4P = 21 - 2P$

$4P = 24 - 2P$

$6P = 24$

$P = 4$

$Q = 13$

25 $Q_S = -3 + 4P;\ Q_D = 21 - 2P$

Price in $ (P)	Quantity demanded (Q_D) $Q_D = 21 - 2P$	Quantity supplied (Q_S) $Q_S = -3 + 4P$
0	21	-3
2	17	5
4	13	13
6	9	21
8	5	29
10	1	37

26

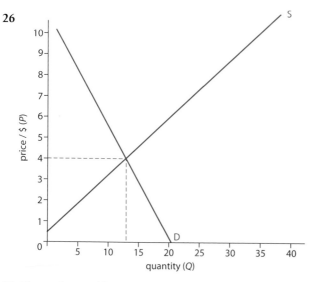

27 The market equilibrium price and quantity are given by the intersection point on the graph above.

28

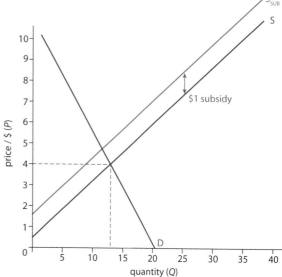

29 $P = 3.33,\ Q = 14.34$, as shown in graph below.

30

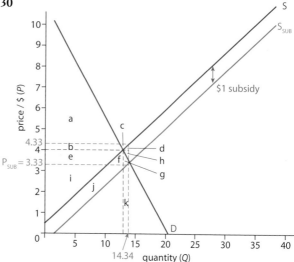

consumer surplus before: a + b

consumer surplus after: a + b + e + f + g

producer surplus before: e + i

producer surplus after: b + c + d + e + f + g + h + i + j

area of the subsidy: b + c + d + e + f + g + h

31 $\$1 \times 14.34 = \$14.34$

32 before subsidy = $52

after subsidy = $47.75

33 before subsidy = $52

after subsidy = $62.09

34 Demand would change at a faster rate, become less steeply sloped.

Demand would become much more elastic.

A given per-unit subsidy would increase the quantity more significantly with more elastic demand. The new quantity would be greater, and the amount of the subsidy would be larger.

Chapter 7

1   When $Q_L = 0$, TP = 0. Without any workers, the firm cannot create any output.

2   a   TP increases at an increasing rate.

   b   TP no longer increases with the seventh worker, and actually decreases with the eighth worker.

   c   By the time the firm employs six or more workers, there is no more capital for them to use and the additional output attributable to those workers stops increasing; it becomes negative, indicating that the eighth worker made the other seven workers less productive overall.

3   Marginal product measures the change in the total product as additional workers are hired.

4   Marginal product begins to decline after the third worker. Since land and capital are fixed, additional workers are less productive than those before them after the firm employs three workers. The declining productivity of labour when it is added to a fixed amount of capital and land is known as the law of diminishing marginal returns.

hire more workers. Labour is a variable resource, so as more workers are hired, total variable cost increases.

7   Fixed costs are the costs of resources that do not vary with output in the short run. Examples include insurance, rent, interest on loans, etc. As output increases in the short run, fixed resources remain fixed, therefore the costs of these resources also remain fixed.

8   Total cost = total fixed costs + total variable costs at every level of output. A firm only faces two types of costs, those for its fixed resources and those for its variable resources. Added together, these equal the firm's total costs.

9   Average total cost tells us the per-unit cost of robotrons.

10 The marginal cost measures the change in total cost whenever output increases by one unit.

11 The number of workers needed to produce one additional robotron decreases at first, indicating that workers actually become more and more productive when the firm starts adding labour to its fixed capital. But beyond three units of output, the number of workers needed to produce additional units gets larger and larger, indicating that labour becomes less and less productive as the firm continues to hire workers to work with its fixed capital. The law of diminishing returns observes that as labour is added to a fixed amount of land and capital, beyond a certain point, the productivity of the variable resource declines.

5

Total output per hour (Q)	Number of workers (Q_L)	Total fixed cost (TFC)	Total variable cost (TVC)	Total cost (TC = TFC + TVC)	Average fixed cost (AFC = TFC ÷ Q)	Average variable cost (AVC = TVC ÷ Q)	Average total cost (ATC = TC ÷ Q)	Marginal cost (MC = ΔTC ÷ ΔQ)
0	0	100	0	100	–	–	–	–
1	6	100	30	130	100	30	130	30
2	10	100	50	150	50	25	75	20
3	13	100	65	165	33.3	21.7	55	15
4	17	100	85	185	25	21.3	46.3	20
5	23	100	115	215	20	23	43	30
6	32	100	160	260	16.7	26.7	43.4	45
7	44	100	220	320	14.3	31.4	45.7	60
8	62	100	310	410	12.5	38.8	51.25	90

6   In order to increase output in the short run, a firm must

12 A firm's total revenue is maximized when the last unit it produced yielded zero marginal revenue. Therefore, at five units of output, this firm is maximizing its total revenue. At six units and beyond, marginal revenue becomes negative, indicating that the firm's total revenue is falling.

13 The revenue the firm earns when it sells just one unit of output is the price it sells that output for. Beyond one unit, however, the firm must accept a lower price to sell additional units (assuming it is a single-price seller). Therefore, at every level of output beyond one unit, the marginal revenue is less than the price of the output, since the firm has to accept less revenue when it lowers the price of all of its output as output increases.

14 Costs would continue to increase. If total revenue decreases and total cost increases, the firm's profits would definitely fall. Since most firms are interested in maximizing profits, producing beyond five units would harm this firm.

15 a Six units. This is where MC is as close as possible to MR, but not greater than MR. At any level of output beyond six units, this firm would reduce its total profits, since the cost of additional units exceeds the revenue earned.

b $40. The firm's total revenue at six units is $300 and its total cost is $260. Economic profit = TR − TC = 300 − 260 = 40.

c At less than three units, this firm's total cost is greater than its total revenues, indicating it would earn losses when producing less than three units.

d Beyond seven units, this firm's total costs exceed its total revenue, indicating the firm would earn losses beyond seven units.

16 The perfectly competitive firm is a price-taker. Since it is one of hundreds or thousands of identical firms, a change in one firm's output has no impact on the market equilibrium price. Therefore, as this firm's output increases, the price remains constant at $50.

17 This firm can sell additional units of output at the constant equilibrium price of $50, so its marginal revenue (the change in total revenue from each additional unit of output) is always $50.

18 a Four units. Beyond four units, the firm's marginal cost is greater than its marginal revenue, indicating that its total profits would decrease beyond this point.

b $815. The firm's total revenue at four units is $1000 but its total cost is only $185. TR − TC = 1000 − 185 = 815.

c Five units. The firm's marginal revenue is zero at five units. At any level of output below five units, the firm can increase its total revenue by increasing its output, but beyond five units MR becomes negative and total revenue begins to decline.

d If the firm produced any more than seven units of output, its total costs would exceed its total revenues, indicating the firm would earn economic losses.

19 This firm produces less output and charges a higher price than the perfectly competitive firm with the same costs.

20 The imperfect competitor must lower its price to sell more output, since it is a price-maker and has significant market power.

21 The firm must sell all its output for the same price (it cannot price-discriminate). Therefore, when it lowers its price to sell additional units, it does so not just for those additional units, but for all of its output, which means the firm's marginal revenue will always be lower than the price of the product.

Chapter 8

1 Because this is where the firm's MR = MC, the profit-maximizing quantity.

2 Total revenue = price × quantity. The firm is producing 100 units at a price of $15 per unit. Therefore, TR = 100 × 15 = $1500

3 Total cost is found by multiplying average total cost (ATC) by level of output. At 100 units, the firm's ATC = $12. Therefore, TC = 100 × 12 = $1200

4 Economic profits = total revenues − total costs. Therefore, economic profits = 1500 − 1200 = $300

5 Firms are profit-seekers. Since there are no barriers to entry, and since firms in this market are earning economic profits, we would expect more firms to enter this market in the long run.

6 TR = P × Q. Therefore, TR = 15 × 100 = $1500

7 TC = ATC × Q. Therefore, TC = 18 × 100 = $1800

8 Losses are another word for negative profits. This firm's profits are $1500 − $1800 = −$300. This firm is losing $300 at the moment.

9 Either demand for the product could have fallen thereby reducing the price, or the firm's costs could have risen thereby increasing ATC and eliminating the firm's profits.

10 Firms are losing money by remaining in this market, therefore, some will wish to leave in the long run.

15 The firm's total revenue = price × quantity; TR = 20 × 50 = 1000. Its total costs = average total cost × quantity; TC = 22 × 50 = 1100. The firm's total costs exceed its total revenues, indicating that this firm is earning losses of $100.

16 a No. The firm is currently earning economic losses of $100, yet it is not producing at its profit-maximizing level of output where MC = MR. Even though we are not given the firm's MR, we know it is $20 because it is a perfect competitor, so MR = P.

b No. The firm is already producing below its profit-maximizing level. Since MC is less than P, we know this firm is producing too little output already.

c No. The firm's current losses of $100 are less than its total fixed cost. We can calculate total fixed costs by determining AFC (ATC – AVC) and multiplying it by the quantity produced. AFC = 22 – 18 = 4. Total fixed cost is therefore 4 × 50 = $200. If the firm shut down, it would lose these fixed costs, which exceed its current losses of only $100.

Alternatively, we could use the simple shut-down rule, which says that if P is less than AVC, the firm should shut down. Clearly, the price of $20 is greater than the firm's AVC of $18, so the firm should not shut down.

d Yes. By increasing its output, the firm will move upwards along its MC curve until MC = P. At that point, we can assume the firm's losses will be smaller, and it may even break even or earn profits.

17 No. If the firm's ATC = 21, the firm is still earning losses of $1 per unit (since the price is only $20). With losses being earned, firms will exit the market in the long run until the firms that remain are only breaking even.

Chapter 9

3

Price (P)	Quantity demanded (Q_D)	Total revenue (TR)	Marginal revenue (MR)
8	3	24	–
7	4	28	4
6	5	30	2
5	6	30	0
4	7	28	–2
3	8	24	–4

4a–d

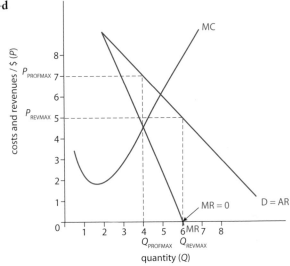

Chapter 11

8 a $C + I + G + (X - M) = GDP$

Government spending on goods and services (G)	900
Gross private domestic investment (I)	410
Consumption (C)	950
Exports (X)	330
Imports (–M)	–150
GDP	2440

b GDP – net income receipts from abroad = GNI

GDP	2440
Income from foreign employment	750
Net property income from abroad	–270
GNI	2920

9 $\dfrac{\$431 \text{ billion}}{115} \times 100 = 374.78 \text{ billion}$

10 $\dfrac{\$1.5 \text{ trillion}}{106.5} \times 100 = 1.408 \text{ trillion}$

11 $\dfrac{\$900 \text{ million}}{97} \times 100 = 927.8 \text{ billion}$

12 GDP growth

year 2: $\dfrac{560 - 543}{543} \times 100 = 3.1$

year 3: $\dfrac{551 - 560}{560} \times 100 = -1.6$

year 4: $\dfrac{559 - 551}{551} \times 100 = 1.45$

year 5: $\dfrac{615 - 559}{559} \times 100 = 10.01$

Inflation rate

year 3: $\dfrac{109 - 105}{105} \times 100 = 3.8$

year 4: $\dfrac{123 - 109}{109} \times 100 = 12.8$

year 5: $\dfrac{104 - 123}{123} \times 100 = -15.4$

Chapter 12

1 **a** MPC = $\Delta C/\Delta Y = 60/100 = 0.6$

MPT = $\Delta T/\Delta Y = 20/100 = 0.2$

MPS = $\Delta S/\Delta Y = 10/100 = 0.1$

MPM = $\Delta M/\Delta Y = 10/100 = 0.1$

(Notice that the change in consumption is only $60 billion, since of the $70 billion increase in household spending, $10 billion went towards the purchase of imports.)

b MRL = MPT + MPS + MPM = 0.2 + 0.1 + 0.1 = 0.4

c Government spending multiplier, $k = 1/(1 - \text{MPC})$ = $1/(1 - 0.6) = 2.5$

d An increase in investment spending of $50 billion will be multiplied 2.5 times through successive increases in consumption and investment spending, ultimately increasing Germany's total output by $125 billion.

Chapter 13

1 **a** Country X's labour force is 42 million people (70% of the 60 million adults). The other 18 million can be assumed to be students, not willing or able to work, prisoners, or other adults who are not part of the labour force.

b Unemployment rate (UR) = % of labour force who are unemployed. Assuming 39 million of the 42 million in the labour force are employed, the unemployed population is 3 million people.

UR = $(3/42) \times 100 = 0.0714 \times 100 = 7.14\%$

2 **a** LFPR = $(44/65) \times 100 = 0.677 \times 100 = 67.7\%$

b UR = number of people unemployed / number of people in the labour force. Therefore, with UR = 9%, number of people unemployed = 9% of labour force.

44m × 0.09 = 3.96m. There are 3.96 million people unemployed.

3 **a** Switzerland's LFPR = 4 264 435.1 / 5 175 054 = 0.824 × 100 = 82.4%

b Switzerland's UR = 153 518 / 4 264 435.1 = 0.036 × 100 = 3.6%

c Spain's LFPR = 21 950 810.9 / 31 141 200 = 0.704 × 100 = 70.4%

d Spain's UR = 1 821 917 / 21 950 810.9 = 0.083 × 100 = 8.3%

Chapter 14

1 **a** South Korea

b Germany, China and Japan

c Q3 2008, Q4 2008, Q1 2009, Q2 2009. In Q3 2009 Germany experienced deflation, and in Q4 2009 returned to inflation.

d In the face of inflation, households prefer to spend rather than save. Inflation reduces the real interest on savings, and means prices will be higher in the future than today, so households wish to spend their money before it loses its value.

2 **a** Q3 2008 – Q4 2008:
$(107.9 - 108.4)/108.4 = -0.0046 \times 100 = -0.46\%$

Q4 2008 – Q1 2009:
$(107.7 - 107.9)/107.9 = -0.0019 \times 100 = -0.19\%$

Q1 2009 – Q2 2009:
$(108.3 - 107.7)/107.7 = 0.0056 \times 100 = 0.56\%$

Q2 2009 – Q3 2009:
$(108.5 - 108.3)/108.3 = 0.0018 \times 100 = 0.18\%$

Q3 2009 – Q4 2009:
$(108.6 - 108.5)/108.5 = 0.00092 \times 100 = 0.10\%$

Q4 2009 – Q1 2010:
$(109.1 - 108.6)/108.6 = 0.0046 \times 100 = 0.46\%$

b Inflation was highest between Q1 2009 and Q2 2009, the average price level rose at its highest rate of 0.56%. The lowest rate of inflation occurred between Q3 2008 and Q4 2008, when the rate of inflation was −0.46%.

c From Q1 2009 until Q4 2009, the country experienced disinflation meaning that the inflation rate was still positive, but lower each quarter than the quarter before.

d The country experienced deflation between Q3 2008 and Q1 2009, during which inflation was negative.

3 **a** Iceland; the inflation rate was 12.7%

b Only Belgium experienced deflation, when the price index fell from 108.3 to 108.2 between 2008 and 2009.

The deflation rate was therefore −0.09%.

c inflation rate 2007–08:
$(126.3 - 112.1)/112.1 = 0.126 \times 100 = 12.6\%$

inflation rate 2008–09:
$(141.5 - 126.3)/126.3 = 0.120 \times 100 = 12.0\%$

Inflation rate was higher between 2007 and 2008 than between 2008 and 2009.

4 a weighted price of the basket of goods for 2010:
(5 × 0.15) + (12.5 × 0.10) + (90 × 0.4) + (8 × 0.15) + (15 × 0.2) = 42.2

price index for 2010 = (42.2/42.2) = 1 × 100 = 100

weighted price of the basket of goods for 2011:
(5.5 × 0.15) + (10 × 0.1) + (105 × 0.4) + (6.5 × 0.15) + (18 × 0.2) = 48.4

price index for 2011 = 48.4/42.2 = 1.15 × 100 = 115

b inflation from 2010 to 2011 = (115 − 100)/100 = 0.15 × 100 = 15%

c Books are weighted at just 15% of the typical household's consumption. So a 10% increase in the price of books must be multiplied by 0.15 to determine its effect on the overall price level: 10% × 0.15 = 1.5%. A 10% increase in the price of books, *ceteris paribus*, will increase the average price level by just 1.5%.

d A 10% increase in the price of rent would have a greater impact on the average price level, because rent is weighted at 40% of the typical household's consumption: 10% × 0.4 = 4%. A 10% increase in rents would increase the average price level by 4%.

e The impact that a change in the price of a particular category of goods has on the overall inflation rate depends how heavily that category is weighted in the price index. Goods like rent and petrol are weighted more heavily than goods like DVDs and hamburgers, so when rent and petrol become more expensive, it increases the overall inflation rate more than when DVDs and hamburgers go up in price.

Chapter 15

4 None of the countries experienced recession between 2004 and 2005. Some of them experienced slowing growth, but for all the countries represented, growth was positive throughout 2004 and 2005.

5 Output increased between 2007 and 2008, but at a much slower rate in 2008 than it did in 2007. In 2007, GDP growth was around 6%, while in 2008 it fell to around 2.4%.

6 Ghana could have experienced an increase in the productivity of its workforce, or there could have been a boost in export sales or government spending, or investment in capital by firms, or consumption spending by households.

7 Generally speaking, countries in which investment makes up a larger percentage of GDP tend to have higher average growth rates. Ghana and the Czech Republic experienced the highest levels of investment, and on average the highest

growth rates. Japan had the lowest levels of investment, and one of the lowest growth rates.

8 The US experienced recession in the early 1930s, then again in the mid-1940s. After 1950, recession became milder, but there were notable periods of negative growth in the early 1970s, early 1980s and again in 2008.

9 The highest rates of growth appear to follow the years in which growth is negative or very low. This can be explained by the business cycle theory. When an economy contracts, or experiences negative growth, it may experience rapid growth during the recovery phase while it races to get back to where it was before the recession started. High growth rates are unsustainable over time, however, because once an economy returns to full employment, resources become increasingly scarce and growth begins to slow again.

10 Since the 1970s, fluctuations in growth rates have become more mild, with lower peaks and milder troughs. This is evidence that macroeconomic policies have been effective at promoting relative stability in the growth of output in the US.

11 a • (669 699 − 631 302)/631 302 = 0.061 × 100 = 6.1%
   • (710 288 − 669 699)/669 699 = 0.061 × 100 = 6.1%
   • (760 212 − 710 288)/710 288 = 0.070 × 100 = 7.0%
   • (798 320 − 760 212)/760 212 = 0.050 × 100 = 5.0%

b Between 2006 and 2007 growth was 7%, its highest rate over the years indicated.

c 2004–05: (149.075 − 145.2)/145.2 = 0.027 × 100 = 2.7%
   2005–06: (154.35 − 149.075)/149.075 = 0.035 × 100 = 3.5%
   2006–07: (157.95 − 154.35)/154.35 = 0.023 × 100 = 2.3%
   2007–08: (164.825 − 157.95)/157.95 = 0.044 × 100 = 4.4%

d real GDP growth rate = nominal growth rate − inflation rate
   2004–05: 6.3% − 2.7% = 3.6%
   2005–06: 6.1% − 3.5% = 2.6%
   2006–07: 7.0% − 2.3% = 4.7%
   2007–08: 5.0% − 4.4% = 0.6%

e Between 2006 and 2007, when the real GDP grew by 4.7%.

Chapter 16

7 a The worker will pay no tax on the first 6000 euros:
6000 × 0 = 0 euros

He or she will pay 5.5% on the next 4000 euros:
4000 × 0.055 = 220 euros in tax

b The worker earning 10 000 euros will pay an average tax rate of 220/10 000 = 0.022 × 100 = 2.2%. The marginal rate of taxation of 5.5% is greater than the worker's average tax rate of 2.2%, because the marginal rate only applies to income earned above and beyond the money he or she earned that was included in the lower tax brackets.

c He or she will pay: $6000 \times 0 = 0$

plus $(12\,000 - 6000) \times 0.055 = 330$

plus $(26\,000 - 12\,000) \times 0.14 = 1960$

plus $(50\,000 - 26\,000) \times 0.30 = 7200$.

total tax paid = $330 + 1960 + 7200 = 9490$ euros

d $27\,490/100\,000 = 0.2749 \times 100 = 27.49\%$

8 a $(20\,000 \times 0.15) + (20\,000 \times 0.25) = \$8000$

b $(20\,000 \times 0.15) + (30\,000 \times 0.25) + (30\,000 \times 0.40) = \$22\,500$

c $(20\,000 \times 0.15) + (30\,000 \times 0.25) + (50\,000 \times 0.4) + (20\,000 \times 0.5) = \$40\,500$

9 a $8000/40\,000 = 0.2 \times 100 = 20\%$

b $22\,500/80\,000 = 0.28125 \times 100 = 28.125\%$

c $40\,500/120\,000 = 0.3375 \times 100 = 33.75\%$

10 a $50\,000 \times 0.2 = \$10\,000$ in tax

b $60\,000 \times 0.2 = \$12\,000$ in tax

11 The direct tax on income is more effective at redistributing income, because it increases as a percentage of income as income increases; it is progressive. The indirect tax, on the other hand, is regressive. The rich pay more than the poor, but the percentage of the rich person's income paid in tax is much lower than the poor person's.

In the above example, the rich person earning $120\,000 pays $12\,000 in tax, or just 10%. With the same 20% indirect tax though, the poor person earning $40\,000 pays $10\,000 in tax, or 25% of his or her income.

Chapter 17

1 a The US government never ran a budget surplus between 2000 and 2010. The national debt grew every year of the decade, indicating that the government ran a deficit in each year.

b In 2010, the national debt grew by nearly $1.6 trillion, indicating that the budget deficit was around $1.6 trillion in 2010.

c During each of the 11 years shown, the US government spent more than it collected in tax revenues.

d It is possible that the government passed tax cuts during this period, or that it simply increased its level of spending more rapidly than it increased its tax receipts.

2 a Between 1978 and 1980 unemployment almost doubled from 7.6% to 13.5%, indicating the US was in a deep recession.

Between 1990 and 1992, unemployment increased by around 2%, indicating that the economy was in a recession, but not one as deep as the one in the late 1970s.

b To address rising unemployment, the US government could have cut taxes or increased government spending. Doing so would increase households' disposable incomes and increase the level of aggregate demand, moving the economy back towards full employment (see figure below).

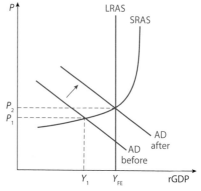

c Using contractionary fiscal policy to reduce inflation may lead to an increase in unemployment. Using expansionary fiscal policy to reduce unemployment may cause inflation.

3 a Spending multiplier, $k = 1/(1 - \text{MPC})$

$k = 1/(1 - 0.6) = 1/0.4 = 2.5$

b The desired change in national income of $60 billion would require an increase in government spending of $60/2.5 = \$24$ billion

4 A tax cut of $24 billion would not have the same expansionary effect as an increase in government spending of $24 billion, because some of the tax cut (40%) will be leaked from the circular flow before it is ever spent in the nation's economy. An increase in government spending, on the other hand, is a direct injection into the nation's circular flow.

5 If the government wishes to reduce AD by $20 billion to reduce inflation, it would only have to cut government spending by $20/2.5 = \$8$ billion.

Chapter 20

1 a

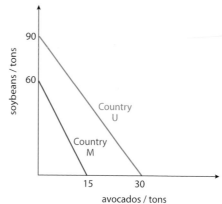

b Country M:

opportunity cost of soybeans = 15 avocados/60 soybeans = 0.25 avocados

opportunity cost of avocados = 60 avocados/15 soybeans = 4 soybeans

Country U:

opportunity cost of soybeans = 30 avocados/90 soybeans = 0.33 avocados

opportunity cost of avocados = 90 soybeans/30 avocados = 3 soybeans

c Country M has comparative advantage in soybeans, with a lower domestic opportunity cost (0.25 avocados) than country U (0.33 avocados).

Country U has comparative advantage in avocados, with a lower domestic opportunity cost (3 soybeans) than Country M (4 soybeans).

d Country M would normally give up 4 soybeans for every avocado. Country U would normally give up 0.33 avocados for each soybean. One rate that would benefit each would be for Country M to trade 3.5 soybeans for 1 avocado from Country U. From Country M's perspective, it would trade 0.285 avocados for every soybean, an improvement over the previous domestic opportunity cost of 0.33. This would make both better off, because the each country has a lower opportunity cost for trading than they did when trying to make both products themselves.

e

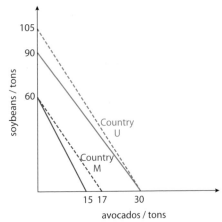

Chapter 21

6

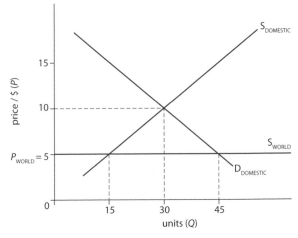

7 Answers may vary, but should approximate the following.

a

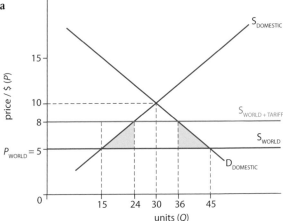

b **i** 5 × 15 = $75

ii 8 × 24 = $192

iii 5 × 30 = $150

iv 5 × 12 = $60

v 3 × 12 = $36

vi ½ (24 − 15) × 3 = ½(9) × 3 = 13.5

½(45 − 36) × 3 = ½(9) × 3 = 13.5

The total area of inefficiency and welfare loss = 13.5 + 13.5 = 27

8 a Results may vary, but should approximate the following.

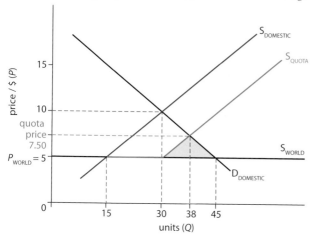

b i 5 × 15 = $75

  ii domestic quantity × price after quota = 23 × 7.5
  = $172.5

  iii 5 × 30 = $150

  iv 7.5 × 15 = $112.50

  v 2.50 × 8 = $20
  2.50 × 7 = $17.50
  $20 + $17.50 = $37.50

9 a Results may vary, but should approximate the following.

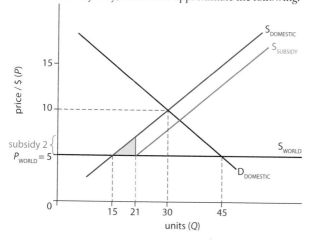

b i 5 × 15 = $75

  ii 5 × 21 = $105

  iii 5 × 24 = $120

  iv ½(2 × 6) = $6

  v 2 × 21 = $42

Chapter 22

14 a $Q_S = 10 + 3P$; $Q_D = 50 - 2P$

  $10 + 3P = 50 - 2P$

  $3P = 40 - 2P$

  $5P = 40$

  $P = 8$ RMB per USD

  $Q = 34$

b

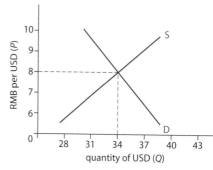

15 a 1 USD/1.6 GBP = 0.625 GBP buys 1 USD

  b 1200/1.6 = 750 GBP

  c 45 × 1.6 = 72 USD

  d 11 GBP/10 GBP = 1.1 GBP (the price has risen 10%)

  The old exchange rate = 0.625 GBP per USD. Now it
  should take 10% more GBP to buy USD (or anything
  priced in USD). So the new exchange rate = 0.625 × 1.1
  = 0.6875 GBP per USD

16 Last year, a 60 RMB jersey cost 720 JPY, therefore, each RMB
  cost 720/60 JPY. The exchange rate of the RMB was 12 JPY.
  One JPY was therefore 1/12 RMB or 0.083 RMB.

  This year, the same 60 RMB jersey costs 780 JPY. More JPY
  are needed to buy the jersey, indicating that the JPY has
  depreciated. The new JPY/RMB exchange rate is 780/60, or 13
  JPY per 1 RMB. One JPY is now therefore 1/13 RMB or 0.077
  RMB.

Chapter 23

1 a i current account balance =

export of goods:	380
+ export of services:	550
− imports of goods:	550
− imports of services:	400
+ income balance:	−130
+ current transfers:	70
	−$80 billion

This country has a current account deficit of $80 billion.

ii financial account balance =

direct investment:	40
+ portfolio investment:	−80
	−$40 billion

This country has a financial account deficit of $40 billion.

iii capital account balance =

capital transfers:	90
+ transactions in non-produced, non-financial assets:	−25
	$65 billion

This country has a capital account surplus of $65 billion.

iv current account + financial account + capital count + change in reserve assets = 0, therefore:

−80 + −40 + 65 + reserve assets = 0

reserve assets = 80 + 40 − 65 = 55

Change in reserve assets is $55 billion.

v balance of payments = current account + financial account + capital account + change in reserve assets

BoP = −80 + −40 + 65 + 55 = 0

b The country has a trade deficit. It purchased more goods and services from the rest of the world than the rest of the world bought of its goods and services.

c The country's reserve assets must have changed by $55 billion. This number is positive because the country overall had a net deficit in its current, capital and financial accounts of $55 billion, meaning that more money left the country for all its international

transactions than came into the country. For this reason, the country's central bank had to sell off $55 billion of its holdings of foreign exchange, which it exchanged for its own currency, resulting in an inflow of $55 billion of its own currency from the rest of the world. This makes up for the net outflow of $55 billion in the three accounts, and allows the country to balance out its balance of payments at zero.

Chapter 25

1 A 95.2 terms of trade value for year 2 means that the average price of imports is greater than the average price of exports. The terms of trade have deteriorated.

2 A 103.8 terms of trade value for year 3 means the average price of exports is greater than the average price of imports. The terms of trade have improved.

3

	TABLE 25.1 CALCULATING TERMS OF TRADE				
Year	Index of average export prices	Index of average import prices	Calculation of terms of trade	Terms of trade	Improvement or deterioration?
Year 1	100	100	$\frac{100}{100} \times 100$	100	index year
Year 2	100	105	$\frac{100}{105} \times 100$	95.2	deterioration
Year 3	109	105	$\frac{109}{105} \times 100$	103.8	improvement
Year 4	116	112	$\frac{116}{112} \times 100$	103.5	deterioration
Year 5	120	110	$\frac{120}{110} \times 100$	109	improvement
Year 6	120	125	$\frac{120}{125} \times 100$	96	deterioration

The arrangement is word by word.

Italic numbers indicate illustrations not included in the text page range. **Bold** numbers indicate interesting facts boxes.

E

M